The Encyclopedia of Vaudeville

The Encyclopedia of Vaudeville_____

Anthony Slide

GREENWOOD PRESS   Westport, Connecticut • London

Library of Congress Cataloging-in-Publication Data

Slide, Anthony.
   The encyclopedia of vaudeville / Anthony Slide.
      p.   cm.
   Includes bibliographical references and index.
   ISBN 0–313–28027–4 (alk. paper)
   1. Vaudeville—United States—Encyclopedias.   2. Entertainers—
United States—Biography.   I. Title.
PN1968.U5S37   1994
792.7′0973—dc20   93–8632

British Library Cataloguing in Publication Data is available.

Library of Congress Catalog Card Number: 93–8632
ISBN: 0–313–28027–4

First published in 1994

Greenwood Press, 88 Post Road West, Westport, CT 06881
An imprint of Greenwood Publishing Group, Inc.

Printed in the United States of America

The paper used in this book complies with the
Permanent Paper Standard issued by the National
Information Standards Organization (Z39.48–1984).

10 9 8 7 6 5 4 3 2

A Presidential Commendation

I like . . . especially good vaudeville when I am seeking
perfect relaxation. . . . If there is a bad act at a vaudeville
show, you can rest reasonably secure that the next
one may not be so bad; but from a bad play, there
is no escape.

President Woodrow Wilson, who was a weekly visitor
to Keith's Theatre in Washington, D.C., until the death
of his wife. Quoted in *The New York Dramatic Mirror*
of January 20, 1915

Contents

Photo essay follows page 291

Preface

This book is the first attempt to provide an encyclopedic guide to vaudeville. Included here are entries not only on the performers, the vaudevillians, but also individuals active behind the scenes in various administrative and creative capacities, major theatres, genres, historical terms, vaudeville houses in individual cities, and much, much more. For individuals, each entry provides complete information as to places and dates of birth and death. Aside from biographical data, entries on vaudevillians may also include contemporary criticism, a sampling of an act's various routines, commentary by the performers themselves or by their contemporaries as well as an appraisal of the performer's place in vaudeville history. Additionally, bibliographies are included where appropriate. The volume concludes with a guide to vaudeville resources and a general bibliography.

Surprisingly little is available on the history of vaudeville, and much that does exist is selective, reprinting a sampling of contemporary commentary, or written by individuals active in the field, whose firsthand memories are important but who have made little or no effort to check their facts and rely too heavily on faulty recollections. The primary source for *The Encyclopedia of Vaudeville* has been articles and reviews in contemporary trade papers such as *The New York Dramatic Mirror* and *Variety*. Over the past twenty years, I have had the opportunity to talk with a number of surviving vaudevillians (virtually all of whom are now, sadly, no longer with us), and I have also welcomed advice from members of the vaudeville audience who have suggested ''names'' that have slipped between the cracks in previous studies and also offered information as to the content of such acts. How I wish I might have been privileged to witness ''Think-a-Drink'' Hoffman!

The Encyclopedia of Vaudeville should prove to be a standard reference source for librarians. As its entries often include sample dialogue, routines and comedy patter, the book is, hopefully, entertaining enough to have appeal beyond that of a serious reference work and should prove enjoyable reading for the casual user. It will transport its readers back to the days before political correctness when vaudeville performers could and did say just about anything, in any guise they wished—but whatever they had to say was always presented with no malice and no vicious intent. Many of the entries here should serve as departure points for additional research by both the student and the serious scholar. While the major vaudevillians who made the transition to radio, television, and motion picture remain "household names," there are many fascinating acts and historical circumstances deserving of wider attention and scholarship. Vaudeville remains very much uncharted territory in the history of American popular entertainment.

The origins of *The Encyclopedia of Vaudeville* lie in my earlier work *The Vaudevillians*. I have revised and corrected, where necessary, the 150 or so entries that appeared there, and this current offering provides more than 500 entries, ranging in length from one paragraph to several pages. The entries cover the entire history of vaudeville from the 1800s and Maggie Cline, Lottie Collins, and Tony Pastor through the 1930s and Cross and Dunn, Señor Wences, and Henny Youngman. In that the entries contain passing references to many other figures in vaudeville, particularly minor acts, the index should be used to track down performers or behind-the-scene players not included in the main A-through-Z section of the encyclopedia. All performers discussed in general subject headings such as "Animal Acts" and "Freak Acts" are, of course, included in the index, and this indexing more than doubles the number of individuals included in the book.

Many institutions and individuals made this work possible. My thanks first to the vaudevillians and those associated with the vaudeville stage with whom I have spoken: Herb Baker, Milton Berle, Jesse Block and Eve Sully, George Burns, Irene D. Caine, Viola Dana, Kitty Doner, Fifi D'Orsay, Mary Foy, S. Linton Hopps, Mrs. Gus Kahn, Liz Kaufman, Nick Lucas, Flo McFadden, Ken Murray, Fayard Nicholas, Robert North, Kathryn Perry, Olga Petrova, Eleanor Powell, Al Rinker, Rose Marie, Virginia Sale, Penny Singleton, Joe Smith, Arthur Tracy, Rudy Vallee, Ted and Priscilla Waldman, and Nancy Welford.

The remembrances of the following members of the vaudeville audience were particularly helpful: Jack Spears, Herb Sterne, William C. Wilson, and especially Robert A. Bloch.

The birth and death information included in this volume was particularly difficult to track down, and I could not have included as much documentation as I have without the overwhelming help and support of Bill H. Doyle.

The following individuals provided help in various areas of research: Irene Atkins, Carmen Boden, Mary Brian, Ned Comstock, Patricia Coward, Eleanor Debus, Madeline Foy, Ron Foy, Alan Gevinson, Sam Gill, Robert Gitt, Herb Graff, Marty Kearns, Robert Knutson, Richard Lamparski, Robert J. Landry (former managing editor of *Variety*), David W. McCain, Polly Miller of the Ted Lewis Museum, Peter J. Mones, Edmund H. North, David Pierce, Brian Taylor, Benny Urlik, and Hans J. Wollstein. Special thanks to Everett and Bill Fields and the entire W. C. Fields family of friends and, for help in researching British music hall, the late Raymond Mander and Joe Mitchenson.

For institutional help, I am grateful to the staffs of the Margaret Herrick Library of the Academy of Motion Picture Arts and Sciences, the Library of Congress, the Literature Department of the Los Angeles Central Library, the New York Public Library at Lincoln Center, and the Doheny Memorial Library of the University of Southern California. Thanks also to the Library of the Museum of the City of New York, the Will Rogers Memorial (Reba Collins), the University of Iowa Libraries (Robert A. McCown, Head Special Collections and Manuscript Librarian), the Harvard Theatre Collection (Jeanne T. Newlin), the Theatre Collection at Princeton University (Mary Ann Jensen), and The Shubert Archive (Maryann Chach).

Vaudeville: An Appreciation ___

For a relatively short period of time, from the mid to late 1800s through the early 1930s, vaudeville was an American institution, as important in its day as radio, the motion picture, and television as *the* people's entertainment. Its early audience, before it became "refined" under B. F. Keith and E. F. Albee, was largely immigrant in makeup, and the performers, the vaudevillians, came from much the same working-class, poor, inner-city background. A comfortable rapport existed between performer and spectator, a relationship that was not equalled in vaudeville's reincarnation in radio or television, where listeners and viewers are all too aware of the financial status of those entertainers who would seek to approach them as social equals.

Just as that relationship is lost, so undocumented and neglected are many of the once-great names from the world of vaudeville. George Burns and Gracie Allen are still a part of our lives, but how many recall a similar husband-and-wife team, Block and Sully, from whom Burns and Allen borrowed many of their routines? Thanks to television, Jack Benny and Milton Berle can amuse us still, but what remembrances remain of Smith and Dale, Lou Holtz, Eddie Foy, or Julius Tannen? Dustin Hoffman was Tootsie, but what of the great female impersonators who were once taken for granted on the vaudeville stage: Bothwell Browne, Julian Eltinge, Bert Errol, or Karyl Norman?

Social conditions have changed. What once passed for entertainment is now considered racist or politically incorrect. Adolf Hitler and the rise of Naziism in Germany put an end to the style of Jewish humor presented by Willie and Eugene Howard, Benny Rubin, and Ben Welch. The blackface antics of Aunt Jemima, Al Jolson, and Moran and Mack have no place in America of the 1990s. The anecdotes of Walter Kelly as the Virginia Judge would no longer find an audience, even in the Southern states.

Vaudevillians were an amazing breed—they had stamina, energy, enthusiasm, fortitude, and, above all, a determination to succeed. Literally, they fought for audience recognition, year after year, town after town, until they became headliners. Their story is also the story of a younger, vibrant America, offering boundless opportunities to poor kids from New York's Lower East Side, such as Eddie Cantor and George Jessel, and a relative escape from racism for black entertainers like Bill Robinson, Ethel Waters, and Josephine Baker. Racial and religious lines might be drawn beyond the footlights, but on the vaudeville stage all men and women were created equal; a young Eleanor Powell could enjoy the companionship of Buck and Bubbles or Bill Robinson; Eddie Cantor could play a sketch with the great black entertainer Bert Williams; and Jews and gentiles knew and shared an equal chance at success. There was no discrimination in the hardships that vaudevillians were forced to endure, and neither was there in the fame that they might achieve.

The word "vaudeville" has its origins in fifteenth-century France, when a miller named Olivier Basselin in the Valley of the Vire in Normandy wrote a series of songs he called *Vaux-de-Vire*. They remained popular for two hundred years, and the name was corrupted to *voix de ville*, or sounds of the town. From that came the French *vaudeville*, meaning a ballad or light form of comedy. As an entertainment form, American vaudeville has its origins in the minstrel shows which developed here in the early 1800s and in British music hall, or variety. Perhaps a desire to remain staunchly independent of Great Britain led to Americans' adopting the French name vaudeville, rather than the more obvious and well-defined British term of variety.

In its American beginnings, vaudeville embraced an all-male audience who came to its early theatres, saloons, and beer gardens as much to smoke and drink as to enjoy the entertainment. As *The New York Dramatic Mirror* pointed out in 1913, "so it may be said that smoking and drinking existed at the birth of the form, making it appear that vaudeville came into the world with all of its teeth, so to speak, including the wisdom, with the full upper and lower." Its curse, as one American clergyman claimed, was the three Ws: wine, women, and tobacco (and while tobacco may not begin with a W, it is a weed). Tony Pastor was the first to try to refine vaudeville, in the 1860s. The man who first succeeded in making the entertainment form respectable was B. F. Keith. Neither pioneer is credited with first using the term vaudeville in the United States; that honor goes to H. L. Sargent, who first billed himself as "Sargent's Great Vaudeville Company" at Weisiger's Hall, Louisville, on February 23, 1871.

There are many similarities between vaudeville and the early motion picture industry. Both were operated as virtual monopolies or "trusts," the latter by the Motion Picture Patents Company and vaudeville by B. F. Keith and his henchman, E. F. Albee. The Motion Picture Patents Company lost its power because it failed to realize that the film industry was advancing into new fields. E. F. Albee and the B. F. Keith organization "killed" vaudeville because of a similar inability to move with the times, a refusal to work with the motion picture, rather than fight it.

Vaudeville has its modern origins with B. F. Keith in Boston, but there was only one home for vaudeville, and that was the Palace Theatre at Broadway and 47th Street in New York, which opened on March 24, 1913. Its closure as a two-a-day vaudeville house in May 1932 marked the beginning of the end for vaudeville. Vaudeville lingered on as an accompaniment to motion pictures in so-called presentation houses, and the Second World War gave it a brief, new lease on life, as many vaudevillians were called upon to entertain the troops through the U.S.O. In the late 1940s and early 1950s, vaudeville was a staple of television—Milton Berle's popular program was no more than a glorified vaudeville bill—but if vaudeville survives at all in that medium today, it is as but an empty shadow of its former self.

Why was vaudeville so popular? Why would audiences, week after week, make routine pilgrimages to their local Orpheum, B. F. Keith, or Pantages theatre? It cannot have been because they always knew that the show would be good, for in many cases it was not—and when vaudeville was bad, it was very, very bad. No, the reason for vaudeville's appeal is a simple one, and it lies in the variety of the acts and the knowledge that acts were never overly long. An audience could sit through fifteen minutes of a second-rate comedy routine, secure in the knowledge that the next act would probably be a good one. E. F. Albee summed up vaudeville's appeal when he wrote in a 1923 edition of *Variety*: "In vaudeville, 'there is always something for everybody,' just as in every state and city, in every county and town in our democratic country, there is opportunity for everybody, a chance for all."

The Encyclopedia of Vaudeville

A

BUD ABBOTT (Asbury Park, N.J., October 2, 1895—Woodland Hills, Ca., 1974) and **LOU COSTELLO** (Paterson, N.J., March 6, 1906—Beverly Hills, Ca., March 3, 1959)

The miracle of the comedy of Abbott and Costello is that it was so antiquated, and yet it entertained a generation of moviegoers; and so much a part of American popular culture did the pair become that they continue to amuse (on film) and be imitated through the present. Writing in *Liberty* in 1941, Howard Sharpe commented, "What the worried, depressed people of America are standing in paying queues to witness is the oldest humor in the world—a fat comedian and his straight man hitting each other over the head, spitting in each other's eyes, falling on their faces, arguing heatedly about a hundred senseless topics. It is a classic brand of entertainment which originated in the music halls, honky tonks, and beer parlors of America, being relegated finally to sidestreets as vaudeville expired."

When Lou asked, "Where do all the little bugs go," and Bud replied, "Search me," audiences laughed in the 1930s and continue to laugh in the 1990s.

Bud Abbott began his career as a treasurer, or box-office manager, for various burlesque houses. In 1918 he met and married a chorus girl named Betty Smith, and with her help produced the tab show *Broadway Flashes*, which toured the Gus Sun circuit. Other shows followed, and gradually Bud began working as a comic straight man. Lou Costello tried entering the film industry in 1927, working as an extra and stuntman. Following a 1928 accident while doubling for leading lady Dolores Del Rio, Lou became a "Dutch" comedian in burlesque. The two men certainly met each other in the early 1930s, possibly as early as 1929, and did occasionally perform together, although by this time Bud was working as a straight man to Harry Evanson and Lou with straight man Joe Lyons.

It was not until January 1936 that Abbott and Costello formally decided to work as a team, hired by the Minsky Brothers for their New York and Brooklyn burlesque theatres. The men worked at Atlantic City's Steel Pier during the 1936 and 1937 summer seasons. Late in 1937 Bud and Lou toured in a vaudeville show titled *Hollywood Bandwagon*, and in February 1938 they appeared at Loew's State, New York. It was at the Loew's State engagement that the pair was seen by Kate Smith's manager, Ted Collins, and they made their radio debut on *The Kate Smith Hour* on February 3, 1938.

Abbott and Costello continued to work on radio with Kate Smith through the summer of 1940. On March 24, 1938, they first performed the "Who's on First?" routine on radio, having used the skit in their act as early as 1936.

As a result of their radio work, Abbott and Costello were starred in the Broadway revue *Streets of Paris*, which opened at the Broadhurst Theatre on June 19, 1939. Reviewing the show in the following day's edition of *The New York Times*, Brooks Atkinson commented that the pair "carry laughter to the point of helpless groaning. . . . Abbott is the overbearing mastermind whose feverish and impatient guidance of the conversation produces the crises. Costello is the short, fat he-who-gets-slapped. He is a moon-face zany with wide, credulous eyes, a high voice and puffy hands that struggle in futile gestures. Both men work themselves up into a state of excitement that is wonderful to behold."

Abbott and Costello made their screen debuts in *One Night in the Tropics*, released in November 1940. It was the first of thirty-six feature films the team made together, all but three of which were produced by Universal. Additionally, Universal produced a 1965 compilation film, *The World of Abbott and Costello*, and Lou appeared in one solo effort, *The 30-Foot Bride of Candy Rock* (1959).

Aside from their work on screen, Abbott and Costello also had their own radio show between 1942 and 1949, initially on NBC and later on ABC. They made their television debut on July 19, 1939, in a fifteen-minute program titled *So This Is New York*, but, of course, are better remembered for their syndicated television series, *The Abbott and Costello* Show (1951–1953), and for their guest appearances from 1951 to 1954 on NBC's *The Colgate Comedy Hour*.

Following a December 1956 appearance at the Sahara, Las Vegas, the two men split up. Lou continued to work as a comedian and actor until his death. Because of problems with the Internal Revenue Service, Bud refused to perform again except for a 1961 television appearance and providing the voice for his cartoon character in Hanna-Barbera's 1967 television series.

The breakup of the pair in the mid 1950s was, in part, an indication of the temporary loss of appeal of their comedic style. They had become a little too broad and a little too familiar for audiences whose tastes were for the humor of Mort Sahl or Lenny Bruce. However, the return to favor of burlesque-style entertainment has resulted in a revival of the appeal of Abbott and Costello, particularly for younger audiences. The two are, without question, American institutions, and thanks to the permanence of their screen appearances, that familiar cry of "Heyyyyyyy Abbott-t-t-t-t" will be heard for many years to come.

BIBLIOGRAPHY

"Abbott, Bud and Costello, Lou." *Current Biography*, October 1941, pp. 1–2.

Anobile, Richard J., ed. *Who's on First?: Verbal and Visual Gems from the Films of Abbott and Costello*. New York: Darien House, 1972.

Costello, Chris, with Raymond Strait. *Lou's on First: A Biography*. New York: St. Martin's Press, 1981.

Cox, Stephen, and John Loftin. *The Official Abbott and Costello Scrapbook*. Chicago: Contemporary Books, 1991.

Furmanek, Bob, and Ron Palumbo. *Abbott and Costello in Hollywood*. New York: Perigree Books, 1991.

Gaver, Jack, and Dave Stanley. "Laborers in the Cornfield: Abbott and Costello." In *There's Laughter in the Air!* New York: Greenberg, 1945, pp. 125–37.

"Lou Costello Remembers," *Screen Guide* 12, no. 12 (December 1947), pp. 67–69.

Marill, Alvin H. "Bud Abbott & Lou Costello." *Screen Facts* 4, no. 4 (1970), pp. 1–20.

Mulholland, Jim. *The Abbott and Costello Book*. New York: Popular Library, 1975.

Peary, Danny. "Abbott and Costello: Top Comics of the Forties." *The Velvet Light Trap* 5 (Summer 1972), pp. 30–32.

Sharpe, Howard. "$1,000,000 for the World's Oldest Humor." *Liberty* 18, no. 37 (September 13, 1941), pp. 48–49.

Thomas, Bob. *Bud & Lou: The Abbott & Costello Story*. Philadelphia: J. B. Lippincott, 1977.

Van Ryn, Frederick. "Abbott, Costello and Hitler." *Liberty* 19, no. 21 (May 23, 1942), pp. 20–22.

ACROBATS

In vaudeville, acrobats were of many different types, but the one thing they all had in common was that they were never booked as anything except the opening or closing act on the bill. One of the earliest female acrobats in vaudeville was Carrie Swain from the 1880s, and, from the same era, the earliest acrobatic clown act was Caron and Herbert. Among the popular acrobatic acts that played the Palace were Dainty Marie, The Three Whirlwinds (who performed on skates), the Rath Brothers, and the Bracks.

Taking a year at random, 1926, the four most highly promoted acrobatic acts were the Six Rockets (six women billed as "the only act of this kind in the world"), the Roma Bros. ("a study in bronze and balancing"), the Three Melvin Brothers ("world's most sensational gymnasts"), and the Three Golfers ("comedy springboard acrobats").

Typical of the ethnic balancing and acrobatic acts was the On Wah Troupe, three Chinese men and two women popular in the late 1920s and early 1930s who engaged in contortions, balancing plates on ends of poles, and similar feats. Apparently the group consisted of a father and his four children, but as *The Billboard* (April 19, 1930) put it, after viewing the act at Fox's Academy, "can't be sure, however, as all Chinese look alike."

ADVANCED VAUDEVILLE. See SHUBERT ADVANCED VAUDEVILLE

AFTERPIECES

"Afterpieces" was the name given to finales in which performers were required to appear in addition to performing their own acts. No extra pay was offered a performer for this additional work, introduced by the B. F. Keith and Orpheum circuits in 1923.

"AFTER THE BALL"

Written at the start of the "golden age" of vaudeville and a seminal song in the history of popular entertainment, "After the Ball" is one of the great sentimental numbers of all time. Its survival in popularity is in part due to Jerome Kern's interpolation of the song into his 1927 musical *Show Boat*. It was written and published in 1892 by Charles K. Harris (Poughkeepsie, N.Y., May 1, 1867— New York, December 22, 1930), who also wrote material for many vaudeville acts and used the song as the title of his autobiography, *After the Ball: 40 Years of Melody*. The song is the story of an old man who caught his sweetheart kissing another man at a ball. Only after her death does he discover that the man was her brother. Now he is a lonely, old man because he broke his sweetheart's heart, after the ball:

> After the ball is over,
> After the break of morn,
> After the dancers' leaving,
> After the stars are gone.
> Many a heart is aching,
> If you can read them all;
> Many the hopes that have vanished,
> After the ball.

WILL AHERN (Waterbury, Ct., October 9, 1896—Burbank, Ca., May 16, 1983)

Following service with the navy during the First World War, Will Ahern entered vaudeville in 1919 with a comedy act in which he appeared in cowboy garb, told jokes, and performed rope tricks. In the mid 1920s, he teamed with chorus girl Gladys Reese, whom he later married, and the pair developed an act that embraced all of Ahern's former activities, but also included Gladys speaking with a Mexican accent and dancing inside a spinning rope to the tune of "Alice Blue Gown" and the couple singing and dancing together with a finale consisting of an acrobatic Russian dance. As Robert Dwan has written, "Their genius was in making these diverse numbers come together into a cohesive act."

Will and Gladys Ahern played the Palace in 1926, 1928, and 1929 and were also featured in the 1927 Broadway production *Sidewalks of New York*. As a solo act, Will Ahern appeared in the 1930 production of *Simple Simon*, while his wife teamed in vaudeville with Will's brother, Dennis. Will and Gladys

Ahern appeared in a number of films from 1929 onward and made their first European tour in 1931. Following U.S.O. tours during the Second World War, the Aherns settled in Hollywood, opening a rehearsal studio. Will Ahern's last professional stage appearance was in a 1980 Los Angeles production of *Guys and Dolls*.

BIBLIOGRAPHY

Dwan, Robert. "A Lifetime of Joy in Vaudeville." *Los Angeles Times Calendar*, May 22, 1983, p. 3.

E. F. ALBEE (Machias, Me., October 8, 1857—Palm Beach, Fl., March 11, 1930)

E. F. Albee was the most influential figure in twentieth-century vaudeville, and also the most disliked. Through his control of the B. F. Keith Vaudeville Circuit, Albee determined the fate of virtually every vaudevillian in the United States. He created a company union, National Vaudeville Artists, Inc., to which all vaudevillians were required to belong, and levied a 5 percent commission on all acts wishing to appear on the Keith circuit. Through either its ownership of the theatres or its control of the booking of the non-Keith vaudeville houses, the latter had a monopoly on vaudeville in the eastern United States, and as its chief executive, E. F. Albee ruled the Keith empire with an iron fist.

From his office on the sixth floor of the Palace Theatre Building in New York, Albee kept a tight control of the Keith interests. He was resolute in his determination that vaudeville should be a respectable form of entertainment. There were to be no profanity, no vulgarity, no scanty costumes, and no improper behavior on stage. He would tolerate no questioning of his authority. When Sime Silverman began editorializing against Albee in *Variety* in 1913, he issued a dictate that no vaudeville act that advertised in the tradepaper, no vaudeville act seen reading *Variety*, would be permitted to appear on the stages of B. F. Keith.

In his autobiography, Fred Allen recalled being called by Albee to appear at the Palace: "It was like God bending from His empyrean throne and summoning an ant into His presence. I had no choice. If I turned Mr. Albee down, I might as well have started pricing brine and gone into the pickle business."

Edward Franklin Albee was the son of Nathaniel S. Albee, a prominent New England shipbuilder. At the age of sixteen, he left home and joined P.T. Barnum's circus, learning the skills of showmanship and traveling on the road with various circus outfits until 1883. He was thoroughly disliked by his fellow circus men and, apparently, often abused and forced to undertake the most menial of tasks. In 1883, Albee became an employee of B. F. Keith in Boston, helping to expand the organization through the supervision of the building of new theatres in Providence, Rhode Island, and Philadelphia. In time, he became general manager of the operation, and by 1891 was in full control of all aspects of the burgeoning B. F. Keith vaudeville empire. As *The New York Dramatic Mirror* commented in 1913, "B. F. Keith is the King of Vaudeville, but E. F. Albee is the Viceroy."

A shrewd businessman, Albee did not seek publicity for himself as his power grew. He was content to remain the power behind the throne; the theatres were Keith theatres and not Albee houses, and few outsiders knew the man who controlled the destiny of American vaudeville. Only after the deaths of B. F. Keith and his son did Albee publicly assert his power and authority. He built magnificent palaces for vaudeville—the E. F. Albee in Brooklyn was the best example—but seemed strangely unaware that what appeared at those theatres was more important than the buildings themselves. His coldness prevented Albee's developing friendships with performers. As Joe Laurie, Jr., commented, "The beautiful houses did a lot to dignify vaudeville, but beautiful theatres can't entertain."

Ultimately, E. F. Albee failed to understand the basic purpose of vaudeville, just as he failed to understand the threat to vaudeville from the motion picture industry. He was uneasy with actors, always desirous of controlling them. When he founded the United Booking Office in 1906, he commented, "All my life actors have been gypping me. Now I am going to gyp them."

Through the manipulations of Joseph P. Kennedy, Albee lost control of his empire to RCA. One day, he came into Kennedy's office to make a suggestion, only to be told, "Didn't you know, Ed? You're washed up, you're through." Although immensely wealthy, with a fortune of more than $14 million, Albee became an embittered man. One of his associates pointed out to him that through his actions, his failure to understand vaudeville, "you killed vaudeville, Mr. Albee." Albee died suddenly in Palm Beach, Florida, and his body was brought back for burial at the Cathedral of St. John the Divine in New York. He had made a fortune from vaudeville, but he left nothing to its charities. One vaudevillian commented, "The funeral played to a small house."

E. F. Albee had one son, Reed, who worked for B. F. Keith. Reed Albee adopted a son who is the playwright and E. F. Albee namesake, Edward Albee.

BIBLIOGRAPHY

Albee, E. F. "E. F. Albee on Vaudeville." *Variety*, September 6, 1923, pp. 1, 18.
Copley, Frank Barkley. "Story of a Great Vaudeville Manager." *American Magazine*, December 1922, pp. 46–47.
"E. F. Albee's Death Leaves Vaude without a Champion." *The Billboard*, March 22, 1930, p. 9.
Kinsley, Walter J. "Edward F. Albee: Viceroy of Vaudeville." *The New York Dramatic Mirror*, August 13, 1913, p. 13.
Laurie, Joe, Jr. "Edward Franklin Albee." In *Vaudeville: From the Honky-Tonks to the Palace*. New York: Henry Holt, 1953, pp. 342–47.

Learny, H. "You Ought to Go on the Stage." *Collier's*, May 1, 1926, pp. 10 + .
McGregor, D. "Supreme Court of the Two a Day." *Collier's*, June 20, 1925, pp. 38 + .

"ALEXANDER'S RAGTIME BAND"

One of the most popular American songs of all time and one closely associated with vaudeville is "Alexander's Ragtime Band," composed by Irving Berlin and published originally by Waterson and Snyder. (The copyright laws in the United States resulted in the song's falling into the public domain prior to Berlin's death.) In the history of popular song, "Alexander's Ragtime Band" is important in that it changed the sixteen-bar chorus prevalent prior to its publication to a standard thirty-two-bar chorus. The use of the name "Alexander" implies a "coon" song, but an element of syncopation and modernity is evident from Berlin's use of the word "Ragtime." Also, the song's line "so natural that you want to go to war" has much the same quality as a military march.

"Alexander's Ragtime Band" was first heard in 1909 at Jesse L. Lasky's *Folies Bergere*, a New York cabaret. It was played as an instrumental number and had no impact. The following year, Berlin wrote lyrics for the number, and it was an immediate hit in the revue *The Merry Whirl*, which opened on May 30, 1910, at the New York Theatre. The song quickly became associated with Emma Carus and Al Jolson, and by the end of 1911, more than one million copies of the sheet music had been sold. It is, of course, one of the most popular of all Irving Berlin songs and was used as the title for the 1938 20th Century–Fox musical that featured lyrics and music by Berlin.

Such was the song's popularity and originality in Berlin's repertoire up to that time that a rumor circulated that "Alexander's Ragtime Band" was written by "a little colored boy" or "a little nigger boy" whom the composer, who could not write music, kept hidden away. The most obvious choice as composer was a pianist named Lukie Johnson. Berlin vehemently denied the rumors and offered $20,000 to any Negro who could compose another "Alexander's Ragtime Band," but the gossip continued throughout Berlin's career.

As a result of the song's success, a vaudeville act appeared in 1912 called Alexander's Rag Time Band. It consisted of an eleven-piece brass band supported by a mixed chorus of singers and dancers. "With the company all clad in red at the finish, the lights from the front working overtime and a great medley of 'rag' airs on the brasses, the turn will rouse any small time audience it appears before," commented "Fred" in *Variety* (February 24, 1912). The group never made it "big" in vaudeville.

BIBLIOGRAPHY

Bergreen, Laurence. *As Thousands Cheer: The Life of Irving Berlin*. New York: Viking, 1992.

HADJI ALI (Egypt, 1892—Wolverhampton, England, November 5, 1937)

Sometimes billed as "The Egyptian Enigma," Hadji Ali performed an extraordinary regurgitation act in which he swallowed and subsequently spat out various objects including nuts and live goldfish. The act culminated in his swallowing water and kerosene. He would spit out the latter, setting fire to a model house, and then regurgitate water to put out the fire. The act has been captured at least twice on film, in the 1930 short subject *Strange as It Seems* and in *Politiquerias*, the Spanish-language version of Laurel and Hardy's *Chickens Come Home* (1931).

Hadji Ali came to the United States in the early 1920s, appearing at fairs, carnivals, and in vaudeville. In 1929, he toured the Pantages circuit, and in 1930 to 1931, he appeared in the prologue to the feature film *Morocco* at Grauman's Chinese Theatre in Hollywood. He died while touring the United Kingdom in a show titled *New Faces*.

While unusual, regurgitation acts involving expansion and contraction of the stomach and control of the throat muscles have been a form of entertainment since the seventeenth century.

FRED ALLEN (Cambridge, Ma., May 31, 1894—New York, March 17, 1956)

Writing in *American Vaudeville*, Douglas Gilbert commented, "In vaudeville, Allen was a carefree, irresponsible performer, a clean nut comic who presented any ridiculous thing that occurred to him. He'd quit off in the middle of a routine, sit flat on the stage almost in the footlights, and read his press notices to the orchestra leader. At one time he used a shapeless and dilapidated ventriloquist's dummy for a purposely atrocious ventriloquial specialty; another time he used a frightful banjo to accompany an equally wretched song. His dead pan was superb, making the foolish things he did get over for riotous laughter." From vaudeville, Fred Allen went into radio—"this drudgery, this sham, this gold mine," as he once called it—and became one of the medium's biggest stars. S. J. Perelman called Allen "the great sourpuss," and his cynical, dour, baggy-eyed style came over to radio listeners through Allen's scripts, for which he was almost entirely responsible.

Born John Florence Sullivan, Fred Allen began his working life in the Boston Public Library before breaking into vaudeville in the early teens. He was initially known as Freddy James and billed—with some justification—as "The World's Worst Juggler." In 1914, Allen toured Australia, juggling and telling jokes like "She was so old when they lit the candles on her birthday cake six people were overcome by the heat" and "I don't have to look up my family tree, because I know that I'm the sap." Returning to the United States, Allen played small-time vaudeville for a while and then, in an attempt to break into the big time, changed his name to Fred Allen, borrowing the last name from the Fox circuit booker Edgar Allen.

As Fred Allen, he played the Fifth Avenue Theatre, New York, in January 1918. Sime Silverman saw him and was devastating in his review, published in the January 4, 1918, issue of *Variety*: "If Fred Allen is his right name he should change it, and if Fred Allen isn't his right name, someone should tell what it was, for this Fred Allen has copped and copped until he may think he has an act. . . . His is a nutty talking juggling turn and if he gets away with it on the big time, then he is not near as nutty as the big time is." Silverman had no problem in recognizing gags and routines "stolen" from a number of other vaudevillians, in particular Felix Adler, Edwin George, and Joe Cook. Back Allen went to the small time, and it was not until 1922 that he became established as a vaudeville headliner. When the comedian played New York's Colonial Theatre in June 1921, *Variety* (June 10, 1921) had changed its opinion of Allen, perhaps because he had disposed of all his paraphernalia such as the ventriloquist's dummy and the juggling and was now relying on his monologue. "Allen's present act is big time and it looks all his own," reported the trade paper.

From vaudeville, Allen went into revue with *The Passing Show of 1922*, which played an important part in his life in that he met his future wife, Portland Hoffa, who was a member of the chorus. They were married in 1927. Allen was also a member of the cast of the 1924 edition of *The Greenwich Village Follies* and later starred with Libby Holman and Clifton Webb in *The Little Show* (1929) and *Three's a Crowd* (1930). He was also featured in *Vogues of 1924* and *Rufus LeMaire's Affairs* (1926). During this period, Allen was also seen on the vaudeville stage, most notably in a twenty-two-minute sketch titled "Disappointments of 1927," in which he was joined by Hoffa. The premise of the sketch was that Allen was the prologue singer about to introduce the rest of the cast, from Paul Whiteman and His Band to a line of voluptuous chorus girls. Unfortunately, a telephone call told him that none of them was able to appear. Allen then proceeded to do the entire show, aided by Hoffa, who wanted to disgrace herself and was thus willing to work with him. In addition to performing with Hoffa, Allen developed a double act with Bert Yorke as his straight man, in which the two appeared at the Palace on October 4, 1926.

Fred Allen's years in vaudeville are recorded in detail in the second volume of his autobiography, *Much Ado about Me*, which is, without question, the finest autobiography of a vaudevillian yet written. Its style and use of comedy validate Herman Wouk's definition of Fred Allen as "a classic humorist."

Radio listeners first heard Fred Allen on CBS on October 23, 1932, on *The Linit Bath Club Revue*. Other radio programs followed, but it was not until 1934 and *Town Hall Tonight* that Allen's radio style became established. In 1939, *Town Hall Tonight* became *The Fred Allen Show*, which continued in popularity for a decade and introduced the famous characters of Allen's Alley: Mrs. Nussbaum (Minerva Pious), Ajax Cassidy (Peter Donald), Titus Moody (Parker Fennelly), and Senator Beauregard Claghorn (Kenny Delmar). On radio, Fred Allen was noted for his running gag feud with Jack Benny and his outspoken attacks on the radio executives, which resulted in frequent censorship of his program. Allen was the great pessimist—or perhaps one should say realist—of the entertainment world, and his radio scripts emphasized this attitude. At the close of his book on the radio years, *Treadmill to Oblivion*, Allen noted, "All that the comedian has to show for his years of work and aggravation is the echo of forgotten laughter."

The Fred Allen Show was last aired on June 26, 1949, and Allen was not heard from on a regular basis until he joined the panel of *What's My Line?*, on which he was a regular on CBS from 1954 to 1956. On television, Allen also appeared in 1950 on *The Colgate Comedy Hour* on NBC and in 1951 to 1952 on *Chesterfield Sound Off Time*, also on NBC. However, Fred Allen was never a major success on TV. As he once explained, "I am not videogenic. After my only video appearance I received fan mail from three undertakers. About my future—I have no illusions. If I live long enough I expect to die." Aside from radio and television, Allen made the occasional film appearance from 1929 onward, most notably in *Thanks a Million* (1935), *Sally, Irene and Mary* (1938), *Love Thy Neighbor* (1940), and *It's in the Bag* (1945). He was last seen on screen in *O. Henry's Full House* (1952).

Fred Allen died while out for a stroll in New York. An apocryphal story had him walking his dog at the time of his death, but, ironically, not only did Allen not have a dog, he did not like dogs. Allen's death did not end an era in radio entertainment, because that era had already passed away some seven years earlier, and television put an end to the type of humor for which he was noted. Allen was an intellectual, and his comedy appealed as much to the highbrow in the audience as the average man in the street. He was a genius at barbed wit and the fast, devastating comeback gag. In the early 1930s, he responded with a riposte to an aggressor against his character: "Tell me, did your parents ever consider birth control?" Fifty years later, that gag was revived by younger comedians, who considered references to birth control as daring and sophisticated. Fred Allen was not simply a man of his time, but a man of all time.

BIBLIOGRAPHY

"A Bah! from the Pooh-Bah." *Time*, October 21, 1946, pp. 66, 68.

Allen, Fred. "Allen's Alibi." *Esquire*, June 1949, p. 69.

————. "The Moderate Life of a Moderator." *Theatre Arts* 37, no. 10 (October 1953), pp. 25–25.

————. *Treadmill to Oblivion.* Boston: Little, Brown, 1954.

————. *Much Ado about Me.* Boston: Little, Brown. 1956.

Collins, Frederick L. "The Other Side of the Benny-Allen Feud." *Liberty* 16, no. 4 (January 28, 1939), pp. 33–34.

Fadiman, Clifton. "Party of One." *Holiday*, December 1954, pp. 6, 8–9, 11.

"Forever Allen." *Newsweek*, September 6, 1948, pp. 46–48.

"Fred Allen." *Current Biography*, February 1941, pp. 19–20.

"Fred Allen Cuts a Slice of Old Vaudeville Ham." *Life*, June 8, 1942, pp. 27–29.

Havig, Alan. *Fred Allen's Radio Comedy.* Philadelphia: Temple University Press, 1990.

Hirschfeld, Al. "Fred Allen: A Grim Success Story." *The New York Times Magazine*, July 2, 1944, pp. 18, 53–54.

Kennedy, John B. "Wisecracker," *Collier's*, June 7, 1930, pp. 19, 64, 66.

McCarthy, Joe. "What Do You Think of Television, Mr. Allen?" *Life*, July 4, 1949, pp. 69–72.

————, ed. *Fred Allen's Letters.* Garden City, N.Y.: Doubleday, 1965.

Minoff, Philip. "Fred Allen: It's No Joke." *Cue*, September 16, 1950, pp. 16, 22.

Perelman, S. J. "The Great Sourpuss or, Should Auld Acquaintance Be Exhumed?" *Holiday*, December 1952, pp. 95, 97–98, 101–102.

"Sad Farewell to a Very Funny Man." *Life*, April 2, 1956, pp. 99, 101.

Smith, H. Allen. "Fred Allen." *Cosmopolitan*, January 1946, pp. 8, 16.

"Speaking of Pictures." *Life*, December 18, 1944, pp. 8–10.

Strakosch, Avery. "The Mighty Allen." *Look*, May 19, 1942, pp. 30–33.

Taylor, Robert. *Fred Allen: His Life and Wit*. Boston: Little, Brown, 1989.

Wallace, Irving. "Fred Allen: Never without a Gag." *Liberty* 19, no. 9 (February 28, 1942), pp. 31–32.

"The World's Worst Juggler." *Time*, April 7, 1947, pp. 71–72, 74.

Zolotow, Maurice. "Fred Allen: Radio's Sour Clown." *Look*, August 2, 1944, pp. 30, 32, 35, 37.

GRACIE ALLEN. See GEORGE BURNS AND GRACIE ALLEN

ALL-GIRL ORCHESTRAS

A novelty presentation in vaudeville and elsewhere, all-girl orchestras became popular at the turn of the century, decades before women's suffrage. They survived and prospered through the 1950s, when the concept seemed to have lost much of its freshness. Curiously, with the advent of the feminist movement, all-girl orchestras (as which they were always described) disappeared.

According to Edward B. Marks in his autobiography *They All Sang*, the first all-women orchestra in the United States played the Atlantic Gardens Music Hall on New York's Bowery at some time in the late 1800s. A popular female orchestra in the Boston area was The Fadettes Woman's Orchestra, directed by Caroline B. Nichols. It played the Keith Theatre as early as June 2, 1902, and even had its own opening march, "The Fadettes of Boston," composed by Pasterneck.

The best known female leader of an all-girl orchestra was a former blond showgirl named Ina Ray Hutton (1916–1984), who was billed as "The Blond Bombshell of Swing." Born Ina Curtis, she had been in vaudeville in the 1920s and in 1926 played the Palace as one of Gus Edwards' Future Stars. She formed her first all-female orchestra in 1935 at the suggestion of agent Johnny Hyde from the William Morris Agency. The orchestra was later disbanded, and from 1940 to 1947, Hutton led an all-male orchestra. She revived the all-female orchestra for television in 1952 and continued to perform with it through the late 1960s. Ina Ray Hutton was featured prominently in two feature films, *Big Broadcast of 1936* (1935) and *Ever Since Venus* (1944), as well as many short subjects. In 1989, Bette Midler announced plans to star in a film biography of the orchestra leader.

The other best known leader of an all-girl orchestra was a man named Phil Spitalny (1889–1970), who came to the United States from his native Ukraine at the age of fifteen. Spitalny had been the conductor of male orchestras when he heard a violinist named Evelyn Kaye perform and conceived the idea of an all-female orchestra. The orchestra came to fame on radio, on *The Hour of Charm*, heard on CBS from 1935 to 1936 and on NBC from 1936 to 1946. It featured Evelyn Kaye as Evelyn and Her Magic Violin, but because of Spitalny's thick Russian accent, he was not permitted to speak. Prior to its radio debut,

Phil Spitalny and His All-Girl Orchestra played the Capitol Theatre, New York, in 1934. Evelyn and Spitalny were married in 1950 and retired in 1955. In 1980, Evelyn donated her "magic violin" to the Smithsonian Institution.

While all-girl orchestras were generally led by women, Phil Spitalny was not the only man with one. In the mid 1930s, Count Berni Vici had a similar combination, and in the fall of 1935, he headed a vaudeville unit playing the Golden Gate Theatre, San Francisco, and the Orpheum Theatre, Los Angeles.

Other female orchestras included the ten-piece Rita Mario Orchestra, which played New York's Fifth Avenue Theatre in April 1918. Writing in *Variety* (May 3, 1918), Sime Silverman described it as "a turn that will grace any bill." He was less enthusiastic about Frankie Cramer and Her Melody Bandits, an eight-piece ensemble, which Silverman (February 9, 1927) thought "might suffice as a novelty in the smaller picture palace presentation houses."

Eve Shirley and Jazz Band achieved success at the Palace in May 1919, when the act was moved from opening to the third spot on the bill. The five women in the band not only performed jazz numbers but also danced and sang. One member of the group even performed a shimmy dance, which *Variety* (May 16, 1919) noted "made the Palace regulars sit up and take notice." In the late 1920s, a large aggregation of female musicians appeared under the name of The Ingenues. They were billed as "The Band Beautiful," but an extant 1928 Vitaphone film short indicates that that claim was something of an exaggeration. In their favor, the members of the orchestra were multitalented, with each playing as many as three instruments; for example, the violinists also performed on the accordion and banjo. The Ingenues were also featured in the 1927 edition of the Ziegfeld *Follies*, accompanying the Brox Sisters in their rendition of "It's Up to the Band," while seated at the keyboards of nineteen white, baby grand pianos.

Aside from the combinations of Ina Ray Hutton and Phil Spitalny, the only other major all-girl orchestra of the 1930s was that led by Babe Eagan, who headlined at the Pantages Theatre, Los Angeles, in January 1934. She claimed to have played not only the United States, but also Britain, France, and Germany, and the Hollywood *Citizen-News* (January 10, 1934) reported, "Every one of her girls is an accomplished soloist and each is an individual entertainer." The first "all-colored," all-girl orchestra was the Harlem Playgirls, which first played vaudeville in 1937.

ALPHONSE

A popular opening act on vaudeville bills in the 1920s and 1930s, Alphonse presented a routine titled "Creations," featuring three attractive young women attired only in skin suits. Alphonse would drape the women in bolts of material which he styled into elegant dresses while keeping up a constant narration, and within five minutes the models were clothed in the latest fashions. From 1926 through 1928, Irene D. Caine (who later became a wardrobe woman and costume designer in the film industry) was one of the models, and she recalls earning a salary of $75 a week, a considerable sum for a showgirl and evidence of Alphonse's popularity and related pay.

Alphonse was the stage name of Alphonse Berg or Berge (the spelling varies), and the performer was the embodiment of a dapper, middle-aged Frenchman with a pencil-thin moustache and elegant afternoon attire. He was featured in the second, 1943, edition of Ken Murray's *Blackouts*, and was also in the cast when the show opened at New York's Ziegfeld Theatre on September 6, 1949. Late in his career, as part of a nightclub act, Ed Wynn performed a routine similar to that of Alphonse. It is also worth contemplating if Charlie Chaplin was paying tribute to Alphonse with a sequence in *A Woman of Paris* (1923), in which a model (played by Bess Flowers) stands on a pedestal clothed in a bolt of fabric, which is slowly removed, leaving her nude. The scene is very much Alphonse's "Creation" sketch in reverse.

AMATEUR NIGHTS

The cheapest form of vaudeville entertainment, amateur nights were first conceived by Henry Clay Miner and introduced at his London and Bowery Theatres in the 1880s. While in later years amateur acts worked without payment, it would appear that initially Miner did pay these performers.

ANIMAL ACTS

Almost always placed as the opening item on vaudeville bills, animal acts held little appeal for audiences. They were equally unpopular with their fellow performers, in that others on the bill had to contend with the smell from the animals who were housed in the dressing rooms and with the smell from the animals' food, which also had to be prepared in the theatres.

There was virtually no animal that could not be trained to appear on the vaudeville stage, although some acts from the turn of the century do not appear to have been able to make the transition from carnivals to theatres. Vaudeville audiences were not given the opportunity to view Muslinger's Troupe of Performing Pigs and Sheep or Prof. L. Sunlin with King Bill, "the only trained bull in the world."

Big cat acts were not restricted to circuses, and among those appearing on the vaudeville stage were Marck's Lions, Bert Nelson and His Lioness, Princess Pat, Arnaldo's Leopard and Panthers, Furtell's Jungle Lions, Richard Herman's Jungle Kings, Dolores Vallecita's Leopards, and Captain Proske's Tigers. The best known of such acts was Adgie and Her Lions, which dates back to the beginning of the twentieth century. Madame Adgie would not only work with her lions, but also perform a Spanish dance, sing "La Paloma," and attempt Delsarte posing surrounded by the animals. "Once seen her marvelous work is never forgotten," commented *The Billboard* (November 5, 1904). At one point, Madame Adgie decided to place mirrors around the cage, only to have to remove them quickly when the lions entered, saw themselves reflected, and went beserk.

Equestrian acts included May Wirth and Family, Professor Buckley's Curriculum, Mme Etoile's Society Horses, the Davenports, Ella Bradna and Fred Derrick, the Duttons, the Five Lloyds, the George St. Leon Troupe, and Bostock's Riding School, featuring Lillian St. Leon. In the 1890s, Guy Leon presented two singing donkeys named Jack and Jill, and a little later came Rossi's Musical Horse, who laughed. In the 1920s, The Sheik was a white horse that specialized in adopting various poses; the act was reviewed in *Variety* on August 30, 1923.

Monkey acts included Wormwood's Monkeys, Alleina's Monkeys, Consul the Great, Galleti's Monkeys, Gillette's Baboons and Monkeys, Jean Clairemont's Circus Monkeys, La Bella Polla, and McCart's Monkeys. The acts were very similar, with the animals performing human-like activities such as cycling, saying their prayers, or performing acrobatics. Corresponding tricks were expected of the bears comprising acts such as Batty's Bears, Spessardy's Bears, Pallenburg's Bears, and Alber's Ten Polar Bears.

One of the most successful monkey acts was Richard the Great, trained by Harry De Rosa, who was billed as "The Monkey Who Made a Man of Himself." In his publicity, it was announced, "Darwin said that he was a Monkey before he was a Man. Richard the Great says he is a Man, no matter what Darwin was." The monkey made his New York debut at the Orpheum on September 10, 1914, and filled every one of the theatre's 2,500 seats twice a day.

Trained birds walked tightropes and performed various tricks in acts such as Swain's Cockatoos, Merle's Cockatoos, Camilla's Pigeons, Conrad's Pigeons, and what Joe Laurie, Jr. claimed was "the best bird act of them all," Olympia DesVall's. In the mid teens, Kurtis' Educated Roosters was billed as "The Only Complete Rooster Act in Vaudeville." It was, apparently, a copy of an earlier act, Torcat's and Flora D'Aliza's Educated Roosters.

Among the more unusual animal acts to be found on the vaudeville stage were Jeff (a boxing kangaroo) and Rhinelander's Pigs. The latter act had the pigs refusing to perform, at which point the trainer would take out a butcher's knife and begin to sharpen it. The pigs immediately resumed the routine. It was generally the animals who suffered humiliation on the vaudeville stage, but occasionally the situation was reversed, as in The Butting Ram, featuring five goats and two pigs, an act that would conclude with the goats butting the trainer around the stage.

The most eccentric animal act did not feature animals at all, but consisted of an elderly lady named Mrs. E. Hathaway Turnbull, who spent twenty-three minutes on the stage of the Palace in the summer of 1921 discussing "Our Animals and How They Help Us." *Variety* (August 1, 1921) considered her "as pulsating as a rainy afternoon in Kenosha." The only competitor in Mrs. Turnbull's class was a monkey impersonator named Nathal, active in the late 1920s, who would clamber over the backs of seats and along the balcony railings of vaudeville houses.

See also DOG ACTS, FINK'S MULES, POODLES HANNEFORD, MAR-

CELLE AND SEA LION, POWER'S DANCING ELEPHANTS, SWAYNE'S
RATS AND CATS.
BIBLIOGRAPHY
Laurie, Joe, Jr. "Animal Acts." In *Vaudeville: From the Honky-Tonks to the Palace*.
    New York: Henry Holt, 1953, pp. 155–70.

DAVE APOLLON (Kiev, Russia, 1898—Las Vegas, May 30, 1972)
    A vaudevillian who transformed mandolin playing into an art form, Dave
Apollon claimed to have formed his own orchestra in his native Russia at the
age of fourteen. He came to the United States in 1921 and was an immediate
success on the vaudeville circuit. With his Filipino Orchestra, Apollon appeared
on the last two-a-day program at the Palace Theatre on May 7, 1932, and the
last vaudeville presentation at New York's State Theatre on December 23, 1947.
At the time of his death, he was in his eighth year appearing with his mandolin
band in the lounge of the Desert Inn, Las Vegas.

ROSCOE ATES (Grange, Mi., January 20, 1896—Los Angeles, March 1,
1962)
    A comedian of the low order, Roscoe Ates possessed a pliable face and pop
eyes, and specialized in portraying a comic, stuttering character in vaudeville.
As a child, he had stammered but broke himself of the habit at the age of
eighteen. As a teenager, Ates studied the violin, and in 1914, he began playing
violin accompaniment to silent films at the Cosy Theatre in Chickasha, Oklahoma. From there, he entered vaudeville, where he remained until embarking
on a film career in 1929. Active on screen through 1961, Ates appeared in two
landmark productions—*Cimarron* (1931) and *Gone with the Wind* (1939)—and
was also a cowboy sidekick to Eddie Dean in a series of Westerns produced
between 1946 and 1948. His marital problems with three wives resulted in many
courtroom appearances and resultant publicity through the years.
BIBLIOGRAPHY
Rothel, David. "Roscoe Ates." In *Those Great Cowboy Sidekicks*. Metuchen, N.J.:
    Scarecrow Press, 1984, pp. 96–101.

AUNT JEMIMA (Wilkes Barre, Pa., 1898—Brooklyn, N.Y., January 3, 1950)
    Equally as famous as the name on a brand of pancake syrup was a vaudevillian
named Aunt Jemima, a plump and jovial singer who was, in reality, a woman
of Italian descent named Tess Gardella, performing in blackface. Following the
death of her miner father, Gardella came to New York and entered show business
in 1918, singing at political rallies, dances, and nightclubs. It was Lew Leslie
of *Blackbirds* fame who changed her name to Aunt Jemima and brought her to
vaudeville.
    As a stage attraction at New York's Bedford Theatre, appearing before the
movie, she proved so popular in February 1920 that fifteen minutes into the film

(*The Clouds Roll By* with Douglas Fairbanks), the lights had to be brought up so she could reappear to take another bow and ask the audience to watch the feature because had no further songs in her repertoire. Aunt Jemima made her Palace debut in 1922; she was not the headliner, but "Ibee" in *Variety* (October 30, 1922) announced she had "a place in big-time vaudeville." By 1924, "the cheery purveyor of pop songs" (as *Variety* dubbed her) was singing "It Had to Be You" and "The Charleston" and was proclaimed the season's biggest hit at the Hippodrome.

Tess Gardella had appeared in the 1921 edition of George White's *Scandals*, but her best known, non-vaudeville appearance was as Queenie in the original Broadway production of *Show Boat*, which opened at the Ziegfeld Theatre on December 27, 1927. She sang "Hey, Feller!," "C'mon Folks," and "Can't Help Lovin' Dat Man." She left the show in March 1930 and the following month was headlining at the Palace. *The Billboard* (April 12, 1930) commented, "She has pipes that are golden, a knack of selling them, and a marvelous sense of humor. A great act anywhere."

In 1949, Tess Gardella played the Palace again as Aunt Jemima. It was her last public performance. As a blackface act, Aunt Jemima was unique and one of the longest running female acts of its type in the history of vaudeville. Her natural conviviality overwhelmed audiences, and as *The Billboard* (March 21, 1931) noted, she was the personification of "the colored mammy." In fact, the secret of her success lay in her being the black mammy of the Ethel Waters type in *A Member of the Wedding*, in whose arms everyone wished to be held and loved. Aunt Jemima represented warmth and joy, and the fact that she was really white doubtless helped to win over those with racial antagonisms.

B _____

BELLE BAKER (New York, December 25, 1893—Los Angeles, April 28, 1957)

Belle Baker was one of vaudeville's great singing stars, remembered for the manner in which she would put over a song with a sob in her voice, but to describe her merely as a masterful torch singer is tantamount to labeling Fanny Brice a singer of comedy numbers. Baker was equally adept at handling both the comic and the melancholic, and as proof of this one need look no further than three songs she introduced, all written by Irving Berlin, the composer with whom she was most associated. In 1913, at her debut at the Palace, Baker sang Berlin's comic number "Cohen Owes Me Ninety-Seven Dollars," the death bed lament of Old Man Rosenthal to his son. Two very different Berlin songs with which she will always be associated are the poignant "What'll I Do?" and the carefree "Blue Skies," which she introduced in the 1926 Ziegfeld show *Betsy.*

"She doesn't croon, nor does she coon shout," wrote *Variety* (November 10, 1931). "She sobs her lyrics with a cry in her voice that's catching." And never was this more evident than in Baker's rendition of the Hebrew chant "Eli, Eli," in which she sang in Yiddish of the troubles and sorrows of the Jewish people. Her recordings run the gamut from "Poor Little Butterfly Is No Fly Gal Now" (1919) and "I've Got the Yes! We Have No Bananas Blues" (1923) to "My Yiddishe Momma" (1925) and "I Cried for You" (1923). One of her lesser known but most pleasant recordings is "I'm Walking with the Moonbeams (Talking to the Stars)" from 1930. The words may be unfamiliar, but Belle Baker's delivery is such that one soon begins to sing along. It was this quality that an anonymous critic in *The New York Dramatic Mirror* (May 15, 1920) noted:

Everybody knows Belle Baker and the sort of songs she sings. She has been one of the most popular of all the singers in the realm of vaudeville for several years, and has been responsible for the popularity of more songs than you can shake a stick at. One of the best numbers which she is using now in her tour of the B. F. Keith Theatres is Stark and Cowan's ballad success, "Everybody's Buddy." It is admirably suited to Miss Baker's methods, and when she sings it everybody leaves the theater whistling it.

Belle Baker was not particularly attractive. She was short and plump, with dark hair and dark features. It was her voice and her mannerisms that made her great, an artful blend of intimacy and clowning, with the hint of her Jewish background never far below the surface. "Belle Baker has a direct appeal," wrote Frederick James Smith in *The New York Dramatic Mirror* (March 17, 1915). "There's a humanness in her ragging—a personality that reaches over with a punch and holds." After her death, Eddie Cantor wrote of Baker: "Her talent was enormous. She was Dinah Shore, Patti Page, Peggy Lee, Judy Garland, all rolled into one. Her voice filled the theatre and her words—every one of them—reached you in the very last row of the gallery. All this, mind you, without the aid of a microphone. She could make you laugh, she could make you cry. She could make you a fan for life."

A product of New York's Lower East Side Jewish ghetto, Belle Baker was born Bella Becker, the daughter of penniless Russian immigrants. After a little schooling and working in sweatshops, the child began to sing at the age of eleven at the Cannon Street Music Hall, where she was heard by Jacob Adler, one of the greatest names in the New York Jewish theatre, and offered a position with his company at the Grand Theatre. Producer and promoter Lew Leslie was the next person in Baker's life. He taught her how to put over a number and began booking her into small theatres in the New York area; eventually Belle Baker made her vaudeville debut at the age of fifteen in Scranton, Pennsylvania. A year later, Baker and Leslie were married, they divorced in 1918.

Belle Baker made her major vaudeville debut at Hammerstein's Victoria Theatre in 1911 and was soundly criticized for the quality of her songs, her dress, and her material. One critic, C. F. Zittell, was particularly scathing, but a few weeks later he telephoned Baker and offered to help her improve the act. Recalling that time in the March 2, 1923, issue of *Zitt's*, the publisher-critic wrote, "I selected songs for the young lady, personally staged her songs, and then obtained an opening for her at the Manhattan Opera House." Within two years, Belle Baker was a vaudeville headliner.

In the teens, Belle Baker developed a close friendship with Irving Berlin, and the composer was to write many songs for her, including "My Wife's Gone to the Country," "Wake Up, America," "Always," and "Prohibish." Explaining her choice of song material, Baker wrote in *Variety* (December 26, 1919):

If I think a number has possibilities, I try it. It would be out of reason to believe I could sing all the songs I hear. But I try to send them all away with a smile for the writer of a bad song today may write a good song tomorrow. The life of any of my songs depends upon the audience. I sing a song as long as I believe the audience wishes to hear it. Often I have discarded a number upon this impression, to later find I am singing it again, by request. Song writers are among the greatest benefactors in the world. They lyrically tell the public in seriousness or laughter those things the public likes to hear, when accompanied by a pretty melody that sends the blues out of your system. Or a ballad hits you just right. The writers give their all for the public, to make them laugh or forget.

By November 1917, it was reported that Belle Baker had outdrawn all "name" headliners in gross receipts in the New York area B. F. Keith theatres. Two years later, the singer married for a second time—Maurice Abrahams, a composer responsible for such hits as "He'd Have to Get Under," "Hitchy Koo," "Ragtime Cowboy Joe," and "America, I Love You." In 1920, Baker gave birth to a son, Herbert, who was to become a prominent Hollywood scriptwriter, and to whom Baker dedicated a number of songs, notably "Ten Little Fingers, Ten Little Toes." In 1924, Baker wrote her first song (with Grace Deagon), the mildly popular "Pretending." Baker left vaudeville briefly to star in Florenz Ziegfeld's production of *Betsy*, which opened at the New Amsterdam Theatre on December 27, 1926, but ran for a mere thirty-nine performances. She returned to vaudeville in April 1927, headlining at the Orpheum, Los Angeles, and the following year starred twice at the Palace, in February and November. In 1929, the singer made her feature-film debut in the Columbia production of *The Song of Love*; she appeared in one other American feature film, *Atlantic City* (1944).

Maurice Abrahams died in New York on April 13, 1931. On September 21, 1937, Baker married Elias H. Sugarman, editor of *The Billboard*, but they were divorced on November 28, 1941. Abrahams's death affected his wife greatly, and for over a year she restricted her performing to radio, before returning to vaudeville in the summer of 1932, when she introduced one of her biggest hits, "All of Me." In 1934, Baker, along with Beatrice Lillie, topped the bill at the London Palladium and also costarred in a British feature film, *Charing Cross Road*, released the following year. On May 22, 1936, she made her American nightclub debut at New York's Versailles Club, after having earlier played the Kit Kat and the Café de Paris in London.

In the 1940s, Belle Baker's stage appearances dwindled, and the performer made her last important public appearance at the Palace in May 1950. In 1955, she was honored on Ralph Edwards's *This Is Your Life*.

BIBLIOGRAPHY
Baker, Belle. "Singing Popular Songs." *Variety*, December 26, 1919, p. 20.

JOSEPHINE BAKER (St. Louis, June 3, 1906—Paris, April 12, 1975)
Josephine Baker was an American Negress with a naturalistic style of dancing and a unique personality. She achieved her greatest success in Paris, becoming a legend in her own lifetime. Born Frida McDonald, Baker was forced to leave school at the age of eight in order to help support her mother, brother, and two sisters. While living with her grandmother in Philadelphia at the age of fifteen or sixteen, she joined a traveling vaudeville troupe. In 1923, she was in the chorus of *Shuffle Along* in New York, and, in hindsight, Langston Hughes wrote of her appearance, in the *New York Post* (March 27, 1964), "There was something about her rhythm, her warmth, her smile, and her impudent grace that made her standout." That same quality was visible the following year when

Baker appeared in *Chocolate Dandies*; ''some quiet inexplicable attraction drew the eyes of the audience to a little girl with flaming eyes, a body that was the epitome of dance and a strange, unbeautiful but fascinating trick of pushing her head forward on her little neck as some young animal might have done when he scented food ahead,'' wrote an anonymous writer in *Theatre Arts*.

Following an engagement at the Plantation Club, Josephine Baker decided to leave New York for Paris, where she appeared in *La Revue Nègre*, opening at the Théâtre des Champs-Elysées in October 1925. From there, she went to the Folies Bergère, creating a sensation dancing nude except for a skirt made of bananas. In the 1930s, Baker consolidated her reputation as an international star. She returned to the United States to headline with Fanny Brice in the 1936 edition of the *Ziegfeld Follies*. George Balanchine choreographed her numbers, which were notable for the blend of black and white chorus boys by whom she was surrounded. The New York press was somewhat negative, and Baker did not stay long with the show. Back in France (where she became a citizen in 1937), Baker starred in her two most important films, *ZouZou* (1934) and *Princess Tam-Tam* (1935).

Josephine Baker spent the war years in France and North Africa, entertaining troops and working for the Resistance movement. She purchased an estate in southwest France called Les Milandes, and there, with her last husband Jo Bouillon, she housed adopted children from all over the world, whom she described as her ''rainbow family.'' She returned to the United States in 1951, and the trip was a mix of success and humiliation. In Los Angeles, for the week ending July 10, 1951, she set the postwar record for any vaudeville attraction in the city, grossing $40,900 at the Hill Street Theatre. In New York, she was refused service at the Stork Club because of the color of her skin. She responded to this insult the following year during a tour of Argentina by telling a reporter, ''The United States is not a free country. . . . They treat Negroes as though they were dogs.'' It was a valid comment, but one that resulted in harassment from immigration officials when next she came to the United States in 1955.

In 1956, Baker announced her retirement from the stage of the Olympia Music Hall in Paris, but she resumed her career at the same theatre in 1961. Three years later, she faced bankruptcy, and in 1969 she was evicted from Les Milandes. Jospehine Baker returned in triumph to her native country in 1973, appearing at Carnegie Hall; she had last visited the United States ten years earlier, joining the Rev. Martin Luther King, Jr. in his march for civil rights in Washington, D.C. On March 25, 1975, Baker returned to the Paris stage, appearing in the lead in her own life story at the Bobino Music Hall. On April 8, 1975, she celebrated her fiftieth anniversary in show business with a party attended by friends, including Princess Grace of Monaco, Sophia Loren, and Jeanne Moreau. Two days later, she was found unconscious at her Paris home, the victim of a stroke and a severe heart condition. She died two days later without regaining consciousness.

Josephine Baker's theme song, ''J'ai Deux Amours,'' was indicative of her love for both Paris and her homeland. However, from the 1920s onward, it was very obvious that only the former really appreciated her unique talent.

BIBLIOGRAPHY
Baker, Josephine, and Jo Bouillon. *Jospehine*. New York: Harper & Row, 1977.
Guild, Leo. *Josephine Baker*. Los Angeles: Holloway House, 1976.
Hammond, Bryan, and Patrick O'Connor. *Josephine Baker*. Boston: Little, Brown, 1988.
Haney, Lynn. *Naked at the Feast: A Biography of Josephine Baker*. New York: Dodd, Mead, 1981.
"Josephine Baker." *Theatre Arts* 26, no. 8 (August 1942), p. 502.
"Josephine Baker." *Current Biography*, July 1964, pp. 19–22.
Kisselgoff, Anna. "Josephine Baker: Dancing through the Jazz Age." *The New York Times*, March 29, 1987, pp. H14, 38.
Rose, Phyllis. *Jazz Cleopatra: Josephine Baker in Her Time*. New York: Doubleday, 1989.
Schroeder, Alan. *Josephine Baker*. New York: Chelsea House, 1991.

PHIL BAKER (Philadelphia, August 24, 1896—Copenhagen, December 1, 1963)

Despite many years in vaudeville, Phil Baker is chiefly known as the host of the CBS radio program *Take It or Leave It*, on which he asked the $64 question from 1941 to 1947. He began his vaudeville career while still a teenager, playing piano accompaniment to a violinist named Ed Janis. At the age of nineteen, Baker broke up with Janis and teamed in a violinist-accordionist act with Ben Bernie, which began as a serious performance and gradually developed into a comedy routine. Following the First World War, Baker built up a solo act, in which he sang, told jokes, and played the accordion, and which featured a heckler in the audience named "Jojo."

Phil Baker was also featured in revues—*Music Box Revue* (1923), *Artists and Models* (1925), and *A Night in Spain* (1927)—and was a frequent headliner at the Palace during 1930 and 1931. He entered radio in 1933 as *The Armour Jester*, sponsored by Armour Packing on the Blue Network, and between 1935 and 1939 had his own program, *The Phil Baker Show*, on CBS. He was also seen occasionally in films, including *The Gang's All Here* (1943) and *Take It or Leave It* (1944).

BIBLIOGRAPHY
Gaver, Jack, and Dave Stanley. "Phil Baker." In *There's Laughter in the Air!* New York: Greenberg, 1945, pp. 231–40.
"Phil Baker." *Current Biography*, November 1946, pp. 24–26.

ERNEST R. BALL (Cleveland, July 21, 1878—Santa Ana, Ca., May 3, 1927)

Ernest R. Ball composed many sentimental ballads, often with Irish themes and often in collaboration with and for singer Chauncey Olcott. Among Ball's best known songs are "Love Me and the World Is Mine," "Mother Machree," "A Little Bit of Heaven," "Let the Rest of the World Go By," "When Irish Eyes Are Smiling," and "Will You Love Me in December as You Do in May?"

He was one of the 1914 charter members of ASCAP (the American Society of Composers, Authors, and Publishers).

A frequent entertainer on the vaudeville stage in the teens and 1920s, one of Ball's earliest appearances was at Hammerstein's Theatre, New York, in May 1911. He sang some of his own songs, accompanying himself on the piano, and *Variety* (May 6, 1911) commented, "As a regular vaudeville act Ernest Ball will do nicely if not placed in too heavy running." Ball worked in vaudeville initially with Maude Lambert and later, in 1922, with George MacFarlane. He appeared at the Palace in 1923 and 1926 and died in his dressing room at the Yost Theatre, Santa Ana, while touring with his act "Ernie Ball and His Gang," the gang being a male octet. In 1944, 20th Century–Fox filmed Ball's life story under the title *Irish Eyes Are Smiling*, with Dick Haymes in the role of the composer.

"BANANA"

A burlesque comedian was always referred to as a "banana," with the lead comedian being the top banana, perhaps because the fruit at the top of the stalk is always the ripest and most desirable. According to Don Wilmeth in *The Language of Popular Entertainment*, the use of the word "banana" may derive from the banana-shaped bladder much in use in burlesque for hitting the comedian over the head. The term "top banana" entered common usage as a result of the 1951 Broadway production of that name, starring Phil Silvers.

BARBETTE (Round Rock, Tx., December 9, 1904—Austin, Tx., August 5, 1973)

Barbette was unique in the art of female impersonation in that he was a superb trapeze artist, thrilling American vaudeville audiences in the teens and delighting Parisian society in the 1920s. He performed aerial acrobatics, often coupled with a slack wire walking routine, and audiences never ceased to be amazed when he removed his wig after taking three or four bows. "It is a real shock as no one would for a moment think he is a man while the act is in progress," reported *The New York Dramatic Mirror* (September 4, 1919).

Born Vander Clyde, Barbette learned his craft in his mother's backyard. After his first visit to a circus in Austin, Barbette was determined to be a performer. Upon graduation from high school at the age of fourteen, he answered an advertisement in *The Billboard* placed by one of the Alfaretta Sisters, who were billed as "World Famous Aerial Queens." One of the sisters had died and the other was looking for a partner. She explained to the young Clyde that audiences were far more impressed by female, rather than male, trapeze artists, and suggested he dress as a girl. After a stint with Alfaretta and later with Erford's Whirling Sensation, Barbette developed a single act, with which it appears he made his New York debut at the Harlem Opera House in 1919. "Barbette is a distinct novelty. She is not a bad looking girl at all," wrote *The New York Dramatic Mirror*. "The first thing she does is a good slack wire walking routine.

Then she performs on rings and lastly on a trapeze. She works hard and fast and her stunts are quite thrilling. She is liked so well, she is called out to make many bows. About the third bow she pulls off her wig and 'she' surprises everyone by being a man.'' At this point, Barbette was just the opening act on the bill, but he quickly became a headliner.

In 1923, Barbette went to Paris, to appear at the Casino de Paris. He was not the star attraction on the bill—that was actor Sessue Hayakawa—but he was the hit of the evening, appearing in a white gown covered with ostrich feathers and ending his act with a *chute d'ange* from the trapeze to the white-carpeted floor of the stage. When he pulled off his wig to show his nearly bald head and took the stance of a professional wrestler, the audience went wild with surprise and delight. In the years to come, Barbette was to be one of France's most popular cabaret stars. He was photographed by Man Ray, and his friend Jean Cocteau wrote of him, ''He walked the tightrope high above the audience without falling, above incongruity, death, bad taste, indecency, imagination. . . . Ten unforgetable minutes. A theatrical masterpiece. An angel, a flower, a bird.'' In 1930, Cocteau had Barbette appear in drag in the writer's film *Blood of a Poet*. Alfred Hitchcock's film *Murder* from the same year features a homosexual female impersonator trapeze artist as the murderer, and there can be little doubt that the character is based on Barbette, even to his stage costume, a parody of that worn by the artist.

While Barbette was being feted by European audiences, he remained, in the words of Milton Berle, ''a hell of a nice guy.'' He headlined at the Palace in 1927, first seen at the head of a grand staircase wearing a long ostrich feather train, which he discarded before beginning his act. *Variety* (February 9, 1927) wrote, ''As an impersonator, Barbette will fool anybody, as an aerial artist, he is superb. A tendency to overaccentuate the feminine gestures in spots should be watched.'' Barbette was one of the featured players in *Billy Rose's Jumbo* (1935). As Jimmy Durante sang of beautiful women, Barbette performed his aerial acrobatics. Upon returning to the ground, he removed his wig at the close of Durante's song, leading the comedian to cry, ''Betrayed!''

While appearing at Loew's State, New York, in 1938, Barbette caught pneumonia, and the long illness that followed put an end to his performing. He continued to train new performers, served as an aerial consultant for the stage show *Disney on Parade*, and was aerial choreographer for *The Big Circus* (1959). He also worked with a number of circuses and was the only female impersonator to be the subject of a *New Yorker* profile (although he was recognized in the article more as Jean Cocteau's inspiration than as a personality in his own right).

At the end of his life, Barbette returned to his home state of Texas, not exactly noted for its liberal attitude toward female impersonators, and to the city of Austin, which Barbette found offensive. When a waitress in a coffee shop there delivered his coffee before Barbette had finished his entree, he is supposed to have shuddered and remarked, ''I've never been able to readjust to crudity.''

BIBLIOGRAPHY

Ray, Man, and Jean Cocteau. *Barbette*. Berlin: Borderline, 1988.

Ray, Man, Jean Cocteau, and Francis Steegmuller. *Le Barbette*. Paris: Jacques Damase, 1980.

Steegmuller, Francis. "Onward and Upward with the Arts: An Angel, a Flower, a Bird." *The New Yorker* no. 32 (September 27, 1969), pp. 130–43.

WILKIE BARD (Manchester, England, March 19, 1870—London, March 5, 1944)

Wilkie Bard was an eccentric British music hall comedian who appeared with a bald forehead and a large black spot painted over each eyebrow. He made his first professional appearance in 1895, singing the cockney song "Never 'ave a Lodger for a Pal," and later developed a series of comic characterizations, the best of which was the woman who proclaimed "I Want to Sing in Opera." Bard first came to the United States in 1913, earning a reported $4,000 a week to appear at Hammerstein's Victoria Theatre. He returned in 1919 to play the Palace but was a major "flop" at the Monday matinee. Disheartened, he planned to cancel the engagement and return to England, but *Variety*'s Sime Silverman persuaded him to change his routine to make it more accessible to American audiences, and the comedian was ultimately successful. Wilkie made a second appearance at the Palace in 1923, and *Variety*'s "Con" reported, "He's a natural anywhere for American audiences." Following the Palace appearance, the comedian toured in vaudeville but did not return to the United States again, although he continued to perform in his native England almost until his death.

ETHEL BARRYMORE (Philadelphia, August 15, 1879—Beverly Hills, Ca., June 18, 1959)

America's best known theatrical family, the Barrymores, were no strangers to vaudeville. Maurice, the father of Ethel, John, and Lionel, made his vaudeville debut in 1897 in a one-act version of the play *A Man of the World* by Augustus Thomas. John and Lionel made an occasional foray onto the vaudeville stage, but it was Ethel Barrymore who can truly be classified as a vaudeville headliner. She made her debut at the Palace the week of April 28, 1913, in the one-act play *Civilization* by Richard Harding Davis and was back again at the Palace in August of the next year.

The one-act play with which Ethel Barrymore is most associated on the vaudeville stage is *The Twelve Pound Look* by J. M. Barrie, in which she first appeared as curtain-raiser to *Alice Sit-by-the-Fire* at New York's Empire Theatre on February 13, 1911. She returned to the Empire with *The Twelve Pound Look* in May 1917, presenting it as part of a program of one-act plays. Having witnessed Sarah Bernhardt's success in vaudeville, Ethel Barrymore decided to present *The Twelve Pound Look* on the Orpheum circuit, and Martin Beck paid her a weekly salary of $3,000. In case American vaudeville audiences were not aware of the value of twelve pounds, the subtitle *The $60 Look* was added to the play's title.

Ethel Barrymore brought *The Twelve Pound Look* to the Palace in June 1921 and September and December 1926. As she recalled in her autobiography, "Anytime I didn't have a play that I could bear to do I went back to vaudeville with *The Twelve Pound Look*, and every time I went it was good for me. Those exacting audiences loved the play, and I played it for years and years."

BIBLIOGRAPHY

Barrymore, Ethel. *Memories: An Autobiography*. New York: Harper & Brothers, 1955.

BARTHOLDI INN

The last major theatrical boarding house in New York was the Bartholdi Inn, which was opened in 1899 by Mme Bartholdi on two upper floors of the building at 1546 Broadway, the ground floor of which was occupied by Child's Restaurant. When Bartholdi became ill, the establishment was taken over by her daughter Polly, and by 1906, it had expanded to one hundred rooms on the upper floors of three buildings at West 45th Street and Broadway. Among the Bartholdi Inn's tenants were Pearl White, D. W. Griffith, Mack Sennett, Charlie Chaplin, Eva Tanguay, Nat Wills, and the chorus girls from the Ziegfeld *Follies*. It was here also that the first motion picture fraternal organization, the Screen Club, was founded on Labor Day 1912.

The establishment closed on February 1, 1920, shortly before the buildings which it occupied were demolished to make way for the new State Theatre. The inn's furnishings were auctioned off on February 4, 1920. At its passing, *Variety* commented, "When the Bartholdi Inn passes into oblivion there will never be another like it. The day of the intimate theatrical boarding house in New York is gone forever, the numerous hotels in the theatrical district supplying everything the Inn could supply perhaps better—but without the spirit of comradeship."

BIBLIOGRAPHY

"Bartholdi Inn Passes Out Feb 1; Last Theatrical Room House." *Variety*, January 31, 1920, p. 9.

JAMES BARTON (Gloucester, N.J., November 1, 1890—Mineola, N.Y., February 19, 1962)

Writing in *Shadowland* (August 1923), Kenneth Macgowan called James Barton "the greatest comic dancer in twenty-five years and two hemispheres, and a rollicking comedian even in blackface." To *Variety*'s Robert J. Landry, "he was perhaps the most singularly talented of all headliners—sang as sensationally as Jolson, danced like Bill Robinson and was a standup comedian like Will Fyffe or whoever else one might name." Barton was all things to vaudeville, and then, at the height of his fame, he embarked on a second career as a legitimate stage actor and won a new set of honors.

James Barton was born into a theatrical family. His mother was an actress, in whose arms he made his first stage appearance at the age of two in *The Silver King*. His father, James, was a comedian and song-and-dance man who worked with the West and Primrose Minstrels. His grandfather was a showman who at one time ran a female baseball club called Barton's Blue Bloomer Girls, and his Uncle Ed was a singer and dancer in vaudeville, one half of the team of Barton and Van Lear. James Barton spoke his first lines on stage—in Louisville, Kentucky—when he was four and from then on worked steadily in small-time vaudeville, burlesque, and stock.

As a monologist, his most famous story concerned a man who could get free drinks in saloons by recounting the story of how he was bitten by a mad dog. He first told the tale in Alexandria, Virginia, in 1909, and it became a renowned part of his act. The character in the monologue was based on Barton's maternal grandfather, and once when the comedian was heckled at the Palace by a woman in the audience who claimed the story libeled the Irish, Barton stepped out of character and said, "Madam, I am doing my grandfather right now."

James Barton made his first Broadway appearance in *The Passing Show of 1919*, which opened at the Winter Garden Theatre on October 23, 1919. It made him a star, and was followed by roles in *The Last Waltz* (1921), *The Rose of Stamboul* (1922), *Dew Drop Inn* (1923), *The Passing Show of 1924*, and *No Foolin'* (1926). Barton was virtually a regular at the Palace from 1928 to 1932; he headlined there in March, April, July, and August 1928; February 1929; May and October 1931; and April 1932. And during that period he also found time to star in *Artists and Models* (1930) and *Sweet and Low* (1930).

The entertainer's career changed course in 1934, when he succeeded Henry Hull as Jeeter Lester in *Tobacco Road* and played the part for 1,899 performances from 1934 to 1939. An even greater success was the role of the reformed alcoholic Theodore Hickman in Eugene O'Neill's *The Iceman Cometh*, in which Barton opened at the Martin Beck Theatre on October 9, 1946. His final stage triumph was as Bert Rumson in *Paint Your Wagon*, which opened in November 1951. James Barton also enjoyed a spasmodic film career, involving roles in seventeen feature films between 1923 and 1961, of which the most important are *Lifeboat* (1944), *The Time of Your Life* (1948), and *The Misfits* (1961).

Outside of the theatre, James Barton's principal enthusiasm was baseball. At his home on Long Island, he had a baseball park that could seat seven thousand fans and his own team, the adult, hardball Night Hawks of the New York Metropolitan Baseball Association. At one time, in the 1940s, he also owned Jim Barton's Star of Tobacco Road Stadium and Cantina in Queens, New York. After each performance of *The Iceman Cometh*, he and his wife would take the subway to the bar, where they remained until three A.M. Barton's eccentricities were as varied as his career in show business.

BIBLIOGRAPHY

Chapman, John. "Song, Dance and Iceman." *Esquire*, June 1947, pp. 64, 149–51.
Gehman, Richard. "James Barton." *Theatre Arts* 36, no. 2 (February 1952), pp. 28–29, 76.
Kennedy, John B. "The Bouncing Barton." *Collier's* 82, no. 6 (August 11, 1928), pp. 19, 47–48.

PEG LEG BATES (Fountain Inn, S.C., 1907—)

The miracle of Peg Leg Bates was not only that he was one of the greatest rhythm tap dancers but also that he performed with only one leg, the peg leg on the other providing him with his stage name. The son of a sharecropper, Clayton Bates lost his leg as a result of an accident in the factory where he was working at the age of eleven. The left leg was amputated at the knee on his mother's kitchen table. Within eighteen months of the accident, Bates had learned both to walk and dance on a peg leg, and soon began performing in touring all-black shows.

In the late 1920s and the 1930s, Peg Leg Bates was a popular entertainer in New York night spots, including the Cotton Club and Connie's Inn, and headlined at the Palace in November 1929. He executed extraordinarily athletic dance routines, and with the peg leg as a base would appear almost to be flying through the air. The peg leg was not a handicap but a prop, with different colored peg legs being used to match the dancer's stage attire. Peg Leg Bates made occasional film and television appearances; he was first seen on *The Ed Sullivan Show* in 1950 and last performed there ten years later.

While performing at one of the Jewish resorts in the Catskill Mountains, Peg Leg Bates realized that such vacation centers were not open to black Americans, and in 1951 he opened the first such establishment catering exclusively to the black community, Peg Leg Bates Country Club at Kerhonkson. When Bates's wife, Alice, died in 1987, he leased the resort to others. By that time, attendance was down, in large part because integration meant that blacks were free to vacation at any hotel or resort.

Peg Leg Bates was not the only "monopede" dancer in vaudeville. Ed Ernie and Emil Honegger worked as a team, and according to Joe Laurie, Jr., "one had the right leg off and the other the left, and they each wore the same size shoe, so they would buy one pair of shoes."

BIBLIOGRAPHY

Frank, Rusty. "Peg Leg Bates." In *Tap!: The Greatest Tap Dance Stars and Their Stories, 1900–1955*. New York: William Morrow, 1990, pp. 46–51.

NORA BAYES (Milwaukee, 1880—Brooklyn, N.Y., March 19, 1928)

Critic Burns Mantle described her simply as "a singer of popular songs," while Douglas Gilbert wrote in *American Vaudeville*, "Nora Bayes was the American [Yvette] Guilbert, mistress of effortless talent in gesture, poise, delivery, and facial work. No-one could outrival her in dramatizing a song. She was entrancing, exasperating, generous, inconsiderate—a split personality; a fascinating figure." Nora Bayes was also one of the biggest names in vaudeville, on a par with Elsie Janis and Eva Tanguay. With a voice that on phonograph recordings sounds far from memorable, she introduced such standards as "Shine on Harvest Moon," "Down Where the Wurtzburger Flows," and "Has Anyone Here Seen Kelly?"

She was born Eleanor or Leonora Goldberg in Milwaukee, although some sources claim her birthplace to be either Chicago or Los Angeles. Nora Bayes's first stage appearance was probably at the Chicago Opera House in 1899, and by 1907 she was appearing successfully at New York's Fifth Avenue Theatre. The following year, Bayes married Jack Norworth, a former blackface comedian, and the couple worked together until their divorce in February 1913. They were known as "The Happiest Married Couple of the Stage," but their billing as "Nora Bayes, Assisted and Admired by Jack Norworth" indicates not only Bayes's difficult, egocentric personality, but also that their marriage was far from an equal partnership.

Jack Norworth (Philadelphia, January 5, 1879—Laguna Beach, Ca., September 1, 1959) had formerly been married to actress Louise Dresser, while Bayes had one previous marriage and was to have three later ones. He was a prolific composer, usually working in association with lyricist Albert Von Tilzer; among his many compositions are "Shine on Harvest Moon," "Take Me Out to the Ball Game," "Meet Me In Apple Blossom Time," and "Since My Mother Was a Girl." The couple's life was filmed in 1944 by Warner Bros. under the title *Shine on Harvest Moon*, with Ann Sheridan playing Bayes and Dennis Morgan as Norworth.

Nora Bayes was brought in as a headliner to play Topsy, a soubrette, with the 1907, and first, Ziegfeld *Follies*, after the show had transferred from the Jardin de Paris on the roof of the New York Theatre to the Liberty Theatre. She and Norworth starred in the 1908 edition of the *Follies*, introducing "Shine on Harvest Moon," which was revived by Ruth Etting in the 1931 edition of the *Follies*. The couple made their last *Follies* appearance in 1909. Bayes quit the show, claiming Ziegfeld wanted her to wear tights and ride a pink elephant, but the real reason may have been because Ziegfeld described Bayes's costar, Lillian Lorraine, as the prettiest little thing he had ever seen.

Besides her vaudeville appearances, Nora Bayes starred in many successful Broadway shows, including *The Jolly Bachelors* (1910), with Jack Norworth, and *Little Miss Fix-It* (1911), in which she and Norworth sang the delightful courting couple's lament, "Mr. Moon-Man, Turn off Your Light." In 1915, she starred in the revue *Maid in America*, with "all kinds of music rewritten by Sigmund Romberg" and "words by the actors and their friends." In *The Cohan Revue of 1918*, described as "a hit and run play batted out by George M. Cohan," Bayes performed a satire on the knitting craze, in which she ceaselessly worked on a sweater for a soldier, heedless of burglary and fire in her household. The musical play *Ladies First* opened at the Broadhurst Theatre in October 1918 and was subsequently moved over to the newly opened Nora Bayes Theatre—to have a theatre named after one must surely be the supreme wish of all egotistical performers—on December 30, 1918. The Nora Bayes Theatre was subsequently renamed the Forty-fourth Street Theatre and is now part of *The New York Times* plant. In 1922, along with Harry Richman and Norma Terriss, Bayes starred in *Queen o' Hearts*, a musical comedy by Lewis Gensler, in which she played the proprietress of a matrimonial agency. (Gensler had written "Black Eyed Susan" for Bayes to sing in vaudeville some years earlier.)

Following her divorce from Norworth, Bayes was modestly billed in vaudeville as "The Greatest Single Woman Singing Comedienne in the World." Typical of her vaudeville repertoire was the 1915 song "I Work Eight Hours a Day, I Sleep Eight Hours a Day, That Leaves Eight Hours for Lovin'." As *Variety* noted, "Miss Bayes had an extensive repertoire of songs which ranged from semi-classics to the comedy types. She had the exceptional knack of putting over a song which continually brought her countless copyists." At the Palace Theatre in May 1916, Bayes introduced, as her baritone partner, Edmund Goulding, who was later to become a prominent Hollywood director. During the First World War, she tirelessly entertained the troops and also introduced, in 1917, the most famous of all wartime songs, George M. Cohan's "Over There."

Her salary was at least $2,500 a week; in September 1921, she played the Winter Garden at $3,500 a week, and shortly before her death was touring at $5,000 a week. Her health began to deteriorate in the early 1920s, and, as it did, her temperamental behavior increased. She was more interested in telling audiences about her adopted children than in providing them with comedy and song, and at one point E. F. Albee refused to have her play any of his houses any longer.

As early as November 1905, Nora Bayes had appeared in London at the Palace Theatre. In 1924 she was back in London, aiming for a comeback by playing the Palladium for a mere $300 a week. Cissie Loftus was on the same stage, doing an impersonation of Bayes, when the real thing appeared and helped her out. So popular was the routine that the two repeated it at the Palace. But it was also at the Palace, a year later, that Nora Bayes's temperament got the better of her again, with disastrous results for her career. She was to appear in a National Vaudeville Artists benefit on a bill that also included Sophie Tucker, who had been promised number five spot on the program. Bayes was to follow Tucker, but she refused, claiming her reputation would be damaged by allowing Tucker to go on before her. The Palace's booker, E. V. Darling, refused to reconsider his decision, and remembering Bayes's past rudeness and temperament, suggested she leave the theatre. Darling then told the show's master of ceremonies, Emmett Keane, to tell the audience what had transpired, leaving out nothing but Bayes's bad language.

In March 1928, Nora Bayes came to Eddie Darling and begged him to put the large photographs of her out in the lobby of the Palace Theatre so that when she drove past she would know they were there—he could take them down when the matinee performance was to begin. Darling did as she requested, and two days later Bayes was dead of cancer. Her last stage appearance had been at the Fox circuit's Audubon Theatre (at 168th Street and Broadway) the week of February 20, 1928. She had told Edgar Allen of the Fox vaudeville staff, "I'd love to play one more week and retire."

BIBLIOGRAPHY
Benchley, Robert C. "Your Loving Son, Nora Bayes." *Everybody's*, May 1921, pp. 52–
    53.
Hackett, Francis. "At Keith's Vaudeville." *The New Republic*, April 6, 1918, p. 297.
"Why People Enjoy Crying in a Theater." *American Magazine*, April 1918, pp. 33–35.
Wolf, Rennold. "Nora Bayes, An Expert in Songs and Matrimony." *The Green Book
    Magazine*, April 1914, pp. 571–580.

GEORGE BEBAN (San Francisco, 1873—Los Angeles, October 5, 1928)

Noted on stage and in silent films for his Italian characterizations, George Beban was in fact of Scottish-Irish descent. He began his career in San Francisco with Reed and Emerson Minstrels and later worked with Weber and Fields. Initially, he was an eccentric French comedian, often cast as French characters in musical comedy and billed as "the artistic French dancing buffoon." Almost as a party piece, he began reciting a tearjerker called "Mia Rosa." Percy G. Williams heard him and was so impressed that he asked Beban to develop the poem into a one-act play for vaudeville, which became *The Sign of the Rose*. After some seven years on the road with the play, Beban wrote a four-act version, which opened at New York's Garrick Theatre on October 11, 1911, running for a mere thirteen performances.

In 1914, Beban was signed to producer Thomas H. Ince to make his film debut in an original motion picture called *The Dago*. The film was subsequently released in January of the following year as *The Italian* and has become a minor classic of the screen. Later in 1915, Beban filmed *The Sign of the Rose* for Ince, under the title *An Alien*, and remade the film in 1922 under its original title. He continued to make films on a regular basis until his death, which was the result of his being thrown from a horse at a dude ranch near Big Pine, California.

BIBLIOGRAPHY
Beban, George. "100% Italian—In Plays." *The New York Dramatic Mirror*, December
    4, 1920, p. 1067.

MARTIN BECK (Lipto Szert Mikols, Czechoslovakia, July 30, 1867—New York, November 16, 1940)

The creator and head of the Orpheum circuit and the builder of the Palace Theatre, Martin Beck was an eccentric and often abusive theatrical entrepreneur who was generally supportive of the acts he booked. In his native Austria, Beck worked as a waiter and a lowly member of a theatrical troupe before coming to the United States at the age of sixteen. Initially, he worked as a waiter at a beer garden in Chicago in the early 1890s before going to San Francisco with the Schiller Vaudeville Company. In San Francisco, he met Gustave Walters, who owned the Orpheum Theatre, and when the theatre was taken over by Morris Meyerfeld in 1899, Beck helped him to expand, with the acquisition of additional theatres, and in 1905, Beck took over the running of the organization. He married Meyerfeld's daughter and became president of the circuit in 1920. In 1913, Martin Beck built and opened the Palace Theatre on Broadway. It was his first venture into vaudeville on the East Coast, but even before the theatre had opened he had lost his controlling interest in it. Nonetheless, Beck continued as the theatre's first booker and was responsible for bringing Sarah Bernhardt to the United States for a triumphant vaudeville tour and engagement at the Palace in 1913.

Martin Beck initiated what became known as the State-Lake (Chicago) policy, named after another theatre he built, whereby he booked nine acts for a seven-act show, and thus could present four shows a day with the performers only having to work in three each.

In 1923, Martin Beck was voted out of the presidency of the Orpheum circuit after the company went public. The following year, he built the Martin Beck Theatre, which opened on November 11, 1924, with *Mme Pompadour*. Built almost entirely of steel and often compared to a fortress, the Martin Beck was the only New York theatre on which there was no mortgage. He returned to vaudeville in 1932 as supervisor of the booking office at RKO. In 1934, he brought the D'Oyly Carte Opera Company to the United States for the first time. Beck remained active in the theatre until his death, holding a financial interest in *Cabin in the Sky*, which was playing at the Martin Beck Theatre at that time.

BEER GARDENS

In the 1880s, 1890s, and early 1900s, open-air beer gardens in New York often provided entertainment for their patrons, at the same time offering opportunities for would-be vaudevillians to perform. The most prominent were Atlantic Gardens (50 The Bowery), Blank's Winter Gardens, later known as the Sans Souci (100 Third Avenue), Bowery Garden (The Bowery), Dietrich's Columbia Casino (2840 Broadway), the East River Casino (1764 Avenue C), and Unter den Linden, also known as Stillegebauer's (2581 Broadway).

JACK BENNY (Waukegan, Ill., February 14, 1894—Beverly Hills, Ca., December 26, 1974)

When Jack Benny died, his age was listed as eighty, but to millions of his radio and television fans, Jack Benny passed away at the age of thirty-nine, a beloved American entertainer, untouched by scandal or hint of egotism, whose beginnings were in vaudeville, but who never really established his familiar style until he started his radio career in the 1930s. In radio, Benny learned how to use silence to his advantage. A lengthy pause would follow a burglar's demand of "Your money or your life," and eventually the comedian's voice would be heard: "I'm thinking it over." Benny used the pause in the opening line of his first radio broadcast on an Ed Sullivan talk show on CBS on March 29, 1932. "Ladies and gentlemen," he said "this is Jack Benny talking. There will be a slight pause while you say 'Who cares?' " On television, he used that famous long, hard stare to add to the impact of the jokes; it was a stare pregnant with meaning. The Jack Benny trademarks, in particular his meanness and his theme song, "Love in Bloom," all came along after the vaudeville days were over, although he had used the pregnant pause to limited effect in vaudeville, together with his "who cares?" philosophy.

Writing in *Life* (June 3, 1926), Robert Benchley noted one of the comedian's early attributes: "Mr. Benny is possessed of that most important attribute for comedy—ease. He has an agreeable, but not too agreeable, manner. His countenance expresses his emotions in some mysterious manner without changing. He ambles on with a very good line of stuff, but whether you like it or not seems a matter of indifference to him."

Born Benjamin Kubelsky, the son of Polish Jewish immigrants, Benny grew up in Waukegan, Illinois, and there at the age of six he was forced to take violin lessons by parents who hoped their son might grow up to be a classical violinist. At the age of fifteen, Benny was earning eight dollars a week, playing in the pit orchestra at Waukegan's Barrison Theatre. Two years later, he entered vaudeville with Cora Salisbury, also from the Barrison Theatre orchestra, as one half of Salisbury and Benny; she played the piano and Benny the violin, and their straight music act was billed as "From Grand Opera to Ragtime." When America entered the First World War, Benny enlisted in the navy; he discovered his talent for comedy entertaining troops at the Great Lakes Naval Training Station with violin solos interspersed with wisecracks.

Benny returned to vaudeville after the war as a solo performer, initially calling himself Ben K. Benny. He changed his name in 1921 because it created confusion with that of another violinist-vaudevillian, Ben Bernie, to whom in terms of style of delivery he bore a certain resemblance. *Variety*'s Sime Silverman saw Benny at New York's Fifth Avenue Theatre and reported in the January 21, 1921, issue of the trade paper that the comedian had "gags, presence and assurance." Among such gags in that era of prohibition was the following: "An optimist is a bartender still paying dues to his union." The only suggestion that Silverman made for an improvement to the act was that Benny discard the violin—the comedian did not.

Aside from vaudeville, Jack Benny worked in nightclubs and in Earl Carroll's *Vanities*. He was frequently at the Palace: in September 1927, November 1928, December 1929, and May and September 1931. His earliest legitimate stage appearance was in *The Great Temptations* in May 1926. In 1927, Benny teamed with a musical group called The New Yorkers, with whom he had been appearing at New York's Little Club, and returned to vaudeville with them in a twenty-one minute act. The running gag was to have Joe Venuti direct the band, which played well until Benny took over, when the result was disastrous. *Variety* (November 30, 1927) reported, "Benny and New Yorkers are a fine layout for vaude or picture houses. Benny scores with his gags, sells his band and the band adds to the sale by its excellent playing."

The somewhat effeminate quality visible in Jack Benny's later work originated in the late 1920s, when it seemed that most masters of ceremonies should appear limp-wristed and effete. Frank Fay worked this way, as did Harry Rose. This effeteness is evident in M-G-M's 1930 two-reel short subject *The Song Writers Revue*, in which Benny appears as master of ceremonies, introduces ten composers, and exchanges jokes with the very amusing Fred Fisher. The exasperated expression is there, but the timing seems a little unsure and the jokes are best forgotten.

Benny's film career began in 1929 with M-G-M's *The Hollywood Revue of 1929*, in which he served as a poor master of ceremonies. His most famous film is *The Horn Blows at Midnight* (1944), which was so poorly received that it became a perennial gag with the comedian. In all, he made more than twenty films, including *Chasing Rainbows* (1930), *Love Thy Neighbor* (1940, which was based on the famous Jack Benny–Fred Allen radio feud), *Charley's Aunt* (1941), and *The Meanest Man in the World* (1942). His favorite role was as the Polish actor forced to impersonate Hitler in Ernst Lubitsch's *To Be or Not to Be* (1942). "I think I'm the only comedian who had Hamlet thrust upon him," he commented in the *Saturday Evening Post* (March 13, 1948).

The first of Jack Benny's radio shows was *The Canada Dry Ginger Ale Program*, which received its first airing on NBC on May 1, 1932. It was followed by *The Chevrolet Program* (1933), *The General Tire Program* (1934), *The Jello Program* (1934), *The Grape Nuts Program* (1942), and eventually *The Jack Benny Program*, sponsored by Lucky Strike, which began on October 1, 1944. Within a few years of Benny's having his own show, all the familiar names had become regulars on the program: announcer Don Wilson, Eddie Anderson as Rochester, singer Dennis Day, and, of course, Benny's wife, Mary Livingstone, whom he had met when she was Sadie Marks, a salesgirl with the May Company in Los Angeles, and married in 1927. Also featured on *The Jack Benny Program* was bandleader Phil Harris and Mel Blanc with his famous cry, "Train now loading on track three—all aboard for Anaheim, Azusa, and Cuc—amonga." In 1949, Benny moved from NBC to CBS and continued with his radio program until May 22, 1955. If nothing else, Jack Benny's show established him in the self-created role of one of the world's meanest men, the exact opposite of his real-life character. The radio image certainly paid off financially, for by January 1955 Benny was receiving $15,000 a week for personal appearances, a far cry from the few hundreds a week that had been his vaudeville salary ten years earlier. Benny's radio and later television success was due in no small part to his writers, for Benny was never great at ad-libbing and stopped providing his own material when his vaudeville career ended. During one of his verbal bickerings with Fred Allen, he said, "You wouldn't dare say that if my writers were here."

Interestingly, most of Jack Benny's character traits developed by accident. In a 1960 interview with gossip columnist Hedda Hopper he recalled:

> I developed characterizations by accident. That wasn't genius on my part. I didn't stop to plan I am going to be stingy, or thirty-nine, or feud with Fred Allen, or own a Maxwell. If Fred Allen and I had sat down with each other and said let's have a feud, it wouldn't have lasted three weeks. But I just happened to hear him say something one week and

I went on and said something about it, and it went on. We were in that feud eight months before we even discussed it with each other on the phone. The way I got to be stingy, we had one or two stingy jokes on the show and they got a big laugh, and the next week we put a few more jokes in, and then we let it go. But we came back to it every so often so that it got beyond us and became a part of the characterization.

Jack Benny made his first television appearance on March 9, 1949, on a variety program with Bing Crosby and others. *The Jack Benny Program* was first televised on October 28, 1950, and continued through April 16, 1965, seen on CBS except for the final season, when it moved to NBC. Benny, of course, continued to appear on television after that date on *Shower of Stars*, *The Jack Benny Hour*, and other programs.

Almost until his death, Jack Benny never stopped working. He would play his violin at charity concerts, raising more than $1 million for the state of Israel. Just prior to his death, it was announced that Benny would star opposite Walter Matthau in the film of *The Sunshine Boys*, a role that ultimately went to Benny's close friend George Burns. Benny's funeral, attended by so many of his colleagues and friends, demonstrated the affection in which he was held by his profession. In his eulogy, Bob Hope said, "The world lost a national treasure. . . . He had the geniousness of a Picasso and a Gershwin. . . . He didn't stand on the stage, he owned it. He was stingy to the end—he only gave us eighty years and that wasn't enough. . . . He never used his sharp wit to injure or belittle anyone." *Newsweek* admirably summed up Jack Benny when it described him as "the ageless fussbudget who played straight man to the world."

BIBLIOGRAPHY

Amory, Cleveland. "Jack Benny's $400 Yaks." *Saturday Evening Post*, November 6, 1948, pp. 25, 81–83, 86, 89.

Beatty, Jerome. "Unhappy Fiddler." *American Magazine*, December 1944, pp. 28–29, 142–44.

Benny, Jack. "What Makes a Perfect Lover." *Esquire*, January 1945, pp. 69, 169–71.

_____. "From Vaudeo to Video via Radio." *Collier's*, March 24, 1951, pp. 13–14, 79–81.

_____. "After 39 Years—I'm Turning 40." *Collier's*, February 19, 1954, pp. 32–34.

_____. Prologue to *I Love Her That's Why* by George Burns. New York: Simon and Schuster, 1955.

_____, and Joan Benny. *Sunday Nights at Seven: The Jack Benny Story*. New York: Warner Books, 1990.

Benny, Mary Livingstone, and Hilliard Marks with Marcia Borie. *Jack Benny*. New York: Doubleday, 1978.

Cantor, Eddie. "The 'Jack' in Benny." *Cosmopolitan*, May 1949, pp. 18, 135–37.

Collins, Frederick L. "Why Jack Benny Is the Highest-Paid Entertainer in the World." *Liberty* 13, no. 13 (March 28, 1936), pp. 18–19.

Davidson, Bill. "Buck$ Benny Rides Again." *Saturday Evening Post*, March 2, 1963, pp. 27–31.

Fein, Irving A. *Jack Benny: An Intimate Biography*. New York: G. P. Putnam's Sons, 1976.

Giddins, Gary. "Inventing Jack Benny." *The Washington Post*, August 3, 1986, pp. B1, B3.

Harrity, Richard, and Ralph G. Martin. "The 39 Years of Jack Benny." *The American Weekly*, June 23, 1963, entire issue.

"It's Benny Two to One." *Newsweek*, March 31, 1947, pp. 66–68.

"Jack Benny." *Current Biography*, August 1941, pp. 67–68.

Josefsberg, Milt. *The Jack Benny Show*. Westport, Ct.: Arlington House, 1977.

Livingstone, Mary, "How to Live with a Comic." *Liberty* 18, no. 6 (February 8, 1941), pp. 56–57.

————, as told to Jane Kesner Ardmore. "I Got Even with Jack Benny: I Married Him." *Woman's Home Companion*, October 1953, pp. 38, 115, 123, 127, 130.

————, as told to Helen Markel. "A Love Letter to Blue Eyes." *Good Housekeeping*, October 1957, pp. 114–15, 178, 180–81.

Marx, Arthur. "No. 1 Master of Timing." *The New York Times Magazine*, February 13, 1955, p. 17.

Millstein, Gilbert. "The Fiddle Squeaks." *TV Guide*, September 23, 1961, pp. 12–15.

Museum of Television and Radio. *Jack Benny: The Radio and Television Work*. New York: Harper-Collins, 1991.

Robinson, Hubbell, and Ted Patrick. "Jack Benny." *Scribner's Magazine* 103, no. 3 (March 1938), pp. 11–15.

Rosten, Leo. "Jack Benny: America's Favorite 'Fall Guy.' " *Look*, May 9, 1950, pp. 53–54, 56, 58, 60.

Saroyan, William. "Jack Benny's 39 Years." *Look*, November 1, 1955, pp. 51–53, 55, 59.

Sharpe, Howard. "Jack Benny's Ten Best Gags." *Liberty* 18, no. 45 (November 8, 1941), pp. 16–17, 61.

Smith, David R. *Jack Benny Checklist: Radio, Television, Motion Pictures, Books and Articles*. Los Angeles: UCLA Library, 1970.

Walker, Waller. "Jack Benny—He Has to Be Loved." *Look*, May 15, 1945, pp. 33–34, 36, 38, 41–42.

Zolotow, Maurice. "The Fiddler from Waukegan." *Cosmopolitan*, October 1947, pp. 49, 50–51, 137–38, 141–46.

MARION BENT. See PAT ROONEY, JR. AND MARION BENT

LEON BERG (Berlin, Germany, November 29, 1866—Dayton, Oh., October 17, 1933)

Leon Berg served as a press agent for many vaudevillians, including Yvette Guilbert, Loie Fuller, and Eva Tanguay. It was Berg who devised the stunt that Anna Held bathed only in milk. He attended the Berlin Conservatory of Music and later composed many songs, including, ironically, the "Liberty Loan March" during the First World War. For more than thirty years, he was associated with the Hurtig and Seamon burlesque organization and, from 1913 to 1929, managed the Lyric Theatre in Dayton.

EDGAR BERGEN (Chicago, February 16, 1903—Las Vegas, September 30, 1978)

While he remains America's most famous ventriloquist, Edgar Bergen was not one of the greatest. Even before his many years in radio, Bergen was incapable of preventing his lips from moving, but somehow audiences were able to overlook this fault and believe that Charlie McCarthy and Bergen's other dummies did indeed have lives of their own. They were in every sense his alter egos, as precious to him as his family, including daughter Candice, an actress best known for her work in the television series *Murphy Brown* (first seen on CBS in 1988). There was a gentleness to Bergen's humor; it might not have created belly laughs, but it made one feel good inside. Audiences sensed that Edgar Bergen really believed in Charlie McCarthy and Mortimer Snerd, and that the conversations between them continued long after the audiences had departed.

Through the years, Bergen's act changed drastically, and the ventriloquist who appeared at the Palace in 1926 bore little resemblance to the star of radio, television, and nightclubs of later years. Born Edgar Berggren, the performer decided to become a ventriloquist after watching the Great Lester in vaudeville and reading a twenty-five-cent book of magic titled *Hermman's Wizard Manual*. The prototype for Charlie McCarthy was fashioned by an Irish woodcarver named Charlie Mack around 1920, and his features were borrowed from an Irish newsboy who used to deliver newspapers to the Berggren family. The name Charlie McCarthy also originated with the wood-carver. The original doll was four feet tall and weighed twenty-four pounds; he was made of Michigan pine, and the head was attached to the body by a shaft approximately nine inches long.

Bergen claimed that he was shy and nervous as a young man and that through Charlie McCarthy's uninhibited personality he was able to express himself. Edgar Bergen and Charlie McCarthy appeared together in small Chicago Theatres and on the Redpath Chautauqua circuit during the summer months. Years later, the ventriloquist remembered his first theatrical engagement: "It was on a Saturday in a suburban theater and the contract price was three dollars for five shows. When the manager paid me off about midnight, he said I'd been a tremendous hit and that he was going to give me something extra. He did—a quarter out of his own pocket. And that's the only time anyone in show business has ever paid me more than I contracted for."

Gradually, Edgar Bergen advanced his career until, in June 1926, he was appearing in a fifteen-minute act at the Palace. It was a sketch that had Bergen and a nurse played by Christine Caldwell finding Charlie McCarthy, as a newsboy and orphan, crying on a park bench. The couple took McCarthy to a doctor, who discussed various operations he wished to perform on the dummy. The sketch closed with Bergen and the nurse becoming engaged and keeping Charlie as an office boy. "Neatly set and well manipulated it clicked heavy here," reported *Variety* (June 30, 1926). From this sketch another developed with Bergen as a doctor about to perform an operation on Charlie McCarthy, which ended with the dummy coming out of the ether and shouting, "Was it a girl?"

In 1930, Edgar Bergen and Charlie McCarthy made their first screen appearances in a series of Vitaphone shorts, produced by Warner Bros. The first two were titled *The Operation* (based on the aforementioned sketch) and *The Office Scandal*. In the latter, also based on a vaudeville routine, McCarthy applies for a job as an office boy, sees the married secretary kiss the boss, and gets the job. Both films also featured Bergen's then human partner Christina Graver (who may perhaps have been the same individual as Christine Caldwell). Both shorts are preserved at the UCLA Film and Television Archive and provide important documentation of Bergen's vaudeville routines, racier than his later work and lacking in warmth.

The major break for Bergen and McCarthy came on December 17, 1936, when they guest-starred on Rudy Vallee's radio show. The two worked on a regular basis with Vallee until April 1937, and the following month—on May 9—they began their own radio program under the sponsorship of Chase and Sanborn coffee. Initially known as *The Chase & Sanborn Hour*, the program quickly became *The Charlie McCarthy Show*, evidence of who was the star attraction of the team. Bergen and McCarthy remained on radio for the next twenty years; as Edgar Bergen commented, "It was absolutely the last place in the world a ventriloquist should go, and sometimes doing the absolutely wrong thing works." He might also have added that with vaudeville virtually dead and a lack of ability to stop his lips from moving, there was no better place for a ventriloquist such as Bergen than radio. The most famous aspect of Bergen and McCarthy's radio work was a long-running feud between W. C. Fields and Charlie McCarthy which lasted from 1938 through 1944 and led to their being partnered together in a feature film, *You Can't Cheat an Honest Man* (1939). Among Charlie McCarthy's best known quips to W. C. Fields are: "Mr. Fields, is that your nose or a new kind of flamethrower?," "Do you mind if I stand in the shade of your nose?," and "Why don't you fill your nose with helium and rent in out for a barrage balloon?"

Other dummies Bergen introduced on radio were Mortimer Snerd, Effie Klinker (who looked like Sneezy in Disney's *Snow White and the Seven Dwarfs*), Ophelia (a querulous old lady), Maisie and Matilda (two barnyard hens), Podine Puffington (a tall, glamorous blond), Lars Lindquist (a Swedish fisherman), and Gloria Graham (who "wouldn't sit still and stop talking . . . she gushed herself right out of show business"). For the record, at this time, Charlie McCarthy weighed 40 pounds and wore size 4 clothes, 2AAA shoes, and a 3 3/8 hat. The head had always remained the same, but the body had been replaced from time to time. Some of Charlie McCarthy's most quoted lines are:

To Admiral Halsey: "Hiya, sailor."

To Paulette Goddard: "Take away your face and figure and what have you got?"

To Marilyn Monroe (who told him she was wearing her wedding dress with "something borrowed"): "You didn't borrow enough!"

Edgar Bergen had the knack of constantly updating his humor to the social climate. When appearing at the Hollywood Palladium, Charlie McCarthy thought it was the London Palladium and demanded to know, "Where's the queen?" Tongue-in-cheek, Bergen replied, "Don't be silly, Charlie, there are no queens in Hollywood."

In 1947, Edgar Bergen deserted Charlie McCarthy to play Mr. Thorkelson in the film version of *I Remember Mama*, which he described as his favorite role because it was one in which he did not have to be Edgar Bergen. The ventriloquist appeared in many other films, including *The Goldwyn Follies* (1938), *Song of the Open Road* (1944), *Fun and Fancy Free* (1947), *Captain China* (1949), and *Don't Make Waves* (1967); his last screen appearance was a cameo in *The Muppet Movie* (1979), which is dedicated to his memory. Edgar Bergen was less successful on television; he made many guest appearances and hosted a quiz show on CBS, *Do You Trust Your Wife?*, from January 1956 through March 1957. On September 21, 1978, Bergen announced he was retiring from show business and that Charlie McCarthy was to be bequeathed to the Smithsonian Institution, to which Charlie responded, "Well, at least I won't be the only dummy in Washington." A month later, while playing a farewell engagement at Caesar's Palace in Las Vegas, Bergen died. He had just ended his show with the words, "All acts have a beginning and an end . . . and I think that time has come for me. So I think I'll just pack up my jokes and my friends." It was a touching farewell from an entertainer whose audiences had always been long-lasting and affectionate, perhaps because as film producer Sam Goldwyn remarked in his own inimitable style, "the popularity of Charlie McCarthy and the Seven Dwarfs proves that people are getting tired of people."

BIBLIOGRAPHY
Bergen, Candice. *Knock Wood*. New York: Linden Press/Simon & Schuster, 1984.
Bergen, Edgar. "The World of Puppetry—Edgar Bergen Has It on a String." *Los Angeles Times Calendar*, January 3, 1965, 15.
"Charlie McCarthy Is the Most Objectionable Young Man in America." *Life* 3, no. 4 (July 26, 1937), pp. 57–58.
Collins, Frederick L. "The Strange Case of Mortimer Snerd and Charlie McCarthy." *Liberty* 17, no. 9 (March 2, 1940), pp. 42–44.
"Cultivated Groaner." *Time*, November 20, 1944, pp. 54, 56–57.
Diehl, Digby. "Q&A Edgar Bergen." *Los Angeles Times West Magazine*, March 5, 1972, pp. 21–22.
"Edgar Bergen." *Current Biography*, May 1945, pp. 42–45.
Lewis, Frederick. "The Private Life of Charlie McCarthy." *Liberty* 14, no. 40 (October 2, 1937), pp. 16–17.
Packer, Eleanor. *A Day with Charlie McCarthy and Edgar Bergen*. Racine, Wi.: Whitman, 1938.
Reynolds, Quentin. "The Man Who Talks to Himself." *Collier's* 99, no. 12 (March 20, 1937), pp. 24, 88–89.
Sharpe, Howard. "Charlie McCarthy's Ten Best Gags." *Liberty* 18, no. 51 (December 20, 1941), pp. 50, 52–53.
Smith, H. Allen. "Charlie McCarthy." *Cosmopolitan*, August 1944, pp. 8, 10.

SAMMY BERK (circa 1894—New York, August 5, 1983)

A novelty dancer who worked with a number of female partners, Sammy Berk began performing as a child with his uncle's Sokoloff Troupe. In 1914, he appeared in the Broadway production of *The Lilac Domino*, and there he met Lillian Broderick. The two teamed as a vaudeville act until Berk enlisted in the navy during the First World War and Broderick married Joe Schenck of Van and Schenck. In 1918, Berk teamed with a woman named Valda, but the act lasted only a short time, and in 1919 he teamed for a third and final time with Juanita Saun. The couple were married in 1920 and as Berk and Saun were a popular team on the vaudeville circuit, billed as "Creators of Snappy Steps." In 1926, they toured the British music halls. With the demise of vaudeville, Berk became a booker for Irving Mills and later an independent agent and personal manager. His son Dick Berk was also a dancer in vaudeville with the act of Berk and Hallow.

BIBLIOGRAPHY

Smith, Bill. "Sammy Berk." In *The Vaudevillians*. New York: Macmillan, 1976, pp. 63–67.

MILTON BERLE (Brooklyn, N.Y., July 12, 1908—   )

As his nickname "Mr. Television" indicates, Milton Berle belongs more in a volume on the history of television than a study of vaudeville, but Berle's early success on TV was thanks entirely to the years of training he spent in vaudeville. The comedian himself has acknowledged that *The Texaco Star Theater*, which was first seen on NBC on June 8, 1948, began as little more than a glorified vaudeville show, with the first program introduced with the words, "Welcome to the Texaco Vaudeville Theater." Milton Berle was the show's master of ceremonies, a role he had played in the late 1920s and 1930s. *The Texaco Star Theater* was full of the sort of wisecracking quips that had assured Berle's success in vaudeville; for example, he would come out at the start of the show and announce, "We had a wonderful show prepared for you—but it won't be ready 'til next week." He was never at a loss for words or a joke, although many of his gags had probably been "borrowed" from other comedians. In the early days of Berle's vaudeville career, one prominent vaudevillian said, "Nobody had any respect for him. He stole everyone's material." It was this easy appropriation of the material of others that led to Berle's becoming known as "The Thief of Bad Gags."

Milton Berle has answered this criticism, explaining, "Material won't do; it's personality. If you don't have a directional point of view or a style, you better toss out what you've got and find yourself. Personality is what people tune in to watch or turn out to see. And funny is funny. Nothing's old if you haven't heard it before and nothing's new if you have."

The Texaco Star Theater also featured Berle's trick of intruding himself into the acts of others, another vaudeville device about which there is some controversy. Berle insists that he has never butted into another performer's act without permission and without rehearsing the situation. Some vaudevillians disagree. Ted Waldman recalled that Berle interrupted Beatrice Lillie's act at the Palace, completely destroying her rapport with the audience. At one point he asked her, "Are you Lady Peel?," to which Lillie responded, in total disregard for the ban on swearing onstage at the Palace, "Goddamn right, I am." Whatever the truth of the matter, Berle has been interrupting since 1924, and it has become one of his trademarks.

Born Milton Berlinger, the entertainer grew up in Harlem. The biggest influence on his life was his mother, Sarah, of whom Berle once said, "She was my mother, but she was also my father, my best friend, my sweetheart." It would be easy to label her aggressive, but that would be unfair because there is no doubt that Berle was happy to follow where his mother led. Legend has it that Berle made his stage debut at the age of five in a Charlie Chaplin look-alike contest at a theatre in Mount Vernon, New York, but as Chaplin did not make his screen debut until Berle was six, this cannot be true. Berle did enter vaudeville as a young child, chaperoned by his mother, who was to witness every performance given by her son until she died in 1954. In the teens, Berle worked in the Philadelphia area for a Gus Edwards—type entrepreneur named E. W. Wolf, who put on "kid" shows with names like *Playmates*, *The Melody of Youth*, *Ting-a-Ling*, and *Tid-Bits*. In 1920, he appeared in a revival of *Florodora*, as part of the Baby Sextette, six small boys and girls who sang a reprise of the show's hit song, "Tell Me, Pretty Maiden." On his mother's advice, he turned the number into a comedy by starting off on the wrong foot, which made him stand out and perhaps taught the young Berle how to steal the show, or, to be more precise, how to steal a gag from the act of others.

In 1921, Berle teamed with Elizabeth Kennedy for a vaudeville act called Kennedy and Berle, with the two appearing in the sketch "Broadway Bound," written and produced by Milton Hockey and Howard Green. It featured the two young players in scenes from Shakespeare's *Romeo and Juliet*, a classic melodrama such as *Orphans of the Storm*, and a popular play such as *Lightnin'*. They played the Palace for the first time on May 2, 1921, opening the second half of the bill. When Berle grew too big to play opposite Kennedy, the act broke up, in 1924. He became a single, offering an opening song, a comedy routine, and more often than not, an impersonation of Eddie Cantor (which he had first given while working for E. W. Wolf).

Berle made his single debut in New York at Loew's State on December 29, 1924. As the years passed, Berle's act changed, and he grew in popularity. In 1927, he was presenting a sketch titled "Memoirs of Milton," in which he sang "I Get the Girls That Get What I Have." The high spot was a routine in which a girl would come on the stage, set as a dockside, and announce she was planning suicide. She would then flirt with Berle and take his money. When a second girl appeared and announced her suicide plans, Berle tipped her into the water. Reviewing the act at the American Theatre, *Variety* (April 27, 1927) was not wildly enthusiastic, noting that "Berle is worthy of something better than he does here."

From vaudeville, Milton Berle graduated to nightclubs, where his gags were deliberately geared to insult the customers. He would turn to one of the men in the audience and comment, "Oh, I see it's novelty night; you're out with your wife." He informed the guests that there were two waiters per person, one to hand them the check and one to revive them. Between 1932 and and 1934, Berle's weekly salary rose from $450 to $2,500 a week.

He appeared in the 1932 edition of Earl Carroll's *Vanities* and was also seen on Broadway in *Saluta* and *Lost Paradise* (both, 1934). Berle also made his radio debut in 1934 and became a regular on that medium in 1936 on CBS's *Community Sing*. Although he was not entirely successful on radio, he was heard on the air almost continuously through 1948; his best known program was the 1944 series *Let Yourself Go*, which encouraged members of the audience to do precisely that, acting out their secret desires. Berle had appeared in silent films as a bit player, in a Pearl White serial and other productions shot in Fort Lee, New Jersey. He made his major screen debut in *New Faces of 1937*, followed by *Sun Valley Serenade* (1941), *Always Leave 'em Laughing* (1949), *Let's Make Love* (1960), *It's a Mad, Mad, Mad, Mad World* (1963), and *The Oscar* (1965), among others.

Milton Berle achieved his greatest success with his 1948 television debut on *The Texaco Star Theater*. He appeared under Texaco sponsorship until 1953, when his program became *The Buick-Berle Show*. A year later, it became *The Milton Berle Show*, and as such it lasted until 1956. Berle returned with a new show in 1958, and that continued, on and off, through 1967. With his theme song, "Near You," he was, unquestionably, the most popular star on television in its early years, and it is claimed that he was responsible for the sale of more TV sets than any other personality or any advertising campaign. *Limelight* (March 16, 1961) claimed that Berle's *Texaco Star Theater* could be credited with selling almost 353,000 sets in use in the New York area in 1950.

The television series also gave Berle an opportunity to appear in drag, a style of entertainment that he acknowledges he learned from some of the great female impersonators of the teens. Why does he dress as a woman? Steve Allen had the answer when he said, "What people say about Milton Berle is true—he will do anything for a laugh. But the important thing, to my mind, is that he always gets the laugh." Drag gave Milton Berle the opportunity to be outrageous. He could appear in female attire, complaining, "What you have to go through for a lousy $15,000 a week." He could turn to a woman in the audience and quip, "Lady, you've got all night to make a fool of yourself; I've only got an hour."

Milton Berle never appeared on television as a glamorous woman. It was not his style, and as he wrote in his autobiography: "For me, drag is another way to get laughs. My drag is too gay to be gay. . . . I get tired of people asking, 'Is Milton or isn't he?' To the best of my knowledge, Milton isn't. And so what?

To me, gay is another way of life. You go to your church, I'll go to mine, okay?"

He appeared in drag as Cinderella in the 1982 Macy's Thanksgiving Parade, but perhaps his best drag appearance was on one of the Smothers Brothers shows, in a scene not even written by Berle. He recalls:

It was a takeoff on Tom Snyder. The camera was supposed to be Tom Snyder, and when we opened up all you saw was a close-up of my hand with a cigar, and the voice said, "Have things changed since you were on television?" They pulled back and I was dressed very chic like Doris Day, complete makeup. And I said, "Well, things have changed for me. I've changed the color of my hair." And the punch line was, "Before we finish this interview, just remember this, fairy tales can come true, it can happen to you if you're young at heart. Or would you rather be a pig?"

Milton Berle reached the zenith of his career on May 16, 1949, when he was featured on the covers of both *Time* and *Newsweek*, the first show business personality to be so honored. (The *Newsweek* cover featured him in a grotesque Carmen Miranda–like outfit.) In 1951, Berle signed an unprecedented thirty-six-year, $6 million–dollar contract with NBC, which remained in force, with some revisions, until 1987. Certainly show business (particularly television) has been kind to Milton Berle, but at the same time he has given back much in the delight he has afforded the millions of members of his audience through the years. Berle himself shrugs off his unique position in entertainment, noting merely that "the milestones weren't milestones at the time, just a chance to work."

BIBLIOGRAPHY

Ace, Goodman. "Berle's Still Berling." *Collier's*, April 7, 1953, pp. 52–54.
Berle, Milton, with Haskel Frenkel. *Milton Berle: An Autobiography*. New York: Delacorte Press, 1974.
————. *B.S. I Love You: Sixty Years with the Famous and the Infamous*. New York: McGraw-Hill, 1988.
Bester, Alfred. "The Good Old Days of Mr. Television." *Holiday*, February 1958, pp. 97, 99–100, 102–3, 105.
"The Child Wonder." *Time*, May 16, 1949, pp. 70–72, 75–77.
James, Edwin H. "Anything for a Laugh." *Redbook*, January 1950, pp. 51, 94–96, 100.
Lindeman, Lawrence. "Conversation with Milton Berle." *Oui*, December 1975, pp. 71–72, 100–116.
"Mama Remembers Milton Berle's 40 Years in Show Business." *Look*, November 3, 1953, pp. 115–19.
"Million Dollar Clown." *Look*, April 29, 1947, pp. 66–69.
"Milton Berle." *Current Biography*, June 1949, pp. 44–46.
Minoff, Philip. "Behind the Scenes with Uncle Miltie." *Cue*, February 6, 1954, pp. 12–13.
Rosten, Leo. "Everything for a Laugh." *Look*, November 21, 1950, pp. 64, 68, 70, 72.
Slide, Anthony. "Uncle Miltie, Uncle Miltie, We Love You." *Emmy*, July-August, 1982, pp. 24, 28.
Smith, Bill. "Milton Berle." In *The Vaudevillians*. New York: Macmillan, 1976, pp. 68–73.

Sylvester, Robert. "The Strange Career of Milton Berle." *Saturday Evening Post*, March 19, 1949, pp. 38–39, 150, 152–53.

"Television's Top." *Newsweek*, May 16, 1949, pp. 56–58.

Weld, Matt. "Witticitizen: Milton Berle." *Pageant*, February 1945, pp. 34–35.

IRVING BERLIN (Mohilev, Russia, May 11, 1888—New York, September 22, 1989)

"Irving Berlin has no place in American music. He *is* American music," said fellow composer Jerome Kern of the man who wrote the lyrics and music for more than fifteen hundred songs, including "Alexander's Ragtime Band," "God Bless America," "Oh! How I Hate to Get up in the Morning," "Cheek to Cheek," "White Christmas," "Always," "Blue Skies," "Easter Parade," and "What'll I Do?" Irving Berlin was also an influential figure in American vaudeville, particularly during the teens years, when not only did he provide many of the songs sung on the stage, but also appeared on it in person.

In a 1920 article in *American Magazine*, Berlin explained why his songs were so popular, and the reasons he gave are also why those songs appealed to vaudevillians: the melody must musically be within the range of the average singer; the title must be simple, easily remembered, and "planted" effectively in the song; the song must be sexless, logically able to be sung by a man or a woman; there must be "heart interest," even if the number is comic; it must be original in idea, words, and music; it must deal with emotions known to everyone in the audience; the lyrics must be euphonious, written in easily singable words; and, finally, the song must be perfectly simple.

Irving Berlin's first major success came in 1909, when he wrote "My Wife's Gone to the Country." It originated after Berlin asked vaudevillian George Whitney to go to a show with him, and Whitney said, "Sure, my wife's gone to the country." That same year, Polly Moran introduced two of Berlin's songs in vaudeville, "Yiddle on Your Fiddle Play Some Rag Time" and "Next to Your Mother, Who Do You Love?" The following year, May Irwin was so taken with Berlin's song "My Wife Bridget" that she paid the composer $1,000 for the exclusive rights.

By the mid teens, it would seem there was no singing act in vaudeville that did not use an Irving Berlin number. In July 1914, Belle Baker and Ruth Roye were both appearing at the Palace, and both were singing ragtime songs composed by Berlin. Baker sang five new songs specially written for her by the composer: "Follow the Crowd," "Treat Her Like a Baby," "Rosenthal's Business Affairs," "Back to the Michigan," and "Come Back from Mexico," which *The Billboard* (July 18, 1914) described as "the best wop song ever written." On May 15, 1915, *The Billboard* reported that the previous week was "surely Irving Berlin's week at the Palace, with three acts using one or more of his songs and another number being played by the orchestra for the exit. At the Monday matinee Fritzi Scheff sang a new Berlin composition and then called upon the author, who marched down to the front and sang two verses, amid great applause."

This was not the first time that Irving Berlin had appeared on a vaudeville stage. As early as September 1911, he played Hammerstein's Victoria Theatre, singing, "Don't Wait until Your Father Comes Home" and "The Mysterious Rag," among others. Despite complaining, as did many in the audience, that the composer did not use a piano onstage, "Jess" in *Variety* (September 16, 1911) thought that Berlin had "a dandy style in delivering a song." In the summer of 1913, Berlin went to England and appeared on stage at the London Hippodrome.

During the First World War, Irving Berlin was busy in the army with his *Yip! Yip! Yaphank* revue, which introduced "Oh! How I Hate to Get up in the Morning," and which Sime Silverman described in *Variety* (August 23, 1918) as "a great show by a great bunch." After the war, Berlin returned to the vaudeville stage, and *The New York Dramatic Mirror* reviewed his act on October 23, 1919:

Irving Berlin has undertaken a vaudeville route that will serve to increase the present popularity of his many songs. He is one of the most facile of present day song writers, and every one is glad to see this stalwart young composer in civies once more, after so nobly springing to arms for the defense of his country. With Harry Akst at the piano, his repertoire includes "Mandy," "Oh! How I Hate to Get up in the Morning," and his latest, "You'd be Surprised!"

Irving Berlin's stage musicals date back to *Watch Your Step* in 1914, and perhaps not surprisingly he returned in the 1920s to the musical comedy and revue genre, writing the music and lyrics for the various editions of the *Music Box Revue* from 1921 to 1924. Later the screen beckoned, and Irving Berlin never returned to vaudeville, but his importance to the medium cannot be overemphasized. In 1919, when *Variety* began publishing a series on "Who's Who" in vaudeville, Irving Berlin was a natural choice of subject. Johnnie O'Connor (*Variety*'s "Wynn") wrote of him, "A little nervous, always on the go, but never forgetful. Russia has given America much in a musical way, but few Berlins. What a regular kid he is! None more regular, no siree!"

BIBLIOGRAPHY

Bergreen, Lawrence. *As Thousands Cheer: The Life of Irving Berlin*. New York: Viking Press, 1990.

Freedland, Michael. *Irving Berlin*. New York: Stein & Day, 1974.

————. *A Salute to Irving Berlin*. London: W. H. Allen, 1986.

O'Connor, Johnnie. "Irving Berlin." *Variety*, August 1, 1919.

O'Malley, Frank Ward. "Irving Berlin Gives Nine Rules for Writing Popular Songs." *American Magazine*, October 1920, pp. 37, 239–46.

Seldes, Gilbert. "Irving Berlin." *The New Republic*, December 12, 1928, pp. 100–102.

Suskin, Steven. *Berlin, Kern, Rodgers, Hart, and Hammerstein: A Complete Song Catalogue*. Jefferson, N.C.: McFarland, 1990.

Woollcott, Alexander. *The Story of Irving Berlin*. New York: G. P. Putnam's Sons, 1925.

GEORGE AND BERT BERNARD

Billed as the Bernard Brothers, George and Bert were neither brothers nor named Bernard. The dominant partner was Bernard George, who reversed his name and in 1935 teamed with Bert Maxwell in a singing and dancing act. In Chicago in 1941, the couple developed an act in which they pantomimed to recordings of the Andrews Sisters and other female acts while dressed in a parody of feminine attire. After the Second World War, they revived the act and for fourteen years were active in England and France. In the United States, they were frequent performers at nightclubs in Las Vegas, New York, and Miami. George Bernard died on October 22, 1967, at the reported age of 55, in Vancouver, Canada, after completing the final show of the night in a revue titled *Vive Les Girls* at the Cave Theatre Restaurant. Following Bernard's death, Bert Maxwell continued the act with Les Bernard (no relation to George Bernard).

SAM BERNARD (Birmingham, England, June 16, 1863—on his way across the Atlantic to Europe, May 18, 1927)

A popular actor specializing in German characaterizations and later becoming a "Dutch" comedian, Sam Bernard made his British music hall debut in 1885. He appeared on the legitimate stage and in revues as well as vaudeville, in which he was featured both as a monologist and the leading actor in various one-act playlets. Bernard made his first appearance at the Palace Theatre in January 1914 and his last in March 1926.

SARAH BERNHARDT (Paris, October 23, 1844—Paris, March 26, 1923)

Dozens of actresses of the legitimate stage took time out to appear in vaudeville, but only one legendary theatrical star ever graced the halls of vaudeville, and that was Sarah Bernhardt. Theatrical promotor Martin Beck arranged for the actress to make what was billed as one of many American farewell tours in the winter of 1912 and the spring of 1913, at a reported salary of $7,000 a week. She performed single acts from her repertoire, and her leading man was Lou Tellegen (1883–1934), who went on to become a minor matinee idol in films and to marry opera singer Geraldine Farrar. According to critic and scholar Gerda Taranow, at this time Bernhardt was concentrating on roles that she liked or which were repetitions or imitations of those she had played from her break with the Comédie Française in 1880 through her direction of Renaissance in 1898. The vaudeville program varied from city to city but might include Bernhardt as the Empress in *Theodora*, as Marion la Vivandière in *Une Nuit de Noel sous le Terreur* (translated for vaudeville audiences as *A Christmas Night under the Terror*), or as Marguerite Gautier in *La Dame aux Camélias*.

Sarah Bernhardt had the right to select the supporting acts. No animal performers were permitted on the same bill. She was extremely relaxed in other respects and would often write letters of recommendation for her fellow artistes. W. C. Fields presented no problem to the actress. He appeared with her at her

Palace Theatre debut and later, on October 11, 1913, supported Bernhardt at a royal command performance for King George V and Queen Mary at the London Coliseum. One act that fared less well was the acrobatic turn of the Heras Family, which was booked to close the Bernhardt program in Chicago. When the actress learned of it, she cabled Beck that she would not be followed by acrobats. She was not! The story is told that Beck was concerned as to the response of his star to the requirement that she give Sunday performances in certain cities, but Bernhardt replied, "Monsieur Beck, the theatre is my life. Of course I shall play on any Sunday!"

The Sarah Bernhardt twenty-two-week vaudeville tour, managed by Eddy Sullivan of the Charles Dillingham organization, opened at the Majestic Theatre, Chicago, on December 2, 1912. It almost got no farther, as Bernhardt became ill during Christmas week, but she recovered sufficiently to continue. The actress traveled by private Pullman car with nineteen members of her company, a chef, a porter, and a maid. Playing the Orpheum circuit, she appeared at theatres in St. Louis, Milwaukee, Winnipeg, Edmonton, Kansas City, Los Angeles, San Francisco, Seattle, Denver, and Omaha, among others.

At the close of her triumphant tour, Bernhardt appeared for three and a half weeks at the Palace Theatre in May 1913. For her first week there, the supporting acts included McMahon, Diamond, and Clemence, performing a scarecrow dance; Harris, Boland, and Holtz, a trio presented by Elsie Janis; the Edison talking films that used sound on cylinder, which were screened out of sync and greeted with derision by an opening night audience; Mlle Fregoleska; and Seldom's Poems in Marble, which closed the program. On her opening night at the Palace, Bernhardt took eighteen bows after appearing in the piece *A Christmas Night under the Terror*. *Variety* (May 9, 1913) reported, "Her vaudeville tour has not improved Mme Bernhardt's physical self for it was noticed she did not display the same confidence in her movements as at her opening in Chicago some few months ago. She moved round more carefully, always making sure to find a prop and did part of her work on a chair. But it was Bernhardt which is enough." The Palace show cost $10,000 to produce, which after Bernhardt's salary left very little for the other performers, and brought in an average of $22,000 a week.

In 1915, one of Bernhardt's legs was amputated. According to Robert Grau, $250,000 was vaudeville's estimate of her worth for twenty-five weeks after the operation, but the actress turned down the proposal. She also rejected an offer from a San Francisco showman to display the amputated leg, with a cable stating, "If you wish my left leg, see the doctors; but if it is my right leg you want, you must see my American impressario, Mr. Connor."

After a legitimate stage tour of North America closed in Montreal in December 1917, Sarah Bernhardt let it be know that, for financial reasons, she would be willing to appear once again in vaudeville. However, because of wartime restrictions on "foreign acts," as Bernhardt was classified, negotiations for the tour broke down. The divine Sarah did play three weeks at the Palace Theatre, beginning on Monday, December 17, 1917. She introduced a new playlet, *Du Théâtre au Champ d'Honneur* (*From the Theatre to the Field of Honor*), and also offered such old favorites as *Camille* and *Jeanne d'Arc*. Belle Baker was one of the supporting acts during Bernhardt's stay at the theatre. "Remarkable what this grand old lady can do in the varieties as against her drawing power on the road at the head of her own company," noted *Variety* (January 4, 1918). "It must be deduced that in vaudeville at lower prices and with an entertaining bill surrounding her, it's just the people who want to see Bernhardt rather than to see her play who are drawn in. And Bernhardt does draw a different crowd from the customary vaudeville attendance."

After her three weeks at the Palace, Bernhardt played a week at New York's Riverside Theatre. *Variety* (January 11, 1918) reported:

That the divine one is still wonderfully possessed with the power of inspiring her audience is the marvel of the stage. Perhaps most mystifying is her retention of voice power. She thrilled the house which after her half-hour playlet applauded for fully two minutes. Mme Bernhardt again played the role of the wounded color bearer in *From the Theatre to the Field of Honor*. The playlet has been slightly changed over the initial Palace presentation. Then the surgeon and stretcher bearers were in French uniforms, but now they wear the khaki of America, which brings the story into fuller tune since Americans were long in the hospital corps even before our entrance into the fray.

Sarah Bernhardt was a remarkable woman, not only in that she could draw vaudeville audiences to hear her speak in a language they did not understand but also in her ability to arouse such audiences with the emotion of her portrayals. Here was a woman in her seventies playing two shows a day and one-night stands in towns and cities of which she had probably never even heard before. Perhaps as Caroline Caffin has suggested, an audience admired a performance by Bernhardt or dances by Ruth St. Denis, but at the same time, "it never loses consciousness that these are exotics, who demand a certain readjustment of its point of view." At the same time, there was a magic to Bernhardt's acting. A *Variety* critic pointed out, "Bernhardt is seventy-three now, but she doesn't look it upon the stage, and played the eighteen-year-old Joan [of Arc] without spoiling the illusion of the young girl."

Whatever the reason, one must agree with the summation of Dorothy L. Sayers's character Lord Peter Wimsey in *Clouds of Witness* (1927): "voice gone, bloom gone, savour gone—but still a classic."

BIBLIOGRAPHY

Arthur, Sir George. *Sarah Bernhardt*. Garden City, N.Y.: Doubleday, 1923.

Baring, Maurice. *Sarah Bernhardt*. New York: Appleton-Century, 1934.

Emboden, William A. *Sarah Bernhardt*. London: Studio Vista, 1974.

Gold, Arthur, and Robert Fizdale. *The Divine Sarah: The Life of Sarah Bernhardt*. New York: Alfred A. Knopf, 1991.

Izard, Forrest. *Sarah Bernhardt: An Appreciation*. New York: Sturgis & Walton, 1915.

Noble, Iris. *Great Lady of the Theatre: Sarah Bernhardt*. New York: Messner, 1960.

Row, Arthur William. *Sarah, the Divine: The Biography of Sarah Bernhardt.* New York: Comet Press, 1957.

Skinner, Cornelia Otis. *Madam Sarah.* Boston: Houghton Mifflin, 1967.

Taranow, Gerda. *Sarah Bernhardt: The Art within the Legend.* Princeton: N.J.: Princeton University Press, 1972.

BEN BERNIE (New York, May 30, 1891—New York, October 20, 1943)

With the nickname of "The Old Maestro" and his familiar greeting of "Yowsah," Ben Bernie enjoyed his greatest success on radio as a master of ceremonies, violinist, and orchestra leader. Born Bernard Anzelvitz, Bernie was a serious student of the violin, making his debut at the age of fourteen at Carnegie Recital Hall. As a teenager, he briefly taught violin and also sold the instrument in a department store until in 1910 he teamed with Charlie Klass in a vaudeville act titled "Fiddle-Up-Boys." *Variety* (February 11, 1912) caught the act at Brooklyn's Academy of Music and reported, "They played both violin and accordion, on the assumption that since each of the instruments had become a riot by itself, collectively, the two must start a panic. Theoretically correct, but Messrs. Klass and Bernie, each young enough to hold down an office boy job, started to play upon the stage before their musical education had been completed. Which only goes to show that if you play ragtime, you must know how to play ragtime."

Initially he was known as Bernard Berni, but in the teens he changed his name to Ben Bernie and developed an act with Phil Baker, in which the latter played the accordion and told jokes and Bernie continued to play the violin. In 1923, Bernie formed his own band, Ben Bernie and All the Lads, which played New York's Roosevelt Hotel for six years. In the early 1930s, he and his band toured vaudeville with Maurice Chevalier, and he also appeared in two Paramount feature films, *Shoot the Works* (1934) and *Stolen Harmony* (1935).

Ben Bernie had been heard on radio as early as 1923; his network radio show was first broadcast by CBS in 1931 and continued almost until his death. It gained popularity when Bernie began a much publicized feud with columnist Walter Winchell. His theme songs were "It's a Lonesome Old Town When You're Not Around" and "Au Revoir, Pleasant Dreams." Both are representative of the sweet, gentle music with which Bernie is associated.

THE BILLBOARD

An important early trade paper covering all aspects of the entertainment industry, *The Billboard* later dropped the definite article and became the primary observer of the music industry. Founded in Cincinnati by W. H. Donaldson and James Hennigan, *The Billboard* was first published on November 1, 1894, as *Billboard Advertising*, catering to the interests of the bill posting, poster printing, and advertising industries. In the late teens and early 1920s, Walter Winchell wrote the "Stage Whispers" column for the paper under the name of "Busybody." In the 1920s and 1930s, *The Billboard* was edited by Elias E. Sugarman, the third husband of vaudevillian Belle Baker. The periodical is available on microfilm from Kraus-Thomson.

BLACK AMERICANS IN VAUDEVILLE

While it is true that a black vaudeville circuit, the Theatre Owners Booking Association, existed to provide segregated entertainment for black audiences in the American South, mainstream vaudeville was remarkably well integrated in comparison to other areas of society. There was some discrimination in most vaudeville houses in that black Americans in the audience were not permitted to sit in the more expensive seats, but onstage a surprising number of black entertainers were billed alongside their white counterparts from the 1890s onward.

When B. F. Keith introduced continuous vaudeville at his Boston theatre on July 6, 1883, one of the acts was the Olympian Quintette, identified as "colored." As early as the mid 1850s, black minstrel shows began to be formed. In 1865, Charles Hicks created the first major all-black minstrel troupe and, supposedly for the first time, introduced the famous line, "Why did the chicken cross the road?" The Georgia Minstrels, as they were called, were reviewed as they appeared at the Tremont Temple, Boston, by the *New York Clipper* (December 23, 1865): "These are real 'nigs,' and they are not only reported as being first rate, but are doing a good business." The troupe continued well into the twentieth century but were not always welcomed in the South; in 1902, one of the minstrels was lynched in New Madrid, Missouri.

A prominent monologist on the vaudeville stage in the 1880s and 1890s was Charlie Case (1858–1916), whose anecdotes revolved around the behavior of his father:

Father was a peculiar man. Us children didn't understand him. Mother understood him. Mother could always tell when father'd been drinking. We couldn't tell. We used to think he was dead. Father was a great hand for finding things. I remember him coming home one night. He picked up something. He couldn't see just what it was, but he brought it home. When he got to the house he found it was an arm-load of wood. Father didn't mean to take anybody else's wood, of course. We already had a lot of our own just exactly like it.

Charles Johnson and Dora Dean were a popular Negro song-and-dance act of the 1890s, billed as the "King and Queen of Colored Aristocracy." Another popular black song-and-dance team of the same era was Bob Cole and Billy Johnson, who played Proctor's 23rd Street Theatre in 1897, and the following year were featured at the Roof Garden of Koster and Bial's Music Hall. At that time, they were billed as "The Kings of Koondom." The Cole and Johnson partnership was dissolved a year or two later, and Cole teamed up with J. Rosamond Johnson; he died in 1911, at which time she began a new partnership with Charlie Hart.

There was opposition within the vaudeville fraternity to black performers. In 1901, the White Rats declared its hostility toward nonwhites. There was minimal fraternization between black and white vaudeville performers, and for that reason, Afro-Americans formed their own social club in 1898, the Greasy Front, run in New York by Charlie Moore. It was followed in 1908 by the Frogs, with Bert Williams as its first president, and in 1909, the Colored Vaudeville Benefit Association was founded in New York.

Bert Williams emphasized his Negroid features on the vaudeville stage with the use of blackface makeup, and this was a fairly common practice among both black men and women. A popular trio of entertainers, the Whitman Sisters (Mabel, Essie, and Alberta), used blackface makeup in part because they were fair-skinned enough to pass for white, and such deception actually hurt their work when they appeared with black male performers. A 1902 critic complained "black men making love to white girls look cheap," and urged all fair-skinned Negro women to wear blackface makeup on stage.

This practice continued among black performers well into the 1920s. Critic Richard Watts, Jr., writing in *The Film Mercury* (March 15, 1929), praised what he considered the natural performance of Steppin' Fetchit in the film *Hearts in Dixie*, and commented:

> It is a strange but, I think, undeniable fact that the only really authentic and believable Negro comedian since the days of Bert Williams has been the white Charles Mack, of the inordinately popular team of Moran and Mack. The Negro has almost invariably been effective as a serious actor, but as soon as he tries to be comic he loses all his racial gift for natural humor and seems only an uneventful white player working blackface. The strange sight of, for example, such a naturally gifted pair of Negro performers as Miller and Lyles, putting burnt cork on their faces and then behaving with all the Afro-American realism of a road company of Eddie Cantor, has always struck me as being both curious and distressing. The trouble apparently is the Negro comedian insists on going to Broadway for his inspiration, rather than to his own race.

The majority of black vaudevillians were in the area of song and dance. Surprisingly, there were at least two black ventriloquists performing in mainstream vaudeville in 1909 and 1910. The first was J. W. Cooper, who appeared at the Bijou Theatre, Brooklyn, in February 1909. "There is some novelty in seeing a colored ventriloquist. Mr. Cooper is progressive," reported *Variety* (February 22, 1909). Frank Rogers appeared at Hammerstein's Victoria Theatre in April 1910 with two "kid" dummies, one black and one white. *The New York Clipper* (February 5, 1910) reported:

> Frank Rogers, a rather good looking young fellow, appeared with two dummies to uphold the cleverness of his race along the lines of ventriloquial work. One of the figures was a little white "tough," while the other was a slow thinking, stammering "coon" kid, who was very funny. The "boys" get into an argument over spelling, and quite a few laughs were aroused over the dispute.
>
> Rogers catches his different intonations nicely, and the changes of voices between the two kids, especially in a rapid, heated argument they indulged in, was excellent. . . . The ventriloquial work finished with the singing of "Here Comes Mah Train" by the black dummy, with the white 'boy' chiming in the responses. A big hand brought Rogers back,

and as an encore number he gave various vocal imitations with good effect, including a moving train and a trolley car, the latter being especially faithful.

As evidence of the number of black entertainers in mainstream vaudeville, in its issue of that same date, February 5, 1910, *Variety* reviewed the male-and-female song-and-dance couple Rastus and Harrison, who pleased audiences at the New York Roof. Black vaudevillians by this time had also traveled to Europe and made a name for themselves long before the "flight" to Britain and France in the 1920s and 1930s of such major American black entertainers as Josephine Baker, Adelaide Hall, and Elizabeth Welch. At the American Theatre in September 1909, Johnson and Dean, a male-and-female, black song-and-dance act, intrigued audiences by recalling their recent success in Budapest with a Hungarian song and their equally successful appearance in London with Johnson's appearing as "Tommy Atkins." *Variety* (October 2, 1909) hailed Johnson and Dean as "the leaders among the colored mixed acts in vaudeville."

Aside from routinely reviewing black acts, *Variety* paid particular attention to Afro-American entertainers in its early years, with articles written by black performers in 1906 and 1907. The first, written by Ernest Hogan (q.v.), pointed out, "That there is no so-called color-line in the vaudeville houses is evidenced by the large number of Negro acts now before the public The sum total of colored acts on the variety stage to-day numbers over fifty, giving employment to over two hundred colored people." While noting that men predominated, Hogan did list the following among black women with "enviable reputations on the vaudeville stage": Abbie Mitchell, Black Patti, Aida Overton Walker, Belle Davis, Alice Mackey, Mattie Wilkes, and Carita Day.

In 1907, Harry Kraton of the vaudeville act The Kratons commented:

"There are great possibilities for the colored artist in vaudeville. I can speak of vaudeville only in the most appreciative terms. I have met with the most courteous reception, square dealings, and have experienced no detriment through being colored. A word of advice, a mere suggestion to my race, is not to overstep any bounds. Be polite, be gentlemanly, be womanly, and you will command and receive due regard from everybody."

According to Joe Laurie, Jr., there were 270 black Americans in principal roles on the American stage, with a total of 1,400 black performers available. The number on the vaudeville stage seems to have diminished by the 1920s. The major, and remembered, names had emerged, but they no sooner were a success in vaudeville than they moved over to the legitimate stage to star in revues or musical comedies. On February 6, 1926, the *Afro American* listed the following black performers on white vaudeville circuits: Plantation Review, Bryston and Jones, Gaines Brothers, Dixie Four, Jones and Pleat, Harrington and Green, Bill Robinson, Glen and Jenkins, the Four Chocolate Dandies, Covan and Ruffin, Harris and Holly, Tabor and Green, Chappelle and Stinnette, Skeftel's Revue, the Black and White Revue, Lucky Sambo, Monkey Shines, Rarin' to Go, Seven-Eleven, and Sliding Billy Watson.

Only Bill Robinson remains a "name" today, but the other acts indicate clearly that black vaudevillians were not the exception in mainstream vaudeville. They may not be familiar figures today, but their contribution to the history of vaudeville was substantial.

See also JOSEPHINE BAKER, PEG LEG BATES, BUCK AND BUBBLES, WILLIE COVAN, ADELAIDE HALL, ERNEST HOGAN, SISSIERETTA JONES, MILLER AND LYLES, FLORENCE MILLS, MILLS BROTHERS, NICHOLAS BROTHERS, BILL ROBINSON, SISSLE AND BLAKE, STEP BROTHERS, THEATRE OWNERS BOOKING ASSOCIATION, GEORGE DEWEY WASHINGTON, ETHEL WATERS, BERT WILLIAMS, EDITH WILSON.

BIBLIOGRAPHY

Hogan, Ernest. "The Negro in Vaudeville." *Variety*, December 15, 1906, p. 22.

Kraton, Harry. "Colored Folk in Vaudeville." *Variety*, December 14, 1907, p. 31.

Laurie, Joe, Jr. "The Negro in Vaudeville." In *Vaudeville: From the Honky-Tonks to the Palace*. New York: Henry Holt, 1953, pp. 201–207.

Sampson, Henry T. *Blacks in Blackface: A Source Book on Early Black Musical Shows*. Metuchen, N.J.: Scarecrow Press, 1980.

————. *The Ghost Walks: A Chronological History of Blacks in Show Business, 1865–1910*. Metuchen, N.J.: Scarecrow Press, 1988.

BLACKFACE.   See AUNT JEMINA, EDDIE CANTOR, LEW DOCK-STADER, DUNCAN SISTERS, "ETHIOPIAN," GEORGE "HONEY BOY" EVANS, JAY C. FLIPPEN, AL HERMAN, AL JOLSON, EDDIE LEONARD, McINTYRE AND HEATH, MORAN AND MACK, GEORGE H. PRIMROSE, FRANK TINNEY

BLACKOUT

A blackout is a short comedy routine, ending on a punch or curtain line as the stage lights quickly go out or the curtain closes. It was more in use in burlesque and revues than in vaudeville and played before a drop curtain as the scenery was changed.

HARRY BLACKSTONE (Chicago, September 27, 1883—Hollywood, Ca., November 17, 1965)

The last of the great twentieth-century magicians, Harry Blackstone was generally billed simply as "Blackstone," and when vaudeville's days were numbered, he created his own magic show which he took on the road. Born Harry Bouton, Blackstone became interested in magic after seeing Harry Kellar perform in 1898, and with his brother Pete developed an act titled "Straight and Crooked Magic." Blackstone's best known trick was the intimate one of making a handkerchief seemingly dance. He could also saw a woman in half, demonstrate levitation, and at one point featured the "Phantom Stallion," a live horse he would make disappear.

EUBIE BLAKE. See SISSLE AND BLAKE

(JESSIE) BLOCK (New York, December 16, 1900—New York, March 22, 1983) and **(EVE) SULLY** (Atlantic City, N.J. 1902—New York, August 7, 1990)

Jesse Block and Eve Sully had a husband-and-wife act—he was the straight man and she the dumb brunette—which was popular in vaudeville at approximately the same time as George Burns and Gracie Allen came to prominence. As the following routine indicates, there was great similarity between the two acts, and both used the same writer, Al Boasberg. However, there was never any animosity between Block and Sully and Burns and Allen, and the two couples remained firm friends.

Block: Why are you late?

Sully: I was watching the show and I had to change my seat six different times.

Block: Why, were you molested?

Sully: Yes, finally.

Block: Where were you born?

Sully: In a hospital.

Block: Why, were you sick?

Sully: No, I wanted to be near my mother.

Block: I saw your sister on the street today, but she didn't see me.

Sully: I know, she told me.

Block: Say, where can I get hold of your sister?

Sully: I don't know, she's awfully ticklish.

Block: I never met anyone as dumb as you.

Sully: My sister's dumber than me.

Block: You mean dumber than I.

Sully: She's dumber than both of us.

Block: Did you hear the story of the Scotsman who found a corn plaster on the street and went out and bought tight shoes?

Sully: No, you didn't tell me about it. Did I ever tell you about the Scotsman who found a corn plaster on the street and went out and bought tight shoes?

Block: I just told you that story.

Sully: That's where I heard it!

As *Variety* (May 14, 1930) commented, it was "smooth, easy dialog that can't miss." Sully would end the routine with a silly giggle, go into the wings, and return with a soft-shoe dance, saying, "Look Ma, I'm dancing." As will be noted, whereas Gracie Allen was forever discussing her brother, Eve Sully's major topic of conversation was her sister. Unlike George Burns with his cigar, Block and Sully had no particular props. They would appear onstage in street clothes, with Block often wearing a straw hat. When they first developed their routine, they would carry a suitcase onstage and sit on it while engaging in cross talk.

Block and Sully paid Al Boasberg $25 a week for material, and other gags were written by "a pimply faced kid of 21" (as Jesse Block described him) named Herman Wouk. Eve Sully would also read short poems, such as the following:

> There once was a butcher named Hutton,
> Whose wife was a glutton for mutton.
> He sneaked up behind her,
> Threw her in the grinder.
> No Hutton, no mutton, no glutton—no nuttin!

Although they may not have been aware of it, the Block and Sully and Burns and Allen routines were interchangeable. Jesse Block recalled a routine he and Eve Sully did with Jack Benny, when the latter was master of ceremonies at the Palace Theatre in Chicago. At the close of the act, Benny appeared:

Benny: Jesse, come here. I always knew you were clever, but that girl you work with, she was wonderful.

Block: Did you ever meet her?

Benny: No, I never met her. I'd love to meet her.
(Eve comes on stage and says hello.)

Benny: You're awfully cute. Do you smoke?

Sully: No.

Benny: Do you drink?

Sully: No.

Benny: Do you go out?

Sully: No.

Benny: What do you do?

Sully: I tell lies.

Benny: I'd like to take you out.

Sully: I can't. I'm married.

Benny: To whom?

Sully: To Jessie.
(Eve goes off giggling, while Benny stands there with his typically exasperated look.)

Block: Sorry Jack, I did the best I could.

This routine, with Bing Crosby substituting for Jack Benny, is performed almost word for word by Burns and Allen in a 1933 Paramount short, *Hollywood on Parade*.

Jesse Block began his career as a child. At the age of fifteen, he auditioned for Gus Edwards, and when an opening came, Edwards sent two of his kids, Jack Weiner and Walter Winchell, down to the East Side of New York where Block lived, to fetch him. Block made his debut in Edwards's *Song Revue of 1915* in Madison, Wisconsin; also in the *Revue* were Georgie Price, Lila Lee, and Arthur Freed. Eventually, Block developed a song-and-dance act with Frances Dunlap titled Block and Dunlap. When the act broke up four years later, he met Eve Sully through Bert Gordon. Except for a sister in the Yiddish theatre, Eve Sully had no theatrical background. She had been touring in a song-and-dance act with Jeanette MacDonald's sister Blossom (who was later professionally known as Blossom Rock).

Block and Sully got together in 1926 and were married in 1930. "We rehearsed for four years," joked Block. He continued:

> Our act always remained the same. A dumb dame and a soft-shoe dance. We immediately clicked. We played all the important theatres in this country, two-a-day. And then, when we went to the presentation houses, were responsible for talking acts coming in to the Chicago Theatre. Up to that time, it had been singing acts and acrobats, but we were the first talking act ever to play there—5,000 seats. In 1930, we went to England and played the Palladium with Burns and Allen—not on the same bill, of course. They played the Holborn Empire and we played the Palladium. Then we played the Holborn Empire and they played the Palladium.

In 1929, Block and Sully played the Palace for the first time and worried about having to put over their act after the Wall Street crash. They need not have been concerned. Block came onstage from one side and Sully from the other. She walked up to him and asked. "Did you vote for Hoover for president?" He replied, "Certainly I did." Eve Sully commenced to hit her partner over the head, and the more she hit him, the more the audience laughed. "From then on we were set," noted Block. Reviewing their act a couple of months later, *Variety* (March 12, 1930) commented, "Jesse Block and Eve Sully have a talk routine with lapses into song and action. Okay on the smart retorts, the girl playing dumb." Block and Sully returned to the Palace in April and October 1930. After jumping from vaudeville to presentation houses, they became headliners.

In the early 1930s, Block and Sully had their own radio program on Monday nights, with Paul Douglas as the announcer, Arlene Francis as Eve's sister, and Gertrude Niesen providing a few songs. In 1941, they were heard on WMCA–New York as the Damon Runyon characters, Joe and Ethel Turp. The couple also appeared in a number of film shorts and were featured, in the roles of Ben Ali and Fanya, in the 1934 Samuel Goldwyn production of *Kid Millions*, starring their friend Eddie Cantor. In 1940, Block and Sully were on Broadway in George Abbott's production of *See My Lawyer*, which also featured former silent screen star Madge Bellamy. Some years earlier, they had worked on the legitimate stage, taking over from Fred and Adele Astaire in the Chicago production of *For Goodness Sake*.

In 1938, with Lou Holtz and Belle Baker, Block and Sully were the last vaudevillians to appear on the stage of the Capitol Theatre.

During the Second World War, they toured with the U.S.O. In June 1939, Block and Sully headlined at Loew's State, with the former emceeing and Sully heckling; "Jesse and Eve are capable of dishing out plenty of laughs even if a large portion of their stuff has whiskers," commented *The Billboard* (June 10, 1939). In 1948, they played their last vaudeville engagement—at Loew's State—and shortly thereafter, Block began a new career as a stockbroker. "I don't think any act played Loew's State as many times as we did," recalled Block. "We'd go from Loew's State to the Paramount, across the street; from the Paramount to the Capitol, up the block on Broadway; from the Capitol to B. S. Moss's Broadway. We played every theatre on Broadway except the Roxy."

BIBLIOGRAPHY

Smith, Bill. "Block and Sully." In *The Vaudevillians*. New York: Macmillan, 1976, pp. 74–82.

LEW BLOOM

Billed as "A Society Tramp," Lew Bloom was a sad-faced comic monologist at the height of his fame in the 1890s. In 1893, he was a busy performer in the New York area, appearing at the Lyceum Theatre, Brooklyn, the week of March 20, the London Theatre the week of June 26, and Proctor's the week of July 3. He was one of the first to appear in a shabby tramp costume, preceding Nat C. Wills and W. C. Fields. In deadpan fashion, he would tell the audience: "I don't spend all my time in saloons. I can't. They have to close up some time. The early closing law is an imposition on people who enjoy club life. The other day, I went into a saloon and the bartender must have mistaken me for somebody else. He let me pour my own drink."

Nothing is known of Bloom's origins or when or where he died.

BEN BLUE (Montreal, September 12, 1901—Hollywood, Ca., March 7, 1975)

A sad-faced comedian who was also a first-rate dancer, Ben Blue was born Benjamin Bernstein and made his show business debut in Baltimore at the age of thirteen. At the age of fifteen, he was a chorus boy in New York shows, and four years later, he opened dance schools in St. Paul and Duluth, Minnesota. Circa 1920, he also originated a skating dance that he took on the vaudeville circuit and which helped gain him popularity. He headlined at the Palace in February and July 1929, April 1930, and January, March, and April 1931. Ben Blue was also the first headliner to succeed Judy Garland, in February 1952, after her record-breaking run. He appeared as well in the 1939, and last, edition of George White's *Scandals*.

Ben Blue was active on screen from 1926 to 1968, and his feature films include *High, Wide and Handsome* (1937), *College Swing* (1938), *My Wild Irish Rose* (1947), and *It's a Mad, Mad, Mad, Mad World* (1963). In the 1940s, he operated Slapsie Maxie's nightclubs in Los Angeles and San Francisco, and in the late 1950s and early 1960s also operated Ben Blue's Night Club in Santa Monica, California.

AL BOASBERG (Buffalo, N.Y., December 5, 1892—Los Angeles, June 18, 1937)

A noted writer of vaudeville material in the 1920s, Al Boasberg provided gags for Bob Hope at the start of his career, and in 1926 wrote the most famous of all Burns and Allen sketches, "Lamb Chops." He entered films in 1925 as a title writer and worked on the following Buster Keaton films: *Battling Butler* (1926), *The General* (1927), *Doughboys* (1930), and *Free and Easy* (1930). Boasberg wrote a number of screenplays, provided the storyline and comic dialogue for the 1929 M-G-M feature *The Hollywood Revue of 1929*, and also wrote many of the gag sequences for the Marx Brothers vehicle *A Day at the Races* (1937). Because of the number of gags for films and radio for which he did not receive credit, Boasberg became known as the "Hollywood Ghost Writer."

In 1929, he turned to production, co-producing a series of two-reel shorts for Radiant Pictures, and in 1934 he directed *Myrt and Marge* for Universal. He also wrote radio material for Eddie Cantor and Block and Sully, and only a day before his death had signed a new one-year contract to provide material for Jack Benny. At his death, he left an estate valued at a mere $5,250.

RAY BOLGER (Dorchester, Ma., January 10, 1904—Los Angeles, January 15, 1987)

Ray Bolger was an eccentric dancer whose legs seemed to be made of rubber, hence his billing in vaudeville as "Rubberlegs" Bolger. He achieved greater fame on screen, primarily as a result of his performance as the scarecrow in *The Wizard of Oz* (1939); other films include *The Great Ziegfeld* (1936), Rosalie (1937), *Sweethearts* (1938), *The Harvey Girls* (1946), *Babes in Toyland* (1961), and *The Runner Stumbles* (1979).

Raymond Wallace Bolger entered show business in 1922 with the Bob Ott Musical Comedy and Repertoire Company, touring the New England states as well as New York, Pennsylvania, and New Jersey. Next, he teamed with Ralph Sanford, developing a vaudeville act involving songs, comedy, and eccentric dancing called Sanford and Bolger, "A Pair of Nifties." The act broke up when the couple reached New York. In 1926, Bolger appeared in two Broadway shows, *The Merry World* and *A Night in Paris*, and the following year he made his Palace debut. Also in 1927, Bolger appeared with Leota and Lola Lane in the vaudeville sketch "Ritz Carlton Nights," presented by Gus Edwards. Other Broadway shows in which Bolger appeared include *Me for You* (1929), *Heads Up!* (1929), the 1931 edition of George White's *Scandals*, *Life Begins at 8:40* (1934), and *On Your Toes* (1936). He was also one of the stars on the opening bill at Radio City Music Hall.

The performer's career received a major boost in 1948, when he starred on Broadway in *Where's Charley?*, the musical version of *Charley's Aunt*, which he also filmed in 1952. He presented his own program, *The Ray Bolger Show*, on CBS radio in 1945, and starred on television in *The Ray Bolger Show* on ABC from 1953 to 1955. He continued working until his death.

BIBLIOGRAPHY

Abramson, Marty. "You're Fired!" *The American Weekly*, January 19, 1950, p. 28.

"Here's Bolger." *Newsweek*, July 18, 1949, pp. 72–73.

Kahn, E. J., Jr. "The Dancing Scarecrow." *Cosmopolitan*, July 1952, pp. 73–75, 129–30.

Oldfield, Col. Barney. "Ray Bolger Was There at Music Hall's Birth." *Variety*, April 12, 1978, pp. 2, 104.

Zolotow, Maurice. "Muscles with a Sense of Humor." *Saturday Evening Post*, July 30, 1949, pp. 32, 74–76.

IRENE BORDONI (Ajaccio, Corsica, January 16, 1895—New York, March 19, 1953)

With her provocative eyes and saucy demeanor, Irene Bordoni was a great chanteuse in revues and vaudeville. She made her stage debut in the chorus at Paris's Théâtre des Variétés at the age of thirteen and was a major French revue star when she was brought to the United States in 1912. That year, she appeared in vaudeville and was also seen in *Broadway to Paris*, which opened at New York's Winter Garden Theatre on November 20, 1912. The following year, she toured the Orpheum circuit with Melville Ellis, who acted as both her pianist and costume/set designer. Bordoni's first song in English was the unlikely "Sweet Adeline," but more appropriate was "Pretty Baby," which she performed in both English and French.

Bordoni returned briefly to Europe in 1914 but was back in the United States for the remainder of the decade, featured on the New York stage in *Miss Information* (1915), *Hitchy-Koo* (1917), *Sleeping Partners* (1918), and *As You Were* (1920). She was equally busy in the 1920s, starring in *The French Doll* (1922), *Little Miss Bluebeard* (1923), *Naughty Cinderella* (1925), *Mozart* (1926), and *Paris* (1928). She also found time for vaudeville appearances, headlining at the Palace in May and November 1927 and September 1930. She played opposite Jack Buchanan in the 1929 screen version of *Paris* and was also seen in the 1929 all-star film revue *The Show of Shows*.

There was a welcome Broadway comeback with *Louisiana Purchase* in 1940, and Bordoni also starred in the 1941 film version. In 1951 and 1952, she toured in the unlikely characterization of Bloody Mary in *South Pacific*. Only two months prior to her death, she played on the road in the musical *Maggie* but dropped out of the cast before the show came to New York. Irene Bordoni's second husband was composer E. Ray Goetz (1886–1954), who produced many of his wife's shows in the 1920s.

BIBLIOGRAPHY

"Mlle Bordoni's Love Affair." *Cosmopolitan*, February 1913, pp. 414–15.

BORSCHT BELT

The Borscht Belt was the name given to an area in the Catskill and Adirondack Mountains where resorts catered to Jewish visitors. The term was invented by *Variety* originally as the Borscht Circuit, and initially considered derogatory. The first priority of the resorts in the Borscht Belt was Kosher food, followed by good, vaudeville-style entertainment, organized by the social director, or *Toomler* (meaning tumult maker). The region was first developed at the turn of the century, when a number of boarding facilities opened, but it was not until the 1920s, that the first entertainers began appearing; at first they were not paid but merely provided with room and board, and when payment was given it was only on the understanding that the entertainers should double as hotel employees. Among those whose careers began in the Borscht Belt were Robert Alda, Jan Peerce (as a violinist at the Breezy Hill Hotel), Danny Kaye (a member of the entertainment staff at the White Roe Lake in 1933), Jackie Mason, Joey Adams, Alan King, and Henny Youngman (who started at the Swan Lake Inn in 1932).

The most important of the Borscht Belt resorts was the Grossinger Hotel at Grossinger, New York, which began in 1914 when Selig and Malke Grossinger purchased a rundown farmhouse. The facility developed from a boarding house to a resort under the guidance of the Grossingers' son Harry (1888–1964) and his wife, Jennie (1892–1972), and the expansion continued under the supervision of their son Paul (1916–1989). At the height of its success, the Grossinger Hotel entertained more than 100,000 visitors annually and later became a year-round operation, catering to conventions and younger people interested in the nearby skiing facilities. Entertainers at the Grossinger Hotel in 1939 included Milton Berle, Eddie Cantor, and Henny Youngman, and Cantor wrote that "when vaudeville faded . . . Grossinger's became the Palace."

Entertainment at the Borscht Belt resorts generally consisted of a dance team, a singer, and a comedian. The Grand Hotel in High Mount, New York, was the first to feature major vaudevillians in 1935, when Ethel Merman, Willie Howard, George E. Price, the Ritz Brothers, and Cab Calloway appeared there. They came as guests and in return presented a free show. The resorts declined in the 1950s, and the death knell was sounded in 1985, when the Grossinger Hotel was sold to a New York investment group.

BIBLIOGRAPHY

Adams, Joey, and Henry Tobias. *The Borscht Belt*. New York: Bobbs-Merrill, 1966.
Cantor, Eddie. "Grossinger's." In *As I Remember Them*. New York: Duell, Sloan and Pearce, 1963, pp. 59–63.

BOSTON

In 1906, there were seven vaudeville houses in Boston: Austin and Stone's Museum, the Columbia Music Hall, the Howard Athenaeum, the Lyceum, B. F. Keith's, the Palace, and Walker's. By 1921, with the city's population at 748,060, there were eleven: the Bourdoin Square Theatre, the Casino, the Howard Athenaeum, B. F. Keith's, Loew's Orpheum, the State, the Boston, the

Franklin, Gardon's Central Square Theatre (Cambridge), the St. James, and the Scollay Square Olympia Theatre.

See also B. F. KEITH

BOSWELL SISTERS

The best known sister trio of their day, the Boswell Sisters were noted for their harmony and rhythmic style that were precursors to the swing music of later years. They gained fame on radio but also played vaudeville. Martha Meldania Boswell (1905–1958), Constance (Connee) Foore Boswell (1907–1976), and Helvetia George Boswell (1911–1988) began their radio career by winning an amateur contest in 1922, which led to their performing on WSMB–New Orleans. During 1929 and 1930, the sisters were in Los Angeles, singing on KFWB, and in February of 1931, they signed with NBC in New York to appear on *Pleasure Hour*. In June 1931, they moved to CBS and got their first commercial sponsor, Baker Chocolate, in October of that year. During 1932, they were heard on *Music That Satisfies*, and in 1934, they costarred with Bing Crosby on *The Woodbury Hour*. To consolidate their radio career, the sisters toured in vaudeville and appeared at the Palace in October 1931 and February 1932. The group broke up in 1936 when Vet (Helvetia) retired to have a child. Connee married the trio's manager, Harry Leedy, in 1935 and continued as a solo act through the 1950s. Because she had been crippled by polio as a child, she generally performed sitting down.

RAY/RAE BOURBON (Texas, 1893—Big Spring, Tx., July 19, 1971)

A flamboyant, homosexual female impersonator, Ray (or Rae, as he preferred to be known) Bourbon was noted for his outrageous material, replete with references to "queens" and suggestive dialogue. He had neither the style nor the dignity of his colleagues and enjoyed little success in vaudeville, concentrating instead on major metropolitan nightclubs, mainly in New York. In the 1920s, he played small-time vaudeville and also claimed to have worked as an extra in a number of silent films. His heyday was the 1930s and 1940s; penniless and out of work in 1956, Bourbon devised a publicity stunt, claiming to have undergone a sex-change operation in Juarez, Mexico. In 1968, he was accused of being an accomplice in the murder of a Texas pet store owner who had been taking care of Bourbon's dogs. Despite a plea of innocence, the female impersonator was sentenced to a ninety-nine year prison term. On June 3, 1970, *Variety* published a letter from Bourdon asking for help—"I seem to have been completely forgotten by everyone"—but no one paid any attention. He suffered a heart attack in the Brown County Jail in Brownwood, Texas, and was transferred to the Big Spring State Hospital, where he died.

BIBLIOGRAPHY

Newlin, Jon. "Unpopular Music: Rae Bourbon . . . Tells All!" *Wavelength*, July 1987, pp. 8–9.

EL BRENDEL (Philadelphia, March 25, 1891—Hollywood, Ca., April 9, 1964)

El Brendel's stock-in-trade was the comic portrayal of a simple minded Swede with ill-fitting clothing. Mispronouncing the letter "j" as "y" in his delivery, he introduced the phrase "yumpin' yimminy," which is still in use today more because of Brendel's many film appearances than his earlier vaudeville work. Brendel had no Swedish ancestry but was of German-Irish extraction. He had entered vaudeville in 1913 as a German dialect comedian, but with America's entry into the First World War, he changed his character to Swedish.

Initially, Brendel worked in vaudeville with his wife, Flo Burt, telling jokes and performing sleight-of-hand tricks. They were not at first successful as a team and split up in 1916, with Burt appearing in *The Suffragette Revue* and Brendel working burlesque houses. The couple reteamed in 1917, introducing a new act in which Burt sang, Brendel performed an eccentric dance, and the two exchanged comic patter as Brendel explained that he earned eight dollars a week, spent seven for board, and the other dollar on women. *The New York Dramatic Mirror* (December 18, 1919) viewed the act at New York's Fifth Avenue Theatre and described it as "an unqualified, uproariously funny act." Brendel and Burt quickly became vaudeville headliners, starring at the Palace in 1927 and 1929 and also appearing in a revue, *The Mimic World of 1921*.

In 1926, El Brendel signed a contract with Famous Players–Lasky, appearing in eight silent feature films during 1926 and 1927, of which the most important is *Wings* (1927). Dissatisfied with the roles he was offered, he returned to vaudeville, but was back on screen in 1929, signing a contract with William Fox with a guaranteed weekly salary of $650, rising by 1931 to $1,000. Brendel's Swedish characterizations became familiar to film audiences and have remained so through the present. Unfortunately, in most of his films, Brendel leaves an impression of comic mediocrity which is at odds with reaction to his earlier work in vaudeville; for example, as early as October 12, 1917, *Variety* hailed him as "genuinely funny." In all, he appeared in some forty sound feature films, including *The Big Trail* (1930), *Just Imagine* (1930), *Mr. Lemon of Orange* (1931), *Little Miss Broadway* (1938), and *If I Had My Way* (1940). He retired briefly from the screen in 1944 but returned for Preston Sturges's *The Beautiful Blonde from Bashful Bend*. That production failed to revive Brendel's screen career and he made only two additional features, *Paris Model* (1953) and *Tobo, the Happy Clown* (1965).

Even while working in Hollywood, El Brendel continued to make vaudeville appearances, and in the late 1930s, he appeared with Flo Burt in a *Hollywood Surprises* show which included the two performing a supposed love scene between Garbo and Stokowski. In the 1950s, Brendel was active on television, most notably playing the father of the Joan Davis character in the situation comedy *I Married Joan* (NBC, 1952–1955).

BIBLIOGRAPHY

Belfrage, Cedric. "The Synthetic Swede." *Motion Picture Classic* 31, no. 3 (May 1930), pp. 52, 98.

JAY BRENNAN. See SAVOY AND BRENNAN

FANNY BRICE (New York, October 29, 1891—Los Angeles, May 29, 1951)

At the time of her death, *Variety* rightly hailed Fanny Brice as "one of the greatest singing comediennes in the history of the American theatre." Her comedy songs, including "Becky Is Back in the Ballet," "I Should Worry," and "Secondhand Rose," have never lost their comic appeal. But humor was only part of her appeal, for Fanny Brice was equally adept with tragic lyrics. Her rendition of "My Man," a French hit from 1920 with English lyrics by Channing Pollock, demonstrates her major talent as a torch singer. To understand how Fanny Brice could handle a lyric, one need only listen to her singing "Cooking Breakfast for the One I Love," which she introduced in a 1930 film, *Be Yourself!* At first, she sings the lyric straight, with warmth and affection; then, as the words begin to get silly, with talk of oatmeal sprinkled with lox, a Yiddish accent begins to creep into her voice. Few singers had such control over a song, an inherent ability drastically to change the impact of the number on the audience.

As a comedienne, Fanny Brice had the advantage of a funny face with expressive eyes and a mouth which, when she grinned, appeared to be an ugly gash in her features. And yet that same face could be poignantly and hauntingly expressive when necessary, although the demand for Brice's brand of pathos disappeared in the 1930s with the rise of her radio career. Her comedy style was distinctly Jewish, with a failure fully to grasp the meaning of the English language. It is interesting that before the statement became a classic Sam Goldwyn remark, Fanny Brice had said, "A verbal agreement is not worth the paper it's written on."

Once when Fanny Brice was asked about her career, she responded:

> Listen, kid! I've done everything in the theatre except marry a property man. I've been a soubrette in burlesque and I've accompanied stereopticon slides. I've acted for Belasco and I've laid 'em out in the rows at the Palace. I've doubled as an alligator; I've worked for the Shuberts; and I've been joined to Billy Rose in the holy bonds. I've painted the house boards and I've sold tickets and I've been fired by George M. Cohan. I've played in London before the king and in Oil City before miners with lanterns in their caps.

It was a remarkable career for a girl named Fannie Borach born on New York's East Side, and one that has not diminished with her death. Audiences still laugh at her Baby Snooks routine with Judy Garland in the 1938 M-G-M film *Everybody Sing*. She has been the subject of three book-length biographies and three biographical feature films. Much Jewish-based comedy seems dated, but Fanny Brice is ageless.

Like most vaudevillians, Fanny Brice always wanted to entertain. Unlike most of her contemporaries, her first name could be spelled two ways, either as Fanny or Fannie, but she preferred the former and tried to stick to it from the 1930s onward. As a child, Brice appeared one amateur night at Kenney's Theatre, Brooklyn, singing—with tears of emotion—"You Know You're Not Forgotten by the Girl You Can't Forget.'' She auditioned for George M. Cohan but was rejected because she could not dance. She toured in burlesque, first in *The Transatlantic Burlesque* and then in *College Girl*, and while appearing in the latter at the Columbia Theatre in New York, she was seen by Florenz Ziegfeld, who was casting the 1910 edition of his *Follies*.

There was no question that when the *Follies* opened at the New York Theatre on June 20, 1910, a new star was born. Despite the presence of Lillian Lorraine and Bert Williams, not to mention over three hours of glamour, no one had any doubt that the real star of the new *Follies* was Fanny Brice. She was ''the individual hit of the show,'' reported *Variety* (June 18, 1910), reviewing the *Follies* during its tryout at the Apollo Theatre in Atlantic City. ''Her first song, 'Lonely Joe,' was a riot, while the second, 'Grizzly Bear,' was nearly so.'' Fanny Brice starred in the 1911, 1916, 1917, 1920, 1921, and 1923 editions of the Ziegfeld *Follies*, but in all she was allowed only to display the comedic side of her character; ''They'll never take you home because of your tears, but because of your laughter,'' Ziegfeld once told her of the audience.

When not in the *Follies*, Fanny Brice was busy in vaudeville and on the musical comedy stage; she starred in *The Honeymoon Express* (1913), *Nobody Home* (1915), *Why Worry?* (1918), *Fanny* (1926, specially written for her by David Belasco), *Fioretta* (1929), and *Sweet and Low* (1930). She became a vaudeville favorite as quickly as she became a *Follies* favorite. On April 27, 1912, *Variety* reported that she was ''unquestionably 'the goods' for vaudeville. Miss Brice is chock full of unction and has a keen sense of travesty.'' She made her first appearance at the Palace in February 1914 and was to be a regular there for the next twenty years. At the Palace in September 1915, she introduced ''Becky Is Back in the Ballet,'' wearing a short ballet skirt and flesh pink stockings to sing about the girl who graduated from a ballet school in the Hester Street neighborhood of New York. She gave impersonations of a salesgirl in a millinery store and a Yiddish mother's boasting of her daughter's cleverness, and concluded her act with a song in male attire. ''When Miss Brice learns to refrain from starting to disrobe before she is out of sight of the audience her new act will be a step—several of them in fact—in the right direction,'' tartly commented *Variety* (September 10, 1915).

A few years later, Fanny Brice was back at the Palace with her torch number ''The Song of the Sewing Machine,'' a lament for the women of the sweatshops. On the same program—between 1915 and 1925 the length of her vaudeville act had grown from twelve to forty minutes, and audiences still wanted more—she presented the marvelous monologue of ''Mrs. Cohen at the Beach,'' with its punch line to the kids, ''Why didn't you do it when you were in the water?'' In March 1930, she gave her classic ''Dying Swan Ballet'' at the Palace, and in order not to stop the show completely, she had to appear at the end of the program as well as in the headliner spot.

Fanny Brice's private life was involved and exciting. She once joked, ''I've been poor and I've been rich. Rich is better!'' A teenage marriage in 1910 to

Frank White was dissolved in 1913. A second marriage to gangster Nicky Arnstein in 1918 ended in divorce in 1927 and produced two children. Arnstein was the inspiration for the song ''My Man.'' In 1930, Fanny Brice married showman Billy Rose but divorced him eight years later. ''She once told me,'' said Rose, ''that she married Frank White, the barber, because he smelled so good; she married Nick Arnstein because he looked so good; and she married me because I thought so good.'' Whatever his faults, Fanny Brice had to admit, ''I was never bored with Billy.'' Fanny Brice's language was as colorful as her marriages, and, offstage, she made no allowances for how she spoke. ''Anyone who can't say f—k is deceitful,'' she told her biographer.

Her memory would sometimes fail her, but never where money was concerned. Jesse Block recalled an incident that took place in the 1930s:

> We played the Oriental Theatre in Chicago with Fanny Brice. She had just closed with the *Follies*. She was a tremendous headliner. This was the first time we met, and we became great friends after that. We were together for a number of years until she moved to California. She had a heart condition. She never went to any place, except to Eddie Cantor's house. Now we come to California, and we haven't seen her for a couple of years. And in the meantime, because of her illness, she became very absentminded. Now out there, Eddie has a dinner party for us, George and Gracie Burns, Jack and Mary Benny, and Fanny Brice. So that night, we're reminiscing. I say, ''Remember, Fanny, when we played on the same bill at the Oriental Theatre?'' She says, ''Kid, I don't remember playing the Oriental Theatre.'' I say, ''Sure, remember we went down to the College Inn and we saw Ben Bernie and His Band?'' ''I don't remember Ben Bernie.'' ''This I'm sure you'll remember. Al Capone gave you a party.'' ''No!'' I say, ''Fanny, I remember everything. I remember you got $7,500 for the week.'' She says, ''I got $8,000.'' That she remembered!

In 1928, Fanny Brice made her film debut for Warner Bros. and the Vitaphone in *My Man*. She appeared in four other feature films: *Be Yourself!* (1930), *The Great Ziegfeld* (1936), *Everybody Sing* (1938), and *Ziegfeld Follies* (1946). Aside from *Be Yourself!*, in which she was given an opportunity to act, the films were chiefly an excuse for re-creations (often unsatisfactory) of her vaudeville and *Follies* sketches. Thanks to radio, Fanny Brice's most famous characterization became Baby Snooks, which had its antecedents in her vaudeville ''Babykins'' skits and which, according to legend, she had first tried out at a party after the opening of the 1910 Ziegfeld *Follies*. Baby Snooks was first heard on radio on February 29, 1936, and continued intermittently until Brice's death. Snooks's lisping voice and inquisitive ''Why, Daddy?'' to actor Hanley Stafford was one of the best known radio phrases of the day. The character was first heard on CBS's *The Ziegfeld Follies of the Air*, then on NBC in *Good News of 1938* and *Maxwell House Coffee Time*; from 1944, Brice returned to CBS on the *Baby Snooks Show* until 1949, when she moved to NBC.

Fanny Brice had planned to end Baby Snooks's career on June 21, 1951, when her NBC contract ended, and to devote herself to her hobby of interior decoration. She announced she wanted to retire because ''it's too much work.''

Sadly, fate took a hand, and Fanny Brice suffered a massive cerebral hemorrhage, leading to her death.

Since her death, Fanny Brice has been played by Barbara Streisand in two feature film biographies, *Funny Girl* (1968) and *Funny Lady* (1975). *Funny Girl* was a tremendous influence in Streisand's career; she played the title role in the original Broadway production and won an Academy Award for best actress for the screen version. Earlier, in 1939, 20th Century–Fox filmed a fictionalized account of Brice's and Nicky Arnstein's romance in *Rose of Washington Square*, starring Alice Faye and Tyrone Power.

Fanny's brother Lew Brice (died June 16, 1966) also played vaudeville as a comedian, and worked onstage in the late 1920s with his then-wife Mae Clark before she became a film actress. Singer Elizabeth Brice, who worked in both musical comedy and vaudeville, is no relation.

BIBLIOGRAPHY

Brice, Fanny, as told to Palma Wayne. "Fannie of the Follies." *Cosmopolitan*, February 1936, pp. 20–23, 138–39; March 1936, pp. 46–49, 106–108; April 1936, pp. 64–64, 101–102.

Collins, Frederick L. "The Private Life of Baby Snooks." *Liberty* 15, no. 34 (August 20, 1938), pp. 11–13.

"Fanny Brice." *Current Biography*, June 1946, pp. 73–75.

"Fannie Brice and Her Adventures." *The New York Dramatic Mirror*, April 22, 1914, p. 20.

"Fannie of the Follies—Five Good Reasons Why Fannie Brice Stops the Winter Garden Show Every Night." *Stage*, March 1936, p. 51.

Goldman, Herbert G. *Fanny Brice: The Original Funny Girl*. New York: Oxford University Press, 1992.

Grossman, Barbara W. *Funny Woman: The Life and Times of Fanny Brice*. Bloomington: Indiana University Press, 1991.

Katkov, Norman. *The Fabulous Fanny: The Story of Fannie Brice*. New York: Alfred A. Knopf, 1953.

Kutner, Nanette. "If You Were Daughter to Baby Snooks." *Good Housekeeping*, March 1943, pp. 38, 168.

Rose, Billy. "A Girl Named Fanny." *McCall's*, September 1963, pp. 52, 190–91.

Zolotow, Maurice. "Baby Snooks." *Cosmpolitan*, September 1946, pp. 25, 168–72; October 1946, pp. 50–51, 124–26.

BRITISH MUSIC HALL

While its origins date back long before the beginnings of American vaudeville, British music hall developed in much the same fashion from entertainment in saloons and taverns with a gradual phasing over to a theatrical environment. Modern British music hall dates from 1860, but the pleasure gardens, out of which it developed, date back to the 1700s, with the most famous being the Vauxhall Gardens (which opened in June 1732). Saloons and supper clubs offering entertainment flourished in the early to mid 1800s but declined in popularity with the passage of the Theatre Act of 1843, which put their entertainment under the jurisdiction of the Lord Chamberlain's Office.

The man most closely associated with the creation of the British music hall is Charles Morton (1819–1904), who was known as "The Father of the Halls," just as Tony Pastor was called "The Father of Vaudeville." In 1848, he acquired the Canterbury Arms in the south London district of Lambeth, and it was the first of three music halls of that name on the site. Unlike vaudeville, British music hall always had a master of ceremonies known as the chairman, who would not only introduce the acts but also banter with the audience and lead it in song. The first major British music hall was the Alhambra Palace Music Hall, which opened on December 10, 1860. It was followed by the Oxford Music Hall (near the junction of London's Oxford Street and Tottenham Court Road), opened by Charles Morton in 1861, but destroyed by fire in 1868. The music halls began in London but quickly spread to the suburbs and then to the rest of the country, until by 1875, there were more than three hundred in London alone. Just as American vaudeville theatres were generally named the B. F. Keith, the Orpheum, or the Pantages, British music halls were usually the Empire or the Hippodrome.

Some of the British music hall performers who appeared in vaudeville in the last century were Bessie Bonehill, Lottie Collins, Dan Leno, Little Tich (Harry Relph), Vesta Tilley, and Vesta Victoria. Charlie Chaplin and Stan Laurel were products of the British music hall, although neither had any impact in vaudeville. Both worked for British showman Fred Karno, whose theatrical comedy company became synonymous with slapstick; Laurel came to the United States with the Karno troupe in 1910, while Chaplin came over in 1910 and 1912. Aside from those who are the subjects of entries, the following British music hall performers also appeared in American vaudeville in the years indicated: Charles Coburn (1900), Gus Elen (1907), Dick Henderson (1924), Lupino Lane (1914), George Lashwood (1909), G. S. Melvin (1908, 1912, 1924), George Mozart (1907), Talbot O'Farrell (1920), Nellie Wallace (1908, 1909), Wilson, Keppel, and Betty (1930), and Robb Wilton (1923).

See also WILKIE BARD, ALBERT CHEVALIER, LOTTIE COLLINS, GRACIE FIELDS, WILL FYFFE, HERSCHEL HENLERE, HETTY KING, HARRY LAUDER, DAN LENO, ALICE LLOYD, MARIE LLOYD, LILY MORRIS, ADA REEVE, ELLA SHIELDS, VESTA TILLEY, VASCO, VESTA VICTORIA, ALBERT WHELAN, WEE GEORGIE WOOD.

BIBLIOGRAPHY
Busby, Roy. *British Music Hall: An Illustrated Who's Who from 1850 to the Present Day*. London: Paul Elek, 1976.
Cheshire, D. F. *Music Hall in Britain*. Rutherford, N.J.: Fairleigh Dickinson University Press, 1974.
Felstead, S. Theodore. *Stars Who Made the Halls: A Hundred Years of English Humor, Harmony and Hilarity*. London: T. Werner Laurie, 1946.
Gammond, Peter. *Your Own, Your Very Own*. London: Ian Allen, 1971.
Green, Benny. *The Last Empires: A Music Hall Companion*. London: Pavilion Books, 1986.

Honri, Peter. *Working the Halls*. Farnborough, England: Saxon House, 1973.
_____. *John Wilton's Music Hall: The Handsomest Room in Town*. Hornchurch,
    England: Ian Henry, 1985.
House, Jack. *Music Hall Memories*. Glasgow, Scotland: Drew, 1986.
Mander, Raymond, and Joe Mitchenson. *British Music Hall: A Story in Pictures*. London:
    Studio Vista, 1965.
Mellor, G. J. *The Northern Music Hall: A Century of Popular Entertainment*. Newcastle-
    upon-Tyne, England: Frank Graham, 1970.
Newton, H. Chance. *Idols of the Halls*. London: Heath Cranton, 1928.
O'Malley, Frank Ward. "In the 'appy London 'alls." *Saturday Evening Post*, March
    17, 1923, p. 15.
Pope, W. Macqueen. *The Melodies Linger On*. London: W. H. Allen, 1950.
Rose, Clarkson. *Red Plush and Greasepaint: A Memory of the Music-Hall and Life and
    Times from the Nineties to the Sixties*. London: Museum Press, 1964.
Scott, Harold. *The Early Doors: Origins of the Music Hall*. London: Nicholson and
    Watson, 1946.
Senelick, Laurence, David Cheshire, and Ulrich Schneider. *British Music Hall, 1840–
    1923: A Bibliography and Guide to Sources with a Supplement on European Music
    Hall*. New York: Shoe String Press, 1981.
Short, Ernest. *Fifty Years of Vaudeville*. London: Eyre and Spottiswoode, 1946.
Speaight, George. *Bawdy Songs of the Early Music Hall*. Newton Abbot, England: David
    & Charles, 1975.

BROADWAY THEATRE

Located at the corner of Broadway and 41st Street in New York, the Broadway
Theatre opened on March 3, 1888, with Sardou's *La Tosca*. From 1908 onward,
it was noted for its musical comedy and vaudeville presentations. It was demolished in 1929. The theatre should not be confused with Tony Pastor's Broadway
Music Hall or the present Broadway Theatre at 52nd Street.

JOE E. (EVANS) BROWN (Holgate, Oh., July 28, 1892—Los Angeles, July 6, 1973)

Joe E. Brown was a comedian whose stock-in-trade was a big mouth, which
he would open to reveal a wide grin, punctuated by siren-like wails. He would
also flap his hands around in a gesture more despairing than effeminate, reminiscent of the classic mannerism of actress ZaSu Pitts.

Becoming proficient at acrobatics as a child, at the age of eleven Brown joined
a troupe called the Five Marvelous Ashtons, first appearing with them at Sells
and Downs Circus in Chanute, Kansas. Four years later, in 1906, he joined the
Bell Prevost Trio as a trampoline artist. From there, he spent ten years in
vaudeville, burlesque, and carnivals, developing an act with Frank Prevost, billed
as "A Few Minutes of Foolishness." Brown made his Broadway debut in 1919
in *Listen Lester*, which had opened in December of the previous year at the
Knickerbocker Theatre. He was moderately successful in the 1920s appearing
in revues and musical comedies, including *Jim Jam Jems* (1920), the *Greenwich
Village Follies* (1923), *Captain Jinks* (1925), and *Twinkle Twinkle* (1926). In

1927, Warner Bros. filmed Brown and actress Perquita Courtney in a ten-minute extract from the last production, and the following year, Joe E. Brown embarked on a major career as a film comedian. The films generally exploited Brown's best known feature, sometimes even in their titles: *You Said a Mouthful* (1932) and *Shut My Big Mouth* (1942).

"The comedian with the infinite grin," as *Time* (July 16, 1973) called him, won the Bronze Star for his efforts in entertaining the troops during the Second World War. He flew more than 200,000 miles and during 1942 and 1943 became the first Hollywood performer to visit China and India. The death of his son, Captain Don E. Brown, on October 8, 1942, was presumably influential in Brown's decision to devote himself so unsparingly to the war effort.

At the end of his career, Joe E. Brown played a role that has become a cult classic, that of the millionaire suitor of Jack Lemmon in *Some Like It Hot* (1959).

BIBLIOGRAPHY

Brown, Joe E. *Your Kids and Mine*. Garden City, N.Y.: Doubleday, Doran, 1945.

_____, as told to Ralph Hancock. *Laughter Is a Wonderful Thing*. New York: A. S. Barnes, 1956.

"Joe E. Brown." *Current Biography*, February 1945, pp. 76–78.

"Joe E. Brown: Favorite Pin-Up Boy of the Army." *Look*, May 30, 1944, p. 55.

Laurie, Joe, Jr. "A Thumbnose Sketch, Joe E. Brown." *Variety*, February 5, 1947, p. 27.

Monroe, Keith. "That Battling Buffoon Named Brown," *Saturday Evening Post*, December 8, 1951, pp. 22–23, 107–108, 111.

"On the Go Joe." *Newsweek*, February 28, 1944, p. 76.

Pearson, Ben. "Nobody's Perfect: Not Even Joe E. Brown." *Daily Variety*, October 29, 1985, pp. 32, 128.

BOTHWELL BROWNE (Copenhagen, March 7, 1877—Los Angeles, December 12, 1947)

Bothwell Browne was one of the best known female impersonators on the vaudeville stage, hailed by *Variety* as early as 1910 as second only to Julian Eltinge. Like most female impersonators of the day, Browne relied on beautiful gowns to put across his act, but he also would generally appear in a playlet or sketch, supported by a number of attractive women, but none more beautiful than he. He was a handsome man (and woman), slimmer and far better looking than Eltinge.

Born in Denmark, Walter Bothwell Bruhm emigrated with his family to San Francisco, where he studied dance. He appears to have started his career with the Cohan and Harris Minstrels. He made his New York debut on September 6, 1908, at the Fifth Avenue Theatre in a sketch titled "Winning a Gibson Girl." Writing in *Variety* (September 12, 1908), Sime Silverman thought him "a decidedly clever female impersonator," but added, "has still to be judged by more than one character." Browne was back at the Fifth Avenue Theatre in September 1910, playing a variety of female roles, including a showgirl, a suffragette, and "The Pantaloon Girl," and closing with a dance as Cleopatra. *Variety* noted that his one weakness was the lack of a strong singing voice. Despite such a debility, Browne did appear in one musical comedy, *Miss Jack*, which opened in New York at the Herald Square Theatre on September 4, 1911, but ran for a mere sixteen performances.

The story line of *Miss Jack* had Browne as a college boy imprisoned in a young ladies seminary. He took on the guise of one of the young women who had run away and carried the characterization through three acts. He did not unwig for the finale. The musical comedy opened on August 14, 1911, in Asbury Park, New Jersey, prior to its New York opening. It was generally assumed that *Miss Jack* opened in New York one week in advance of Julian Eltinge's *The Fascinating Widow* in order to take advantage of the latter's publicity.

Despite these early New York appearances, Bothwell Browne proved more popular on the West Coast and throughout the teens tended to concentrate his vaudeville appearances in San Francisco, Los Angles, Spokane, and Seattle. In 1913, he produced a sketch titled "The Serpent of the Nile," featuring his cousin Frances Young as Cleopatra, which opened at the Pantages Theatre, Spokane, on September 22. Following a tambourine dance by eight harem girls, the queen's messenger (played by Phyllis Lambert) appeared, performed a sword dance, and then told Cleopatra of Marc Antony's death. A snake was called for, and Cleopatra proceeded to remove various veils. Only at the fifteen-minute presentation's close was the audience apprised of the sex of Cleopatra with the removal of "her" wig.

Frances Young was also featured in Bothwell Browne's "Exotic Art Dances," which opened at the San Francisco Hippodrome on September 4, 1916. It began with Browne, dressed in a gold cloth, introducing Young, who performed a dance as an ancient Persian swordsman. *Variety* (September 15, 1916) reported, "This lad is about as handsome a built boy as one wants to see and he danced so easily and gracefully his efforts met with good results." Browne then reappeared to perform "The Dance of Vanity" in the guise of a Japanese maid. The act closed with Young, as a scantily clad Egyptian slave, ministering to the needs of Browne as Cleopatra. From today's viewpoint, the whole thing sounds somewhat effete, but *Variety* called it "the best staged, produced, costumed and elaborate dancing turn that ever left the Pacific Coast."

In 1919, comedy film producer Mack Sennett starred Browne in a vulgar, anti-German comedy titled *Yankee Doodle in Berlin*, which had Browne as an American aviator donning female attire in order to obtain German secrets. *Photoplay*'s critic Julian Johnson thought Browne's impersonation "very creditable and inoffensive." As a result of the film's popularity, Browne put together a vaudeville act with a group of Mack Sennett Bathing Beauties and headlined with them at the Palace in December 1919.

Bothwell Browne was adept at publicity. He was featured on the front cover of *Variety* for December 12, 1919, dressed in both male and female costumes, and made the covers of *The New York Dramatic Mirror* on October 30, 1919, and January 21, 1920. The last announced that he was topping the B. F. Keith bills with his Bathing Beauties in a *20th Century Revue*, assisted by the Browne Sisters. (The latter were, in reality, his brother Nicholas's children, Dorothy and Flavilla.)

Browne's popularity declined in the 1920s, as his act tended toward repetition. On October 24, 1923, he opened at the Hill Street Theatre, Los Angeles, in an Egyptian sketch with six girls and himself as the queen (!). In later years, he taught dance and produced revues at nightclubs such as the Half Moon on New York's West 80th Street. No hint of scandal ever attached itself to his name. Supposedly, as a child, he asked his mother plaintively, "Do I have to get married?" The answer was no, and Bothwell Browne died a bachelor.

BIBLIOGRAPHY

Hardeman, Paul D. "Walter Bothwell Browne." *California Voice*, June 3, 1983, pp. 16–17.

Slide, Anthony. *Great Pretenders: A History of Female and Male Impersonation in the Performing Arts*. Lombard, Il.: Wallace-Homestead, 1986.

BROX SISTERS

The Brox Sisters were a singing trio, consisting of Dagmar and Loraine (both born in Memphis, Tennessee) and Kathlyn (born in Winchester, Kentucky). They were featured on the New York stage from the early 1920s, appearing in both the 1923 and 1924 editions of the *Music Box Revue*, as well as *The Cocoanuts* (1926) and the 1927 edition of the Ziegfeld *Follies*. They entered vaudeville in Los Angeles in the summer of 1928, having already made a name for themselves locally in radio, and Arthur Ungar in *Variety* (July 11, 1928) hailed them as "a welcome asset." The sisters played the Palace in November 1930 and in the summer of 1931 were featured on NBC, probably replacing the Boswell Sisters, who had just moved over to CBS.

On screen, it was the Brox Sisters who introduced "Singin' in the Rain" in M-G-M's *The Hollywood Revue of 1929*. The following year, they were featured in *The King of Jazz* and *Spring Is Near*. They also made three Vitaphone short subjects for Warner Bros. in the late 1920s.

GENE BUCK (Detroit, August 8, 1885—Great Neck, N.Y., February 25, 1957)

Under the name Gene Buck, Edward Eugene Buck was a major figure in the New York revue field in the teens and 1920s. Educated at the University of Detroit and the Detroit Art School, his first involvement in show business was in the cover design for sheet music. In 1907, he came to New York and designed and directed Lillian Russell's vaudeville act. He became chief writer and assistant to Florenz Ziegfeld for thirteen editions of the *Follies* from 1912 to 1926, and also originated and oversaw the production of eleven editions of Ziegfeld's *Midnight Frolics* (1915–1922). Buck was also involved with other Broadway shows, including *No Foolin'* (1926), *Yours Truly* (1927), *Take the Air* (1927), and *Ringside* (1928). He returned to help Ziegfeld mount the last *Follies* of his lifetime in 1931, and with Mark Hellinger created a "Broadway Reverie" sequence featuring Ruth Etting singing "Shine on Harvest Moon." Gene Buck was one of the 1914 charter members of ASCAP (the American Society of Composers, Authors, and Publishers), a member of its board of directors from 1920 until his death, and its president from 1924 to 1941.

BUCK AND BUBBLES

Ford Lee (Buck) Washington (Louisville, Ky., October 16, 1903—New York, January 31, 1955) and John W. (Bubbles) Sublett were two talented black vaudevillians whose creativity helped them transcend racial barriers. "They were a tremendous act," recalled Jesse Block. "John Bubbles is one of the most talented boys. He can sing better than anyone. He can dance better than anyone." Eleanor Powell remembered:

I think Bubbles is fantastic. He did things with his feet. . . . I don't know how many times Buck and Bubbles and I played the Paramount together. When Bubbles was on, I'd be in the wings, on my stomach, watching the feet, and it got so he was playing to me, not to the audience. And I'm doing the same thing when he's on. And after the show, we'd go down to the basement and knock our brains out jamming around.

While Buck vamped at the piano, Bubbles would dance up a storm, proving himself one of the greatest exponents of syncopated tap dancing and one of the creators of rhythm tap dancing. "I took the white boys' steps and the colored boys' steps and mixed 'em up all together so you couldn't tell 'em, white or colored," he explained. At the same time, there was nothing unrehearsed to his performances: "I'd just listen to the music and feel what I could do with it. Then I'd put it together in my head. I didn't often just get up and dance without planning it first; that's a waste of energy. When I figure I've got it, I get up and do it. Then it's all synchronized together."

Buck and Bubbles got together in Louisville, Kentucky, when Buck was nine and Bubbles thirteen. After four years, the two made it to the stage of B. F. Keith's Mary Anderson Theatre in Louisville, the first Blacks to play there, dancing and singing "Curse of an Aching Heart" and "Somebody Loves Me." They came to New York to play the Columbia Theatre at 47th Street and Seventh Avenue and within a few months were appearing at the Palace. As headliners, Buck and Bubbles toured the Keith circuit, and in 1923, they headed their own revue, with five girls and two boys, which opened in New York in July of that year at the City Theatre. There was comedy, singing, dancing, and first-rate impersonation of Williams and Walker. "The revue has plenty of entertainment," reported *Variety* (July 26, 1923).

Bucks and Bubbles headlined at the Palace in September 1928 and December 1929. One of their last vaudeville appearances in New York was at Loew's State in July 1932.

Aside from vaudeville, the couple were featured in Lew Leslie's *Blackbirds of 1930* and the 1930 edition of the *Ziegfeld Follies*. Their films include *Variety*

Show (1937), *Atlantic City* (1944), and *A Song Is Born* (1948). They sang "Breakfast in Harlem" in the 1936 London revue *Transatlantic Rhythm*, which also featured Ruth Etting, Lupe Velez, and Lou Holtz. Most importantly, Buck played Mingo and Bubbles portrayed Sportin' Life in George Gershwin's *Porgy and Bess*, which opened at Boston's Colonial Theatre on September 30, 1935. It is claimed by those privileged to have seen and heard it that Bubbles's rendition of "It Ain't Necessarily So" and "There's a Boat Dat's Leavin' for New York" has never been surpassed.

Following Buck's death, Bubbles returned to the Palace as a single act in August 1967, as part of the *Judy Garland Show*. That same year, he retired when a stroke left him partially paralyzed. He did, however, return to the New York stage in May 1980 to appear in the revue *Black Broadway*, leading the audience in singing "It Ain't Necessarily So" and closing the show with Eubie Blake's "Memories of You."

BIBLIOGRAPHY

"Bubbles." *The New Yorker*, August 26, 1967, pp. 21–23.

Goldberg, Jane. "John Bubbles: A Hoofer's Homage." *Village Voice*, December 4, 1978, p. 112.

Smith, Bill. "John Bubbles." In *The Vaudevillians*. New York: Macmillan, 1976, pp. 56–62.

Wheelock, Julie. "Bubbles, the Rhythm Tap King." *Los Angeles Times Calendar*. December 19, 1982, pp. 82–83.

BURLESQUE

An offshoot of vaudeville, burlesque provided a training ground for a number of popular comedians, including Abbott and Costello and Phil Silvers, but only a handful of women—Ann Corio, Margie Hart, Gypsy Rose Lee—in burlesque made names for themselves outside of the medium. Probably adapted from the Latin word *Burla*, meaning a trifle or a bit of nonsense, burlesque had two distinct meanings as regards American popular entertainment. The first was as a burlesque of a popular musical comedy or legitimate drama, and in such form it was dominated by Tony Pastor and Weber and Fields. The second, which is generally dated from the arrival in the United States in the 1860s of Lydia Thompson and her British Blondes, was as an entertainment featuring young women displaying as much leg as the law would allow, with the leg often encased in flesh-colored tights, and usually performing a cancan type of dance. The first American burlesque show was probably Mme Rentz's Female Minstrels, presented by M. B. Leavitt, which developed into the Rentz-Santley combination.

Until the 1890s, women in burlesque shows were not slim but rather hefty and short. The best example of their kind, and one of the first stars of American burlesque, was May Howard, who headed her own burlesque company after performing with the Rentz-Santley troupe and as one of the "birds" in *Bob Manchester's Night Owls* in 1886 and 1887. Cootch dancing, a precursor of the shimmy, which involved much wriggling of the body in time to musical accompaniment, became the norm in burlesque houses of the 1890s, and the best known exponent of the dance was Little Egypt, who created a sensation at the 1893 Chicago World's Fair. One of New York's first burlesque houses was Robinson Hall on 16th Street between Broadway and Fifth Avenue; it was supplanted in popularity by the Columbia Theatre, which opened on Broadway in 1904. Between 1890 and 1900, many theatre managers converted their variety houses to burlesque by adding chorus girls to appear between acts. The first two major burlesque circuits were the Columbia Amusement Company and the Empire Circuit of Burlesque Theatres and Companies (later taken over by Columbia).

The first major burlesque star of the twentieth century was Millie De Leon, noted for her cootch dancing and named "The Girl in Blue," after she had appeared circa 1903 in a company of that name. A typical burlesque show of the period was described by John B. Kennedy:

The pattern of the old shows was always the same. Opening chorus in which the girls appeared in knee-skirts. Then the comedians—an Irishman with a red nose, a Dutch comic with an enormous stomach and a Semite with an apostolic beard. These gentlemen immediately became embroiled in a love tangle with a lady, usually an hour-glass soubrette referred to as "the lady widow." Each schemed to marry her. Each wore baggy clothes in contrast to the smart attire of the wise-guy or straight man who also paid court to the lady widow. The racial roughnecks punctuated their wooings with kicks fore and aft and coarse gibes, and were, in turn, punctuated by the ladies of the chorus who gamboled on in gradually minimized costumes, bawling popular songs totally unrelated to the plot.

Striptease became an established, and to the audience the most important, part of burlesque in the 1920s. The comics remained, but the humor became bawdier and more sexually oriented. In 1937, Fiorello La Guardia was instrumental in closing all burlesque houses in New York, and the decline of the entertainment form can be dated from that year. On March 26, 1942, a petition was filed in the New York Supreme Court, signed by 28,500 individuals, including Fanny Brice, Al Jolson, and Jay C. Flippen, asking for the retention of burlesque in the state and continuation of the burlesque policy at the Gaiety Theatre, whose renewal license was under review. The renewal was denied the following month. Burlesque did, of course, continue in other parts of the United States and was revived in New York under other names and in parodies of itself. For example, striptease performer Ann Corio appeared on the New York stage in a black dress with an attached padlock and sang "I Would If I Could, but I Can't." The proliferation of porno theatres further hurt burlesque, and its ultimate death came with the easy availability of pornographic and similar fare on videotapes intended for home consumption.

See also MINSKY BROTHERS, STRIPTEASE.

BIBLIOGRAPHY
"The Church Wars on Burlesque. *Life* 2, no. 22 (May 31, 1937), p. 20.
Corio, Ann, and Joe DiMona. *This Was Burlesque*. New York: Grosset and Dunlap, 1968.

Grau, Robert. "The Evolution of Burlesque." *The New York Dramatic Mirror*, April 30, 1913, p. 5.

Kennedy, John B. "Revised Version." *Collier's* 90, no. 20 (November 12, 1932), pp. 14, 45–47.

Minsky, Morton, and Milt Machlin. *Minsky's Burlesque: A Fast and Funny Look at America's Bawdiest Era*. New York: Arbor House, 1986.

Sobel, Bernard. *Burleycue: An Underground History of Burlesque Days*. New York: Farrer & Rinhart, 1931.

Zeidman, Irving. *The American Burlesque Show*. New York: Hawthorn Books, 1967.

GEORGE BURNS (New York, January 20, 1896—   ) and **GRACIE ALLEN** (San Francisco, July 26, 1906—Hollywood, Ca., August 27, 1964)

If the man or woman in the street was asked to name the one act symbolizing all that was great about vaudeville, an act that has endured in popularity for more than fifty years, there is no question that the answer would be Burns and Allen. As a comedy team, they were unrivaled in the annals of show business, and now that Gracie Allen is gone, George Burns has found new success as a leading man in films and on the nightclub circuit. The reason for the lasting fame of Burns and Allen is not difficult to ascertain. It was not simply talent, although they certainly had that, but rather the ability to grasp and prosper with each new medium of entertainment that came along. First they rose to the top in vaudeville, then radio, followed by movies, and eventually television.

The routines of George Burns and Gracie Allen do not need repeating here, for there can be no one who is not familiar with George's straight-man questions and Gracie's dizzy responses—dialogue that was, more often than not, concerned with Gracie's family and, in particular, her brother:

Gracie: Did you know my brother was held up by two men last night?

George: For how much?

Gracie: Oh, all the way home!

Whatever George Burns had to say, Gracie had a response. When, as her boss, George commented angrily, "You should have been here two hours ago," secretary Gracie replied with innocent sweetness, "Why, what happened!" Gracie would always misunderstand with hilarious results. On a bus tour of New York City that included Grant's Tomb and the George Washington Bridge, she was outraged that the nation could find a tomb for Grant, while the father of country was consigned to his final resting place under a bridge.

In an interview with *The New York Times*, George Burns once noted that he considered the reason for the pair's success: "We were kicking around for eight years telling the same jokes before anything happened. Suddenly people got the idea that Gracie's crazy and needs protection. We had nothing to do with the things that happened to us. The public makes and breaks people like us too fast.'' The public may make or break a vaudevillian, but it can also come to adore and cherish an act, and such was the case with Burns and Allen.

Born Nathan Birnbaum, George Burns first tried his hand at show business at the age of seven when, after his father died, he formed the Pee Wee Quartette. Later, he joined forces with Abie Kaplan, and because the two of them followed the truck of the Burns Brothers coal yard, in the hopes of picking up any coal that might drop on the street, they became known as the Burns Brothers. The first name of George the comedian took from an elder brother, Isidore, whom he admired and who was called George by his friends. At the age of thirteen, George Burns linked up with an entertainer named Mac Fry, becoming Mac Fry and Company. Next came a partnership with Sam Brown as Brown and Williams (after a former member of the act), and so it went on. Burns was Glide in Goldie, Fields and Glide, followed by participation in an act called The Fourth of July Kids. In his autobiography, *I Love Her, That's Why!*, George Burns wrote that he often changed his name because the booker of a specific theatre threatened not to give him another job if he knew who he was. To add to confusion, at one time, George Burns was playing in an act titled Burns and Links—and he was Links!

Eventually, at the age of twenty-four, Burns's vaudeville fortunes began to improve. He found a new partner in Sid Gary, who was later popular on radio and noted for his high soprano voice. Two years later, Burns and Gary split up, and the former joined forces with Billy Lorraine, with an act called Burns and Lorraine—Two Broadway Thieves, so titled because the act consisted of imitations of Broadway stars such as Al Jolson and Eddie Cantor. In his autobiography, Fred Allen recalled some of the dialogue from the Burns and Lorraine act:

Burns: I had a fight with my wife last night.

Lorraine: What happened?

Burns: She chased me around the house with a red-hot poker. I finally ran into a closet and shut the door.

Lorraine: And then?

Burns: My wife started knocking on the closet door and yelling, ''Come out of that closet, you coward! Come out of that closet, you coward!''

Lorraine: Did you come out of the closet?

Burns: Not me. In my house, I'm boss!

While working with Lorraine, Burns was also developing an act of his own. The last place that Burns and Lorraine played was the Union Hill Theatre in New Jersey, and while there, Burns told the headliner, Rena Arnold, of his plans; at the same time, he told her a risqué story. Miss Arnold was offended by the story but told her friend Gracie Allen that she should approach Lorraine, who was looking for a new partner. Gracie Allen saw the act, confused Burns with Lorraine, and asked him for a job. It was three days before she discovered the mistake!

Born in San Francisco, Gracie Allen was the daughter of song-and-dance man Edward Allen, whom she described as "the first and best clog and minstrel man in San Francisco." Of her birth, she said, "I was so surprised I couldn't talk for a year and a half." Gracie Allen first worked on stage as a child with her father. Later, she appeared with her sisters, Bessie, Pearl, and Hazel, in an act called Larry Reilly and Company, in which she danced an Irish jig and sang. Burns and Allen made their first appearance together in 1922 at the Hill Street Theatre in Newark, New Jersey; they were married four years later on January 7, 1926, in Cleveland. The initial billing was George N. Burns and Grace Allen, and at first Gracie played the straight role and Burns was the comedian, but in a matter of months, the roles had been reversed, and Burns was established as the cigar-chomping straight man, with Allen as his dizzy partner.

Gracie: All great singers have their trials; look at Caruso. Thirty years on a desert island with all those cannibals.

George: You've got the wrong man.

Gracie: No, you're the man for me.

George: But they say I'm through as a singer. I'm extinct.

Gracie: You do not!

Variety (April 12, 1923) saw Burns and Allen at New York's Fifth Avenue Theatre and reported, "He has a good delivery for this style of talk and the girl is an excellent foil. They have more than average personalities. The act lets down in spots, due to the dialog, and can be strengthened in this respect." *Variety* also noted the act was similar in style to that of an earlier team called Matthews and Ayres. Of course the trade paper was not always impressed with Burns and Allen; a few months later on July 28, 1923, it commented, "A brighter and smarter vehicle will have to be secured if they expect to advance."

Burns and Allen's first great success was with a sketch titled "Lamb Chops," written for them by Al Boasberg. Abel Green saw the pair perform at the Palace and wrote in *Variety* (August 25, 1926), "George N. Burns and Gracie Allen have a new skit in Lamb Chops, by Al Boasberg; funny stuff, almost actor proof, but further enhanced by the team's individual contributions. Miss Allen is an adorable 'dizzy' with an ingratiating prattle. Burns foils and wisecracks in turn and the laugh returns are fast and many. They dance off before the routine encore, which brings him back for a bit wherein he reclines on a prop mat on the stage, 'feeding' his partner. A tip-top comedy interlude for the best vaudeville."

The dialogue for "Lamb Chops," which became so well known to vaudeville audiences that they would often join in, included the following repartee:

George: What did you take up at school?

Gracie: Anything that wasn't nailed down.

George: Do you care about love?

Gracie: No.

George: Do you care about kisses?

Gracie: No.

George: What do you care about?

Gracie: Lamb chops.

George: I bet you couldn't eat two big lamb chops alone.

Gracie: No, not alone I couldn't. With mashed potatoes and peas I could.

In the summer of 1929, Burns and Allen filmed "Lamb Chops" for Warner Bros./Vitaphone, featuring a delightful song "Do You Believe Me?" The nine-minute short was advertised as "popular song and dance team in an offering of snappy steps and stories," and is preserved at the UCLA Film and Television Archive. Burns and Allen returned to the Palace in August and December 1930 and April 1931.

Also in the summer of 1929, the couple went to England for a total of twenty-one weeks, several of which were spent in London, alternating performances between the Holborn Empire and the London Palladium. They were billed as "The Famous American Comedy Couple," and the English took Gracie in particular to their hearts. One critic wrote, "Excepting Beatrice Lillie, she is perhaps the most adroit female laugh-getter in vaudeville. . . . Sweet simplicity gushes from her eyes and her lips though it is obvious from the first that she is full of guile." While in England Burns and Allen made a series of radio broadcasts for the BBC, happy precursors of what lay ahead.

When Burns and Allen returned to the United States, there was no question as to their popularity. Their film career began with *Lamb Chops*, and the couple then began appearing in a series of Paramount features, including *The Big Broadcast* (1932), *International House* (1933), *Six of a Kind* (1934), *We're Not Dressing* (1934), *The Big Broadcast of 1936*, *The Big Broadcast of 1937*, *Damsel in Distress* (1937), and *Honolulu* (1939). Gracie was also featured in a few films on her own, most notably *The Gracie Allen Murder Case* (1939).

Burns and Allen became radio regulars on CBS in 1932, when they were signed to appear on the Guy Lombardo program, sponsored by Robert Burns Cigars; soon after, *The Burns and Allen Show* made its appearance. It began as a vaudeville-style entertainment and did not develop into a situation comedy until the early 1940s. Of course, the running gag in the show in the early 1930s was Gracie's search for her lost brother (in reality, an employee of Standard Oil in San Francisco). CBS would have Burns and Allen wander in and out of other radio programs asking about Gracie's daft brother, who had hurt his leg falling off an ironing board while pressing his pants. *Time* (January 30, 1933) commented, "Burns and Allen have shot into first place as the most annoying broadcast on the air—the climax of sub-moronic radio drivel.'' In 1940, Allen declared her candidacy for president on the ''Surprise Party'' ticket, campaigning for the repeal of prohibition. When told this had already been accomplished, she replied, ''Oh really? I can hardly wait for my brother to sober up so I can tell him about it.''

On October 12, 1950, *The George Burns and Gracie Allen Show* made a successful transition to television—on CBS—after eighteen years on the radio. The program's thirty-minute format was that of situation comedy, with the pair playing themselves, aided by Harry Von Zell (the announcer as himself), Ronnie Burns (the couple's adopted son as himself), Bea Benaderet (as Blanche Morton, Gracie's friend and neighbor), and Larry Keating (as Blanche's husband, Harry). One of the show's sponsors was Carnation Milk, and Gracie would say sweetly, ''I never will understand how they get milk from carnations.'' Each episode ended with George and Gracie's performing one of their vaudeville routines, and the close, George's ''Say goodnight, Gracie,'' was one of the best known in the history of television. The show ended in September 1958, when Allen announced her retirement. George Burns carried on for another year with his own program, featuring the same characters as the original.

Gracie Allen died in 1964, and at her funeral, Jack Benny said, ''Her love was so great it never waned in a span of forty years. . . . Gracie Allen was an institution. Her timing and delivery was the most natural I have ever known.'' George Burns continued to work, with his career blossoming. In 1975, he won the Academy Award for best supporting actor for his work in *The Sunshine Boys*. He recorded his first album, *I Wish I Was 18 Again* in 1980, with the title cut becoming a hit single. In 1982, he recorded a second album, *As Time Goes By*, with Bobby Vinton. In July 1992, Burns announced a long-term commitment with Caesar's Palace in Las Vegas, including an appearance in his one hundredth birthday year. His only other commitment for his one hundredth birthday is an appearance at the London Palladium.

BIBLIOGRAPHY

Allen, Gracie. *How To Become President*. New York: Duell, Sloan and Pearce, 1940.
_____. ''My Life with George Burns.'' *Look*, December 16, 1952, pp. 17, 19–20.
_____, as told to Jane Kesner Morris. ''Gracie Allen's Own Story 'Inside Me.' '' *Woman's Home Companion*, March 1953, pp. 40–41, 100, 102, 109, 112, 116, 119, 122–24, 126–27.
Benny, Jack. ''George Burns and Me.'' *Coronet*, October 1966, pp. 18–24.
Beranger, Clara. ''How Dumb Is Gracie Allen?'' *Liberty*, 11, no. 35 (September 1, 1934), pp. 15–17.
Blythe, Cheryl, and Susan Sackett. *Say Goodnight, Gracie!: The Story of Burns and Allen*. New York: E. P. Dutton, 1986.
Burns, George, with Cynthia Hobart Lindsay. *I Love Her, That's Why!* New York: Simon and Schuster, 1955.
_____. *Living It Up or They Still Love Me in Altoona!* New York: G. P. Putnam's Sons, 1976.
_____. *Third Time Around*. New York: G. P. Putnam's Sons, 1980.

————. *How To Live To Be 100—or More: The Ultimate Diet, Sex and Exercise Book*. New York: G. P. Putnam's Sons, 1983.

————. *Dr. Burns' Prescription for Happiness*. New York: G. P. Putnam's Sons, 1984.

————. *Gracie: A Love Story*. New York: G. P. Putnam's Sons, 1988.

————, with David Fisher. *All My Best Friends*. New York: G. P. Putnam's Sons, 1989.

————. Foreword to *Sunday Nights at Seven: The Jack Benny Story* by Jack Benny and Joan Benny. New York: Warner Books, 1990.

"Burns." *The New Yorker*, March 22, 1976, pp. 29–30.

Champlin, Charles. "The World's Youngest 92-Year-Old Man." *Los Angeles Times Calendar*, April 3, 1988, pp. 21, 32.

Clarke, Gerald. "Going in Style with George Burns." *Time*, August 6, 1979, pp. 59–60.

"George Burns and Gracie Allen." *Current Biography*, March 1951, pp. 75–77.

Krebs, Albin. "Gracie Allen—Just the Name Evoked a Smile." *New York Herald Tribune*, August 29, 1964, p. 8.

O'Leary, Susan. "The George Burns and Gracie Allen Show: Life in a Domestic Comedy." *Emmy*, January/February 1984, pp. 44–51.

"Playboy Interview: George Burns." *Playboy*, June 1978, pp. 85–106.

Rader, Dotson. "The Jewish Comedian." *Esquire*, December 1975, pp. 106–109, 192, 196–98.

Rochlin, Margy. "Golden Oldie." *Los Angeles Times Magazine*, January 8, 1989, pp. 8–14, 37–38.

Schraub, Susan. "George Burns: From Vaudeville to Nashville." *Harper's Bazaar*, December 1980, pp. 81, 134–35.

Zolotow, Maurice. " . . . Say Goodnight, George." *Los Angeles*, December 1979, pp. 256–59, 472–75.

SADIE BURT. See GEORGE WHITING AND SADIE BURT

C

MARIE CAHILL (Brooklyn, N.Y., February 7, 1870—New York, August 23, 1933)

A popular comedienne and singer on the legitimate stage, Marie Cahill made infrequent forays into vaudeville from 1919 onward. She was born into a strict Roman Catholic family who insisted that she wear extremely full costumes when appearing onstage. Her first appearance was in Brooklyn in the late 1880s as a soubrette in the romantic Irish melodrama *Kathleen Mavourneen*; her New York debut was in *C.O.D.*, which opened at Poole's Eighth Street Theatre on July 1, 1889, and later that same year Cahill appeared in her first musical, *A Tin Soldier*. After appearances for three years in the productions of Augustin Daly, Cahill enjoyed a major success in 1902 with *The Wild Rose*, produced by George Lederer, in which she sang "Nancy Brown." That song became the title for a musical comedy written by George Broadhurst and Frederick Rankin, with music by Silvio Hein and George Hadley, which made Cahill a star in 1903. By this time, she was under the personal management of Daniel V. Arthur, whom she later married. Possibly the greatest success in Marie Cahill's early career was *Marrying Mary*, which opened at Daly's Theatre in August 1906.

The comedienne did not make her vaudeville debut until March 1919, when she headlined at the Palace. Her songs included "As Long as the Congo Flows" and "If You Like Me and I Like You." She also performed a telephone sketch, carrying on a monolog with her friend Ethel. Her vaudeville debut was, in the words of *The New York Dramatic Mirror* (March 25, 1919), "a theatrical function of importance," and the trade paper continued:

"Miss Cahill's dates in vaudeville are as assured as was from the first the United States' and the Allies' victory against the Hun. Hereafter she will be a distinctive vaudeville institution of a status which will have the admiration of the whole family. Each member of the family, too, will attend her performances which fact will make her one of the best drawing cards on the Big Time."

Interestingly, despite her religious background, some of her numbers were slightly risqué, such as her 1920 hit "It's Right Here for You (If You Don't

Get It 'Taint No Fault o' Mine)." Cahill returned frequently to the Palace in the 1920s, headlining in February 1924, October 1925, and October 1926. She was one of the stars on the theatre's April 1925 old-timers bill. Her last stage role was as Gloria Wentworth in *The New Yorkers*, which opened at the Broadway Theatre in December 1930. At the time of her death, she was still revered as one of the great musical comedy stars of the day.

MRS. PATRICK CAMPBELL (London, February 9, 1865—Pau, France, April 9, 1940)

"No, I'm not dreaming of appearing at any music hall," the great British dramatic actress Ellen Terry told *Variety* in October 1910, after receiving several offers to appear in vaudeville upon her arrival in the United States. "No actors in their senses should, in my opinion, at least not while the regulations and privileges are so different for the different places. . . . I don't think actors show to advantage in a music hall. They cannot entertain the visitors as some to the manner born (of music halls can do). To be sandwiched in between past masters of the art of vaudeville entertainment, such as Paul Cinquevalli and Alice Lloyd, really shows off an actor to ill advantage. Music hall artists are out of place in a theatre—actors are out of place in a music hall—at least, that is my opinion."

Ethel Barrymore was one actress who did not agree with Ellen Terry's position, and another was Britain's Mrs. Patrick Campbell (born Beatrice Rose Stella Tanner, who took her stage name from her first husband). In need of money, a constant problem for the actress, Mrs. Campbell arrived in New York in 1910 and telephoned a friend to announce, "Here I am. I have a good one-act play and a lovely frock, and I would be glad of a vaudeville engagement. What shall I do?" She was told to telephone E. F. Albee, who gave her ten weeks of work at a salary that Mrs. Pat claims in her autobiography was $500 a week and that Douglas Gilbert in *American Vaudeville* states was $2,500. Legend has it that in the middle of her conversation with Albee (when she was setting down her rule of two performances a day, no work on Sundays, and no obligation to speak to any other performers on the same bill), she asked for a telephone, rang her hotel suite, and apologized to Pinkie, her Pekinese, for being late. "I am," she explained, "with those horrible men in the vaudeville business."

The one-act play in which Mrs. Pat starred on the vaudeville stage was titled *Expiation!*; she had originally planned to appear in it in England. In her autobiography, the actress recalled, "Oh, those two performances of *Expiation!* I had to kill a man twice a day and shriek—and it had to be done from the heart—the Americans see through 'bluff'—and I was advertised as a 'Great tragic actress'!" *Variety* (February 19, 1910) reviewed *Expiation!* and commented, "Any legitimate of rank who enters vaudeville, and gives a little for the money received has done something. In comparison, Mrs. Pat has done a lot."

Variety was not as kind about Mrs. Campbell's second vaudeville offering, *The Ambassador's Wife*, a twenty-four-minute playlet by her son Alan Patrick Campbell, which opened at the Majestic Theatre, Chicago, in May 1910. The paper thought it unfair that the actress's son was allowed to practice as a storyteller while the audience was forced to suffer. As to Mrs. Pat herself, according to Douglas Gilbert, she complained about everything and "a hundred and forty-six Tanguays couldn't tie her for temperament."

While appearing in Hollywood productions in the early 1930s, Mrs. Patrick Campbell found time to appear at vaudeville theatres, concert halls, and other venues to lecture on "Diction in Dramatic Art," a subject on which she had first spoken at the Lyric Theatre in Hammersmith, London, in July 1927. To listen to Mrs. Pat talk of "beautiful speech," and to hear her impersonate a man of the cloth preaching a sermon with and without the correct vocal intonations was devastating. Her voice could have the power of a volcano, the crispness of water from a mountain spring, or the warmth of a log fire, and, of course, she was much too good for American audiences, whether in movie houses or vaudeville theatres.

BIBLIOGRAPHY

Campbell, Mrs. Patrick. *My Life and Some Letters*. New York: Dodd, Mead, 1922.

Dent, Alan. *Mrs. Patrick Campbell*. Westport, Ct.: Greenwood Press, 1973.

Peters, Margot. *Mrs. Pat: The Life of Mrs. Patrick Campbell*. New York: Alfred A. Knopf, 1984.

Slide, Anthony. "Mrs. Patrick Campbell." *Films in Review* 40, no. 3 (March 1989), pp. 163–67.

EDDIE CANTOR (New York, January 31, 1892—Beverly Hills, Ca., October 10, 1964)

In his 1929 book *Caught Short! A Saga of Wailing Wall Street*, there is a cartoon that typifies the questionable taste of Cantor's humor. He is in blackface, knocking on industrialist J. P. Morgan's door, and announcing, "I am the Kuhn of Kuhn, Loeb and Company." That same brand of humor also spread over into his Jewish jokes, although in view of his own religion, such comedy seems less offensive by today's standards. As a Jewish aviator who named his plane Mosquito—the Spirit of New Jersey, Cantor could not emulate Lindberg's crossing of the Atlantic because he couldn't eat ham sandwiches. He changed his name to Ginsberg from Levey, explaining, "I was in the South, around Mississippi during the floods, and I read headlines in the papers that they were going to blow up all the levees." He announced that "I'd go to war for my mother country, Russia—darkest Russia—for all my relatives there, General Walkowitch, Itzkowitch, Eczema." When queried on eczema, he replied, "Yes, that's another itch."

Eddie Cantor's stage characterizations, if not effeminate, were at least effete. In *Whoopee!*, he is weak and a chronic hypochondriac; when not running away from his strong and domineering female nurse, he is commenting to the hero as to how cute he looks without his shirt. When that same hero, a half-breed Indian, confides, "I went to your schools," Cantor asks in surprise, "You went to a Hebrew school?" In one highly suggestive scene in *Whoopee!*, he discusses operations with another man, and both begin pulling up their shirts and pulling down their trousers to display their various scars. The sequence ends with both rolling around together on the floor. In a famous sketch from the 1919 edition of the Ziegfeld *Follies*, Cantor plays the effeminate, college-educated son of railway porter Bert Williams, complete with horn-rimmed glasses and a mincing walk. The tough old Negro porter is horrified that his son has not, at least, turned into a football hero, and is about to hit him when Cantor exclaims in a girlish voice, "Remember, Daddy, I have a temper." Williams replies, "I'll show you where you got it from!" The sketch concludes with Williams putting his porter's cap on Cantor's head and saying, "Pick up them bags! This is my graduation and your commencement."

In the introduction to his anthology of the *World's Book of Best Jokes*, Eddie Cantor explained that he preferred humorous insults to all other types of jokes, because ordinary jokes are forgotten ten minutes after delivery but insults are repeated until they become classics. Cantor also confessed to having used more than twenty thousand jokes over an eleven-year period on radio. He had first embraced blackface humor in 1910, figuring it would help get his material over. With the addition of horn-rimmed glasses, he became more than the average vaudeville blackface minstrel; the glasses added a hint of intelligence and brought the characterization away from the Southern cotton field and into the twentieth century and the liberated life of a Northern Negro. The comedian was a great defender of blackface and ethnic humor. "When this kind of harmless humor was barred," he told the *Los Angeles Times*, "it took half of the fun out of show business."

Dancing, clapping his hands, eyes popping, the energetic comedian sang songs with which he will always be associated—"Making Whoopee," "My Baby Just Cares for Me," "If You Knew Susie," "Hungry Women," "You'd Be Surprised," and "We're Having a Baby, My Baby and Me," which NBC considered too risqué for Cantor to sing on network television. His recordings were always immensely popular. In 1920, Cantor signed a new contract with Brunswick Records for $220,000 over a five-year period, the largest contract of its kind, easily surmounting those offered to such well-known, international stars as Enrico Caruso and John McCormack.

Eddie Cantor was born Isidore Itzkowitz and raised by his grandmother Esther Kantrowitz. When he enrolled in school at the age of six, he started to give his grandmother's name and never finished it. The school registrar told him that Isidore Kantor was sufficient. Soon after, the "K" became a "C," and his wife-to-be persuaded him to adopt Eddie as his first name because it sounded "cute." Cantor's entry into vaudeville was typical of others of his generation, including amateur shows and burlesque appearances that led to abortive partnerships with Al Lee and Sam Kessler in 1914, and even an unsuccessful 1914 engagement in an André Charlot show in London, *Not Likely*. The first break in Cantor's career came in 1912, when he was signed by Gus Edwards to appear with George Jessel, Eddie Buzzel, George Price, and Lila Lee in *Kid Kabaret*. "It was not first class vaudeville," wrote Cantor, "but the best and only acting school of its kind, where poor young boys and girls could learn the art of entertainment in all its forms and get paid for learning." A close friendship developed between Cantor and Jessel, which endured through the rest of Cantor's life. In 1931 the two enjoyed a highly successful joint engagement at the Palace Theatre. When Jessel appeared on Cantor's television show in the 1950s, the two would sing a song called "Pals" that dated back to the Palace days.

Cantor's second big break came in 1916, when he left an engagement with the Oliver Morosco production of *Canary Cottage* in Los Angeles to return to New York and a tryout with Florenz Ziegfeld. The comedian made a big hit in Ziegfeld's *Midnight Frolics* and as a result was put into the 1917 edition of the Ziegfeld *Follies*. The 1918 and 1919 editions followed, and Cantor might have continued in the revue through the 1920s had he not walked out of the 1919 *Follies* to join the Actors' Equity Strike. Ziegfeld announced that he would have nothing more to do with Cantor, and the performer began a new alliance, with the Shubert Brothers, for whom he appeared in *Broadway Brevities of 1920* (1920) and *Make It Snappy* (1922). Happily, Cantor and Ziegfeld patched up their differences, and Cantor returned to star for the producer in the two most important musical comedies of his career, *Kid Boots* (1923) and *Whoopee!* (1928), plus the 1927 edition of the *Follies*. In 1954, Eddie Cantor reminisced:

Those never-to-be forgotten Ziegfeld nights when the entrances were crowded with the stars and the showgirls listening to the devastating, cheer-provoking lines of Will Rogers!—lines that would be just as big today. "We never lost a war or won a conference," he drawled. "America is an open book—a checkbook," he'd say, and nothing could follow his act—nothing but the finale. The pantomime of Bert Williams, the robust humor of W. C. Fields, the songs of Fanny Brice, they're all gone now, but I have my memories. Today, with television, a fellow can have a big time, a big salary, a big rating and security—but the satisfaction, the joy of being part of the Ziegfeld tradition is no more. I could cry.

Eddie Cantor returned to vaudeville in 1923 and proved he was still as popular with vaudeville audiences as he was with those for musical comedy. He opened his tour at the Orpheum Theatre, Brooklyn, delivering such popular songs as "How Ya Gonna Keep Your Mind on Dancing," "Oh, Gee! Oh, Gosh!," and "Yes, We Have No Bananas." *Variety* (June 7, 1923) reported, "Eddie Cantor is an entertainer with a capital 'E.' He is value received for vaudeville."

In 1926, Eddie Cantor made his film debut in the screen version of *Kid Boots*, but it was not until 1930 and the film version of *Whoopee!* that he made his mark in motion pictures. Among Cantor's best known features, the early ones made under contact to producer Samuel Goldwyn, are *Palmy Days* (1931), *The Kid from Spain* (1932), *Roman Scandals* (1933), *Kid Millions* (1934), *Ali Baba Goes to Town* (1937), *Thank Your Lucky Stars* (1943), and *If You Knew Susie* (1948, which he also produced).

Cantor was an early performer on radio and came into his own on *The Chase and Sanborn Hour* on NBC in 1931. As *The Eddie Cantor Show*, the program was heard on CBS from 1935, and Cantor became known for his radio discoveries, including Deanna Durbin, Bobby Breen, and Dinah Shore. In 1939, he was blacklisted for his outspoken criticism of certain government officials as fascists, but he came back on NBC in 1940. In 1944, he raised $40 million for war bonds during a twenty-four hour marathon radio show. Cantor moved over to television in September 1950 with NBC's *The Colgate Comedy Hour*. He left the program in 1954 and that same year began his own syndicated television series, *Eddie Cantor Comedy Theatre*, which was produced through 1955.

Aside from his work on radio, television, stage, and screen, Eddie Cantor was a distinguished and prolific author, writing two autobiographical works and a number of shorter, comic volumes: *Caught Short!*, *You Hoo Prosperity*, *Your Next President*, *Between the Acts*, and *Who's Hooey?* He also took a great interest in political and social activities. In the 1930s, he was the most outspoken of major leftist-leaning entertainers. He was a founder of Actors' Equity, the American Federation of Radio and Television Artists (AFTRA), and the Screen Actors Guild. To Eddie Cantor goes the credit for the creation of the March of Dimes. He was an outspoken leader in Jewish affairs, so much so that in 1935, the neofascist Catholic priest Father Coughlin said, "Jews have only three enemies to fear—Bernard Baruch, Eddie Cantor, and the Motion Picture Industry." The State of Israel awarded Cantor the Medallion of Valor in 1962 for his "extraordinary achievements" on behalf of that nation. In 1956, the Academy of Motion Picture Arts and Sciences presented him with a special Oscar "for the distinguished service to the film industry," and in 1964, President Lyndon Johnson gave Cantor the U.S. Service Medal in recognition of his humanitarian work.

A 1952 heart attack slowed Cantor down considerably, and he never fully recovered from the death of his wife, Ida, on August 8, 1962—they were married on June 9, 1914, and had five daughters. Two years after Ida's death, the great entertainer and humanitarian was also gone.

BIBLIOGRAPHY

Bleeden, Joe. "Makin' Whoopee." *Emmy* 14, no. 1 (January/February 1992).

Bowes, Vivian. "His Brother's Keeper." *Collier's*, December 4, 1948, pp. 50, 80.

Cantor, Eddie. *Caught Short: A Sage of Wailing Wall Street*. New York: Simon and Schuster, 1929.

————. *Between the Acts*. New York: Simon and Schuster, 1930.

————, as told to David Freedman. *My Life Is in Your Hands*. New York: Blue Ribbon Books, 1932.

————. "The Ten Best Gags of Eddie Cantor." *Liberty* 18, no. 43 (October 25, 1941), pp. 43–44.

————, ed. *World's Book of the Best Jokes*. Cleveland: World, 1943.

————. "I Remember the Ziegfeld Follies." *Esquire*, July 1947, p. 72.

————. "Those Ziegfeld Days—and Nights!" *Variety*, January 6, 1954, p. 271.

————, with Jane Kesner Ardmore. *Take My Life*. New York: Doubleday, 1957.

————. *As I Remember Them*. New York: Duell, Sloan and Pearce, 1963.

"Eddie Cantor." *Current Biography*, November 1941, pp. 132–34.

Mullett, Mary B. "We All Like the Medicine Doctor Eddie Cantor Gives." *American Magazine*, July 1924, pp. 34–35.

Smith, Frederick James. "Eddie Cantor Had Six Months to Live." *Liberty* 14, no. 30 (July 24, 1937), p. 11.

Stumpf, Charles K. "Banjo-Eyes—Eddie Cantor." *The World of Yesterday*, December 1980, pp. 39–44.

CARDINI (Wales, 1894—Kingston, N.Y., November 11, 1973)

Cardini was the stage name of Richard Valentine Pitchford, a smooth-talking, sleight-of-hand magician, who made a successful transition from vaudeville to nightclubs. Tricks with a lighted cigarette and playing cards were the specialty of his act, which was introduced by his wife, Susan Walker, who would appear dressed as a page boy, shouting, "Paging Mr. Cardini." Cardini would then appear elegantly attired in evening dress, top hat, and monocle. He made his first appearance in Wales in 1918 and adopted the name Cardini on a 1920 variety tour of Australia. He first appeared in vaudeville in 1926 and made a number of appearances at the Palace in the late 1920s.

LA CARMENCITA

A Spanish danger noted for her fiery, often defiant style, La Carmencita was a vaudeville headliner briefly taken up by New York society in the 1890s. She was painted by John Singer Sargent, and a ball in her honor was held at Madison Square Garden on January 30, 1891. She was first seen in New York at Niblo's Gardens on August 17, 1889, featured with Mlle Paris in "a spectacular ballet extravaganza" titled *Antiope*, but made little impact. It was not until she appeared at Koster and Bial's Music Hall on February 10, 1890, in "The Pearl of Seville" and accompanied by her Spanish Students that she became an immediate success, returning many times to Koster and Bial's. In December 1892, she danced after the second act of *The Prodigal Father* by Glen Macdonough at the Broadway Theatre, and that was her last major appearance; according to George C. D. Odell in *Annals of the New York Stage* (Columbia University Press, 1949), "she was passé, her glory withered. She danced out with *The Prodigal Father*." In reality, she was still to be seen in New York vaudeville for the next couple of years, appearing at Koster and Bial's in September 1893 and at the American Theatre Roof Garden in August 1894.

LEO CARRILLO (Los Angeles, August 6, 1881—Santa Monica, Ca., September 10, 1961)

Most Americans know Leo Carrillo as a character actor, specializing in semi-sleazy ethnic types with only a rudimentary knowledge of the English language. His image as Pancho to Duncan Renaldo as the title character in the television series *The Cisco Kid* (syndicated, 1950–1956) is a part of American popular culture. In reality, Leo Carrillo was a member of one of California's oldest and most venerated families, heir to a dynasty founded by a companion to Father Juniper Serra, José Raimundo Carrillo, in the 1700s.

While working as a sketch artist in the art department of the *San Francisco Examiner*, Carrillo made his vaudeville debut in 1896 at a matinee performance at the city's Orpheum Theatre, delivering a monologue as he sketched. He left the newspaper and embarked on a vaudeville career in which he became a headliner. Carrillo made the transition from vaudeville to the legitimate stage on March 8, 1915, when he appeared as Giovanni Gassolini in *Fads and Fancies*. While he is generally recognized to be of Spanish descent, it was in Italian roles that he prospered. In 1916, he was featured in *Upstairs and Down*, and in 1917, he achieved his greatest success in *Lombardi, Ltd.*, in which he also toured. While extremely busy on the legitimate stage in the 1920s, he still found time to headline at the Palace Theatre in March 1926.

Leo Carrillo recognized the value of his years in vaudeville, telling *The New York Dramatic Mirror* in 1920, "The vaudeville training is of untold benefit to the artist when he reaches the legitimate. His 'sense of time,' learned through the vaudeville process, demonstrates its value in divers ways. By gauging himself in this respect he can restrain from doing his 'time' to excess and prevent his style from becoming 'stocky.' Nothing is more annoying than the actor who becomes stereotyped in a stock mold and this rut proves the downfall of many a man in the legitimate."

The actor entered films in 1928, appearing in some seventy-five features through 1952. He retired in 1959. Leo Carrillo is, with Will Rogers, the only Hollywood star to have a Southern California beach named in his honor, and, of course, both Rogers and Carrillo began their careers in vaudeville.

BIBLIOGRAPHY

Carrillo, Leo. *The California I Love*. Englewood Cliffs, N.J.: Prentice-Hall, 1961.

May, Dale Ballou. *The Adobe Is My Birthstone: Leo Carrillo's Rancho de los Quintes, a Reflection of the Man, His Era, and His Career*. Carlsbad, Ca.: City of Carlsbad, 1988.

Taylor, Frank J. "Leo the Caballero." *Saturday Evening Post*, July 6, 1946, pp. 26–27, 86, 88–89.

HARRY CARROLL (Atlantic City, N.J., November 28, 1892—Santa Barbara, Ca., December 26, 1962)

A charter member of ASCAP (American Society of Composers, Authors, and Publishers), Harry Carroll was a prolific composer, with his best known songs being "Trail of the Lonesome Pine," "I'm Always Chasing Rainbows," and "By the Beautiful Sea." He was a frequent entertainer on the vaudeville stage, playing the piano and singing his own songs, often assisted by a female partner. At the Palace in February 1922 that was Anna Wheaton. At his last appearance at the Palace in December 1930, it was Maxine Lewis. In between, Carroll was at the Palace (seldom as the headliner) in March 1923, October 1923, January 1927, August 1928, and June 1929.

A professional pianist as a child, Carroll played at New York night spots prior to entering vaudeville. He was composer or musical director for many Broadway shows, including *The Passing Show of 1914*, *Dancing Around* (1914), *Maid in America* (1915), *Oh! Look!* (1918), *The Little Blue Devil* (1919), and Ziegfeld's *Midnight Frolic* (1920). He put together a number of revue-style vaudeville acts and toured the Keith circuit in 1920 with "Varieties of 1920." In March 1924, he and Joe Donohue played the Hippodrome with a revue act called "Everything Will Be All Right." In 1928, he toured the Keith circuit with the "Harry Carroll Revue," featuring twenty performers, led by comedian Ken Murray in "One Big Artistic, Fast, Humorous Production." In the 1940s, Carroll appeared at a number of West Coast nightclubs with his wife, Polly.

EMMA CARUS (Berlin, Germany, March 18, 1879—New York, November 18, 1927)

Because she had a good voice combined with unattractive features, Emma Carus made her name in vaudeville as a singing comedienne. She would usually begin her act with the line, "I'm not pretty, but I'm good to my family." Grace, the wife of legendary composer Gus Kahn, recalled, "She had a beautiful baby face, but she was quite stout. And Gus and I wrote a song for her called 'Henry, Oh Henry, Your Mother Is Looking for You'—a little kid's song. And it was kind of strange seeing this big, fat woman standing up there singing a song like a child."

The daughter of the noted prima donna Henrietta Rolland, Carus first sang publicly at the age of six. According to Edward B. Marks in his 1935 auto-biography, *They All Sang*, she was discovered by a singer and songwriter named Monroe "Rosie" Rosenfeld (the man who supposedly gave Tin Pan Alley its name). Rosenfeld heard Emma Carus when she was working at a hotel and noticed a valuable timbre in her speaking voice. The entertainer made her New York debut in 1894 and became a popular favorite in musical comedy, staring in such shows as *The Giddy Throng* (1900), *The Wild Rose* (1902), *45 Minutes from Broadway* (1907, succeeding Fay Templeton), *Up and Down Broadway* (1910), and *The Wife Hunters* (1911). During part of its run, Emma Carus was featured in the original, 1907 production of the Ziegfeld *Follies*, and later that same year, she appeared for the first time on the vaudeville stage. From 1915 onward, she was exclusively a vaudeville headliner.

PAT CASEY (Springfield, Ma., 1874—Hollywood, Ca., February 7, 1962)

Pat Casey is a shadowy but important figure in vaudeville, an early agent who became involved in labor relations on the side of management, founding the Vaudeville Managers Protective Association to fight the strike activities of the White Rats. After an early involvement in theatre management at the Parlor Theatre, Springfield, in 1894, Casey became a New York theatrical agent at the turn of the century. In the teens, he became an executive with B. F. Keith, serving as right-hand man to E. F. Albee. With the demise of vaudeville, he became the head of labor relations for the Association of Motion Picture Producers. He retired in 1947 but continued with the association in a consultancy capacity.

As Robert J. Landry wrote in *Variety*, "Pat Casey . . . was a showman whose biography will elude full telling for the simple reason that so much of it was and is hidden. He was a deft negotiator, a go-between and private emissary for innumerable individuals, organizations and trade causes."

BIBLIOGRAPHY

Landry, Robert J. "Pat Casey: Man Behind the Scenes." *Variety*, February 14, 1962, p. 4.

IRENE CASTLE (New Rochelle, N.Y., April 7, 1893—Eureka Springs, Ak., January 25, 1969) and **VERNON CASTLE** (Norwich, England, May 2, 1887—Fort Worth, Tx., February 15, 1918)

While Mrs. Castle claimed in her autobiography that "we only went into vaudeville when we were hard up," there is no question that she and her husband were popular headliners from 1914 through 1916. As Frederick James Smith wrote in *The New York Dramatic Mirror* (June 30, 1915), "The dance craze is dead—but the popularity of the Castles goes on."

Born Irene Foote, Irene Castle met her future husband, a stage actor for more than six years, at a rowing club in 1910. They were married in New Rochelle in May 1911. Later that same year, Vernon and Irene Castle went to Paris to star in a revue whose opening was so delayed, until March 1912, that when it did commence, it was titled *Enfin—Une Revue*. The pair returned to the United States in 1914 and were the stars of the Irving Berlin musical *Watch Your Step*, which opened at the New Amsterdam Theatre on December 8, 1914. The success of that show led the Castles to open Castle House on New York's 46th Street, where they taught the latest dances to society.

Vernon and Irene Castle first appeared before the motion picture camera for a 1914 short subject, in which they showed off various dance steps. They made one feature film together, *The Whirl of Life* (1915), and between 1916 and 1922, Irene Castle starred in seventeen additional feature films and one serial, *Patria* (1916–1917). The couple's life, *The Story of Vernon and Irene Castle*, was filmed by RKO in 1939 as a vehicle for Fred Astaire and Ginger Rogers.

Following the outbreak of the First World War, Vernon Castle, a British subject, joined the Royal Flying Corps. He was killed while training Canadian pilots at an airfield near Fort Worth, Texas. Following his death, Irene Castle remarried three times. She returned to vaudeville, dancing at the Palace with a new partner, William Reardon, for the week of January 9, 1922. *The New York Dramatic Mirror* (February 1922) complained that "Miss Castle is not offering anything new in the dance line."

BIBLIOGRAPHY

Castle, Irene. "My Memories of Vernon Castle." *Everybody's*, November 1918, pp. 22–27; December 1918, pp. 36–41; January 1919, pp. 38–42; February 1919, pp. 50–55; March 1919, pp. 39–42.

_____, as told to Bob and Wanda Duncan. *Castles in the Air*. Garden City, N.Y.: Doubleday, 1958.

Stainton, Walter H. "Irene Castle." *Films in Review* 13, no. 6 (June–July 1962), pp. 347–55.

CHAZ CHASE (1902—Hollywood, Ca., August 4, 1983)

Chaz Chase was a diminutive and silent comic who would appear onstage dressed in an outfit somewhere between that of a dandy and a tramp. He would then proceed to eat anything he could lay his hands (or rather his mouth) on, including lighted matches, cigarettes, a rose, and the cardboard dickey that he always wore. The act would generally conclude with a comic striptease. George Burns once told the joke of meeting Chase in a restaurant and his complaining that he could find nothing on the menu to eat.

This exponent of the gustatory binge enjoyed an extensive career, stretching from the 1925 edition of the Ziegfeld *Follies* to a 1982 engagement in the Mickey Rooney/Ann Miller revue *Sugar Babies*. He played the Palace in 1926 and was also seen on Broadway in *Ballyhoo* (1930), *Saluta* (1934), *Laughter over Broadway* (1939), and *High Kickers* (1941). Chase was also a frequent nightclub entertainer, notably at the Latin Quarter in New York and the Crazy Horse Saloon in Paris.

Chaz Chase was featured in a couple of short film subjects, but he should not be confused with the comedian Charlie Chase.

DAVE CHASEN (Odessa, Russia, July 18, 1898—Los Angeles, June 16, 1973)

A legendary Beverly Hills restauranteur, Dave Chasen had earlier made his name in vaudeville as one of the great, silent stooges. He was primarily known for a gesture called "The Idiot's Salute," which film director Frank Capra described as "a salute that started with the sudden raising of both arms chin-high, as if to fend off a blow. Then a quick expression change from mock fright to the widest-eyed, most open-mouthed gargoylish smile ever seen on any face, followed by the right hand—fingers spread wide and palm toward viewer—crossed in front of his fixed idiot's smile like a slowly opening fan."

Dave Chasen came to the United States with his parents in the early years of the century and grew up in Port Chester, New York. He is most closely associated as a stooge with Joe Cook, working with the comedian not only in vaudeville but also in the 1924 edition of Earl Carroll's *Vanities*, *Rain or Shine* (1928), *Fine and Dandy* (1930), and *Hold Your Horses* (1933). He also appeared in a few films: *Rain or Shine* (1930), *Old Man Rhythm* (1935), *Millions in the Air* (1935), and *Arizona Mahoney* (1937). In 1936, Harold Ross, editor of *The New Yorker*, suggested that Chasen open a restaurant and provided an initial $3,500 investment for the Southern Barbecue Pit, which later became simply Chasen's, and which continues in operation to the present under the direction of Chasen's widow, Maude.

BIBLIOGRAPHY

Capra, Frank. "The Priceless Ingredient That Was Dave Chasen." *Los Angeles Times Calendar*, August 26, 1973, pp. 16, 23, 77.

Christy, George. "Reminiscing with Dave Chasen." *Los Angeles*, August 1979, pp. 44–47.

Ford, Corey. "The Stars Are Dave's Dish." *Collier's*, July 9, 1949, pp. 27, 72–73.

Sayre, Joel. "How to Eat Like a Movie Star." *Saturday Evening Post*, April 6, 1957, pp. 28–29, 140, 142, 144–46.

Schulberg, Bud. "See You at Dave's." *Holiday*, April 1951, pp. 64–65, 67, 70, 135, 137–38.

"CHASER"

The "chaser" was the last act on the vaudeville bill, designed to chase the audience from the theatre. When films lost their novelty appeal as vaudeville attractions, they were often used as chasers between 1900 and 1903.

CHAUTAUQUA

In many respects, Chautauqua was a wholesome, outdoor form of vaudeville that flourished from 1874 through 1924. Throughout the United States, brown tents went up in cities and towns as lecturers and respectable entertainers spent the summer months touring on a circuit that was as controlled and financially successful as anything that the vaudeville industry could contrive. The concept of Chautauqua originated with a minister named John H. Vincent of Camptown, New York, who, with a friend named Lewis Miller of Akron, Ohio, decided to start a summer school to teach religious values. Miller was a trustee of a summer camp at Lake Chautauqua, New York, and it was there that the first meeting, titled the Sunday-School Teachers' Assembly, was held in the summer of 1874. Soon the meetings became nondenominational and attracted speakers as varied as Booker T. Washington, Carry Nation, and Eugene V. Debs. In 1881, the Chautauqua School of Theology was formed, followed in 1883 by the Chautauqua University and in 1900 by the Chautauqua Press. The movement also published a monthly magazine, *Chautauquan*.

The idea quickly spread, with a similar group forming at Lakeside, Ohio, in 1876, and by 1900, two hundred Chautauqua assemblies were in operation. The notion of presenting Chautauqua in tents had its origin in the Lyceum movement, founded in 1826 by Josiah Holbrook of Millburg, Massachusetts. An association for mutual intellectual improvement, Lyceum groups met in the winter months in community halls and heard lecturers who were booked as part of a circuit. The most popular was Ralph Waldo Emerson, but his popularity was soon eclipsed on both the Lyceum and Chautauqua circuits by William Jennings Bryan (who spoke without the aid of a microphone to 100,000 listeners in San Francisco).

The Lyceum lectures were booked through the Redpath Lyceum Bureau of Keith Vawter, and he soon became established as the chief circuit booker for Chautauqua, with his only major competitor being J. Roy Ellison's Ellison—

White Chautauqua and Lyceum System, which booked "acts" west of the Rockies and was also active in Canada. As Chautauqua grew, small-time vaudeville performers found employment there, and some of the more "sanitized" major performers became equally at home on both the vaudeville stage and in Chautauqua tents. Will Rogers was one vaudevillian that Chautauqua was most anxious to book, but he always turned down the offers. Benjamin Chapin was a popular celebrity, impersonating Abraham Lincoln in both media, as was Frederick Warde with his recitations from Shakespeare. Virtually any vaudeville act was considered appropriate provided it represented culture, inspiration, or uplift.

Chautauqua celebrated its golden jubilee in 1924 with thirty-five million persons attending programs at tents in twelve thousand cities and towns nationwide. It was also the last year in which Chautauqua flourished. Vaudeville, motion pictures, and radio had stolen away the Chautauqua audiences for good.

BIBLIOGRAPHY

Case, Victoria, and Robert Ormond Case. *We Called It Culture: The Story of Chautauqua*. Garden City, N.Y.: Doubleday, 1948.

Gould, Joseph E. *The Chautauqua Movement: An Episode in the Continuing American Revolution*. Albany: State University of New York Press, 1961.

Harrison, Harry P., as told to Karl Detzer. *Culture under Canvas: The Story of Tent Chautauqua*. New York: Hastings House, 1958.

Hurlbut, Jesse Lyman. *The Story of Chautauqua*. New York: G. P. Putnam's Sons, 1921.

Irwin, Alfreda L. *Three Taps of the Gavel: The Chautauqua Story*. Westfield, N.Y.: The Westfield Republican, 1970.

MacLaren, Gary. *Morally We Roll Along*. Boston: Little, Brown, 1938.

Morrison, Theodore. *Chautauqua: A Center for Education, Religion, and the Arts in America*. Chicago: University of Chicago Press, 1974.

Richmond, Rebecca. *Chautauqua: An American Place*. New York: Duell, Sloan and Pearce, 1943.

CHERRY SISTERS

The best contemporary description of the Cherry Sisters is given by Robert Grau in his 1910 volume on *The Business Man in the Amusement World*:

"They were just a quartette of incompetents, and they were so indifferent to their reception by the public, that they were in demand for many years, at a salary far higher than would have been accorded them if they had possessed any real ability. There was, though, something approaching cruelty in the spectacle which these poor females presented, night after night, in exhibiting their crudities to howling, insulting audiences."

The Cherry Sisters, whose names have become synonymous with any act devoid of talent, were originally five in number: Effie (Indian Creek, Ia., 1878—Cedar Rapids, Ia., August 5, 1944), Jessie (Indian Creek, Ia., ?—1903), Lizzie (Indian Creek, Ia., ?—Grand Rapids, Ia., May 12, 1936), Addie (Wheaton, Il., 1859—Cedar Rapids, Ia., October 25, 1942), and Ella (birth and death dates unavailable). To raise money to attend the 1893 Chicago World's Fair, the sisters put on shows for their friends, and because such friends were so uncritical, the sisters were persuaded, when they reached Chicago, to approach a vaudeville agent and become professional entertainers. The agent was quick to realize the potential he had with an act that was so bad, and he signed them to appear in one-act melodramas such as *The Gypsy's Warning*, interspersed with songs, with the sisters touring through Iowa, Kansas, and Illinois.

Oscar Hammerstein read of them and realized the enjoyment they would bring to a sophisticated New York audience. He sent his stage manager, Al Aarons, to Chicago to locate them, and on November 28, 1896, the sisters made their New York debut at Hammerstein's Olympia Theatre Roof Garden. A net was placed in front of the stage, and Oscar Hammerstein and his son Willie encouraged the audience to hurl vegetables and fish at the women, who were dressed in red calico. They were billed as "The Cherry Sisters—Something Good, Something Sad," with the emphasis on the latter. When the rotten vegetables started to be thrown before Effie had even finished her first song, "Three Cheers for the Railroad Boys," Hammerstein explained to the sisters that other star performers, jealous of their talents, had hired the throwers.

"Chicot" reviewed the Cherry Sisters' act when they played Proctor's Pleasure Palace and reported the women had received golden horseshoes as a tribute to their talent; he continued, "If arrangements could be made, I should be glad to present them with a horseshoe attached to the business end of an able-bodied and hard-working jackass." When *Variety* panned their act in 1908, the sisters responded with a letter that read in part, "In your issue of March 21, you had an article which was one of the most malicious, violent and untruthful writings we have ever read. The person who wrote it is not deserving the name of man, but is instead a contemptible cur. You said in your paper that we advertised ourselves 'the worst show on earth,' which makes you a liar, point blank. We have always advertised ourselves as one of the best, and we would not be far from the truth if we said the best."

The Cherry Sisters retired after Jessie's death in 1903 but made a number of comebacks. None of the sisters married. Effie was the most active, twice running unsuccessfully for mayor of Cedar Rapids. She even considered running for Congress on an anti-liquor, anti-tobacco platform. Of a May 1924 comeback at the Orpheum, Des Moines, *Variety*'s local reviewer commented, "If it were not for a reputation for being a bad act gained 30 years ago, the Cherry Sisters could not get a hearing. . . . As terribleness, their skit is perfection." In 1935, Addie and Effie Cherry were invited to appear at a New York nightclub, The Gay Nineties, with their manager, Carl Whyte, at the piano, but audiences by this time were frankly embarrassed by the pitiful sight of two old ladies unaware of their shortcomings.

BIBLIOGRAPHY

Gartner, Michael. "Fair Comment." *American Heritage*, October/November 1982, pp. 28–31.
Hale, Avery. "So Bad They Were Good." *Coronet*, December 1944, pp. 92–96.

ALBERT CHEVALIER (London, March 21, 1861—London, July 11, 1923)

The coster comedian—the performer with a cockney accent born within the sound of London's Bow Bells—has been an integral part of British music hall from Gus Elen through Flanagan and Allen to Max Bygraves. Flanagan and Allen never appeared in the United States, while Gus Elen made his vaudeville debut in 1907, and Max Bygraves played the Palace in October 1951, but they were relatively unsuccessful compared to Albert Chevalier, who earned $1,750 a week in American vaudeville and delighted American audiences despite his heavy accent and the strong English characteristics of his songs and monologes.

The songs, which he usually wrote himself, were, and are, gems of working-class English life. Once heard, audiences never forgot "Mrs. 'enry 'awkins," "Knocked 'em in the Old Kent Road" (usually associated with Marie Lloyd), and "My Old Dutch," in which an elderly cockney recalls the forty years spent with his wife, his Old Dutch: "She's stuck to me through thick and thin, when luck was out, when luck was in; Oh, what a wife to me she's bin and what a pal." The song could never fail to move an audience to tears—particularly when Chevalier asked that death might take him first in order that he might prepare the way in Heaven for his Old Dutch. Similarly, in the spoken song "The Fallen Star," Chevalier enumerated in perfect theatrical English the woes of a stage actor down on his luck, who remembers yet again forty years ago—a cherished period of time for Chevalier—when he was a "favorite of the Vic. . . . But now I pass unrecognized in crowded streets and bars. The firmament of fame holds no record of my name; the name of a fallen star." These songs were never really sung by Albert Chevalier, but rather recited in much the same style as Rex Harrison adopted to play Professor Higgins in *My Fair Lady*.

The son of a French father and English mother, Chevalier was on the legitimate stage for many years before moving over to music hall and vaudeville. No doubt the years spent with such prominent British actors as Arthur Roberts, Squire Bancroft, and John Hare helped him tremendously when it came to the conception of his vaudeville characterizations. Most reference sources agree that Chevalier first sang a cockney song, "Our 'armonic club," in London's Strand Theatre's production of the pantomime *Aladdin* in 1889. His first music hall appearance was at London's Tivoli Theatre in 1891.

Albert Chevalier was both arrogant and pompous in discussing his origins and his attitude toward the music hall:

You know I am not of the music halls. When I opened at the London Pavilion, I had come straight from the legitimate. That opening night I shall never forget. I fancied the audience were paying no attention whatever to me. The din was hideous. I was on pins and needles all the time I was on the stage. When I came off, the stage manager said to me, "How quiet they were tonight. I never knew them to be so peaceful." Peaceful! To me it seemed pandemonium.

A music-hall atmosphere is really not propitious for artistic work. The wonder is that anybody is able to accomplish anything. I have known artists—genuine artists—fail ignominously in a music hall, where in a theatre they would take the house by storm. But a music hall audience doesn't come to be amused; it comes to amuse itself.

Albert Chevalier made his vaudeville debut at Koster and Bial's Music Hall in 1896. In Europe, he worked frequently with Yvette Guilbert—a strange combination—and joined her on a triumphant six-week tour of American vaudeville in 1906. The following year, he returned to the legitimate stage in the Theatre Royal, Drury Lane, production of *The Sins of Society*. From that point onward, he alternated legitimate stage work with appearances in music hall and vaudeville. In 1909, he returned to the United States, opening in vaudeville at New York's Colonial Theatre. "Rush" saw him there and commented in *Variety* (October 2, 1909):

Chevalier has several new songs, the best being "The Workhouse Man," in which he tells the touching story of an aged pauper separated from his wife by the rules of the poorhouse. He opened with "A Fallen Star," sung over here not long since by Ralph Herz. "I've Got 'er 'at" is a comic in the Cockney dialect. "Wot vor De'er Love Oi" brings the singer forward in the role of a loutish Yorkshire farmer, a character which, with its accompanying dialect, is most unfamiliar to Americans. Chevalier is the same finished artist. His characters are made convincing without trickery or the slightest touch of exaggeration.

In 1915, Chevalier starred opposite the American actress Florence Turner in a British film, *My Old Dutch*, based on the song. That same song was also used as the basis for a stage play by Chevalier, presented at New York's Lyceum Theatre in July 1920.

At the time of his death, after he had announced his final retirement from the stage, *Variety* (July 26, 1923) hailed him as "the greatest of all coster comedians," but that is a title that does not do justice to a vaudevillian whose characterizations were always uniquely English yet which, through his artistry, transcended the barriers of nationality.

BIBLIOGRAPHY

Chevalier, Albert. *Before I Forget*. London: T. Fisher Unwin, 1902.
"Cockney Laureate." *Living Age*, August 25, 1923, pp. 380–81.
Daly, Brian, ed. *Albert Chevalier*. London: Macqueen, 1895.
"A Man of Magnetism." *The New York Dramatic Mirror*, October 13, 1896, p. 17.

CHICAGO

In 1906, the following vaudeville houses were in operation in the city: the Haymarket, the Clark Street Museum, the Olympic, the Majestic, the Folly, the London Dime Museum, Howard's, the International, the Metropolitan Music Hall, the Pekin (black-owned and catering to black audiences), the Trocadero, and Sid Euson's. By 1921, at which time Chicago had a population of 2,701,212, it had five major vaudeville theatres: McVicker's, the Majestic, the Palace Music Hall, the Rialto, and the State Lake (opened in 1919 and seating 3100).

See also KOHL and CASTLE.

CHORUS GIRLS

While not an integral part of vaudeville, chorus girls are worthy of attention, as male audiences through the decades will confirm. The concept of the chorus girl dates back to England in the 1840s, when the dance routines were taken from the ballet. Even then, chorus girls were noted for their skimpy costuming, causing W. Davenport Adams to write in 1882, "There can be charming ballets without reducing the coryphées almost to nudity." One of the first U.S. shows to utilize chorus girls was *The Black Crook* in 1866. It was, of course, usual to have vaudeville shows begin with an animal act, acrobatics, or a similar "dumb" routine. Curiously, the one major exception was the opening bill at the Palace Theatre in March 1913, when the program began with the Eight Palace Girls. *The Billboard* (April 5, 1913) commented, "The girls are good to look upon and have a routine of dance steps which they show in a snappy manner. There is no change of costume and taken as a whole the act would not get far in regular vaudeville theaters."

Showman Florenz Ziegfeld took the idea of the chorus line, but instead of having his women dance, he posed them in settings and with lighting effects to dramatize their individual beauty. With the first edition of the Ziegfeld *Follies* in 1907, he created the showgirl. Ziegfeld created her, and George White (in his *Scandals* from 1919 onward) and Earl Carroll (in his *Vanities* from 1923 onward) continued the tradition. A favorite vaudeville joke was the question to a mother as to whether she wanted her daughter to be glorified by Ziegfeld or scandalized by White.

Many of Ziegfeld's showgirls became as famous as the stars of the *Follies*. They were photographed by Alfred Cheney Johnston and in the 1920s painted by Albert Vargas. Some, such as Dolores (who was at the height of her fame during the First World War) became legends in show business history; others, including Kathryn Perry, Mary Hay, Marion Davies, Justine Johnstone, Lilyan Tashman, Billie Dove, Claudia Dell, and Virginia Bruce, enjoyed later success on screen. Quite a few, including Peggy Hopkins Joyce and Peaches Browning, married millionaires. In 1928, Peaches Browning was billed as "The Most Noted Woman in the World," following her marriage to an ecentric multimillionaire owner of real estate. She was the first entertainer to play the RKO vaudeville circuit on a percentage basis, singing "I'm All Alone in a Palace of Stone."

Kathryn Perry recalled that showgirls would refer to the bracelets given to them by admirers as "service stripes." "I got three of the prettiest bracelets, a little ruby one, a little diamond one, and a little sapphire one. And I didn't have to do a damn thing. When those boys drove me home and kissed me goodnight, they kissed me on the cheek. I went to this man's house alone for dinner one night. He was very dignified looking with a white moustache, all curled up. He didn't get fresh with me but he asked if I'd like to stay overnight and sleep at the foot of the bed." The routine was always the same: "Mornings you'd go down there at 10:30 to rehearse. My mother would meet me for dinner after the matinee. Then back to do a night show, and afterwards we'd do a show on the

Roof. Then we'd go on to a party at Delmonico's. You had to be tough and healthy."

The most prominent group of chorus girls in the world were the Tiller Girls. They came from a dancing school in England founded by John Tiller (who died in New York on October 22, 1925, at the age of seventy-one). Tiller sent over many units of eight or sixteen chorus girls to work in American shows, and the Tiller Girls were an institution in Europe long after their creator's death. In Paris, the best known chorus women were the Bluebell Girls at the Folies Bergère. They took their name from an Irish orphan named Bluebell Murphy, who began dancing in the chorus of the Jackson Girls in the mid 1920s. She created the Bluebell Girls in the early 1930s, and they took over the spot at the Folies Bergère formerly occupied by the Buddy Bradley Girls from England.

In the United States, the best known chorus line is the Rockettes at Radio City Music Hall in New York. The group was founded in St. Louis in 1925 by Russell Markert as the Missouri Rockets, after he had seen the Tiller Girls in the 1922 edition of the Ziegfeld *Follies*. S. L. Rothafel featured the Rockets in 1927 at the Roxy Theatre in New York. Later, Markert created two other groups of chorus girls, one to play in Broadway shows and the other in vaudeville. Because of an implied connection with the Roxy Theatre, the name of the chorus girls at Radio City was changed to the Rockettes.

BIBLIOGRAPHY

Bacon, George Vaux. "Chorus Girls in the Making." *The Green Book Magazine*, October 1913, pp. 571–579.

Francisco, Charles. *The Radio City Music Hall: An Affectionate History of the World's Greatest Theater*. New York: E. P. Dutton, 1979.

Parker, Derek, and Julia Parker. *The Natural History of the Chorus Girl*. Indianapolis: Bobbs-Merrill, 1975.

CINCINNATI

In 1906, there were three vaudeville houses in Cincinnati: the Columbia, the People's, and the Casino. By 1921, with the city's population at 401,247, there were four: the Columbia, B. F. Keith's, the Liberty, and the Palace.

PAUL CINQUEVALLI (Lissa, Poland, June 30, 1859—London, July 14, 1918)

Paul Cinquevalli was one of the greatest classical jugglers in vaudeville and British music hall. At the time of his death, *Variety* (July 19, 1918) wrote of him, "Cinquevalli was a model for gracefulness in juggling, which he made an art through his deft manipulation of all sorts of articles, light and heavy." Born Paul Kesner, the juggler was educated in Berlin and at the age of thirteen became apprenticed to a gymnast and aerialist named Cinquevalli, whose name the young student adopted. He went to England in 1885 and soon became billed as "The Human Billiard Table" because of the manner in which he could play billiards or pool on his own back.

Cinquevalli first came to the United States in 1888 with Rich and Harris's Howard Athenaeum Company. He made a triumphant return visit in 1901, playing the Keith circuit and appearing for ten consecutive weeks at New York's Union Square Theatre. According to *The New York Dramatic Mirror* (November 16, 1901), "Australia, South Africa, India, Mexico, and the South American countries alike bowed down in amazement at his marvelous work, so much better was he than these who had preceded him that they were forgotten." He was back again in 1904, at which time the *New York Clipper* provided the following description of him: "Cinquevalli is of medium size, but is the personification of muscular development and graceful action."

A final appearance in Britain in 1912 was followed by a tour of Australia, but the outbreak of the First World War led to his erroneously being branded a German, and he was forced into early retirement in 1915. He died at his home in Brixton, a south London suburb, which was a popular residential area for British music hall artists.

(BOBBY) CLARK (Springfield, Oh., June 16, 1888—New York, February 12, 1960) and **(PAUL) McCULLOUGH** (Springfield, Oh., 1883—Boston, March 25, 1936)

It is an irony of fate that while generations continue to thrive on the comedy of the Marx Brothers, imitating the walk, leer, and voice of Groucho, few recall the humor of Clark and McCullough, who were just as amusing, with the outrageous comedy of Bobby Clark still worthy of imitation. Clark was the funny man, with black glasses painted on his face, a cigar in one hand, and a leer and walk that were all his own. On his head was a porkpie hat, offset by a short topcoat and a cane which, sooner or later, would be used to smack the bottom of a retreating chorus girl. Like Groucho Marx, Bobby Clark was both witty and intelligent, announcing, for example, that the team's motto was "Omnia Cafeteria Rex" (We Eat All We Can Carry). The act might well have been called Clark and Who?, in that McCullough was the straight man/stooge, although he could and did crack a joke when required. As a team, Clark and McCullough delighted vaudeville, burlesque, and revue audiences from 1912 through the 1930s, at which time they made occasional excursions into films, transferring some of their better sketches from the transcience of the stage to the semipermanence of motion pictures.

No matter what production in which he appeared, Clark would completely take over the show. While playing the comedy lead in a 1947 revival of Victor Herbert's *Sweethearts*, he provided his own gags and at one point confided to the audience, "Never was a thin plot so complicated." When appearing in the 1946 production of Molière's *The Would-Be Gentleman*, Clark was told that the alphabet was divided into vowels and consonants, to which he responded, "That's only fair." In a 1942 production of *The Rivals*, directed by Eva Le Gallienne, he refused to stand still on stage for a moment; while the other actors were delivering their lines, Clark was clambering over the furniture, deploring the pictures, leering and winking at the rest of the company, and carrying on imaginary conversations. Eventually, Le Gallienne said to him, "I've never worked with anybody like you, Mr. Clark. I think you'd do a better job by yourself. I'll just try to keep the other actors out of your way." Bobby Clark's favorite dramatist was William Shakespeare, "because the clowns never get killed."

Both Clark and McCullough were born in Springfield, Ohio, where Clark made his stage debut in May 1902 at the Grand Opera House, as an attendant in *Mrs. Jarley's Waxworks*. The two met while in grammar school and also attended tumbling classes at the local Y.M.C.A. Continuing their acrobatics in each other's backyards, McCullough suggested in 1900, "I'll tell you what. Let's become partners. Maybe we can go into show business or something." They did. After placing advertisements for their act in *The Billboard* and the *New York Clipper*, the two were invited to join first the Culhane, Chace and Weston Minstrel Show and, later, Kalbfield's Greater California Minstrels. Eventually, the pair joined Ringling Brothers' Circus. A story is told of Al Ringling complaining of the amount of luggage that Clark carried with him and constantly added to. Clark responded that he was traveling with so much luggage only because he had noticed the circus was advertised as "bigger and better." For six years, between 1906 and 1912, Clark and McCullough worked in various circuses as clowns and musical performers, billed variously as the Jazzbo Brothers, the Prosit Trio, and Sunshine and Roses.

Clark and McCullough (unlike most comedy duos, the funny man's name was first in their billing) entered vaudeville on December 2, 1912, at the Opera House in New Brunswick, New Jersey, with an act consisting chiefly of trying to set a chair on top of a table. In those early years, the act was primarily pantomime with little or no dialogue. Later, the pair developed a sketch in which Clark volunteered to act as a lion tamer in a circus if McCullough would wear a lion skin and substitute for an escaped lion. In the meantime, unbeknown to Clark, the lion returned, and he played out the sketch with such comments as "Great, boy, great! You're doing a grand job"; "Put some life into it! We're getting fifty cents for this job" and "This is one of the classic performances of history. You even smell like a lion!"

Clark and McCullough toured in vaudeville for five years until the 1917 White Rats strike against the vaudeville management, which the two supported. The strike ended with management's barring any vaudeville act that had participated in the strike. To continue working, Clark and McCullough entered burlesque and there achieved their greatest success to date. Clark once reminisced about burlesque comedy, noting, "We had a lot of good people then. It would be hard to pick out the best. Maybe Joe Welch with his Jewish comedy, or his brother Ben Welch, or Dave Marion, or maybe Frank Tinney. I used to catch them all whenever I could. They were good—better than anybody today, I think. Real funny fellows. Make you laugh like you meant it." A classic Clark and Mc-Cullough burlesque sketch was titled "The Courtroom" and had Clark as a judge at the trial of a striptease performer. Every time an attorney spoke, Clark would hit him with a bladder and shout, "You're trying to inject hokum into this case!" Eventually, a fight broke out involving everyone in the courtroom and was stopped only by the suggestion that the stripper demonstrate her act for the judge in his chambers. Clark soon returned to announce, "Case settled out of court!"

Critic Howard Lindsay recalled:

> The core of their vaudeville act was pantomime, but they learned the use of dialogue, the value of the feed line and the timing of the comedy line. They learned another lesson vaudeville could teach better than any branch of the entertainment field—economy. In the eighteen or twenty minutes a vaudeville act was allowed, there could not be a wasted word or an insignificant movement.

As burlesque stars, Clark and McCullough were featured in *Puss Puss*, which opened at the Columbia Theatre, New York, on December 9, 1918. Clark played Count Rolling No Moss, while McCullough was Baron Few Clothes, and the two sang "They Go Wild over Us" and "Spanish Onions," described as "a strong specialty." In addition, the pair made their London debut in *Chuckles of 1922*, which opened at the New Oxford Theatre on June 19, 1922. From *Chuckles of 1922*, the pair went into the 1922 edition of *The Music Box Revue*. Irving Berlin had seen Clark and McCullough in London and immediately wanted them for the revue, which made the couple Broadway stars. *The Music Box Revue* led to appearances at both the Palace and the Hippodrome in 1924. Clark and McCullough also appeared in the 1924 edition of *The Music Box Revue*, *Strike Up the Band* (1929), *Music in the Air* (1932), and *Walk a Little Faster* (1932).

Surprisingly, despite their fame on Broadway, Clark and McCullough were not major headliners in vaudeville as yet. They played New York's Capitol Theatre—which featured both vaudeville and films—in January 1928, and *Variety* (January 11, 1928) reported that few in the audience knew who they were. However, it was not long before the audience was roaring with laughter because, as *Variety* noted, "they cash in heavily on ability rather than on laurels gained through past successes." Within two months, the pair were headlining at the Palace.

A return trip to England was far less successful. Clark and McCullough were in the 1931 edition of *C. B. Cochran's Review*, which opened at the Palace Theatre, Manchester, on February 18, 1931. Audiences in that northern city loved Clark and McCullough, but when the *Review* opened at the London Pavilion in March 1931, the comedy duo were greeted with a slow handclap, and the show closed within two weeks.

Clark and McCullough made a number of film appearances between 1929 and 1935, notably in two-reel short subjects for RKO. The shorts were shot quickly at the studio, with three days allowed for rehearsal and three for actual shooting. They received a flat salary of $7,500 a week, which even divided between the two was a fairly substantial amount in that another star of RKO comedy shorts, Edgar Kennedy, received a flat salary of only $2,250 a week.

In the spring of 1936, the partners were resting: Clark in New York and McCullough in a sanitarium in Massachusetts. They had just finished touring in a version of the revue *Thumbs Up*, in which the pair had appeared on Broadway the previous year. On March 23, 1936, McCullough walked into a barber shop in Medford, Massachusetts, and ordered a shave. After the shave was completed, he picked up the razor and slashed his throat and wrists. He died two days later in a Boston hospital. "I think it was just something Paul couldn't help. Something that had been with him all the time and he didn't even know," said Clark. *Variety* (April 1, 1936) noted that McCullough might have been only a straight man, but "the fact that he was a vital part of the noted team was never doubted, least of all by Bobby Clark."

Clark remained in seclusion for several months, but he reappeared to play solo for the first time in the 1936 version of *The Ziegfeld Follies*. He sang "I Can't Get Started" with Gypsy Rose Lee and also appeared with Fanny Brice in a sketch titled "The Sweepstakes Ticket." Even without his partner, he was as funny as ever, and he was to continue working through the years, appearing in *Streets of Paris* (1939), *Star and Garter* (1942), *Mexican Hayride* (1944), *As the Girls Go* (1948), and *Jollyana* (1952), among others. In 1956, he toured as Mephisto in *Damn Yankees*, playing it straight except for the cigar—"It seems to me that the devil would smoke cigars," he explained.

For the last few years of his life, Clark lived in retirement in New York with his wife, Angele Gaignat, whom he had married in 1923. With his death, the leer "that lit up the whole theatre" was no more.

BIBLIOGRAPHY

"Bobby Clark." *Current Biography*, May 1949, pp. 111–13.

Taylor, Robert Lewis. "Enter Crouching Low and Smoking a Cigar." *The New Yorker* 23, no. 30 (September 13, 1947), pp. 37–42, 45.

————. "Minstrel and Circus Days." Ibid., no. 31 (September 20, 1947), pp. 32–36, 38–40.

————. "Up from Jaw Moose." Ibid., no. 32 (September 27, 1947), pp. 36–46.

BESSIE CLAYTON (Philadelphia, circa 1878—Long Branch, N.J., July 21, 1948)

Bessie Clayton was a dancer on the vaudeville stage who began her career at the end of the last century. Writing in *Vaudeville* in 1914, Caroline Caffin commented, "Among the foremost of our dancing favorites is Bessie Clayton, the sportive, laughing, elfin creature, whose dazzling whirl of energy seems to come from an inexhaustible dynamo of youth and merriment. Her recent dance with a pierrot-like company was a revel of dainty mischief and frolic, wooing all to join her in a spirit of infectious joy." Clayton's first husband was Julian Mitchell, who staged shows for Weber and Fields and Florenz Ziegfeld; after his death in 1924, she married Bert Cooper (died 1946). The dancer graduated from vaudeville to Weber and Fields but later returned to the vaudeville stage. She took her dancing very seriously and was happier with European rather than

American audiences, complaining, "The little Moonlight Dance that I open with is the best thing I do, but it is the hilarious number after it that pleases the spectators. We are ragtime crazy. We want ragtime in our music and turkey trotting in our dancing—anything to startle us, and sometimes shock us. That is America, but it isn't art." Bessie Clayton gave her last stage performance in 1924.

BIBLIOGRAPHY

Parsons, Chauncey L. "American and European Danseuse—Bessie Clayton." *The New York Dramatic Mirror*, May 22, 1912, pp. 5, 11.

CLEVELAND

In 1906, there were five vaudeville houses in Cleveland: the Lyric, the Empire, B. F. Keith's, the Arch Hall, and the Star. By 1921, with the city's population at 800,000, there were four: B. F. Keith's Hippodrome, B. F. Keith's 105th Street, B. F. Keith's 17th Street, and Loew's State.

LADDIE CLIFF (Bristol, England, September 13, 1891—Crans-Montana, Switzerland, December 8, 1937)

The New York Dramatic Mirror (September 16, 1914) hailed Laddie Cliff as "the best eccentric dancer of the English type in the varieties." He was a popular favorite in American vaudeville in the early teens, playing at the Palace (but not as a headliner) in 1913 and 1914, and also appearing in the opening program at the Folies Bergere in 1911. Cliff made his stage debut in his native England at the age of eight in a concert party and three years later made his London debut. He first came to the United States in 1907, making his debut at New York's Colonial Theatre. He was active onstage as both a performer and a producer until his death, and he also appeared in a number of British films: *Sleeping Car* (1933), *Happy* (1934), *Sporting Love* (1936), and *Over She Goes* (1937).

KATHLEEN CLIFFORD (Charlottesville, Va., February 16, 1887—Los Angeles, January 11, 1963)

A male impersonator who was often described as the American answer to Vesta Tilley, Kathleen Clifford would appear dressed as a very dapper man, even sporting a monocle to go with her top hat and tails, billed as "The Smartest Chap in Town." Because British male impersonators were held in such high regard in vaudeville, Clifford would generally pretend to have been born in England. She was active on the vaudeville stage as a male impersonator as early as 1910, when *Variety*'s Sime Silverman hailed her as "a dandy looking boy," although he did complain, "she doesn't carry herself over well, in bearing, or the wearing of her clothes, including hats."

Kathleen Clifford began her career as a straight musical comedy performer and was featured as a teenager in the 1907 musical extravaganza *The Top o' the' World*. It was a characterization as a young girl that appealed to legitimate theatre audiences for the latter, but it was as a male impersonator that Clifford was known to vaudeville audiences. In a 1914 interview, she described how she went about creating her male persona:

When I don my masculine attire I am a man—for a moment. The first thing I know—without realizing it—I find myself searching my clothes for my cigarette case. Now I never smoke cigarettes off stage. Not that I have any prudish ideas against women smoking, but I simply don't care for them. Yet, in my masculine make-up, I find a cigarette in my hands before I know it. It's intuition, I guess, for there isn't a thing masculine about me off stage.

In making my quick change behind my shadow screen, I never look at a mirror to adjust my tie or put on my hat. I've been told that men do it in the careless way—that any way they put on their hat is the right way.

Aside from her work on stage, Kathleen Clifford appeared in films from 1917 to 1928, but not always in male roles or in parts involving male disguise. She continued in vaudeville through the early 1930s, but it was very clear that her vogue as a headliner had ended almost a decade earlier, and by the late 1920s Clifford was pursuing a new occupation—that of a Hollywood florist.

Following retirement, she wrote a novel of her Hollywood years titled *It's April... Remember*. Following her death, Clifford's body was shipped to Belgrade, Yugoslavia, the former home of her husband, where she was buried.

BIBLIOGRAPHY

"The Gentle Art of Being a Man." *The New York Dramatic Mirror*, March 4, 1914, p. 23.

HERBERT CLIFTON (London, October 19, 1885—Hollywood, Ca., September 26, 1947)

A female impersonator, Herbert Clifton was billed as "The Male Soprano" and advertised as having a voice worth one thousand pounds. He made his American debut at New York's Alhambra Theatre in January 1910, appearing as a ragged street urchin and singing "Love Me and the World Is Mine," "The Holy City," and "Stop Your Tickling, Jock," the last in his natural voice. Contemporary critics were not impressed, but audiences liked him, and after a brief return to England in March 1910, Clifton was back in the United States in September for a second vaudeville tour.

He was featured in the 1914 edition of the Ziegfeld *Follies*, and the New York *American* reported, "His wonderful portrayal brought tears to the eyes of many." Clifton's act was varied. First he appeared as a scrub lady singing Tosti's "Good-Bye." He performed a quick change to sing and dance as a chorus girl, and followed that by lifting his skirts to reveal a pair of trousers and performing a somewhat suggestive burlesque dance. To close his act, Clifton gave his impersonation of Geraldine Farrar singing "One Fine Day" from *Madame Butterfly*. In view of his somewhat plump appearance, Clifton did well to rely on characterizations rather than attractive clothes, as in his 1920 vaudeville act "Travesties of the Weaker Sex." Accompanying the impersonator at the piano was his wife, who sang while Clifton made his quick changes and who was also responsible for musical arrangements.

With the demise of vaudeville, Clifton entered films as a minor character actor. His last screen appearance was in *Ivy* (1947).

MAGGIE CLINE (Haverhill, Ma., January 1, 1857—Fair Haven, N.J., June 11, 1934)

Arguably the first female solo singer in vaudeville, Maggie Cline was noted for one comic Irish song, "Throw Him Down, McCloskey," which it is reported she purchased from J. W. Kelly for $1. She was a rabble rouser whose anti-English comments delighted the New York Irish immigrant audiences of her day. Once she drove the horse and cab that nightly took her from her Irving Place home directly onto the stage at Hyde and Beaman's Theatre. Her official billing was "The Irish Queen," but one critic labeled her "The Brunhilde of the Bowery."

She began her working life in a shoe factory, but after five years ran away with a burlesque troupe in Boston. Her initial songs were sentimental in style, including the Irish ballad "Mary Ann Kehoe." It is claimed she made her first New York vaudeville appearance in 1879. Certainly, she was on the stage at Hyde and Beaman's Theatre on February 14, 1881. Her first appearance at Tony Pastor's Music Hall was on November 14 of the same year. She married a cafe owner named John Ryan in 1888 and retired in the early teens, but not before playing the Palace in January 1914. Her last public appearance was in December 1928 at the opening night of Proctor's 58th Street Theatre; she declined all efforts to persuade her to sing.

GEORGE M. (MICHAEL) COHAN (Providence, R.I., July 4, 1878—New York, November 5, 1942)

"The first president—he can be a king and emperor if he chooses—of the republic of Broadway" was the description of George M. Cohan coined by *The New York Dramatic Mirror* (February 8, 1919). It is a fitting label for the man who symbolized American popular entertainment in the first third of the twentieth century. Cohan may not have participated in vaudeville during its heyday from 1900 through 1925, but there can be little question about his importance in the vaudeville field in view of the eight-foot-tall bronze statue of him, unveiled on September 11, 1959, which stands as the dominant feature in New York's theatre district, directly opposite the home of American vaudeville, the Palace Theatre.

As the composer of "Yankee Doodle Dandy," "Over There," and "You're a Grand Old Flag," it is appropriate that George M. Cohan should have been born on the 4th of July (although in recent years there has been some question that the correct birth date may have been the 3rd). The son of two minor variety artists, Jerry and Nellie Cohan, George M. Cohen learned to play the violin at the age of eight, and by the age of twelve he was playing the title role in *Peck's Bad Boy*. Even before then, Cohan had become part of the family vaudeville act—in the spring of 1889—billed along with his parents and sister, Josie, as The Cohan Mirth Makers, "The Celebrated Family of Singers, Dancers, and Comedians with Their Silver Plated Band and Symphony Orchestra." (Depending upon the family finances, the last was usually augmented to eight members.) Under the management of B. F. Keith—"We were always welcome at Keith's," Cohan noted in his autobiography—the family toured America, singing, dancing, and joking until, as the Four Cohans, they became the highest paid act of their number in vaudeville. George M. Cohan began to provide the material for the family act, notably a playlet titled *Running for Office*, while at the same time providing material for other vaudeville performers. The youngster also contributed enthusiasm to the act, explaining, "I am not a comedian, and I can't get laughs. So I try for enthusiasm."

At the turn of the century, George M. Cohan and his family left vaudeville, not of their own accord, but as a result of a dispute with B. F. Keith over billing. When Cohan complained to Keith, the latter accused him of manufacturing the complaint in order to force Keith to pay more money for the act. In anger, Cohan told Keith, "I'll make you a promise right now—that no member of the Cohan family will ever play for you again as long as you are in the theatrical business." Because of his anger with Keith and a quarrel with Keith's booker, Edward V. Darling, Cohan was never to play the Palace Theatre, although the stage version of his life story, *George M!*, starring Joel Grey, opened there in 1968. As it transpired, the break with vaudeville was for the best, for on February 25, 1901, Cohan's first play, *The Governor's Wife*, opened on Broadway, starring the Four Cohans. It was followed by *Running for Office* (a play-length adaptation of Cohan's earlier vaudeville sketch, produced in 1903), *Little Johnny Jones* (1904), *45 Minutes from Broadway* (1906), and *George Washington, Jr.* (1906).

In 1906, the producing partnership of Sam Harris and George M. Cohan came into being, and together the two men presented forty-five plays by Cohan and others, including *The Honeymooners* (1907), *The Man Who Owns Broadway* (1909), *The Cohan and Harris Minstrels (1909), Get-Rich-Quick Wallingford* (1910), *The Little Millionaire* (1911), *Broadway Jones* (1912), *Seven Keys to Baldpate* (1913), *The Miracle Man* (1914), *Hello Broadway!* (1914), *Hit-the-Trail Holliday* (1915), *The Cohan Revue of 1916*, *The Cohan Revue of 1918* (1917), and *A Prince There Was* (1918), all written by Cohan. His lack of support for the 1919 Actors' Equity Strike (in fact, he opposed it) damaged Cohan's reputation in the theatre, and even to the present time he has his detractors within Equity. But this did not prevent Cohan's continuing a distinguished theatrical career as an author, producer, and actor. In 1922, he produced and wrote *Little Nellie Kelly*. In 1923, he produced, wrote, and starred in *The Song and Dance Man*, an appropriate title for the little man with big talent, and one of the more than thirty plays he produced between 1920 and 1937, when he and Sam Harris were reunited for the production of *Fulton of Oak Falls*, written by and starring Cohan. In 1933, Cohan surprised everyone by starring successfully in the Theatre Guild production of Eugene O'Neill's *Ah, Wilderness!* George M. Cohan's last great stage success was as F.D.R. in the Rodgers and

Hart musical *I'd Rather Be Right*, which opened at New York's Alvin Theatre on November 2, 1937, and ran for 266 performances. Whatever his critics may have said, there is no question that Cohan was an extraordinarily gifted man of boundless energy and talent.

Thanks to his plays and his songs—which include, aside from those already mentioned, "Give My Regards to Broadway," "Harrigan," "45 Minutes from Broadway," and "Mary's a Grand Old Name"—George M. Cohan became a national institution, the male Betsy Ross, as Joe Laurie, Jr. called him. *Vogue* (March 15, 1933) noted that Noël Coward was the George Cohan of England, after production of the former's patriotic drama *Cavalcade*. In 1936, Congress awarded Cohan the Medal of Honor. Hollywood filmed his life, with James Cagney as Cohan, under the title *Yankee Doodle Dandy* in 1942. Cohan had also appeared, not too successfully, in a number of films, including *Seven Keys to Baldpate* (1917), *Broadway Jones* (1918), *Hit-the-Trail Holliday* (1918), *The Phantom President* (1932), and *Gambling* (1934). Additionally, from 1917 onward, many of his stage plays were adapted for the screen.

As to what George M. Cohan considered the most interesting period of his life, Gilbert Seldes wrote in 1934: "He seriously says today that the only theatre he really loved was the theatre which was essentially his father's, the theatre of one-night stands, of six performances a day, of small houses in small towns, of Brooklyn and Coney Island, the theatre in which he had grown up and his father had grown up."

BIBLIOGRAPHY

Cohan, George M. *Twenty Years on Broadway, and the Years It Took to Get There: The True Story of a Trouper's Life from the Cradle to the "Closed Shop."* New York: Harper and Brothers, 1925.

————. "Dance and Stay Young." *Liberty* 8, no. 43 (October 24, 1931), pp. 32–36.

————. "A Comedian Stops to Think." Ibid., no. 44 (October 31, 1931), pp. 26–32.

————. "Dirt for Dough's Sake." *Liberty* 13, no. 23 (June 6, 1936), pp. 21–24.

Dale, Alan. "Real George M. Cohan." *Cosmopolitan*, March 1913, pp. 547–49.

"Is George M. Cohan to Be Regarded as a Joke or a Genius?" *Current Opinion*, March 1914, pp. 192–93.

McCabe, John. *George M. Cohan: The Man Who Owned Broadway*. Garden City, N.Y.: Doubleday, 1973.

"Mechanics of Emotion." *McClure's Magazine*, November 1913, pp. 69–77.

Morehouse, Ward. *George M. Cohan: Prince of the American Theater*. Philadelphia: J. B. Lippincott, 1943.

Seldes, Gilbert. "Song and Dance Man." In *Profiles from the New Yorker*. New York: Alfred A. Knopf, 1938, pp. 342–61.

"COHEN ON THE TELEPHONE"

The most famous of Jewish monologues on the vaudeville stage and in early recordings is "Cohen on the Telephone," introduced in British music halls in 1912 by Joe Hayman (of the vaudeville team of Hayman and Franklin). The Samuel Cohen character quickly became popular in the United States as depicted by Barney Bernard, George L. Thompson, Louis Mann, Harry Marks, and the best known delineator, Monroe Silver. The last took Silver away from the telephone and introduced monologues in which he was at the opera, a picnic, listened to the radio, discussed prohibition, and visited the movies. With Billy Murray, Monroe Silver made his last "Cohen" recording, "Casey and Cohen in the Army," in 1942.

The following is the basic "Cohen on the Telephone" (sometimes known as "Cohen at the Telephone") monologue:

"Hello! Hello! Are you dere? Hello! Vot number do I vant? Vell, vot numbers have you got? Oh, excuse me, my mistook. I vant Central 248, please. Yes, dot's right, 248. I say, Miss, am I supposed to keep on saying, 'Hello!' and 'Are you dere?' until you come back again? Vell, don't be long. Hello! Are you dere? Yes. Are you de benk. Yes, I vant to see de manager, please. I say, I vant to see de manager, please. Vot do you say? This is not a telescope, it is a telephone? Say, you tink you're very clever, ain't it? Vell, du mehr favor. Just hang a small piece of crepe on your nose, your brains are dead, and if I have any more of your impertinence, I'll speak to de manager about you. I said I'll sp ... Oh, I am speakin' to de ... Oh, you're de manager. Oh, I beg your pardink. Much obliged.

"Say, Mister Manager, I rang you up to tell you I'm your tenant Cohen. I said, I'm your tenant Cohen. I ain't going, I'm stopping here. I'm your tenant—no—not Lieutenant Cohen. I vant to tell you dot last night de vind came unt blew down de shutter outside my house, and I vant you to send ... I say last night de vind came unt ... de vind, de vind. No, not de devil, de vind. You know (makes a loud blowing sound), vell dot blew down de shutter outside mine house, and I vant you ... I say it blew de shutter out. The shutter. No, I didn't say 'Shut up.' No, de shutter—de ting vot comes down de front of de shop, and I vant you to send a car-pen-ter to mend de shutter, to men ... no, not two men. No! Hello! Are you dere? Yes, last night de vind came und blew down de shutter outside mine house, and I vant you to send a car-pen-ter, a vorkman, yes, you know ... one of dose fellows vot hits de hammer vid de nails. Yes, dot's it, a vorkman. I vant you to send a vorkman to mend de damaged shutter. I say, I vant you to send a vorkman to mend, to ... no, not two men, von man to mend de damaged shutter, de dam ... I'm not svearink at you, I'm only tellink you. Are you dere? Last night de vind came unt blew down de shutter outside mine house, and I vant you to send a car-pen-ter—a carp. Oh, never mind, I'll have it fixed myself."

BIBLIOGRAPHY

Corenthal, Michael G. *Cohen on the telephone: A History of Jewish Recorded Humor and Popular Music 1892–1942*. Milwaukee, Wi.: Yesterday's Memories, 1984.

LOTTIE COLLINS (London, 1866—London, May 1, 1910)

One of the most popular singer-comediennes of British music hall, Lottie Collins gained international fame with the song "Ta-Ra-Ra-Boom-De-Ay!," to which she performed a dance in a semi-cancan style. For its day, the song was considered risqué, with the lyrics of its verse in quiet contrast to the rowdiness of its chorus:

A smart and stylish girl you see,
The belle of good society.
Fond of fun as fond could be,
When it's on the strict QT.

I'm not too young, not too old,
Not too timid, not too bold.
But just the very thing I'm told
That in your arms you'd like to hold.

Lottie Collins first heard the song on an inauspicious American vaudeville tour in 1891. It originated some years earlier at a brothel known as Babe Connors in St. Louis, which specialized in an all-Negro roster of ladies and which was frequented by the members of various minstrel troupes. The song was considerably cleaned up by composer-lyricist Henry J. Sayers and first published in 1891. Collins brought "Ta-Ra-Ra-Boom-De-Ay" back to the United States in 1892, when she was presented by Charles Frohman and paid a salary of $1,000 a week. Her other major success, also a chorus song in which the audience might join, was "Daddy Wouldn't Buy Me a Bow-Bow," but it never had much of an impact in America. In fact, the Joseph Tabrar song was more of a success for Vesta Victoria than Collins.

Lottie Collins first appeared on the British music hall stage in 1877 as a dancer with a skipping-rope number, appearing with her sisters Lizzie and Marie in a sketch titled "Skiptomania." She became a solo act in 1886, concentrating on "coon" songs. She was a favorite in both Britain and the United States throughout the 1890s, also appearing in pantomime and musical comedy. Her third husband, James W. Tate, appeared in music hall with Clarice Mayne, and her daughter Jose Collins (1887–1958) was a major star of musical comedy, best remembered as the original leading lady of *The Maid of the Mountains*.

COMPOSERS

Aside from Ernest R. Ball and Irving Berlin (both q.v.), many other composers appeared on the vaudeville stage, usually prior to success in their chosen field. Many vaudevillians, of whom Gus Edwards and Joseph E. Howard are two notable examples, also enjoyed secondary careers as composers. Among composers who appeared on the vaudeville stage are Con Conrad (1891–1938), Buddy Pepper (1922–   ), Harry Ruby (1895–1974), Charles Tobias (1898–1970), and Eugene West (1883–1949). His work as a composer ("This Could Be the Start of Something Big," etc.) may be secondary to his career as an entertainer, but there is little doubt that Steve Allen (1921–   ) learned much of his comedy technique while touring in vaudeville with his parents, Belle Montrose and Billy Allen. The great Harold Arlen (1905–1986) had already written the music and lyrics for *The Nine Fifteen Revue* (1930) and the 1930 edition of Earl Carroll's *Vanities* before appearing at the Palace in July 1931 and February 1932.

Robert Wilcox Bigelow (1890–1965) was the composer of "Hard-Hearted Hannah." He also spent fourteen years in vaudeville, from 1909 to 1923, as half of the piano act Bigelow and Campbell, and later in the 1920s spent three years with Texas Guinan as her pianist. Aside from writing such classics of Americana as "The Perfect Day," "Just A-Wearyin' for You," and "I Love You Truly," Carrie Jacobs Bond (1862–1946) also toured in vaudeville.

Novelist Theodore Dreiser's brother Paul Dresser (1857–1906) joined a medicine show at the age of sixteen, toured in vaudeville as a singer and monologist, and in 1885 was the end man with Billy Rice's Minstrels. He later wrote such poular songs as "On the Banks of the Wabash" and "The Blue and the Gray." In 1942, 20th Century–Fox filmed his life story as *My Gal Sal*, with Victor Mature as the composer.

Clarence Gaskill (1892–1947) wrote "Minnie the Moocher" with Cab Calloway, and immediately after the First World War had toured vaudeville as the Melody Monarch in a single piano-playing act. (Cab Calloway was around for the end of vaudeville, headlining at the Palace in June 1931 and at Loew's State, New York, in June 1932.) Mack Gordon (1904–1959) wrote some marvelous songs with Harry Revel, including "Did You Ever See a Dream Walking?," "Stay as Sweet as You Are," and "May I Have the Next Romance with You?" Prior to joining up with Revel in 1930, Gordon had toured vaudeville for a number of years in an act titled Three Jacks and a Queen. Charles K. Harris (1867–1930) was the composer of "After the Ball," which is also the title of his autobiography. He had commenced his career playing the banjo in minstrel shows and vaudeville and also contributed special material to various vaudeville acts. Before he became part of the composing team of DeSylva, Brown, and Henderson in 1925, Ray Henderson (1896–1970) had toured in vaudeville. In 1924, Roger Wolfe Kahn (1907–1962) toured vaudeville with his orchestra. He also headlined at the Palace in February 1929.

Before he composed the scores for *Where's Charley?*, *Guys and Dolls*, and *The Most Happy Fella*, Frank Loesser (1910–1969) had worked in vaudeville as a caricaturist. The composer of "Hey, Mr. Banjo," Freddy Morgan (1910–1971), had, appropriately enough, worked in vaudeville in the 1920s as part of the banjo duo Morgan and Stone. Between 1909 and 1918, J. Russel Robinson (1892–1963) worked in vaudeville as a member of the Robinson Brothers; later, he appeared as a single and was one of the original members of the Original Dixieland Jazz Band.

Marion Sunshine (1894–1963) wrote many songs with a Latin-American beat and took credit for introducing that music genre to the United States. She had begun her stage career at the age of five in the melodrama *Two Little Waifs* and subsequently entered vaudeville. Her career in revue and musical comedy began with an appearance in the first, 1907, edition of the Ziegfeld *Follies*. She was a frequent attraction at the Palace, appearing there in November 1926, March 1928, October 1929, September 1930, and April 1931.

The composer of "I'm Forever Blowing Bubbles," Nathaniel Hawthorne Vincent (1889–1979), was a member of the vaudeville teams of Tracey and Vincent and Franklyn and Vincent, and later became a recording and radio entertainer in the late 1920s with Fred Howard as The Happy Chappies. Clarence

Williams (1893–1965), who worked for many years with Jelly Roll Morton, became a professional entertainer with a minstrel show at the age of twelve. He was musical director for Harry Belafonte when the singer opened at the Palace on December 15, 1959.

Erno Rapee (1891–1945) made his vaudeville debut in 1914, playing classical numbers and patriotic medleys on the piano. "The pianist hasn't yet found out how to get his hair cut in the American style" was the chief criticism from Sime Silverman in *Variety* (January 9, 1914). The trade paper was far kinder to Rapee when he became an important composer for silent films, including *What Price Glory* (1926), for which he wrote the theme song, "Charmaine." Harry Von Tilzer (1872–1946) wrote many songs for vaudevillians, including "A Bird in a Gilded Cage," "Wait till the Sun Shines Nellie" and "Under the Anheuser Busch." He made his own vaudeville debut at Hammerstein's in October 1907, singing other songs of his own composition, including "Just Help Yourself," "Lulu and La La La," "Top o' the Morning," and "Dearie."

Von Tilzer was typical of many composers who provided material for select vaudeville headliners or worked on the vaudeville stage as piano accompanists. Maurice Abrahams (1883–1931) wrote songs for his wife, Belle Baker. Prior to the First World War, Milton Ager (1893–1979) worked as an accompanist. Louis Alter (1902–1980) accompanied Nora Bayes and also wrote special material for Irene Bordoni, Beatrice Lillie, and Helen Morgan. Grant Clarke (1891–1931) wrote special material for Nora Bayes, Fanny Brice, Al Jolson, Eva Tanguay, and Bert Williams. His comic song "Secondhand Rose" will always be associated with Fanny Brice. Dave Dreyer (1894–1967) was accompanist to Belle Baker, Frank Fay, Al Jolson, and Sophie Tucker. Arthur Freed (1894–1973) and Louis Silvers (1889–1954) worked together in vaudeville and also provided material for Gus Edwards. Cliff Friend (1893–1974) was an accompanist for Harry Richman and also appeared on the British music hall stage. George Gershwin (1898–1937) accompanied Nora Bayes and Louise Dresser. Harry Harris (1901–) wrote special material for Jimmy Durante, Ted Lewis, and Sophie Tucker. Will J. Harris (1900–1967) was active from 1921 to 1934 directing vaudeville shows. Gus Kahn (1886–1941) wrote special material for many vaudeville acts, usually in association with his wife, Grace. Ted Koehler (1894–1973) provided material for a number of vaudeville singers. Blanche Merrill (1895–1966) wrote for Belle Baker, Nora Bayes, Fanny Brice, Willie Howard, and Eva Tanguay. Her "Becky Is Back in the Ballet" proved a great audience-pleaser for Fanny Brice. Melville Morris (1888–?) worked as a vaudeville entertainer in his own right and also provided piano accompaniment for Al Jolson and Blossom Seeley. Harry Pease (1886–1945) was known in vaudeville as the "Boy with the Golden Voice" and also wrote special material for many vaudevillians. Lew Pollack (1895–1946) played piano in vaudeville. Max Rich (1897–1970) accompanied a number of singers, including Belle Baker. Herbert Spencer (1878–1944) studied voice with Caruso and then sang for twelve years on the vaudeville stage. He was music arranger for Lillian Russell. Sam H. Stept (1897–

1964) accompanied both Jack Norworth and Mae West. Roy Turk (1892–1934) wrote special material for Nora Bayes, Rock and White, and Sophie Tucker.

See also ERNEST R. BALL, IRVING BERLIN, GENE BUCK, HARRY CARROLL, JOSEPH E. HOWARD, LIEUTENANT GITZ RICE.

JOHN W. CONSIDINE (Chicago, 1863—Hollywood, Ca., February 11, 1943)

John W. Considine controlled an early vaudeville circuit on the West Coast and was also general manager of the Northwest Orpheum circuit. He moved from Chicago to Seattle in 1889, opening his first vaudeville house, the People's Theatre, there. In partnership with "Big Tim" Sullivan, Considine created the Sullivan and Considine circuit, beginning with the Orpheum Theatre in Seattle and followed by Orpheum theatres in Spokane and Portland. In 1916, Considine sold out his interest to Marcus Loew. In 1932, his son John Considine, Jr. married Carmen, the daughter of Alexander Pantages, ending a bitter rivalry between the two entrepreneurs.

CONTORTIONISTS

Contortionists were generally relegated to circuses and dime museums, but a few made the transition to vaudeville. If a contortionist could prove himself a "freak" act, there was a possibility of headliner billing, but usually contortionists were members of the vaudeville group known as "dumb acts," assigned to opening or closing the program. International theatrical agent H. B. Marinelli began his career as a contortionist, as did Harry Houdini. According to Joe Laurie, Jr., the earliest recorded contortionist in vaudeville was Walter Wentworth, who dates back to 1872. The most unusual was "Yuma." Unable to obtain an appointment with booker J. J. Murdock, "Yuma" had himself delivered to Murdock in a small box. When the box was opened, "Yuma" appeared dressed as the devil and received a week's booking at Chicago's Masonic Temple. "Dracula," a contortionist from 1907, sounds interesting, as does "Kola, the Human Frog," who spent a great deal of time in 1918 leaping about on various vaudeville stages.

JACK CONWAY (Albany, N.Y., 1898—Bermuda, October 2, 1928)

Jack Conway was a reviewer of vaudeville, musical comedy, and burlesque for *Variety*, who wrote under the name "Con." He was noted for his use of slang—*American Mercury* described him as "America's master of slang"—and for the many phrases which he invented, such as "palooka" and "scram." He described the legs of an aging chorus girl as "varicose alley." As *Variety* (October 10, 1928) commented at the time of his death, "There is no question that during Jack's 15 years with *Variety*, he contributed most liberally to the present vogue of slang, not through *Variety* which held him down, but through the writing thieves who stole from him." At the age of five, Conway came with his widowed mother to New York, where she became a schoolteacher. Circa

1911, he joined *Variety* as an advertising solicitor but quickly changed over to reporting. He left the paper in 1926 to work as a comedy title writer in Hollywood, where he was employed at the time of his death—from heart failure.

JOE COOK (Evansville, In., 1890—Poughkeepsie, N.Y., May 15, 1959)

Joe Cook's comedy was of a transcendental variety, above and beyond analysis. Cook would ask his stooge, "How's your uncle?" Back came the reply, "I have no uncle." Undeterred, Cook insisted, "How is he?" And back came the final reply, "Oh he's fine." The comedian's unique place in vaudeville is explained by two advertisements, one from 1909 and the other from 1920. The first introduces Cook as the "Master of All Trades. Introducing in a fifteen-minute act, juggling, unicycling, magic, hand-balancing, ragtime piano and violin playing, dancing, globe-rolling, wirewalking, talking, and cartooning. Something original in each line—Some Entertainment." By 1920, Cook had refined his description simply to what he was, a humorist with a one-man vaudeville show. As *Variety* as early as December 18, 1909, described him, "A doer of many things is Joe Cook," and as a funny man he had few peers in the history of American vaudeville.

Joe Cook's real name was Joseph Lopez, and he took the surname Cook from the family that raised him after the death of his parents. *Variety* once suggested that there should be a marker at the Cook house on the corner of Fourth and Oak streets in Evansville, Indiana, where Joe Cook learned the tricks that were to bring good clean fun to millions. Initially, he worked with his brother in an act titled the Juggling Kids, but he appeared as a single turn at Proctor's 125th Street Theatre as early as July 1907. Within two years, he was a vaudeville headliner whose classic routine featured an imitation of four Hawaiians. Before he began, Cook would explain that he was actually imitating only two Hawaiians; he could imitate four Hawaiians but did not wish to do so because that would put out of work all performers who could only imitate two Hawaiians. Cook would appear onstage with a ukelele in his hand and begin:

I will give an imitation of four Hawaiians. This is one [whistles]; this is another [plays ukelele]; and this is the third [marks time with his foot]. I could imitate four Hawaiians just as easily, but I will tell you the reason why I don't do it. You see, I bought a horse for $50 and it turned out to be a running horse. I was offered $15,000 for him, and I took it. I built a house with the $15,000, and when it was finished, a neighbor offered me $100,000 for it. He said my house stood right where he wanted to dig a well. So I took the $100,000 to accommodate him. I invested the $100,000 on peanuts, and that year, there was a peanut famine, so I sold the peanuts for $350,000. Now why should a man with $350,000 bother to imitate four Hawaiians?

Another vaudeville gag had Cook as a landlord attempting to collect rent on a miniature cottage. After arguing with the imaginary tenant, Cook would walk off with the cottage under his arm. An Indian lecture had a stooge holding up a beer mug as a sample of early Indian pottery, while the chief's collection of bows and arrows consisted of bow ties and Arrow collars. A stooge from the audience would be invited to drink a bottle of beer while blindfolded, with the blindfold misplaced over his mouth instead of his eyes. Joe Cook would enter with three papier mâché figures of gymnasts on his shoulders, and stagger around pretending to be under a terrible strain in supporting them. The act always included numerous contraptions, such as one that dropped a weight on an assistant's head to remind him when to ring a bell during the performance. Few would disagree with a 1925 *Variety* review: "The act is as it always was one of the greatest comedy novelties in vaudeville. Cook is as versatile as he is clever and is blessed with a gift for travesty and a whimsical personality that would bring him laughs at an undertakers' convention."

Aside from vaudeville, Joe Cook appeared on stage in *Hitchy-Koo* (1919) and starred in the first edition of Earl Carroll's *Vanities* in 1923, as well as the 1924, 1925, and 1926 editions. He was immensely successful as "Smiley" Johnson in *Rain or Shine* (1928), which he filmed in 1930; in *Fine and Dandy* (1930) and *Hold Your Horses* (1933), he appeared with his long-time stooge, Dave Chasen (later of restaurant fame). Surprisingly, even without the visuals that the stage offered, Joe Cook was equally popular on radio as a guest artiste in the 1930s. He returned to Broadway in *Off to Buffalo!* in 1939 and the following year made his last stage appearance in *It Happens on Ice*, the first of the ice shows at New York's Center Theatre.

In 1942, Joe Cook was stricken with Parkinson's disease, which became progressively worse through the years. In that so little of his humor is preserved on film, Joe Cook's reputation has diminished through the years since his death, but those who had the privilege of witnessing his act in vaudeville will echo the sentiments of critic Brooks Atkinson in his review of *Rain or Shine* in *The New York Times*; he was "the greatest man in the world."

BIBLIOGRAPHY
Allvine, Glendon. "Greatest Man in the World." *Variety*, May 20, 1959, pp. 1, 68.
Green, Stanley. "Joe Cook." In *The Great Clowns of Broadway*. New York: Oxford University Press, 1984, pp. 38–49.
Landry, Robert J. "Death of an Amazing Performer." *Variety*, May 20, 1959, p. 64.
"What Makes 'Em Laugh." *The American Magazine*, February 1931, pp. 38–39, 153.

"COON" SONGS

Very popular on the vaudeville stage at the turn of the century, "coon" songs featured ragtime melodies and black-oriented lyrics. They were often written by black Americans but almost always performed by white vaudevillians, sometimes in blackface. Female performers of such songs were billed as "coon" shouters (and among their number were Louise Dresser, Marie Dresser, and Sophie Tucker), and they were often supported by two or three young black children called "picks" (an abbreviations of pickaninnies).

The most famous of all "coon" songs was "All Coons Look Alike to Me," written in 1896 by Ernest Hogan. Its chorus was:

All coons look alike to me,
I've got another beau, you see,
And he's just as good to me as you, nig!
ever tried to be,
He spends his money free,
I know we can't agree,
So I don't like you no how,
All coons look alike to me.

Paul Dresser, the brother of novelist Theodore Dreiser, wrote a number of "coon" songs, including "I'se Your Nigger If You Wants Me, Liza Jane" (1898), "You'se Just a Little Nigger, Still You're Mine, All Mine" (1898), and "Niggah Loves His Possum or Deed He Do, Do, Do" (1904), which was sung with great success by Eddie Leonard. Other "coon" songs include "That Nigger Treated Me Allright" (1899) by Walter Hawley; "Every Race Has a Flag but the Coon" (1900) by Will A. Heelan and J. Fred Helf; "Ghost of a Coon" (1900) by Bert Williams and George Walker; "Coon! Coon! Coon!" (1901) by Leo Friedman; "Nobody's Lookin' but de Owl and de Moon" (1901) by Bob Cole, James Weldon Johnson, and J. Rosamond Johnson; and "If the Man in the Moon Were a Coon" (1905) by Fred Fisher.

Not all "coon" songs contained the word "coon," and, initially, they were also popular with black performers. In 1898, Bert Williams and George Walker featured three "coon" songs: "I Don't Like No Cheap Man," "In a Cooler for the Warmest Coon in Town," and "Not a Coon Went Out the Way He Came In." At least one black American performer, Billy Miller, parodied "coon" songs with his "All Spaniards Look Alike to Me."

There is no question that "coon" songs did much to fuel negative stereotypes of black Americans and to encourage the use of "coon" and "nigger" as commonplace words in American society. However, they evoked little criticism from most black Americans. Writing in the Afro-American newspaper the *Indianapolis Freeman* on October 7, 1905, Bob Cole opined that "the word 'coon' is very insulting," but at the same time argued, "There is no harm in the words Negro, Darkey, Colored, or Afro-American." It was not until January 2, 1909, that the *Indianapolis Freeman* editorialized that "coon" songs must go, pointing out:

"Williams and Walker are a great deal to blame for being the originators and establishing the name 'coon' upon our race . . . the Negro has not changed his name: He is no longer human, but a 'coon.' . . . Abraham Lincoln once wrote a harsh letter to a man and after considering how the man might feel over it he threw the letter in the stove. Every composer who writes a song with the word 'coon' in it should do the same."

In reality, "coon" songs enjoyed a brief revival in 1912, but by 1915 they had disappeared from the vaudeville stage as a new type of ragtime music was introduced, its composers and lyricists providing words that seemed determined to prove that ragtime had no connection with the American Negro. Ragtime music might be traced back to black Americans in the mid–1890s, but twentieth-century composers presented it as their innovation, and any black-oriented lyric had the wrong connotation.

BIBLIOGRAPHY

Sampson, Henry T. *The Ghost Walks: A Chronological History of Blacks in Show Business, 1865–1910*. Metuchen, N.J.: Scarecrow Press, 1988.

LOU COSTELLO.   See BUD ABBOTT AND LOU COSTELLO

WILLIE COVAN (Savannah, Ga., 1896—Los Angeles, May 7, 1989)

A leading black American tap dancer, Willie Covan began his vaudeville career at the age of twelve as one of the pickaninnies or Picks supporting a minor vaudevillian named Cozy Smith. In the 1920s, he put together a vaudeville act with his wife, Flo, his brother Dewey, and Corita Harbert, known as the Four Covans. In 1924, he appeared in a London revue, *Dover Street to Dixie*, and when it opened in New York in October 1924, it was retitled *Dixie to Broadway*. Shortly thereafter, he teamed with Leonard Ruffin, and as Covan and Ruffin the two men appeared at the Palace in July 1926.

He came to Los Angeles in the late 1920s, opening a club there, and in 1936 opened the Covan School of Dance. At the insistence of Eleanor Powell, he was hired by M-G-M to provide private lessons for various leading players. He also appeared in a number of films. Semiretired by 1973, Willie Covan continued to give private lessons to a few professionals, and his last pupil in 1985 was Debbie Allen.

BIBLIOGRAPHY

Dwan, Robert. "A Legend in His Own Feet." *Los Angeles Times Calendar*, July 26, 1981, pp. 6–7.

Frank, Rusty. "Willie Covan." In *Tap!: The Greatest Tap Dance Stars and Their Stories, 1900–1955*. New York: William Morrow, 1990, pp. 23–29.

WILL CRESSY (Bradford, N.H., October 20, 1863—St. Petersburg, Fl., May 7, 1930)

Prominent as both a performer and a writer of vaudeville sketches, Will Cressy was noted for his gentle rube character and the rural sketches that he wrote almost on a yearly basis for himself and his wife, Blanche Dayne. Cressy's family ran a flour, feed, hay, and grazing business (which he and his brothers later inherited and operated), but Will ran away from home to join a theatrical touring company. He first came to prominence in New York in 1906, and his skill as a writer led to his earning a steady income from his fellow vaudevillians. On the legitimate New York stage, Cressy appeared in *The Old Homestead* (1898), *A Village Lawyer* (1902, which he also wrote), and *Lightnin'* (1919).

(ALAN) CROSS (circa 1895—North Hollywood, Ca., March 4, 1993) and **(HARRY) DUNN** (Boston, circa 1899—Las Vegas, February 11, 1965)

Cross and Dunn were a very funny comedy team who joined forces in 1932 and whose act consisted of parodies of popular songs. Both had worked as single acts in vaudeville in the 1920s, with Cross playing the Palace as early as October 1923, and Dunn appearing there (billed as Henry Dunn) in July 1929. In 1924, Dunn had teamed up with Joe Rome, and the two appeared in that year's edition of Earl Carroll's *Vanities*. In the 1940s, Dunn moved to Las Vegas, where he handled public relations at the Dunes Hotel; at the time of his death, he was entertainment director at the Tropicana Hotel. When Alan Cross died, he was reportedly the oldest living vaudevillian.

FRANK CRUMIT (Jackson, Oh., September 26, 1888—New York, September 7, 1943) and **JULIA SANDERSON** (Springfield, Ma., August 20, 1887—Springfield, Ma., January 27, 1975)

Few singing couples endeared themselves so much to vaudeville and radio audiences as did Frank Crumit and Julia Sanderson. Their relaxed style of delivery and charm of manner added much to any vaudeville bill, for, as *Variety* noted in 1925, "an abundance of 'class' surrounds the couple to the extent they unquestionably tone up any vaudeville bill besides which their mild and unassuming manner of delivery is restful."

Julia Sanderson's career predates that of her husband by many years. The daughter of a well-known actor, Albert Sackett, she appeared as a child in Philadelphia with Forepaugh's Stock Company, and in 1903 was appearing as a member of the chorus and an understudy to Paula Edwardes in *Winsome Winnie*. In April 1904, Sanderson opened in *A Chinese Honeymoon* at New York's Lyric Theatre in the role of Mrs. Pineapple, and later that same year, she supported DeWolf Hopper in *Wang*. Later stage successes included *The Tourists* (1906), *The Dairymaids* (1907), *The Arcadians* (1910), *The Sunshine Girl* (1913), *The Girl from Utah* (1914), *Sybil* (1916), *The Canary* (1918), and *Hitchy-Koo* (1920). She made her London stage debut as Suzanne in *The Hon'ble Phil*, in October 1908.

Julia Sanderson made her vaudeville debut in January 1907 at Keeney's Theatre, New York. *Variety* (January 12, 1907) noted that "Miss Sanderson has a delightful full, rich voice and an altogether charming stage presence." Both the voice and the presence were to delight vaudeville audiences for many years to come.

Frank Crumit was educated at the University of Ohio and wrote the school football song, "The Buckeye Battle Cry." After graduation he toured in vaudeville as a singer and ukelele player and was billed as "A Comedian Who Can Sing, Play Instruments and Tell a Story." He also began to write songs, many of which have stood the test of time as mild-mannered comic numbers of considerable humor: "Song of the Prune," "A Parlor Is a Pleasant Place to Sit

In," "There Is No One with Endurance Like the Man Who Sells Insurance," and "Abdul Abulbul Emir."

On August 9, 1921, *Tangerine*, a musical comedy about a South Seas island where women do all the work and the man's place is in the home, opened at New York's Casino Theatre. It starred Julia Sanderson as Shirley Dalton and, in a lesser role, Frank Crumit as Dick Owens. From this first meeting, a romance developed, and the couple teamed up, first professionally and later in private life. Crumit was Julia Sanderson's third husband; her first marriage had been to the well-known jockey James Todhunter Sloan and the second to Lt. Bradford Barnette. Crumit and Sanderson were regular headliners on the vaudeville stage in the mid 1920s, and they appeared together at the Palace in February 1924. In January 1928, they took over the leads from Gertrude Lawrence and Oscar Shaw in the original Broadway production of George and Ira Gershwin's *Oh, Kay!*

Before his teaming with Julia Sanderson, Frank Crumit had built up quite a reputation in vaudeville; *Variety* (November 15, 1923) commented, "For vaudeville Crumit is as sure as rent day." Thanks largely to his many phonograph recordings, he was also fast becoming a radio personality. In 1928, he and Sanderson made their radio debut as a team, and the following year they were signed to star in *Blackstone Plantation*, sponsored by Blackstone Cigars and initially broadcast over the CBS network. When that show expired in 1933, the couple returned briefly to vaudeville but were soon back on the air, guesting on a number of variety shows until 1938, when they were signed by NBC to star in the quiz program *The Battle of the Sexes*. In 1942, they hosted *The Crumit and Sanderson Quiz* on Saturday nights on CBS.

When Frank Crumit died, he and his wife had two radio programs on the air, a daily entertainment show sponsored by the Southern Cotton Oil Company, and a weekly quiz show for the Lewis Howe Company. After her husband's death, Sanderson appeared for a while on the Mutual network with her program *Let's Be Charming*, then announced her retirement.

D

CHARLIE DALE. See SMITH AND DALE

DANCERS

In all combinations, varieties, and styles, dancers were a fixture on the vaudeville stage, most notably in the teens, when they helped popularize the latest dance steps. It was primarily from vaudevillians that Americans first learned of the Pavlova Gavotte, the fox-trot, the hesitation waltz, the maxixe, the toddle, and the tango. From the 1926 edition of George White's *Scandals*, Ann Pennington brought the black bottom to vaudeville, and the Lindy hop, named in honor of aviator Charles Lindbergh, livened up vaudeville in the late 1920s, a predecessor to the jive dancing of the 1930s and 1940s.

With Lew Quinn, Joan Sawyer introduced the rumba, created for them by J. Tim Brymn. Described in 1916 as "the peerless queen of the modern dance," Sawyer surprised her fans in 1919 by teaming with Arthur Ashley to present a series of scenes from popular plays to vaudeville audiences. In October 1914, she appeared at the Palace, partnered by Nigel Barrie, performing the Aeroplane Waltz.

Other dancers at the Palace included ballerina Adeline Genée in 1914; Margaret and Dorothy Cameron in 1915; the Metropolitan Opera Ballet, also in 1915; and Doralinda, billed in 1916 as "The World's Most Versatile Dancer." Ballerina Lydia Lopokova made her vaudeville debut at the Palace in April 1915, onstage with the Morgan Dancers. "Lydia is pretty—so few dancers are," commented Frederick James Smith in *The New York Dramatic Mirror* (April 21, 1915). In June 1915, Miss Swan Wood and her Ballet Divertissement company of eight girls appeared on the Palace stage. Evan-Burrows Fontaine presented "decorative dance pantomimes" at the Palace in July 1916, and assisting her was Kenneth Harlan, who later became a leading man in silent films.

Basil Napier Durant and Margaret Hawkesworth played the Palace in April 1916 after a successful nightclub engagement at the Plaza Hotel. They performed the Valse Fantasy, Pre-Catalan Tango, Plaza Trot, and Piping Rock One Step.

Ruth St. Denis and Ted Shawn headlined at the Palace in March 1917. Adelaide and J. J. Hughes opened the 1917–1918 season at the Palace and were described by *The New York Dramatic Mirror* (September 8, 1917) as "one of the most popular dancing teams of our stage." Their specialty was a Pierrot and Pierette balletic dance.

Jack Mason and Lois Whitney presented a program of tango demonstrations at the Palace in May 1914, but it was their "colored orchestra" from the Folies Marigny in Paris that gained the most attention. The same happened to Bonnie Glass in 1915, when she danced the gavotte and the cakewalk at the Palace, and audiences were more intrigued by her all-Negro orchestra.

On the opening bill at the Palace on March 24, 1913 was La Napierkowska, a pantomimist and dancer. *The Billboard* (April 5, 1913) commented:

> The truth of the matter is that La Napierkowska is a mighty good-looking and shapely dancer of the 'cooch' variety, formerly so often seen in the Oriental shows on the midway of a fair. But the young lady is some dancer of the kind. There isn't a portion of her body that she cannot make wiggle at will and there is very little of it that isn't constantly wiggling during the time which she spends on the stage in her offering, *The Captive*. She is supposed—so the story of the program runs—to have been stung by a bee and the gyrations that follow the stinging are consequent of the pain she feels. It must be some pain, for such wriggling has never before been seen on a high-grade vaudeville stage.

La Napierkowska was held over for a second week, at which time she was joined by a second dancer on the bill, Ruth St. Denis.

The majority of dancers and dance partnerships have been forgotten. In the late teens, Bryan and Broderick presented an act titled "Let's Dance." "Their technique was well grounded," reported *The New York Dramatic Mirror* (March 1, 1919), "and when they become better molded in the design of their numbers, the inspiration and poetry strongly evident at present will add continuity and charm to their act." From England came Ted Trevor and Diane Harris, with an eleven-minute act of ballroom dancing. Reviewing their performance at New York's Riverside Theatre, *Variety* (October 29, 1924) reported, "The first impression is that the dancers are lightning fast, but subsequent numbers, of which there are three, detract from that through a certain tenor of similarity which prevails through the dances. Each is executed with no mean sense of showmanship, and to this, which must be added, the likable appearance of the pair, may be attributed the foundation upon which the team rests." From France, in 1922, came Mitty and Tillo, billed as "France's Greatest Dancers" (Mitty being described as a former member of the Folies Bergère company).

Percy Oakes began dancing in Chicago in 1913 and was noted for twirling his partner in the air, high above his head. From 1923 onward, Sammy Lewis and his wife and partner, Patti Moore, presented a dance routine billed as "Dancing with a Sense of Humor." Radice Furman was not only a vaudeville dancer but also the daughter of Professor A. P. Furman, a noted dance instructor of the teens and 1920s. In 1924, a vaudeville act called "The Realm of Fantasy" featured Stasia Ledova, "the incomparable premier danseuse," W. Wania, "the pioneer of all Russian dancers," and the Eight English Rockets, a female precision dance troupe. In 1926, Deno and Rochelle originated the Charleston Apache dance. That same year, adagio dancers Naro and Zita Lockford (brother and sister) were popular. Playing the Hippodrome in May 1926 was Vera Fokine and the Fokine Ballet. In the late 1920s, Dorothea Rogers and five female colleagues danced on roller skates.

Before their respective screen careers, Mae Murray and Clifton Webb worked in vaudeville as a dance team, presenting "society dances." Five black musicians accompanied the couple onstage as they performed the "D'Arlequin Waltz," "Brazilian Maxine," a tango titled "Cinquante Cinquante," and "Barcarole Waltz," which was claimed as a creation of Murray's. *Variety* (March 20, 1914) reported, "In a becoming pink charmeuse outfit over chiffon Miss Murray's pretty arms, hands and feet seemed set to music. That Palace audience Monday night went plumb daffy over her dancing. In praising her splendid dancing Webb should not be overlooked." As her film career died, Mae Murray returned to vaudeville in 1929. The *Vaudeville News and New York Star* (April 20, 1929) caught her act in Chicago and commented, "She dances a tango that is a tango, with seductive charm and Latin fire."

Clifton Webb was a prominent dancer on the New York stage for a number of years. In the 1920s, he and Mary Hay (a former Ziegfeld *Follies* showgirl featured in D. W. Griffith's film *Way Down East* and one-time wife of actor Richard Barthelmess) were a popular dancing team in vaudeville and in *Sunny* (1925). In January 1929, they headlined at the Palace with an act that featured two pianos played by Victor Arden and Phil Ohman; the latter, of course, went on to become a popular band leader in the 1930s. *Variety* (January 23, 1929) commented, "As mixed comedy dancers, and dancers who do not exert themselves, Webb-Hay could dance twice as long as they do at present and still please. As class dancers and names, they seem to condescend in doing comedy, but if attempted by others the same comedy would appear amateurish."

In the teens, Ivy and Douglas Crane were dancing headliners on the Orpheum circuit, known as the Irene and Vernon Castle of the West. In later years, Ivy Crane Wilson became a fan magazine writer and Hollywood columnist for a British Newspaper; she died in Woodland Hills, California, on December 7, 1977, at the age of ninety. Another early husband-and-wife dancing partnership was Dorothy Dickson and Carl Hyson. They were two of America's leading exponents of ballroom dancing, featured in vaudeville and, in 1919, at New York's Palais Royal Dance Club. Dickson appeared in *Oh Boy!* (1917) and the 1918 edition of the Ziegfeld *Follies*. She went to London in 1921 to star with Carl Hyson (whom she was later to divorce) in *London, Paris and New York* at the London Pavilion. From that point on, she appeared almost continuously on the London stage through the 1950s.

Emma Haig was popular in vaudeville both as a solo dancer and in partnership with various male dancers. Before George White created his famous *Scandals*, he was one of Haig's partners, replaced in 1919 by Jack Waldon. Haig and Waldon appeared together at Henderson's, Coney Island, in June 1919, and *Variety* (June 6, 1919) commented that she "is just the same clever little dancing girl that she has always been." Reviewing Emma Haig's solo act at the Palace in the summer of 1919, the paper (June 27, 1919) described her as "a whirlwind of speed, a gifted kicker, and a tireless worker," but noted that without a partner "that touch of gracefulness and team rhythm is missing." Haig was back at the Palace in March 1923, working with a young tenor named George Griffin; she tried a little singing herself, but it was marred by a noticeable lisp. For fifteen minutes, Haig performed a variety of dances, including a Spanish number and a Jackie Coogan impersonation. "The finale, with her most difficult steps gets the tiny lady off heartily liked. There is no straining for recognition and the several bows are healthy and called for. This is the first rate number for any bill and a headliner for the average big-time house, especially West, where Miss Haig is a favorite," reported *Variety* (March 29, 1923). Emma Haig died in Los Angeles on June 9, 1939, at the age of 41.

Fred and Adele Astaire claimed to have made their professional debut in vaudeville at Paterson, New Jersey, in 1910, but as early as October 17, 1908, *Variety* saw them perform at New York's Hudson Theatre, and commented:

The Astaire children are a nice looking pair of youngsters, prettily dressed, and they work in an easy style, without the predominating "freshness" which usually stands out above everything else with "prodigies." Dancing is the feature. It ranges from toe to the more popular (in vaudeville) hard-shoe. The singing falls almost entirely to the boy, who has a surprisingly powerful voice for a lad of his years. . . . The toe-dance following the song could be replaced to advantage. It has a tendency to make the boy appear girlish, something to be guarded against. His actions throughout are a trifle too polite, which is probably no fault of his own, as he appears to be a manly little chap with the making of a good performer.

In 1918, Fred and Adele Astaire were featured in *The Passing Show*, and Heywood Broun wrote in the *New York Tribune*, "In an evening in which there was an abundance of good dancing, Fred Astaire stood out. He and his partner, Adele Astaire, made the show pause early in the evening with a beautiful, careless, loose-limbed dance in which the right foot never seemed to know just what the left foot was going to do, or cared either. It almost seemed as though the two young persons had been poured into the dance." After *The Passing Show of 1918*, Fred and Adele Astaire were marked as major revue and musical comedy stars; they never returned to vaudeville.

See also SAMMY BERK, RAY BOLGER, LA CARMENCITA, IRENE AND VERNON CASTLE, BESSIE CLAYTON, LADDIE CLIFF, WILLIE COVAN, MLLE DAZIE, GABY DESLYS, ROSIE AND JENNY DOLLY, JACK DONAHUE, BUDDY EBSEN, LOÏE FULLER, JANETTE JACKETT, PAUL AND GRACE HARTMAN, GERTRUDE HOFFMAN, BUDDY HOWE, MOSCONI BROTHERS, NICHOLAS BROTHERS, ANN PENNINGTON, ALBERTINA

RASCH, BILL ROBINSON, PAT RONEY, JR. AND MARION BENT, "SA-LOME" DANCE CRAZE, STEP BROTHERS, TAP DANCING, GERTRUDE VANDERBILT, FLORENCE WALTON, NED WAYBURN, GEORGE WHITE, ANNABELLE WHITFORD.

EDWARD V. (VALENTINE) DARLING (1891—New York, July 29, 1951)

Edward V. Darling, or Eddie Darling, as he was generally known, was one of the most influential figures in the Keith-Albee organization, being its chief booker and the man responsible for booking acts at the Palace Theatre. In that he had to deal with the egos of headliners, his was not always an easy job, and some of the fights in which he became involved lasted a generation. For example, because of a quarrel between Darling and George M. Cohan, the latter never played the Palace. According to Joe Laurie, Jr., writing in *Vaudeville*, "Eddie Darling had a sense of humor and especially loved to 'rib' single women. He would drop in to visit them backstage and repeat some piece of gossip he heard about them, etc., and in no time he'd have created an upheaval. The actors liked him, as he was a fair man in his dealings with them."

Darling came to work for E. F. Albee in 1905 and soon became his confidential secretary. In 1909, he was promoted to head booker, a position he held until 1930, when he retired shortly after Albee's death. In the 1920s, Darling was noted for importing European acts to the Palace and, in particular, for the presentation of all-British bills. He was succeeded as booker for the Palace by George Godfrey.

HAZEL DAWN (Ogden City, Ut., March 23, 1890—New York, August 28, 1988)

On March 13, 1911, Hazel Dawn appeared for the first time at New York's New Amsterdam Theatre as Claudine in *The Pink Lady* by Ivan Caryll and C.M.S. McLellan. The musical comedy established Dawn as a Broadway star, and the show's title and its hit song, "My Beautiful Lady," became synonymous with the actress. The success of *The Pink Lady* led to Dawn's being starred in a series of Broadway farces, including *Up in Mabel's Room* (1919) and *Getting Gertie's Garter* (1921), and also to a brief vaudeville career in the mid 1920s.

Dawn was born Hazel Tout into a strict Mormon family. When it was suggested that her sister should study singing, the entire family moved to London, where Hazel studied the violin and also made her stage debut in *Dear Little Denmark* in 1909. The following year, she appeared in London in *The Balkan Princess* and also made her New York debut in *The Dollar Princess*. (She may also have appeared in an early version of the Ziegfeld *Follies*.) Following *The Pink Lady*, Dawn starred in Victor Herbert's *The Debutante*; the composer had seen her in the earlier production and thought her "an apparition of beauty, sweetness and talent." The Famous Players Film Company was equally impressed with Hazel Dawn, and she was starred in eleven feature films between 1914 and 1917.

Hazel Dawn made her vaudeville debut in November 1923 at New York's

Alhambra Theatre in a sketch titled *The Little Pink Lady*. The twenty-three-minute act was described by *Variety* (November 29, 1923):

Miss Dawn in a morning negligee is an eye-filling vision upon her first entrance as the mistress of a young society businessman with whom she has been intimate for five months. The couple breakfast together, the dialog developing that he absents himself every two weeks on "business trips." His ejaculation [sic!] at discovering his wife's picture in the morning paper leads to a confession to his mistress that he is a divorced man. His wife is the leader of the "big sister" movement fostered to save fallen women.

A social worker enters after the lover has left. She turns out to be the wife. The mistress upbraids her and scoffs at her pretensions. The cynical one, goaded by 'good woman's' smug superiority, confesses her "affair" with the husband. He returns looking for his cigarette case and is face to face with both women.

Forced to make a choice and threatened with poverty by his wife, who handles the money bags, he repudiates his mistress. The "pink lady" forces the wife to promise to divorce him by threatening a scandal, then orders her former lover from the apartment for his lack of courage when forced to choose between them and for his lies about divorcing his wife.

Variety's Jack Conway praised the sketch, which also featured Eleanor Dawn as the wife and George Drury Hart as the husband. Audiences also liked the act, but the theatre management did not, and within a few days it was taken off the bill, being declared too risqué.

Hazel Dawn returned to vaudeville the following year in a twenty-two-minute playlet by Edgar Allan Woolf titled *The Land of Love*. She played a chorus girl on the verge of stardom who must decide between her career or her husband and seven-year-old son. A novel presentation had the actress appear as she would look in old age had she embraced a career or acknowledged mother love. The act opened at the Palace in January 1924, and according to *Variety* (January 31, 1924), "Miss Dawn was at no time convincing."

Following a 1927 marriage to mining engineer Charles Grunell, Hazel Dawn basically retired from the stage, returning only in 1931 to play in *Wonder Boy*. Following the 1941 death of her husband, she worked in the casting department of the J. Walter Thompson advertising agency. In 1946, she appeared in the film *Margie*, and in 1947, she returned to Broadway in *I Gotta Get Out*. The following year, she toured with her daughter Hazel Dawn, Jr. in *Years Ago*.

BIBLIOGRAPHY

"Dawn of a Bright Era." *Theatre Arts* 43, no. 9 (September 1959), pp. 29–32.

"Hazel Dawn Returns in New Comedy." *Cue*, September 13, 1947, pp. 10–11.

St. John-Brenon, Aileen. "Shot at Dawn." *Motion Picture Classic* 8, no. 4 (June 1919), pp. 31, 69.

"Setting the Record Straight." *Theatre Arts* 43, no. 10 (October 1959), pp. 94–95.

MLLE DAZIE (St. Louis, September 16, 1884—Miami Beach, Fl., August 12, 1952)

Born Daisy Peterkin, Mlle Dazie was a leading exponent of contemporary dance on the vaudeville stage. In her 1914 study of *Vaudeville*, Caroline Caffin wrote, "She has all the accomplishments of the toe-dancer, the pirouettes and airy flights of the classic ballet; but with them the elusive sprightliness, piquant and varying, which saves them from becoming mechanical or stilted. She uses these devices, not for their own sake, but as graceful phrases of expression.''

When Dazie first appeared on the vaudeville stage, she was billed as ''Le Domino Rouge,'' and sported a red mask. Later, she dropped the mask and was billed simply as Mlle Dazie, under which name she appeared in the 1907, and first, edition of the Ziegfeld *Follies*. On June 5, 1909, she opened a tour of the Keith theatres in Boston, playing New York, at the Fifth Avenue Theatre, beginning July 5. Her act featured a pantomime titled ''L'Amour d'Artist,'' written expressly for her by Signor G. Molasso, and in which she was partnered by a male dancer known simply as Bonsfligio. Dazie claimed that, in ''L'Amour d'Artist,'' she was the first American dancer on the vaudeville stage to attempt to interpret a story without words.

In February 1917, Dazie headlined at the Palace in a ballet pantomime titled ''The Garden of Punchinello,'' in which she was directed by Herbert Brenon (who later became a distinguished film director). She made her last stage appearance in the 1919 production of *Aphrodite*.

BIBLIOGRAPHY

Dazie, Mlle. ''Turkey Trots and Chorus Girls.'' *The Green Book Magazine*, February 1913, pp. 217–220.

CARTER De HAVEN (Chicago, October 5, 1886—Woodland Hills, Ca., July 20, 1977)

Carter De Haven's career on screen was as a comedian and later production executive, but in vaudeville he was known for his work as a dancer and singer. It was while he was singing in a church choir in Chicago that Martin Beck heard him and booked De Haven for the Orpheum circuit. In 1907, De Haven married Flora Parker (Perth Amboy, N.J., September 1, 1883—Hollywood, Ca., September 9, 1950), and as De Haven and Parker the pair soon became headliners. They were at Hammerstein's Victoria Theatre in January 1909 with an act that featured dancing and a blend of comic and romantic songs, and *The New York Dramatic Mirror* (January 23, 1909) reported, ''From start to finish it is a delightfully entertaining offering.'' In 1914, De Haven and Parker played the Palace and also put together a new act, a musical skit titled ''The Masker.'' *The New York Dramatic Mirror* (October 14, 1914) again endorsed Carter De Haven as ''a nimble dancer, an agreeable vocalist of the American nasal musical comedy school, and he possesses a dapper Broadwayesque personality.''

It was probably the last quality that helped De Haven and Parker enter films. As De Haven recalled, ''It was a man who saw me, heard me on the Orpheum circuit, and asked how I'd like to be in pictures. I laughed at the idea. I said, 'That's silly. What could I be in pictures?' To be a star in motion pictures you got to be tall, handsome and something like that. I said, 'I'm not any of them.' But I said okay. They hired me at Universal in 1915 and I made a hit.''

With his wife, Carter De Haven was starred in a series of short domestic comedies, in which the couple was billed as Mr. and Mrs. Carter De Haven. From short subjects, they graduated to feature films, including *The College Orphan* (1915), *The Wrong Door* (1916), *A Youth of Fortune* (1916), *Twin Beds* (1920), *The Girl in the Taxi* (1921), *Marry the Poor Girl* (1921), and *My Lady Friends* (1921). The couple divorced in 1928.

Carter De Haven also worked as a director in silent films. He was an assistant to Charlie Chaplin on *Modern Times* (1936) and also appeared in the comedian's 1940 feature *The Great Dictator*. In 1927, Carter De Haven opened a legitimate theatre, the Hollywood Music Box Theatre, at 6126 Hollywood Boulevard; it is now the Henry Fonda Theatre. His son Carter De Haven was a producer, and his daughter is actress Gloria De Haven.

BIBLIOGRAPHY

Slide, Anthony. "Carter De Haven." *The Silent Picture* no. 15 (Summer 1972), pp. 26–27.

VAUGHN DeLEATH (Mount Pulaski, Il., September 26, 1896—Buffalo, N.Y., May 28, 1943)

Vaughn DeLeath was one of the great names in early radio. Billed as the "First Lady of Radio," the medium's first crooner, her voice was selected by Dr. Lee De Forest as that best suited to the radio microphone. She was also a radio executive and a song writer, best remembered for "I Wasn't Lying When I Said I Love You," who made literally hundreds of popular recordings in the 1920s.

Her large size and warm, engaging personality made her a natural for occasional vaudeville appearances in the 1920s and 1930s. She was also seen on the stage, as Signora Calvaro, in *Laugh, Clown, Laugh*, which opened at the Belasco Theatre, New York, on November 28, 1923. In 1938, DeLeath and Kate Smith began litigation to determine which had the right to bill herself as "The First Lady of Radio." Temporarily, Smith reluctantly agreed to permit DeLeath to retain the title.

WILLIAM DEMAREST (St. Paul, Mn., February 27, 1892—Palm Springs, Ca., December 28, 1983)

The comedian who never smiled and who later became a popular character actor in films, William Demarest entered vaudeville while still a child, with his brothers Reuben and George, performing a mixture of comedy and soft-shoe dancing in blackface under the name the Demarestio Brothers, "European Comedy Stars." In 1904, the boys' mother took them to New York for minor vaudeville appearances, and William Demarest developed a single act. He teamed up with Estelle Collett, and in 1917 the couple married in Los Angeles, where Demarest enlisted for the First World War. After demobilization, Demarest continued to perform as a minor vaudeville comedian, with a slapstick routine involving pratfalls and his playing the cello.

In an interview with the *Los Angeles Times*, he described his act:

The audience settles back and says, "Here comes another straight musical act." I could play the hell out of that cello, and I get going good on "Zigeunerweisen." All of a sudden I stop, put the cello down, lie down on the floor and try to do a nip-up. It looks like I'm going to make it, but I don't. I snap way up in the air and come down flat on my back like a sack of cement. You'd think I'd broke my neck. I don't say a damn thing, just pick up the cello, sit down and go on with "Zigeunerweisen" where I left off.

In 1927, Demarest was signed to a contract by Warner Bros. and appeared in a number of Vitaphone films. After a few years on screen, he decided to return to vaudeville, and in May 1932, he was one of the acts on the closing bill at the Palace as a two-a-day house. He appeared with Estelle Collett; she played the violin, he the cello, and both told a few jokes. "Demarest is not quite as refined as he might be, but he is almost always funny," was the comment of Elias E. Sugarman in *The Billboard* (May 14, 1932). There is further evidence of Demarest's vulgarity in a sketch which Demarest performed in the 1931 edition of Earl Carroll's *Vanities*. Demarest is a producer, who welcomes star Lillian Roth in his office. She puts her dog down on the desk and it begins to urinate. Told to leave, she does so, picking up the dog, which continues to urinate. A couple of stooges appear as writers, argue with Demarest, and as they do so strike his desk, sending urine flying all over the stage.

In the 1930s, Demarest became an agent but continued to make occasional screen appearances. In 1940, director/writer Preston Sturges persuaded him to appear in *The Great McGinty*, and the actor became a member of Sturges's stock company, most notably playing Mr. Kockenlocker in *The Miracle of Morgan's Creek* (1944). He continued to appear in films through the 1970s and was also prominent on television as Uncle Charley O'Casey in *My Three Sons* (CBS, 1965–1972).

BIBLIOGRAPHY

Dwan, Robert. "William Demarest: On Finding the Laughs." *Los Angeles Times Calendar*, May 3, 1981, pp. 4–5.

Franchey, John. "Dead-Pan Demarest." *Modern Screen*, February 1945, pp. 79–80.

Muir, Florabel. "Sourpuss Bill." *Saturday Evening Post*, February 23, 1946, pp. 17, 127, 133.

GABY DESLYS (Marseilles, France, September 4, 1881—Montrouge, France, February 11, 1920)

A legendary singing and dancing star of the first two decades of the twentieth century, Gaby Deslys had a scandalous reputation even greater than her talent. Even before she had made her American debut, she was the subject of a burlesque at the Folies Bergere in New York, in which her much publicized romance with King Manuel of Portugal was featured. She made her New York debut at the Winter Garden Theatre on September 27, 1911, in *Les Debuts de Chichine*, but it was her second Winter Garden show, *Vera Violetta*, which opened on November 20, 1911, that delighted audiences more. It was followed by *The Belle of Bond Street*, which opened at the Shubert Theatre on March 30, 1914, and

Irving Berlin's *Stop! Look! Listen!*, which opened at the Globe Theatre on December 25, 1915.

Born Gabrielle Caire, Gaby Deslys spent many years on the Paris Stage before delighting London audiences in *The New Aladdin*, which opened at the Gaiety Theatre on September 29, 1906. From the United States, Gaby Deslys brought jazz to Europe, filling her songs with Americanisms. She returned to America in the fall of 1919, trying to arrange a vaudeville tour, but no manager was willing to meet her salary demand of $25,000 a week.

Gaby Deslys's dancing partner in the United States was an interesting character named Harry Pilcer (New York, April 29, 1885—Cannes, France, January 14, 1961). He had been a male prostitute prior to becoming a dancer, and he was every bit as beautiful as Gaby Deslys, for whom he choreographed the "Gaby Glide." In the 1917 Parisian revue *Laissez-Les Tomber*, Pilcer and Deslys danced a complicated number involving their moving up and down ladders. Gaby Deslys and Harry Pilcer were first seen together on screen in the 1915 feature *Her Triumph*, produced in Paris by the Famous Players Film Co. It featured the "Dance Deslys." The couple also appeared in *Infatuation*, directed by Louis Mercanton, produced by Eclipse, and released in America by Pathé on December 1, 1918. When Jacques Charles wrote "Mon Homme" for Mistinguett (made famous in the United States by Fanny Brice as "My Man"), he made it no secret that the song was dedicated to Harry Pilcer. In the mid teens, Pilcer presented his sister Elsie Pilcer with Dudley Douglas in a vaudeville act titled "Smart Songs, Sayings, Dances, and Gowns."

Wracked with consumption, Gaby Deslys died in Pilcer's arms. The dancer later worked with Mistinguett (who made two American theatrical appearances but did not perform in vaudeville).

BIBLIOGRAPHY
Gardiner, James. *Gaby Deslys: A Fatal Attraction*. London: Sidgwick & Jackson, 1986.

DETROIT

In 1906, the Crystal and the Temple were the only vaudeville houses in Detroit. By 1921, with the city's population at 993,739, there were five vaudeville theatres: the Temple, Columbia, La Salle Garden, Miles Regent, and Palace.

MAX DILL.   See KOLB And DILL

HENRY E. DIXEY (Boston, January 6, 1859—Atlantic City, N.J., February 25, 1943)

A distinguished actor of the legitimate stage, Henry E. Dixey worked frequently in vaudeville, not only appearing in playlets and sketches, but also demonstrating his talents as a dancer and comedian. He made his stage debut in melodrama in Boston at the age of nine; he gained fame in the title role of the burlesque *Adonis*, which opened at New York's Bijou Opera House on September 4, 1884. "Henry E. Dixey . . . literally crammed the piece with irrelevant but laughable and effective performance,'' reported the critic for *The New York Times* (September 5, 1884). The production helped Dixey become a leading matinee idol of the day, and he revived it in 1886, 1889, 1893, 1894, and 1900. Dixey's other Broadway productions include *A Modern Magdalene* (1902), *The Man on the Box* (1905), *Becky Sharp (1911), The Deluge* (1917), and *The Two Orphans* (1926). His last Broadway appearance was in *The Beaux's Stratagem* in 1929.

With his handsome looks and stylish dancing, Dixey was very much a theatrical personality. He enjoyed a long-running feud with fellow actor Wilton Lackaye and also had strong views on alcohol. He explained, ''When I drink, I think, and when I think, I drink.'' He was opposed to mixed drinks and took his liquor straight, commenting, ''The continual use of ice cubes in drinks will develop a race of people with black and blue upper lips.''

BIBLIOGRAPHY

Reynolds, Walter. ''A Duplex Interview with Dixey.'' *The Green Book Magazine*, April 1914, pp. 668–675.

LEW DOCKSTADER (Hartford, Ct., 1856—New York, October 26, 1924)

Lew Dockstader was one of the last and one of the greatest blackface minstrels. Born George Alfred Clapp, he came to New York in 1873 and joined the Earl, Emmett and Wilde Minstrels. The following year, still known as Clapp, he toured the country with the Whitmore and Clark Minstrels, gaining great popularity with his song ''Peter, You're in Luck This Morning.'' Dockstader made his first vaudeville appearance in the 1890s, and on Labor Day 1895 was one of the headliners on the opening bill at Proctor's Pleasure Palace in New York. Rather than continue in vaudeville, in 1898, Dockstader teamed with George Primrose to form the Primrose and Dockstader Minstrel Men, which became America's best known blackface troupe. When the couple split in 1904, Lew Dockstader's Minstrels, with a company of forty artists, was formed.

In 1905, Lew Dockstader was filmed by the American Mutoscope and Biograph Company performing his most popular song to date, ''Everybody Works but Father.'' Two versions of the song, one in whiteface and one in blackface, were filmed, with an entreaty for audiences to join in the chorus:

> Everybody works but Father, he sits around all day,
> Feet in front of the fire, smoking his pipe of clay.
> Mother takes in washing, so does sister Ann,
> Everybody works in our house, but my old man.

Lew Dockstader's vaudeville act consisted of blackface characterizations of prominent figures of the day and was apparently based on an earlier blackface act by Frank Bell. As he grew older and more portly, Dockstader abandoned blackface and became a monologist, but he continued to poke mild fun at the personalities of the day. *The New York Dramatic Mirror* (September 18, 1920) reported, ''He is the only monologist today who can skillfully touch upon the [political] campaign candidates and do it in just the humorous, satirical manner that an audience will take kindly to." Lew Dockstader remained active until his death, appearing on Broadway in *Some Party* (1922) and *The Black and White Revue* (1923). He appeared in only one feature-length film production, *Dan* (1914), in the title role of a Southern slave, played in blackface.

DOG ACTS

Like most animal performers in vaudeville, dog acts were booked either as opening acts or as chasers, the last act on the bill, intended to chase the audience out of the theatre. There was more than a hint of truth to the opinion that it was a dog's life in vaudeville if your only place on the bill was at its start or close. What is amazing is not so much the number of dog acts, but their variety. In the 1890s, leaping dogs were very popular, presented by Meehan's Leaping Dogs, Fred Gerner and Co., and others. In 1906, M. Ferreros presented his Dog Musician, which played the bells, while acrobatic tricks were performed by Braatz's Dogs. In 1924, Sylvia Loyal presented Heinie, her French poodle with "His Original Trick-Catching Boomerang Hats." Most dog owners might scoff at the originality of such an act, but Loyal announced that Heinie was the "only existing dog doing this trick."

In April 1910, Uno the Mind Reading Dog made his New York debut at the Fifth Avenue Theatre. He appeared on stage, fully clothed in feminine attire, which the trainer removed, one garment at a time. The dog was then asked to pick out selected items off the stage and bring his owner coins of various denominations. "A selection on the bells concludes the offering, making a nice finish to a good entertaining opener," commented *Variety* (April 23, 1910).

Talking dogs were little more than freak attractions. Prelle's Talking Dogs had a minor vogue in 1904. The best remembered talking dog was Don, a very popular act of 1912, but the problem was that he spoke only German. With considerable effort, audiences could be persuaded that Don had actually said *Küchen* (kitchen) and similar words. Don was also quite temperamental and would not appear at roof gardens, finding the noise from the traffic too distracting.

Following his success on screen, Rin Tin Tin was brought to the vaudeville stage in 1930, playing the Palace as a headliner (not an opening act) in May of that year. While Sime Silverman in *Variety* (May 21, 1930) was persuaded to agree that the act was "interesting," he had to admit, "perhaps more so for lovers of dogs."

Many dog acts featured a generic assortment of animals, such as Sheldman's Educated Dogs, presented by Mlle Marjorie (1901); Herr Techow's Cats and Dogs (1901); D'Alma's Dogs and Monkeys, first seen at the Keith Theatre, Boston, in 1901, but not asked to return until 1905; Herbert's Dogs, featuring "Precocious Canines in Many Clever Stunts" (1921); Bury's Four Footed Thespians (1927); and Whitey the Canine Star, who was featured with his master, Ed Ford, in a February 1931 sketch at the Palace Theatre titled "Benevolence."

Among the specific breeds of dogs to be found in vaudeville, bulldogs seemed high in popularity. May Barkley's Bulldog Music Hall featured not only live dogs but also dummies, with the audiences unable to differentiate between the two groups. Of Al Rayno's Famous Bull Dogs, *The New York Dramatic Mirror* (September 11, 1909) commented, "Seldom is an animal act seen that is as pleasing as this one." In 1905, Rosina Casselli presented a pack of wild chihuahuas. Madame A. Strakai appeared "with her Siberian canine friends" and claimed to be making her U.S. debut in 1924.

The highest paid dog act in the golden age of vaudeville was Barnold's Drunken Dog, whose depiction of alcoholic stupor was compared favorably to that of James Barton, and who received $1,000 a week from Klaw and Erlanger. Writing in *Vaudeville*, Joe Laurie, Jr. rated Barnold's Drunken Dog a "great novelty act." In his autobiography, *They All Sang*, Edward B. Marks names Professor Parker's Dogs as the "best dog act of their time."

One dog act that made the transition from vaudeville to television was Al Mardo, who developed an act in 1921 in which his dog did nothing. The first dog was named Flash, and as Mardo ordered the dog to perform various tricks, it would merely sit still with a bored expression on its considerably ugly face. In the 1940s, Al Mardo entertained a new generation as a featured performer in Ken Murray's *Blackouts* with the successor to Flash, a bulldog named Mr. Chips. In the 1950s, he brought the act to television. (Al Mardo began his career in 1912, appearing with Gus Edwards and later in minstrel shows.) Mardo had a number of imitators, including one unidentified act that featured a dog sitting lifeless on a pedestal throughout the performance. The curtain would come down at the act's close and rise as the dog jumped off the pedestal to take a bow. What the audience did not realize was that the dog seated on the pedestal for the first fifteen minutes was a dummy.

BIBLIOGRAPHY

Dwan, Robert. "Al Mardo and the Dog That Did Nothing." *Los Angeles Times Calendar*, October 2, 1983, pp. 6, 7.
Laurie, Joe, Jr. "Animal Acts." In *Vaudeville: From the Honky-Tonks to the Palace*. New York: Henry Holt, 1953, pp. 155–70.

ROSIE/ROSZIKA (Hungary, October 25, 1892—New York, February 1, 1970) and **JENNY/YANCSI** (Hungary, October 25, 1892—Hollywood, Ca., June 1, 1941) **DOLLY**

Reviewing the Dolly Sisters at the Palace, Sime Silverman wrote in *Variety* (February 24, 1922), "As two dandy looking twins who cannot be told apart, with class and who can dance if they want to, the Dolly Sisters are always worth the price of admission just to look at." They were as much a part of the 1920s as Art Deco, which in some mysterious way they resembled, and yet their career goes back well before 1920, to 1909, when they first played vaudeville as a dance team at Keith's Union Square Theatre.

The Dolly Sisters were, as one commentator put it, the Gabors of their era. They married well and often and were at home in all the world's glamour spots, from Westhampton, Long Island, to Monte Carlo (where Roszika once claimed to have won $400,000 in one evening at roulette). They were elegant and they were beautiful, and in their company one might find the world's most eligible bachelors, from the Prince of Wales to Diamond Jim Brady (who Roszika said once gave her a Rolls-Royce, "not merely a Rolls-Royce, but one wrapped in ribbons").

They were born Roszika and Yancsi Dutsch, identical twins from Hungary, but to American audiences they were known always as Rosie and Jenny Dolly. From vaudeville, the pair went into the 1911 edition of the Ziegfeld *Follies*, in which they performed a dance routine as Siamese twins. They also starred in *His Bridal Night*, a farce by Lawrence Rising, revised and elaborated by Margaret Mayo, which opened at the Republic Theatre, New York, on August 19, 1916. They starred together again in one feature film, *The Million Dollar Dollies*, released by Metro in 1917, and separately, Roszika was seen in *The Lily and the Rose* (1915) and Yancsi in *The Call of the Dance* (1915). From 1916 onward, the Dolly Sisters were regulars at the Palace, although critics often complained that their singing abilities were nonexistent and that they seldom bothered to change their dance routines. For example, James Metcalfe in *Life* (August 31, 1916) described them as "certainly more eloquent with their feet than in speech or the art of acting. They are so dainty to the sight that they should never make the mistake of appealing to the sense of hearing." The reality was that dancing and singing were minor considerations compared to how the Dollys would dress for their vaudeville appearances or how many costume changes they would make. As *Variety* (July 20, 1917) noted, "The Dollys are the Dollys, and people accept them in that way."

In the 1920s, the Dolly Sisters were to be seen more in Paris and London music halls than on the New York stage; one of their last major French revues was *Broadway à Paris*, the most popular show of 1928. They starred, along with Moran and Mack and Vincent Lopez and His Orchestra, in *The Greenwich Village Follies*, which opened at the Shubert Theatre on September 16, 1924, with lyrics and music by Cole Porter. The high spot of the show was a routine featuring the sisters with Jud Brady's Dogs impersonating them.

After retirement in the late 1920s, the Dolly Sisters concentrated on the social scene. On June 1, 1941, Yancsi was found dead in her Hollywood apartment, where she had formed a noose from the drapes and hanged herself. Eight years previously, she had been seriously injured in a motoring accident in France, necessitating major plastic surgery, and had never fully recovered from the trauma of losing her beauty. In 1945, George Jessel produced a feature film at 20th Century–Fox, loosely based on the lives of the sisters, titled *The Dolly Sisters*, starring Betty Grable and June Haver. When Roszika died in 1970, *Variety* reported that her one philosophy in life had been, "If you drink Scotch, make it Black and White. It will never hang you over.'

BIBLIOGRAPHY

Tyrrell, Henry. "Delectable Dollys." *Cosmopolitan*, September 1912, pp. 549–51.

JACK DONAHUE (Charleston, Ma., 1892—New York, October 1, 1930)

By his own definition, Jack Donahue was "just a hoofer" who became a star. He entered show business at the age of eleven with a medicine show and next joined the Young and Adams Repertory Company, performing specialty dance numbers between the acts. When the company was stranded in Chicago, Donahue joined a burlesque company, then entered vaudeville.

On the vaudeville stage, he worked initially with his wife, Alice Stewart, in an act called Donahue and Stewart. It was a mixture of dance and comedy, with Donahue as the straight man and his wife appearing as an eccentric male dancer. When she retired, Donahue worked as a single—appearing at the Palace as early as 1915—alternating dance numbers with light comedy, and later, in the 1920s, also working as a master of ceremonies. He made his first Broadway appearance in *The Woman Haters* in 1912, but his first prominent parts were in *Hitchy-Koo* (1917) and *Angel Face* (1919). He appeared in the 1920 edition of the Ziegfeld *Follies* and was also featured on the Broadway stage in *Molly Darling* (1922), *Be Yourself!* (1924), *Sunny* (1925), *Rosalie* (1927), and *Carry On* (1929). He would still return to vaudeville and headlined at the Palace in June 1921 and August 1927.

In November 1929, Donahue opened in New York in *Sons o' Guns*. The following year, he took the show on the road, and while playing in Cincinnati was taken ill. He returned to New York, where he died of heart failure. He should not be confused with chorus boy turned Hollywood director Jack Donohue.

BIBLIOGRAPHY

Donahue, Jack. *Letters of a Hoofer to His Ma.* New York: Cosmopolitan, 1931.

KITTY DONER (Chicago, 1895—Los Angeles, August 26, 1988)

Male impersonation was very much a prerogative of the British as far as vaudeville was concerned, with Vesta Tilley and Ella Shields being the best known exponents of the art. The best known American male impersonator and the only one on a par with Tilley and Shields was Kitty Doner. Reviewing her act on November 26, 1924, *Variety* commented, "If our cousins across the pond think they have a patent on the raising of male impersonators, they ought to get a load of this baby. In male clothes, she is as masculine as a Notre Dame guard, and in female togs as feminine as bare legs. As a dancer, she is in a class by herself."

Perhaps not surprisingly, both of Doner's parents were British. Her father, Joe Doner, was born in Manchester on September 25, 1864, and her mother, Nellie, in London on December 15, 1874. Nellie was a popular principal boy in British pantomime before joining up with Joe Doner in an act titled "The Escaped Lunatics." One of Doner's routines was to play Dr. Jekyll and Mr. Hyde, and his daughter recalled, "My dad was a very fine actor and a beautiful dancer. He wanted to be a prize fighter and he trained but his brother, who was a very fine actor and a top star who changed his name from Doner to John D.

Gilbert, didn't want Dad to be a prize fighter. He said, 'He's a good mimic and a good actor, and he's got to go on the stage.' ''

The reasons why Kitty Doner first dressed as a boy are fascinating from a purely psychological viewpoint. ''I was the first-born,'' she recalled, ''and my dad was very, very disappointed that I wasn't a boy, and as I grew I turned out sort of gawky. I wasn't considered a pretty girl. I was very boyish, and because my dad taught me dancing, my dancing was manish. The story goes that my father and mother were in various shows, and when the time came for me to go into a show, they put me in an act with them, and dad dressed me as a boy. He said, 'She might as well get started dressed as a boy because she's not pretty enough to compete with the beautiful girls in show business.' '' Kitty Doner was to appear also in other guises; in 1905, she appeared as a canary in the children's bird ballet at the New York Hippodrome. In 1909, she made her vaudeville debut with Brady's Dancing Dogs as one of the four girls featured with the four collies in the act.

In 1912, Kitty Doner appeared in her first show, *The Candy Shop*, which opened Broncho Billy Anderson's Gaiety Theatre in San Francisco. Kitty appeared in both male and female attire in the show and made a reputation for herself, at least as far as the West Coast was concerned. As a result, she was invited to join the cast of *The Passing Show of 1913*. Her father took over her management and brought her to see Florenz Ziegfeld, whom she begged to allow her to play a female role (at least until she learned that she would have to do pratfalls and would not wear the beautiful clothes of the showgirls). Kitty Doner was in the Ziegfeld *Follies* for one night—and then her father took her out of the show and decided that from that point on she would always play a boy.

Kitty Doner's biggest break came in 1914, when she was signed to play opposite Al Jolson in *Dancing Around*, a revue that also featured Clifton Webb and was based on a popular song of the period, with music by Sigmund Romberg. The show opened at the Winter Garden Theatre on October 10, 1914. Kitty was to play with Al Jolson, with whom she was romantically involved, in two further revues: *Robinson Crusoe, Jr.*, which opened at the Winter Garden on February 17, 1916, again with music by Sigmund Romberg, and *Sinbad*, which opened at the Winter Garden on February 14, 1918, with music by Romberg and Jolson.

During the run of *Dancing Around*, Doner began perfecting her male impersonation routine. She would study the men in the cast. ''I followed them around until the men in the show were just nuts,'' she remembered. ''I was under their tail; I was under their feet. I was mimicking everything they would do, the way they would twirl their moustaches or the way they would brush their hair back.'' This stood her in good stead when she returned to vaudeville in the late teens. Reviewing her act, *The New York Dramatic Mirror* (October 30, 1919) commented,

It's a real delight to watch a clever little artiste like Kitty Doner in action. And when it comes to dancing steps with the soft shoes in the masculine attire, Kitty is head and shoulders above the majority of men and women cracked up as dancing stars. Kitty Doner is a graceful dancing dynamo and isn't a bit afraid of hard work. Other feminine vaudevillians should watch her and profit accordingly.

Kitty's vaudeville act, "A League of Song Steps," gained for her the title of "The Best Dressed Man on the American Stage." It also landed her an engagement in the home of male impersonation, England, where she topped the bill at London's Victoria Palace in 1922.

Kitty Doner's brother Ted (1896–1979) and sister Rose were also in show business, and the three appeared together often on the vaudeville stage. Ted and Kitty took over the Fred and Adele Astaire roles in the touring company production of *Lady Be Good* in the mid 1920s. At that time, she was offered a film contract by Joseph Schenck but turned it down; she was to make only one screen appearance, in a 1928 Warner Bros. short, *A Bit of Scotch*, for which she was paid $1,750. Throughout the 1920s, Kitty Doner's weekly vaudeville salary averaged $1,000; when she toured on the William Fox circuit in 1927, she was paid $1,500 a week, and when she performed at the Hill Street Theatre, Los Angeles, that same year, she received $1,200.

In May 1926, Kitty Doner was at the Palace (where she first appeared in 1919) with an act that typified her vaudeville appearances at that time. With Jack Carroll at the piano, she appeared first in evening dress, followed by a song as a French dandy. Next came an appearance in skirts to perform some high kicking. Then, onstage, she stripped down to a pair of briefs and a bra for a fast change to a Scotsman. Doner recalled that a pink floodlight was used for her strip change, which gave the audience the distinct impression that she was naked and caused great concern to E. F. Albee. Reviewing that act, "Sisk" wrote in *Variety* (May 5, 1926):

Monday night she appeared to fine advantage, combining the enthusiasm and infectious pleasure of working with the already good material which helps her attractive and unique talents. She rivals Ella Shields in the male impersonations and that is no scant praise. What makes her an even more important figure is that marvellous dancing stuff. Kitty Doner, then, is not just a headliner—she's a headliner who offers not only a well known name but some honest-to-John entertainment.

Kitty Doner never gave impressions of well-known men, but rather her male impersonations were unique unto themselves. Equally unique were her female impersonations, such as Tillie from Tenth Avenue, with her opening line, "Yes, this is the joint. My gang hangs out here."

She was a performer who moved with the times, and when her style of old-fashioned vaudeville died, she was the first to admit it, telling the *San Francisco Chronicle* in a headline story on November 25, 1934, "There ain't any vaudeville, but some people won't believe it." She developed a nightclub act with Harold Stern and His Orchestra. In the 1940s, she became show director with *Holiday on Ice*, and during 1950 and 1951, Kitty Doner was responsible for auditioning talent for *Ted Mack's Amateur Hour*. It was not her first involvement with television; on August 1, 1931, she had performed her act in front of a television camera at the CBS studios on the top of New York's Vanderbilt Hotel, the first complete stage act to be televised over a radius of more than one hundred miles. She had also been involved with television in the 1940s, teaming with

Pauline Koner to create what was called "television dance," expressly choreographed for the medium.

Throughout her career, Kitty Doner lived up to the title given her by *The New York Dramatic Mirror* (August 7, 1920): "Just another name for pep."
BIBLIOGRAPHY

Doner, Kitty. "A Star Is Reborn." *Liberty* 15, no. 26 (June 25, 1938), pp. 53–55.

BILLY DOOLEY (Chicago, February 8, 1893—Hollywood, Ca., August 4, 1938)

A tall comedian with a rubber-like body and large, round eyes, Billy Dooley entered vaudeville with his sister Ethel and brother Jed, working as trick cyclists and billed as the 3 Dooleys. As a solo act, he was billed variously as The Scotch Comedian, The Six Cylinder Comedian, and The Cowboy Cyclist, and developed a routine that included small talk and trick roping in the style of Will Rogers. Through the years, Billy Dooley worked with a number of partners. In 1914, he was working with Evelyn Robson as Dooley and Robson, and the pair presented "Vaudeville of Today," an act that was a vaudeville bill in itself, including singing, dancing, bike riding, an imitation of Harry Lauder, and a rope dance in the style of Fred Stone. In 1917, he was teamed as Dooley and Nelson in an eccentric dancing act with Eddie Nelson. Later in the decade, he joined forces with Helen Storey as Dooley and Storey in a novelty act called "Vaudeville à la Carte." A *Variety* critic caught the act at the Orpheum Theatre, Oakland, and commented (July 23, 1920), "Dooley's versatility naturally dominates the act, which makes a strong bid for comedy and can be classified as a good novelty offering. They registered a good-sized hit in second position, but can easily hold down a later spot." In 1922, Dooley and Storey toured British music halls.

Early in the 1920s, Dooley developed the character of a sailor named Goofy-Gob. Comedy film producer Al Christie saw Dooley as the character in a sketch titled "The Misfit Sailor," signed him to a contract, and in the summer of 1925, Dooley began starring in Christie Comedies. He continued on screen in minor roles through the 1930s. Brother Jeb Dooley (1884–1973) was also reasonably successful in vaudeville.

RAY DOOLEY (Glasgow, Scotland, October 30, 1890—East Hampton, N.Y., January 28, 1984)

A vaudeville headliner known primarily for her baby impersonations, Ray Dooley was also a popular star of revues, appearing in the 1920, 1921, and 1925 editions of the Ziegfeld *Follies* and the 1928 edition of Earl Carroll's *Vanities*. She began her career in a Philadelphia minstrel show headed by her father, Robert Rogers Dooley, but at the age of fifteen, she eloped with entertainer Eddie Dowling, with whom she would frequently appear onstage. Born Rachel Rice Dooley, Ray made her Palace debut in 1917, and her last appearance there, with Eddie Dowling, was in 1932. When not appearing on the vaudeville stage with her husband, she would perform with her Metropolitan Minstrels.

For the 1920 edition of the Ziegfeld *Follies*, W. C. Fields wrote a sketch titled "The Family Ford," in which Ray Dooley was his spoiled child, and it was a characterization with which she was stuck for the rest of her career. After appearing in her husband's revue, *Thumbs Up*, which opened in December 1934, Dooley retired, devoting herself to the rearing of her one daughter. She returned to the stage in 1948 for a series of three one-act plays, under the collective title *Hope's the Thing*, in which Eddie Dowling also appeared, as well as produced and directed.

FIFI D'ORSAY (Montreal, April 16, 1907—Woodland Hills, Ca., December 2, 1983)

The saucy French bombshell from Montreal is better known for her screen appearances in early talkies than for her work onstage, but it was in vaudeville that she began her career, and that was where she learned her craft. In a 1980 interview, she was quick to point out that there is a major difference between being a movie actress and being an entertainer. "As I sit here talking to you now," she commented, "I can say I'm both. And I'm a comedienne and I can be a dramatic actress. I have a lot of tricks under my belt. I work to everybody—that's the secret of my success. Maurice Chevalier taught me that—not to work just to the people in front of you; turn to everybody, work the circumference of the room."

Born Yvonne Lussier, the entertainer-to-be worked as a secretary in Montreal in order to raise sufficient money to come to the United States and make her ambition to become an actress a reality. She came to New York in 1924 and was met by Helen Morgan, whom Fifi had known in Canada. Morgan let Fifi stay in her apartment and advised her to check the adverts for jobs in show business. This she did, and she spotted a notice that director John Murray Anderson was auditioning for the touring company of *The Greenwich Village Follies*. "I was singing 'My Man' in French and in English, too," recalled Fifi, "and I was singing 'Yes, We Have No Bananas' in French, and then I sang 'Chicago.' Well, John Murray Anderson liked me, and right away he chose me to be in the show. He said, 'Where do you come from?' and straight away I told him the Folies Bergère in Paris. I wanted to make myself important! Do you know that he chose me to be a chorus girl, but then, when we started rehearsing, he gave me a specialty to do." That specialty was an apache dance, which later had to be dropped because dancing was not among D'Orsay's many talents.

The original star of this version of *The Greenwich Village Follies* was Karyl Norman, the "Creole Fashion Plate," but because he proved to be too poor a draw on the road, he was replaced after a month by Jane and Katherine Lee. They also failed to draw, and, finally, Gallagher and Shean joined the show, and they were its stars for a year. With charming frankness, Fifi recalled:

I became Mr. Gallagher's little sweetheart. He was thirty-seven years older than me, but it was good for me because he knew all the little tricks of the business and I was a beginner. I wanted to learn everything about show business and he taught me—believe me! He was the greatest straight man in the business. Mr. Shean was the comic, but without Mr. Gallagher he couldn't have done very well. He was always talking to me with a highball in his hand. He was drinking all the time!

John Murray Anderson named Yvonne Lussier Fifi, and her billing in *The Greenwich Village Follies* was "Mademoiselle Fifi," a name she took when she left the show and worked in a vaudeville act with Ed Gallagher. "I was his guardian, I was his nurse, I was his lover, I was like a wife, but I wasn't his wife. I would be the one to dress him before he went on the stage. I would stand him on the stage. He was always drunk, but, boy, when he got on the stage, he could say his lines. But I was proud to do it, because he was my teacher. I helped him because he was helping me, although it was no fun," remembered D'Orsay.

After two years with Gallagher, Fifi D'Orsay was living with her aunt, who rented out rooms in her New York apartment, and among the tenants was Charlie Butterworth. It was Butterworth who sent Fifi over to see Herman Timberg. At eight o'clock in the morning, Fifi arrived, full of pep, sat down at the piano, and began to sing "Chicago." Timberg was suitably impressed and teamed her with Herman Berrens in a vaudeville sketch titled "Ten Dollars a Lesson," in which Berrens was a professor giving piano lessons to the saucy Mademoiselle Fifi, who sang "Everything Is Hotsy Totsy Now." Fifi wore a striking red outfit, had her hair cut in boyish style, and dyed it black. She made her first entrance with a ukelele under her arm, and when she told Berrens that her ukelele teacher had given it to her, Berrens would cast anxious glances at his piano. The sketch ended with the two singing "We're So in Love." Berrens and Fifi became a popular vaudeville act, booked on the Orpheum circuit for forty-five weeks of the year.

Eventually, Fifi decided that she would like to work as a solo act, which she did, first as a mistress of ceremonies on the Publix circuit. While playing at the Harris Theatre, Pittsburgh, on a bill headlined by Rubinoff, Fifi received a telegram asking her to come to New York and make a screen test for William Fox. She was engaged to marry Herman Berrens's brother Freddie, who had a musical act in vaudeville, but decided that a career in motion pictures was more important. For her test, she sang the same group of songs she had performed for John Murray Anderson, and the result was a seven-year contract. Fifi's first film was *They Had to See Paris*, which starred Will Rogers in his first sound feature. (It was Rogers who had recommended Fifi, having met her in 1925 with Ed Gallagher.) To Rogers, she was "Froggie," but by now she had added the name of D'Orsay, because she liked the perfume of the same name. "Now they think my name is spelled Dorsey," she commented, "and they asked me if I'm Jimmy Dorsey's mother!"

Fifi D'Orsay played opposite Will Rogers again in *Young as You Feel* (1931), with her "French" sophistication working as a natural foil to Rogers's down-home Americanism. Fifi D'Orsay's later films include *Hot for Paris* (1930), *Those Three French Girls* (1930), *Mr. Lemon of Orange* (1931), *Going Hollywood* (1933), *Wonder Bar* (1934), *The Gangster* (1947), and *What a Way To Go!* (1964). While starring in films of the early 1930s, D'Orsay was also appearing in presentation houses with her vaudeville act, earning as much as $5,000 a week. "After I became a film star, I was busy all the time," she remembered. She played the Paramount, the Capitol, and the Roxy, and headlined at the Palace in January 1932. At one point, she had a vaudeville act with Edmund Lowe and Victor McLaglen, with whom she had also appeared on-screen. In 1933, D'Orsay obtained a release from her Fox contract in order to concentrate on her stage appearances.

When the Palace returned to a policy of presenting vaudeville acts together with feature films in the 1950s, Fifi D'Orsay also returned, proving that her act still had "oomph" and that audiences had not forgotten her. Along with that marvelous musical comedy star Ethel Shutta, D'Orsay brought the sparkle that once lit up the vaudeville and revue stages to the Stephen Sondheim musical *Follies*, during 1971 and 1972. In her sixties, she still displayed the energy and vitality for which she was known—and also displayed a fair share of temperament, complaining of her billing below, rather than above, the title. Throughout the 1970s, Fifi D'Orsay continued to perform in an act titled "I'm Glad I'm Not Young Anymore." She would tell jokes, such as "I'm no chicken anymore . . . I'm an old hen," "years ago, they used to call me a sexpot, now I'm a sexagenarian," and "I'm old enough for Medicare but not too old for men to care." To the end, she remained an ageless, vital reminder of the exhilaration that was vaudeville.

BIBLIOGRAPHY

McMillan, Penelope. "A Bombshell of Her Old Self." *Los Angeles Times*, April 18, 1982, part II, pp. 1, 6.
Stanke, Don. "Fifi D'Orsay." *Film Fan Monthly* no. 128 (February 1972), pp. 21–29.

EDDIE DOWLING (Woonsocket, R.I., December 9, 1894—Smithfield, R.I., February 18, 1976)

An extraordinarily versatile figure in the history of popular entertainment, Eddie Dowling's career encompassed vaudeville, musical comedy, and the legitimate stage, with his working as an actor, director, and producer. Born Joseph Nelson Goucher, Dowling adopted his mother's maiden name when he entered vaudeville as a child performer in the early 1900s. Following a 1914 marriage to headliner Ray Dooley, Dowling developed a vaudeville sketch titled "The Stowaway," concerning a young immigrant about to be deported. In its pathos, the sketch was indicative of the quality of serious acting Dowling was to pursue in later years.

Eddie Dowling made his Broadway debut in *The Velvet Lady* in 1919 and later that same year was featured in the Ziegfeld *Follies*. He made a major transition in his career in 1922 by codirecting, coproducing, and starring in the musical comedy *Sally, Irene and Mary*. At the same time, he continued to work in vaudeville, headlining on tour with his wife from 1931 to 1932; they also appeared together in *Sidewalks of New York* (1927) and *Thumbs Up!* (1934). Dowling made his debut as a serious dramatic actor in Philip Barry's *Here Come the Clowns* (1938), and around the same time became a major Broadway producer, responsible for, among others, *King Richard II* (1937) with Maurice Evans, William Saroyan's *The Time of Your Life* (1939), and Tennessee Williams's *The Glass Menagerie* (1945). He remained active in the theatre through the 1960s.

BIBLIOGRAPHY

"Eddie Dowling." *Current Biography*, February 1946, pp. 153–57.

Gresham, William Lindsay. "Eddie Dowling." *Theatre Arts* 30, no. 11 (November 1946), pp. 632–39.

LOUISE DRESSER (Evansville, In., October 5, 1878—Woodland Hills, Ca., April 24, 1965)

A statuesque blond beauty who was once nominated as the natural successor to Lillian Russell, Louise Dresser was a star of both musical comedy and vaudeville, renowned as a singer and an actress. Born Louise Josephine Kerlin, Dresser joined a burlesque show at the age of fifteen, following the death of her father, a railroad engineer. At the age of eighteen, she met composer Paul Dresser (1857–1906), who had known her father. The young woman became Dresser's protegée, and he suggested that she adopt the name Dresser and pretend to be his sister. As a result of this subterfuge, it was generally believed that not only was Louise Dresser the sister of Paul Dresser, but also the sister of Dresser's brother Theodore Dreiser. Louise Josephine Kerlin became Louise Dresser in Chicago, and there, for the first time, she began singing two of Paul Dresser's best known songs, "On the Banks of the Wabash" and "My Gal Sal."

Louise Dresser appeared in vaudeville at the turn of the century as a singer, backed by a group of Negro children, and billed as Louise Dresser and Her Picks (short for pickaninnies). She made her first New York vaudeville appearance in the spring of 1906 and first played the Palace in 1914. That same year, she enlarged her talent as a vaudeville performer by appearing in the playlet *A Turn of the Knob*. At the height of her vaudeville career, Dresser earned $1,750 a week. On the legitimate stage, Dresser played Mrs. Burton in *A Matinee Idol* (1910), Leonora Longacre in *Broadway to Paris* (1912), Ruth Snyder in *Potash and Perlmutter* (1913), and Patsy Pygmalion in *Hello Broadway!* (1914).

A first marriage in 1898 to composer and vaudevillian Jack Norworth ended in divorce in 1908. Two years later, Dresser married actor Jack Gardner, the original star of the operatta *The Chocolate Soldier*, and they remained married until his death in 1950. Dresser began her screen career in 1922 and gave many memorable performances, including Catherine the Great in *The Eagle* (1925), the title role in *The Goose Woman* (1925), Al Jolson's mother in *Mammy* (1930), and the Empress Elizabeth in *The Scarlet Empress* (1934). She retired from the screen in 1937, and announced plans for a comeback following the death of her husband failed to materialize.

BIBLIOGRAPHY

Albert, Katherine. "Two True Troupers: Louise and Marie." *Photoplay* 37, no. 4 (March 1930), pp. 34–35.

Dresser, Louise. "Vaudeville's the Hardest." *Variety*, December 14, 1907, p. 25.

Gebhart, Myrtle. "The Mothering Heart." *Picture Play*, January 1930, pp. 22–24, 110.

Patterson, Ada. "I Am Thirty-Six and Proud of It." *The Green Book Magazine*, January 1916, pp. 161–68.

Tully, Jim. "On the Banks of the Wabash." *Photoplay* 27, no. 6 (May 1925), pp. 43, 106–107.

MARIE DRESSLER (Cobourg, Canada, November 9, 1869—Santa Barbara, Ca., July 28, 1934)

There are few comediennes as fondly remembered or as well known from vaudeville and the golden age of the motion picture as buxom Marie Dressler. She was, as *Variety* (August 22, 1919) commented, "A great scout with the mob, loves a good story and knows how to tell one, and a tireless worker. A good woman, that's all."

Born Leila Koerber, the daughter of an itinerant musician who moved his family from town to town with sickening regularity, Marie Dressler was a natural-born clown, in part because of her weight and her lack of beauty. "I was born homely," she wrote in her autobiography. At the age of fourteen, she joined the Nevada Stock Company against the wishes of her parents and took the name of Marie Dressler from an aunt. She moved from stock company to stock company, eventually arriving in New York and singing at the Atlantic Garden on the Bowery and Koster and Bial's Twenty-third Street Theatre. Her first major success came with her role as Flo Honeydew of the Music Halls in an operatic comedy titled *The Lady Slavey*, which opened in Washington, D.C., in September 1896.

She became a favorite in vaudeville and burlesque at the turn of the century, noted for her "coon" songs and impersonations. "She is a very shapely woman, large and heavy, and her ways immediately captivate an audience," wrote *The Billboard* (April 4, 1903). After Joe Weber split with Lew Fields in 1904, the former asked Dressler to join his company, which included Anna Held, in *Higgledy-Piggledy*. She was to remain with Weber for a number of years, gaining the somewhat unglamorous title of "Joe Weber's Amazon." Dressler appeared at New York's Colonial Theatre in January 1907, offering impersonations of Mrs. Leslie Carter and Blanche Bates from the legitimate stage, and singing what was almost her theme song, "A Great Big Girl Like Me." She returned to the Colonial in April 1908, portraying a chesty elocutionist and a classy prima donna. *Variety* (April 25, 1908) commented, "There is just enough accuracy and truth in her burlesques to make the picture ridiculously plain."

Marie Dressler introduced her character Tillie Blobbs, a Broadway house drudge, in *Tillie's Nightmare*, "a mélange of mirth and melody," which opened at New York's Herald Square Theatre on May 5, 1910. The show featured Dressler singing "Heaven Will Protect the Working Girl," a classic of lower-class mentality and middle-class morality, with a final chorus:

> Stand back there, villain, go your way.
> Here I will no longer stay;
> Although you were a marquis or an earl
> You may tempt the upper classes
> With your villainous demitasses,
> But Heaven will protect the working girl!

As a result of the success of *Tillie's Nightmare*, Dressler was invited by Mack Sennett to star in the 1914 feature-length film *Tillie's Punctured Romance*. The production did more to help the careers of Dressler's costars, Charlie Chaplin and Mabel Normand, but she did appear in the two sequel films, *Tillie's Tomato Surprise* (1915) and *Tillie Wakes Up* (1917).

Aside from these screen appearances, Marie Dressler was active through the decade in musical comedy and vaudeville; she also participated in the 1917 and 1918 Liberty Loan drives and the Actors' Equity Strike of 1919, in which she headed the chorus girls' division. In April 1919, Dressler headlined at the Palace, receiving the surprisingly small weekly salary of $1,500. *The New York Dramatic Mirror* (April 8, 1919) commented:

> Marie Dressler, one of the greatest institutions of burlesque on the American stage—not of the ten-twenty-thirty standard but of the strata that demands talent and brains—has returned to vaudeville. This is an occasion to make Broadway sit up and take notice. . . . She was in all her cut-up glory, exactly like the old days of Weber and Fields. She satisfied everyone. In doing so she made herself a matter of importance to the Associated Press. Few actresses, even considering those who play Ibsen and other queer fellows' scribbling are quoted by the transcontinental press as much as she for the reason that she has always some to say that even college professors can understand as well as servant girls.

The Palace appearance was almost a swan song for Dressler in that her career began falling apart in the 1920s. Stage engagements dwindled, although she did appear on the October 1925 old-timers bill at Palace. By 1927, Dressler was contemplating leaving the United States for good and opening a small hotel in Paris, something she had considered as early as 1901. However, she was offered a supporting role in a 1927 Fox film, *The Joy Girl*, and this led to other parts in silent films, thanks in large part to the efforts of M-G-M screenwriter Frances Marion. With the coming of sound, Dressler proved her value as an actress, notably opposite Greta Garbo in the latter's first talkie, *Anna Christie* (1930). She played opposite Polly Moran in a series of comedy shorts and feature films, and in 1930, she received the Academy Award for best actress for her work opposite Wallace Beery in *Min and Bill*.

In the final years of her life, Marie Dressler became once again one of America's favorite entertainers, one of the biggest box-office attractions of the early 1930s. In a radio tribute to her shortly after her death, Will Rogers described her fittingly as "a marvelous personality and a great heart."

Playright Zoë Akins wrote a fictionalized version of Marie Dressler's lifer, *O Evening Star*, which opened at New York's Empire Theatre on January 8, 1936, with Jobyna Howland as the Dressler character, here called Amy Bellaire. In the 1940s, plans were announced to film a biography of the comedienne, starring Gracie Fields, but nothing came of the project.

BIBLIOGRAPHY

Dressler, Marie. *The Life Story of an Ugly Duckling*. New York: Robert M. McBride, 1924.

———, as told to Mildred Harrington. *My Own Story*. Boston: Little, Brown, 1934.

Janis, Elsie. "Magnificent Marie." *The New Movie Magazine* 6, no. 5 (November 1932), pp. 36–37, 104–105.

Mason, Vera. "Nobody Wanted Dressler." *Shadowplay* 2, no. 5 (January 1934), pp. 28, 76.

Rimaldi, Oscar. "The Irrepressible Marie Dressler." *Hollywood Studio Magazine*, September 1986, pp. 30–32.

St. Johns, Adela Rogers. "The Private Life of Marie Dressler: Part One—The Ugly Duckling." *Liberty* 10, no. 19 (May 13, 1933), pp. 20–25.

———. "The Private Life of Marie Dressler: Part Two—The Rising Star." *Liberty* 10, no. 20 (May 20, 1933), pp. 10–15.

———. "The Private Life of Marie Dressler: Part Three—I'm Through." *Liberty* 10, no. 21 (May 27, 1933), pp. 32–37.

———. "The Private Life of Marie Dressler: Part Four—Conclusion." *Liberty* 10, no. 22 (June 3, 1933), pp. 32–38.

(JAMES TERENCE) DUFFY (1889—New York, March 30, 1939) and **(FREDERICK CHASE) SWEENEY** (1894—Los Angeles, December 10, 1954)

Unfortunately, no record of their act survives on film, but everyone agrees that Duffy and Sweeney was one of the funniest knockabout comedy acts in vaudeville. It involved a great deal of slapping about the face and backside and repartee in which the two men addressed each other as "Mr. Duffy" and "Mr. Sweeney," and which may have influenced Gallagher and Shean. The two were unpredictable onstage, in large part because of the amount of liquor they consumed between performances. At one theatre in Memphis, Duffy became so infuriated with the lack of response from the audience that he ended the act with an impromptu speech: "And now, ladies and gentlemen, my partner will go through the aisles with a baseball bat and beat the bejesus out of you."

Jimmy Duffy began his career working as a song-and-dance man with his mother and father in an act called Duffy, Sawtelle and Duffy. He later teamed with Mercedes Lorenz before joining forces with Fred Sweeney, who had been working with a traveling stock company. Were it not for his alcoholism, Duffy would have been a major success as a writer of comedy material; between bouts of alcoholism he provided material for the 1923 and 1925 editions of Earl Carroll's *Vanities* and *Keep It Clean* (1929). Jimmy Duffy was found dead, a victim of alcoholism, at the corner of Eighth Avenue and 47th Street in New York in 1939; shortly before his death he had been working as a comedy writer for NBC. Sweeney ended his career working as a "bit" actor in Hollywood.

"DUMB ACT"

"Dumb Act" is the term used to describe a nonverbal act on a vaudeville bill, such as performing animals or acrobats. Such acts had to be strictly visual because they were either the first or last on the bill, onstage while the audience was either noisily seating itself or noisily exiting the theatre.

DUNCAN SISTERS

One of the greatest sister acts on the vaudeville stage, the Duncan Sisters harmonized and laughed their way through the years, although behind the good humor were the dual problems of Rosetta Duncan's frequent bouts with alcoholism brought on, in part, by the effort of trying to hide her lesbianism. Vivian also had her problems, including an unhappy marriage to actor Nils Asther, a closet homosexual, who tried to persuade his wife to indulge him in three-way sex scenes involving a second man.

Despite it all, Vivian (Los Angeles, June 17, 1899—Los Angeles, September 19, 1986) and Rosetta (Los Angeles, November 23, 1896—Acero, Il., December 4, 1959) represented vaudeville at its most entertaining, singing straight songs such as "Remembering," "Baby's Feet Go Pitter Patter 'Cross My Heart," "I'm Following You," and "Side by Side" or comic numbers like "I Gotta a Code in By Dose," "It Must Be an Old Spanish Custom," "In Sweet Onion Time," "The Prune Song," and "The Cuspidor My Father Left to Me." They had a presence and a sense of timing, and, as *Variety* once commented, they were performers in the full sense of the word.

The daughters of a Los Angeles real estate agent, Hymie and Jake (as Rosetta and Vivian were affectionately known) took to the stage around 1916 with a yodeling act. They worked briefly for Gus Edwards, who is generally credited with having discovered them, and by May 1917, the sisters had their own act, twelve minutes long, in which they first appeared in New York at the Fifth Avenue Theatre. *Variety* (May 11, 1917) commented:

"The Duncan Sisters are two blonde girls presenting what should be termed a stereotyped sister-act. The girls possess a restricted song routine, with the possible exception of a patriotic number used as an encore. One is a pianist, accompanying her sister, who leads all the numbers, with the exception of two duets, in which the girls lack harmony. The number leader has not been sufficiently groomed to handle character songs and it would be advisable to drop the one number of this order. The Duncan Sisters are not ripe as yet for the big time."

The Duncans gradually perfected their vaudeville act, with Rosetta very much the leader of the team, providing most of the comedy, and Vivian as the pretty ingenue. They appeared in the Palace in November 1922 with an act titled " 'S That All Right!'' After a couple of stints in musical comedy, the sisters developed an idea for a show of their own. They took *Uncle Tom's Cabin*, jazzed it up a little, added a lot of comedy, and the result was *Topsy and Eva*, which opened at San Francisco's Alcazar Theatre on July 9, 1923. The book was by Catherine Chisholm Cushing, with the music and lyrics by the Duncan Sisters. Vivian appeared as the sweet, innocent, peaches-and-cream heroine, Little Eva, while Rosetta donned blackface to clown, quite brilliantly, as Topsy.

Outrageous is the only description that can be given to Rosetta's impudent Topsy, with her philosophy, "I'se mean an 'ornery, I is, mean an' ornery. I hate everybody in the world, and I only wish there were more people in the world so I could hate them too." Even Vivian, despite the sweetness of of her character, would kid around during the show. Others in the production included Basil Ruysdael (as Uncle Tom), Frank W. Wallace (as Simon Legree), and Myrtle Ferguson, whose Aunt Ophelia St. Clair was a perfect foil to Rosetta Duncan's Topsy. It would be easy to brand Rosetta's portrayal as an insult to black Americans, but as *Variety* (December 9, 1959) noted, "Memory does not suggest that there was anything invidious racially in Rosetta Duncan's Topsy, though in that more innocent long-ago before Adolph Hitler brought racial 'stereotypes' in worldwide bad odor, there was not the same quickness to take notice which prevails today."

Topsy and Eva opened in Chicago in December 1923. During its twenty-three-week run at the Selwyn Theatre, it grossed $462,387, despite distinguished critic Burns Mantle's description of the show as "a freak of the season . . . purports to be a musical comedy version of *Uncle Tom's Cabin*; and it is a terrible thing." The show opened in New York at the Sam Harris Theatre on December 23, 1924, and after it closed there, the Duncans were forever taking it on the road, particularly on the West Coast, where they remained tremendously popular. They even took *Topsy and Eva* to England, France, Germany, and South America, playing the roles in the languages of the particular countries in which they were appearing.

The Duncan Sisters filmed *Topsy and Eva* as a silent feature in 1927, but the film was not particularly successful, for one needed to hear the girls as well as see them in order totally to appreciate their talents. The sisters appeared in two other feature films, *Two Flaming Youths* (1927), in which they had a cameo, and *It's a Great Life* (1929), which introduced "I'm Following You" plus a somewhat risqué version of "Tell Me Pretty Maiden." In the late 1920s, Rosetta and Vivian were back on the vaudeville stage, singing some of the songs from *Topsy and Eva*, together with numbers such as "Sittin' on the Curbstone Blues" (wearing children's clothes). *Variety* (January 23, 1929) reported, "The Duncans are a vaudeville act, in or out of picture houses. . . . There are many who insist the Duncan Sisters could entertain with bows only."

In the summer of 1932, the Duncan Sisters announced plans for a series of short comedies to be called *Adventures of Topsy and Eva*, but nothing came of the proposal. "You cannot keep the Duncans down," reported Louella Parsons in her gossip column on June 4, 1932. "They go on and on like Tennyson's proverbial brook."

In 1942, the Duncan Sisters announced their retirement, but they returned ten years later, chiefly playing nightclubs. On December 11, 1959, while driving home from a nightclub engagement at Mangam's Chateau in Lyons, on the outskirts of Chicago, Rosetta Duncan's car struck a bridge; she died three days later. At that time, Charlotte Greenwood described her as "the greatest clown on the American stage." For a while, Vivian Duncan worked as a solo act; she made her Los Angeles debut at Billy Gray's Bandbox in December 1960, joining comedienne Alice Tyrrell to sing one of the more outrageous numbers from *Topsy and Eva*, Topsy's lament of "I Never Had a Mammy." She lived in retirement for the last twenty years of her life.

Literary scholar Edward Wagenknecht has always had a peculiar fondness for *Topsy and Eva*, and of its stars he wrote:

"The Duncan Sisters suggested a fresh wholesomeness which was not the quality most frequently encountered in the musical comedy stars of their time, but they also had a good deal of tart commentary on hypocrisy and pretension, much of which was no less effective for being implicit rather than explicit. . . . Their career was a record of splendid generosity; they always gave freely of their means and of themselves, and I am sure many theatregoers must remember them, as I do, with great affection."

BIBLIOGRAPHY

Kendall, Robert. "The Fabulous Duncan Sisters." *Hollywood Studio Magazine*, May 1976, pp. 28–29.

Spensley, Dorothy. "The Song and Patter Kids." *Photoplay*, September 1929, pp. 35, 129–30.

Stevens, Ashton. "The Duncan Sisters." In *Actorviews*. Chicago: Covici-McGee, 1923, pp. 69–74.

Wagenknecht, Edward. "Topsy and Eva." In *As Far as Yesterday*. Norman: University of Oklahoma Press, 1968, pp. 119–25.

HARRY DUNN.   See CROSS AND DUNN

JACK DURANT (New York, April 12, 1905—Miami, January 7, 1984)

Jack Durant enjoyed two vaudeville careers, first as half of an acrobatic comedy act with Frank Mitchell, later as a solo comedian. He entered vaudeville at the age of nine in a small-time acrobatic act with Bud Aarons, in which he was forced to dress as a girl. In the mid 1920s, Durant met dancer Frank Mitchell (New York, May 13, 1905—North Hollywood, Ca., January 21, 1991), and a partnership began that lasted through the late 1930s. The couple appeared at the Palace in December 1928 and were featured in the 1931 edition of Earl Carroll's *Vanities*. In 1934, the two men signed a contract with 20th Century–Fox and appeared together in a number of screen musicals; in 1935, Durant married former silent film actress Molly O'Day.

Durant and Mitchell split in 1938, with the latter continuing in films and Durant returning to the stage. The following year, he served as master of ceremonies at the Casa Mañana in New York, and in 1940, Durant was back on Broadway in *Pal Joey*. He was also in the 1963 revival of the show, as well as in *The Girl from Nantucket* (1945).

BIBLIOGRAPHY

Maltin, Leonard. "Mitchell and Durant." In *Movie Comedy Teams*. New York: New American Library, 1970, pp. 331–33.

Smith, Bill. "Jack Durant." In *The Vaudevillians*. New York: Macmillan, 1976, pp. 103–20.

JIMMY DURANTE (New York, February 10, 1893—Santa Monica, Ca., January 29, 1980)

Jimmy Durante's appeal is one involving personality rather than performance. As journalist Quentin Reynolds wrote in *Show* magazine, he was "a piano player with no great talent—a comedian whose jokes are offbeat and unfunny in the retelling—a satirist who is unconscious of what he is doing." His is a comedic style which is impossible to analyze because there is no style. "He is essentially a clown," commented *The New York Times* (March 26, 1944). "He doesn't dazzle you with jokes; he overwhelms you with the sheer power of his exuberant good nature and a tumultuous sense of the ridiculous." Equally incomprehensible is an audience's fascination with Durante's singing voice, which as Fred Allen said, "can only be described as a dull rasp calling its mate." And yet who else could present such songs as " I Can Do without Broadway, But Can Broadway Do without Me?," "Toscanini, Stokowski and Me," "Who Will You Be with When I'm Far Away?," and, of course, "Inka Dinka Doo."

Durante's craggy face, huge nose, wide grin, and exuberant personality were an essential part of show business for more than sixty years. He may have mangled the English language, but many of his sayings have become part of the vocabulary of the twentieth century: "That's my boy," "Stop the music," "I got a million of 'em," and "Goodnight Mrs. Calabash, wherever you are." A typical Durante joke relied both on his destruction of the English language and his misunderstanding of it: "An operetta? That ain't music. It's a dame that woiks for the phone company." In and of itself, the line is not particularly amusing, but as delivered by Durante, an audience had no choice but to laugh. And unlike many modern comedians who find humor in the cruelty of their jokes toward others, Jimmy Durante's biggest joke concerned the outstanding part of his own physique—his nose. He first began joking about it in 1923 at the Club Durant: "Here it is, folks! Yes, it's real! It ain't gonna bite you, and it ain't gonna fall off!"

"I got my nose from my mother, a piano from my father and I got a taste for outdoor plumbing from the jernt where we lived. The bathroom was out inna backyard.'' Thus Durante would recall his early years on New York's Lower East Side, where he was born James Francis Durante, and where he first began playing the piano at neighborhood parties. In 1916, he organized a five-piece novelty band for the Club Alamo in Harlem, and joined forces with a singing waiter named Eddie Jackson and a young girl named Jeanne Olsen. Durante formed a partnership onstage with Jackson and married Olsen.

According to Durante, shortly after their marriage, he and Olsen stayed at a rooming house in Chicago, owned by a Mrs. Calabash. She was ''a truly wonderful woman and we loved her,'' and years later, Durante began calling his wife Mrs. Calabash as an affectionate nickname. After Jeannie's death in 1943, Durante was on a television program with Gary Moore, and at the show's close, he ad-libbed, ''Goodnight, Mrs. Calabash.'' The next time he said it, he added, ''wherever you are.'' So well-known did the line become that the public would argue as to its meaning, but the secret of Mrs. Calabash's identity was not revealed until Durante spoke at a National Press Club luncheon in Washington, D.C., on March 7, 1966.

In 1923, Durante and Jackson opened a speakeasy called the Club Durant at 232 West 58th Street in New York. There they were joined by a tap dancer and comic named Lou Clayton, and thus began the team of Clayton, Jackson and Durante. It was Clayton who nicknamed Durante ''Schnozzola'' and also coined the phrase, ''If that's the way you want it, that's the way it's gonna be.'' *Variety*'s editor and publisher, Sime Silverman, blatantly promoted the club in the pages of his trade paper to such an extent that prohibition officers had no alternative but to move in and close the place down. Undaunted, the trio opened a new club, the Parody, and from there moved on into big-time vaudeville.

With Harry Donnelly's Parody Club Orchestra, Lou Clayton, Eddie Jackson, and Jimmy Durante made their vaudeville debut as a trio at Loew's State, New York, in March 1927. The act was titled ''Jest for a Laugh'' and included five songs: ''Yucatán,'' ''I'm Going to Tell a Story,'' ''The Noose,'' ''She's Just a Cow,'' and ''Jimmy, the Well-Dressed Man.'' Most of the comedy was handled by Durante, who brought down the house with his humorous direction of the onstage orchestra. Sime Silverman was in the audience on opening night and reported in Variety (March 16, 1927):

Here's a tough break, because it is necessary to say that those boys went over to a hit Monday night at the State. . . . It's tough because this was the chance awaited to send over a receipt in full for the many checks at their various sawdust joints. . . . Lou Clayton, Eddie Jackson, and Jimmy Durante are cafe entertainers, by training, instinct, nature, good nature, ability, disposition, love (of coin), and anything else you may want to add. New to vaude . . . the boys did exceptionally well in routining by the Monday night performance. They clipped down to thirty-four minutes from forty-four at the matinee.

In April 1928, the trio headlined at the Palace, breaking the theatre's box-office record and earning $3,000 a week. In a reference to the trade paper's love of debasing the English language, a critic for *Variety* (April 18, 1928) described them as ''those three cafe spirits who talk like *Variety* writes.'' Jimmy Durante loved working in vaudeville: "I like to see 'em on a Sunday night changin' da billin' on da Loew's State, changin' dat billin', takin' dose letters down and puttin' dose new letters up. You can't get nuttin' more excitin' den dat."

Clayton, Jackson, and Durante made their Broadway debut in Florenz Ziegfeld's production of *Show Girl*, with music and lyrics by George and Ira Gershwin and Gus Kahn, which opened at the Ziegfeld Theatre on July 2, 1929. Also in the cast of the show, which ran for 111 performances, were Ruby Keeler, Eddie Foy, Jr., and Harriet Hoctor. The trio's next Broadway appearance was also their last together, in *The New Yorker*, with music by Cole Porter, which opened at the Broadway Theatre on December 8, 1930. Ann Pennington and Marie Cahill were also in the cast. *The New Yorkers* was a revue-style musical comedy centered on Hope Williams, a tired and disgusted society girl from Park Avenue ("where bad women walk good dogs"), who dreamed up acts of foolishness.

In 1930, Jimmy Durante made his feature film debut in *Roadhouse Nights*, and the following year, when he decided to sign a five-year contract with M-G-M, the trio split up. There was no animosity in the breakup. Clayton said of Durante, "You can warm your hands on this man," and for many years he was his partner's manager. Lou Clayton died in Santa Monica, California, on September 12, 1950, at the age of sixty-three. Eddie Jackson continued to appear, on and off, with Durante for many, many years, usually performing "Won't You Come Home, Bill Bailey?" The two men had a tiff in October 1958 while appearing in Las Vegas, with Jackson's claiming that Durante had slighted him, but they made up in April of the following year, and Jackson was present at Durante's funeral. Eddie Jackson died in Los Angeles on July 16, 1980, at the age of eighty-four.

In the 1930s, Durante alternated film work with Broadway appearances. On the stage he was seen in *Strike Me Pink* (1933), *Policy* (1936), *Red Hot and Blue* (1937), and *Stars in Your Eyes* (1939). In 1935, he appeared as Claudius B. Bowers in *Billy Rose's Jumbo*, a role he repeated for the 1962 film version. In addition, Durante made his first English appearance, at the London Palladium, on June 1, 1936, and what might have seemed very American humor proved equally appealing to the British public. Durante found the English very polite, recalling, "One joinalist—from da London *Times*—tries to kill me wit' politeness. He asks if I minds if he mentions my nose. I'm surrounded by assassins! 'If ya don't mention it,' I says to him, 'you puts me outa business.' " Jimmy Durante was featured in more than thirty motion pictures released between 1930 and 1963, but few did justice to his talents, with film scripts proving too restrictive for his humor. Among the comedian's better known films are *The Cuban Love Song* (1931), *Blondie of the Follies* (1932), *The Phantom President* (1932), *George White's Scandals* (1934), *Hollywood Party* (1934), *Sally, Irene and Mary* (1938), *Little Miss Broadway* (1938), *You're in the Army Now* (1941), *The Man Who Came to Dinner* (1942), *It Happened in Brooklyn* (1947), *Pepe* (1960), and *It's a Mad, Mad, Mad, Mad World* (1963). While in the United Kingdom, he starred opposite tenor Richard Tauber in the 1936 film musical *Land without Music* (released in America as *Forbidden Music*).

Jimmy Durante had been starred on radio as early as 1934, but he came to prominence in that medium with *The Camel Comedy Caravan*, on which he used his theme song, "Ya Gotta Start Off Each Day with a Song." Durante was costarred with a young Gary Moore. Because of his crewcut, the latter was called "The Haircut," while for obvious reasons, Durante became known as "The Nose." The partnership split up in 1947, and Durante continued to broadcast solo on NBC through 1950, when he made his television debut in *Four Star Revue*.

In 1951, *Four Star Revue* was renamed *All Star Revue*, and Durante was one of this popular NBC Saturday night show's four alternating stars through 1953. From 1953 to 1954, Durante was a regular host on NBC's *The Colgate Comedy Hour*. Eddie Jackson and Jimmy Durante were reunited on *The Jimmy Durante Show*, seen on NBC from 1954 to 1956 and repeated in 1957 on CBS. The show was set at the Club Durant and is perhaps best remembered for Durante's duets with Margaret Truman. Durante's last television series was *Jimmy Durante Presents the Lennon Sisters*, seen on ABC from 1969 to 1970, in which the comedian costarred with the singing group made popular by Lawrence Welk.

"As long as they laugh, as long as they want me to sing, I'll stay" was Durante's motto, but in 1972, a stroke put an end to his performing career. Younger generations may have difficulty in understanding his popularity, but for those old enough to have seen him on stage or television, it is as Gene Fowler wrote, "The great clown stays on with us, as great clowns always stay on in the hearts of men and women and children who seek in the refuge of merriment an hour of escape from the scowls of the day."

BIBLIOGRAPHY

Adler, Irene. *I Remember Jimmy: The Life and Times of Jimmy Durante*. Westport, Ct.: Arlington House, 1980.

"America's Greatest Nose. . . . " *Life* 1, no. 5 (December 21, 1936), p. 7. [Durante was the first vaudevillian to be featured in *Life* magazine.]

Beranger, Clara. "The Private Life of Jimmy Durante." *Liberty* 11., n. 51 (December 22, 1934), pp. 15–17.

Berg, Louis. "Gentleman Jimmy." *Los Angeles Times: This Week Magazine*, January 28, 1951, pp. 14–15.

Cahn, William. *Good Night, Mrs. Calabash: The Secret of Jimmy Durante*. New York: Duell, Sloan and Pearce, 1963.

Durante, Jimmy, and Jack Kofoed. *Night Clubs*. New York: Alfred A. Knopf, 1931.

—————. Introduction to *Without Rhyme or Reason* by L. Wolfe Gilbert. New York: Vantage Press, 1956.

Fowler, Gene. *Schnozzola: The Story of Jimmy Durante*. New York: Viking Press, 1951.

"Jimmy Durante." *Current Biography*, September 1946, pp. 166–168.

Kennedy, John B. "Tough Dollar." *Collier's* 92, no. 4 (July 22, 1933), pp. 19, 39–40.

Mangel, Charles. "Pinocchio Lives!" *Look*, March 4, 1969, pp. 93–98.

McCarthy, Joe. "Jimmy the Well-Dressed Man." *Holiday*, January 1962, pp. 113–14, 116, 118–19.

Perelman, S. J. "Jimmy Durante." *Life* 100, no. 2577 (April 1933), pp. 21–23.

Reynolds, Quentin. "The Indestructible Enigma." *Show* 2, no. 2 (February 1962), pp. 60–63.

Robbins, Jhan. *Inka Dinka Doo: The Life of Jimmy Durante*. New York: Paragon House, 1991.

Seldes, Gilbert. "Jimmie [sic] Is Exhubilant." *The New Republic*, January 16, 1929, pp. 247–48.

Zolotow, Maurice. "The Great Schnozzola." *Saturday Evening Post*, July 15, 1950, pp. 22–23, 122–28.

E

BUDDY EBSEN (Belleville, Il., April 2, 1908–   )

Christian (Buddy) Ebsen began his dancing career as a chorus boy in *Whoopee!* in 1928, and the following year understudied Will Philbrick in the road company of the show. When *Whoopee!* closed, Ebsen brought his sister, Vilma, to New York and formed a dance partnership with her. He appeared at the Palace Theatre in September 1930 and with his sister in *Flying Colors* (1932) and the 1934 edition of the *Ziegfeld Follies*.

In 1935, Ebsen was offered a contract by M-G-M and made his screen debut in *Broadway Melody of 1936* (1935). Following supporting roles in a number of film musicals, including *Captain January* (1936) and *Broadway Melody of 1938* (1937), Ebsen returned to Broadway in 1939 to appear in *Yokel Boy*. He also appeared in the 1946 Broadway revival of *Show Boat*. Ebsen's screen appearances in the 1940s through the 1960s were limited to a couple per decade, usually in supporting, nonmusical roles. The actor gained new popularity on television with his roles as Jed Clampett in *The Beverly Hillbillies* (CBS, 1962–1971) and as the title character in *Barnaby Jones* (CBS, 1973–1980).

BIBLIOGRAPHY

Barber, Rowland. "The Family That Hoofs Together." *TV Guide*, August 9, 1975, pp. 9–11.

"Buddy and Vilma Ebsen." *Vanity Fair*, August 1990, p. 94.

Ebsen, Buddy, with George A. Gunston. *Polynesian Concept*. Englewood Cliffs, N.J.: Prentice-Hall, 1972.

Essoe, Gabe. "The Star Who Became a Puppet Who Became a Star." *TV Guide*, October 11, 1969, pp. 40–42, 44, 46–47.

Hopper, Hedda. "Davy Crockett's Pal." Syndicated column, October 2, 1955.

Lewis, Richard Warren. "The Golden Hillbillies." *The Saturday Evening Post*, February 2, 1963, pp. 30, 32–34.

O'Hallaren, Bill. "Even Buddy Ebsen Can't Solve This Mystery." *TV Guide*, May 6, 1978, pp. 16–20.

Whitney, Dwight. "Too Rich to Work?" *TV Guide*, August 25, 1973, pp. 21–26.

EDEN MUSÉE

The Eden Musée, located on 23rd Street in New York, between Fifth and Sixth Avenues, was opened in 1883 by the Eden Musée American Co. as a waxworks exhibit, which also included a Winter Garden wherein visitors might listen to concerts by the Eden Musée Orchestra. As explained in contemporary literature, "The founders of the Eden Musée had a higher object in view than that alone of establishing a profitable commercial enterprise. It was their intention to open a Temple of Art without a rival in this country, affording to all an opportunity for instruction, amusement and recreation, without risk of coming into contact with anything or anybody that was vulgar or offensive. . . . The Eden Musée is an immense step toward a realistic representation of nature and life."

With the passing of time, other amusements, including vaudeville acts, were added to the delights of the Eden Musée. In 1894, for six months, two kinetoscopes were installed, enabling visitors to view moving pictures through a peephole device. The French Lumière films were first presented in the United States at the Eden Musée in 1896. In November 1897, Richard B. Hollaman, who had succeeded the company first president Theodore Hellman in 1895, formed a company to produce a film of *The Passion Play*, at a reported cost of $16,000, which was exhibited for six months at the Eden Musée. The Eden Musée closed its doors in the summer of 1915.

CLIFF EDWARDS (Hannibal, Mo., June 14, 1895—Hollywood, Ca., July 17, 1971)

Cliff Edwards was a prominent singer and recording star who accompanied himself on the ukelele and gained the nickname "Ukelele Ike." In 1940, he was the off-screen voice for Jiminy Cricket in Walt Disney's *Pinocchio*, and the number he sang in that film, "When You Wish upon a Star," became his theme song. When the television series *Disneyland* began on ABC in 1954, it was Edwards's recording of the song that was used to introduce the program.

Edwards first began playing the ukelele while a newspaper boy in St. Louis and New York, using the instrument to increase his sales. In the late teens, he teamed with songwriter Bob Carleton, and the two introduced the song "Ja Da" to vaudeville audiences. In 1920, Edwards teamed with singer/dancer Pierce Keegan in an act titled "Jazz as Is." Edwards headlined at the Palace as a single act in April 1924 and August 1932, and appeared on Broadway in *The Mimic World of 1921* (1922), *Lady Be Good* (1924), *Sunny* (1925), and the 1935 edition of George White's *Scandals*. In the 1920s, he developed as a recording artist, began making records in 1922, and had his biggest hit with "June Night."

In 1928, Edwards played the Orpheum in Los Angeles and was signed to a film contract by M-G-M's Irving Thalberg. He made his feature film debut in

The Hollywood Revue of 1929, introducing the song "Singin' in the Rain." The entertainer appeared in more than eighty films, including a considerable number of Westerns in the late 1930s and early 1940s. His first radio series, *Cliff Edwards, Ukelele Ike*, was heard on NBC in 1932, and he was also the star of two early television programs, *The Cliff Edwards Show* and *The 54th Street Revue*, both aired on CBS in 1949.

Despite a worldwide reputation—he first played London night spots in 1925 and toured Australia as late as 1951—and a considerable income from recordings—he claimed to have sold a total of seventy-four million records—Cliff Edwards was always in financial trouble. He filed for bankruptcy at least three times: in March 1933, March 1941, and June 1949. The man whom *Daily Variety* (July 21, 1971) described as "small of stature but mighty of melodic accomplishments" died alone and penniless. After his death, it was revealed that Walt Disney Productions had been making payments to the Actors Fund for his support.

BIBLIOGRAPHY

Parish, James Robert, and Michael R. Pitts. "Cliff Edwards." In *Hollywood Songsters: A Biographical Dictionary*. New York: Garland, 1991, pp. 239–44.

GUS EDWARDS (Hohensalza, Germany, August 18, 1879—Los Angeles, November 7, 1945)

To describe Gus Edwards as a vaudevillian is a misnomer, for his career on the vaudeville stage is relatively unimportant compared to his careers as a composer, a producer of vaudeville and nightclub acts, and a discoverer of new talent. He was called "The Star Maker"—the title of a 1939 Paramount film biography in which he was portrayed by Bing Crosby—in that he was responsible for the careers of Eddie Cantor, the Duncan Sisters, George Jessel, Eleanor Powell, Walter Winchell, Ray Bolger, Larry Adler, Hildegarde, Ona Munson, Lila Lee, and many others.

While Gus Edwards started these people on a show business career, it should not be assumed that he was always the major force in their lives onstage. For example, Eleanor Powell recalled that in 1925, when she was in Atlantic City with her parents:

I was on the beach and I was eleven years old. And the person who ended up being a baby sitter for me on the beach was Johnny Weissmuller. One day I was doing these cartwheels and splits—just a kid you know—and this man walks over. Now remember, I don't know the name Gus Edwards; I don't know the name Al Jolson; I've never been to a show. He says, "You're pretty good," and he says he's Gus Edwards. Now Johnny knew who he was. He said, "I'd like to speak to your mother. I'd like you to come up and work at the Ritz Grill." So I tease my mother that night, "Please . . . " And I did an acrobatic dance to "The Japanese Sandman." The big stars of the show were Lola and Leota Lane. Well, I made seven dollars a night, three nights a week. I came back the next summer when I was twelve. Then, in the winter I went back to Springfield, Massachusetts, and dancing school. When we finally saved a little money, my mother and I went back to New York, and Ben Bernie put me to work in his club.

In New York, Powell took it upon herself to seek representation by the William Morris Agency and to get into a show at the Capitol Theatre. As she noted, Gus Edwards was not her mentor. He saw her and put her into her first show, but that, basically, was it.

As a child, Gus Edwards came to the United States from his native Germany. With his fine soprano voice, he attracted the attention of Tony Pastor, who had the notion of having the fourteen-year-old Edwards sing from one of the balcony boxes of his 14th Street Theatre. Before he was twenty, Gus Edwards had become a songwriter and established his own publishing company. He wrote one of the hit songs from the Spanish-American War, "Goodbye Little Girl, Goodbye," and among his other compositions are "Meet Me under the Wisteria," "By the Light of the Silvery Moon," "I Can't Tell Why I Love You but I Do," "I Just Can't Make My Eyes Behave," "In My Merry Oldsmobile," "Jimmy Valentine," "If a Girl Like You Loved a Boy Like Me," "I'll Be with You When the Roses Bloom Again," "Sunbonnet Sue," "If I Was a Millionaire," and "He's My Pal." Edwards's most famous song was "Schooldays," which became his theme song and which he used in the various kiddie shows that he produced for vaudeville.

These kiddie acts, the earliest of which appears to be "The Newsboy Quintet" (dating back to the 1890s and including Edwards himself), really became popular in 1905. They had titles such as "Kid Kabaret," "The Nine Country Kids," "School Boys and School Girls," and "Juvenile Frolic," and featured children such as Herman Timberg, Walter Winchell, Georgie Price, Eddie Cantor, and Lila Lee, who was later to become a silent screen star but was then known as "Cuddles." George Price recalled for *Variety* that the kids called Edwards "Woof," because his favorite trick was to stick his head through the door and growl like a dog to frighten the children. "We lived like the royal family," reminisced Price. "Cuddles and I had a governess. We had our schooling on the road. One of the chorus boys would get extra money for teaching us. One of our teachers was Arthur Freed, now the Metro producer." Another who had fond memories of Edwards was Eddie Cantor, who wrote, "I sat on his knee, and he taught me how to sing."

Typical of Edwards's productions was his "Song Revue," a fifty-minute vaudeville act which played the Palace in October 1914. There were four principals, Gus Edwards, George Jessel, Lilyan Tashman (later a leading lady in films), and Sallie Seeley, plus a chorus of boys and girls, who provided nonstop songs such as "You Gotta Stop Pickin' on My Little Pickanniny," "The Bohemian Rag," "Shadowland," "Just around the Corner from Broadway," and "I Love You, California." In addition, George Jessel gave impersonations of Bert Williams, Eddie Foy, and Raymond Hitchcock. *Variety* (October 3, 1914) noted, "Jessel has apparently a fund of undeveloped talent. . . . He should be instructed to cover up his self-consciousness." *Variety* also singled out a member of the chorus, Lila Lee, whom it noted was billed merely as "Cutey Cuddles," and ended its review by stating, "Edwards has given every detail especial attention and may be credited with one of vaudeville's biggest productions."

Edwards came to Hollywood in 1929. He wrote a number of songs for M-G-M's *the Hollywood Revue of 1929*, including "Your Mother and Mine" and "Lon Chaney Will Get You If You Don't Watch Out," and also contributed material to M-G-M's *Chasing Rainbows* (1930). As a result of his experiences in the film capital, he returned to vaudeville in 1930 with an act titled "Gus Edwards and His Hollywood Protégés." Forty-five minutes in length, it was seen by the audience at the Palace in April 1930. The leading protégé was one Armida, a Mexican singer and dancer who had appeared in a number of early talkies. The remainder of the program is reminiscent of a Major Bowes Amateur Hour, with tap dancers, a violinist, and a boy who gave an impersonation of Ted Lewis. Sime Silverman reported in *Variety* (April 16, 1930) that Edwards was paid $4,250, and that his return to vaudeville was not worth the effort he had put into its preparation.

Sometimes Gus Edwards would work as a solo act in vaudeville. In May 1909, he was at Hammerstein's, New York, singing some of his own compositions, including "My Old Lady," "My Cousin Caruso" and "Up in My Aeroplane." "Quite apart from the fact that his own compositions have made him a widely familiar name, he is a decidedly skillful entertainer," reported *Variety* (May 22, 1909). Just prior to the First World War, Edwards produced what was remembered as one of New York's best cabaret entertainments at Reisenweber's. Additionally, he wrote the scores for many Broadway stage successes, including *When We Were Forty-One* (1905, which featured Elsie Janis, whom he had managed), *Hip! Hip! Hooray!* (1907), *School Days* (1908), *The Merry-Go-Round* (1908), and the 1910 edition of the Ziegfeld *Follies*.

Extant papers indicate how Edwards would finance his productions. In September 1920, he announced plans for *The Gus Edwards Review* of 1920, which was to cost $100,000. It was to feature Eddie Cantor, Lila Lee, Rosa Ponselle (who had already left vaudeville), George Jessel, the Duncan Sisters, and Herman Timberg. Investors were asked to each contribute $500. Edwards announced a weekly expense of $8,000 with the company receiving 65 percent of the gross in New York and 75 percent elsewhere. Investors would share in the estimated profits of $5,000 a week.

In the mid 1930s, Edwards produced an amateur talent show on radio from Los Angeles station KFWB. For the last eight years of his life, he was an invalid cared for by his wife, Lillian, whom he had married on November 28, 1905.

BIBLIOGRAPHY

Cantor, Eddie. "Gus Edwards." In *As I Remember Them*. New York: Duell, Sloan and Pearce, 1963, pp. 11–15.

Edwards, Lillian. "My Husband, Gus Edwards." *American Weekly*, December 5, 1948, p. 16.

Price, Georgie. "Geo. Price Recalls His School Days of Show Biz with Gus Edwards." *Variety*, November 14, 1945, p. 48.

Woolf, S. J. "Gus Edward's Academy." *The New York Times Magazine*, March 23, 1941, pp. 12, 19.

KATE ELINORE (?—Indianapolis, December 30, 1924)

A singing comedienne, Kate Elinore was featured in the original 1910 production of the Victor Herbert comic opera *Naughty Marietta* in the role of Lizette. She began her career in vaudeville in the mid 1890s in a comic act with her sister May. In 1909, she teamed with Sam Williams, whom she married, and they made their vaudeville debut together at the American Music Hall, New York, in September 1909. Sam Williams (1884–1961) had worked in vaudeville as a pianist since 1904; he wrote songs for his wife and also composed such patriotic First World War numbers as "Just Like Washington Crossed the Delaware, Pershing Will Cross the Rhine" and "When I Fought for the U.S.A." Following his wife's death, he became a stockbroker. Kate Elinore played the Palace in January 1924, and later that same year, she was the headliner at the Orpheum in Los Angeles. While there, she contracted a mysterious illness and died a short time later.

JULIAN ELTINGE (Newtonville, Ma., May 14, 1883—New York, March 7, 1941)

The most famous female impersonator of his day, Julian Eltinge's beauty caused him to be dubbed "Mr. Lillian Russell." According to W. C. Fields, "Women went into ecstacies over him. Men went into the smoking room." Eltinge always handled his act with exquisite good taste, no hint of scandal ever attached itself to the name of this perennial bachelor, and he was well liked by all within the vaudeville fraternity; "Julian Eltinge is as great in his work as the late Richard Mansfield was in his," commented George M. Cohan in 1909.

Julian Eltinge first donned feminine attire at the age of ten, when he appeared in the annual revue of the Boston Cadets, and, apparently, he was so successful in the female role that the following year, the revue was written around him. Word of his success reached the ears of a number of theatrical managers, and soon Eltinge was appearing in a number of minor productions around the country. His first major success came in 1904, when he appeared in *Mr. Wix of Wickham*, a musical comedy with music by Jerome Kern and others.

Eltinge was already making vaudeville appearances, and as early as May 14, 1906, he made his London debut at the Palace Theatre. His New York vaudeville debut came in September 1907, when he appeared at the Alhambra Theatre in an act that included "The Sampson Girl," a skit on the Gibson Girl vogue, and "Willie Green," in which he appeared in kid's clothes. He was billed simply as Eltinge in order to give his act an air of mystery, and *Variety* (September 21, 1907) reported, "The audience was completely deceived as to Eltinge's sex until he removed his wig after the second song. Eltinge will be liked. He is artistic in everything he does, and his act is far and away above what is described as female impersonation.'' His vaudeville success can be attributed in large part to the glamorous costumes he used, which apparently won over completely the female members of the audience, and to a creditable singing voice, far superior to that possessed by other female impersonators of the period.

In a 1909 interview, Eltinge explained that he spent two hours transforming himself into a woman with the help of his male Japanese dresser, Shima. Almost an hour would be devoted to his makeup, and Eltinge noted, ''It depends on where you put the paint, not how much you splash on.''

Aside from solo vaudeville appearances, between 1908 and 1909, Eltinge toured with the Cohan and Harris Minstrels. On September 11, 1911, *The Fascinating Widow* opened at New York's Liberty Theatre. As in later plays and films, Eltinge was featured in a dual role, that of Mrs. Monte and Hal Blake, and although the play had only a short run in New York, Eltinge was able to tour with it for the next couple of years. (Interestingly, also in the cast was June Mathis, who was to become a well-known silent screenwriter, and who is generally credited with having discovered Rudolph Valentino for *The Four Horsemen of the Apocalypse*. Before he became a star, Valentino worked with Eltinge in a 1920 film titled *The Adventurers*, which was reedited and reissued in 1922 as *The Isle of Love*.) Two other farces that had short runs in New York, but in which Eltinge toured successfully, were *The Crinoline Girl*, which opened at the Knickerbocker Theatre on March 16, 1914, and *Cousin Lucy* (with music by Jerome Kern), which opened at the Cohan Theatre on August 27, 1915.

After a small cameo role in the 1915 film *How Molly Malone Made Good*, Julian Eltinge embarked on a short but profitable screen career in 1917 with *The Countess Charming*, in which he again played a dual role, and in a stage version of it in which he later toured. Reviewing the film in the December 1917 issue of *Photoplay*, Randolph Bartlett noticed that Eltinge was beginning to show his age and to have weight problems:

Enter Julian Eltinge, female impersonator, as they miscall him in vodeveel. . . . There is nothing female about Eltinge, and in these days he is now barely able to appear the grande dame, whereas not many years ago he could do you an ingenue that you would find yourself making eyes at. But his picture, *The Countess Charming*, is great fun. The story is not especially important, the entertainment consisting in the swift transitions from masculine to feminine and back again. Here Eltinge has an opportunity that the stage denied him, and it is too bad that he failed to realize it until he had lost his beauty. The film gives an instantaneous change of costume in a flash-back; a similar change in a stage performance would occupy so much time that the value of the juxtaposition would be lost.

Aside from the aforementioned *The Adventurers*, Eltinge appeared in *The Clever Mrs. Carfax* (1917) and *The Widow's Might* (1918). In 1925, he returned to the screen to star in *Madame Behave*, which also featured Ann Pennington. While appearing in films, Eltinge also found time to write, cast, and produce vaudeville sketches for his Julian Eltinge Players. He, himself, returned to vaudeville in 1918 after an absence of several years in January 1918, with an eighteen-minute act at the Palace, involving four songs and four costume changes, from widow's weeds to a bathing suit. A year later, he starred in a new vaudeville show, produced by William Morris, which opened at the Mason Theatre, Los Angeles. Eltinge had lost twenty pounds through a strenuous course of exercise and dieting and appeared in many different costumes designed by Cora Mc-Geachy, while the scenery was designed by Erté. Frederick James Smith in *The New York Dramatic Mirror* (January 11, 1919) reported:

Cleverly removing the stigma of "female impersonations," Eltinge's impersonations are always a subtle and good-humored satire on feminine mannerisms and foibles. In his new show, he has several numbers which are really brilliant and penetrating satire, especially the vampire number, in which he satires the screen vampires. . . . There is a one-act play, a little farce written by Eltinge and June Mathis, which is a gem of fun, in which Eltinge plays the star part. Motion pictures and spoken lines are artistically combined in this. He presents also a bride number and a bathing girl who wears six different costumes.

Supporting Eltinge were Dainty Marie in her aerial act, the Dancing Lavars, and the Arnaut Brothers, who were billed as musical clowns.

Eltinge continued to tour in vaudeville through the mid 1920s. In February 1921, while appearing at the Majestic Theatre, Chicago, he confided to the audience that his corsets were hurting him, a problem with which many women in the theatre sympathized. When he returned to the Palace in April 1923, *Variety* (April 19, 1923) found him "as welcome as the flowers in May." He was back again at the Palace in November 1927. A year later, Eltinge was advertising himself as "an institution in the American theatre. Foremost impersonator of the fair sex."

The performer had the ultimate honor of having a New York theatre named after him. Al H. Woods, who had produced *The Fascinating Widow*, told Eltinge, "Sweetheart, you're a big money maker for me, and I'm going to name my theatre for you." A year to the day from the opening of *The Fascinating Widow*, on September 11, 1912, the Eltinge Theatre opened on 42nd Street with *Within the Law*. It was later renamed the Empire and became a movie theatre.

Julian Eltinge went to extraordinary lengths to stress his masculinity; there were endless stories of his beating up stagehands, members of the audience, and fellow vaudevillians who made suggestive remarks with regard to his sexual preference. Certainly, there was never a public hint that he was homosexual, and if he had a lover, male or female, there is no record of that person's existence. He never married and for the last years of his life lived with his mother on his ranch in Southern California. The fixation with proving his masculinity does, of course, suggest the need to cover up something in that area. Both Jesse Block and Milton Berle were of the opinion that Eltinge was homosexual, but this was vehemently denied by actress Ruth Gordin, who, in a *New York Times* article, described Eltinge as "as virile as anybody virile."

In the 1930s, Julian Eltinge toured with his own company, and in July 1932, he opened in *The Nine O'Clock Revue* at the Music Box Theatre in Hollywood. That same year, he starred in a grade B talkie, *Maid to Order*, directed by Elmer Clifton. Also in Los Angeles, Eltinge appeared at a sleazy nightclub, the White Horse, on Cahuenga Boulevard, but a Los Angeles ordinance, created to crack down on homosexual hangouts, prohibited men from wearing female attire in public. Thus, in January 1940, Eltinge appeared at the White Horse with his costumes on display on a clothes rack and had to stand by each to give the appropriate impersonation. Herb Sterne, the theatre and film critic for *Rob Wagner's Script*, was at the opening night and remembered it as a pathetic affair with barely a dozen people in the audience. Eltinge closed after a few nights.

He was not seen on the New York stage from 1927 until 1940, when he appeared, along with Blanche Ring, Eddie Leonard, and Pat Rooney in Billy Rose's *Diamond Horshoe Jubilee*. Also in 1940, Eltinge appeared in the Universal feature film *If I Had My Way*.

BIBLIOGRAPHY

Eltinge, Julian. "How I Portray a Woman on the Stage." *Theatre*, August 1913, pp. 56, 58.

"Eltinge Says He Didn't." *Variety*, January 6, 1906, p. 12.

"Julian Eltinge—A Dressing Room Marvel." *Variety*, December 11, 1909, pp. 28, 153.

Slide, Anthony. *Great Pretenders: A History of Female and Male Impersonation in the Performing Arts*. Lombard, Il.: Wallace-Homestead, 1986.

"Troubles of a Man Who Wears Skirts." *Green Book Magazine*, May 1915, pp. 813–17.

KNUTE ERICKSON (Ogden, Ut., May 27, 1872—Los Angeles, December 31, 1945)

A minor-league version of Swedish comedian El Brendel, Knute Erickson was born Carl Erickson and unlike Brendel was the son of Swedish immigrants. In the early 1900s, he developed a vaudeville act featuring the character of "Daffy Dan," which he introduced to the screen in 1915 in a series of two-reel comedies. Erickson continued in films, almost always in supporting roles, through 1933, while also working in vaudeville at least through the 1920s.

BERT ERROL (Birmingham, England, August 11, 1883—Brighton, England, November 28, 1949)

The most successful female impersonator in British music hall, Bert Errol was a familiar figure in American vaudeville from 1910 to 1921. Errol worked in concert parties and British minstrel shows before making his first London solo appearance in 1909, billed as "The Famous Male Soprano and Double-Voiced Vocalist." He first came to the United States in June 1910 and created something of a sensation when it was revealed he had paid $1,000 customs duty on his gowns, many of which he had purchased from the estate of the marquis of Anglesey. (Despite a military moustache, the marquis was very fond of dressing up as a woman and entertaining his guests in theatrical presentations.) Due to some confusion, the impersonator was billed as "Erroll Burt," but he generated considerable publicity and was featured on the front cover of the May 28, 1910, issue of *The New York Dramatic Mirror*.

Bert Errol returned to America in the fall of 1913. The high spot of his performance at New York's Alhambra Theatre was a rendition of "My Hero" in falsetto. "Mark" in *Variety* (November 14, 1913) commented:

Errol sings better than any of the female impersonators yet seen in New York and depends much on his voice to carry him along. He could have helped out with his deception by using a different stage monicker. Replying to an encore he doffed his wig and made a speech that brought forth a boo and bah and he should guard certain words hereafter if he makes any more remarks. Female impersonators as a rule have the audience against them and certain mannerisms or speeches can do a lot of harm. Errol may not have the class or showmanship of Eltinge but he works along a different line and you have to give him credit. He arrives late with the glory about worn threadbare, but he will get his share.

Bert Errol was back again exactly a year later, touring the Orpheum and Keith circuits for some seven months. He returned frequently to vaudeville through 1921. For fear of any suspicion of homosexuality, Errol would always have his wife, Ray Hartley, appear with him at the end of the act. In later years, he appeared as a pantomime dame in his native England and became known for his parodies of musical comedy stars.

LEON ERROL (Sydney, Australia, July 3, 1881—Hollywood, Ca., October 12, 1951)

With his acrobatic clowning, his "rubber legs," and his depiction of a comic drunk, Leon Errol was well-known in revue and in motion pictures, but he also contributed much to the vaudeville scene. He did not rely too heavily on spoken gags; his approach was purely physical. If he was in bed and needed covers, Errol would not simply add them to the bed. He would spread the covers on the floor with the pillow at the head, roll himself in the material, and then make a dive for the bed. His "rubber legs" were so called because of the way he walked. *Vanity Fair* (June 1925) called them "comic and talented underpinnings." As *Esquire* commented in 1947, "It was a walk that was half punch drunk, half plain drunk; it was a stagger, a wobble, it was both legs seeming to give way at the same time but never quite buckling completely." In his day, the Leon Errol walk was as famous as the shuffling step of Charlie Chaplin's tramp character.

A native Australian, Leon Errol originally planned to be a surgeon, until college dramatics lured him away from that field. From the age of twenty through thirty, he toured Australia, New Zealand, and England, appearing in vaudeville, stock companies, and musical comedy. Errol came to New York in 1911, at which time he met Florenz Ziegfeld and was signed to appear in that year's edition of the *Follies*, which opened on June 26. (Many sources claim that Errol was in the 1910 edition of the *Follies*, which is simply not true, although certainly he had appeared on the American stage prior to 1911.) In the 1911 *Follies*, Leon Errol was featured in a sketch with Bert Williams and also performed a dancing skit of Hazel Dawn's *The Pink Lady* with his wife, Stella Chatelaine. (Errol and Chatelaine were married on August 10, 1907, and appeared frequently together onstage; she died on November 7, 1946.) Of the comedian's *Follies* debut, *Variety* (July 1, 1911) wrote, "Errol had plenty to attend to during the evening. Allowing for . . . nervousness, he did it all with credit." Leon Errol was a regular feature at the *Follies* through 1915, and also helped stage the 1914 and 1915 editions.

The comedian's U.S. vaudeville debut came at New York's Brighton Theatre in July 1916, with an eighteen-minute act in which he played a drunk at a railway station, adapted from a sketch that he and Bert Williams had performed in the 1915 *Follies*. Assisting Errol were May Hennessy as a newsgirl, Frank Mc-Dermott as a ticket collector, Alf P. James as a detective, Walter Felton as the ticket seller, and Harry McBride as the porter (created by Williams). Sime Silverman, writing in *Variety* (July 21, 1916), was somewhat critical:

If an audience can believe Mr. Errol's "souse" is funny for sixteen minutes, then they will like him in this skit. . . . While the Errol turn has nothing sensationally funny, this comedian carries it over as a summer attraction, but does so mostly through his reputation gained as a member of the *Follies*. In actualities there is too much of the same thing; Errol does not do enough dancing, and the turn has a very poor finish at present.

Following his years with the *Follies*, Leon Errol was featured in *The Century Girl* (1916), *Hitchy-Koo* (1917), and its sequel, *Hitchy-Koo 1918*. On March 25, 1919, *Joy Bells* opened at the London Hippodrome, starring Errol and George Robey, a popular British comedian-singer. A rivalry broke out between the two which, of course, did nothing to hurt the show at the box office. Having recently been named a Commander of the British Empire by King George V, George Robey would sign for his salary each week, adding the initials "C.B.E." to his name. Not to be outdone, Errol added to his own name "C.E.W.," meaning "Collect Every Week." As evidence of Errol's popularity in vaudeville, prior to his leaving for England, he headlined at both the Palace and Riverside theatres in January 1919. He would close the first half of the bill at the Palace, then take a taxi to the Riverside for the second-to-closing position. On his return from England, Errol toured in a vaudeville sketch titled "The Guest" with Jed Prouty.

In the 1920s, Leon Errol was seen on the Broadway stage in *Sally* (1920), *Louie the 14th* (1925), *Yours Truly* (1927), and *Fioretta* (1929). He became an American citizen in 1923. In 1927, he contributed a vaudeville sketch titled "Partners" to fellow performer William Gaxton. From 1924 onward, Errol was primarily to be seen on-screen. He appeared in literally dozens of productions, including *Yolanda* (1924), *Paramount on Parade* (1930), *Her Majesty Love* (1931), *Alice in Wonderland* (1933), *We're Not Dressing* (1934), *Make a Wish* (1937), *Six Lessons from Madame La Zonga* (1941), *Higher and Higher* (1943),

Joe Palooka (1946), and *Footlight Varieties* (1951). In films, he was best known for the "Mexican Spitfire" series of features he made with Lupe Velez in the late 1930s and early 1940s.

BIBLIOGRAPHY

Maltin, Leonard. "Leon Errol." *Film Fan Monthly*, no. 109/110 (July/August 1970), pp. 3–19, 26–31.
"The Man with the Rubber Legs." *Esquire*, September 1947, p. 54.
Mullett, Mary B. "Leon Errol Tells What It Is to Be a Comic Actor." *American Magazine*, January 1922, p. 18.
Smith, Frederick J. "Broadway Favorites." *The New York Dramatic Mirror*, July 16, 1913, p. 9.

"ETHIOPIAN"

Blackface acts on both the minstrel stage and in vaudeville were often described as "Ethiopian" entertainers. The term was not initially used to describe a Negro performer until the early twentieth century, when it was generally utilized as a euphemism for black American. For example, W. C. Fields would make reference to "an Ethiopian in the woodpile."

RUTH ETTING (David City, Nebr., November 23, 1896—Colorado Springs, Co., September 24, 1978)

In the early 1930s, Ruth Etting was one of America's most popular singers, a torch singer par excellence, a happy singer of sad songs, with an emotional style that hid a somewhat limited range. She became known as the "Sweetheart of Song," and her popularity as a Columbia recording artist and radio singer was unsurpassed. Etting was also a prominent vaudeville performer, first in Chicago, later in New York.

Ruth Etting had originally intended to be a costume designer and took courses at the Chicago Art Institute in 1918. The date of her Chicago debut as an entertainer is unclear, but it was certainly a number of years prior to her 1925 appearance in a revue at the Marigold Garden Theatre, which the singer claimed as her first. In 1922, Etting had married Martin Snyder, a gangster commonly referred to as Moe the Gimp, who was to manage her career. She divorced Snyder in 1937 and married her pianist, Myrl Alderman, who was the victim of a shooting incident involving the former husband. The tempestuous Etting-Snyder-Alderman relationship was the chief subject of a very poor 1954 film biography, *Love Me or Leave Me*, which features Doris Day as Etting and James Cagney as Snyder.

Ruth Etting became a popular singer in Chicago nightclubs and vaudeville houses in the mid 1920s. *Variety* (March 10, 1926) reviewed her act at the Chicago Palace and noted, "Here is a single, schooled and developed in the cabarets of Chicago, that big-time vaudeville should not miss." In little over a year, Etting was making her New York vaudeville debut at the Paramount Theatre, backed by Paul Whiteman and His Orchestra. Sime Silverman reviewed her act in *Variety* (June 15, 1927) and commented, "Miss Etting's quiet delivery leaves a likeable impression right away. She more croons than throws her songs over, and her ballad, 'I See You Sally' clinched her. 'She did Moonbeams' nicely, and for 'Sam, the Accordion Man' for the encore was furnished an effect of an accordian player, also under the spot to the side.''

On August 16, 1927, the twenty-first edition of the Ziegfeld *Follies* opened at the New Amsterdam Theatre, and one of its stars was Ruth Etting, now billed as "The Sweetheart of Columbia Records." She sang "Shaking the Blues Away." Etting was to star in the next, and last, *Follies* presented by Flo Ziegfeld in 1931, singing "Shine on Harvest Moon" and "Cigars, Cigarettes." "I'd go out in front of the curtain dressed in one of those luscious creations that Ziegfeld always had for his girls," she recalled. "I was no actress, and I knew it. But I could sell a song." Etting also appeared with Eddie Cantor and Ethel Shutta in *Whoopee!*, which opened at the New Amsterdam Theatre on December 4, 1928, and with Ed Wynn in *Simple Simon*, which opened at the Ziegfeld Theatre in February 1930. In the last she introduced perhaps her most famous song, "Ten Cents a Dance," while from *Whoopee!* came "Love Me or Leave Me." Other famous songs associated with Ruth Etting include "It All Depends on You," "Mean to Me," and "Everybody Loves My Baby."

In the early 1930s, Ruth Etting was featured on a number of radio programs. She also appeared in three feature films, *Roman Scandals* (1933), *Hips, Hips, Hooray* (1934), and *Gift of Gab* (1934), plus more than thirty short subjects for Paramount and Warner Bros. between 1928 and 1936. She announced her retirement in 1936, claiming "there wasn't much satisfaction in singing into a microphone, that the stage lost its glamour when Ziegfeld died, and she didn't think much of the pictures." Ruth Etting did, however, make a reasonably successful comeback on radio and in nightclubs in the 1940s.

BIBLIOGRAPHY

Eells, George. "Ruth Etting." *Films in Review* 27, no. 9 (November 1976), pp. 539–
    46.
Moshier, W. Franklyn. "Ruth Etting Today." *Film Fan Monthly*, September 1974,
    pp. 19–25.

GEORGE "HONEY BOY" EVANS (Pontotlyn, Wales, March 10, 1870— New York, March 12, 1915)

One of the greatest American blackface minstrels was not a product of the South, but a native of Wales. He made his first stage appearance at Balser's Music Hall in Canton, Ohio, in 1891, as a member of the Columbia Quartette. In 1892, he joined the Haverly minstrel troupe in Chicago. The following year, he worked with Cleveland's Minstrels and Primrose and West's Minstrels, but returned to Haverly in 1894. Shortly thereafter, he entered vaudeville as a singing blackface comedian and was immensely popular. Evans returned to minstrels on July 27, 1908, opening in Atlantic City with the Cohan and Harris Minstrels, of which he took over ownership in March 1910. As a blackface act, he had commenced his vaudeville career earning $50 a week; by 1908, his salary was $1,500 a week. The minstrel continued to work almost to his death, making his last appearance, in Birmingham, Alabama, three weeks before his demise.

George "Honey Boy" Evans was also a songwriter, coauthoring "In the Good Old Summertime." His nickname "Honey Boy" comes from the song of that title, written for him by Jack Norworth.

F

FANCHON AND MARCO

Fanchon and Marco were a sister and brother who used their first names only throughout their careers as vaudeville performers and later as producers of highly successful vaudeville acts and vaudeville-style prologues to motion pictures in presentation houses across the United States. Fanchon, who was the dominant member of the partnership, and Marco, who was born in Los Angeles on April 21, 1894, Wolff began their show business career playing in an orchestra organized by their parents, Wolff's Juvenile Orchestra, and in the teens appeared in vaudeville as a dancing partnership. They began producing revues in 1919 with the *Fanchon and Marco Revue*; it was followed by *The Fanchon and Marco Satires of 1920* and their first major success, a 1921 touring show titled *Sunkist*. The couple began producing prologues with their own company in 1922, and variously operated under the name of Fanchon and Marco Stageshows, Inc., and the Fanchon and Marco Service Corporation.

The prologues featured beautiful showgirls in exotic settings, and the flagship theatre for the Fanchon and Marco operation was the Paramount in Los Angeles. Among the performers who worked with Fanchon and Marco early in their careers were Dorothy Lamour, Janet Gaynor, Lupe Velez, Bing Crosby, Judy Garland, and Mary Martin. Two major Hollywood costume designers, Helen Rose and Bonnie Cashin, were under contract to Fanchon and Marco, and the major choreographer was Carlos Romero. An average of fifty hour-long musical prologues were produced each year, and as of 1931, the organization had a staff of six thousand. The number dropped to two thousand in 1933, but Fanchon and Marco continued in operation through the 1930s, and as late as 1935, former silent screen star Mae Murray toured in a Fanchon and Marco show.

In 1929, Fox West Coast Theatres acquired a 50 percent interest in the Fanchon and Marco organization, but in 1933, the couple purchased the former's holdings. Aside from the production company, Fanchon and Marco operated the Fanchon and Marco Costume Co. in Los Angeles and also had a school of ballet, one of whose pupils was Cyd Charisse. They also owned the Pavo Real nightclub in

San Francisco. Fanchon and Marco's production activities were not limited to prologues, and they produced a number of vaudeville acts, including "Gobs of Joy," a forty-minute presentation that played the Palace in July 1929.

In 1937, Fanchon became a producer at Paramount and was later active at Republic. During the Second World War, Marco administered the Hollywood Victory Committee. On March 2, 1944, Marco produced the Academy Awards show at Grauman's Chinese Theatre. Fanchon's major contribution to the war effort was production of *All Star Bond Rally* (1945) for 20th Century-Fox. In March 1950, the Paramount Theatre, Los Angeles, which had been closed for nine years, reopened, and Fanchon and Marco revived stage productions there. The first presentation featured orchestra conductor Rube Wolf (who had worked at the Paramount in the 1930s), dancing comedian Gil Lamb, singers Herb Jeffries and Ronnie Gibson, and the twenty Fanchonette dancers.

Fanchon and Marco disappeared from the scene in the 1960s, and no record of their deaths has ever been published. A Fanchon and Marco Collection is part of the Shubert Archive in New York.

BIBLIOGRAPHY

Calvin, Kenneth W. "The Big Idea of Fanchon and Marco." *Dance*, March 1929, pp. 14–16; April 1929, pp. 42–43, 56–58.

FAST-CHANGE ACTS. See LEOPOLDO FREGOLI, OWEN McGIVENEY, PROTEAN ACTS

ANNA EVA FAY (Southampton, Oh., ?—Melrose Highland, Ma., May 12, 1927)

The greatest of all "mental" and "mind-reading" acts in vaudeville was that of Anna Eva Fay, who introduced spiritualism to the vaudeville stage and also to millions of Americans who were influenced by her supposed psychic powers. Her act extended well beyond mere mind reading and would involve psychic phenomena and "manifestations" onstage while Fay was supposedly bound hand and foot. Writing of her in 1891, magician H. J. Burlingame commented, "There is no living person who has created such a furor in the Spiritualistic world. A slender, almost fragile creature, grey eyes, flaxen hair, always richly dressed, and with a score of rings set with glittering diamonds, she invariably has made a most bewildering sensation. No woman ever trod the stage who possessed more confidence in herself and her language than this little, vivacious, almost enchanting person."

While twentieth-century audiences may have accepted Anna Eva Fay's vaudeville act with some skepticism, small-town audiences in the mid nineteenth century were most impressed by her, and when her act was exposed as a fraud in April 1876, there was extensive coverage in the pages of the *New York Daily Graphic*. She continued to perform through the early 1920s, making her last public appearance in Milwaukee in 1924, and was managed in vaudeville by her husband, David H. Pingree (married 1889, died 1932).

Her son John T. Fay was part of his mother's act until the turn of the century, when he developed his own, similar act with his wife, Eva Fay. Like her mother-in-law, Eva Fay would appear blindfolded onstage and use a variety of tricks to identify objects held up by members of the audience or answer questions, some of a highly personal nature. The act relied heavily on her staff, so-called "aisle men," who worked the audience and sold booklets dealing with psychic power and spiritualism.

ELFIE FAY (1881—Hollywood, Ca. September 18, 1927)

Elfie Fay was a popular comedic singer on the vaudeville stage at the turn of the century, with her best known number being "The Belle of Avenue A," by which title she was best known. Her father, Hugh Faye, was part of the Irish comedy act of Barry and Faye, and later Elfie Fay joined with her father's partner, Lydia Barry, to continue the vaudeville team of Barry and Faye.

FRANK FAY (San Francisco, November 17, 1897—Santa Monica, Ca., September 25, 1961)

"Showbiz has a name for the likes of Frank Fay—a trouper's trouper," wrote *Variety* at the performer's death. There were many others with less complimentary names for Frank Fay, whose arrogance, drinking, and sharp tongue made him many enemies in show business. In vaudeville, he was the monologist supreme, who could deliver a deadly ad lib with an insouciant Irish charm. When Milton Berle challenged him to a duel of wits, Fay responded, "I never fight with an unarmed man." He once introduced Rudy Vallee as "certainly the oldest adolescent in existence." With his acid tongue, he could destroy a popular song such as "Tea for Two" by asking his audience, "A dame getting out of bed before the sun comes up—and what for? To bake a sugar cake." His style of humor reached its zenith in the 1920s, as he became one of vaudeville's first regular masters of ceremonies. In this role he could dominate an entire vaudeville bill. He would exchange patter with other acts, fill in time when necessary, interrupt other performers, and trade barbs with any hecklers in the audience.

Francis Anthony Fay was the son of stock company players and made his stage debut at the age of three in a Chicago production of *Quo Vadis?* In 1903, he played the role of the Teddy Bear in *Babes in Toyland*, and later that same year made his first New York appearance as an extra in Sir Henry Irving's production of *The Merchant of Venice*. Appropriately, Frank Fay once responded to a reporter's question as to when he had entered show business with the comment, "Good Lord—I've never been out of it." After many years on the legitimate stage, always in minor roles and almost always in minor productions, Fay teamed with Johnny Dyer and started the comedy act of Dyer and Fay, which was rough and crude, and which Fay apparently loathed.

By 1918, he was established as a solo monologist, and on March 15 of that year, *Variety* commented, "There is something about Fay's work that gets over easily and makes him a favorite." Even at this early stage in Fay's career, he was beginning to show signs of the arrogance that was to become his trademark. While appearing at the Orpheum, Brooklyn, in May 1918, he claimed to be having trouble tying his necktie, and four minutes into his scheduled appearance, he was still in his dressing room wrestling with the tie and assuring onlookers that he was certain the tie would behave itself sooner or later. Eventually the stage manager came to tell Fay of the audience's impatience, to which the performer responded, "Let 'em wait." When word of this behavior got back to the United Booking Office, the remainder of Fay's engagement on the Orpheum circuit was cancelled. In February 1919, he was at the Palace with a skit on prohibition titled "The Face on the Drug Store Floor," and even then he was not above burlesqueing the headliner, who happened to be Olga Petrova. However, *The New York Dramatic Mirror* (March 9, 1919) was quick to note, "Fay is headed straight toward a headline position. And when he gets there he'll be a drawing card too."

Within a couple of years, Frank Fay was indeed a headliner. He was at the Palace in October 1924, performing card tricks with the aid of two stooges, Lou Mann and George Haggerty, who were invited up from the audience, insulted, and hit over the head. "If the laugh is there Fay takes it and if it isn't he doesn't go back after it," commented Sime Silverman in *Variety* (October 15, 1924). At this time, Fay was billed as "Broadway's Favorite Son," although Silverman had to wonder who had made the appointment. Onstage, Fay always appeared neatly groomed, elegantly attired, with very much the air of the dashing Irish-American playboy, but behind the refinement there was, as *Variety* (February 11, 1925) noted, "a whole power house."

After two marriages—to Lee Buchanan and Frances White—ended in divorce, Frank Fay asked Barbara Stanwyck, who in 1927 was making a name for herself opposite Hal Skelly in *Burlesque*, to become his wife. It was a marriage that was to last until 1935, when Stanwyck was riding high with a major career in motion pictures and her husband was on the way down. As Fay and Stanwyck, the couple appeared in a dramatic sketch, *The Conflict*, by Vincent Lawrence, at the Palace in February 1929. It was the story of a young couple, bored with life and each other, who pretend to be happy and discover that they are. It was not a success. "Here's your chance, and probably your last chance, for a view of Frank Fay as a dramatic actor. Don't miss it. You'll die," commented *Variety* (February 13, 1929). "Miss Stanwyck looks very cute in three-piece black and white pajamas with flared coat, looks better than she acts, dramatically."

Fay entered films in 1929 but was relatively unsuccessful. It is interesting to see him as the master of ceremonies in the 1929 Warner Bros. production of *Show of Shows* (a role in which he excelled onstage) and see how dismally he handles the chore. Possibly the only good thing to come from Fay's Hollywood years was his talking Columbia Pictures into hiring his wife.

The crossover to motion pictures was a significant indicator of the problem Fay was encountering in playing vaudeville dates outside of major cities. He was too sophisticated for most rural communities. Once he was playing a small-town vaudeville house when Lindbergh landed in France. Fay came onstage and made the announcement of the event to very mild applause. He said, "Perhaps you didn't hear me," and repeated the news, again to only mild applause. A third announcement was greeted with the same response, at which point Fay said, "If you have never heard of Lindbergh I'm too sophisticated for you," and walked off the stage.

While appearing in vaudeville, Fay had appeared in revues such as *The Passing Show of 1918* and *Jim Jam Jems* (1920). He had even tried his hand at producing his own shows, first with the disastrous *Frank Fay's Fables* in 1922 and later with *Frank Fay Vaudeville* in 1939, which featured Eva Le Gallienne and Elsie Janis. After the divorce from Stanwyck, Fay retired to his $250,000 Hollywood estate and did relatively little. He had no servants and no water in his swimming pool, having not bothered to pay the water bill. However, he did give up alcohol and became addicted to coffee, drinking as many as seventy-seven cups in a five-hour period.

The Frank Fay story might have ended there had it not been for a six-foot, one-and-a-half-inch rabbit named *Harvey*, the subject of a play by Mary Chase. Brock Pemberton was casting the leading role of Elwood P. Dowd, and he wanted Harold Lloyd for the part, but Lloyd did not find the play remotely funny and turned him down. While Fay was in New York for one of his occasional nightclub appearances, Pemberton met with him and decided that here was the perfect Elwood P. Dowd. *Harvey* opened at New York's 48th Street Theatre on November 1, 1944, and Frank Fay embarked on a new career which was to include more than two thousand appearances in the play. "Elwood, as Frank Fay plays him—timing everything faultlessly and giving his screwiness the effect of drollery—is immense," wrote Louis Kronenberger in *PM* (November 2, 1944). "Fay's job is a tightrope walk over Niagara, in which one false move could easily be fatal. But every move is right, and a few seem magical. There is a long scene at the end of the second act where Elwood, questioned by the psychiatrist, talks about himself and Harvey, and sometimes only sits and looks. It introduces a new and dangerous mood, and it could be awful. Somehow Fay manages to transfix the audience and touch them."

Frank Fay's origins in vaudeville had much to do with his success in *Harvey*, and, as he commented to Maurice Zolotow, "How could I help getting along with a rabbit when I was named after St. Francis of Assisi, who was brother to all the birds and beasts?"

It was comments such as that, rather than past behavior on the vaudeville stage, that resulted in *Time* describing Frank Fay as "the gentle man of deadly humor" at the time of his death.

BIBLIOGRAPHY

Fay, Frank. *How to Be Poor*. New York: Prentice-Hall, 1945.
"Frank Fay." *Current Biography*, August 1945, pp. 176–79.
"Frank Fay and Friends." *Newsweek*, January 28, 1946, p. 78.

York, Cal. "Mixed Doubles—with a Dash of Mexican." *Photoplay*, February 1930,
     p. 57.
Zolotow, Maurice. "Frank Fay." *Life*, January 8, 1945, pp. 55–58, 60, 63.

FEMALE IMPERSONATORS

While most women in the audience enjoyed female impersonators, in large
part because of the glamorous clothing they wore, the response of the majority
of men must have been similar to that of critic Frederick James Smith writing
in *The New York Dramatic Mirror* (May 19, 1915): "Considering female impersonators, we've always maintained that we'd rather see one than be one."

Female impersonation is as old as the theatre itself, and in the field of American
popular entertainment, female impersonation dates back to the minstrel shows
of the nineteenth century, where one of the most famous female impersonators
was Francis Leon (billed simply as "Leon"). One critic of the period wrote,
"Just as a white man makes the best stage Negro, so a man gives more photographic interpretation of femininity than the average woman is able to give."
In England, particularly in pantomime, it was the norm to have buxom young
women with shapely legs appear as principal boys while the leading comedians
of the day—from Dan Leno to Arthur Askey—starred as the ladies. There was
never anything improper in female impersonation, no hint of homosexuality or
transvestism, as there is in much contemporary female impersonation.

In vaudeville, female impersonators were careful to appear suitably manly
offstage and, with the obvious exception of Bert Savoy, never "swished" around
onstage. *Variety* was extremely anti-gay and watchful for any hint of homosexuality in female impersonation. Frederick M. McCloy editorialized in the October
1, 1915 issue of the trade paper: "The offensive, disgusting effeminate male or
'fairy' impersonator is now in line for expurgation. And the same influences
that banish the 'cooch' may be relied upon to kick this odious creature through
the stage door into the gutter, where it belongs."

One of the earliest female impersonators in vaudeville was Pete Shaw, who,
with his song "You May Look, but You Musn't Touch," was described as the
prettiest "girl" of the 1890s. When "The Great Crowley" appeared at Miner's
Theatre, New York, in January 1886, the program commented, "This gentleman
has been a puzzle to the community at large as to his sex. He outwomans a
woman."

With their operatic falsetto voices, the first major female impersonators in
vaudeville were all compared to Adelina Patti, the coloratura soprano. The best
known was Everett Stewart, who was billed simply as "Stuart, the Male Patti."
He was discovered working in a post office in Wichita, Kansas, by Tom Heath
of the minstrel team of McIntyre and Heath. Stuart first blacked up as a member
of the McIntyre and Heath Minstrels in the fall of 1887. It is amusing in view
of the entertainer's previous career that his best known song was "The Letter
That Never Came." His work with the postal service also gave rise to the joke
that he was "The Mail Patti."

"There are a good many real female sopranos who would be glad if they could sing as well as Stuart," commented *The New York Dramatic Mirror* (April 17, 1897). Stuart first visited Europe in 1899, and so successful was he in Paris and Berlin that he returned to both cities on an almost annual basis through 1908. On visits to Europe, he always spent time purchasing the latest Paris gowns for his act, and he caused great excitement among the female members of his audience when he began wearing an ankle bracelet. By 1904, *The New York Dramatic Mirror* was hailing Stuart as "the premiere impersonator of the fair sex of the present day." However, he was beginning to show his age, and the lines on his face required more and more makeup as the years progressed. Despite his grace and cultured high soprano voice, Stuart, it is recorded, failed to shave under his armpits, something which, by 1909, "all the best ladies on stage were doing."

Stuart's closest rival was Tacianu, who was also known as Tacino and Tacius, and originally hailed from Italy. His good, clear soprano voice was praised by contemporary critics, who also applauded the fine, baritone voice he would also use.

In direct contrast to the female impersonators of Madame Patti were those who continued the comic tradition from the minstrel stages, and those who claimed to be nothing more than attractive young girls with dubious talents. In the former class was Earl Gillihan, who usually appeared in a double act as Gillihan and Murray, and who was billed from 1892 onward as "Vaudeville's Greatest Wench." Far better known than Gillihan was Gilbert Sarony, who specialized in portraying a grotesque, elderly woman. He died in Pittsburgh— of acute indigestion!—on December 15, 1910, and in its obituary, *Variety* (December 24, 1910) wrote, "Sarony was one of the first female impersonators of the old maid type. He was considered one of the funniest men in the show business." Hal Johnson, who looked remarkably like Lillian Gish, demonstrated just how pretty a female impersonator might be. "There is nothing whatsoever suggestive about his work and he never fails to please," commented *The New York Dramatic Mirror* in 1903.

Female impersonators proliferated in the teens to such an extent that hardly a week went by that a new act was not being reviewed by *Variety*. There was Herbert Charles, who took off his wig after the second song and adopted a gruff voice. "The Divine Dodson" publicized the fact that he was wearing $3,000 worth of costumes, and when not appearing onstage, he operated a millinery establishment, The Man Milliner, in Los Angeles. Vardaman had the dubious distinction of being one of the bulkiest of female impersonators, whom *Variety* thought deserved praise simply for his ability to squeeze himself into a corset, and who had the audacity to end his act performing in a bathing costume. Francis Yates performed two songs in female attire, then changed behind a transparent screen into gentleman's clothing for a final number. Ray Lawrence had a Chinese assistant and also ended his act in male attire, reciting a poem by Robert Service. "Princess Ka" performed classical dances, assisted by a young woman partner, and a slide between numbers announced that he could speak no English. After seeing Reine perform in 1914, *Variety*'s publisher, Sime Silverman, opined that there were too many female impersonators cropping up. Francis and Nord appeared in blond and dark wigs, sang and danced a little, and fooled their audiences until removing their wigs at the act's close.

Clemons and Rodgers played up the obesity of one member of the act, wearing outrageous costumes and adopting effeminate voices, the term for which was a "nance" voice. Alvora performed exotic dances, changing costumes behind a transparent screen. Another dancer was Auremia, whose high spot was "The Dance of Death." Balaban was a heavy-set impersonator who sported a blond wig and sang falsetto, accompanying himself at the piano. He was well liked when appearing at the Victoria Theatre Roof in the summer of 1914. Biscauex sang two straight songs as a woman before changing into male evening dress. Unfortunately, even after changing into male attire, there were those in the audience who doubted he was really a man! George East performed a number of "rags" and gave a creditable impersonation of vaudeville headliner Bessie Clayton.

And in the 1920s, there were still more, including Tommy Martelle and Jean Barrios. According to *Variety* (August 5, 1921), Cecil Grey "presented an appearance that might easily excite the envy of the best dressed society women of America." Arthur Alexander reintroduced blackface to female impersonation in 1922. There were double acts such as Dale and DeLane and Scotch and Bourbon, who arrived on the scene in 1929. It was little wonder that *Variety* (March 8, 1923) complained, "There are more female impersonators in vaudeville this season than ever before. . . . Three impersonators on one bill at a split-week house recently is viewed as a record."

Typical of female impersonators in the 1920s was Du Nord, whom *Variety* (March 12, 1920) saw at the State-Congress in Chicago:

Du Nord works in a neat eye, full stage, with transparent section which permits the audience to see the maid dressing him as he changes. He does three dances—a Spanish, a toe, and an Egyptian dance. Not using his voice, and giving the house a glimpse of the maid, has the tendency to heighten the surprise when he takes off his wig at the finish. The maid, rather, does this for him, which is an unusual twist, and then she takes off her wig.

Presumably audiences could accept a man dressed as a woman, dressing another man, dressed as a woman, but would they have been equally unconcerned if the maid was really a woman dressing and undressing a man onstage?

The demise of vaudeville is coincidental to the demise of female impersonation. The 1930s was a decade in which Americans for the first time became more aware of homosexuality which, of course, equates with female impersonation. To most Americans of that generation, homosexuality was frightening and had no place in popular entertainment. Homosexuality and female impersonation went underground for a couple of decades or more.

See also BARBETTE, GEORGE AND BERT BERNARD, RAY/RAE BOURBON, BOTHWELL BROWNE, HERBERT CLIFTON, JULIAN ELTINGE, BERT ERROL, KARYL NORMAN, FRANCIS RENAULT, SAVOY AND BRENNAN, MALCOLM SCOTT.

BIBLIOGRAPHY

Ackroyd, Peter. *Dressing Up*. London: Thames and Hudson, 1979.

Baker, Roger. *Drag*. London: Paul Elek, 1968.

Bulliet, C. J. *Venus Castina*. New York: Bonanza Books, 1956.

Newton, Esther. *Mother Camp: Female Impersonation in America*. Chicago: University of Chicago Press, 1979.

Slide, Anthony. *Great Pretenders: A History of Female and Male Impersonation in the Performing Arts*. Lombard, Il.: Wallace-Homestead, 1986.

BENNY FIELDS. See BLOSSOM SEELEY AND BENNY FIELDS

GRACIE FIELDS (Rochdale, England, January 9, 1898—Capri, Italy, September 27, 1979)

"Our Gracie," as she was affectionately known, was a legendary figure in British music hall and British films, once described by *The New York Times* (May 31, 1942) as "The Poor Man's Beatrice Lillie." Her style was decidedly working class, as she sang such popular numbers as "Sally" (her theme song), "I Took My Harp to a Party," "In My Little Bottom Drawer," and "The Biggest Aspidistra in the World." Born Grace Stansfield in the north of England, Gracie made her first stage appearance at the age of seven, and her first London appearance at the Middlesex Music Hall in 1915. In shows produced by her first husband, Archie Pitt, she became a star in the mid 1920s. When the Duncan Sisters were playing *Topsy and Eva* in London and Rosetta became ill, Fields donned blackface and essayed the role of Topsy. In 1928, she made her first appearance at the Palace, but was not successful in that audiences could not understand either her humor or her accent. She described this experience as the only flop in her long career, and somewhat compensated for it with a successful 1930 return to the theatre.

Gracie Fields began her screen career in 1931 with *Sally in Our Alley*, and in her 1933 British feature *Sing as We Go* helped revive the British working class laid low by the depression. The film's title became a national anthem of the depression. So popular were Gracie Fields's films that, in 1935, she was signed to an American contract by 20th Century–Fox, and in 1937 brought to the United States with great fanfare. Her most memorable American film is *Holy Matrimony* (1943); plans to have the comedienne star in a 1944 film biography of Marie Dressler came to nothing. Something of Fields's international appeal at this time may be gauged from her being featured in *Stage Door Canteen* (1943), singing "The Lord's Prayer."

She made her British television debut in 1947, and in the 1950s was often featured on American television. Gracie Fields had made her U.S. radio debut on April 30, 1937, on Campbell Soups's *Hollywood Hotel*, at which time Variety (May 5, 1937) opined, "She sounds like Polly Moran with a voice."

BIBLIOGRAPHY

Fields, Gracie. *Sing as We Go*. Garden City, N.Y.: Doubleday, 1961.

Minoff, Philip. "Gracie Goes 'Legit.' " *Cue*, May 19, 1956, p. 17.

Richards, Jeffrey. "Gracie Fields: The Lancashire Britannia." *Focus on Film* no. 33 (August 1979), pp. 27–35; no. 34 (December 1979), pp. 23–28.

Wilson, Elizabeth. "The Aspidastra [sic] Girl." *Liberty*, May 12, 1945, pp. 23, 64–67.

LEW FIELDS. See WEBER AND FIELDS

W. C. FIELDS (Philadelphia, April 9, 1879—Pasadena, Ca., December 25, 1946)

The unique status of W. C. Fields in American entertainment is evidenced by his being the only vaudevillian aside from Will Rogers to have been honored with a commemorative stamp from the U.S. postal service, issued on the one-hundredth anniversary of his birth. He was a master juggler with a caustic wit and a mastery of the euphemism. Phrases such as "drat," "Godfrey Daniels," and "Mother of Pearl" testify to his grandiloquence. He was, in the words of Robert Benchley, writing in *Life* (April 2, 1925), "just about as grand as a comedian could possibly be." British novelist J. B. Priestley recognized another of Fields's unique qualities: "Nobody could suggest the malice of objects better than Fields. At his best moments, an ordinary room, empty of other human beings, could turn itself into a mined mountain pass."

W. C. Fields was also one of the few vaudevillians able to transfer virtually all of his vaudeville routines to film, and by so doing not only create a new, financially successful career for himself but also ensure that his vaudeville act is preserved for posterity. To view the films of W. C. Fields, particularly those he made for Paramount from the early through mid 1930s, is to understand the essence and creativity of Fields, the vaudevillian. His crooked poker game, with aces appearing like flies, may be seen in *Mississippi* (1935). The pool table sketch is preserved in *Six of a Kind* (1934). The juggling routine with cigar boxes is there in *The Old Fashioned Way* (1934), while classic visual and verbal gags are captured in *International House* (1933) and *It's a Gift* (1934), which is surely the finest of Fields's features. (The marvelous sequence in the film in which Fields is trying to sleep on the front porch in the early morning, disturbed by everyone from the milkman to an insurance salesman, was apparently based on an experience in his mother's home when, as a young vaudeville performer, he was trying to sleep late. The same routine also appears in Fields's 1926 silent film *It's the Old Army Game*, which took its title from a phrase Fields popularized in his 1923 stage success *Poppy*.)

William Claude Dukenfield was born in Philadelphia, about which he had much to say, all negative. At the age of fourteen, he became entranced with the juggling of a circus clown and decided where his future lay. His first professional appearance in vaudeville was in the spring of 1896 at an Atlantic City beer hall. He toured in vaudeville and in 1899 joined the Irwin Burlesquers, where he met a chorus girl named Hattie Hughes (whom he married the following year). She worked with him through 1904, when they separated both as a vaudeville act and as husband and wife, although the two remained married and Hattie outlived Fields.

By 1900, W. C. Fields had added comedy to his juggling act, and the "Eccentric Juggler," as he was billed, was a familiar and well-liked figure on American vaudeville stages. In 1901, he made the first of many world tours and was particularly successful in Europe and South Africa. *The New York Telegraph* (October 24, 1901) reported that Fields's "comedy juggling is steadier now than when he first appeared in New York after his return from Europe. He makes few misses and his style, different from the others, amuses. His wife helps dress the stage and the black satin panties have not yet given way." Hattie's "window dressing" was replaced in 1904 by liveried footmen on whom Fields could play such tricks as bouncing balls off their hats (similar to the routine performed in the film *The Old Fashioned Way*). For his costume, Fields appeared as a well-dressed tramp with a stubble of beard.

When Fields starred at London's Palace Theatre in 1902, his act consisted simply of juggling, but when he returned to London in 1904 to star at the Hippodrome, he had added the pool table. The theatre program noted:

Now the Philadelphia comique has come again among us, and the good opinion he then won is now not only maintained but strengthened, for his new billiard absurdity, in which he pockets no less than fifteen balls in one stroke, is one of those extremely clever things which would alone make the reputation of any juggler. His three chief moves on the green cloth are a trio of triumphs, and those interested in the art made famous by Roberts, Peall, and others, must make a point of seeing Fields 'play the game.' The fantastic way he handles his cue, the smart manner in which he pockets the balls, and his little bits of humor intervening all the while, make his turn the most lively and interesting juggling entertainment before the public.

Despite a certain crudity and vulgarity apparent in some of his films—most notably, *International House* (1933)—such traits were not part of Fields's vaudeville act, and it is not surprising that in May 1913, Sarah Bernhardt permitted him to appear with her on the same bill at the Palace. He was third on the program, and *Variety* (May 23, 1913) reported, "The Palace Theatre maintains a certain atmosphere by the magnificence of its construction and appointments. Fields, with his high art pantomimic comedy juggling, belonged to that atmosphere as much as the marble base of the box seats."

After many years on the vaudeville stage, Fields's career took a new turn in 1915, when he made his first appearance in one of the Ziegfeld *Follies*. He appeared in a sketch with Ed Wynn, and at one point hit his fellow comedian over the head with a billiard cue, claiming Wynn was stealing his laughs. Fields was to be part of the *Follies* team through 1918, and again in 1920, 1921, and

1925. The last featured a drugstore sketch which Fields transferred to film in *The Pharmacist* (a 1933 short subject) and also the "Back Porch" sketch. When Fields starred in the 1927 edition of Earl Carroll's *Vanities*, he introduced the sketch of a prospector in a snowbound cabin, with its famous line, "It's not a fit night out for man or beast," while the stagehands threw paper snow. That sketch was the basis for another 1933 short film, *The Fatal Glass of Beer*. And from the same show came a dentist sketch filmed as yet another 1933 short subject, *The Dentist*. Fields's most important stage production of the 1920s was the musical comedy *Poppy*, costarring Madge Kennedy, which opened at the New Apollo Theatre on September 3, 1923. Fields filmed it twice, in 1925 as *Sally of the Sawdust* and in 1936 as *Poppy*.

W. C. Fields made two short films in 1915, *Pool Sharks* and *His Lordship's Dilemma*. In 1924, he appeared in a cameo role, as a drunken British soldier, in the Marion Davies vehicle *Janice Meredith*. His film career began in earnest in 1925 with *Sally of the Sawdust*, followed by *That Royle Girl* (1926), *Tillie's Punctured Romance* (1928), *Her Majesty Love* (1931, Fields's first talkie), *Tillie and Gus* (1933), *Mrs. Wiggs of the Cabbage Patch* (1934), *David Copperfield* (1935), *You Can't Cheat an Honest Man* (1939), *My Little Chickadee* (1940), *Bank Dick* (1940), *Never Give a Sucker an Even Break* (1941), and many others. Once he was ensconced as a film star in Los Angeles, there was to be no return for Fields to vaudeville and the revue stage.

Fields was, without question, a complex individual. He was intelligent and perhaps introspective, but he was certainly not the drunken child-hater that he is so often depicted to have been. While he was estranged from his wife and son, there was a reconciliation when W. C. Fields, Jr., married, and Fields displayed great affection for his grandson. Perhaps the best description of the comedian is given by the writer of the program for the London Hippodrome in 1904: "He is a twentieth-century man, devotes himself entirely to his work, and is satisfied to live on the earth without wanting to own it." The world of entertainment has benefited much from Fields's participation in it.

BIBLIOGRAPHY

Anobile, Richard J., ed. *Drat! Being the Encapsulated View of Life by W. C. Fields in His Own Words*. New York: New American Library, 1968.

————, ed. *A Flask of Fields: Verbal and Visual Gems from the Films of W. C. Fields*. New York: Darien House, 1972.

————, ed. *"Godfrey Daniels": Verbal and Visual Gems from the Short Films of W. C. Fields*. New York: Darien House, 1975.

Beranger, Clara. "The Most Melancholy Funny Man on the Screen." *Liberty* 13, no. 7 (February 15, 1936), pp. 30–31.

Brooks, Louise. "The Other Face of W. C. Fields." *Sight and Sound* 40, no. 2 (Spring 1971), pp. 92–96.

Denby, David. "Diary of a Mean Man." *Premiere* 3, no. 1 (September 1989), pp. 32–33, 40.

Deschner, Donald. *The Films of W. C. Fields*. New York: Citadel Press, 1966.

Everson, William K. *The Art of W. C. Fields*. Indianapolis: Bobbs-Merrill, 1967.

Fields, Ronald J., ed. *W. C. Fields by Himself*. Englewood Cliffs, N.J.: Prentice-Hall, 1973.

————. *W. C. Fields: A Life in Film*. New York: St. Martin's Press, 1984.

Fields, W. C. "My Rules of Etiquette." *Los Angeles Times: This Week Magazine*, December 4, 1938, pp. 6, 15.

————. "My Views on Marriage." *Los Angeles Times: This Week Magazine*, October 15, 1939, pp. 7, 19.

————. *Fields for President*. New York: Dodd, Mead, 1940.

Fowler, Gene. *Minutes of the Last Meeting*. New York: Viking Press, 1954.

Gehring, Wes D. *W. C. Fields: A Bio-Bibliography*. Westport, Ct.: Greenwood Press, 1984.

Lewis, Martin, ed. *The Quotations of W. C. Fields*. New York: Drake, 1976.

Mason, Paul. *W. C. Fields: I Never Met a Kid I Liked*. Los Angeles: Stanyan Books, 1970.

McCarthy, Charlie, as told to Dorothy Spensley. "The Man I Hate." *Radio Mirror* 9, no. 2 (December 1937), pp. 18–19, 67–70.

Miller, Don. "W. C. Fields, The Bank Dick and Me." *Applause* 1, no. 3 (September 22, 1971), pp. 4–5.

Monti, Carlotta, with Cy Rice. *W. C. Fields and Me*. Englewood Cliffs, N.J.: Prentice-Hall, 1971.

Priestley, J. B. "W. C. Fields." *The Atlantic* 179, no. 3 (March 1947), pp. 43–44.

Robinson, David. "Dunkinfield Meets McGargle: Creation of a Character." *Sight and Sound* 38, no. 3 (Summer 1967), pp. 125–29.

Smith, Frederick James. "Is His Nose Red?" *Liberty* 14, no. 36 (September 4, 1937), pp. 37–38.

Taylor, Robert Lewis. *W. C. Fields: His Follies and Fortunes*. New York; Doubleday, 1949.

Walker, Helen Louise. "The Fields You Ought to Know." *Picture Play* 44, no. 3 (May 1936), pp. 52–53, 64.

The W. C. Fields Book. Brooklyn, N.Y.: Wonderful Publishing Company, 1973.

Yanni, Nicholas. *W. C. Fields*. New York: Pyramid, 1974.

FILM STARS IN VAUDEVILLE

The flood of film stars to vaudeville with the coming of sound in 1928 is not difficult to understand. First, vaudeville offered film celebrities an opportunity to prove to their studio heads that they could indeed speak, sing, and dance, and thus were prime material for talkies. Second, vaudeville was a means of bolstering a sagging, and in many cases doomed, career.

However, even before the premiere of *The Jazz Singer* in 1927, with its ramifications for the film community, an occasional silent screen star had tried his or her hand at vaudeville, largely to promote a career or gauge appeal with fans. As early as December 1914, Crane Wilbur, who had been serial queen Pearl White's leading man, appeared on stage at Poli's Theatre in Springfield, Massachusetts, telling of the trials and tribulations of a picture hero. In the summer of 1923, Wilbur again returned to vaudeville, but this time as a film actor whose days of stardom were ended. Francis X. Bushman and Beverly

Bayne, a popular romantic screen duo of the teens, appeared in the comedy sketch *Poor Rich Man* at the Palace in February 1921. In January 1922, Flora Finch, who had partnered comedian John Bunny in the early teens, tried her hand at vaudeville, but *Variety* (January 27, 1922) thought her act slovenly. Henry B. Walthall, one of the stars of D. W. Griffith's *The Birth of a Nation* (1915), made his vaudeville debut at the Hill Street Theatre, Los Angeles, in May 1922 in a twenty-two minute playlet, *The Unknown*, in which he played the dual role of father and son.

The Fairbanks Twins had commenced their film career in the early teens as the Thanhouser Twins, named after the studio to which they were contracted, and in March 1923 appeared at the Palace. *Variety* did not care for them, despite their already having appeared in the Ziegfeld *Follies* and *The Music Box* revues. Although it was to be another decade before she costarred in a series of comedies with Marie Dressler, Polly Moran was already a well-known screen comedienne, thanks to her work with Mack Sennett, when she introduced a vaudeville act in 1918. As part of the presentation, she screened an extract from her film *Sheriff Nell*, and Sime Silverman in *Variety* liked "her semi-nut impromptu way." Child star Wesley Barry, who had played opposite Mary Pickford, made his vaudeville debut in September 1922 at the Orpheum Theatre, San Francisco, in a sketch titled "Welcome Home." As he toured the country with the sketch, he tried to dispel rumors of moral laxity in the film industry, brought on by the William Desmond Taylor murder, the Roscoe "Fatty" Arbucke rape scandal, and Wallace Reid's death from drug addiction, claiming, "Hollywood is so tame that wild flowers won't grow there."

Arbuckle's career ended in 1921 after he was accused of raping starlet Virginia Rappe, and he had no alternative but to turn to vaudeville, hoping to ingratiate himself with the public. He first played vaudeville in San Francisco in June 1924. He was back, at Loew's State, New York, in January 1928. He described Los Angeles as the City of Los Angels and told the audience, "I ain't got nothing now," adding it did not matter as long as he still had his friends and his health. Writing in *Variety* (January 18, 1928), Abel Green commented:

> Arbuckle as a name is still an attraction. One good opening movie featuring the same unsophisticated character he has been associated with in the past will do much to re-establish the rotund comic with the flicker fans who can't but help hold a soft spot in their memory for this engaging funster. But on the stage, Arbuckle misses, although he's a name that can once-around-it in anybody's theatre and do business.

Mildred Harris used films as an integral part of her fifteen-minute playlet *Getting the Money* at New York's Royal Theatre in February 1922. She played an innocent country girl attempting to enter films, and *The New York Dramatic Mirror* (April 1922) reported, "The audience wasn't dissatisfied at the end of her offering—in fact, very much pleased. And this is really unusual for a motion picture star who had entered vaudeville." Dorothy Gish turned down an offer of $2,500 a week to appear in vaudeville in 1921—she would apparently have accepted $5,000—but Bebe Daniels, a major Paramount star, did play vaudeville dates in Buffalo and Detroit in the summer of 1923 at a reported salary of $3,000 a week. She had asked for $4,500. Daniels sang, danced, and told stories of the "How to Get into the Movies" type. *Variety* found her act condescending and patronizing, and wondered why vaudeville audiences would sit through such performances with polite tolerance. Bebe Daniels was back in vaudeville in April 1934, at the Chicago Theatre, Chicago, accompanied by her husband, Ben Lyon. *Variety* (April 10, 1934) thought them "a swell couple for vaude."

Baby Peggy, a typical child star of the movies, headlined at the Hippodrome in February 1925 with an eighteen-minute revue titled "From Hollywood to Hippodrome." The child actress proved remarkably self-assured in this and future vaudeville engagements, and her voice apparently carried, without the aid of microphones, to all parts of the house. In March of the same year, Louise Glaum, a screen vamp, made her vaudeville debut at New York's 81st Street Theatre with a telephone monolog titled "The Web." "Miss Glaum is not impossible to vaudeville if her name means anything, but she does need assistance," reported *Variety* (April 1, 1925). Betty Blythe, whose career was already slipping, headlined at the Palace in August 1926 with songs and impressions. Abel Green commented in *Variety* (August 25, 1926), "Fair voice and okay considering she is Betty Blythe of the silent drama."

Anita Stewart, a popular film favorite of the teens, was scheduled to tour in the vaudeville sketch "Modes of the Moment," but it closed in November 1923 after a ten-day run. Another early favorite, Clara Kimball Young, had better luck with a sketch called "The Adorable Wife," in which she headlined at the Palace in April 1925.

There was a disastrous vaudeville tour by a group of silent stars in the spring of 1925. Bryant Washburn, Cullen Landis, Ruth Stonehouse, Phyllis Haver, Anna May Wong, Helen Holmes, and other second-rate stars were booked to appear at the Kansas City Convention Hall. Seats were $2 each, and the audience was promised the opportunity to dance with the stars after the show. On opening night, the company drove to the hall, accompanied by a police escort and marching band, only to be confronted with eighteen thousand empty seats. There was an immediate display of temperament until the stars realized that reporters were present, at which point they decided to present their show anyway. Their misfortunes had only just begun, for before they could leave town for their next booking in Atchison, Kansas, the local agent for the show filed an attachment on the admittedly very small box office receipts. After that was straightened out, the troupe left for Atchison and Omaha, where the final blow was struck. The orchestra conductor's paycheck bounced, and he attached the receipts. Discouraged, the stars returned to the safety of Hollywood, where such dramas were played out only on the screen.

When the talkies hit, silent screen stars panicked. On February 1, 1928, *Variety* carried a headline announcing, "Film Names Stampede towards Vaudeville," including in that number George Walsh, Ben Turpin, Ian Keith, Ethal Clayton,

Irene Rich, and Renée Adorée. On April 1, 1928, *Variety* listed Ralph Graves, Viola Dana, Shirley Mason, Ruth Clifford, Cullen Landis, Snub Pollard, Agnes Ayres, Lila Lee, William Desmond, and Hank Mann among the "25 Players on Coast Available as Vaude Acts." *Variety* also sounded the death knell for silent stars anxious to embrace vaudeville in its issue of December 24, 1929, with the headline, "Fading Stars Not Wanted by Keith's." One star who did make it big in vaudeville, and also continued his film career, was Tom Mix, who broke the attendance records at the Hippodrome. *Variety* (May 23, 1928) hailed him as "the one man who can do more for vaudeville than vaudeville has done, or could do, by itself for itself."

The onslaught toward vaudeville was such that on February 22, 1928, *Variety* reviewed two sketches featuring former silent stars. Husband-and-wife team John Bowers and Marguerite de la Motte were in the comedy sketch "Dear Doctor" at the Los Angeles Orpheum. Ethel Clayton and Ian Keith were in the dramatic sketch "Clipped" at the Riverside Theatre, New York. *Variety* was not impressed with either act. Claire Windsor entertained at the Los Angeles Orpheum in May 1928; "Miss Windsor's cinema name may draw in some of the key cities. After that it is a matter of conjecture," commented *Variety* (May 9, 1928). Anita Stewart was back again in vaudeville at the Granada, San Francisco. "Her screen charm and personality of the Old Vitagraph days have not deserted her," wrote a sympathetic critic in *Variety* (January 16, 1929). Paramount star Ether Ralston headlined at the Palace the week of June 14, 1930. In March 1930, debonair leading man Nils Asther was at the Chicago Theatre, but *Variety* (March 12, 1930) found him "dull and boring for everyone except the flaps [flappers]."

Silent serial queen Ruth Roland had a pleasing singing voice and became a popular favorite in vaudeville. *The Billboard* (January 24, 1931), noting that she had "a sweet personality that immediately ingratiates her with the audience," saw her at the New Palace in Chicago, where she gave an impersonation of Ted Lewis impersonating Ruth Roland impersonating Ted Lewis singing "Me and My Shadow." Ricardo Cortez, of the "Latin lover" school of silent stars, appeared at the Palace in March 1930 in the playlet *Wanted* by Edwin Burke. *The Billboard* (March 22, 1930) reported, "The screen 'name' scored a personal hit, and not only was his choice of vehicle a smart one, but good taste was also used in the selection of a supporting cast." Even animal stars went into vaudeville. In 1928, cowboy star Buck Jones introduced his horse, Silver, to vaudeville audiences, and in May 1930, Rin Tin Tin played the Palace for $1,200 a week.

Viola Dana (1898–1987) is both atypical and untypical in that prior to entering films in 1910, she had worked extensively on the stage and, in fact, left films after a year to star in *The Poor Little Rich Girl* on Broadway. When talkies appeared, she was surprised that producers failed to recognize that she was fully equipped for the new medium. "To tell the truth," she recalled, "I was fed up with this town. There was a different element coming in." Her vaudeville debut was in June 1929 in a playlet titled *There Goes the Bride* at Proctor's 86th Street

Theatre, New York. Variety (June 27, 1928), unaware of Dana's earlier stage experience, commented unkindly, "As a line reader, Miss Dana does as well as might be expected from a deaf—and dumb—racket alumna." Viola Dana remembered, "Oh God, that was a terrible thing with an awful leading man. On opening night the audience roared with laughter. The leading man had come on stage with his fly open!"

The actress was more successful with her second vaudeville offering, "The Inkwell," a sketch written by Anita Loos, in which Dana was supported by Edward Arnold. Viola Dana recalled it was "a cute sketch suitable for the kind of things I had been doing," and she toured in it for forty weeks, playing three shows a day and four on Saturdays and Sundays, except at the notorious Harris Theatre in Pittsburgh, where five shows a day were demanded. Dana and "The Inkwell" were successful, although it must be noted that The Billboard's Cincinnati critic called it—when the sketch opened at the Albee Theatre there on April 13, 1930—"about the weakest and most inane piece of business we have looked at in this house in a long, long time."

Viola Dana experienced no unpleasantness or animosity from her fellow performers because of her movie star status, and had nothing but praise for vaudevillians. She did run into one problem in that she worked full stage, which annoyed magician Fred Keating, one of whose tricks was to swallow needles and pull them, threaded, from his mouth. Keating would not speak to Dana, so she gathered together a dozen large darning needles, stuck them into a card, and had her maid deliver them to Keating's dressing room with a note asking if he would care to swallow those.

Vaudeville also provided opportunity for a number a new screen stars to enhance their reputation. Paramount leading man Charles "Buddy" Rogers made his first stage appearance at the Chicago Theatre in July 1929, and Variety reported he was well liked by the female members of the audience. He sang a couple of songs and performed what was to become his standard routine of playing the various instruments of the orchestra. Another Paramount contract player, comedian Jack Oakie, entertained at Brooklyn's Paramount Theatre in June and July 1930. Also from Paramount, Helen Kane was at the New York Paramount in May 1928; "Helen Kane sings, looks and sells. Remember the name," wrote Variety (May 23, 1928). The voice of cartoon character Betty Boop was based on Helen Kane's and spoken by Mae Questelle, who also appeared in vaudeville in the summer of 1930.

In July 1932, Jack Benny, Una Merkel, Jean Hersholt, Lew Cody, Anna May Wong, Armida, and Abe Lyman and His Hollywood Orchestra were brought to New York to appear onstage at the Capitol Theatre with the M-G-M feature film Unashamed. Jack Benny served as master of ceremonies, Anna May Wong sang (very badly, according to Variety), and Lew Cody and Una Merkel proved their talents as comics. "The Capitol never has offered a stage show as elaborate and as entertaining as its current Hollywood on Parade," wrote Bland Johaneson in

The New York Mirror (July 15, 1932). "It's a $5.50 review, brisk, tuneful, colorful, loaded with laughs, rich in personalities."

Throughout the 1930s, film stars continued to make occasional appearances in vaudeville. Maurice Chevalier was at the New York Paramount in 1932 with a twenty-five minute act of songs and clowning. He also gave impersonations of Rudy Vallee and Willie Howard, told the plot line of his new film, and earned $10,000 a week and a reported percentage of the gross receipts. "Bige" in *Variety* (November 15, 1932) called him "a cinch single for any theatre that can afford to play and pay him." There were not many. During the run of the feature film *The Cat and the Fiddle* at the Capitol Theatre in February 1934, Ramon Novarro was onstage nightly. Clark Gable played the Century Theatre, Baltimore, in February 1934, and in April of the same year, Gloria Swanson played the New York Paramount.

In December 1933, Gary Cooper, supported by Sari Maritza and Raquel Torres, played a week at the New York Paramount. He was paid $4,000 a week, far less than Lou Holtz could have demanded to appear in the same sketch, "The Eternal Triangle," which had the two female stars battling over Cooper, who eventually walked off with the maid. That same month, Bela Lugosi played the Loew's State, New York, in an eighteen-minute version of *Dracula*.

Christmas week of 1933 had Mary Pickford appearing at the New York Paramount in the nineteen-minute playlet *The Church Mouse*, by Ladislaus Fodor. It was Pickford's first formal stage appearance since performing in David Belasco's *The Good Little Devil*, twenty-five years earlier; for her trouble, the actress was paid $10,000 a week and a percentage of the gross receipts. She was well worth the money, as standing-room-only crowds gathered to see her as a poor little stenographer who melts the stony heart of a big banker. *Variety* thought her performance a combination of Pickford's roles in *Tess of the Storm Country*, *Kiki*, and *Daddy-Long-Legs*, and hailed the vaudeville debut of a national institution as an occasion, if not an event.

Pickford's second and best known husband, Douglas Fairbanks, had played vaudeville before entering films in 1915. His 1914 vaudeville vehicle *All at Sea* was described by *The New York Dramatic Mirror* (May 27, 1914) "as exciting as an ice cream soda. In other words it was frothy and mild and not in the least dramatically intoxicating." Two years earlier, Fairbanks had toured vaudeville with a comedy playlet, *A Regular Business Man*, by John Stokes. Sime Silverman called him, in *Variety* (February 24, 1912), "one of the best light comedians who ever played in vaudeville."

There were others whose vaudeville careers were slight in comparison to later screen or stage, careers. Patricia Collinge made her vaudeville debut at New York's Fifth Avenue Theatre on September 27, 1908, billed as "A Little Girl From Dublin." Ina Claire, "The Singing Comedienne," appeared in vaudeville in the spring of 1909. Vivienne Segal, who starred in a number of early Warner Bros. musical features, appeared at the Palace in June 1922; "as a straight singing single she is an acquisition," reported *Variety* (June 30, 1922). Jane and Ginger Rogers were a sister act at New York's American Theatre in May 1928. "Nice looking girls who haven't much of a chance," commented *Variety* (May 16, 1928). "Just a pair without the professional touch and nothing to suggest that they will attain it." Ethel Merman teamed with Al Siegal in a 1930 act titled "Modern Songs in Modern Style," and *Variety* (July 9, 1930) reported, "She is a good looking girl with a fair enough voice that might carry much further with special stuff."

Eleanor Powell had worked in vaudeville in the 1920s and early 1930s before entering films in 1935. Her career came full circle when she took a hiatus from the screen in 1939 to tour the vaudeville circuit with an act that included four dance numbers and impersonations of Katharine Hepburn and James Stewart. "Her work was tops," reported *The Billboard* (May 6, 1939), upon seeing her act at Loew's State, New York.

BIBLIOGRAPHY

"12 Film Stars in Bloomer." *Variety*, March 4, 1925, pp. 1, 34.

FINK'S MULES

Fink's Mules is, without question, the most famous opening act in the history of vaudeville, an act that has taken on mythological proportions despite the almost total lack of documentation on its existence. It is recalled with fondness by every vaudevillian, and yet nothing is known of Fink or his origins. Despite the name, Fink's Mules was not an act entirely made up of mules, but also included ponies, dogs, and monkeys. Nor was it the only act of its type, having been preceded by Cliff Berzac's animals. (According to Joe Laurie, Jr., in his book *Vaudeville*, the latter was a very funny act; "people from the audience were invited to ride [a bucking mule] for a reward and of course the stooges came up and were very funny. This had been done for years in vaude and in circuses, but Berzac was the first to have a turntable to try to ride and it really had the customers in hysterics!").

Fink's Mules was a comedy act featuring a stereotypical stupid Negro attempting to ride a mule, and it first came to the attention of the critics when it played the opening ten minutes of the Palace bill in April 1918. Why do people remember Fink's Mules? Perhaps because, as Ken Murray recalled, it is quite a task to train a mule. Or perhaps because, as Sime Silverman wrote in *Variety* (April 19, 1918), "The trainer is middle-aged, the setting and apparatus are bright looking, also clean, with the animals the same, and the act may be counted upon as a comedy number in any program."

Aside from playing the Palace in New York, Fink's Mules was also featured at the Hippodrome in April 1926.

JAY C. FLIPPEN (Little Rock, Ak., March 6, 1898—Hollywood, Ca., February 3, 1971)

Jay C. Flippen worked in vaudeville as both a white and blackface comedian, but critics and audiences alike seemed to prefer him in the latter makeup. When he was in whiteface, *Variety* (March 26, 1930) wrote, "His blackface was always one of the best among many." Three months later, with Flippen back in blackface, *Variety* (June 11, 1930) commented, "Flip's style, delivery voice, diction, face and every gesture are built for cork." Flippen's background was decidedly blackface. At the age of fourteen, he had joined a minstrel show; he understudied Al Jolson and worked in tab shows and burlesque before becoming a vaudeville comedian billed as "The Ham What Am." From the mid 1920s onward, Flippen was active on the Broadway stage, appearing in *June Days* (1925), *Hello, Lola!* (1926), *The Great Temptations* (1926), *Padlocks of 1927* (1927), and *The Second Little Show* (1930), among other productions. He was a frequent headliner at the Palace, starring there in March and September 1926, May 1927, January 1928, January 1929, and February 1931.

The comedian appeared briefly in films in the 1930s, but it was not until a decade later than he made his mark as a craggy-faced character actor in *Brute Force* (1947), *They Live by Night* (1950), *Oklahoma!* (1955), *The Killing* (1956), *How the West Was Won* (1962), and other productions. During the filming of *Cat Ballou* in 1964, his right leg became infected and was later amputated, but he continued to work from a wheelchair in both films and television. His best known work in the latter medium was as Chief Petty Officer Homer Nelson in *Ensign O'Toole* (NBC, 1962–1963). At his funeral, Milton Berle described Flippen as "one of the greatest standup comedians I ever saw."

FOLIES BERGERE

The first attempt in the United States to present vaudeville in a supper club atmosphere was the Folies Bergere. This first cabaret-style theatre-restaurant was opened by Jesse L. Lasky and Henry B. Harris on April 16, 1911. It was located at 210 West 46th Street, New York. Two performances an evening were presented, with the first featuring two burlesques and a ballet, and the second a "cabaret" or vaudeville performance, which began at 11 P.M. and ran until 1 A.M. Diners were served between 6 and 8:15, to the accompaniment of a live orchestra. Seating prices ranged from $1 and $2 in the balcony through $2.50 in the restaurant section, and $20 for a box seating six for the first show and $12 in the same location for the second.

The opening show began with a burlesque titled *Hell*, written by Renold Wolf, followed by a second burlesque, *Gaby*, based on the much publicized love affair between Gaby Deslys and King Manuel of Portugal. Ethel Levey played Gaby and English comedian Laddie Cliff was the king. Among those appearing in *Hell* were Otis Harlan, Mayme Kelso, Arthur Lipson, Taylor Holmes, and Kathleen Clifford. The cabaret program was not overly exciting, featuring a French singing comedienne named Jeanette Denarber, singer Maude Tiffany with Ted Snyder at the piano, the Pender Troupe, Brice and King, Moffett and Clare, Mlle Simone de Bergi, and the Roberty Dancers. The opening night program began with a near disaster, when, at the close of the *Hell* presentation, the head of a standpipe blew off, releasing five thousand gallons of water, which came crashing through the ceiling over the theatre's east entrance. Many in the audience were drenched, but according to Sime Silverman in *Variety*, "The people behaved splendidly. The excitement quickly subsided when it was announced from the stage the cause and effect.''

Silverman was quite enthused over the project:

''The conception certainly never equaled the magnificence of the completion. Messrs. Harris and Lasky have gone the limit. This they have done in every respect, from the restaurant to the cabaret, taking in the theatre itself, and not forgetting other little innovations for theatre-goers, such as, for instance, a call boy inquiring of patrons shortly before the ending of the evening whether they wish a taxi giving a numbered card to those who do, the card becoming the person's carriage call. An interpreter is another new feature. The waiters are distinguished from the guests by uniforms of grey, following the dress style. Even the 'captains' of the waiters, though wearing the regulation evening clothes, have silver buttons on their coats. Some of the better known restaurants in New York could learn a few things at the Folies Bergere, both in the service and the cooking of the food.''

The Folies Bergere was not a success. Lasky and Harris brought over Madame Olga Petrova from England in August 1911, but she failed to please at that time. Within a few months, the Folies Bergere closed its doors for good. In October 1911, the building reopened as a legitimate theatre, the Fulton, under which name it continued to operate until 1955, when it was renamed the Helen Hayes Theatre.

FOURTEENTH STREET THEATRE. See TONY PASTOR

HARRY FOX (Pomona, Ca., May 25, 1882—Woodland Hills, Ca., July 20, 1959)

Harry Fox boasted an ingratiating personality that made him a natural juvenile favorite on the vaudeville stage. His comic songs were often enhanced with a chirping whistle and what seemed to be a perpetual smile. He epitomized the youthful, relaxed leading man, and had he not been a comedian, could easily have found employment as a lightweight star of musical comedies.

Born Arthur Carrington, the comedian adopted the surname of one of his ancestors, George L. Fox, a noted clown. Determining to follow in the latter's tradition, Harry Fox ran away from home at the age of fifteen and joined a circus. From there, he moved to burlesque and stock companies. In the early years of the twentieth century, he teamed with the Millership Sisters, and with them was reasonably successful on the vaudeville stage. One of his first important appearances in revue was in *The Passing Show of 1912*. He supported Gaby Deslys in *The Honeymoon Express* (1913) and *Stop! Look! Listen!* (1915); the former show also featured Yansci Dolly of the Dolly Sisters, who became Mrs. Harry Fox.

In the 1920s, Fox appeared in *All Star Jamboree* (1921) and *Round the Town* (1924), but his most important show was the 1925 edition of George White's *Scandals*. Harry Fox first appeared at the Palace in March 1914 with Yansci

Dolly (minus her sister). He was a frequent visitor in the 1920s, headlining there in June and December 1926, October 1927, and November 1928. He blended comedy patter with lightweight songs such as "Halfway to Heaven" and "Belles of Hotels" (whose subtitle, "Towels! Towels! Towels!", gives some indication of the number's story line).

Harry Fox had entered films in 1916, playing in the serial *Beatrice Fairfax*, and also made a handful of comedy shorts for Essanay in the mid teens. In 1920, he announced his plan to leave the stage for motion pictures, but Fox was never more than a lowly supporting, or bit, player on-screen, with his last known credit being *Easter Parade* (1948).

Prior to his marriage to Yansci Dolly, Fox had been married to Beatrice Curtis (died 1936) and appeared with her in vaudeville, continuing to do so in the 1920s. Following his divorce from Yansci Dolly in 1931, Fox married screen actress Evelyn Brent. He ended his working life as a photo laboratory technician with Douglas Aircraft Company in Los Angeles, before illness forced his retirement in 1956.

It has been suggested that the dance the foxtrot originated with and was named after Harry Fox in 1913; the dance was later modified and made famous by Oscar Duryea.

BIBLIOGRAPHY

"Harry Fox Tells Story of Success." *The New York Dramatic Mirror*, July 3, 1920, p. 18.

EDDIE FOY (New York, March 9, 1854—Kansas City, Mo., February 16, 1928)

Eddie Foy came to vaudeville somewhat late in his career, but when he arrived on the scene, he was welcomed and loved by audiences and management alike. After his death, E. F. Albee wrote in *Vaudeville News and New York Star* (February 25, 1928):

"There is no doubt that Eddie Foy brought as much wholesome happiness to the American public as any artist of the stage. With his humorous and witty clowning throughout his long career, literally he made millions laugh without ever affronting the good taste or sensibilities of anyone in his audience. Unlike most comedians, Eddie Foy's droll antics, absurd pantomime, and farcical singing and dancing captured and kept the young as well as the old, the innocent as well as the wise. Probably he was the favorite of more entire American families than any other stage artist. His last vehicle, a sketch called 'The Fallen Star,' booked as his farewell tour as a fitting climax to his fifty-six years on the stage, was a complete success from its start but when Eddie Foy looked over the long itinerary ahead of him he said with his quaint smile, 'That is certainly the longest continuous tour that I ever started on. I doubt if I will live to finish it.' Well it is finished, sooner than anyone could guess, but probably in the manner he might have chosen—in working to the last, happy in his beloved profession, and giving of his best to make others happy. He was an inspiration to all his countrymen and an honor to the N.V.A. and to his profession. . . . I shall miss his hearty salutation whenever he left. I shall always remember his kindly and humane qualities. I have lost a real friend.''

The comedian was born Edward Fitzgerald in New York's Greenwich Village, the son of a tailor from Dublin. When his father died in 1862, the young Eddie took to singing, dancing, and performing acrobatics in local saloons to help his impoverished family. Sometimes, he would appear in blackface, singing:

I'm happy little Ned;
I earn my daily bread
By doing chores for white folks 'round the town.
I was never known to shirk
From any kind of work,
At blacking boots there's none can take me down.

In 1865, the family moved to Chicago, just in time for the great fire. At the age of sixteen, Eddie teamed with another boy, Jack Finnegan, but because Finnegan and Foy sounded too Irish, they billed themselves as Edwards and Foy. The two played beer halls, singing and dancing, and appearing in blackface. Later, Eddie Foy teamed with Ben Collins in a similar act, and he also began to work as a ''super'' at McVicker's Theatre and the Academy of Music in Chicago. Circuses and minstrel shows followed, and it was a tough, uphill climb until Foy became known as ''a Western variety artist,'' playing everywhere in the West, from Butte, Montana, to Denver, and from Dodge City, Kansas, to San Francisco. From 1888 through 1894, Foy appeared under the management of David Henderson in fantasies such as *Cinderella*, *Ali Baba*, and *Sinbad the Sailor*, performing in Chicago and on tour. As Foy recalled them, they were ''years of unqualified success, even of triumph; years of freedom from business or financial worry.''

Eddie Foy became a Broadway star thanks to his mimicry, pantomime clowning, and eccentric dancing in *The Strollers* in 1901. His greatest stage success was as Sister Anne, singing ''I'm a Poor Unhappy Maid'' and ''Hamlet Was a Melancholy Dane'' in *Mr. Bluebeard*, which opened at the Iroquois Theatre, Chicago, on November 23, 1903. Foy was appearing in *Mr. Bluebeard* (which had originally been a Theatre Royal, Drury Lane, production) when the tragic fire occurred at the theatre on December 30, 1903.

There was a natural Irish complexion to Foy's features, but in most of his stage productions, he appeared in eccentric costumes or, in the case of *Mr. Bluebeard*, in drag. In 1903, *Vanity Fair* wrote of him, ''Every movement of his facial muscles tells a complete story of his prevailing emotions.'' Offstage, he was apparently very different, and according to *The Billboard* in 1911, ''Eddie Foy, who is so dry, arch, and ludicrous on the stage, is rather quiet in private life and converses in a low tone with little laughter. He has, however, a kindly smile which flickers across his face when something amusing occurs to him.'' Foy was married four times. In 1879, he wed an actress named Rose Holland, by whom he had two children, both of whom died. After Holland's death, he married another actress, Lola Sefton, and when she died in 1896, he married Madeleine Morande, a member of the Chicago Opera House ballet. Morande died in 1918, and in 1923, Foy married Marie Reilly. By Madeleine Morande, he had eleven children, of whom only seven lived. But those seven—Charles, Richard, Irving, Bryan, Madeline, Mary, and Eddie, Jr.—were to play an important part in the comedian's career after 1910.

Eddie Foy had played major vaudeville in the early years of the century, giving impersonations of President Theodore Roosevelt, John D. Rockefeller, and Elsie Janis. "He is one of the funniest acts in vaudeville at the present time," commented Sime Silverman in *Variety* (May 19, 1906). On August 12, 1910, Eddie Foy made his first appearance with his children, the Seven Little Foys, at a Lambs Club picnic. Within two years, Eddie Foy and the Seven Little Foys were established vaudevillians, and Eddie never really returned to the legitimate stage, content with his "happy family and happy act," as *Variety* (August 23, 1912) described them. They appeared in sketches titled "Fun in the Foy Family," "The Old Woman Who Lived in a Shoe," and "Slumwhere in New York," most of them written by Will Jerome. In any town that Foy was appearing, he would joke that if he and his family lived there, it would be a city. Eddie Foy, Jr., would imitate his father, and there would be dialogue such as the following between Madeline and her father. "Bring me a home a doll," she asked. "What kind of doll?" "Oh, mamma says you know all about dolls," answered Madeline. "I know enough about them not to bring them home," responded Foy. At the end of the act, Mrs. Foy would often appear and take—in view of the offspring—a well-deserved bow.

Madeline Foy (who died in Los Angeles on July 5, 1988, at the age of eighty) recalled, "We had a private tutor and our aunt. We had a lot of people taking care of us. We sang and danced. We had very good voices. We'd come out all in a line, and my father would bring out a little suitcase in which was my brother Irving, who was two years old. Then we'd sing a medley; each one would step down and sing a song. Then Eddie, Charlie, and Mary would dance. We used to do a march at the finish of the act. Old-fashioned and corney, I guess, but it was cute." Madeline Foy doubted the story that her father went into vaudeville because of a fight with theatrical entrepreneur Lee Shubert, that resulted in Foy's pushing Shubert into a theatre pit and the later banning of the comedian from Shubert theatres for all time.

B. F. Keith's *Theatre News* in Washington, D.C., commented on September 15, 1919: "The Foy family in vaudeville presents a simple problem in arithmetic. If one Foy is funny, how funny are eight Foys? Those who have followed Eddie Foy and the younger Foys throughout their stage career know the answer. Eddie Foy has been and still is one of the brightest spots in American amusement. His peculiar methods have set a fashion in humor these many years, and his family is each and every one a chip off the old block. The family has been working together in a humanitarian effort to bring more cheer into the world for several years. In stature, one of the elder Foys is larger than his pater. But the stature has nothing whatever to do with fun, as shown by the fact that the smallest of the Foy progeny is generally conceded the best comedian of them all, not even excluding poppa Foy.''

As the children grew, the act split up. Bryan went into the film industry, becoming one of the pioneers of the sound motion picture at Warner Bros. After Eddie Foy's 1923 marriage, there was a brief period of animosity between father and children, and in time the younger Foys developed their own vaudeville act. Eddie Foy died in Kansas City, while appearing on the Orpheum circuit in the title role of the sketch ''The Fallen Star,'' by Tom Barry. He signed himself off with the words, ''On the whole, life has been a pretty jolly affair. I have no complaints to make, and few regrets.''

Eddie Foy, Jr. (1905–1983), appeared at the Palace in September and December 1927 and made his Broadway debut two years later in *Show Girl*. That same year, he made his feature film debut in *Queen of the Night Clubs*. He was featured in many Broadway shows, including *The Cat and the Fiddle* (1931), *At Home Abroad* (1945) and *The Pajama Game* (1954), as well as countless films through the 1960s. He played his father in *Lillian Russell* (1940), *Yankee Doodle Dandy* (1942), and *Wilson* (1944). His father was portrayed by Bob Hope in the 1955 film *The Seven Little Foys*.

IRENE FRANKLIN (New York, June 13, 1876—Englewood, N.J., June 16, 1941)

In 1908, in a popularity contest organized by Percy Williams to find the Most Popular Woman Vaudeville Artist, the winner was impressionist and singing comedienne Irene Franklin, who easily beat out Eva Tanguay, Vesta Victoria, and Marie Dressler. Her songs, such as ''Be Your Age,'' are works of original satire, laced with venom. Reviewing Franklin's act in *The New York Dramatic Mirror* (May 12, 1915), Frederick James Smith wrote, ''She injects so much humor, she touches such a vibrant note of pathos that she is quite irresistible. Her 'kid' songs are unforgettable, and her slangy dissertation of a chorus girl invading the Great White Way was a little masterpiece of characterization.'' A year later—on April 29, 1916—Smith returned to his subject: ''She combines an almost O. Henry understanding of everyday life with a Eugene Field sense of childhood. And, aside from her creation of lyrics, as Will Cressy has said, she can tell a story with a single movement of her hands.''

Irene Franklin claimed to have made her stage debut at the age of six months; certainly she played all the usual child roles of the period, from *Shore Acres* to *Editha's Burglar*, before embarking on a vaudeville tour of Australia at the age of fifteen. In 1894, she appeared in London variety theatres, and the following year made her American vaudeville debut. At the age of twenty, Irene Franklin was an established vaudeville performer, usually providing her own material consisting of kiddie songs such as ''I'm Nobody's Baby Now'' and satires on such social phenomena as the feminist movement, lampooned in ''The Woman

Policeman.'' She sang the plight of the unmarried woman in ''If I Don't Lock My Father Up, It's the Old Maid's Home for Me.'' With the advent of prohibition, Franklin sang of the man who didn't carry a hip flask in the risqué number, ''What Have You Got on Your Hip? You Don't Seem to Bulge Where a Gentleman Ought to.'' The teens craze of the *thé dansant* was parodied in ''At the Dansant.'' ''Help! Help! Help!'' was the lament of the fireman's wife who did not understand why the showgirls whom her husband had to rescue always had to wear such skimpy attire.

In the brilliant 1907 song ''Expression,'' Franklin illustrated all the human emotions by facial expressions. A year later, she introduced ''Red Head,'' in which she portrayed a little, red-headed schoolgirl who tells of the names she is called by the other children. Sime Silverman wrote in *Variety* (October 10, 1908), ''It is a work of art in character study, and Miss Franklin's delivery could not be improved upon.'' ''Red Head'' was composed by Burton Green, who was for many years Irene Franklin's pianist, filling in onstage while she executed her various costume changes. The couple first met when the singer played Tony Pastor's where Green was the resident pianist at $75 a week. Green divorced his wife, writer Helen Van Campen, and he and Irene Franklin became a team in private life and on the vaudeville stage until Green's death on November 17, 1922. The couple entertained the troops in France during the First World War, and were the first vaudeville artists to have a paid advertisement on the front cover of *Variety* on December 19, 1913.

A few years earlier, on December 4, 1909, Franklin and Green had placed another advertisement in *Variety*, noting that all of the entertainers' songs were copyrighted and that their attorney, Nathan Burkan, would take action against anyone attempting to imitate Irene Franklin or sing Burt Green's songs. ''Persons wanting to give an imitation of Miss Franklin can use 'Red Head,' '' the advertisement continued. ''The song will go no matter how badly you sing it.''

After Green's death, Franklin married another pianist, Jerry Jarnigan, who died in 1934. She continued in vaudeville and also returned to the legitimate stage, appearing in shows in New York, Los Angeles, and San Francisco. She had made her legitimate stage debut in New York as Josephine Zaccary in *The Orchid* at the Herald Square Theatre in 1907; her other non-vaudeville shows include *Hands Up* (1915) and *The Passing Show of 1917* (1917). With the demise of vaudeville, Franklin entered films in 1933, appearing in *Lazy River* (1934), *Change of Heart* (1934), *The President Vanishes* (1934), *Timothy's Quest* (1936), *Song and Dance Man* (1936), *Midnight Madonna* (1937), *Married before Breakfast* (1937), and *Fixer Dugan* (1939), among others. She died in poverty at the Actors Fund Home in Englewood, New Jersey. Only three days earlier, she had celebrated her sixty-fifth birthday, and *The New York Times* reported she had written a friend, ''Another of my Friday the Thirteenth birthdays is upon me, but I don't think there are many who will remember me or who care.''

It is hard to analyze or describe the work of this red-headed comedienne. At the time of her death, some writers compared her to Beatrice Lillie, but it is clear that Irene Franklin's songs and impersonations were less subtle than those of Lillie. Take, for example, the tale of a passenger asking the conductor to put him off at Watt Street. The play on the word Watt—"What street?" "Yes, Watt Street," etc.—is amusing, but hardly original. Possibly the best comment on the art of Irene Franklin comes from "Rush" in *Variety* (February 9, 1907): "a style that is smooth and quiet but which baffles accurate description." One thing is very clear. In an age when vaudeville performers generally impersonated other celebrities, Irene Franklin impersonated the ordinary working woman and child— in other words, her audience—and in this her comic style is most closely approximated today by that of Lily Tomlin.

BIBLIOGRAPHY

Franklin, Irene. "How Not to Write Lyrics—Being an Exposition of Curious Phenomena, as Observed by a Collector of Crippled and Destitute Story Compositions." *Variety*, December 14, 1907, pp. 20, 65.

―――――. "Making Songs Tell a Story." *The New York Dramatic Mirror*, December 16, 1914, p. 19.

WILLIAM FRAWLEY (Burlington, Ia., February 26, 1887—Hollywood, Ca., March 3, 1966)

Adept at portraying gruff characters with soft hearts, William Frawley's chief claim to immortality is for his role as neighbor Fred Mertz on *I Love Lucy* (CBS, 1951–1957) and as Michael Francis "Bub" O' Casey on *My Three Sons* (ABC, 1960–1964). Frawley entered vaudeville at the age of twenty in a singing and comedy act with his brother Paul. With his wife, Edna (married 1914; divorced 1927), he performed a dancing and singing act; they played the Hippodrome, San Francisco, in September 1918, when the featured number was "I'm Going to Hang Around till I Make You Care for Me." Although his screen career did not start in earnest until 1931, Frawley was a fixture in Southern California in the teens, working as an unbilled player at the American "Flying A" Company in Santa Barbara, and also dancing with his wife at Al Levy's Spring Street Cafe in Los Angeles. He began appearing in Broadway musicals in the mid 1920s, and had his first straight role on Broadway in *20th Century* (1932). Frawley died of a heart attack while taking an evening stroll down Hollywood Boulevard.

BIBLIOGRAPHY

Nash, Jay Robert. "William Frawley." In *Zanies*. Piscataway, N.J.: New Century, 1932, pp. 140–42.

Conlon, Scoop. "Bill Frawley." *Photoplay* vol. 47, no. 2 (January 1935), pp. 58, 116.

FREAK ACTS

Freak acts in vaudeville were primarily limited to the stage of Willie Hammerstein's Victoria Theatre and were generally short-lived. They chiefly comprised those with unusual physical deformities or individuals who had become instant celebrities in the popular press. Evelyn Nesbit Thaw, who survived longer than most freak acts, became a vaudeville headliner because her husband shot and killed her lover, architect Stanford White. Peaches Browning embarked on a vaudeville career in 1926 when the fifteen-year-old schoolgirl split up from her fifty-one-year-old millionaire husband, Edward "Daddy" Browning. The Victoria Theatre was no longer in operation for freak acts such as Peaches Browning, but there was still a market in vaudeville. Indeed, Edward Browning, dubbed by the tabloids as "High Priest of the Daddy Cult," could equally have been successful on the vaudeville stage, had he so desired.

Some freak acts, such as the Cherry Sisters, never understood that they were so labeled. Others quickly learned the reality of the situation, and the story is often told of a would-be suicide who volunteered to kill himself on the stage of the Victoria Theatre, only to be asked by Willie Hammerstein what he would do for an encore. The closest Hammerstein came to a suicide onstage was a playlet titled *Electrocution*, presented in May 1914, in which a murderer was shown dying in the electric chair, complete with sparks, crackling, and electric flashes. Objection to the playlet was such that it was taken off after two performances, with *The New York Dramatic Mirror* (May 27, 1914) opining, "Electrocution could appeal only to an exceedingly morbid minded person."

Of the genuine freak acts, one of the most revolting, but popular, was Willard, the Man Who Grows, billed as "the star attraction of the Wintergarten, Berlin." Clarence E. Willard was featured in vaudeville during 1913 and 1914, and could add 7½ inches to his height of 5 feet, 9-3/4 inches. He could extend his arms to anywhere from 8 to 15 inches, and could make one leg 4 inches longer than the other. As "Wynn" noted in *Variety* (October 17, 1914), "Willard is one of that strange species of novelty that one must see to appreciate."

If Willard sounds repulsive, consider Doss, who was similarly billed as "The Man That Grows." *Variety*'s "Wynn" also reported on his act, at the American Roof, on December 8, 1916:

Entirely devoid of personality, appearance or general stage ability and entirely valueless for entertaining, since there is not even an atom of mystery surrounding his speciality, "Major" Doss billed at Loew's American as "The Man That Grows," comes under the natural classification of a museum act. Doss is introduced by an announcer who gives a brief history of his life. Among other things he explained that during an attempted balloon ascension some years ago Doss suffered a fall which resulted in curvature of the spine. Doss is a hunchback and the disfiguration naturally leads one to the solution of the growth mystery. During the turn Doss squirms the hunch around from his back to his chest, one of the most disgusting "bits" ever shown on a stage, and any manager who would permit the exhibition before an audience of women should have his brain examined.

In the fall of 1912, the Women's Suffrage Party of Greater New York gave a seventeen-minute performance at Hammerstein's Victoria Theatre. *Variety* (September 13, 1912) reported that their reception was cool, largely because too many of their sisters were where they should be, at home taking care of the laundry and kids. Paul Swann was a somewhat effeminate dancer of the Isadore Duncan school, who billed himself as "The Most Beautiful Man in the World" when he played Hammerstein's Victoria Theatre in October 1914. He was subjected to a certain amount of ribaldry and jeering from the audience, and Sime

Silverman commented in *Variety* (November 1, 1914), "He died in the final dance, and it's tough to die at Hammerstein's."

Mr. and Mrs. General Tom Thumb played Hammerstein's Victoria in September 1914, helped by Loney Haskins, who revealed to the audience that Mrs. Thumb was seventy-three years of age, but neglected to document her husband's age. Sime Silverman commented in *Variety* (October 3, 1914):

> The little set these miniature people use, together with their small voices made the "sketch" they are trying to present look like a marionette show.... The midgets are recalled by name and fame as freak attractions, having exhibited in side shows and museums for years, if not all of the present troupe, some of them. They are not to be seriously considered as actors, and what they did doesn't matter—it is the sight of these very little people who are so well known by reputation. But for vaudeville that means little now, as midgets are employed who are real entertainers, something the Thumbs probably have never aspired to.... It just drew curiosity, satisfied at first sight. The program billed the people as Count, Countess and Baron Magri, quite some nobility in the reading.

From the world of fashion, Lucile, otherwise known as Lady Duff Gordon, presented her fashion show at the Palace in December 1917, and proved so popular that she was held over for a second week. Another member of the British aristocracy who tried vaudeville was Lady Aberdeen, whose 1918 act was assured of success by her singing of "America" at its close. From the criminal world, vaudeville presented famed outlaw Al Jennings, who talked to audiences in 1921. Reviewing his act, *Variety* (February 11, 1921) commented, "His monolog is a preachment against outlawry.... As it stands, it is rather dull and Jennings falls into the freak class."

The sports and the associated world provided many freak acts. In December 1909, Sam Mahoney expounded on the value of cold water bathing at New York's Fifth Avenue Theatre. He spent six minutes in an ice-cold water tank and then delivered his speech seated on a block of ice. "Like other 'freak' offerings, this one will hold the interest as long as the public yearns for frapped amusements," commented *The New York Dramatic Mirror* (December 25, 1909). In the fall of 1926, Babe Ruth played vaudeville houses in San Francisco and Minneapolis as a monologist. That same year, Gertrude Ederle, the first woman to swim the English Channel, proved fairly popular on the vaudeville stage. She earned $1,000 a day at Brooklyn's Mark Strand Theatre with an act similar to that of Annette Kellermann, which included waltzing underwater. One of the most popular sporting acts to play vaudeville was Jack Dempsey; in February and March 1922, he played the New York Hippodrome for four weeks at a guarantee of $5,000 a week, and in the first week he earned $7,000 as his percentage of the gross. Dempsey's act consisted primarily of a dialogue with his manager, Jack Kearns, with jokes such as, "They [the girls] calls me honey; I get stung so often." With references to his knocking out Georges Carpentier in the fourth round, he talked of French and American national holidays and punned, "But we Americans all celebrate the fourth." So popular did Jack

Dempsey prove to be in vaudeville that he returned, again with manager Kearns, to play the Loew's circuit in October 1924.

Earlier, in March and April 1909, world heavyweight champion Jack Johnson had played vaudeville at Hammerstein's Victoria, fighting and winning a three-round contest with white boxer Kid Cutler. "Johnson is a drawing card, and seems to attract even those hostile to him through his color," reported *Variety* (April 3, 1909). In August of the following year, Johnson embarked on a thirty-week vaudeville tour.

An unusual freak act that played New York's 86th Street Theatre in October 1928 was a group of Hopi Indians, who performed a snake and other tribal dances. Audiences were not enthusiastic. One of the most extraordinary and certainly most moving of freak acts was Helen Keller, who played the Palace in February 1920. With her mentor, Annie Sullivan, she demonstrated lip-reading and answered questions from the audience. When asked what she thought of Sullivan, Keller did not reply but placed her head on Annie Sullivan's shoulder and gave her a hug. "It was a throb scene," commented Sime Silverman in *Variety* (February 27, 1920). Helen Keller was billed as "Deaf but not Dumb."

The freak act of all time came late in vaudeville's life when, in September 1933, Aimee Semple MacPherson played New York's Capitol Theatre. For $5,000 a week, MacPherson, wearing a white dress with a large cross dangling in front of her bosom, told audiences of her life and her religion. When she thanked God for His kindness in providing her with a steady income, there were hoots of derision from the audience, but nothing disturbed the evangelist. What disturbed the management was the scarcity of people in the audience, for, as *Variety* (September 26, 1933) pointed out, "As a box office attraction it looked like the founder and general manager of 226 churches was a washout."

See also HADJI ALI, CHERRY SISTERS, LONEY HASKELL, VIOLET AND DAISY HILTON, ALFRED LATELL, CARRY AMELIA MOORE NATION, POLAIRE, EVELYN NESBIT THAW.

LEOPOLDO FREGOLI (Rome, July 2, 1867—Viareggio, Italy, November 26, 1936)

Leopoldo Fregoli was a fast-change artist, who was extremely successful on his first New York appearance on the roof of the Olympia Theatre in the summer of 1896. Writing in *The Illustrated American* (July 25, 1896), Julian Jerrold commented:

" 'El Dorado,' his latest creation, is a perfect bewilderment. A ballet-dancer, an ingenue, an aged woman with remnants of a voice and memories of the rest of it, an impressario, a juggler, a hypnotist, a prestidigitateur, a musician playing half a dozen musical instruments, a magician, a series of orchestra conductors, an exposer of magician's tricks, and other personalities to the number of sixty, are included in the gamut of changes presented by this remarkable artist. The rapidity and completeness of the transitions from one impersonation to another, and the truthfulness that marks them all, are incredible unless seen. His performance lasts over an hour, and to the audience it seems as though sixty different men and women were engaged in giving an evening's entertainment. His impersonation of Herrmann is perfect, and the exposure of the famous tricks of the magician always provokes laughter.''

A superior fast-change artist, Fregoli was not a great actor, and there were often complaints that he mumbled his lines. *Variety* first reported his death in Paris on December 10, 1910, but it proved to be false. Fregoli retired in 1922.

THE FRIARS CLUB

The Friars Club is the common name by which the leading fraternal association of variety entertainers, the Friars National Association, Inc., is known. It was organized in New York on November 15, 1904, as the Press Agents' Association by Charles Emerson Cook, Channing Pollock, and John S. Flaherty to identify and eliminate individuals who used fraudulent means to obtain ''free passes'' to theatre presentations. The organization expanded in 1906 to include press agents from throughout the country, and on November 16, 1907, it was incorporated as the Friars, which was considered simpler and more expressive than the association's original name.

In 1907, Wells Hawks was elected the first president, or abbot, of the Friars. Others who have served long terms as abbots are George M. Cohan (1912–1919, 1928–1932), George Jessel (1933–1935), Jay C. Flippen (1936–1938), Milton Berle (1940–1945, 1947–1953), Joe E. Lewis (1954–1971), Ed Sullivan (1972–1974), and Frank Sinatra (1975—present).

The Friars moved to its first clubhouse, at 107 West 45th Street, on May 9, 1908. At the first election held there, it was decided that the clubhouse should be known as the Monastery. An annual Frolic, held by the Friars since 1907, raised funds in June 1911 to acquire the site for a new club house at 106–110 West 48th Street, and on October 21, 1915, George M. Cohan led a march of the members to the new location, where the cornerstone was laid. The new Monastery opened on May 22, 1916, with Cohan again leading the members in a march to the building. After entering the clubhouse, Cohan threw the key to the front door into the street, symbolizing that the building would never be closed. However, that impossibility happened in 1932 as a result of the depression and the end of vaudeville. A small group of members continued to meet at various locations, and in 1948, Milton Berle was able to arrange for the acquisition of a new clubhouse at 123 West 56th Street, which opened the following year. In 1956, the membership voted to move to yet a new clubhouse at 57 East 55th Street, 10022, the former home of investment banker Martin Erdmann. The new Monastery was formally opened in November 1957.

As early as 1907, the Friars had hosted dinners honoring major figures in the theatre, beginning with Clyde Fitch. In 1950, it began annual testimonial dinners and celebrity luncheons, with the first honorees being Joe E. Lewis and Sam Levenson.

A Los Angeles branch of the Friars Club was founded in 1947. As early as

1949, it hosted a Friars Frolic at the Shrine Auditorium, and out of this event grew the Friars "roasts," noted for the bawdy language of their speakers and the large sums of money raised for charity. Milton Berle was abbot of the Los Angeles Friars Club from 1962–1992, when he was succeeded by Steve Allen. That last year, the club announced plans to increase its failing membership by recruiting new, younger comedians.

Address: 9900 Little Santa Monica Boulevard, Beverly Hills, Ca. 90212.

BIBLIOGRAPHY

Adams, Joey. *Here's to the Friars: The Heart of Show Business*. New York: Crown, 1976.

Frolick, Billy. "Take Our Club, Please." *Los Angeles Times Calendar*, August 9, 1992, pp. 5, 28–30.

Jones, D. M. "The Friars—A Unique Theatrical Club—Its Beginnings and Its Present Status." *New York Star* 1, no. 25 (March 20, 1909), pp. 14–15, 20.

TRIXIE FRIGANZA (Grenola, Ks., November 29, 1870—Flintridge, Ca., February 27, 1955)

Trixie Friganza was credited with having a unique comic sense and a gentle humor she used chiefly on herself. She was a large woman, made even larger by the innumerable costumes she would discard one at a time during the performance, and her weight was one source of her humor. Trixie described herself as a "perfect forty-six," sang songs like "I'm Not Having Birthdays Anymore," and told 1920 audiences that "the way for a fat woman to do the shimmy is to walk fast and stop short." She announced that her favorite stone was a brick and told of the village belle who spurned the livery stable keeper for a greenhouse worker because of atmospheric reasons. She was always on the lookout for a suitor, be it only "my garbageman," whom she sang about in 1918; three years earlier she had been lamenting "Won't Someone Kindly Stake Me to a Man?"

Born Delia O'Callahan, Trixie Friganza was educated at St. Patrick's School, Cincinnatti. She took her mother's maiden name for her first stage appearance in the chorus of *The Pearl of Pekin* on October 23, 1889. In 1892, she was introduced to audiences in *The Mascot*, starring Henry E. Dixey, and by the mid 1890s, Friganza had become a popular star performer, making her London debut in 1901 in *The Belle of Bohemia*. Her first vaudeville appearance was at Hammerstein's Theatre, New York, in the summer of 1906. Sime Silverman reported in *Variety* (June 2, 1906), "In the imitations Miss Friganza did, the most pronounced and important of which was that of Marie Dressler, there is really nothing discernible showing a studied effort in preparation. . . . There is no reason why Miss Friganza, with a well laid out offering, should not become a valuable attraction in vaudeville. She has the requisites otherwise. With her present material it will be a gamble."

Among Trixie Friganza's many early stage successes were *The Girl from Paris* (1901), *Sally in Our Alley* (1902), *The Prince of Pilsen* (1904), *Twiddle Twaddle* (1906), *The Orchid* (1908), *The American Idea* (1908), and *The Passing Show of 1912*. In the last, as part of a parody of *Oliver Twist*, Friganza played Nancy to the Bill Sikes of Charles J. Judels. From 1912 onward, Trixie was primarily active on the vaudeville stage. With her act ''My Little Bag o' Trix,'' she was always, as *Variety* wrote of her March 1920 appearance at the Palace, ''a riotous hit.''

In the 1920s, she headlined at the Palace in April 1924, May 1927, April and September 1928, and April 1929, and was also featured in *Murray Anderson's Almanac* (1929). At the same time, she also embarked on a film career as a character actress, easily making the transition from silents to sound, and appearing in, among other films, *The Coming of Amos* (1925), *The Road to Yesterday* (1925), *Monte Carlo* (1926), *Gentlemen Prefer Blondes* (1928), *Free and Easy* (1930), *Myrt and Marge* (1934), *Wanderer of the Wasteland* (1935), and *If I Had My Way* (1940). However, ''the Perpetual Flapper,'' as *The Billboard* dubbed her in 1931, was beginning to suffer more and more from arthritis. In 1940, she turned over her considerable fortune to the Flintridge (California) Academy of the Sacred Heart, and, despite some opposition from convent authorities, made her home there, occupying a room from which she could watch the Rose Bowl games in Pasadena at the foot of the hill. She also taught a drama class for the girls at the convent school until she became totally bedridden.

''The Champagne Girl,'' as she was sometimes called, gave an interview to the *Los Angeles Times* on the occasion of her seventy-ninth birthday. She told of her delight in watching television: ''You should hear me talk back to those actors. 'You still telling those old jokes and getting by with it?' I ask 'em. But they keep right on and pay no attention to me at all. Say, that's where vaudeville has gone—into television.''

JOE FRISCO (Milan, Il., 1889—Woodland Hills, Ca., February 12, 1958)

Joe Frisco was the comedian's comedian, of whom his fellow vaudevillians have always spoken with affection and often awe. At the same time, Frisco was not above trashing his colleagues as the following comments on Irving Berlin and Milton Berle indicate:

''That B-B-Berlin's got a h-h-hell of a voice, b-b-but you g-g-gotta hug him to hear him.''

''That B-B-Berle, when they m-m-made him they threw away the sh-sh-shovel.''

Those remarks also illustrate one of Frisco's trademarks, his acute stutter, which, apparently, was not an affectation. Joe Frisco was a small man, who always sported a derby hat and a cigar. His humor was as famous as his gambling, which kept him continually short of funds. The lack of money was another source of Frisco humor. An agent called, telling the comedian he could get him top billing at the Palace at $3,000 a week. ''Are you k-k-kiddin?'' stuttered Frisco on the telephone, ''you know my p-p-price is $3,500 and not a n-n-nickel less.'' The agent suggested Frisco come to his office and discuss the matter, to which came back the reply, ''W-w-what! And get locked out of my room?''

Born Louis W. Joseph, Joe Frisco began in vaudeville in 1903 with a soft-shoe routine in partnership with Andrew Coffee, in an act titled "Coffee and Doughnuts." The pair broke up in 1906, and Frisco came to Chicago, taking whatever employment was available, and even working for a while the following year as a stagehand for the Ziegfeld *Follies* when it played the city. He continued to dance in vaudeville, perfecting a routine called the "Frisco Dance," a soft-shoe shuffle performed to the music of the Dark Town Strutter's Ball. In 1917, he was in New York, performing in cabaret at Rector's Restaurant, and for the first time adding a monolog to his act. In 1920, he was featured in the Ziegfeld *Midnight Frolic*, and within a few years was a major star of vaudeville, headlining at the Palace in September 1927, June 1929, and December 1930, and also appearing in the 1928 edition of Earl Carroll's *Vanities*. He still danced, and even introduced a Jewish version of the Charleston.

Frisco seemed to tire of the effort needed to perform in vaudeville, and settled down to being the court jester to the vaudeville fraternity, performing more offstage than on. He made a number of films, including *The Gorilla* (1931), *Western Jamboree* (1938), *Ride Tenderfoot, Ride* (1940), *Atlantic City* (1944), *Shady Lady* (1945), *That's My Man* (1947), and *Sweet Smell of Success* (1957).

BIBLIOGRAPHY

Adams, Joey. "Happiness Was a Thing Called F-F-Frisco." *Coronet*, April 1968, pp. 50–54.

Hayes, Peter Lind. "M-M-Meet J-J-J-Joe F-F-F-Frisco." *Collier's*, December 1, 1951, pp. 20–21, 50, 52.

————. "A Character Called Frisco." *Variety*, January 4, 1967, p. 34.

Irwin, Ben. "Joe Frisco: He Stuttered to the Top." *Los Angeles Times Calendar*, April 19, 1981, p. 4.

LOÏE FULLER (Fullersburg, Il., January 15, 1862 or 1870—Paris, France, January 1, 1928)

Before Isadore Duncan appeared on the scene, Loïe Fuller (born Mary Louise Fuller) was probably the best known of American modern dancers, making her debut at the age of two-and-a-half and her first New York appearance in 1886. She introduced her famous "Serpentine Dance" at the Columbia Theatre, New York, on October 20, 1891, and was the hit of the 1900 Paris Exposition. Miss Fuller made a number of appearances on the vaudeville circuit, most notably in 1910. In January of that year, she introduced her new, seventeen-minute act, "Ballet of Light," at Keith's Theatre in Boston. Utilizing her own electricians and directing in person, she presented seven girls in flimsy white costumes dancing to the illumination of lights thrown from the proscenium arch, the rear of the theatre and the floor of the stage. Boston audiences liked the act, and on opening night she received four curtain calls. When the act played the Fifth Avenue Theatre, New York, *Variety* (February 26, 1910) was less enthusiastic: "Her new offering for beauty and color has it all over anything lately in the barefoot dancing line. But it will scarcely become a big box office attraction. The New York public has become sated with barefoot dancing."

Barefoot modern dancing enjoyed a brief vogue on the vaudeville stage, but it was very much a fad. As *Variety* (April 21, 1937) acidly remarked, "When Miss Fuller played with scarfs and lights there was a reason for it—she was blazing trails. There is no reason for it today."

BIBLIOGRAPHY

Anet, Claude. "Loïe Fuller in French Sculpture." *Architectural Record*, March 1903, pp. 270–78.
Kermode, Frank, "Loïe Fuller and the Dance before Diaghilev." *Theatre Arts* 46, no. 9 (September 1962), pp. 6–21.

WILL FYFFE (Dundee, Scotland, February 16, 1885–St. Andrews, Scotland, December 14, 1947)

A comedian and singer who typified the Scottish working man as he performed "I Belong to Glasgow" and "Ninety-Four Today," Will Fyffe was hailed in the United States as the best known Scotsman in show business after Harry Lauder. After more than twenty-five years on the stage, he made his first music hall appearance in London in 1916, but did not become a star until a 1921 performance at the London Palladium. In the late 1920s, he became a frequent entertainer at the Palace, appearing there in April 1927, February and March 1928, and January 1929. He was featured in the last, 1932, edition of Earl Carroll's *Vanities*. A plump, affable character comedian on-screen, Fyffe appeared in some twenty-two British feature films between 1930 and 1947; he made only one American film, *Rulers of the Sea*, for Paramount in 1939. Will Fyffe died as a result of falling from a hotel room window.

J. AUSTIN FYNES (Boston, 1859—Jackson Heights, N.Y., July 20, 1928)

James Austin Fynes was active in vaudeville management at the turn of the century. He began his career in Boston as a journalist, coming to New York to write drama criticism for the *New York Sun* and later editing the *New York Clipper*. When B. F. Keith opened his first New York theatre, the Union Square, in 1893, he appointed Fynes its manager. The latter adopted a policy of bringing, for the first time, legitimate performers to the vaudeville stage, and this proved a tremendously successful tactic. However, E. F. Albee became resentful of Fynes's independence, and Fynes left the B. F. Keith organization to join F. F. Proctor as his general manager. In 1906, Fynes acquired sites in Jersey City and at 125th Street and announced he was creating a new vaudeville circuit, but the project failed to materialize.

When B. F. Keith's Opera House opened in Providence, Rhode Island, in 1894, the manager was Fynes's brother, John T. Fynes.

BIBLIOGRAPHY

Laurie, Joe, Jr. "James Austin Fynes." In *Vaudeville: From the Honky-Tonks to the Palace*. New York: Henry Holt, 1953, pp. 403–406.

G

(EDWARD) GALLAGHER (San Francisco, 1876—Astoria, N.Y., May 28, 1929) and **(AL) SHEAN** (Dornum, Germany, May 12, 1868—New York, August 12, 1949)

In the annals of vaudeville, Gallagher and Shean are probably unique in being known for one song and one song only, "Absolutely, Mr. Gallagher? Positively, Mr. Shean." Through the years, it has been the subject of endless parodies, a number for which there are any amount of topical variations. Because Ed Gallagher and Al Shean had first appeared together in a sketch called "Mr. Gallagher and Mr. Shean in Egypt," the song was always performed with Gallagher wearing a straw hat and Shean wearing a fez, with the pyramids as a painted backdrop. It was first introduced by Gallagher and Shean in vaudeville in 1921, and was the hit number of the 1922 edition of the Ziegfeld *Follies.*

The origins of "Absolutely, Mr. Gallagher? Positively, Mr. Shean" are somewhat obscure. The words and music are generally credited to the partners, although in June 1922, Bryan Foy filed a lawsuit claiming that he wrote the song in May of the previous year, while Gallagher and Shean and Eddie Foy and the Seven Little Foys were appearing at Keith's Theatre, Indianapolis. Foy argued, " 'Mr. Gallagher and Mr. Shean' is unique in that it has done the unusual of elevating a two-man song act into one of vaudeville's greatest drawing cards and from there into the acme of production aspirations, a feature in a Ziegfeld *Follies* on the strength of that one song alone." Gallagher and Shean were quick to point out that others had used the idea of a "Mister" song before they did, particularly Major J. Orrin Donovan, who performed a "Mister Dooley" routine from 1903 onward. In fact, the song obviously has its origins in minstrel shows and their "Mister Bones" routines. Ed Gallagher revealed that the music that is credited to him was "doctored" by Ernest R. Ball and adapted from "old familiar strains." The truth would appear to be that Bryan Foy did indeed come up with the basic idea for the song, and that Gallagher and Shean purchased the idea from him outright for an undisclosed sum of money.

Edward Gallagher was known as one of the best comics in vaudeville and burlesque. For fifteen years, he had a partnership with Joe Barrett. Gallagher and Barrett were known for a series of sketches of military travesties, the best known of which was "The Battle of Too Soon." Al Shean began his vaudeville career in 1890 with the Manhattan Comedy Four—the other three members of the act were Sam Curtis, Arthur Williams, and Ed Mack—which was noted for its knockabout comedy and harmonizing in such songs as "It Isn't What You Used to Be, It's What You Are Today." When the Manhattan Comedy Four disbanded in 1900, Shean teamed up with Charles L. Warren in a sketch titled "Crovadus Upside Down" (a parody on the popular stage melodrama *Quo Vadis?*). Shean and Warren split up in July 1904.

In the early teens, Al Shean and Ed Gallagher decided to join forces for the operetta *The Rose Maid*, which opened at the Globe Theatre, New York, on April 22, 1912, and ran for 176 performances. Then, in April 1914, for reasons unknown, the two split up and did not speak to each other for six years. Gallagher continued in vaudeville, while Shean appeared in a couple of musical shows: *The Princess Pat* (1915) and *Flo-Flo* (1917). He also revived his partnership with Charles L. Warren. Sime Silverman saw the two together and commented in *Variety* (February 5, 1915), "Al Shean was a funny German comedian six years ago, and he's funnier now."

One day, Al Shean casually mentioned to his sister Minnie, mother of the Marx Brothers, that "Ed and I could do a great act together, only he won't talk to me." Minnie set about getting the pair back together, and in April 1920, the new Gallagher and Shean vaudeville act opened at the Fox Crotona Theatre on Long Island. They appear to have sung "Positively, Mr. Gallagher? Absolutely, Mr. Shean" for the first time on the New York stage at the Fifth Avenue Theatre in August 1921. *Variety* (August 12, 1921) described them as "one of the strongest two-man comedy acts in vaudeville," and continued, "The dialog is all timely, and was good for a continuous roll of staccato laughs that punctuated the pauses like machine gun fire.... These youngsters look set for anything short of a typhoon."

Gallagher and Shean billed their act as "By, about and for Themselves," but the title was short-lived. After their hit performance in the 1922 Ziegfeld *Follies*, they signed with the Shuberts, with whom they soon quarelled. The couple decided not to work at all rather than tour for the Shuberts, but when Jones and Green purchased their contract, Gallagher and Shean went into the 1924 edition of *The Greenwich Village Follies*. While appearing in a 1925 touring edition of the show, Gallagher and Shean had another difference of opinion. Again history does not record the cause of the dispute. Shean announced he would continue in *The Greenwich Village Follies*, while Gallagher said he would return to vaudeville with a new partner, Fifi Lussier, who had been a chorus girl in the show and later became known as Fifi D'Orsay (q.v.).

At the height of his career, Ed Gallagher suffered a nervous breakdown, brought on by the legal dispute concerning "Positively, Mr. Gallagher? Absolutely, Mr. Shean,'' the breakup with Al Shean, and marital problems with his fourth wife, Ann Luther, who divorced him. In 1927, he was committed to the Rivercrest Sanitarium in Astoria, New York, where he died two years later.

Al Shean continued as a solo act onstage and later in films. Among his many screen appearances were roles in *Music in the Air* (1934), *Page Miss Glory* (1935), *San Francisco* (1936), *It Could Happen to You* (1937), *The Prisoner of Zenda* (1937), *Too Hot to Handle* (1938), *The Great Waltz* (1938), *Joe and Ethel Turp Call on the President* (1939), *The Blue Bird* (1940), *Atlantic City* (1944), and *People Are Funny* (1946). Shean's biggest critical success on the stage was in the title role of Brian Doherty's comedy *Father Malachy's Miracle*, which opened at New York's St. James Theatre on November 17, 1937.

In later years, he would continue to perform "Positively, Mr. Gallagher? Absolutely, Mr. Shean,'' playing both himself and Ed Gallagher and changing hats and voices for each character. In the fall of 1943, he took on a new partner, Joe Kenney, to play the Gallagher role.

TESS GARDELLA. See AUNT JEMIMA

WILLIAM GAXTON (San Francisco, December 2, 1893—New York, February 2, 1963)

A singer and comedian—"A sort of man who sings through his toes as well as his oral cavity,'' according to Brooks Atkinson in *The New York Times*— William Gaxton began his career in vaudeville but gained wider fame for his performances in musical comedy. Born Arturo Antonio Gaxiola, William Gaxton may have been a cousin of Leo Carrillo. He entered vaudeville as a song and patter man, teamed with Anna Laughlin before going solo. In the late teens, he starred in vaudeville sketches written for him by S. Jay Kaufman and Rupert Hughes. He made his Broadway debut in the 1922 edition of the *Music Box Revue*, but his performance was eclipsed by that of Clark and McCullough. He appeared in many other Broadway shows, including *A Connecticut Yankee* (1927), *Fifty Million Frenchman* (1929), *Anything Goes* (1934), *White Horse Inn* (1936), and *Louisiana Purchase* (1940), but his greatest success was as President John P. Wintergreen in George Gershwin's *Of Thee I Sing* (1931).

William Gaxton appeared in a handful of films, including *It's the Old Army Game* (1926), *Fifty Million Frenchmen* (1931), *Something to Shout About* (1943), and *Best Foot Forward* (1943). He was also a businessman who marketed his own line of perfume called, appropriately enough, "De Toi Je Chante." His wife, Madeline (who died on May 23, 1990), was one of the Cameron Sisters, a dance team in vaudeville in the 1930s. Gaxton's last appearances, in 1961 and 1962, were in Guy Lombardo's summer production of *Paradise Island* at the Marine Theatre, Jones Beach, N.Y.

GLADYS GEORGE (Patten, Me., September 13, 1904—Los Angeles, December 8, 1954)

Born Gladys Anna Clare, Gladys George was the daughter of touring actors, and she joined their act shortly before first grade. The initial billing of The Three Clares changed as audiences responded to Gladys's performances, and the act soon became Little Gladys George and Company. The family's biggest success on the vaudeville stage was in a playlet titled *The Doll's Dream*.

In 1918, Gladys George left vaudeville to appear on the legitimate stage in *The Betrothal* for Winthrop Ames. The following year, she was in Los Angeles on tour with *The Better 'Ole*, and here she was seen and signed to a film contract by producer Thomas H. Ince. She made five films between 1919 and 1921, with the first being *Red Hot Dollars*, directed by Jerome Storm and starring Charles Ray. In 1921, George returned to the legitimate stage, where she was a fixture until 1934 when, during the New York run of *Queer People*, she made a screen test for Paramount. The test led to a contract with M-G-M, and George's first sound film, *Straight Is the Way* (1934). Between 1934 and 1953, the actress appeared in thirty-two features, of which the most memorable are *Valiant Is the Word for Carrie* (1936, for which she was nominated for an Academy Award), *The Roaring Twenties* (1939), and *The Maltese Falcon* (1941). She ended her career with *It Happens Every Thursday* (1953).

Gladys George was married four times. There was a suggestion that her death was suicide, but an autopsy revealed natural causes. She left an estate valued at less than $500.

BIBLIOGRAPHY

Brunas, John. "Gladys George." *Film Fan Monthly* no. 129 (March 1972), pp. 9–19.
Crichton, Charles. "Life on the Strand." *Collier's* 95, no. 10 (March 9), 1935, pp. 19, 39.
Rinehart, Mary Roberts. "A Valiant Picture for a Valiant Star." *Photoplay* 5, no. 4 (October 1936), p. 13.

LOTTIE GILSON (Pennsylvania, 1867—New York, June 10, 1912)

Billed as "The Little Magnet," Lottie Gilson was the leading soubrette of the vaudeville stage from the 1880s through the early 1900s. Her repertoire included both tear-jerkers and risqué numbers, and the song most associated with her is "The Sunshine of Paradise Alley." It is believed she was one of the first entertainers to accept payment from composers and publishers for singing (and thus popularizing) their songs. She is also credited as the first to use a singing stooge in her act. Circa 1885, while she was singing at Hyde and Behman's Brooklyn Theatre, a boy in the gallery took up the song. The interruption was such a success that Lottie Gilson incorporated it into her act. Around the same time, she also devised the idea of taking a mirror and using it to shine a light on the head of a bald man, to whom she would then sing. In *American Vaudeville*, Douglas Gilbert hailed her as "a melodic rabble rouser and . . . versatile."

In the 1880s, Lottie Gilson was a regular at both the Miner's Theatre on the Bowery and Tony Pastor's. In February 1893, Gilson was discharged by the management of the Imperial Music Hall for pretending to have had a cold and lost her voice, and thus breaking an engagement. She returned to the Imperial in May of the same year. From June to July 1894, the entertainer was the star attraction at the Madison Square Garden Roof.

Little is known of the entertainer's background. She was born Lydia Deagon. Her first husband was named Gilson, the second was J. K. Emmett, Jr., and the third, Salvatore De Nufrio. Prior to her early death, she "had passed through several periods of depression and illness."

BILLY GLASON (Boston, September 10, 1904–   )

Billy Glason was a singing comedian who would intersperse his monologue with popular songs of the day. He billed himself as "Just Songs and Sayings," and claims to have the distinction of being the only performer whom no headliner was willing to follow. "Look, you bring them in—I'll entertain them," he used to say—and he did.

At the age of ten, Glason began work selling newspapers. From that he graduated to plugging songs in the Boston area. He added a few jokes to his songs and became a vaudevillian. As he recalled for Bill Smith in *The Vaudevillians*:

"I had an act and I'm in demand. Abe Montague, who later was a Columbia Pictures vice-president, owned a theater in Boston, the Bay Square, and he booked me to sing with slides. I stayed there for three years. Then I was booked into the Beacon Theater, a well-known vaudeville house on Boston's Tremont Street. They used to book thirty acts on Monday. Ten were always fired. There was no protection. When I first started I was doing a Jew act with the beard and derby. I borrowed my father's derby and a red bandana handkerchief and I played South Boston, strictly an Irish neighborhood. After the first show the manager came in and handed me my pictures. Murder—I was fired."

Lou Walters discovered Glason and booked him on the Poli circuit in the Boston area and later, in the 1920s, on the Keith circuit. Glason was a mainstay of vaudeville in the 1930s, and in 1939 hosted his own comedy show, Bill Glason and His Gang on WMCA–New York; the show featured his wife, Paula (married 1939; died 1978 at the age of 76).

Billy Glason was also a songwriter—"Why Do They Always Say No?," "Sing a Song," "Croon a Tune," "He'll Always Be One of Those Guys," etc.—and since the 1940s has been active selling gags to after-dinner speakers and comedians (including Steve Allen, Johnny Carson, Bob Hope, and Ed Sullivan). Glason's boast was that he could take an old gag such as "Who was that lady I saw you with last night?" and switch it around to become a new joke:

"Who was that lady I saw you with at the sidewalk cafe last night?"

"That was no sidewalk cafe, that was our furniture."

BIBLIOGRAPHY
Smith, Bill. "Billy Glason." In *The Vaudevillians*. New York: Macmillan, 1976, pp. 30–
   37.

GEORGE FULLER GOLDEN (Alabaster, Mi., 1868—Los Angeles, February 17, 1912)

A good-looking young man, George Fuller Golden was described by Douglas Gilbert in *American Vaudeville* as "a rough, tough pugilist; a lover of poetry, a voracious reader of the classics; a radical idealist." When not prizefighting, Golden loved to dance, and he teamed with a friend, James (Gypsy) Dolan, in a song-and-double-clog act and in a sketch titled "The High-Toned Burglar." When the pair split up, Golden worked as a monologist, telling a series of "Casey" stories. A classic monolog concerned Golden and Casey in London, with the former extolling the chimes ringing from Westminster Abbey. As Golden spoke more and more eloquently of the sound of the bells, his friend Casey kept asking him to repeat himself. Eventually, Casey put his mouth close to Golden's ear and shouted, "Those damn bells are making such a hell of a racket, George, I can't hear you!"

In 1899, he made his first visit to London—he returned in 1905—but was not successful in music hall. Penniless, Golden was helped by the British theatrical and charitable organization the Water Rats. When he returned to New York, he persuaded his vaudeville colleagues to found a similar organization, the White Rats (q.v.). At the height of his success in vaudeville, Golden contracted tuberculosis. As had his British colleagues, Golden's American friends rallied round and financed his writing a book, *My Lady Vaudeville and Her White Rats*, on the history of the organization. (Supposedly, George M. Cohan donated $10,000.)

George Fuller Golden's daughter Olive married Western screen star Harry Carey and enjoyed a long career in films as a character actress. At his death, *Variety* (February 24, 1912) wrote of Golden:

> George Fuller Golden was probably the best known and most beloved actor who ever appeared in vaudevile. He devoted more time and accomplished more for his brother and sister artists than any fifty people that ever interested themselves in the various movements for the betterment of vaudeville conditions.

HORACE GOLDIN (Vilna, Poland, December 17, 1867—London, August 22, 1939)

Horace Goldin was a magician who popularized the illusion of sawing a woman in half; by 1921, so closely associated had his name become with the trick that he operated half-a-dozen road companies presenting the act. Later, he modified the illusion with the woman's torso no longer in a box but visible to the audience, with a buzz saw supposedly slicing it in two. As a gag, Goldin would often have an ambulance parked outside the theatre with a sign, "In Case the Saw Slips." Born Hyman Goldstein in Poland, the magician came to the United

States as a child. As early as 1902, Golden gave a royal command performance in England, and thereafter billed himself as "The Royal Illusionist." Unlike his fellow magicians, who required a ninety-minute show in which to present their routines, Goldin moved along at such a frenetic pace that he could handle the same number of illusions in a twenty-minute vaudeville act. "Don't blink or you'll miss a trick," he would tell his audience.

NAT C. GOODWIN (Boston, July 25, 1857—New York, January 31, 1919)

One of the most popular actors of the American stage from the 1870s through the mid teens, Nat C. Goodwin was at his best in comedy roles. He began his career in vaudeville and made three later forays into the medium in 1909, 1911, and 1916. Goodwin made his first stage appearance as a newsboy in *Law in New York* at the Howard Atheneum in Boston on March 3, 1874. His New York debut and his first major success was at Tony Pastor's Broadway Theatre in December 1875, in a sketch titled "Ned Stryker," with Goodwin's adopting the billing of "Actor, Author, and Mimic."

On the legitimate stage, Nat C. Goodwin played almost everything, from *An American Citizen* (first performed in 1897) and *The Cowboy and the Lady* (1899) to *Nathan Hale* (1899) and *Cameo Kirby* (1908). Like most comedians, he yearned to play tragedy, which he did at least once to great effect in *Nathan Hale*, which opened at New York's Knickerbocker Theatre on January 2, 1899. Goodwin starred with one of his wives, Maxine Elliott, in *When We Were Twenty-One* in 1900, but his best known role was that of Fagin in a 1912 stage adaptation of Charles Dickens's *Oliver Twist*, which also featured Marie Doro and Constance Collier. The actor played the same role on screen, almost simultaneously with the New York opening, in a five-reel production by the General Film and Sales Co., released on a states rights basis in May 1912. The film is now lost. Goodwin also appeared in four other early feature films: *Business Is Business* (1915), *The Master Hand* (1915), *The Marriage Bond* (1916), and *Wall Street Tragedy* (1916).

Reviewing Nat C. Goodwin's career in 1919, *The New York Dramatic Mirror* commented, "The range of his parts ran the entire gamut of dramatic construction. His greatest ambition was to play Shakespeare and he made productions of *The Merchant of Venice* and *A Midsummer Night's Dream*, but Shylock and Bottom did not bring him the fame he received in modern roles."

In the fall of 1916, Goodwin was a headliner at the Palace, billed as a monologist, telling stories to the audience with a gentle and quiet humor. *Variety* (October 6, 1916) thought that as a vaudevillian he was "a glittering entertainer." Critics of his theatrical performances were often harsher in their evaluations.

Nat C. Goodwin died in New York after leaving the touring company of *Why Marry?* prematurely in Philadelphia.

BIBLIOGRAPHY

"Appreciation," *The Nation*, February 8, 1919, pp. 205–206.

Goodwin, Nat C. *Nat Goodwin's Book*. Boston: Richard G. Badger/The Gorham Press, 1914.

"Nat Goodwin Almost a Great American Actor." *Literary Digest*, February 15, 1919,
    pp. 88–92.

BERT GORDON (New York, April 8, 1895—Duarte, Ca., November 30, 1974)

The "Mad Russian" comedian of radio and occasional films, Bert Gordon
was born Barney Gorodetsky. He started in vaudeville at the age of twelve with
an act titled "Stage Struck Kids," and later teamed with his brother Harry. He
first came to prominence in the 1921 edition of George White's *Scandals*; his
only other Broadway appearance was in *Hold on to Your Hats* in 1940. With
his thick Slavic accent and his dialect greeting of "How dooo you dooo," Bert
Gordon delighted radio listeners when he first appeared on *The Eddie Cantor
Show* in 1935; the "Mad Russian" was introduced the following year, and
Gordon stayed with Cantor on radio through 1949. (He also worked on radio
with Milton Berle.) Gordon's film appearances include *She Gets Her Man* (1935),
New Faces of 1937, *Outside of Paradise* (1938), and *Sing for Your Supper*
(1941).

Bert Gordon was not a comedian who appealed to intellectuals. Yet critic
Richard Watts, Jr., wrote of him in 1941 in *The New York Herald-Tribune* as
"a genuinely funny man, a fellow to be accepted among the authentic comedians
of this day."

NILS T. GRANLUND (Korpilombolo, Sweden, 1882—Las Vegas, April 21, 1957)

With his many shows for nightclubs and the vaudeville stage featuring attractive, young showgirls, Nils T. Granlund became, in the words of Lee Mortimer in *The New York Daily Mirror* "the conceiver, inventor and creator of
modern night life." Generally known to the public as "N.T.G." and to his
friends as "Granny," Nils Thor Granlund was born in a village in Swedish
Lapland and came to the United States at the age of nine, when his parents
migrated to Providence, Rhode Island. Upon graduation from high school, Granlund got a job as a newspaper reporter, and in 1912 became press agent for the
road tour of *Hanky Panky*. With that show he came to New York, and also came
to realize an audience's fascination with showgirls. In New York, Granlund was
hired by Marcus Loew as a press agent, and eventually became director of
publicity for the Loew theaters.

He became involved in radio with WHN–New York in 1922, and by 1924,
after he had announced a number of boxing bouts, Granlund was in demand as
a master of ceremonies. He began producing a number of nightclub acts, many
for Texas Guinan, for which he would also serve as master of ceremonies. In
the late 1920s, he acquired a 150-acre property at Ramsey, New Jersey, which
became known as "Granny's Farm" and was a popular retreat for many show
business personalities. In April 1932, Granlund made it to the Palace with what
was described as "The Biggest Act in Vaudeville," and featured forty of the

"World's Loveliest Girls." The critic for *The New York Times* (April 18, 1932) commented, "While it is an entertainment not entirely at home within the confines of even so elastic a stage as the Palace's, it does present, in varying degrees of undress, an assortment of Times Square eyefuls."

Granlund was also able to achieve what would seem the impossible, presenting showgirls on radio. In the summer of 1935, his program *Nils T. Granlund Girls* began airing on WEAF, sponsored by Bromo-Seltzer. *Variety* (July 17, 1935) commented, "The program and N.T.G., rather than any of the girls, stood out on the inaugural broadcast. It opened and closed with the girls rehearsing a tap dance, nicely conveyed by sound effects."

The showman appeared as himself on-screen in the 1930s and 1940s in a handful of films, and prior to the Second World War, he relocated to Los Angeles, where he was to be active on radio and television and also to manage the Florentine Gardens on Hollywood Boulevard from 1940 to 1948. He died in an automobile accident in Las Vegas, and arrangements for his funeral were made by Yvonne De Carlo, one of his discoveries.

BIBLIOGRAPHY

Granlund, Nils T., with Sid Feder and Ralph Hancock. *Blondes, Brunettes, Bullets*. New York: David McKay, 1957.

CARY GRANT (Bristol, England, January 18, 1904—Davenport, Ia., November 29, 1986)

Cary Grant was one of the great romantic stars of American film—*Bringing Up Baby* (1938), *The Philadelphia Story* (1941), *To Catch a Thief* (1955), *Charade* (1963), etc.—but few acknowledge his many years in vaudeville prior to the commencement of his film career in 1932. Born Archibald Leach, Grant was fascinated by British music hall and the circus, and at the age of sixteen, he joined the Penders, a troupe of acrobatic dancers and stilt walkers, organized by Robert and Margaret Lomas. With an act called "The Long and Short of It: A Screaming Absurdity," the Penders toured Britain, France, and Germany. In April 1911, they made their U.S. debut with a stilt-walking act at the Folies Bergere. They returned to the United States in 1920 to appear in the revue *Good Times*, which opened on August 9 of that year at the New York Hippodrome. The following year, the Penders made an American vaudeville tour. In 1923, Robert Lomas retired, and Archibald Leach, Jack and Doris Hartman, and Tom and Jim Lomas formed the Lomas Troupe, which began a tour on the Pantages circuit in September 1923. The group split up in 1925, at which time Leach became leading man to Jean Dalrymple, touring vaudeville as a member of the Jack Janis Company in various playlets. Two years later, he became a legitimate actor, but for the rest of his life, Cary Grant never lost his love for all forms of variety entertainment.

BIBLIOGRAPHY

Higham, Charles, and Roy Mosely. *Cary Grant: The Lonely Heart*. New York: Harcourt, Brace, Jovanovich, 1989.

ROBERT GRAU (circa 1854—Mount Vernon, N.Y., August 9, 1916)

An important early chronicler of all aspects of early twentieth-century entertainment, Robert Grau was also an agent and booker for vaudeville in the 1890s. He helped promote Loïe Fuller as an international star, and was responsible for bringing Maurice Barrymore to vaudeville, at the New Union Square Theatre, New York, in March 1897. Robert Grau authored three major historical texts, *The Business Man in the Amusement World* (1910), *The Stage in the Twentieth Century* (1912) and *The Theatre of Science: A Volume of Progress and Achievement in the Motion Picture Industry* (1914), all published by the Broadway Publishing Company. At the time of his death, Grau was a publicity representative for Thomas H. Ince and F. F. Proctor. His brother Maurice Grau was general manager of the Metropolitan Opera.

THE GREAT LESTER (circa 1881—Los Angeles, July 14, 1956)

Ventriloquist Harry Lester billed himself as "The Great Lester" in a vaudeville career dating back to the early years of the twentieth century. Working in the days prior to the use of the microphone, Lester would walk through the audience with a handkerchief stuffed in his mouth while his dummy whistled a tune. He also claimed to be the first ventriloquist to have his dummy talk while drinking a glass of water (although Joe Laurie, Jr., claims this stunt dates back to 1821), and also perfected an act in which he talked on the telephone to heaven and hell, trying to locate his sister, emulating the noise of the telephone being lifted off the hook, the busy signal, and so forth. With his dummy, Frank Byron, The Great Lester was an early influence on Edgar Bergen. For the last few years of his life he operated a studio in Hollywood.

ABEL GREEN (New York, June 3, 1900—New York, May 10, 1973)

Abel Green continued the comprehensive reporting of the American vaudeville scene in *Variety* begun by Sime Silverman. He began his career at *Variety* as a reporter in 1918 and became its second editor, succeeding Silverman, in 1933. Like his mentor, Silverman, Abel Green always wore a bow tie. *New York Times* critic Vincent Canby, whom Green had hired to work for *Variety* in 1959, described him as "the man whose style was his content." It is an appropriate definition of the man who is credited with creating such show business terms as "boffo," "biz," "obit," "webs," "biopic," "payola," "plugger," "socko," "eatery," "pix," and "flick." Green also was responsible for the classic *Variety* headline "Sticks Nix Hick Pix," meaning audiences in rural areas stay away from motion pictures dealing with country life. On a more serious level, it was Abel Green who, in 1919, set up *Variety*'s network of European correspondents. He appeared as himself in the 1947 film *Copacabana*.

Abel Green edited *The Spice of Variety* (New York: Henry Holt, 1952) and also coauthored, with Joe Laurie, Jr., *Show Biz: From Vaude to Video* (New York: Henry Holt, 1951).

BIBLIOGRAPHY
Brownell, Richard B. "There's No Green Like Abel Green." *Good Housekeeping*, October 1954, pp. 67, 197–201.
Canby, Vincent. "The Greening of Show Biz." *The New York Times*, May 20, 1973, pp. 1, 38.

BURTON GREEN. See IRENE FRANKLIN

CHARLOTTE GREENWOOD (Philadelphia, June 25, 1893—Beverly Hills, Ca., January 18, 1978)

"She has the distinction of looking like no one else in the world," wrote Robert Benchley in *Life* (April 27, 1922) of this tall, long-legged, and awkwardly graceful entertainer, who is chiefly known for her work as a character actress in such films as *Palmy Days* (1931), *Down Argentine Way* (1940), *The Gang's All Here* (1943), and, of course, *Oklahoma!* (1955). (The role of Aunt Eller in *Oklahoma!* was written by Rodgers and Hammerstein with Greenwood in mind, but she never got to play it in the original Broadway production of the musical.) It is films that have assured Charlotte Greenwood immortality, but it was in vaudeville that she first came to prominence, with an act called "Two Girls and a Piano."

The two girls in question were Charlotte Greenwood and Eunice Burnham, and together they toured the United States between 1909 and 1912, delighting small-time vaudeville audiences everywhere and earning a mere $25 a week. The svelte Greenwood was an excellent foil for the plump Burnham, and while the latter performed at the piano, Greenwood did comic dances and sang about her girlish laughter:

> I may not be so pretty,
> And I don't dress like a queen.
> I may not be so witty;
> I am over sweet sixteen.
> My face is not my fortune
> (It looks like the morning after),
> But I still maintain
> That I retain
> (Bing! Bing!)
> My girlish laughter!

"Miss Greenwood is the tall, awkward girl whose limbs seemed to take involuntary excursions to all portions of the stage, and who is described as being loose jointed as the latest toy from the toy factory," wrote one critic. Another, unkindly and somewhat unfairly, wrote, "Her face is nearly as ugly as that of Polaire." It was Alan Dale, writing in 1913, who summed up the secret of Charlotte Greenwood's success through the years: "Miss Greenwood is undiluted joy. She is funny all over. Her face is a comic mirror for every laugh."

Charlotte Greenwood made her first stage appearance at the New Amsterdam

Theatre in New York on November 2, 1905, in the chorus of *The White Cat*. As Lottie Greenwood, she received her first featured role—albeit a very minor one—as Lola in *The Rodgers Brothers in Panama*, which played the Casino, New York, in 1908. After years of touring with Eunice Burnham, during which she was more and more billed above her partner, Greenwood was invited to appear in *The Passing Show of 1912*, which featured Willie and Eugene Howard and Trixie Friganza. *The Passing Show of 1913*, *The Tik-Tok Man of Oz*, and *Town Topics* followed before Charlotte Greenwood gained her most famous stage role in 1915, that of Letty in *So Long Letty* (in which she was costarred with Walter Catlett). This was followed by a series of "Letty" shows: *Linger Longer Letty* (1919), *Let 'er Go Letty* (1921), *Letty Pepper* (1922), and *Leaning on Letty* (1935). Actually, Letitia Proudfoot was first introduced in *Pretty Mrs. Smith* (1914), but it was not until *So Long Letty* and the Earl Carroll tune of the same name that Greenwood became permanently identified with the character.

Throughout the 1920s and 1930s, Charlotte Greenwood was very much in demand for musicals and revues, including *The Music Box Revue* (1922), *Hazzard Short's Ritz Revue* (1924), with songs by Martin Brooner, whom Greenwood married on December 22, 1924, and *Rufus LeMarie's Affairs* (1927). In 1930, Greenwood appeared in her first nonmusical comedy *Mebbe*, and in 1932, she made her London debut in *Wild Violets* at the Theatre Royal, Drury Lane. Between stage appearances, she worked as a solo turn in vaudeville in the 1920s—headlining at the Palace in May 1926 and January 1927—and also embarked on a lengthy screen career (that had actually begun in 1915 with *Jane*). The performer was also active on radio in the 1930s.

Charlotte Greenwood's stage career continued through the 1950s, and from 1947 to 1949, she toured as Mama in *I Remember Mama*. After an absence of twenty-three years, she returned triumphantly to the Broadway stage as Juno in Cole Porter's *Out of This World*, which opened at the Century Theatre in December 1950. As an ardent Christian Scientist, Greenwood objected strenuously to the risqué lyrics of the show. She made her last screen appearance in 1956, in *The Opposite Sex*.

When Charlotte Greenwood appeared with Eunice Burnham at Hammerstein's Victoria Theatre the week of September 26, 1909, she was billed as "The Laughing Hit of the Season." It was a description that could have been applied to her for the next forty years.

BIBLIOGRAPHY

Crichton, Kyle. "Lady Longlegs." *Collier's* 101, no. 3 (January 15, 1938), pp. 15, 43.

Hopper, Hedda. "An Oscar for 'Letty'?" Syndicated Column, February 19, 1956.

"Long-Legged Letty Makes Money Striding across Country's Stages." *Newsweek*, October 18, 1937, p. 24.

Metcalfe, James S. "High-Kicking Ability." *Life*, November 27, 1919, p. 899.

Mullett, Mary B. "Tall, Thin, Awkward Girl Becomes a Broadway Star." *American Magazine*, December 1923, p. 34.

Parsons, Louella. "Charlotte Greenwood." Syndicated Column, June 17, 1951.

Renaud, Ralph E. "The Secret of the Greenwood Kick." *San Francisco Chronicle*, February 25, 1912, p. 21.

GROCK (Moulin de Loveresse, Switzerland, January 10, 1880—Imperia, Italy, July 14, 1959)

One of the most famous of all international clowns, Grock's career was centered in Europe, but he did appear in American vaudeville at the end of 1919 and the beginning of 1920. Born Adrian Wettach, Grock worked in various circuses until deciding to become a clown in 1906. In the teens, William Morris, Charles Dillingham, and others tried to persuade Grock to come to the United States, but to no avail. Eventually, in 1919, Grock agreed to play one week in vaudeville for $1,000, thanks to the efforts of Eddie Darling. He opened at New York's Riverside Theatre billed simply as an "extra" addition to the bill. *Variety* critic "Josh" saw him and in a lengthy discussion commented:

> By this time you may be chafing a bit and asking, "Well, what does he do?" He does acrobatics, plays the piano, concertina, talks, sings, dances and—oh, it's no use trying to describe him. The dramatic editor of the London *Times* recently wrote a very learned article on clowns and devoted a good deal of its space to Grock. He confessed himself unable to describe this individual and wound up by declaring that probably Grock pleases because he is Grock.

From the Riverside, Grock was brought over to headline at the Palace, and he became the first headliner to be held over there for a second week as the headliner.

Grock always worked with an assistant, who served as a straight man and violinist. The first was Antoinette, at which time the act was billed as Antoinette and Grock. While maintaining a villa on the Italian Riviera, Grock made his home base in Paris, where he was a frequent entertainer at the Cirque Medrano. After the Second World War, he operated his own circus, retiring in 1955.

BIBLIOGRAPHY

Grock. "My Colleague Charlie Chaplin." *Living Age*, March 1931, pp. 43–45.
"Grock Retires." *Living Age*, January 1931, pp. 538–39.

YVETTE GUILBERT (Paris, January 20, 1865—Aix-en-Provence, February 2, 1944)

A great French *chansonneuse*, noted for her expressive song presentations, Yvette Guilbert was no stranger to American vaudeville, touring here in 1906 and 1909. Guilbert made her first appearance at Variétés, Paris, on June 21, 1888; subsequently, she made frequent appearances on the London stage, and her dramatic debut, also at Variétés, was on October 24, 1907, in *L'Amour en Banque*.

Yvette Guilbert's American debut was as the opening attraction at Oscar Hammerstein's Music Hall Theatre in the Olympia complex on December 17, 1895. She was paid $4,000 a week, and was tremendously successful with American audiences with an act that was comprised entirely of French language songs with the exception of two "coon" songs she was persuaded to include in her repertoire, "My Gal's a High Born Lady" and "I Want You, My Honey, Yes, I Do." Guilbert returned to the United States in the spring of 1906 with a vaudeville act titled "Chansons Crinoline." She encountered some resistance on her opening night in April 1906 at New York's 23rd Street Theatre, as members of the gallery audience complained loudly that her songs were in French only. Subsequently, she alternated French and English numbers, providing translations of the former. "Chicot" wrote in *Variety* (April 28, 1906):

Mme Guilbert is vastly different from the black gloved motionless woman whose uplifted eyebrow was an extravagance of gesture and whose songs were for the better (or worse) part surcharged with suggestion. In her present work she employs to advantage a wonderfully mobile face and her every gesture is pregnant with meaning. She selected old time songs of French and English ancestry and those who were unable to follow the French songs were at least able to appreciate the wealth of expression, the flexibility of voice and the vivacity of her manner.

Percy G. Williams brought Guilbert back to vaudeville in October 1909, when she opened at New York's Colonial Theatre, wearing a hoop skirt and singing three English songs and only one French number. "There is a demureness, a certain delicate and underlying humor, and a power of facial expression that makes Madame Guilbert's work most delightful," wrote *The New York Dramatic Mirror* (October 23, 1909). "And then her power of suggestion or the wave of a hand! It is the art of the pantomimist combined with the art of the singer."

Yvette Guilbert returned to the United States in 1919, making her legitimate stage debut in the title role of *Guibour* at the New York's Neighborhood Theatre. She was back again in June 1928 with a one-woman show. Ten years later, in June 1938, Yvette Guilbert celebrated her golden jubilee with a gala concert at the Salle Pleyel in Paris.

BIBLIOGRAPHY

Geffroy, Gustave. *Yvette Guilbert*. New York: Walker, 1968.

Guilbert, Yvette, *How to Sing a Song*. New York: Macmillan, 1918.

————. *The Song of My Life*. London: George Harrap, 1929.

————, and Harold Simpson. *Yvette Guilbert: Struggles and Victories*. London: Mills and Boon, 1910.

Knapp, Bettina Liebowitz, and Myra Chipman. *That Was Yvette: The Biography of Yvette Guilbert, the Great Diseuse*. New York: Holt, Rinehart and Winston, 1964.

TEXAS GUINAN (Waco, Tx., January 12, 1884—Vancouver, Canada, November 5, 1933)

If any individual symbolizes the prohibition era in the United States it is Texas Guinan, whose nightclubs were the only places to be if one wanted to enjoy life in New York in the 1920s. Americans were willing to spend money as if there was no tomorrow, and Texas Guinan was there with her famous cry of "Hello, Sucker!" to take the cash. However, despite her close ties to the more sophisticated aspects of New York night life, it was in vaudeville that Texas Guinan came to fame, and in vaudeville where she ended her all-too-brief life.

Born Mary Louise Cecilia Guinan, Texas began her show business career as a rodeo driver. In his 1927 book *Behind the Curtains of Broadway's Beauty Trust*, Will A. Page wrote, "When I first meet her she was the prima donna of a touring musical comedy company in Little Rock, Arkansas. The manager of the company, the late John Slocum, told me that some day she would be a big star on Broadway. He was right. She is; not in musical comedy but in the night clubs." In May 1909, Texas Guinan was performing sixteen minutes of song at New York's Fifth Avenue Theatre, where *Variety* (May 29, 1909) saw her and commented, "Miss Guinan has looks, and dresses well. Her well-trained soprano does the rest." On October 16, 1909, the performer was featured on the cover of *The New York Dramatic Mirror*.

Within a year, Texas Guinan had become a popular singer of popular songs in vaudeville, and it is claimed that she was the first songstress to deliver her numbers from a swing suspended over the stage. In 1913, she was self-billed as "God's Masterpiece," and that same year Guinan was featured in *The Passing Show of 1913*. In 1916, she toured vaudeville with musical comedy star Billy Gibson, performing a comedy sketch and singing "Do What Your Mother Did, I'll Do the Same as Your Dad." Around this time, she also introduced a second catch phrase, "Give the little girl a big hand," which was perhaps suggested to her by Jack Osterman.

In 1917, Guinan embarked on a film career as a sort of female version of William S. Hart. Unlike Hart, she had a Western background, and as she pointed out, "I could twirl a lariat, rope a steer, ride—and shoot to beat any tobacco-chewin' cowpoke." She made her first film, a short subject for Balboa titled *The Wildcat*, early in 1917. It was followed by a handful of feature films—*The Fuel of Life* (1917), *The Gun Woman* (1918), *The Love Brokers* (1918), *The She Wolf* (1919), *I Am the Woman* (1921), and *The Stampede* (1921), as well as many two-reel Western shorts. At this time, she was also married to the distinguished film critic Julian Johnson. They had met in 1909, married the following year, and divorced in 1920. As Guinan put it, "He was my idea of a good scout, a regular fellow. As husbands went he was all right—and he went!" A second marriage to George E. Townley was short-lived. In 1929, Warner Bros. starred Guinan in an early sound feature film, *Queen of the Night Clubs*. Her last screen appearance was in 20th Century's *Broadway thru a Keyhole* (1933). Texas Guinan has been portrayed on film by Glenda Farrell, as Missouri Martin, in *Lady for a Day* (1933), by Betty Hutton in *Incendiary Blonde*, a film biography from Paramount (1945), and by Barbara Nichols in *The George Raft Story* (1961).

In the 1920s, the first New York night spot with which Texas Guinan was associated was the El Fay Club, backed by a former taxi operator named Larry Fay. The El Fay was followed by the Club Moritz and the Three Hundred Club. As Will A. Page wrote, "In a few weeks Texas had them standing in line, because she inaugurated the novel idea of the personal hostess sitting down at the table and even bringing her little cuties to be introduced to the rich patrons of the place. But though she introduced the girls to the patrons, she had one invariable rule: the girls always had to leave her place alone and were never allowed to go on to 'parties' under penalty of losing their engagements.''

In each of her clubs, Texas acted as hostess and mistress of ceremonies for the entertainment, which was often produced by Nils T. Granlund. She was also a born press agent, constantly inventing stories and promoting herself. She had Harry K. Thaw engaged to one of her dancers at one point, and even had a reconciliation between him and Evelyn Nesbit to be announced at one of her clubs.

When her clubs were shuttered by prohibition law enforcement officers, Texas Guinan put together a forty-one-minute vaudeville act, Texas Guinan and Her Mob, which opened at the New York Hippodrome in May 1925. The act featured a jazz sextet, a group of singers billed as the Texas Strollers, and, of course, Guinan's famous showgirls, including Ruby Keeler and Peggy Shannon, both of whom were to make names for themselves in the film industry. At this stage of her vaudeville career, Texas Guinan did nothing except introduce the members of her company, the females of whom she described, in an obvious dig at Florenz Ziegfeld, as "glorious girls who don't need glorifying." The entire company joined in the song "Oh, Mr. Buckner," an unflattering tribute to the U.S. attorney general responsible for carrying out the edicts of the Volstead Act. "Plenty of superlatives in connection with this act," commented Abel Green in *Variety* (May 6, 1925).

Texas Guinan was eventually arrested in February 1927 for violation of the prohibition laws at her Three Hundred Club at 151 West 54th Street. She protested that she was merely the club's hostess, helping everyone have a good time, and apparently the jury agreed with her, for she was acquitted. After her brush with the law, Guinan appeared on Broadway in what has been described as one of the worst Shubert revues, *Padlocks of 1927*. With the end of prohibition, Texas Guinan returned to vaudeville. She headlined at the Palace in March 1932, and the following year toured with her own company in a show titled *Too Hot for Paris*. While playing the Beacon Theatre in Vancouver, Canada, and, incidentially, establishing a new house record for attendance, she collapsed backstage after the fourth show on Saturday, November 4, 1933. Texas Guinan died the following morning. A reported ten thousand people viewed her body at Campbell's Funeral Parlor in New York, in the same room where Rudolph Valentino's body had been exhibited a few years earlier.

The last word on Texas Guinan should be left to Will A. Page, who described her as "a breezy blonde and entertaining hostess; a good fellow, with a smile and a joke for everyone and a glad handshake. She made everyone feel at home whether they had ever met her or not.''

BIBLIOGRAPHY
Berliner, Louise. *Texas Guinan: Queen of the Nightclubs*. Austin: University of Texas Press, 1993.
Bolitho, William. "Two Stars," *The Delineator*, January 1931, p. 15.

Doherty, James. "Texas Guinan, Queen of Whoopee!" *Chicago Sunday Tribune*, March 4, 1951, pp. 4–6.

Green, Abel. "Texas Guinan Helped Make B'way History during the Volstead Era." *Variety*, January 4, 1956, p. 423.

Guinan, Texas. "How to Keep Your Husband Out of My Night Club." *Liberty* 9, no. 18 (April 30, 1932), pp. 50–51.

Page, Will A. *Behind the Curtains of Broadway's Beauty Trust.* New York: Edward A. Miller, 1927, pp. 182–86.

Shirley, Glenn. *Hello Sucker!: The Story of "Texas" Guinan.* Austin, Tx.: Eakin Press, 1989.

H

JANETTE HACKETT (1898—New York, August 16, 1979)

Janette (sometimes billed as Jeanette) Hackett came from a well-known theatrical family, her brothers being Raymond and Albert Hackett and her mother, Florence Hackett. (Raymond's wife, silent screen actress Blanche Sweet, also played vaudeville briefly with an act titled "Sweet and Lovely.") Janette had always been interested in dancing, and after stints in the chorus of *The Passing Show* and as a solo dancer in a nightclub, she replaced Billie Shaw in the vaudeville act of Seabury and Shaw in the late teens.

When Seabury and Shaw decided to retire, they gave their act to Janette Hackett. She teamed up with Harry Delmar (September 9, 1892—Los Angeles, August 29, 1984), whom she was later to marry and formed Hackett and Delmar. The act made its New York debut at the 125th Street Theatre in March 1919, and based on contemporary reviews it is surprising the couple went any further. *Variety* (March 7, 1919) noted that Delmar could neither sing nor dance and seemed lost in handling jazz and eccentric dances. The trade paper concluded, "The act is splendidly set, nicely costumed and splendidly routined. The girl looks big time."

Hackett and Delmar persevered and each year produced a new dance revue for vaudeville, unquestionably the creative work of Janette Hackett. The twenty-minute act would feature chorus girls, a variety of dance routines, including an acrobatic number by Delmar, and Hackett in a scanty costume. ("Most all of Miss Hackett's frocks are designed to show a good deal of skin," reported *Variety*.) Reviewing the fourth Hackett and Delmar dance revue, titled "Dance Madness," *Variety* (September 6, 1923) wrote, "It is . . . one that cannot fail to carry them far along the brightest lanes in vaudeville."

In the late 1920s, Hackett and Delmar split, both on- and offstage, and Janette Hackett went solo with a fifteen-minute act featuring dramatic dance numbers in which she was supported by three male dancers, Jose Shalitta, Dan Hurwyn, and Wally Davis. *Variety*'s Abel Green saw Hackett at the 81st Street Theatre in February 1929, and after comparing her looks to those of Garbo reported, "She can take this act into anybody's playhouse and click." The climax of the act had Janette Hackett tear off her partner's mask and discover he was Death, whereupon she would rush to the top of a flight of stairs, pull down a drape, and topple down the stairs, dragging the curtain behind her. Death looked on triumphantly. In its dramatic choreography, the number had the same shock effect as Busby Berkeley's "Lullaby of Broadway" routine from the film *Gold Diggers of 1935*.

In 1930, Hackett married John Steel (who had introduced "A Pretty Girl Is Like Melody" in the 1919 edition of the Ziegfeld *Follies*, and was also a regular on the vaudeville stage). She continued to work as a dancer and choreographer, with her later partners including Cesar Romero and Ivan Triesault.

BIBLIOGRAPHY

Smith Bill. "Janette Hackett." In *The Vaudevillians*. New York: Macmillan, 1976, pp. 182–87.

JACK HALEY (Boston, August 10, 1898—Los Angeles, June 6, 1979)

Never was the continual crossover between vaudeville and musical comedy and revue more apparent than in the case of Jack Haley. An actor, singer, and comedian who began his career in vaudeville, he was to rise to fame in musical comedies and revues such as *Gay Paree* (1925), *Follow Thru* (1929), *Free for All* (1931), and *Take a Chance* (1932). His trademark of popping his eyes and gazing around in a simple act of wonder as if to ask, "What's funny?," later became as famous in films as it had been on the stage.

Haley's father, a ship's navigator, encouraged his son to find employment at sea. A compromise was reached whereby the young man apprenticed as an electrician, but as soon as he had enough money saved, he ran away from home, planning to enter vaudeville in Philadelphia. Instead, Haley began work as a song plugger for the McCarthy Fischer Music Publishing Co. Finally, he did enter vaudeville in partnership with another young man named Charlie Crafts. "Every job was temporary until I got the one I wanted," recalled Haley. He has compared the team of Crafts and Haley to Dean Martin and Jerry Lewis, and certainly there is a vague resemblance in style between Lewis and Haley. While working with Crafts, Haley toured with the Lightner Sisters and Alexander. One of the so-called Lightner Sisters was Flo McFadden, whom Haley later married and worked with in vaudeville.

Crafts and Haley made it to the Palace in February 1924. The following year, Haley was back at the Palace with a new partner, Helen Eby Rock, the widow of William Rock, who played a dumb straight woman to Haley's comedy. The two opened the second half of the Palace bill in April 1925, and *Variety* (April 15, 1925) commented, "The gags and laugh material are ideally bunched to make for spontaneous comedy throughout and is spaced by songs which also help nicely." Jack Haley last played the Palace, as a solo turn, in April 1932.

Jack Haley came to films in 1930 with *Follow Thru*, singing with Zelma O'Neal the song that he had made famous in the original 1929 stage production, "Button Up Your Overcoat." Other films followed, including *Sitting Pretty* (1933), *Poor Little Rich Girl* (1936), *Alexander's Ragtime Band* (1938), *Moon over Miami* (1941), and *George White's Scandals* (1945). Of course, Jack Haley gained screen immortality as the Tin Woodsman in the 1939 M-G-M screen adaptation of *The Wizard of Oz*. Haley's last great stage success was as Zachary Ash in the 1940 production of *Higher and Higher*, a role he re-created in the 1943 film version. When the original stage play opened, Brooks Atkinson noted with deep affection, "There are many things wrong with show business, and with the whole world, as far as that goes, but Jack Haley is not one of them. Haley has a lot of friends who admire his talent for skylarking."

In the 1940s, Haley announced his retirement from show business and decided to devote himself to his real estate interests. He explained, "Fortunately I never had to perform; I was not one of those extroverts who needed to have an audience. I found I could get just as much enjoyment from a real estate deal. I also found that you couldn't take your reviews to the grocery store." He did come out of retirement in 1972 to appear in *Norwood*, a film directed by his son Jack Haley, Jr. In addition to his stage and screen work, Haley was also featured on radio frequently in the 1930s and had his own show from 1937 to 1939 (at first on NBC, later on CBS).

By a happy coincidence, Jack Haley made his last public apperance in company with Ray Bolger (his costar from *The Wizard of Oz*) at the April 9, 1979, Academy Awards presentation, produced by his son. Penny Singleton, who had worked with Haley in the touring versions of *Good News* and *Follow Thru*, and who, like Haley, was a past president of the American Guild of Variety Artists (AGVA), paid tribute to the much-liked comedian: "I learned so much from Jack Haley, about acting, about presence, and about getting laughs."

BIBLIOGRAPHY

Catsos, Gregory M. "An In-Depth Interview with Margaret Hamilton, Jack Haley, and Ray Bolger." *Hollywood Studio Magazine*, April 1989, pp. 10–16.

Hopper, Hedda. "Looking at Hollywood: Jack Haley." Syndicated Column, September 29, 1946.

Maltin, Leonard. "Jack Haley Today." *Film Fan Monthly* no. 123 (September 1971), pp. 3–5.

Savoy, Maggie. "The Tin Man of 'Oz' Really Does Have a Heart." *Los Angeles Times*, August 16, 1970, pp. E1, E10.

Scully, Frank. "Catechist from the Land of Oz." *Catholic Digest*, February 1961, pp. 78–81.

Smith, Bill. "Jack Haley." In *The Vaudevillians*. New York: Macmillan, 1976, pp. 129–34.

ADELAIDE HALL (Brooklyn, N.Y., October 20, 1904–London, November 7, 1993)

Adelaide Hall was far more than one of the great black jazz singers of the twentieth century; she is best described as a diva, a songstress with a voice both operatic and modernistic, as exemplified by her 1927 recording of "Creole Love Song" by and with Duke Ellington. She is best remembered in the United States for featured roles in *Shuffle Along* (1922), *Runnin' Wild* (1923), and *Blackbirds of 1928*, but Adelaide Hall also had a brief career as a vaudeville headliner.

She made her Broadway debut in *Shuffle Along*; it was followed by *Chocolate Kiddies* (1925), *Desires of 1927* (1927), and *Brown Buddies* (1930). She starred, along with Bill Robinson, in Lew Leslie's *Blackbirds of 1928*, which opened at the Liberty Theatre on May 9, 1928, but ran for a mere forty-three performances. In the show, she introduced ''Digga Digga Do'' and ''I Can't Give You Anything but Love, Baby.'' From *Blackbirds of 1928*, Hall went into vaudeville, although Lew Leslie refused to permit her to sing any of the songs that she had performed in the show. She made her New York vaudeville debut in February 1930 at the Palace with an act titled ''Singing Songs—and How,'' conceived by Cecil Mack and with Messrs. Dandridge and Tate at two pianos. On a bill that also included Fanny Brice and Phil Baker, Hall made a considerable impact; of course, she was helped at the Monday matinee by having Bill Robinson join her onstage. *Variety* (February 12, 1930) hailed her as ''a bet for vaudeville,'' noting that ''the colored singer and dancer had poise, apperance and ability.'' She returned to the Palace in August 1930 and in April and July 1931.

In 1927, Adelaide Hall worked in vaudeville with Duke Ellington, and as she recalled:

I was touring the RKO theatre circuit, closing the first half of the show, and Duke's band was opening the second half. One night, standing backstage, I heard him playing ''Creole Love Song'' and began humming to fill in those spaces in the melody. Duke heard me after the show and said, ''Hey, I like that! Let's keep it in!'' A few days later he had me in the recording studio, singing that tune and another wordless vocal in ''Blues I Love to Sing.''

Hall reprised the song at a 1974 memorial service for Duke Ellington at London's St. Martin's in the Fields.

Adelaide Hall toured successfully in American vaudeville. Seeing her at the E. F. Albee Theatre in Cincinnati, *The Billboard* (March 7, 1931) reported, ''She has heaps of personality, a fair enough repertoire of song numbers, and sells it all with a bang.'' While touring in 1932, she heard a young pianist from Toledo, and Art Tatum joined her as coaccompanist, along with Joe Turner. She recorded her first songs with Tatum in August 1932.

In 1925, Adelaide Hall married a former sailor from Trinidad named Bert Hicks, and he became her manager. She made her first visit to Europe in 1925 and toured there in the 1930s. In 1938, she and Hicks decided to make their permanent home in London. That same year, she costarred with Todd Duncan in *The Sun Never Sets* and appeared in *Keep Shufflin'*. Hall and Hicks operated a number of nightclubs in London, including the Florida Club and the Calypso. He died in 1962.

In May 1980, Adelaide Hall returned to New York in *Black Broadway*, a splendid re-creation of the great black revues of the 1920s, which also featured Elizabeth Welch (who had been with Hall in *Blackbirds of 1928*), John Bubbles, and Edith Wilson. She had put on a few pounds since the 1920s, but Hall was still a great singer and entertainer.

Adelaide Hall appeared in a few short subjects, as well as *The Thief of Bagdad* (1940). In 1989, David Robinson and David Mingay produced and directed a documentary of her in a performance titled *Sophisticated Lady*.

(In its issue of September 22, 1916, *Variety* carried a review of a young dancer named Adelaide Hall, whose "good looks and youth help her other accomplishments." She was appearing in New York at Rector's, but this does not appear to have been the same Adelaide Hall.)

BIBLIOGRAPHY

"Do You Remember Adelaide Hall?" *Negro Digest*, May 1951, pp. 73–74.

Feather, Leonard. "2 Expatriates Do It Their Way in Britain." *Los Angeles Times Calendar*, July 30, 1989, p. 59.

Holly, Elestine P. "Adelaide Hall." In *Notable Black American Women*, Jessie Carney Smith, ed. Detroit: Gale Research, 1992, pp. 438–39.

NAN HALPERIN (Odessa, Russia, 1898—Long Island, N.Y., May 30, 1963)

Nan Halperin was a singing comedienne who became known as America's "Famous Satirist." What she satirized was never politics or religion or those genres so popular with today's satirists, but rather the behavior and life-styles of ordinary American women. In a typical Nan Halperin vaudeville routine— from 1918—she presented the epochal periods in a woman's life. First she appeared in pigtails and a calico dress as a precocious ten-year-old, bemoaning the arrival of a new baby in the household and her sudden drop from her special place as the youngest in the family. She was next seen as a young woman attending her first ball and asking, "Why must I have so many clothes to capture just one man?" On her wedding eve, the character was busily disposing of the photographs and letters that reminded her of her romances. Finally, she appeared as a military bride awaiting the return of her aviator husband from his war triumphs. (After the close of the First World War, the last character became a blasé divorcée.) "This is dramatic satire effectively done," commented *The New York Dramatic Mirror* (December 21, 1918).

Born in Russia, Nan Halperin arrived with her parents in Minneapolis and was raised and educated there; although Jewish, she was sent to a Catholic convent, where she studied vocal music and piano. After a number of amateur appearances, Halperin appeared on the vaudeville stage at the age of fifteen, giving child impersonations. She later teamed with other women to present a skit titled "Nan Halperin and Her Suffragettes." She married composer William Barr Friedlander, and he composed all the songs that she used in her act.

By 1915, Nan Halperin had a repertoire of three hundred songs. "They're all intimate, personal songs—distinctly a part of me. They would never do until audiences really began to know me. Once I'm accepted, I can begin drawing upon them," she told *The New York Dramatic Mirror*. "I want to succeed just as myself. But I want to succeed," she continued. Success came in February 1915, when she played the Palace as a headliner, and the following year, Halperin became the first vaudeville performer to receive a three-year contract from the United Booking Office, to be under the direct management of E. F. Albee.

Aside from vaudeville, Nan Halperin is best known for her appearance, along with Miriam Hopkins, in the musical farce *Little Jessie James*, which opened at the Longacre Theatre, New York, on August 15, 1923. As late as June 1932, she was the headliner at the Orpheum Theatre in Los Angeles, telling the *Los Angeles Examiner* (June 4, 1932), "The vaudeville entertainer today has to compete with the greatest stars of the world, through talking motion pictures." Aside from Nan, two brothers were also active in show business: Hal was manager of the Chicago office of *Variety*, and Max was a vaudeville agent in the same city.

BIBLIOGRAPHY
"Nan from Odessa." *The New York Dramatic Mirror*, January 27, 1915, p. 31.

OSCAR HAMMERSTEIN (Berlin, Germany, May 8, 1847—New York, August 1, 1919)

Oscar Hammerstein was an eccentric theatrical entrepreneur whose chief love in life was opera. but who was also heavily involved in vaudeville. His biographer Vincent Sheean wrote, "The name and personality of Oscar Hammerstein became as familiar to the nation as if he had been its elected President. His distinctive appearance was universally recognized. Each of his doings and sayings was chronicled. His legend, expressed in stories, songs, cartoons, and all the apparatus of legend, was spread across the land. In a period when the present use of familiar names had not yet come into fashion he was known to millions as 'Oscar.' "

Born into an affluent Jewish family, Oscar Hammerstein came to the United States in 1862 and discovered the magic of the theatre. Between 1874 and 1877, he wrote five short plays for the Germania Theatre, and during the same period began investing in real estate in Harlem, utilizing income from the *United States Tobacco Journal*, which he had founded in 1874. On September 30, 1889, he opened his first theatre, the Harlem Opera House. It was followed in October 1890 by the Columbus Theatre. On November 14, 1892, Hammerstein opened the Manhattan Opera House, later renamed the Manhattan Theatre. Because of its size—two thousand, six hundred seats—the theatre was too large for plays, and in 1893, Hammerstein turned its operation over to Koster and Bial, at which time it became the new Koster and Bial's Music Hall.

It has been claimed that Oscar Hammerstein created the theatrical district of Times Square by opening the first theatre complex there, the Olympia, on November 25, 1895. The theatre was a financial failure and sold at auction in 1898. Hammerstein's next theatrical venture was the Victoria Theatre, which opened on March 2, 1899, as a legitimate concern, but which was renamed the Victoria Theatre of Varieties on February 8, 1904, and became a vaudeville house operated by Hammerstein's son Willie. The theatre was generally known simply as Hammerstein's or Hammerstein's Victoria. On an adjacent lot, Hammerstein built a second, smaller theatre, the Republic (which opened on September 27, 1900), and the roofs of the two theatres became the Paradise Roof, a summer extension of the Victoria's vaudeville entertainment.

Oscar Hammerstein remained determined to build an opera house for New York, which he did with the Manhattan Opera House, a three thousand, one hundred-seat auditorium located at 34th Street and Eighth Avenue, which opened on December 3, 1906. The Manhattan Opera House was Hammerstein's answer to the Metropolitan Opera House, with whose management he had a long-running feud. To the Manhattan, he brought Nellie Melba, and also presented the American debuts of Mary Garden and Luisa Tetrazzini.

In the spring of 1908, Hammerstein began to present performances of the Manhattan Opera Company in Philadelphia, and perhaps not surprisingly, on November 17, 1908, he opened the Philadelphia Opera House. The latter venue was not successful, and in 1910, with funding provided by Otto Kahn, the Metropolitan Opera House was able to put Hammerstein out of the opera business, taking over the Philadelphia house and forcing Hammerstein to agree not to produce operas in New York for a ten-year period.

Undaunted, Hammerstein turned to musical comedy, producing Victor Herbert's *Naughty Marietta* in 1910. He also opened the London Opera House in November 1911. Hammerstein tried to open the Lexington Opera House in New York in 1914, but the Metropolitan successfully brought an injunction against him. Hammerstein's final years were spent in frustration at projects that never came to fruition, and in 1914, he lost three of his sons, Abe, Willie, and Harry, a shock from which he never fully recovered. He was the grandfather of lyricist Oscar Hammerstein II.

BIBLIOGRAPHY

Sheean, Vincent. *Oscar Hammerstein I: The Life and Exploits of an Impressario*. New York: Simon and Schuster, 1956.

WILLIE HAMMERSTEIN (New York, 1874—New York, June 10, 1914)

The son of Oscar Hammerstein, Willie Hammerstein's name is synonymous with New York's Victoria Theatre and the exploitation of freak attractions in vaudeville. Shortly after his death, Morris Gest wrote of him:

During twenty years he brought more new ideas to vaudeville than any other manager of the present generation. He was a peculiar genius, who violated most of the traditions about theatrical managers by always beginning work at eight o'clock in the morning, and by quitting promptly at nine-thirty every night, when he returned to his home, which he loved dearly. He never participated in the so-called night life of Broadway. His home was entirely separate and distinct from the stage. Though he was one of the best known men on Broadway, he never invited anyone to visit at his home. . . . His two sons had been trained for other pursuits, and it was his wish that they keep away from theatrical life. Yet he loved his own theatre, and in fourteen years never saw a play at any other theatre. His only office was the lobby of his theatre, and there he would spend most of his time, sitting on a crooked chair, and surrounded by a small company of cronies—

among them 'Doc' Steiner, who was always playing childish tricks on Willie; Walter Rosenberg, a manager who made him laugh with funny stories; and a boy tenor named Bell, whose specialty was standing on one foot and singing with one eye closed.

Willie Hammerstein learned his craft of theatre management at the Olympia Theatre before taking over management of the Victoria, on behalf of his father, in 1904. Presenting freak acts such as Evelyn Nesbit Thaw and Don the Talking Dog, he made the Victoria the most successful vaudeville house in New York. The acts cost little, but always drew large crowds. Aside from the "freak" attractions, Willie Hammerstein had a number of favorites that he booked frequently into the Victoria, most notably British music hall comedian Harry Tate (1872–1940) with his "Motoring" sketch.

In the summer of 1912, Willie and his father quarreled, and the former was temporarily removed from management of the Victoria Theatre, but he returned in November of the same year. The return was celebrated by a verse in *Variety* titled "Willie's on the Job Again":

> Willie's on the job again, and Hammerstein's looks great,
> All of Huber's old time freaks are goin' to celebrate,
> To show that he was still there, and that the news was real,
> He rushed to the U.B.O. and booked "The Diving Seal."
> Willie's on the job again, there's joy along Broadway.

Willie Hammerstein's premature death was the result of Bright's disease. His son was the celebrated lyricist and musical comedy writer Oscar Hammerstein II.

See also FREAK ACTS, VICTORIA THEATRE.

BIBLIOGRAPHY

Gest, Morris. "The Famous Freaks of Hammerstein's." *The Green Book Magazine*, September 1914, pp. 551–57.
Gray, Thomas J. "Willie's on the Job Again." *Variety*, November 29, 1912, p. 9.
O'Connor, Johnny. "Willie Hammerstein." *Variety*, June 20, 1919, p. 9.
"Willie Hammerstein." *The New York Dramatic Mirror*, June 17, 1914, p. 21.

POODLES HANNEFORD (Barnsley, England, 1892—Catskill Bay, N.Y., December 9, 1967)

Edwin "Poodles" Hanneford was one of the great clowns and bareback riders of the circus, who made many excursions to the vaudeville stage (or at least to those stages large enough to accommodate his act). His favorite vaudeville venue was the New York Hippodrome, to which he returned many times with his family and wife, Grace, who acted as ring mistress. Hanneford's act was spectacular and dangerously funny. He would pretend to fall off his horse's back, ending up on the ground directly beneath the animal; then he would proceed to climb back on the horse through its back legs, prying them apart with his head. Hanneford's greatest success came at the Hippodrome, when he was one of the featured acts in *Billy Rose's Jumbo*, which opened there on November 16, 1935, and ran for 233 performances.

Born into a famous British circus family in the north of England, Hanneford learned to ride at the age of five. He was blindfolded by his father in order to teach him to rely on the horse's instinct rather than his own sight. In 1915, Hanneford emigrated to the United States, where he was to remain active through the 1960s, appearing on *The Ed Sullivan Show* and the *Hollywood Palace*. For many years, he was a beloved member of the Ringling Brothers and Barnum and Bailey Circus.

As early as 1919, Poodles Hanneford and his family appeared at the Hippodrome in a show titled *Happy Days*. They were back in 1924, by which time, in recognition of the star attraction, the name of the act had been changed from The Hanneford Family to Poodles Hanneford and Co. "Back again and funnier than ever," commented *Variety* (October 29, 1924). "This Poodles Hanneford comes pretty near being a wonder in the ring, whether as a clown comic or a bareback rider. An audience will give Poodles the percentage as a funny man and he is all of that, but his funniments take away from the layman that he's a remarkable rider of a ring horse. Even the audience finally gets that angle toward the finish, despite Poodles' funmaking and his burlesque dressing." In 1928, Hanneford headlined at the Palace, but really, as *Variety*'s Sime Silverman commented in 1924, Poodles Hanneford was "an act for vaudeville, just built for the Hip."

The essence of Poodles Hanneford's success was that he made his equestrian efforts seem easy. The comic attire and the clowning, such as having his suspenders come loose and flap in his face, resulting in his trousers falling down, was not the act. It was the window-dressing to the true genius of his riding techniques.

The only other equestrienne act on the vaudeville stage with the same appeal as that of Poodles Hanneford was May Wirth, who also appeared with her family. As far as Joe Laurie, Jr., was concerned, May Wirth was the greatest straight rider and Poodles Hanneford the greatest clown rider.

HARRIGAN AND HART

Ethnic characterizations of Germans, Jews, Italians, Negroes, and the Irish were developed on the American stage in the 1870s by Harrigan and Hart. The dominant partner in the team, who both wrote, produced, and starred in the couple's productions, was Edward Harrigan (New York, October 26, 1845— New York, June 6, 1911). He was, in the words of William Dean Howells, "the Dickens of America." Harrigan began his stage career singing with Lotta Crabtree in San Francisco in 1861, and made his New York debut in *A Little Fraud* at the Globe Theatre on November 21, 1870. Two years later, he teamed with Tony Hart. Born Anthony Cannon, Hart (Worcester, Ma., July 25, 1855— Worcester, Ma., November 4, 1891) had sung and danced in saloons and toured with circuses before joining Madam Rentz's Female Minstrels in 1870. He was a talented comedian noted for his wench characterizations; of Hart's performances, Nat C. Goodwin wrote, "He sang like a nightingale, danced like a fairy, and acted like a master comedian."

Harrigan and Hart were the stars of the Theatre Comique, which Harrigan later managed until 1881, when it was demolished. Between 1870 and 1879, Harrigan wrote and produced almost eighty vaudeville sketches of topics as varied as politics, life insurance, and baseball. His most famous production, *The Mulligan Guard*, was first produced in Chicago in 1873, and it was followed by *The Mulligan Guard and the Skidmover* (1875) and *The Mulligan Guard Ball* (1879). In all, Harrigan wrote thirty-nine plays, and as biographer E. J. Kahn wrote, "To many out-of-towners, Harrigan and Hart were a New York landmark equal in stature to Broadway."

The couple opened the New Theatre Comique in New York on August 29, 1881, with *The Major*, but it was destroyed by fire on December 23, 1884. Harrigan and Hart severed their partnership in May of the following year. Tony Hart gave his last stage appearance at the Howard Athenaeum, Boston, in May 1887. Later he was committed to an insane asylum, where he died. Edward "Ned" Harrigan continued to perform until October 1908, making his last stage appearance in *His Wife's Family*, a legitimate drama at Wallack's Theatre, New York.

BIBLIOGRAPHY

Kahn, E. J., Jr. *The Merry Partners: The Age and Stage of Harrigan and Hart*. New York: Random House, 1955.

MARION HARRIS (Henderson, Ky., ?—New York, April 23, 1944)

A popular singer of syncopated songs in both vaudeville and on the nightclub circuit, Marion Harris came to fame in the mid 1920s. Her first husband, Phil Goldberg, would often accompany her on the piano. She headlined at the Palace in July 1926, July 1927, March 1928, December 1928, December 1930, and January 1931, and was also seen on Broadway in *Yours Truly* (1927) and *Great Day!* (1929). In the 1930s Marion Harris moved to London, where she enjoyed considerable success at the Café de Paris. On a visit to New York, she was burned to death in a hotel fire.

TONY HART. *See* HARRIGAN AND HART

PAUL HARTMAN (San Francisco, March 1, 1904—Los Angeles, October 2, 1973) and **GRACE HARTMAN** (San Francisco, January, 7, 1907—Van Nuys, Ca., August 8, 1955)

Arguably the greatest comedy dance team in vaudeville, Paul and Grace Hartman specialized in satirizing ballroom dancing, billing themselves as "Satirists of the Dance." Unlike other dancers, they considered facial expressions to be as important as the dance steps, for, as Paul Hartman once explained, "many people think that to mug all you have to do is make faces, cross your eyes, wiggle your ears, or do something equally obvious and ridiculous. But mugging is a gentle art. The version which pays off for us is just a thought or an idea projected from the mugger to the audience with only a slightly exaggerated expression. If this exaggeration is minutely overdone, the expression becomes a grimace. There is nothing grimmer in show business than a grimace.''

Paul Hartman was the son of actress Josie Hart and producer-director-actor Ferris Hartman, a theatrical entrepreneur of the old school who was known as "The Ziegfeld of the West." He allowed his son to make his first stage appearance at the age of six at the Tivoli Opera House in San Francisco. Paul and Grace Barrett were married when she was fifteen and he was seventeen. At that time, they were billed as Hartman and Barrett, touring throughout the West Coast—"We were never able to get east of the Rockies," explained Paul Hartman—and embarking on an extensive tour of the Middle East and Asia, before becoming national vaudeville favorites in the late 1920s. Broadway audiences got to know the Hartmans in *Red, Hot and Blue*, the Cole Porter musical, which opened at the Alvin Theatre on October 29, 1936, and which also featured Jimmy Durante, Bob Hope, Ethel Merman, and Vivian Vance. Their style of dancing was farcical, but at the same time was meticulously conceived and executed.

The Hartmans made their screen debut in *Forty-Five Fathers* in 1937 and were also featured in *Sunny* (1937) and *Higher and Higher* (1943). They were seen on NBC television in 1949 in the early situation comedy series *The Hartmans at Home*. Presumably, some of the trials and tribulations they suffered in their program as a suburban New York couple spilled over into their private lives, for Paul and Grace Hartman were divorced in 1951. Paul Hartman became a successful character actor on television, featured in *The Pride of the Family* (ABC, 1953–1954), *The Andy Griffith Show* (CBS, 1960–1968), and *Mayberry R.F.D.* (CBS, 1968–1971).

BIBLIOGRAPHY

Copeland, Robert. "The Hartman Mugs." *Liberty*, June 15, 1946, pp. 20–21, 73–74.
Raddatz, Leslie. "He's Not Going Anyplace." *TV Guide*, March 23, 1968, pp. 29–30, 32.

LONEY HASKELL (Newark, N.J., 1870—New York, October 20, 1933)

A monologist, Loney Haskell was master of ceremonies of Hammerstein's Victoria Theatre, introducing the freak acts and often keeping up a running commentary if, as was often the case, the acts had nothing to say. Born Lorne Levy, Haskell began his career as a librettist and a performer with Hurtig and Seamon's Burlesque Company. B. F. Keith heard him perform in Boston and urged him to learn to control his inclination to shout his lines, commenting, "If that man could keep his voice down, he would be worth $100 more a week." One of the classic stories introduced by Loney Haskell concerned a man with a stutter who asks a newsboy the way to the railroad station. The boy will not reply, and the man goes off in a rage. Another man standing close by asks the newsboy why he refused to answer the stuttering man, and the boy replied, "Wh-wh-wh-what? And g-g-g-get my h-h-h-head kn-kn-kn-knocked off?''

Haskell made his name at the Victoria Theatre when he was signed to introduce Don the Talking Dog in the summer of 1912. "Dash" in *Variety* (July 19, 1912) described the act:

'Don' and Loney Haskell should divide the billing. The program doesn't even mention Loney, which isn't quite fair, for of the twelve minutes consumed by the show, nine were utilized by the actor. There were those present Monday evening who were rude enough to interrupt his speech at various times, but then one must expect all manner of people to drift into a public roof garden. It was rather strange that they let Loney go as far as he did before they got after him. 'Don' knew what he was up against and sulked through his performance, passing over his vowels without emphasis and little apparent heed. This was the first time that Don had ever appeared on a roof and as someone had foolishly told him in the afternoon it was pretty tough for a talking act up in the air, he was probably a bit nervous. He refused to go until all the windows were closed. 'Don's' voice can be heard quite clearly in the rear of the roof. If one has ever lived on the eighth or tenth floor of an apartment house, it is easy to understand how a dog's voice will carry. It is a question of talking at random with 'Don.' He is a quiet retiring animal, and, unlike a great many children, speaks, only when spoken to. 'Don' answers questions only; he never asks one. The system is this: Loney asks the question in German, explains it in English to the audience, and then Miss Habaleen (who puts 'Don;' through its paces) asks the dog the question. 'Don' answers 'Kuchen,' 'Ruhe,' 'Don,' 'Unger,' etc., as the case may be. 'Don' has never get given the wrong answer. Still 'Don' is going to get over. The trained growls which emanate from his throat can readily be mistaken for words. On the roof the audience, skeptical in the first place, became more so at Loney's speech, but after the dog had made its first try they became interested and later enthusiastic. 'Don' is a novelty. He should not be kidded, and may cause talk. There is little reason to doubt but that Willie Hammerstein will exercise his option after the first two weeks have expired.

Loney Haskell also served as assistant manager of the Victoria Theatre and, following Willie Hammerstein's death, worked with Arthur Hammerstein in operating the theatre. In 1923, Haskell became secretary of the Jewish Actors' Guild, and it was at the organization's offices that he died.

GRACE HAYES (San Francisco, August 23, 1895—February 1, 1989)

Grace Hayes was a popular singer in nightclubs and vaudeville, who became a headliner in the late 1920s. She made her debut at the Palace in July 1929, as the new partner of Neville Fleeson. Despite the billing of Grace Hayes and Neville Fleeson, the latter was the star of the act, playing the piano and introducing the songs that he wrote and Hayes sang. Writing in *Variety* (July 17, 1929), "Bite" hailed Grace Hayes as "as good a singer of comedy as can be found anywhere today," and that opinion was echoed by Mae West, who was in the audience and applauded the singer's impersonation of her as Diamond Lil. Miss Hayes returned to the Palace in May 1932, by which time she had gained a wider audience thanks to her own radio program on NBC. Despite her newfound stardom in radio, she did not use a microphone, and delighted her fans by singing, "You've Got Me in between the Devil and the NBC." She also gave an impersonation of Pola Negri in the film *Paradise* and introduced her son Peter Lind Hayes, calling him simply Peter Lind, as her agent thought it unwise for her to admit to having a teenage son. "The comedienne who as ever, can best be described as being of stately stature, is still an attractive personality with an accomplished conception of stage values," reported *Variety* (May 24, 1932).

The singer made a few film appearances: *King of Jazz* (1929), *Rainbow over Broadway* (1933) and *Babes in Arms* (1939). In the 1930s, she hosted and sang at the Grace Hayes Lodge in the San Fernando Valley area of Los Angeles. Early in the following decade, she took over the Red Rooster in Las Vegas, changing its name to the Grace Hayes Lodge and later the Patio. She built a home at the back of the property, and it became the only residence on the Las Vegas Strip, eventually purchased for $2 million as the site of the Mirage resort. Grace Hayes was married three times; to Joseph Conrad Lind, Charley Foy (of the Seven Little Foys), and Bob Hopkins.

HEADLINER

Headliner was the standard vaudeville term for the star of the show, whose name would appear at the head of the bill. The headliner would always be featured as the next-to-last performer on the program, in what was usually the number eight spot. If there were two headliners on the same bill, one would occupy the aforementioned spot, while the other would be forced to accept the secondary spot immediately prior to intermission, usually number five. The headliner would always expect the theatre's star dressing room, which would be on the main floor, rather than one story or more above the stage. With two headliners on the same bill, theatre managers would often find it more convenient to pretend the star dressing room was being refurbished, thus resulting in both headliners having to occupy a secondary dressing room.

TED HEALY (Houston, Tx., October 1, 1896—Los Angeles, December 19, 1937)

Ted Healy's career is an interesting one—the story of a vaudevillian who entered films with his supporting company and saw those players rise to fame while his career slipped away. Born Charles Earnest Lee Nash, Ted Healy entered show business as a blackface comedian while in his mid teens. In 1922, he teamed with dancer-singer Betty Brown, whom he later married (divorced 1932), and the pair broke into big-time vaudeville, telling jokes and singing a couple of songs in the style of Al Jolson and Eddie Cantor. Reviewing Healy's act at Shea's Theatre, Buffalo, *Variety* (September 1, 1922) commented, "He shows himself possessed of a nimble wit and carries himself with the confidence and poise of a veteran."

The comedian began writing comedy sketches emphasizing physical, slapstick humor, and in 1922 invited two childhood friends, Moe and Shemp Howard, to join the act as stooges. In 1925, Larry Fine, from the vaudeville act of the Haney Sisters and Fine, was also invited to participate. The act was variously known as Ted Healy and His Racketeers, Ted Healy and His Three Southern Gentleman, or Ted Healy and His Gang. It was never billed as Ted Healy and the Three Stooges. From vaudeville, the quartet moved to musical comedy and revue with Healy and Shemp Howard appearing in *A Night in Spain* (1927) and Healy and the three stooges appearing in *A Night in Venice* (1929).

While appearing in the latter show, the men were seen by a talent scout for the William Fox film company and signed to a contract. They were first seen on screen in the feature-length production *Soup to Nuts* (1930). Writing in *Variety* (October 29, 1930), Sime Silverman was not impressed: "Not only is Healy, a comedian whom the New York Palace pays $6,000 a week for headlining in that ace vaude house, made a straight man, but he is turned into a flip romantic juvenile with a girl as unfunny as he is here hanging onto his neck all the while." Interestingly, Healy received a billing and the critical attention, while his stooges were ignored.

This happened not only on-screen but also behind the scenes, as Healy commandeered the bulk of the cash from the Fox contract and refused to push for adequate billing for his colleagues. In 1931 the disgruntled stooges left for New York to play in vaudeville as the Three Lost Souls. A reconciliation took place in 1932, and Healy and his three partners were back together in vaudeville at New York's Broadway Theatre in December 1932. Shemp Howard left the act, and he was replaced by Jerry "Curly" Howard when the group was signed by M-G-M. In 1934, Jules White invited the three stooges to come to Columbia Pictures and star in a series of comedies that he was producing. It was widely rumored that Ted Healy thought it beneath him to leave a prestigious studio such as M-G-M for the Poverty Row outfit of Columbia. The rest, of course, is history, as the Three Stooges became one of the most famous comedy acts to appear in film shorts. "Curly" Howard died in 1952, Shemp in 1955, and Larry Fine and Moe Howard in 1975.

Ted Healy continued to appear in films, with his last production being *Hollywood Hotel* (1937). He died penniless, apparently of heart failure. The night before his death, he had been involved in a fight outside the Trocadero nightclub, and it was thought at the time that his death might have been from brain concussion related to the melée.

Ken Murray remembered Ted Healy as his favorite comedian and his idol:

He was master of throwing things away. I remember one time he was playing the Keith's in Philadelphia, and he followed Vincent Lopez and His Orchestra. Vincent Lopez had about a fifty-piece orchestra on stage, and they used rear projection even in those days. The finish of his act, the lights would dim down and, using the screen, it was as if you were on an airplane coming down the Hudson and circling the Statue of Liberty. The music is playing 'The Stars and Stripes' and it was thrilling. A big finish was tremendous applause. Next act, Ted Healy, and he walks out as he used to, in corduroy pants, old jacket, and the oddest kinda tie. He walks out on stage and says, "Wasn't that a great act with those fellows sitting there in their tuxedos? Look at me, I look like a bum, but what the hell, it's only a week." He was the throwaway master of them all. He was a great comedian.

BIBLIOGRAPHY
Hempstead, Susan. "Healy and His Hooligans." *Shadowplay* 3, no. 1 (March 1934), pp. 26–27, 71–72.
Lenburg, Jeff, Joan Howard Mauer, and Greg Lenburg. *The Three Stooges Scrapbook.* Secaucus, N.J.: Citadel Press, 1982.

LEW HEARN (Poland, February 15, 1882—February 1965)

Lew Hearn was one of the great comic straight men in vaudeville. His whining voice was described by Frederick James Smith in *The New York Dramatic Mirror* (June 16, 1915) as "weird" and "phonographic." He was a perfect foil to Eddie Cantor in *Midnight Rounders* (1920) and *Make It Snappy* (1922) as the customer in the sketch "Joe's Blue Front," attempting to buy a suit from tailor Cantor and demanding "a belt in the back." The sketch is captured on film with both Cantor and Hearn in *Glorifying the American Girl* (1929), and Lew Hearn also gives a delightful cameo performance in *The Specter of the Rose* (1946).

No biographical information on Lew Hearn is available. With his wife, Bonita, he had a vaudeville act in the teens, embracing both comedy and songs, and apparently Florence Mills worked with them at one time. In 1925, Hearn appeared as a rube comedian at New York's Fifth Avenue Theatre, and *Variety* (April 15, 1925) reported, "The act can hold a spot on the best of big time bills." Lew Hearn was frequently seen in revues, with one of the earliest being *Town Topics.* which opened at New York's Century Theatre on September 23, 1915, and was nothing more than a glorified vaudeville show featuring Will Rogers, Trixie Friganza, Clifton Webb, and Blossom Seeley. Other Broadway shows in which Hearn appeared were the 1923 edition of the Ziegfeld *Follies*, *Innocent Eyes* (1924), *Lady Do* (1927), *Ned Wayburn's Gambols* (1929), *Bet Your Life* (1937), *Yodel Boy* (1939), and *The Walking Gentleman* (1942). He was at the Palace in November 1927 and January 1931.

THOMAS HEATH.   See McINTYRE AND HEATH

ANNA HELD (Paris, March 8, 1873—New York, August 12, 1918)

Thanks to Luise Rainer's portrayal of her in the 1936 M-G-M feature film *The Great Ziegfeld*, an image has been created of Anna Held as a slight, ethereal vision of dark loveliness. In reality, Miss Held was somewhat buxom, despite an eighteen-inch waist that had expanded considerably by the mid teens. She was not beautiful in the modern sense, possessing a plump face with fringed and abundant red-brown hair. Her large and expressive brown eyes were her most distinctive features, and it is no surprise that her theme song was "I Just Can't Make My Eyes Behave," written by Will D. Cobb and Gus Edwards, with its famous chorus:

For I just can't make my eyes behave
Two bad brown eyes I am their slave,
My lips may say run away from me
But my eyes say come and play with me.
And you won't blame poor little me, I'm sure,
Cuz I just can't make my eyes behave.

There is little doubt that much of Anna Held's success was thanks to the energetic efforts of her husband, Florenz Ziegfeld, who produced many of the shows in which she starred. He set her up in an apartment at New York's Ansonia Hotel, "heavy with the scent of one thousand American beauty roses," and his publicist, Leon Berg, circulated the famous story of her taking milk baths. Berg's daughter Carmen recalled:

Ziegfeld chose him as one of the men to meet the tug-boat on which she arrived. In those days, milk was delivered to the grocery stores in large metal cans and Dad hurriedly got some empty cans, had them sent to the hotel and put outside her reserved room to make it look legit to the newsmen when they arrived.

The youngest of seven children—the other six died young—Anna Held had French parents, despite her Germanic name. Held was eleven years old when her father died, and her mother brought her to England in search of relatives. The two women took a room next to the Princess Theatre on London's Oxford Street, and, pretending to be sixteen, Anna Held obtained a job in the chorus there. Her mother died when Anna was twelve, and the young girl had no alternative but to continue on the stage, singing in music halls in the Netherlands, Germany, Poland, and Spain. Florenz Ziegfeld first saw Anna Held at London's Palace Theatre in 1895, when, in halting English, she sang a saucy number titled "Won't You Come and Play wiz Me?" That was apparently precisely what Ziegfeld had in mind. He brought her to New York, where she made her debut at the Herald Square Theatre on September 21, 1896, in *A Parlor Match*, again singing "Won't You Come and Play wiz Me?"

A year later, Held and Ziegfeld were married, and the producer starred her in *Papa's Wife*, *The Little Duchess*, *Mlle Napoleon*, and *The Parisien Model*. The last opened at New York's Broadway Theatre on November 26, 1906, and here Anna Held introduced "I Just Can't Make My Eyes Behave." Ziegfeld also arranged for his wife to appear, with great success, on the stage at Koster and Bial's Music Hall for several seasons in the late 1890s. Anna Held is often credited with giving Ziegfeld the idea for his *Follies*, with their emphasis on beautiful girls, but Ziegfeld featured his wife in only one edition of the revue— in 1910—and then she was seen only in a film interlude. In fact, by that time, relations were severely strained between the two. In 1908, Ziegfeld had forced his wife to submit to an abortion rather than permit her pregnancy to interfere with the opening of *Miss Innocence*, and there were also reports that Miss Held was becoming increasingly agitated by her husband's extramarital activities. Finally, they were divorced in 1912.

In November 1910, Anna Held returned to London's Palace Theatre at a salary of $2,500 a week, proving that even without Ziegfeld's aid she was a star earning a star's salary. When she had first played the Palace fifteen years earlier, she had been helped in her act by W. E. Ritchie, an American "tramp" bicyclist who added humor to her numbers by riding around the stage, but now she needed no one to help sell her to an audience. In the spring of 1912, Held toured vaudeville in a skit, and again drew a salary of $2,500 a week. A year later, she was starring in *Mlle Baby*, singing "Roll Those Eyes," "Je Suis Grise," and "Buzzing Time in Beetown."

After a successful European tour, Held returned to American vaudeville and the Palace in October 1915; she had first played there in February 1914. "Jolo" in *Variety* (October 29, 1915) reported, "She is still utilizing her talents in projecting rolling eyes, rhapsodic warbling, and exaggerated Frenchy hip-strolling back and forth. After three brief numbers and the passing of flowers across the footlights, Miss Held obliged with one verse of 'I Just Can't Make My Eyes Behave.' It was all very well received."

Anna Held appeared in only one feature-length film, *Madame la Presidente*, produced by the Oliver Morosco Company in 1916 and based on the play *Madam President*, which had starred Fannie Ward when it opened at the Garrick Theatre on September 15, 1913. As Mlle Gobette, Held seems very much at home in this French farce of mistaken identities (preserved at the UCLA Film and Television Archive). Despite advancing plumpness and a face that was showing signs of Gallic homeliness, she was totally the star. Her large expressive eyes made Anna Held perfectly suited to silent films, and it is unfortunate that she was not allowed to appear in more of them. Before *Madame la Presidente*, she was featured in a 1913 Kinemacolor short.

In the summer of 1917, as her contribution to the war effort, Anna Held created but did not star in "Anna Held's Visions—Military Tableaux," a vaudeville sketch glorifying the gallant French, British, and American allies, for which *Variety* did not care. A year later, she was dead at the early age of 45.

Anna Held's daughter had appeared in vaudeville while her mother was alive under the name of Liane Carrera. After her mother's death, she billed herself as Anna Held, Jr.

BIBLIOGRAPHY

Carrera, Liane. *Anna Held and Flo Ziegfeld*. Hicksville, N.Y.: Exposition Press, 1979.

Held, Anna. "My Beginnings." *Theatre*, July 1907, pp. 180, 182–83.

————. "Don't Do It!" *The Green Book Magazine*, March 1914, pp. 381–386.

————. *Mémoires: Une Étoile française au ciel de l'Amérique*. Paris: La Nef de Paris, 1954.

HERSCHEL HENLERE (Galt, Waterloo, Canada, December 14, 1890—London, January 13, 1968)

Sometimes known as Herschel Hendler—although the family name was Steinberg—Herschel Henlere billed himself as "The Poet of the Piano" while appearing on the vaudeville stage in the teens. In 1912, he toured as an accompanist to Anna Held, and in 1914, he performed "A Musical Mix-Up" act with Texas Guinan. Later, Henlere added comedy to his performance, becoming "The Mad Musician," an act he filmed for the British Pathé Company in 1935. Henlere appeared at the Palace Theatre in March 1920 and February 1925, but from 1921 was primarily active in Europe. As Bert Hendler, he appeared in three American Biograph shorts directed by D. W. Griffith in 1912: *A Temporary Truce*, *The School Teacher and the Waif*, and *An Indian Summer*. As Herschel Henlere, he appeared in the 1933 British musical *Soldiers of the King* (released in America as *The Woman in Command*).

AL HERMAN (1886—Los Angeles, July 2, 1967)

Al Herman was a blackface vaudeville comedian, well regarded by his contemporaries, who was billed either as "The Black Assassin of Grief" or "The Assassin of Grief and Remorse." Unlike other blackface monologists, he would utilize a prop cigar as part of his act. He was featured in the 1921 edition of *The Greenwich Village Follies*, and he was also an occasional screen actor— minor roles only—from the 1920s through the 1950s.

ALEXANDER HERRMANN (Paris, February 11, 1843—between Rochester, N.Y., and Bradford, Pa., December 11, 1896)

A magician noted for his grandiloquent style and his sleight of hand, Alexander Herrmann had a wraithlike appearance, with his thin, angular face offset by a waxed moustache and goatee. He became a magician at the age of fourteen, working with his older brother, Carl. He came to the United States in 1861 and was dubbed "Herrmann the Great" by the American press. He died in his private railroad car en route from Rochester, New York, to Bradford, Pennsylvania, and after his death, his wife, Adelaide, took over the act, assisted by nephew Leon (1867–1909). Carl Herrmann (1816–1887) was possibly a greater magician than his younger brother, but he concentrated on playing the countries of the Eastern Hemisphere after the two men had decided to carve up the world between them.

"HIGHER VAUDEVILLE"

This was a term devised by Vachel Lindsay (1879–1931) to describe performances by poets, whom he likened to street troubadours, reading their works from platforms at colleges, universities, and elsewhere. First used in 1912, the phrase was applied to Alfred Kreymborg, Carl Sandburg, Amy Lowell, and, of course, Lindsay himself. British poets John Masefield and Edith, Osbert, and Sacheverell Sitwell were also considered by Lindsay to be members of the group.

BIBLIOGRAPHY

Lindsay, Vachel. "What Is Beauty in Word and Rhythm?" *Liberty* 7, no. 3 (January 18, 1930), pp. 44–46.

"Poetry Invades the Vaudeville." *Current Opinion*. June 1913, p. 470.

"The Spectator." *The Outlook*, February 1, 1913, pp. 275–76.

GUS HILL (New York, circa 1860—New York, April 20, 1937)

A prominent manager of vaudeville shows, Gus Hill was born Gustave Metz and took his last name from Harry Hill's, a New York sporting resort at Broadway and Crosby Street. Here, Hill gained for himself the title of "Champion Club Swinger of the World." In the 1880s, he headed Gus Hill's Novelties, a touring vaudeville show, and in the following decade began to present a vaudeville act based on "The Yellow Kid" cartoons in the *New York Sunday World*. Later, other cartoon characters, including "Mutt and Jeff" and "The Happy Hooligan," were added to the act. Also in the 1890s, he operated Gus Hill's Minstrels. Hill is often credited with having discovered Montgomery and Stone and Weber and Fields; he also persuaded Billy Reeves to leave Fred Karno's "A Night in an English Music Hall" and tour with Hill's "Around the Clock" vaudeville company. As of 1910, he was one of the largest stockholders in the Columbia Amusement Company.

VIOLET AND DAISY HILTON (Brighton, England, February 5, 1908— Charlotte, N.C., January 4, 1969)

Violet and Daisy Hilton were Siamese Twins joined at the base of the spine. They started as a freak act exhibited in fairgrounds and circuses in Europe and America, and developed into serviceable vaudeville performers, relying on talent rather than sympathy from their audiences. Some sources suggest the twins were born in San Antonio, Texas, but this would appear to be a story circulated to justify their vaudeville billing as "The American Siamese Twins," with the reality being they were from southern England. Vaudeville manager Terry Turner realized the Hilton sisters had more potential than as mere sideshow attractions and brought them into vaudeville, booking them on the Loew's circuit in 1925 at $2,500 per week. They made their vaudeville debut at Loew's State, Newark, in February of that year.

In vaudeville, the twins played the clarinet and saxophone, and gave a reasonable impersonation of the Duncan Sisters. To close the act, two youths would appear on stage and dance with them. They were an immediate hit with long lines waiting outside the theatre to see this vaudeville curiosity. *Variety* (February 25, 1925) reported, "The girls are pretty brunettes, tastefully dressed. Their motivation is as natural and easy as two people strolling arm in arm. One sister walks backward then the other walks forward. . . . It could be played in any vaudeville theatre in the country regardless of the clientele and will duplicate its pulling power in any spot on any bill in America. . . . The act contains nothing repellant or gruesome."

Billed as "The Eighth Wonder of the World," Violet and Daisy Hilton tried to live normal lives despite their physical handicap. They reported that when one had a date, the other would sleep or read. There were problems in getting permission to marry, but in 1936 Violet married dancer James Moore. That marriage was later annulled, and Daisy married vaudevillian Buddy Sawyer. In 1951, the girls were starred in an extremely low-budget feature film, *Chained for Life*, which purported to be loosely based on their lives. The high spot of the production was a dream sequence in which each pictured life without the other, accomplished by one sister at a time bending down low to be hidden behind a strategically placed bush. Aside from *Chained for Life*, the Hiltons had also been seen on-screen as one of the acts in M-G-M's 1932 production *Freaks*.

After retiring from show business, Violet and Daisy Hilton managed a fruit stand in Florida and later worked at a supermarket in Charlotte, North Carolina. They died of complications brought on by a Hong Kong flu epidemic.

The only other Siamese twins act to have any major success in vaudeville were the Gibb Sisters, Mary and Marguerite. Like the Hiltons, they were managed by Terry Turner, and made their vaudeville debut in 1927.

THE HIPPODROME

Stretching an entire New York City block from 43rd to 44th Streets on Sixth Avenue, the Hippodrome was the ultimate in theatrical establishments. Seating five thousand two hundred, its stage facilities included a water tank and hydraulic lifts that could raise or lower fourteen different sections of the stage. It was the brainchild of showmen Frederic Thompson and Elmer S. "Skip" Dundy, who had also built Luna Park at Coney Island. Construction began in July 1904, and the Hippodrome opened on April 12, 1905, with *A Yankee Circus on Mars*. Starring Bessie McCoy, the show featured a thirty-foot airship that landed on stage with a troupe of 250 chorus girls. Thompson and Dundy retired from management of the theatre in the summer of 1906, and the Hippodrome was taken over by the Shubert Brothers. Charles Dillingham took over the operation in 1916, opening his first show there, *The Big Show*, on August 31 of that year. The last Dillingham production there was *Better Times*, and when it closed on April 28, 1923, so did the Hippodrome.

In July 1923, the theatre was taken over by the B. F. Keith Vaudeville Circuit. The technical equipment necessary for the elaborate spectacles for which the Hippodrome was known was removed, the size of the stage was diminished through the use of a false proscenium, and on December 17, 1923, the Hippodrome reopened as a regular vaudeville theatre. In July 1930, the Hippodrome closed again, and remained closed until November 17, 1935, when it reopened with *Billy Rose's Jumbo*. It was the last production at the Hippodrome; it was later converted into a basketball court and on September 1, 1939, demolition of the building began.

One of the highlights of *A Yankee Circus on Mars* was the slapstick comedy of clown Marceline, who became a fixture at the Hippodrome through 1917. There was little interest in Marceline Orbes (his full name) in the 1920s, and he committed suicide on November 5, 1927, at the age of 55. As the presentation of *Billy Rose's Jumbo* at the Hippodrome indicates, the theatre had strong connections to the circus, and among the performers there through the years who entertained in the circus tradition were Poodles Hanneford, Joe Jackson, and Powers Elephants. A Lilliputain village known as Toytown was opened in the

Hippodrome's basement. It included both little people and little animals, and audiences were encouraged to visit Toytown before and after the shows and during intermission. After the Hippodrome was taken over by B. F. Keith, Cliff Friend and Walter Donaldson composed an "At the Hippodrome" overture which was played before each performance.

BIBLIOGRAPHY

Clarke, Norman. *The Mighty Hippodrome*. New York: A. S. Barnes, 1968.

RAYMOND HITCHCOCK (Auburn, N.Y., October 22, 1865—Beverly Hills, Ca., November 24, 1929)

Raymond Hitchcock was a monologist on the vaudeville stage who enjoyed great success in musical comedy and revue. According to Joe Laurie, Jr., "You just had to see and hear him to appreciate him. . . . It wasn't what he said but the way he said it. . . . He would speak about almost anything, topics of the day, and during prohibition he did a monologue on booze, and he always looked as if he was half stewed, without playing the part of a drunk."

After some success in amateur theatricals at an early age, Hitchcock was engaged by a roadshow company in 1890. However, audiences and management found him unsatisfactory, and he ended the tour in Philadelphia, where he spent a year as a shoe salesman at Wanamaker's Department Store. Eventually, Hitchcock returned to the stage, singing in the chorus of *The Brigand* at $16 a week. When the show's star, Charles A. Bigelow, fell ill in Montreal, Hitchcock was given the opportunity to take over the leading role. Other engagements followed in such productions as *The Golden Wedding* (1893), *Charley's Aunt* (1894), *The Night Clerk* (1895), *Paul Jones* (1898), *A Dangerous Maid* (1899), *The Bell of Bridgeport* (1900), and *Vienna Life* (1901). He became a star under the management of Henry W. Savage in *King Dodo*, which opened in Chicago in 1902 and subsequently transferred to the Daly Theatre in New York.

Hitchcock's greatest success in the early years of the twentieth century was in *The Yankee Consul*, a comic opera by Henry M. Blossom, Jr., and Alfred G. Robyn. It opened at the Tremont Theatre, Boston, on September 21, 1903, and subsequently transferred to the Broadway Theatre, New York, on February 27, 1904. Many hit shows followed, including *Easy Dawson* (1904), *The Man Who Owns Broadway* (1909), *The Red Widow* (1911), *The Beauty Shop* (1913), and *Betty* (1916). In 1916, Raymond Hitchcock also made his British debut in *Mr. Manhattan*.

"Hitchy," as he was affectionately known, had his greatest triumph with *Hitchy-Koo*, which he both produced and starred in, and which opened at the Cohan and Harris Theatre, New York, in June 1917. It was little more than a glorified vaudeville show, featuring Frances White and William Rock, Grace La Rue, Irene Bordoni, and Leon Errol. It contained comedy sketches, including a satire on Billy Sunday, and songs by the three female stars of the show. Hitchcock acted as master of ceremonies, sometimes introducing the acts from the stage and sometimes from the front row of the orchestra seats; he even took time out to greet friends in the audience personally. The comedian had a song in the show, written by George M. Cohan and titled "Since I Became a Manager," in which Cohan promised never again to criticize his manager. As Sime Silverman wrote in *Variety* (June 15, 1917), "It's not the kind of show you expect but it's the kind you like." Not unexpectedly, *Hitchy-Koo* was followed by a number of sequels: *Hitchy-Koo 1918, Hitchy-Koo 1919*, and *Hitchy-Koo 1920*.

Raymond Hitchcock continued to star in musicals and revues throughout the 1920s, including the 1921 edition of the Ziegfeld *Follies, Raymond Hitchcock's Pinwheel* (1922), *The Old Soak* (1923), *The Caliph* (1924), *The Ritz Revue* (1924), and *Just Fancy* (1927). He also appeared in a number of films, including *My Valet* (1915, produced by Mack Sennett and his most famous screen appearance), *The Beauty Shop* (1922), *Broadway after Dark* (1924), *Redheads Preferred* (1926), and *The Money Talks* (1927).

By the 1920s, Hitchcock had also become firmly entrenched on the vaudeville stage, although he was not always successful; *Variety* (December 15, 1922) reviewed him at the Palace and commented, "Hitchy is a natural comedian and a natural monologist, but like others he is likely to be dull at times." Hitchcock returned to the Palace in March 1927, and was also on the opening night bill that same month at the Roxy Theatre.

While appearing in *Your Uncle Dudley* in Chicago in May 1929, Hitchcock suffered a heart attack and died a few months later at his Beverly Hills home. At his side was his wife, Flora Zabelle, who had appeared with her husband in many of his shows from *The Yankee Consul* onward.

BIBLIOGRAPHY
Hitchcock, Raymond. "The Art of the Curtain Speech." *Theatre*, October 1917, p. 192.

GERTRUDE HOFFMAN (San Francisco, 1886—Hollywood, Ca., October 2, 1966)

An interpretive dancer on the vaudeville stage, Gertrude Hoffman (real name, Kitty Hayes) introduced Russian dance dramas to American audiences. "Her plastic mobility is always picturesque, suggesting ideas, which, however, are never quite expressed or grasped," commented Caroline Caffin in *Vaudeville* (1914). Hoffman first appeared at the Palace at the close of 1915. She was married to Max Hoffman (died May 1963, at the age of eighty), who was also her manager, and her son Max Hoffman, Jr., also appeared in vaudeville as a dancer. In the 1920s, she had her own dance troupe, the Gertrude Hoffman Girls, and after the demise of vaudeville, Hoffman worked as a dance teacher and also as a choreographer.

ERNEST HOGAN (Bowling Green, Ky., circa 1859—New York, May 20, 1909)

Billed as "The Unbleached America," Ernest Hogan was a major early black performer in mainstream vaudeville. In 1896, he wrote "All Coons Look Alike to Me," which began the vogue for such "coon" songs, and which was prominently featured in the show *The Widow Jones*. Hogan was always very careful to appear reticent and subservient in the company of white Americans, but this did not prevent his being attacked by an angry mob during a race riot in New York in September 1900.

In 1891, he formed Eaton and Hogan's Colored Minstrels with Harry S. Eaton, and that was the beginning of his success. In 1897, Hogan joined Black Patti's Troubadours, and the following year, on July 5, 1898, he starred in Will Marion Cook and Paul Laurence Dunbar's *Clorindy, or the Origin of the Cake Walk* at New York's Casino Roof Garden. In the 1890s, he first began appearing with nonblack productions, and in 1899 was the only Negro in the Philadelphia cast of E. E. Rice's Captain Kidd's Company. That same year, Hogan successfully toured Australia, and on his return stopped in Honolulu briefly to manage the Orpheum Theatre there. He returned to Honolulu again in 1902. Hogan was a frequent performer at New York roof gardens, headlining at the Casino Roof in July 1900, and at the Paradise Garden in July 1903, and June, July, and August 1905. He appeared at the New York Theatre as early as August 1901, drawing a weekly salary of $300, and was back there again in May 1907.

Aside from frequent vaudeville appearances, Ernest Hogan starred in a number of black shows: *The Cannibal King* (1901), *Uncle Eph's Christmas* (1901), *Rufus Rastus* (1905), and *The Oyster Man* (1907). In June 1908, he left the cast of the last show, which he also wrote with Flournoy E. Miller and Aubrey Lyles, because of "a general physical breakdown." He died shortly thereafter.

BIBLIOGRAPHY

Hogan, Ernest. "The Negro in Vaudeville." *Variety*, December 15, 1906, p. 22.

Sampson, Henry T. *The Ghost Walks: A Chronological History of Blacks in Show Business, 1865–1910*. Metuchen, N.J.: Scarecrow Press, 1988.

HOLLYWOOD COMEDY CLUB

The Hollywood Comedy Club is a fraternal organization founded in March 1947 "by a group of great and near great from the wonderful era of vaudeville." The membership roster would appear to indicate an emphasis on the latter category.

Address: 649 North Rossmore Avenue, Los Angeles, Ca. 90004.

TAYLOR HOLMES (Newark, N.J., May 16, 1878—Hollywood, Ca., September 30, 1959)

Before becoming a prominent figure on the legitimate stage and on-screen, Taylor Holmes had commenced his career as a lightweight actor in vaudeville. He made his debut at Keith's Theatre, Boston, in May 1899, and later that same year journeyed to England and appeared in British music hall. His first important role on the legitimate stage was as Rosencrantz to E. H. Sothern's *Hamlet* at New York's Garden Theatre in September 1901. Except for the opening day matinee, Taylor Holmes played the first week of the Palace Theatre in March 1913; *The Billboard* (April 5, 1913) reported, "The applause that greeted his efforts on Tuesday night was barely sufficient to cover a single legitimate bow." He enjoyed an extensive stage career from 1917 to 1958.

Taylor Holmes outlived both of his actor sons, Ralph (1889–1945) and Phillips (1909–1942).

BIBLIOGRAPHY

Brewster, Eleanor. "Taylor Holmes Has Struck Twelve." *Motion Picture Magazine* 15, no. 4 (May 1918), pp. 72–74.

LOU HOLTZ (San Francisco, April 11, 1893—Beverly Hills, Ca., September 22, 1980)

One of the great dialect comedians of vaudeville, no one could tell a good Jewish joke as well as Lou Holtz. He introduced the Jewish character Sam Lapidus, who wore size-eight shoes, but size nine felt so comfortable, he always bought size ten. When Lapidus went to the dentist with a toothache and the dentist asked which tooth hurt, Lapidus would respond, "You're the dentist— you tell me." Lou Holtz would tell convoluted stories peppered with snatches from clichéd poems and verses; one such story is brilliantly preserved (at the UCLA Film and Television Archive) in the 1929 Warner Bros./Vitaphone short *Idle Chatter*. (The short begins with the call boy entering Holtz's dressing room with the words, "You're on," to which the comedian responds, "Oh, how am I doing?") He was known for singing his jokes to "O Sole Mio," and a typical verse would go:

> A fat lady tried to get on the streetcar.
> She didn't know whether to get in front or behind.
> The conductor said, "Which end will you get in, madam?"
> She said, "I'll get them both in at the same time if you don't mind."
> O sole mio . . .

In many ways, Lou Holtz was the stereotypical stage Jew. When he was in someone's office and saw a telephone, he would ask, "Who can I call long distance?" If told by a gentile, many of his gags would have been offensive, but from Holtz they were a delight to hear.

The diminutive comedian held a variety of jobs before taking to singing in the style of entertainer Gus Chandler. He worked as a double act with Fred Weiss and as part of the trio of Boland, Holtz, and Harris. At the age of fifteen, while playing at a popular San Francisco night spot, the Crest, Boland, Holtz, and Harris were spotted by Elsie Janis's mother, and she brought them East to work with her daughter as the Elsie Janis Trio. In time, Holtz married Rita Boland, but they were divorced, and with the breakup of his marriage, Holtz became a single act in more ways than one.

As a solo performer, Holtz did not become successful until he began working in blackface. Presumably he was patterning his act after Al Jolson (for whom he once understudied) and Eddie Cantor, both of whom he resembled in the teens according to *Variety*. The trade paper's issue of November 30, 1917, commented, "It looks as though Holtz with his present material could hold a big-time spot and improve." He did both, and by April 1919 was holding his own on a Palace bill that also included Van and Schenck and Jack Norworth. *Variety* (April 4, 1919) reported, "Lou Holtz in blackface was somewhat of a surprise. Holtz had some excellent material, and while without a positive individual style, his delivery is natural and the impression scored is due solely to his own personality. His gestures are not unlike [Frank] Fay, and the interrupted sentences unmistakably those of Jolson, but Holtz has original material, and were he to eradicate his style, his personality would suffer. His closing number makes a capital finish to the act and he was voted a genuine hit. This chap, industrious to a degree, has been striving for some time to connect, and with this act he seems to have landed. He is ready for any big-time program."

As early as 1915, Holtz had appeared on the musical comedy stage in *A World of Pleasure*, with music by Sigmund Romberg, which opened at the Winter Garden Theatre on October 14, 1915. However, his career took a new turn in 1919, when he was featured with comic Lester Allen, supporting Ann Pennington and Yvette Rugel in the first edition of George White's *Scandals*. The show opened at the Liberty Theatre on June 2, 1919, and ran for 128 performances. Holtz appeared in the 1920 and 1921 editions of the *Scandals*; and no doubt it was in one of those shows that he uttered the memorable question to a mother whose daughter wished to go on the stage, "Would she like to be glorified by Ziegfeld or scandalized by White?" The comedian was also to be seen in three revues at the Winter Garden, together with *Tell Me More* (1925), written especially for him by Buddy DeSylva and George and Ira Gershwin, *Manhattan Mary* (1927) and *You Said It* (1931).

By the mid 1920s, Lou Holtz had come to be recognized as the greatest dialect comedian on the vaudeville stage, although his humor at the time was apparently too New York–oriented. When he played the presentation house, the Chicago, in Chicago in June 1928, Windy City audiences were only polite in their response. *Variety* (June 6, 1928) described him as "too smart for the families. Holtz is unknown to the majority at the Chicago. Drawing power dubious." Also in the 1920s, Lou Holtz developed into a fine master of ceremonies for vaudeville. Douglas Gilbert wrote of him, "He was an extraordinary comic with immediate reactions that made him superb as a master of ceremonies, but he continually stepped over the blue line into vulgarity that often destroyed his effectiveness." Holtz was popular as a master of ceremonies at the Palace, and also gave that theatre plenty to worry about in 1932 when he opened in a vaudeville revue at the competing Hollywood Theatre, and which easily outgrossed the Palace, where the master of ceremonies at the time was Frank Fay. At the Palace in 1930, Lou Holtz introduced Benny Baker as his stooge.

Lou Holtz made his feature film debut in 1930 in *Follow the Leader* with Ed Wynn, but some years later, he reminisced that the experience had not been a happy one, with Wynn ordering most of his scenes deleted from the film. With Block and Sully and Belle Baker, Lou Holtz was held over—an unprecedented move—at Loew's State in September 1935. The following year, he starred in two London revues, *Transatlantic Rhythm* at the Adelphi and *Laughter over London* at the Palace. In the 1940s, he retired to Los Angeles where, in 1951 he produced and starred in a short-lived musical revue at the Belmont Theatre. He had invested well in the stock market and did not need to work, although he made occasional appearances on *The Ed Sullivan Show* and *The Merv Griffin Show*. He was well liked by Jack Paar and appeared on his television program some eighteen times. In 1961, Lou Holtz remarried, and in his 70s sired two sons. He once commented that he could not understand why George Burns should want to keep working, and at his death, that entertainer commented, "In vaudeville, they cancel you and give you back your publicity pictures. I guess it was Lou's turn to get back his pictures."

BIBLIOGRAPHY
Smith, Bill. "Lou Holtz." In *The Vaudevillians*. New York: Macmillan, 1976, pp. 121–28.

"THE HOOK"

The notion of using a hook to remove unpopular performers from the vaudeville stage is probably more legend than reality. The first hook was used at Miner's Bowery Theatre, New York, in October 1903. During an amateur night performance, a tenor refused to leave the stage despite the hisses and jeers of the audience. The theatre's owner, Tom Miner, took an old-fashioned crook-handled cane and had his property man, Charles Guthinger, attach it to a long pole. Miner then reached out, hooked the singer by the neck, and removed him from the stage. Apparently, the audience was so amused by this device that when the next hapless performer arrived onstage, a boy in the gallery shouted, "Get the hook." The legend was born, and by 1908, *The New York Dramatic Mirror* reported that the hook was a standard prop in every theatre featuring amateur nights.

BIBLIOGRAPHY
"History of 'The Hook.' " *The New York Dramatic Mirror*, May 16, 1908, p. 16.

BOB HOPE (Eltham, England, May 29, 1903—   )

Bob Hope is a graduate of American vaudeville who became a show business icon of the American establishment. He is venerated by many as an exemplary figure in American popular culture, a man who since the Second World War has devoted much time and energy to entertaining U.S. troops abroad at times of conflict. He is the individual most associated with that peculiarly American of institutions, the Academy Awards; since the late 1930s, he has served as master of ceremonies for many of the presentations and, despite making a running gag of the refusal of the academy to recognize his acting abilities, has received five special Academy Awards, beginning with a 1940 commendation "in recognition of his unselfish services to the motion picture industry."

While he is revered, Bob Hope has also been the subject of controversy, notably for his right-wing political views, but equally for his failure to entertain in recent years. His television specials on NBC are notable for their singular lack of humor. Hope is a comedian who has always relied heavily on writers to provide him with material, but for the past two decades, it would appear that he has been unable to distinguish between comic writers with an understanding of contemporary humor and those whose talents have long since faded away. The one critic who has been most outspoken in his commentary on Bob Hope is Dwight Macdonald, who wrote in *Esquire* (July 1962), "What is disturbing about Mr. Hope is not the etiolation of his humor, which has been going on for years, but a sinister quality in his presentation. He has developed a gliding, swooping Dracula-like walk and his expression, as he waits for the audience to respond to his tired gags, also reminded me of the Count: a self-congratulatory smirk that often became a positive sneer—hello suckers!''

Contemporary audiences watching Bob Hope who must rely on the laugh track for a response to his humor must wonder if there was ever a time when the comedian was funny. The answer, of course, is yes. At the same time, it is very obvious just from a screening of the "Road" comedies Hope made with Bing Crosby that the former's early humor, in fact throughout virtually his entire film career, has failed to stand the passage of time.

The comedian was born Leslie Townes Hope in the southern English community of Eltham. He adopted the name Bob when children at school began calling him "Hopeless." The family came to the United States in 1907 and settled in Cleveland, where the young Hope, while still a child, sold newspapers and won a contest for his Charlie Chaplin imitation. After graduation from high school, Hope was an amateur boxer and a dance instructor before deciding to go on the stage. With friend Lloyd Durbin, Hope developed an act in which the two young men sang and danced in blackface, which played Cleveland's Bandbox Theatre and toured the Gus Sun circuit as part of [Fred] *Hurley's Jolly Follies*. When Durbin became ill in Huntington, West Virginia, he was replaced by George Byrne, by which time the act was billed as "Two Diamonds in the Rough." As a specialty act, the two were featured in a 1927 Broadway show called *The Sidewalks of New York*, but made little if any impact.

The following year, Bob Hope decided to become a solo vaudeville entertainer and dropped the blackface. He did, however, hire Louise Troxell to appear as his stooge. *Variety* saw him at Proctor's 88th Street Theatre in 1929 and commented, "He sings 'True Blue' for laughs and 'Pagan Love Song' straight—both very good." On May 29, 1932, Hope began a week at the Palace, and as a result of his performance there, he was signed to star in *Ballyhoo of 1932*, which opened in September of that year. (1932 is also an important year in that Hope met Crosby for the first, when both played the Capitol in New York.)

In November 1933, Bob Hope opened in *Roberta*, the Jerome Kern musical, playing the role of Huckleberry Haines. It was while he was in *Roberta* that Hope met and married Dolores Reade. The following year, the comedian was seen on Broadway in *Say When*, and on December 30, 1935, he opened in the 1936 edition of the *Ziegfeld Follies*. He acted as the show's master of ceremonies, sang "I Can't Get Started," and clowned with Fanny Brice. No sooner had he left the *Ziegfeld Follies* than Hope was starred, along with Ethel Merman and Jimmy Durante, in Cole Porter's *Red, Hot and Blue!*, which opened in October 1936.

Bob Hope had appeared in eight short subjects released between 1934 and 1938, but his film career really got underway in earnest with *The Big Broadcast of 1938*, in which he sang "Thanks for the Memory" to Shirley Ross. The song was to become his signature tune. With Bing Crosby and Dorothy Lamour, Hope starred in seven "Road" pictures: *Road to Singapore* (1940), *Road to Zanzibar* (1942), *Road to Morocco* (1942), *Road to Utopia* (1945), *Road to Rio* (1948), *Road to Bali* (1953), and *Road to Hong Kong* (1962). Among the comedian's other major films are *They Got Me Covered* (1943), *Monsieur Beaucaire* (1946), *My Favorite Brunette* (1947), *The Paleface* (1948), *Son of Paleface* (1952), and *Alias Jesse James* (1959). Hope played fellow vaudevillian Eddie Foy in *The Seven Little Foys* (1955).

Bob Hope was first heard on radio on January 4, 1935, on *The Intimate Revue*, which aired on the NBC Blue network. His own program, *The Pepsodent Show*, was first heard on NBC on September 27, 1938, and lasted through 1950. Bob Hope made his first television appearance on *The Star Spangled Revue* in 1950. From 1952 to 1953, he was one of the regular hosts on *The Colgate Comedy Hour* (NBC), and from 1963 to 1967, he hosted *Bob Hope Presents the Chrysler Theatre* (NBC).

After 1932, Bob Hope was too busy to return to American vaudeville, but he did make a vaudeville tour through the United Kingdom in the spring of 1951, and in September 1952, he topped the bill at the London Palladium.

On May 14, 1993, NBC (to which Hope had been under contract for 55 years) celebrated the comedian's 90th birthday with a three-hour tribute, *Bob Hope: The First 90 Years*. Participants included Johnny Carson, Walter Cronkite, Angela Lansbury, and Tom Selleck.

BIBLIOGRAPHY

"Bob Hope." *Current Biography*, June 1941, pp. 402–404.

Collins, Frederick L. "How Bob Hope Got That Way." *Liberty* 16, no. 40 (October 7, 1939), pp. 27–30.

Faith, William Robert. *Bob Hope: A Life in Comedy*. New York: G. P. Putnam's Sons, 1982.

Hope, Bob. *I Never Left Home*. New York: Simon & Schuster, 1944.

————, with Pete Martin. *Have Tux, Will Travel*. New York: Simon & Schuster, 1954.

————. *I Owe Russia $1200*. Garden City, N.Y.: Doubleday, 1963.

————. *Five Women I Love: Bob Hope's Vietnam Story*. Garden City, N.Y.: Doubleday, 1966.

————, with Pete Martin. *The Last Christmas Show*. Garden City, N.Y.: Doubleday, 1974.

————, and Bob Thomas. *The Road to Hollywood: My 40-Year Love Affair with the Movies*. Garden City, N.Y.: Doubleday, 1977.

————, with Dwayne Netland. *Bob Hope's Confessions of a Hooker: My Lifelong Love Affair with Golf*. Garden City, N.Y.: Doubleday, 1985.

————, with Melville Shavelson. *Don't Shoot, It's Only Me: Bob Hope's Comedy History of the United States*. New York: G. P. Putnam's Sons, 1990.

Kaplan, Peter W. "On the Road with Bob Hope." *Film Comment* 14, no. 1 (January–February 1978), pp. 18–20.

Linderman, Lawrence. "Idol Chat." *Emmy* 15, no. 3 (May/June 1993), pp. 18–23.

McVay, Douglas. "In a Dirty Glass: A Tribute to Bob Hope." *Focus on Film* no. 1 (January/February 1970), pp. 15–29.

Morella, Joe, Edward Z. Epstein, and Eleanor Clark. *The Amazing Careers of Bob Hope*. New Rochelle, N.Y.: Arlington House, 1973.

Thompson, Charles. *Bob Hope: Portrait of a Superstar*. New York: St. Martin's Press, 1981.

Trescott, Pamela. *Bob Hope: A Comic Life*. London: W. H. Allen, 1987.

DeWOLF HOPPER (New York, March 30, 1858—Kansas City, Mo., September 23, 1935)

A major comedian of the legitimate theatre, DeWolf Hopper would occasionally appear on the vaudeville stage, always reciting "Casey at the Bat." Born William Hopper, the actor recalled, "DeWolf was born of the vanity of youth. I despised the Quaker plainness of Hopper, and William had a plebeian sound to my fastidious ears." He made his first stage appearance in *Our Boys* at New Haven, Connecticut, on November 4, 1878, and his first New York stage appearance at Haverly's Theatre, in *Our Daughters*, on September 15, 1879. He became a star with *Castles in the Air*, which opened at New York's Broadway Theatre on May 5, 1890, and an international celebrity with his first London appearance, in *El Capitan*, at the Lyric Theatre on July 10, 1899. He was associated with Weber and Fields at the turn of the century, and in 1911 began a long association with the operettas of Gilbert and Sullivan, playing Dick Deadeye in a revival of *H.M.S. Pinafore*.

DeWolf Hopper first recited "Casey at the Bat" at Wallack's Theatre, New York, on May 13, 1888. It was interpolated into a scene in the second act of *Prince Methusalem* and became, in the words of Hopper, "the only great American comic poem." Hopper starred in a screen version of the poem in 1916, produced by the Fine Arts Company. It was not his film debut; that was made three films earlier and in the same year in *Don Quixote*, also produced by the Fine Arts Company. Hopper left the motion picture industry in 1916 to return to the New York stage and the 1917 edition of *The Passing Show*. He made an abortive attempt to return to films in 1929; perhaps he should have listened to film critic Julian Johnson, who described him in *Photoplay* (September 1916), as "that delightful gentleman, grand curtain-speaker, and footlight veteran— also that celluloid lemon and shadow ruin."

DeWolf Hopper never stopped working. He was on the opening night bill at Radio City Music Hall in 1932. On September 22, 1935, he introduced the broadcast of a concert by the Kansas City Rhythm Orchestra; he died early the following morning. He was, as *Variety* (September 25, 1935) commented,

"More than any other actor of his time, perhaps . . . the symbol of the transition of entertainment."

BIBLIOGRAPHY
Hopper, DeWolf. "If I Had Never Been an Actor." *Theatre*, January 1914, pp. 9–10, 44.
————, with Wesley Winans Stout. *Once a Clown, Always a Clown*. Boston: Little, Brown, 1927.
Parsons, Chauncey L. "De Wolf Hopper: The Heavy-Weight Comedian." *The New York Dramatic Mirror*, May 10, 1911, p. 11.
Slide, Anthony. "DeWolf Hopper." In *The Kindergarten of the Movies: A History of the Fine Arts Company*. Metuchen, N.J.: Scarecrow Press, 1980, pp. 32–43.
Wolf, Rennold. "De Wolf Hopper, That Justly Celebrated Husband." *The Green Book Magazine*. March 1914, pp. 396–404.

HARRY HOUDINI (Budapest, March 24, 1874—Detroit, October 31, 1926)

Houdini was the greatest of all escapologists, a vaudevillian whose name has become synonymous with the art of evasion and escape. He was also a magician who could make an elephant vanish from the stage of the New York Hippodrome, and claimed to present the smallest of all magic acts, "The East Indian Needle Mystery," wherein he swallowed seventy needles and twenty yards of thread, and regurgitated the by-now threaded needles. Houdini was a master entertainer; as Frederick James Smith commented in *The New York Dramatic Mirror* (April 8, 1916). "Houdini is a showman of the old school. He does baffling things and he gets every ounce of value out of them."

All of Houdini's exploits, escaping from strait jackets, chains, manacles, jails, barrels of water, and the like—both on- and offstage—were heavily publicized, as were his numerous exposés of fake spiritualism. In the late teens, he also entered film production with the formation of the Houdini Film Development Corporation, assuring a lasting record of his exploits in productions such as *The Soul of Bronze* (1921), *The Man from Beyond* (1922), and *Haldane of the Secret Service* (1923). He also starred in one serial, *The Master Mystery* (1919), and made two feature films for Famous Players—Lasky: *The Grim Game* (1919) and *Terror Island* (1920). Later, he was to be the subject of a film biography, *Houdini* (1953), in which he was played by Tony Curtis.

Harry Houdini was born Erik Weisz in Hungary, and as a child emigrated with his parents to Appleton, Wisconsin, where his father became a rabbi. Houdini began his stage career in 1891, first with a friend named Jacob Hyman in an act called The Brothers Houdini. He chose the name Houdini from an early admiration for the French magician Robert-Houdin. In 1893, Houdini entertained at the Chicago World's Fair, and later worked in dime museums and traveling circuses, performing card tricks and billing himself as "The King of Cards." By 1900, he had become an established vaudeville headliner, billed as "The Undisputed King of Handcuffs," "Monarch of Leg Shackles," and "Champion Jail Breaker," thanks to his ability to escape from anywhere or anything. From a $15-a-week dime museum entertainer, Houdini became a $12,500-a-week vaudeville star, although *Variety* once pointed out that he was worth and could have demanded far more had he ever been able to forget his humble beginnings in show business. When the Keith circuit raised his salary to $1,500 a week, Houdini was quoted as saying, "I feel as though I'm stealing something. Think of $1,500 a week for me and the time when I got $15 a week for playing twenty shows a day." Surprisingly, Houdini was not the highest paid magician of his day, Howard Thurston was considered more commercially successful and able to demand higher fees.

In 1900, Houdini went to England, and within a year, he was the strongest vaudeville attraction in Europe. There were stories of his escape from a prison van bound for Siberia and from a jail cell in Leicester, England, built by Oliver Cromwell. He performed every type of ecapology on stage; he was tied to a ladder, sealed in a galvanized iron boiler, handcuffed inside a rolltop desk. He escaped from all the best jails. One of his best known tricks was to push a long steel needle through his cheek without drawing blood. On January 7, 1918, on the stage of the New York Hippodrome, Houdini made a live, ten thousand-pound elephant disappear. "Mr. Houdini has provided a headache for every child in New York," wrote Sime Silverman in *Variety*. "The matinee crowds will worry themselves into sleep nightly wondering what Houdini did with his elephant."

In January and February 1925, Houdini was to establish a record for being held over for six weeks at the Hippodrome in an act that consisted chiefly of exposing fake spiritualists and explaining how they could make spirits materialize at seances. Spiritualism became a fixation of Houdini's in the early 1920s, and after his death, there were endless attempts to make contact with him in the spirit world. Houdini's wife, Bess, who had worked with him in the early days of vaudeville, participated in many such seances.

At the time of his 1925 Hippodrome appearance, Sime Silverman wrote in *Variety*, "Houdini is an intellectual and, besides that, among showmen he is the peer of all actor-showmen everywhere. Houdini as an actor is a showman on and off—more so, perhaps off than on. As an intellectual Houdini should be an educator upon the stage, for he has dove into the ultra-gullible—the thing that has made monkeys of wise men and fools—spiritualism."

Despite his frequent posing in the near nude—a necessity in proving he had no keys or other means of escape hidden on his person—Houdini was not a handsome or imposing figure, and yet he was the idol of millions of his generation, and millions more in later years. There was little question that Houdini welcomed the adulation, for he was, in some ways, arrogant and egotistical. It was these failings that were, indirectly, to lead to his death. On October 22, 1926, in his dressing room at the Princess Theatre in Montreal, Houdini was asked by a student from McGill University if it was true that he could sustain heavy punches to his abdomen without injury. Houdini agreed, but before he could brace himself for the blows, the student hit him hard three times. Houdini valiantly carried on as if nothing was wrong, but he was in excruciating pain.

His appendix became inflamed, poison entered the blood stream, and a few days later, Houdini died in a Detroit hospital following two operations for peritonitis. As fate would have it, he died on Halloween.

Variety summed up Houdini's unique appeal, noting, "It's not the tricks, illusions, or disappearances that make a successful magician outstanding; it's showmanship, personality, and oftimes creation. . . . For a magical act, tricks and apparatus may be purchased, but the requisite attributes are not on sale anywhere."

BIBLIOGRAPHY

(Houdini authored more than two hundred books and articles; a two-page listing of major items appears in Milbourne Christopher's biography, and a detailed bibliography compiled by Manuel Weltman was published in the October, November, and December 1967 issues of *Genii*.)

"Afterthoughts on Houdini." *Variety*, November 10, 1926, p. 20.

Brandon, Ruth. *The Life and Many Deaths of Harry Houdini*. London: Secker & Warburg, 1993.

Cannell, J. C. *The Secrets of Houdini*. London: Hutchinson, 1932.

Christopher, Milbourne. *Houdini: The Untold Story*. New York: Thomas Y. Crowell, 1969.

Ernst, Bernard M. L., and Hereward Carrington. *Houdini and Conan Doyle: The Story of a Strange Friendship*. New York: Albert and Charles Boni, 1932.

Gibson, Waller B., and Morris M. Young, eds. *Houdini on Magic*. New York: Dover, 1953.

Gresham, William, Lindsay. *Houdini: The Man Who Walked through Walls*. New York: Henry Holt, 1959.

"Handcuff Releases under Difficulties: The Remarkable Feats of Harry Houdini." *Scientific American*, July 20, 1912, p. 58.

Kellock, Harold. *Houdini: His Life Story, from the Recollections and Documents of Beatrice Houdini*. New York: Harcourt, Brace, 1929.

Kendall, Lace. *Houdini: Master of Escape*. Philadelphia: Macrae Smith, 1960.

"Magician Who Mistrusts Spirits and All Their Works." *Literary Digest* June 3, 1922, p. 54.

"Thrills in the Life of a Magician." *American Magazine*, September 1918, pp. 36–37.

Williams, Beryl, and Samuel Epstein. *The Great Houdini*. New York: Julian Messner, 1950.

JOSEPH E. HOWARD (New York, February 12, 1867—Chicago, May 19, 1961)

Joseph E. Howard was noted as both a singer and a composer. Working usually with Will Hough, he wrote the music for such perennial favorites as "Hello, My Baby," "Goodbye, My Lady Love," and "I Wonder Who's Kissing Her Now." In addition to his songs, Howard wrote the music for a number of early Broadway shows, including *The Time, the Place and the Girl* (1907), *The Land of Nod* (1907), *A Stubborn Cinderella* (1909), and *The Goddess of Liberty* (1909). *The Time, the Place and the Girl* was revived in 1942.

At the age of eleven, Howard entered vaudeville as a soprano. He was very much a ragtime entertainer, and one of his first hits on the vaudeville stage was the "Handicap March," written by George Rosey, whose lyrics concerned a horse race, and in the performance of which Howard played the roles of fifteen horses, fifteen jockeys, the crowd in the stands, and two bookmakers. In the teens, Joseph E. Howard adopted the elegant evening attire that became his trademark, together with his claim to being very much a ladies' man. He often teamed on the vaudeville stage with female partners; in 1916 to 1917, he toured in a musical revue with Ethelyn Clark, and in 1926, he was working with Anita Case. "They are sure fire in front of any audience" was *Variety*'s (August 25, 1926) opinion of the latter combination.

In 1947, George Jessel produced a glamorized version of Howard's life for 20th Century–Fox. Titled *I Wonder Who's Kissing Her Now*, the film starred Mark Stevens as Joseph E. Howard. The feature had unforeseen complications for Howard when its release resulted in a lawsuit claiming that he had not composed the title song but rather purchased it from another composer. The accusation seemed to prove the validity of the opinion of many in vaudeville that Howard should have been dubbed the "opportunist of song." Certainly, he continued to perform his "latest successes" decades after they had first been introduced.

WILLIE HOWARD (Germany, April 13, 1886—New York, January 14, 1949) and **EUGENE HOWARD** (Neustadt, Germany, November 7, 1881—New York, August 1, 1965)

Eugene was the straight man and Willie the comic, and as a Jewish comedy team, they were regarded by their contemporaries and their audiences as one of the best. Sime Silverman wrote in *Variety* (May 16, 1913), "If there is a Hebrew comedian in the world who can touch Willie Howard, trot him out. And Willie can give his challenger all those things a Hebrew comedian is supposed to have, including crepe hair, for Willie has none of these, nor does he need them." George Jessel, whose singing of "My Mother's Eyes" Willie Howard would often imitate in the 1930s, commented simply, "Willie Howard was the best of all the revue comics, bar none."

The brothers were as much at home on the vaudeville stage as they were in George White's *Scandals* or *The Passing Show*. There would be rapid-fire comedy cross talk, often followed by a travesty of an operatic medley, and, of course, Willie's impressions of Harry Lauder, Eddie Cantor, or Al Jolson. The classic Willie Howard line was "Come the Revolution, you'll eat strawberries and cream." Often, Willie would parody a popular song; for example, in 1913, he sang "Snooky Ookums" with the line "All night long he's smoking opium." One of the secrets of the act's success was that Willie Howard possessed a good baritone voice, which always added much to the operatic travesties.

Born in Germany, the two brothers grew up on New York's Lower East Side. They began their show business careers separately; Eugene made his first appearance onstage at the Casino Theatre on September 28, 1897, in the chorus of *The Belle of New York*, while Willie made his debut as a boy soprano at Proctor's 125th Street Theatre, also in 1897. Willie first came to attention as the small boy singing to Anna Held from the gallery in *The Little Duchess* in the summer of 1901.

The following year, the brothers joined forces with a vaudeville act titled "The Messenger Boy [Willie] and the Thespian [Eugene]." At approximately the same time, Willie began doing his impressions. The boys toured in vaudeville through 1912, when they were signed by the Shuberts to star in the first edition of *The Passing Show* at the Winter Garden Theatre. They were to be regulars in *The Passing Show*, almost without a break, until 1922. Sime Silverman in *Variety* (May 16, 1913) noted, "The Howards never fail to become a riot at the Garden. They were that in vaudeville before entering musical comedy, and can go back to vaudeville with this act, duplicating their former successes here." Audiences loved their send-up of the Metropolitan Opera star in "The Galli-Gurci Rag" and their travesty of *Rigoletto*. They made reference to two Irish tenors, John McCormack and Alma Gluck, and called Madame Schumann-Heink Schumann-Kyke. The classic routine, "Between the Acts at the Opera," is preserved on film (at the UCLA Film and Television Archive) in a 1926 Warner Bros./Vitaphone short subject.

"The Howard Brothers, Gene and Willie, have long been missing from vaudeville," sighed *The New York Dramatic Mirror* (January 1, 1920), "and oh, what joy there would be if they only returned to the varieties." Eventually, the Howards did leave *The Passing Show*—in 1922—and spent the next couple of years or so on the vaudeville stage. In October 1924, they headlined at the Palace, and *Variety* (October 22, 1924) reported, "The Howards now wear evening clothes with Eugene's the last word in sartorial elegance. Willie's is a comedy assortment of near misfits topped by a high hat. The Howards open with crossfire in which there is never a dull moment. Eugene's straighting in this portion is flawless. Willie's snappy retorts have the laughs popping like machine guns. Some of the gags will no doubt be heard around from now on for they are 'naturals.'" At this time, the brothers were earning $2,500 a week in vaudeville.

In 1926, it was back to the revue stage with George White's *Scandals*, in which the Howards appeared through 1929. They were also to return for the 1935 edition of the show. The pair headlined at the Palace in May 1930, billed as "Two Hebrew Humorists Who Hail from Harlem," but from this point on, Willie and Eugene Howard were almost exclusively on the musical comedy stage, appearing in *Girl Crazy* (1930, Willie only), *Ballyhoo of 1932*, *The Ziegfeld Follies* (1933, and back to the Winter Garden, which must have made them feel at home), *The Show Is On* (1937), and *Crazy with Heat* (1941, Willie only). Willie and Eugene were also appearing in films from 1927 to 1938, chiefly as the stars of short subjects.

In 1940, Eugene retired from the act, concentrating on writing material and acting as manager for his brother. Al Kelly replaced him as Willie's stooge. Willie Howard continued to perform almost until the day he died, featured in nightclubs, on radio, and in the occasional revue. On December 8, 1948, ill health forced Willie to leave the cast of the revue *Along Fifth Avenue* during its Philadelphia tryout; he died in New York on the same day the show opened on Broadway. He was, as one obituary writer commented, "one of the great comedians of this generation."

BIBLIOGRAPHY
Green, Stanley. "Willie Howard." In *The Great Clowns of Broadway*. New York: Oxford University Press, 1984, pp. 83–101.
"In Support of the Moon-Struck." *Literary Digest*, June 2, 1934, p. 20.

BUDDY HOWE (Brooklyn, N.Y., circa 1910—Miami, March 4, 1981)

An acrobatic dancer, Buddy Howe teamed with Jean Carroll and formed a comedy dance act with Carroll as the comedienne and Howe the straight man. Born Buddy Zolitan, the performer changed his name to Howe at the suggestion of a master of ceremonies at a theatre in Rock Island, Illinois, in 1929. He entered vaudeville in 1925 as "Bud" in Patti Moore and Band with Sammy Lewis and Bud and Buddy. The act played small-time vaudeville, and within a couple of years, Howe was working as a solo acrobatic dancer. In the early 1930s, he teamed with Jean Carroll, and the couple married in 1936. That same year, they began an extensive tour of British theatres, which lasted through 1939. In 1945, Howe joined the General Amusements Corp. in Chicago as an agent, and remained with the organization as it expanded to become International Creative Management, of which he was vice-chairman until shortly before his death. Jean Carroll continued to work as a solo performer after 1945.

BIBLIOGRAPHY
Smith, Bill. "Buddy Howe" and "Jean Carroll." In *The Vaudevillians*. New York: Macmillan, 1976, pp. 18–22, 252–59.

HUBER'S

Located at 106–108 East 14th Street, Huber's was the best known of the various dime museums in New York that presented an assortment of freak attractions as well as a selection of vaudeville acts. As far as can be ascertained, the establishment was opened by George Huber in 1881 as Huber's Prospect Garden. According to Edward B. Marks in his autobiography, *They All Sang*, Huber's was modeled on an English music hall, with the prima donna being the proprietor's wife, Minnie Schult. With no air conditioning, Huber's was forced to close each summer, and it did so for good in July 1910, following the retirement of manager John C. Anderson, who had been with Huber's for twenty-two years. The lease was taken over by Luchow's Restaurant. According to *Variety* (July 23, 1910) in an announcement of the closure, Huber's "has played many of the stars who are now established on Broadway as standard musical comedy successes."

Aside from Huber's, other major dime museums in New York were Bunnell's Museum at Broadway and 9th Street (opened in December 1880), Worth's

Museum at 101 Broadway (opened in 1880), and the Globe Dime Museum at 298 Bowery (opened in October 1881).

WALTER HUSTON (Toronto, Canada, April 6, 1884—Beverly Hills, Ca., April 7, 1950)

A major actor of the legitimate stage and screen, Walter Huston learned his craft on the vaudeville stage. He made his first stage appearance in Toronto in 1902 and his first New York stage appearance in 1905 in Hal Reid's *In Convict Stripes*. Between 1909 and 1924, Huston worked exclusively in vaudeville, teamed with his second wife, Bayonne Whipple, as Whipple and Huston. (They were married in 1914 and divorced in 1931.) The first vaudeville sketch in which the pair appeared was titled "Spooks," and featured Huston singing "I Haven't Got the Do-Re-Mi." A second sketch called "Shoes" (and later retitled "Boots") had Huston as a shoe clerk with Whipple as a customer. The third and final sketch, which was put together for the Shubert Brothers, featured the two singing and dancing with a jazz band backing and was called "Time."

In Bill Smith's *The Vaudevillians*, Jack Haley remembered, "They did a comedy sketch. He was a shoe salesman and the entire stage was like a shoe store. This woman came in to buy a pair of shoes. There was funny dialogue. He got the laughs. They did a song and dance. The curtain dropped and they came back again in one to do more song and dance." Huston's ability to deliver a song did not disappear as he grew as a serious actor as is evidenced by his performance of "September Song" in the 1938 Broadway hit *Knickerbocker Holiday*.

Walter Huston returned to the legitimate stage in January 1924, playing Marshall Pitt in *Mr. Pitt*. In November of the same year, he played Ephraim Cabot in *Desire under the Elms* and quickly established himself as a major stage presence. Huston was on-screen from 1929 through 1950, with his major films including *Gentlemen of the Press* (1929 and first), *The Criminal Code* (1931), *Rhodes of Africa* (1936), *Dodsworth* (1936), *Yankee Doodle Dandy* (1942), and *The Treasure of Sierra Madre* (1948). His son, John, became a distinguished director and his granddaughter Angelica a well-known screen actress.

BIBLIOGRAPHY

Grobel, Lawrence. *The Hustons*. New York: Charles Scribner's Sons, 1989.

Kennedy, John B. "Shrinking Star." *Collier's*, May 2, 1931, pp. 14, 16.

Vermilye, Jerry. "Walter Huston." *Films in Review* 11, no. 2, February 1960, pp. 70–83, 100.

JOHN HYAMS (Syracuse, N.Y., June 6, 1869—Hollywood, Ca., December 9, 1940) and **LEILA McINTYRE** (New York, December 20, 1882—Los Angeles, January 9, 1953)

John Hyams and his wife, Leila McIntyre, appeared in a comedy sketch utilizing a photographic studio as a backdrop. It was, according to Douglas Gilbert in *American Vaudeville*, "Livened with subtle crossfire, dainty flirtation, and interpolated single and double specialties.'' Prior to their marriage, Hyams had worked as a blackface minstrel, and McIntyre had appeared as half of Linton and McIntyre, singing, dancing, and playing the banjo. The couple were together in vaudeville for more than thirty years and also appeared in the 1911 musical comedy *The Girl of My Dreams*. They made their screen debut together in the 1927 short *All in Fun*. The couple's daughter was screen star Leila Hyams (1905–1977).

I

ROGER IMHOF (Rock Island, Il., January 15, 1875—Hollywood, Ca., April 15, 1958)

Active on both the legitimate stage and vaudeville, Roger Imhof began his career as a circus clown and Irish comic. With his wife, Marcelle Coreene (died 1977), he developed two classic comedy sketches "The Pest House" and "Surgeon Louder," which delighted vaudeville audiences. Imhof played the Palace on many occasions, including November 1926 and March 1929. He was a character actor on screen from 1930 to 1945, appearing in all the Will Rogers films of 1934 and 1935, as well as many others, including *Hoopla* (1933), *San Francisco* (1936), *Young Mr. Lincoln* (1939), *The Grapes of Wrath* (1940), *This Gun for Hire* (1942), and *Wilson* (1945).

"IN ONE"

There are many references in vaudeville to a performer appearing "in one." This means that his or her act takes place in the approximate six-foot area immediately behind the edge of the stage or footlights. This first six-foot area and the next six feet beyond were known as "in two," and so on in six-foot increments to "in four."

INTERSTATE CIRCUIT

The Interstate Circuit was a small, Texas-based vaudeville circuit comprising the following theatres:

Arkansas

Joie Theatre (Fort Smith; Fridays and Saturdays only)

Majestic (Little Rock; Mondays and Tuesdays only)

Pine Bluff Theatre (Pine Bluff; Thursdays only)

Texarkana Theatre (Texarkana; Fridays only)

Louisiana

Rapieds (Alexandria; Tuesday only)

Columbia (Baton Rouge; Sundays and Mondays only)

Sasenger (Monroe; Wednesdays only)

Orpheum (New Orleans)

Strand (Shreveport; Saturdays and Sundays only)

Oklahoma

Busby (McAllister; Fridays and Saturdays only)

Palace (Muskogee; Sundays and Mondays only)

Orpheum (Oklahoma City)

Orpheum (Tulsa)

Texas

Majestic (Dallas)

Majestic (Fort Worth)

Mertini (Galveston; Fridays and Saturdays only)

Majestic (San Antonio)

Majestic (Wichita Falls; Wednesdays, Thursdays, and Fridays only)

"IN THE BAGGAGE COACH AHEAD"

One of the greatest sentimental ballads ever heard on the vaudeville stage was "In the Baggage Coach Ahead," written in 1896 by black American composer Gussie Davis, who learned his craft at the Cincinnati Conservatory of Music— sweeping its floors. Davis wrote many songs for vaudeville performers, including "Send Back the Picture and the Old Wedding ring," introduced by Helene Mora circa 1890. She was billed as a "female baritone"—the Victorian term for contralto—as was Imogene Comer, who popularized "In the Baggage Coach Ahead." Davis had been a railroad porter, and the incident described in the song had actually taken place. The tune stayed in the memory of Eugene O'Neill, who has his hero in *A Moon for the Misbegotten* comment, "I remembered the last two lines of a lousy tear-jerker song I'd heard when I was a kid kept singing over and over in my brain, 'And baby's cries can't waken her/ in the baggage coach ahead.' "

> On a dark stormy night, as the train rattled on,
> all the passengers had gone to bed,
> Except one young man with a babe in his arms
> who sat there with a bowed-down head,
> The innocent one began crying just then,
> As though its poor heart would break,
> One angry man said, "Make that child stop its noise,
> for it's keeping all of us awake,"
> "Put it down," said another, "Don't keep it in here,
> We've paid for our berths and want rest."
> But never a word said the man with the child,

As he fondled it close to his breast,
"Where is its mother go take it to her,"
this a lady then softly said,
"I wish that I could" was the man's sad reply,
"But she's dead, in the coach ahead."
   While the train rolled onward,
   A husband sat in tears,
   Thinking of the happiness
   Of just a few short years,
   For baby's face brings pictures of
   A cherished hope that's dead,
   But baby's cries can't waken her,
   In the baggage coach ahead.
Ev'ry eye filled with tears, when his story he told,
of a wife who was faithful and true,
He told how he'd saved all his earnings for years,
Just to build up a home for two,
How, when Heaven had sent them this sweet little babe,
Their young happy lives were blessed,
His heart seemed to break when he mentioned her name,
And in tears tried to tell them the rest.
Ev'ry woman arose to assist with the child,
There were mothers and wives on the train,
And soon was the little one sleeping in peace,
With no tho't of sorrow or pain,
Next morn at a station, he bade all goodbye,
"God bless you," he softly said,
Each one had a story to tell in their home,
Of the baggage coach ahead.

IROQUOIS THEATRE FIRE

On the afternoon of Wednesday, December 30, 1903, Eddie Foy was appearing in *Mr. Bluebeard* at the Iroquois Theatre, Chicago, when the stage curtain caught fire. An audience of one thousand eight hundred, chiefly children, was present, and despite Foy's appearance onstage to try to calm the audience, there was panic in the theatre, resulting in the deaths of more than six hundred individuals, half of them children. The worst theatrical fire in American history resulted in a tightening of safety regulations in theatres across the country.

Prior to the Iroquois Theatre fire, 289 members of the audience had died at a fire at the Brooklyn Theatre on December 6, 1876, during a performance of *The Two Orphans* starring Kate Claxton. A backstage fire on May 9, 1911, at a British music hall, the Palace Theatre, Edinburgh, resulted in the deaths of eleven performers and stagehands, among whose number was "The Great Lafayette" (Siegmund Neuberger), who had frequently toured in American vaudeville.

BIBLIOGRAPHY
Everett, Marshall. *The Great Chicago Theater Disaster: The Complete Story Told by the Survivors*. Chicago: Publishers Union of America, 1904.
Northrop, Henry Davenport. *World's Greatest Calamities: The Baltimore Fire and Chicago Theater Horror*. Beaver Spring, Pa.: American, 1984.

MAY IRWIN (Whitby, Canada, June 27, 1862—New York, October 22, 1938)
"Though a great portion of her career was spent in musical and farce comedy, it is as a vaudevillian that she will be remembered," wrote Robert Grau of May Irwin in his 1910 book, *The Business Man in the Amusement World*. A legend of the legitimate stage and vaudeville, May Irwin was known as "The Dean of Comediennes." During the First World War, when she gave a solo command performance before President Woodrow Wilson—to give him a good laugh and keep his mind off war worries—she was created unofficial secretary of laughter.

She began singing in the church choir, and with her sister Flo first went on the vaudeville stage at Daniel Shelby's Adelphi Variety Theatre in Buffalo. They performed throughout the Midwest as "coon shouters," singing Negro melodies such as "Don't You Hear dem Bells?" She was seen by Tony Pastor in Detroit, and he brought May and Flo Irwin to New York to perform at the Metropolitan Theatre in 1877. The sisters split up in 1883, when Augustin Daly offered May a job with his company. May Irwin's first starring role was as Beatrice Byke in *The Widow Jones*, opposite John Rice, in 1895. The kissing scene from this farce was filmed by the Edison Company, and known as *The Kiss*, it has become one of the most famous early film clips in motion picture history. In its review of *The Widow Jones*, *The New York Times* (September 17, 1895) said of May Irwin, "She is as round, as blonde, as innocent looking—when her mood is not reckless—as pink and white and as blue-eyed as ever. . . . Her fund of personal humor is prodigious."

It was not until November 1907 that May Irwin returned to the vaudeville stage at New York's Orpheum Theatre. She had put on some weight—*Variety* unkindly said that at her entrance she looked like a sister team—and began her act by describing the pathos of becoming fat and bemoaning the fact that she no longer had a visible waistline. Throughout the teens, Irwin alternated vaudeville appearances with stage roles in *She Knows No Better* (1911), *A Widow by Proxy* (1913), and *Number 13 Washington Square* (1915), among others. Reviewing her 1917 Palace appearance, Sime Silverman wrote in *Variety* (April 6, 1917), "As often as May Irwin may wish to return to vaudeville just so often will vaudeville always welcome her with open arms, for vaudeville audiences, regardless of what else may be said of them, never fail to recognize an artist."

May Irwin had previously topped the bill at the Palace in February 1915, singing "Kentucky Home" and "Those Were the Happy Days," and reciting "Father's Old Red Beard," especially written for her by Irving Berlin. She closed her act with a recitation complaining that her "waistline will never be what it uster [sic]." "There's real art—a mellow and sincere and healthy art—

in Miss Irwin's comedy," wrote Frederick James Smith in *The New York Dramatic Mirror* (March 3, 1915). "No one is quite like her."

Vaudevillian's greatest low comedienne retired in 1920 to her farm in the Thousand Islands area of New York State with her second husband and manager, Kurt Eisfeldt. If May Irwin is remembered at all, it is not as a vaudevillian or a star of the legitimate stage but rather as a plump, somewhat unattractive actress, bestowing an amorous kiss in a flickering silent film from the cinema's infancy. In making *The Kiss*, little did Irwin realize that she was participating in the birth of one art form and the beginning of the end of another.

BIBLIOGRAPHY

Patterson, Ada. "Home Life of May Irwin." *Green Book Album*, March 1911, pp. 520–25.

———. "Twenty Years a Star." *Theatre*, November 1915, p. 236.

J _____

JOE JACKSON (Vienna, 1875—New York, May 14, 1942)

Comic trick cyclist Joe Jackson was described by *Variety*'s Sime Silverman as "one of the best comedy acts ever in vaudeville." Born Josef Francis Jiranek, Joe Jackson took up cycling as a sport and became champion of his native Austria. While touring with a team in England, Jackson ran into financial difficulties and took a job as a truck rider in a circus. There, for the first time, he put on clown makeup and developed an act in which the cycle came apart as he rode it. Jackson made his U.S. debut at the Fifth Avenue Theatre, New York, in June 1911. For the remainder of his life, Jackson's act remained basically the same, as described by a contemporary reporter in *Variety*:

Jackson's entrance on a stage was always the same. A jolly tramp whose furtive efforts to steal a bicycle, usually parked in front of a rich residence, got the audience laughing. He would shush to the audience, and finally mount the bicycle for a joy ride. The horn came off and Jackson would step on it, fearfully looking around to see if he had alarmed the bike's owner; then the handlebars would come off; then one of the pedals; then the seat, and it was always a big laugh when Jackson sat down where the seat was supposed to be. And when the clown went into his trick riding finish his nonsense had usually completely captivated his audience.

Not everyone witnessing Jackson's act realized wherein lay the comedy. The story is told of the manager of the Keith Theatre in Washington, D.C., reporting back to his home office that "Jackson is a pretty good comedian, but he'll never learn to ride a bicycle."

Joe Jackson had his imitators, including Downey and Claridge and Sam Barton (who died in October 1941 while appearing in *It Happens on Ice* at New York's Center Theatre). Jackson also taught his act to his son Joe Jackson, Jr., who so closely resembled his father that he was able to go on in his place, without recognition, during a 1939 engagement at Radio City Music Hall. Joe Jackson, Jr., adapted the act for presentation on ice, appearing in the New York productions of *Icetime* (1947) and *Ice Capades* (1947), as well as a 1942 West Coast production of the latter.

Joe Jackson, Sr., was also seen on the New York stage in *Good Times* (1920) and *American Jubilee* (1940). He was somewhat of a comic inventor, responsible for a miniature toothbrush and toothpaste holder for those who liked to travel light, and weights which could be applied to eyelids to induce sleep.

He died while appearing at New York's Roxy Theatre. After giving the first performance of the day, he took five curtain calls, commented to a stagehand, "My, they're still applauding," and as he walked toward his dressing room, dropped dead.

BIBLIOGRAPHY

"Joe Jackson Drops Dead at N.Y. Roxy after 5 Bows; Started as Speed Cyclist." *Variety*,
    May 20, 1942, pp. 46, 48.

ELSIE JANIS (Columbus, Oh., March 16, 1889—Beverly Hills, Ca., February 27, 1956)

"Elsie Janis!," wrote Sime Silverman in *Variety* (September 22, 1922). "What Bernardt is to the stage, Elsie Janis is to vaudeville. They like her in musical comedy, and they have liked her on two continents, but to vaudeville she is its queen. . . . Miss Janis in vaudeville is the most natural person in vaudeville." With her winning combination of songs, impersonations, pep, and personality, Janis was one of the great vaudeville headliners of the first three decades of the twentieth century. She was loved by audiences in both the United States and Europe, and the darling of society on both continents.

Born Elsie Bierbower, Elsie Janis owned her fame and success to her mother, a woman who was the ultimate stage mother. She may not have always worried about financial trusts for the future, as her daughter recalled in her autobiography, but she did ensure that Elsie (a name suggested by a theatrical photographer) had a good time while embarking on a stage career second to none in the history of vaudeville and revue. Little Elsie made her stage debut on December 24, 1897, in Columbus, Ohio, as Cain in *The Charity Ball*, and she rarely stopped working from that day on. William McKinley learned of her talents when he was governor of Ohio, and when he became president, he invited the eleven-year-old girl to entertain at the White House. In the summer of 1900, she made her New York debut at the Casino Roof Garden, giving impersonations of Weber and Fields, Fay Templeton, and Lillian Russell. At the age of fourteen, she toured in revivals of *The Belle of New York*, *The Fortune Teller*, and *The Little Duchess*. By 1905, Elsie Janis was a major star, and her impersonations at the New York Theatre Roof Garden in the summer of that year were the most talked of entertainment in the city.

That summer season may well be considered the start of Elsie Janis's career as a vaudeville headliner, leading to her acclamation as "America's Wonder Child," "The Cleverest Girl in the World," and "The Princess Royal of Vaudeville." In a 1916 interview, Janis explained, "I loved vaudeville. Of course, that sounds trite and conventional, but while two performances each day are hard, the response of the variety audience is an electrical encouragement.'' The Elsie Janis vaudeville routine remained basically the same, with impersonations and comic songs, but those whom she impersonated (always without the use of makeup or accessories) did vary. In 1907, at the Colonial Theatre, she was impersonating Vesta Victoria singing "Poor John," Eddie Foy, Eva Tanguay, Ethel Barrymore, and Anna Held. In 1911, she introduced her own composition, "I'd Rather Love What I Cannot Have Than Have What I Cannot Love," and gave impersonations of Irene Franklin, Pat Rooney, Anna Held, Ethel Barrymore, Eddie Foy, and Harry Lauder. As Sime Silverman so aptly noted in *Variety* (April 27, 1907), "Miss Janis, taken by herself and considering her youth, pleases any number of people with her impressions."

Elsie Janis made her first appearance at the Palace on January 3, 1916; reviewing her act, Frederick James Smith wrote in *The New York Dramatic Mirror* (January 15, 1916), "Miss Janis offers little caricatures, vividly drawn with a keen and intelligent sense of humor and deftly exaggerating just a few of a player's peculiarities of style and personality." At that time, the star was offering glimpses of Ethel Barrymore, Frank Tinney, Nazimova singing "I Didn't Raise My Boy to Be a Soldier," Eddie Foy, Harry Lauder, George M. Cohan, and Sarah Bernhardt singing "Tipperary." "You caught a splendid semblance of the divine fire—enough to truly thrill you," wrote Smith of the last impersonation. In 1916, Janis drew the Palace Theatre's first Monday night capacity crowd in months, causing *Variety* (January 7, 1916) to comment, "Elsie Janis in vaudeville evidently means something substantial." In September 1922, she was back at the Palace with impersonations of Bert Williams, Ethel Barrymore as Fanny Brice, and George M. Cohan. One impersonation which Elsie Janis enjoyed giving through the years and which delighted audiences in both America and Europe was of Will Rogers with his lariat.

In 1924, Elsie Janis, or rather her mother, had a dispute over billing at the Palace. Janis threatened to walk out if the name of comedian James Barton continued to be billed beside hers in front of the theatre. Barton's name remained, and Janis did indeed walk out. In her autobiography, she claims the fault was not that of E. F. Albee, who was sick at the time, and that when Albee learned of it he insisted on paying her in full for the uncompleted engagement. However, Elsie Janis was banned from working at the Palace again until the late 1920s.

Elsie Janis was vaudeville, but she was also of musical comedy and revue, and in both of these media she was tremendously popular with London and Paris audiences. Janis's first Broadway success was in *The Vanderbilt Cup* in 1906, which made her a star. It was followed through the years by *The Fair Co-Ed* (1908), *The Slim Princess* (1910), *The Lady of the Slipper* (1912), *The Passing Show* (which opened on April 20, 1914, at London's Palace Theatre and made Elsie Janis a British star), *Miss Information* (1915), *The Century Girl* (1917), *Puzzles of 1925* (1925), *Oh, Kay!* (1927), and many others. In these shows, Janis introduced many popular songs, including "Fo de Lawd's Sake, Play a

Waltz'' (from *The Slim Princes*) and "Florrie Was a Flapper" (from *The Passing Show*).

Elsie Janis's work in entertaining the troops during the First World War is legendary, winning for her the title of "Sweetheart of the A.E.F." (the American Expeditionary Force). On May 31, 1918, *Variety* reviewed her act, "Elsie Janis Over There," as if it were a regular theatrical event rather than a makeshift show for the troops, sponsored by the Y.M.C.A. "Wherever she may go," wrote *Variety*, "Miss Janis scores her usual knockout, and from the soldier's point of view is the biggest thing that ever came down the pike. . . . Elsie Janis may be cited as having done her bit." After the war, Janis came to the George M. Cohan Theatre on Broadway with her revue, *Elsie Janis and Her Gang*, which opened on December 1, 1919, and featured a number of ex-servicemen together with several of the women who had worked with her during the war, including actress Eva Le Gallienne.

In August 1926, Janis made a unique film record of the songs she sang during the war in a short subject for the Vitaphone Company titled *Elsie Janis in "Behind the Lines."* The film, which is preserved at the UCLA Film and Television Archive, features Janis, assisted by "a chorus from the 107th Regiment," performing "When Yankee Doodle Learns To Parley-Vous," "Madelon," "In the Army," and "Good-bye-e-e."

The motion picture played only a small part in Elsie Janis's career. She starred in four feature films produced by the Bosworth Company for release by Paramount in 1915: *The Caprices of Kitty*, *Betty in Search of a Thrill*, *Nearly a Lady*, and *'Twas Ever Thus*. In 1919, Selznick starred her in *A Regular Girl* and *The Imp*. As Janis's stage career wound down in the 1920s, the actress turned to the cinema, working not as an actress but behind the scenes. She adapted *Oh, Kay!* for Colleen Moore in 1928, and the following year she provided a story, *Close Harmony*, for two of Paramount's top musical stars, Charles "Buddy" Rogers and Nancy Carroll. Also for Paramount, Elsie Janis came up with the idea of a revue film, *Paramount on Parade*, which she also supervised and for which she provided song lyrics. For the film, Janis persuaded Paramount to sign a young vaudevillian named Mitzi Green, with a talent for mimicry which reminded Janis of herself when young.

Cecil B. DeMille hired Janis in 1930 to provide dialogue and lyrics for his feature *Madam Satan*. She also wrote the lyrics for a song from Paramount's *Slightly Scarlet* (1930) and, with Edmund Goulding, provided the lyrics for Gloria Swanson's big hit "Love, Your Magic Spell Is Everywhere," in *The Trespasser* (1929). In 1939, Elsie Janis was starred by Republic Pictures in *Women in War*, but by that time she considered armed conflict to be far from the exciting adventure it had been for her in 1917 and 1918, and she agreed to appear in the production only on the understanding that she might be allowed to remark frequently on the horrors of war.

To all intents and purposes, Elsie Janis's career ended in 1932 with the death of her mother. The two had been inseparable and had lived for each other's well-being. "There are Elsie Janises born every day, but not mothers to give up their whole lives to them," said Mrs. Bierbower in 1916:

I can understand how many girls of cleverness, or real ability, never find their way to light. Opportunity is necessary, of course. But behind all success are years of hard work and self-sacrifice. Without understanding care a wonderful plant will fade and its beautiful fruit will be lost. I know people say that I keep Elsie from love and companionship. But they don't guess our closeness and devotion. They don't realize how we fought our way through the years. That's why we are inseparable, and that's why we go everywhere together. But the world doesn't understand.

Elsie Janis did not marry until after her mother's death; within a matter of months, she married actor Gilbert Watson, sixteen years her junior. The couple was soon separated. In her charming and literate autobiography, *So Far, So Good!*, Janis suggested that her epitaph might read, "Here lies Elsie Janis, still sleeping alone." When death came on February 26, 1956, at Elsie Janis's bedside was Mary Pickford, who had known the entertainer since they were both children onstage in the late 1890s. It was Pickford who pronounced the definitive epitaph for Elsie Janis: "This ends the vaudeville era."

BIBLIOGRAPHY

"Is Imitation the Sincerest Flattery?" *Saturday Evening Post*, September 26, 1925, pp. 14–15.

Janis, Elsie. *The Big Show: My Six Months with the American Expeditionary Forces.* New York: Cosmopolitan, 1919.

————. "Ex-Actress." *Liberty* 8, no. 20 (May 16, 1931), pp. 12–14.

————. *So Far, So Good!* New York: E. P. Dutton, 1932.

————. "Back to Broadway." *Liberty* 11, no. 38 (September 22, 1934), pp. 40–41.

————. "Give These Little Girls the Air," *Liberty* 11, no. 40 (October 6, 1934), pp. 41–42.

————. "This Is Station WORK." *Liberty* 12, no. 21 (May 25, 1935), pp. 58–59.

"Janis Turns Back on Mammon." *Newsweek*, July 18, 1936, p. 26.

"Orders from G.H.Q." *Time*, July 20, 1936, p. 37.

St. Johns, Adela Rogers. "Is Elsie Janis Guided by Her Dead Mother's Voice?" *Liberty* 13, no. 48 (November 28, 1936), pp. 15–18.

Smith, Frederick James. "Our Elsie's Own Story." *The New York Dramatic Mirror*, January 29, 1916, p. 27.

————. "The Daughter of the Regiment." *Motion Picture Magazine* 9, no. 2 (October 1919), pp. 16–17.

GEORGE JESSEL (New York, April 3, 1898—Los Angeles, May 23, 1981)

As the years have passed since George Jessel's death, it has become more and more difficult to understand his onetime importance in show business. To younger generations of Americans, he seemed nothing more than a bitter right-winger, an aging entertainer whose arrogance was matched only by the turgidity of what he had to say. Reviewing Jessel's local Los Angeles television debut in 1958, Leo Kovner in *Daily Variety* (September 11, 1958) commented that "he came across alternately stiff and floridly verbose.'' It was an image that remained with Jessel for the rest of his days.

George Jessel was a man of many talents. He was a vaudevillian, and actor on both stage and screen, and a television personality. Franklin Delano Roosevelt dubbed him "America's Toastmaster General." He was also the master of the eulogy. (There is a story, probably apocryphal, of Jessel's delivering a eulogy for James Mason's cat, and after the funeral, a sobbing Jack Benny said, "I never knew cats were so good to Israel.") George Jessel was a humanitarian, and on April 7, 1970, the Academy of Motion Picture Arts and Science awarded him with its Jean Hersholt Humanitarian Award.

He has been a film producer, responsible for *The Dolly Sisters* (1945), *I Wonder Who's Kissing Her Now* (1947), *Oh, You Beautiful Doll* (1949), and *Tonight We Sing* (1953). He was an ardent supporter of Jewish charities and the rights of the state of Israel. He was a staunch conservative. Above all, he was a personality. You might hate him, you might hate what he said, you might hate his politics, but one had to admit that he was a unique human being. Groucho Marx once said that "Jessel is the only man I would rather listen to than myself," and it was an opinion shared by most of Marx's generation of entertainers.

Jessel was not a stereotypical vaudeville performer, but his beginnings were typical of most Jewish entertainers of his day. Born on 118th Street in Harlem, George Albert Jessel's grandfather had emigrated to the United States not from Eastern Europe, as did so many families at the time, but from England. He took to entertaining in 1907 to raise money for the family after his father became ill. With two other boys, Jack Wiener (who later became a Hollywood agent) and Walter Winchell, he formed the Imperial Trio to accompany song slides at a local nickelodeon. With Winchell, he joined Gus Edwards's company as part of a vaudeville act called "School Boys and Girls." Also in the company was Eddie Cantor, and an enduring friendship formed which culminated in a historic 1915 Cantor-Jessel engagement at the Palace.

After leaving Edwards, Jessel put together an act called "Two Patches from a Crazy Quilt" with another Edwards alumnus, Lou Edwards. In 1914, the pair took the act to England. Back in the United States, Jessel appeared with an act titled "A Ray of Sunshine," written for him by Henry Bergman and Sam Lewis, in which he played a man who believed he was George Washington. Jessel continued to build up a reputation in vaudeville, which he actively promoted by taking out a full-page advertisement in the June 20, 1919, edition of *Variety*. The ad quoted Percy Hammond's opinion that "George Jessel is in the front ranks of America's lyric comedians," and that of a Detroit critic who compared Jessel to Chaplin. Jessel also boasted that he was the author of the "big comedy hit song" titled "Oo La La, Oui, Oui." (He was also the author of many other songs, including "Stop Kicking My Heart Around," "Rose in December," and "Oh, How I Laugh When I Think How I Cried about You.")

In the summer of 1920, Jessel put together his own revue, complete with chorus girls and a vaudeville team called Holmes and Welles. Jessel supplied the songs, including the aforementioned "Oh How I Laugh When I Think How I Cried about You" and "I'm Satisfied to Be My Mother's Baby," and cowrote the script with Andy Lewis. *The New York Dramatic Mirror* (September 18, 1920), reporting on the revue when it played the Palace, commented, "There are sections that amble along with others putting it in the tempo necessary to send a big act over. Jessel has tried hard. He works hard. . . . The act will set right anywhere 'big-time' vaudeville is played."

The 1920s saw the emergence of George Jessel's classic monolog in which he talked on the telephone to his mother, assuring her he knew nothing about the money missing from the bureau or the cake from the cupboard. The "Hello, Mama" routine seems funnier in the remembrances of those who heard it than in the reality of its extant recordings. In *The Passing Show of 1923*, Jessel performed a similar routine with his old Jewish mother (played by Annie Lovenworth) sitting in a stage box and talking back to him.

Reviewing Jessel's act at the Palace, *The New York Dramatic Mirror* (September 25, 1920) wrote, "It would not be surprising to see this kid climb into the Broadway spotlights of a musical show before he is many seasons older." Jessel did indeed move on from vaudeville to revue, appearing in Shubert's *Troubles of 1922*, but his greatest success in the 1920s was in the musical play *The Jazz Singer* by Samson Raphaelson, which opened in New York at the Fulton Theatre on September 14, 1925. Jessel played Jack Robin in *The Jazz Singer* more than a thousand times in New York and on the road. In addition, he appeared in *The War Song* (1928), which he cowrote, *Sweet and Low* (1930), and *High Kickers* (1931), which he also cowrote and presented.

Because of what appears to have been a dispute over money, Jessel was preempted by Al Jolson for the screen version of *The Jazz Singer*, which became a landmark in motion picture history as the film which, more than any other, forced the changeover from silent to sound production. Jessel had already made some sound shorts for Warner Bros., the producers of *The Jazz Singer*, but for his talkie debut in a feature film he went over to the Poverty Row studios of the Tiffany Company to star in *Lucky Boy*. Sime Silverman reviewed the film in *Variety* (January 9, 1929) and commented, "George Jessel is a finished actor, on the stage or screen. He has a personality and a naturalness here of performance, whether acting, singing or talking, that sends itself over. This talker squares Jessel for any of his other and easier ones, including shorts." The film introduced one of Jessel's best known songs, "My Mother's Eyes," with which Willie Nelson has enjoyed success in more recent years. That song, along with "When the Curtain Comes Down," was featured on Jessel's first Victor recording, about which *Variety* (February 29, 1929) reported, "Jessel discloses a rich, vibrant baritone, clean and clear as to diction and replete with the necessary dramatic pathos for the proper interpretation of songs of this calibre." Jessel appeared in other films as an actor, but his contribution to the motion picture industry was more importantly as a producer of film biographies of vaudeville personalities.

When vaudeville died, George Jessel was able to adapt, "flitting casually about with easy adaptation'' (as Douglas Gilbert wrote in *American Vaudeville*). He was married four times to three women (with his second wife being film star Norma Talmadge), and he had three children (two out of wedlock). He continued to work until he died, accepting a speaking engagement only two weeks before his death. "Why not?," he was quoted in the *Los Angeles Times* (May 25, 1981). "What else should I do with my time—collect stamps?" The master eulogist was eulogized at his funeral by Milton Berle.

The dust jacket for Jessel's first autobiography, *So Help Me*, includes a description that more than adequately sums up his career: "Master Showman, Raconteur, Movie Producer, T.V. and Radio Speechmaker and Toastmaster General of the United States."

BIBLIOGRAPHY

"George Jessel." *Current Biography*, March 1943, pp. 343–45.

Hopper, Hedda. "Jessel, Mot-Master." Sunday syndicated column, February 19, 1950.

Jessel, George. *So Help Me*. New York: Random House, 1943.

_____. "My Private War with Eddie Cantor." *Los Angeles Times: This Week Magazine*, July 19, 1953, p. 10.

_____. *This Way, Miss*. New York: Henry Holt, 1955.

_____. *You Too Can Make a Speech*. New York: Grayson, 1956.

_____. *Jessel, Anyone?* Englewood Cliffs, N.J.: Prentice-Hall, 1960.

_____. *Elegy in Manhattan*. New York: Avon, 1961.

_____. Foreword to *A Pictorial History of Vaudeville* by Bernard Sobel. New York: Citadel Press, 1961.

_____. *Halo over Hollywood*. Van Nuys, Ca: Toastmaster Publishing Co., 1963.

_____, with John Austin. *The World I Lived In*. Chicago: Henry Regnery, 1975.

Mullett, Mary B. "Be Yourself, George, Be Yourself!" *American Magazine*, November 1927, pp. 38–39.

Perelman, S. J. "Say a Few Words, Georgie." *Holiday*, September 1952, pp. 77–79, 116, 119–20.

Zolotow, Maurice. "Funniest Man at the Table." *Saturday Evening Post* October 17, 1953, pp. 42–43, 131, 133–34.

JOE MILLER'S JOKE BOOK

Whenever a stale or corny joke is told, it is always claimed that it originated in Joe Miller's joke book. The reference is to an English comedian of the eighteenth century, Joe Miller (1684–1738), whose name was attached to a jest book published in 1739 by John Mottley. In the argot of *Variety*, an old joke is a "Joe Miller."

CHIC JOHNSON. See OLSEN AND JOHNSON

AL JOLSON (Strednicke, Russia, May 26, 1886—San Francisco, October 23, 1950)

Al Jolson was not a vaudeville star per se in that his stage career was limited to minstrel shows, revues, and musical comedies. He belongs to that small and exclusive group of performers that includes Will Rogers, George M. Cohan, and Harry Lauder, who never played the Palace, although in September 1930 Jolson turned down $12,000 a week to headline there, the highest vaudeville salary offer on record. Jolson is here because, as Eddie Cantor wrote, "Al Jolson wasn't just a musical comedy star. The great Al was an American institution. He was even more than that—he was what all other musical comedy stars thought they were." It is doubtful that any other performer has introduced so many songs that have become standards: "April Showers," "Rock-a-Bye Your Baby with a Dixie Melody," "You Are Too Beautiful," "Hallelujah! I'm a Bum," "Toot Toot, Tootsie," "Where Did Robinson Crusoe Go with Friday on Saturday Night?," "Let Me Sing and I'm Happy," "There's a Rainbow 'round My Shoulder," "Sonny Boy," "When the Red, Red Robin," "Dirty Hands, Dirty Face," "Home in Pasadena," "I'm Just Wild about Harry," "Liza," and so many more. Jolson had no illusions as to the reasons why these songs were successful; many times he would insist the composers list his name along with theirs as coauthor of the compositions.

Jolson's date of birth is uncertain, but he selected May 26, 1886. He was born Asa Yoelson, the son of Cantor Yoelson, in Russia, from where his parents emigrated to the United States when Jolson was a small child. He became fascinated with the stage after hearing Fay Templeton sing "Rosie, You Are My Posie," and received encouragement from minstrel Eddie Leonard. Jolson's first stage appearance is generally considered to have been in *The Children of the Ghetto*, which opened at New York's Herald Square Theatre on October 16, 1899. For a while he worked in burlesque with his brother Harry, in an act titled "The Hebrew and the Cadet" (Al was the latter). In 1901, the two brothers teamed with an older vaudevillian named Joe Palmer. They were initially billed as Joelson, Palmer, and Joelson, but because the name was so long, the "e" was dropped, and the act became Jolson, Palmer, and Jolson. When Palmer became sick, the act split up, and Al Jolson journeyed to San Francisco shortly after the 1906 earthquake and began to make a name for himself.

As a single, Jolson first appeared in whiteface. His reasons for adopting blackface are given in this outrageous story, which appeared in the souvenir program for *The Jazz Singer*:

The turning tide was a chance conversation one night with an old darky. The man was a Southern Negro who assisted the comedian when he dressed. Jolson was extremely fond of him and appreciative of his loyalty through the lean years of his vaudeville tours. In Washington, Al had acquired a sympathetic interest in Negro life and had learned to mimic the accent of the race. One night when the two were preparing for a performance in a small theatre in Brooklyn, the actor confided to his old dresser his misgivings as to the merits of his act. "How am I going to get them to laugh more?" he mused. The darky shook his head knowingly. "Boss, if yo' skin am black they always laugh." The idea struck Jolson as plausible and he decided to try it. He got some burnt cork, blacked up, and rehearsed before the Negro. When he finished he heard a chuckle followed by the verdict. "Mistah Jolson, yo' is just as funny as me."

Long after it went out of vogue, Jolson continued to use blackface. In the 1930 Warner Bros. film *Big Boy*, he played throughout in blackface as a Negro character.

Jolson was signed to appear as a member of Lew Dockstader's Minstrels and soon became the star of the show, supplanting even Dockstader in popularity with the audience. "As a singer of coon songs," reported *Variety* (March 6, 1909), "Jolson has a method of his own by which lyrics and melody are given their full value. Al Jolson would be welcome to vaudeville."

It was not vaudeville, however, that won Al Jolson, but musical comedy, and throughout the teens, it was a bad year when Jolson was not seen on the stage of New York's Winter Garden Theatre in shows such as *La Belle Paris* (1911), *Vera Violetta* (1911), *The Whirl of Society* (1912), *The Honeymoon Express* (1913), *Dancin' Around* (1914), *Robinson Crusoe, Jr.* (1916), and *Sinbad* (1918). In many respects, these shows were part vaudeville, for there was never a time when Jolson would not stop the proceedings to present ten or fifteen minutes of his favorite songs. He would assure his audience, "You ain't heard nothing yet," a phrase that became part of cinema history when Jolson uttered it in *The Jazz Singer*, the first words spoken in a film which is—incorrectly—regarded as the screen's first talkie. By 1922, there was no one who would argue with Jolson's claim that he was "The World's Greatest Drawing Card." When *Bombo* opened in October 1921, it was at Jolson's 59th Street Theatre in New York.

Reviewers were unanimous in their praise for Jolson's ability to hold an audience. Alexander Woollcott wrote, "There is no other performer who holds such an absolute dictatorship over his audience." "They call him the world's greatest entertainer," wrote Alan Dale. "It doesn't seem exaggerated." O. O. McIntyre commented that "Jolson has the same magnetic qualities that lifted Mansfield, Duse, Tree, and Jefferson to the heights," while George Jean Nathan noted, "The power of Jolson over an audience I have seldom seen equalled." In private life, Jolson was a curiously mixed personality. "He was really pretty complex. He could be marvelous and he could be pretty terrible," remembered Mrs. Gus Kahn. George Jessel wrote, "He was cruel most of the time. . . . But, God, what a great artist he was." Jolson's wife, Ruby Keeler, was once bothered by one of her husband's fans who kept insistently asking her, "Did you know you were married to the greatest entertainer in the world." In the end, an exasperated Keeler replied, "Yes, I do. He told me so himself every morning."

In 1927, Warner Bros. decided to transfer Samson Raphaelson's popular Broadway play *The Jazz Singer* to the screen, utilizing its new Vitaphone sound-on-disc process. George Jessel had been the star of the play and was initially signed for the role, but for reasons unclear, perhaps because Jolson agreed to a percentage of the profits instead of a hefty salary, Jessel was replaced by Jolson. As the story line was supposedly based in part on Jolson's life, he would seem to be the logical choice for the lead. Writing in the old humor magazine *Life*, Robert Benchley noted, "When Jolson enters, it is as if an electric current had been run along the wires under the seats where the hats are stuck. The house comes to tumultuous attention. He speaks, rolls his eyes, compresses his lips, and it is all over. . . . He trembles under his lip, and your hearts break with a snap. He sings, and you totter out to send a night letter to your mother.''

The Jazz Singer started Al Jolson on a new career as a film star. It was followed by *The Singing Fool* (1928), *Say It with Songs* (1929), *Sonny Boy* (1929), *Mammy* (1930), *Hallelujah! I'm a Bum* (1933), *Wonder Bar* (1934), *The Singing Kid* (1936), *Rose of Washington Square* (1939), and many others. Jolson also became immensely popular on radio, at first with *Presenting Al Jolson* in 1932, then with the *Kraft Music Hall* in 1934, and later with *Shell Chateau* in 1935. As the career of his third wife, Ruby Keeler, grew, Jolson's fame began to diminish. However, his career was given a tremendous boost in 1946, when Columbia produced *The Jolson Story*, with Larry Parks playing Jolson and miming to a playback of Jolson's own voice for the songs. *The Jolson Story* was followed the next year by *Jolson Sings Again*. Morose out of the limelight, Al Jolson once more regained his old vitality, embarking on a number of tours to entertain the troops in the Korean War. He was again at the top of the heap when he died. Ironically, just before the news of his death was made public, Danny Thomas had kidded on his television program, ''Larry Parks would be buried in the event of Jolson's death.''

BIBLIOGRAPHY

''Al Jolson,'' *Current biography*, November 1940, pp. 436–38.

Fleming, William J. ''King of Cork.'' *Illustrated World*, January 1923, pp. 663–65.

Freedland, Michael. *Jolson*. New York: Stein and Day, 1972.

Goldman, Herbert G. *Jolson: The Legend Comes to Life*. New York: Oxford University Press, 1988.

Jolson, Harry, as told to Alban Emley. *Mistah Jolson*. Hollywood, Ca.: House-Warren, 1951.

Lee, Kenyon. ''It's Raining Violets for Al.'' *Screen Guide* 12, no. 12 (December 1947), pp. 72–73, 94–95.

McClelland, Doug. *Blackface to Blacklist: Al Jolson, Larry Parks and ''The Jolson Story.''* Metuchen, N.J.: Scarecrow Press, 1987.

Oberfirst, Robert. *Al Jolson: You Ain't Heard Nothing Yet*. San Diego: A. S. Barnes, 1980.

Seldes, Gilbert. ''Demoniac in the American Theatre.'' *Dial*, September 1923, pp. 303–308.

Sharpe, Howard. ''The Ten Best Gags of Al Jolson,'' *Liberty* 18, no. 41 (October 11, 1941), pp. 32–33.

Sieben, Pearl. *The Immortal Al Jolson: His Life and Times*. New York: Frederick Fell, 1962.

Skinner, Richard Dana. ''Al Jolson Again.'' *The Commonweal*, April 23, 1930, p. 715.

SISSIERETTA JONES (Portsmouth, Va., January 5, 1869—Providence, R.I., June 24, 1933)

One of the first Negro opera singers, Sissieretta Jones was dubbed the ''Black Patti,'' in reference to Italian prima donna Adelina Patti, and sang at the White House in 1892 for President Benjamin Harrison. Born Matilda Sissieretta Joyner, the singer married mulatto David Richard Jones at the age of fourteen, and he became her manager. She gave her first principal concert at the Music Hall, Boston, in 1887, and the following year appeared at New York's Steinway Hall. She was the star of the Grand Negro Jubilee at Madison Square Garden in April 1892, and in 1893, she appeared at the Chicago World's Fair.

In 1896, Black Patti's Troubadors, "the Greatest Colored Show on Earth," was created to highlight her singing on the vaudeville circuits. Amid comedy sketches, acrobatics, and dances, Jones sang operatic arias. The Troubadors were renamed the Black Patti Musical Comedy Company in 1908 and continued in existence through 1916. Sissieretta Jones died in poverty, with her funeral expenses paid by friends.

BIBLIOGRAPHY

Mercier, Denis. "Sissieretta Jones." In *Notable Black American Women*, ed. Jessie Carney Smith. Detroit: Gale Research, 1992, pp. 600–605.

K

BEATRICE KAY (New York, April 21, 1907—North Hollywood, Ca., November 8, 1986)

Beatrice Kay was not a vaudevillian, but she helped keep vaudeville alive long after others had reported its demise. Born Hannah Beatrice Kuper, she was onstage as a child, working in various stock companies and in silent films. In 1939, she opened at Billy Rose's Diamond Horseshoe Restaurant in New York, singing songs popular on the vaudeville stage at the turn of the century, and continued with this form of entertainment on radio with *The Gay Nineties Revue*, produced by Al Rinker and heard on CBS from 1940 to 1944. Kay left the show in 1943, in the hope of a Hollywood career, but returned to radio the following year with NBC's *Gaslight Gaieties*. Beatrice Kay made many recordings, of which the most famous is "Mention My Name in Sheboygan," and also made occasional screen appearances, including *Diamond Horseshoe* (1945) and *Underworld U.S.A.* (1961). In the 1970s, she was the star attraction at the Mayfair Music Hall in Santa Monica, California, an attempt to re-create a British music hall from the turn of the century.

BUSTER KEATON. See THE THREE KEATONS

FRANK KEENAN (Dubuque, Ia., April 8, 1858—Hollywood, Ca., February 24, 1929)

A legitimate actor of some stature, Frank Keenan made his first stage appearance with the Boston Museum Stock Company in 1880. He became a leading man in the 1890s, and his most prominent Broadway roles were as Brother Paul in *The Christian* (1898), Jack Rance in *The Girl of the Golden West* (1905), General Warren in *The Warrens of Virginia* (1909), and the title role in *John Ferguson* (1920). He began his film career in 1915 with *The Coward*, and remained a popular leading character actor on-screen until his death, appearing in some thirty-six feature-length productions.

Frank Keenan alternated appearances on the legitimate stage with performances in vaudeville, starring in two one-act dramas, *Man to Man* and *Vindication*. He was the headliner on the second week's bill at the Palace Theatre in April 1913. In *Vindication*, he played an aging Confederate soldier whose son has been sentenced to death. In pleading for his son's life, the soldier declaims, "Governor, don't hang my boy. I don't think you know how it happened. This man, this man, he spit on the picture of Robert E. Lee, and Goddamn him—my boy shot him!" It caused a considerable stir at the Palace, where blasphemy and any form of swearing were prohibited, but so important an actor was Keenan that he was permitted to perform the sketch without censorship.

Frank Keenan was the father-in-law of comedian Ed Wynn.

BIBLIOGRAPHY

Remont, Fritzi. "Ideals and Idols—Past and Present." *Motion Picture Classic* 8, no. 6 (August 1919), pp. 56–57, 62.

B. (BENJAMIN) F. (FRANKLIN) KEITH (Hillsboro Bridge, N.H., January 26, 1846—Palm Beach, Fl., March 26, 1914)

B. F. Keith vies for the title of "Father of American Vaudeville" with Tony Pastor. Certainly, Keith was the "Father of the American Vaudeville Industry" and the creator of the vaudeville circuit. According to Joe Laurie, Jr., Keith was a little man, both in stature and mentality, who was cold, colorless, and petty. Whatever personality Keith may have had, it is not discernible from contemporary articles on him and his career. As a showman, he appears to have been singularly lacking in an understanding of self-promotion. In photographs, he looks stern and forbidding, very much a harsh father rather than a kindly guardian of vaudeville. One of the few innovations he brought to vaudeville was a sense of decency and an insistence that no act use profanity on stage. The latter rule was chiefly enforced by his first wife, Mary Catherine Branley, whom he married in 1873 and who died in 1910. Douglas Gilbert claims in *American Vaudeville* that Mrs. Keith would visit the Keith theatres wearing an apron and bandanna, behaving as if a housekeeper, while her husband carried a hammer in his belt, and was happiest taking care of minor repairs to the fabric of his buildings.

Of Scottish descent, Benjamin Franklin Keith worked on a farm in western Massachusetts from the age of seven to eighteen, acquiring whatever education he could at the district school. At seventeen, he attended a visiting circus and became fascinated with the field of entertainment. He worked with Bunnell's Museum in New York for two year, and also for P. T. Barnum and Doris and Forepaugh before coming to Boston in 1882. Having gained some experience with small shows on the road, he decided to rent a vacant storefront and open a dime museum in partnership with a Colonel William Austin. The Hub Museum, as it was initially called, opened on January 8, 1885, with its first attraction being Baby Alice. According to *The New York Dramatic Mirror* (November 26, 1913), her "principal claim to distinction lay in the fact that at the age of three months she weighed but one and one-half pounds. The admission fee to gaze upon this tiny morsel of humanity was 10 cents, and for two weeks the little one held the boards alone.'' As Baby Alice grew in size, other freak attractions were added to the museum, which also grew, taking over the storefront next door and an upstairs room. The latter was used for vaudeville-style entertainment, with some of the earliest performers being Mrs. Tom Thumb and Fred Kyle with his dog, cat, baby, and bird shows. The name of the museum was changed to the New York Museum, and later the Gaiety Museum.

The upper floor of the museum was expanded, and Keith decided to introduce continuous performances in the room in order to keep crowds waiting to enter the museum below entertained from 10:30 A.M. through 10:30 P.M. The first continuous performance was given on July 6, 1883, and according to *The New York Dramatic Mirror*:

As the number of attractions was limited, it was necessary at that time to have six performances daily, each of two hours' duration. The participants on the first day of the continuous performance were the Durville Family, the youngest of which was a remarkably clever prodigy; an illusion called Rolla; Olympian Quintette (colored), who have since met with great success abroad; the Arctic Moon, which was lectured upon by S. K. Hogdon; Marion Fisk, vocalist; Murray and Monarch; Ainsley Brothers, Hughes and West, with John Barker, the famous bone soloist, and Mr. Hogdon, in an amusing sketch.

In the winter of 1883, E. F. Albee became associated with Keith as his manager, but at this time Keith's partner was George H. Batcheller (1829–1913). It was with Batcheller that Keith opened the Bijou Theatre, Boston, on August 1, 1886, with the opening program consisting of Lillian Lewis in *The Creole*. In 1887, Batcheller sold his interest in the partnership to Keith, and on July 30 of that year the Gaiety Museum closed down. On August 1, 1887, the Bijou Theatre began presenting continuous vaudeville, and so identified with Keith had the name Gaiety become that the Bijou was renamed the Gaiety and Bijou.

With Batcheller gone, Keith began a partnership with E. F. Albee, and the two men began to expand, opening a Gaiety Museum in Providence, Rhode Island, in 1887, and a theatre in Philadelphia. In 1893, the two men opened their first theatre in New York, the Union Square Theatre, and a new Boston theatre, the Colonial. Vaudeville had come of age, and the B. F. Keith circuit was born.

In 1906, B. F. Keith began to lose interest in his vaudeville empire and ceased personal supervision of the bookings for his theatres. Three years later, he withdrew from personal involvement in all his business activities, turning them over to his son Andrew Paul Keith (who died in 1918). On October 29, 1913, Keith married Ethel Bird Chase and embarked firmly on a life of leisure. His death was unexpected, and the showman was buried at Newton Cemetery, Boston. On the day of the funeral, all B. F. Keith theatres were closed until the evening performance.

BIBLIOGRAPHY

''B. F. Keith, Dean of American Vaudeville, Dies Suddenly.'' *The New York Dramatic Mirror*, April 1, 1914, p. 25.

''Father of Modern Vaudeville.'' *Literary Digest*, April 18, 1914, p. 929.

Grau, Robert. "Greatest Vaudeville Manager in the World." *American Magazine*, May 1914, p. 86.

Kingsley, Walter J. "Thirty Years of Vaudeville." *The New York Dramatic Mirror*, November 26, 1913, pp. 4–5.

Laurie, Joe, Jr. "Benjamin Franklin Keith." In *Vaudeville: From the Honky-Tonks to the Palace*. New York: Henry Holt, 1953, pp. 337–47.

B. F. KEITH VAUDEVILLE CIRCUIT

Through either ownership of the theatres themselves or control of the booking of acts into non–Keith-owned houses, the B. F. Keith Vaudeville circuit controlled vaudeville in the Eastern United States and operated as a monopoly. The circuit was known under various names and through much of its existence was known as the United Booking Office (q.v.). It was founded by B. F. Keith (q.v.) and managed by E. F. Albee (q.v.). The latter gained total control of the circuit in 1918, following the death of Keith's son Andrew Paul Keith. The B. F. Keith circuit faced setbacks in the 1920s in large part because of the popularity of the motion picture, and to try to bolster the circuit, E. F. Albee arranged a merger in 1927 with the Orpheum circuit, forming the Keith-Albee-Orpheum circuit.

In 1926, the B. F. Keith circuit became more actively involved in the film industry, presenting films as well as vaudeville acts at many of its theatres (although the practice dated back well into the teens). In May of that year, B. F. Keith acquired a 50 percent interest in Producers Distributing Corporation and announced plans to enter film production. In July 1926, the Keith-Albee-DeMille Exchange, Inc., was created to handle film bookings for the Keith-Albee theatres. (Cecil B. DeMille had a large financial interest in Producers Distributing Corporation.) In 1927, the attitude of B. F. Keith toward motion pictures was somewhat blurred. In March of that year, it announced that it would ban all "name acts" from appearing in sound films. In a counterattack against the motion picture industry, on August 23, 1927, Keith-Albee reported the signing of fifteen Hollywood players to appear in two-a-day vaudeville.

Meanwhile, a meeting had taken place at the Grand Central Oyster Bar in New York in October 1927 between David Sarnoff, general manager of the Radio Corporation of America, and Joseph P. Kennedy, whose holdings included Film Booking Offices of America, Inc. RCA agreed to acquire the latter's stock, and encouraged Kennedy to purchase stock owned by John J. Murdock in Keith-Albee-Orpheum. In the summer of 1928, Kennedy approached E. F. Albee with a view to acquiring Albee's stock in the B. F. Keith circuit but was turned down. Through stock manipulation, Kennedy was able to outmaneuver Albee, and in October 1928, RCA acquired Keith-Albee-Orpheum. On October 23, 1928, RKO Radio Pictures (Radio-Keith-Orpheum) was founded, with Hiram S. Brown as its first president.

Through the acquisition of the Keith-Albee-Orpheum circuit, the new film company was assured of theatrical outlets for its motion pictures. The bitterness of the takeover is evident from the dropping of Albee's name from the new company. Albee's ouster from the company he had controlled for more than thirty years was total, and when he tried to make a suggestion to Kennedy, the latter responded, "Didn't you know, Ed? You're washed up, you're through." At the time of the formation of RKO, the B. F. Keith circuit had controlling or minority interest in 450 theatres and booked vaudeville into a total of 775 theatres.

At the height of its power in the 1920s, the B. F. Keith circuit comprised the following vaudeville theatres:

Alabama

Lyric (Birmingham)

Lyric (Mobile)

Grand (Montgomery)

Canada

Lyric (Hamilton)

New Princess (Montreal)

St. Dennis (Montreal)

Dominion (Ottawa)

Shea's (Toronto)

Shea's Hippodrome (Toronto)

Shea's (Toronto)

Connecticut

Plaza (Bridgeport)

Poli (Bridgeport)

Palace (Hartford)

Poli (Hartford)

Grand (Middletown)

Palace (New Britain)

Bijou (New Haven)

Poli (New Haven)

Lyceum (New London)

Strand (Norwich)

Alhambra (Stamford)

Poli (Waterbury)

Delaware

Garrick (Wilmington)

District of Columbia

B. F. Keith's

Florida

Palace (Jacksonville)

Georgia

Lyric (Atlanta)

Imperial (Augusta)

Grand (Macon)

Bijou (Savannah)

Indiana

B. F. Keith's (Indianapolis)

Kentucky

B. F. Keith's National (Louisville)

Keith's Mary Anderson (Louisville)

Louisiana

Palace (New Orleans)

Maine

B. F. Keith's (Portland)

Maryland

Maryland (Baltimore)

Massachusetts

B. F. Keith's (Boston)

Victoria (Greenfield)

B. F. Keith's (Lowell)

Empire (North Adams)

Majestic (Pittsfield)

Poli (Springfield)

Plaza (Worcester)

Poli (Worcester)

Michigan

Temple (Detroit)

Empress (Grand Rapids)

New Jersey

Tower's (Camden)

Keith's (Jersey City)

Regent (Kearney)

Proctor's (Newark)

Playhouse (Passaic)

Majestic (Paterson)

Pastime (Union Hill)

New York

Proctor's (Albany)

Jefferson (Auburn)

Stone Opera House (Binghampton)

Shea's (Buffalo)

Majestic (Elmira)

Empire (Glen Falls)

Star (Ithaca)

Proctor's (Mount Vernon)

Victoria (Ossining)

Temple (Rochester)

Congress (Saratoga Springs)

Proctor's (Schenectady)

B. F. Keith's (Syracuse)

Crescent (Syracuse)

Temple (Syracuse)

Proctor's (Troy)

Colonial (Utica)

Proctor's (Yonkers)

New York City

B. F. Keith's Alhambra

B. F. Keith's Colonial

B. F. Keith's Palace

B. F. Keith's Riverside

B. F. Keith's Royal

58th Street

Grand

Harlem Opera House

125th Street

Proctor's Fifth Avenue

23rd Street

Winter Garden

New Brighton Theatre (Brighton Beach)

B. F. Keith's Bushwick (Brooklyn)

B. F. Keith's Orpheum (Brooklyn)

Greenpoint (Brooklyn)

Halsey (Brooklyn)

Prospect (Brooklyn)

Henderson's (Coney Island)

Port Richmond (Staten Island)

North Carolina

Academy (Charlotte)

Ohio

Lyceum (Canton)

B. F. Keith's (Cincinnati)

Palace (Cincinnati)

B. F. Keith's Hippodrome (Cleveland)

B. F. Keith's (Columbus)

B. F. Keith's (Dayton)

B. F. Keith's (Toledo)

Hippodrome (Youngstown)

Pennsylvania

Orpheum (Allentown)

Orpheum (Altoona)

Edgmont (Chester)

Able Opera House (Easton)

Colonial (Erie)

Majestic (Harrisburg)

Felley's (Hazelton)

Majestic (Johnstown)

White's Hippodrome (McKeesport)

Allegheny (Philadelphia)

B. F. Keith's (Philadelphia)

Broadway (Philadelphia)

Colonial (Philadelphia)

Grand Opera House (Philadelphia)

Keystone (Philadelphia)

Nixon (Philadelphia)

William Penn (Philadelphia)

Davis (Pittsburgh)

Harris (Pittsburgh)

Sheridan Square (Pittsburgh)

Hippodrome (Reading)

Poli (Scranton)

Poli (Wilkes-Barre)

York Opera House (York)

Rhode Island

Scenic (Pawtucket)

E. F. Albee (Providence)

Bijou (Woonsocket)

South Carolina

Victory (Charleston)

Columbia (Columbia)

Tennessee

Bijou (Chatanooga)

Bijou (Knoxville)

Princess (Nashville)

Virginia

Olympia (Newport News)

Academy of Music (Norfolk)

Century (Petersburg)

Lyric (Richmond)

Roanoke (Roanoke)

B. F. KEITH'S VAUDEVILLE EXCHANGE.   See UNITED BOOKING OFFICE

HARRY KELLAR (Erie, Pa., July 11, 1849—New York, March 10, 1922)
   America's best known magician of his day, Kellar also toured the world, presenting his illusions in Europe, South America, South Africa, and India. He was as much a showman as a magician, and his illusions ranged from the small—changing water into ink—to the magnificent, involving human and animal transformations. He would present seances onstage and in private, in which he was bound in a locked cabinet but was able to move objects. Born Heinrich Keller, the magician toured while still a child as an assistant to I. Harris Hughes, who billed himself as "The Fakir of Ava." On December 15, 1884, he opened his own theatre, Kellar's Egyptian Hall, in Philadelphia, modeled after the original Egyptian Hall in London, where John Nevil Maskelyne and George A. Cooke presented their illusions. Kellar officially retired in May 1908, but he gave his last public performance at the New York Hippodrome on November 11, 1917.

ANNETTE KELLERMANN (Sydney, Australia, July 6, 1887—Southport, Australia, November 5, 1975)
   Annette Kellermann made a career out of swimming and appearing in a one-piece bathing costume. She might have been little more than a freak act, but talent and originality led to her achieving a prominent place in vaudeville history to such an extent that one early commentator, Robert Grau, hailed her in 1910 as "The Queen of Modern Vaudeville." He continued, "Annette Kellermann's appearance in a vaudeville theatre at this time is an event of such importance that at the opening of the sale of seats in any auditorium where she is announced,

one would suppose a Bernhardt or a Patti was scheduled to appear. Either Annette Kellermann is the greatest box office attraction the stage has ever known, or else her manager is the most compelling genius of modern theatrical achievement, and the writer is inclined to the belief that both statements qualify.'' Certainly, much of Annette Kellerman's success must be attributed to her husband and manager, Jim Sullivan, who guided her career through vaudeville houses in England, Australia, and the United States, and also in films. But credit must also go to Annette Kellermann's father, who ambitiously pushed his daughter into show business in the first place.

Born in Sydney, Australia, to parents who were both musicians, as a child, Kellermann was crippled with what appears in hindsight to have been polio. In a 1917 interview, she recalled:

My baby-legs were badly deformed, and I had to wear leg-braces to correct the deformity. As I hobbled about—a frail and sickly child—no one thought that I would ever amount to anything, and even my fondest relations believed that I was not very long for this world. I gradually began to improve, however. The braces helped to straighten my crooked limbs, and I found I could get about more easily and more rapidly. At this point the family doctor recommended swimming exercises to develop my frail underpinnings and facilitate the cure he had started. On his advice, I was taken to Cavell's Baths. Here, somehow or other, in the course of a few lessons I learned to swim. The limbs which had served me so ill on dry land found their true congenial element in the water. At the age of fifteen, I was the champion girl swimmer of Australia. I had attained a fine physical development, and I enjoyed the output of bodily energy with every fiber of my being. Yes, it is true that Mamma, devoted as she was to her artistic profession, wished to make a musician of me. I had a good singing voice, and I was an expert on the violin, having been brought up in the atmosphere of the conservatory, where musicianship was easy. Mother felt that I could win fame and fortune in the distant, more settled lands with the bow and strings. It was planned for me that I should go to Paris, her old home, and there be tutored to perfection by the best violin masters. But, almost before I knew it, I was doing professional swimming work in Sydney, Melbourne, and Adelaide. Such a demand rose for my exhibitions that, almost perforce, I cast aside the thought of musical fame.

Annette Kellermann's father took her on what can best be described as a swimming tour of European capitals; she swam down the Seine, the Rhine, and the Danube. After attracting attention by swimming down the River Thames from Putney Bridge to Blackwall, Kellermann began starring in British music hall, performing an act in which she dived into a large, glass-enclosed tank onstage and performed various water ballets. When she came to the United States, she created a sensation (presumably designed to win her still greater publicity) by appearing at Boston's Revere Beach in 1907, dressed in a one-piece bathing costume. Her vaudeville career took off shortly thereafter. E. F. Albee signed her up, and refurbished her British act by placing mirrors in strategic positions around her tank so that audiences were treated to multi-views of Kellermann's body. At this point, it should be noted that it was the lady's body that was her chief attraction; she had a remarkably unappealing face.

(Incidentally, in *American Vaudeville*, Douglas Gilbert notes that Annette

Kellermann was long preceded by a freak act named "Blatz, the Human Fish," who spent long periods of time underwater, eating, reading a newspaper, and playing the trombone. In 1909, "Enoch, the Man Fish," smoked, played the trombone, and sang underwater. Those who saw Kellermann's act report that, in later years, she would eat a banana underwater.)

On December 26, 1908, Annette Kellermann was featured on the cover of *Variety*, and later that same week she introduced her new act, "On the Beach at Boulogne," at New York's Fifth Avenue Theatre. It began with her entering onstage in a light summer frock, which she discarded inside a bathing machine to reveal a short-skirted bathing suit. While a young man tried to photograph her, Kellermann engaged in some skillful and artistic diabolo throwing. She then climbed a diving board and made a graceful entry into the water tank, at the same time removing the bathing suit to expose a black union suit. The act then proceeded with a series of dives. "The arrangement is a capital example of the right way to build a setting for an individual specialty" commented "Rush" in *Variety* (January 2, 1909). In 1916, Annette Kellermann, now billed as "The Divine Venus," replaced Anna Pavlova in *The Big Show of 1916* at the New York Hippodrome. One of the revue's big production numbers featured an enchanted waterfall, peopled by two hundred mermaids, and Kellermann performing a sensational high dive. In January 1918, she introduced "Annette Kellermann's Big Show," a forty-one-minute extravaganza in which she sang, danced, walked a tightrope, and changed her clothes frequently at the Palace Theatre. Of her figure, Sime Silverman wrote in *Variety* (February 1, 1918), "It's worth looking at twice or more daily."

In December 1918, Annette Kellermann headlined at the Palace in what was described as her "farewell appearance on the first lap of her journey around the world." She was yet again not only presenting high dives but also dancing, singing, and walking a tightrope. "There is too much of what the star does indifferently or fairly well and too little of what she does admirably," complained *The New York Dramatic Mirror* (December 21, 1918).

By this time, Kellermann was also a movie star. As early as August 1909, she had visited the Brooklyn studios of the Vitagraph Company to perform "her daring feats as well as her physical culture exercises and diabolo playing" on film. This footage was screened not only in movie theatres but also as an introduction to her vaudeville act. Annette Kellermann starred in *Neptune's Daughter* (1914), *A Daughter of the Gods* (1916), *Queen of the Sea* (1918), *What Women Love* (1920), and *Venus of the South Seas* (1924). In 1952, Esther Williams played Kellermann in M-G-M's film biography *Million Dollar Mermaid*.

Annette Kellermann officially retired in the 1930s, but she continued to swim one-half-mile a day through her eightieth birthday.

WALTER C. KELLY (Mineville, N.Y., October 29, 1873—Philadelphia, January 6, 1939)

Billed as "The Virginia Judge," Walter Kelly was a popular monologuist who built his act around stories of judicial commentaries from the South, generally of a racist nature. A typical routine would be:

"You here agin, Lem? What did you do this time?"

"Ah didn't do nothin', Jedge. The railroad run over my mule and killed him and they won't pay me. They won't even give me back my rope."

"What rope?"

"Why, Jedge, de rope ah done tied de mule on the track wif."

The act would conclude with Kelly's imitating a Negro boy coming into the court and saying, "Say, Jedge, Colonel Stevens wants to know if you want to go fishin'; he sez they bitin' pretty good." To which the judge responded, "All right, tell him I'll be right along. Court adjourned!" In hindsight, the act closely resembles the character of Judge Priest, played on-screen by Will Rogers in 1934 and Charles Winninger in 1953.

From his birthplace in Mineville, New York, Kelly's parents took him to Philadelphia and Newport News, Virginia. In the latter community, he worked as a shipyard worker, and circa 1895 attended the local police court of a Judge Brown, whose treatment of Negro prisoners fascinated Kelly and after whose talk and mannerisms he modeled his act. Years later, he recalled his first visit to Judge Brown's courtroom.

"The jailer, echoing the clerk, called out the name of William Gaylor, first prisoner. As the heavy barred door creaked back, a very black and stupid little darky emerged from the pack and pranced up to the prisoner's dock. He stood there helplessly while the judge, without looking up from the docket, mumbled:

" 'Willie Gaylor, where is he?'

" 'Yessuh, Mistuh Judge—Willie Gaylor, thass me,' drawled the darkie.

" 'Ten days, Willie. . . . That's me!' snapped the judge as he rapped for the next case."

Shortly thereafter, Kelly opened the Mecca Cafe, Pool Room and Restaurant in Newport News, where he entertained shipyard workers. He came to New York and was invited by Big Jim Sullivan to entertain at the Eagles Club, where he took over from star Marie Dressler when she became ill. On May 24, 1909, Kelly played the Palace Theatre, London, and was soon an international star, welcome not only in Europe and America, but also in Australia. Between 1911 and 1913, Kelly was touring the world with his act. Additionally, he claimed to have made more than five hundred recordings for the Victor record label.

Kelly was back in New York in November 1913, headlining at the 44th Street Music Hall. He introduced a new story involving a Negro accused of stealing chickens. "Judge, the Lord may strike me dead if I stole." "Stand over there for five minute," replied the judge, "and if you are still living I'll give you ninety days." "His humor is the brand that anyone who understands English must laugh at," commented Sime Silverman in *Variety* (November 14, 1913). "Walter Kelly is the kind of an entertainer who should be held in one theatre for a run. You never tire of Kelly. As a single-handed character story teller he is without peer."

The entertainer brought his character to the screen in a 1935 Paramount feature, *The Virginia Judge*. "The older generation who have laughed at Walter Kelly's stories for thirty years will thank Edward Sedgwick, director, for presenting him so faithfully on the screen,'' commented Herb Sterne in *Rob Wagner's Script* (November 25, 1935). Kelly made his screen debut in *Seas Beneath* (1931), and was also seen in *McFadden's Flats* (1935) and *Laughing Irish Eyes* (1936).

By all accounts, Kelly was as racist in person as his monologs read. In December 1905, he refused to appear on the same bill at Hammerstein's Victoria Theatre as Bert Williams and George Walker. Kelly announced he was a Southerner and would not appear on the same stage with Negroes. Walker responded, ''With all due regard to Mr. Kelly, we are paid more money in a week for our work than he gets in three months for his. The man is lacking in brains, that's what's the matter with him.''

A great fight fan, Walter Kelly lost his middle finger when it was bitten off by a fan, with whom he had an argument after the Jeffries-Johnson boxing match. One of his close friends was James J. Corbett. He died as a result of head injuries sustained when hit by a truck in Hollywood. Walter C. Kelly was the brother of playwright George C. Kelly and prominent Democratic politician John B. Kelly (the father of actress Grace Kelly).

BIBLIOGRAPHY

Kelly, Walter C. *Of Me I Sing: An Informal Autobiography*. New York: Dial Press, 1935.

PERT KELTON (Great Falls, Mt., October 14, 1907—Ridgewood, N.J., October 30, 1968)

As her name suggests, Pert Kelton was a bright and vicacious comedienne, whose parents, Ed and Susan Kelton, were also vaudeville performers. Pert joined the family act at the age of four while on tour in South Africa. Later, she teamed with her mother as a sister act, Pert and Sue Kelton, in which Pert played the trombone and Sue the clarinet, both danced, and Pert also gave impersonations of Charlie Chaplin and William S. Hart. The act concluded with the two women providing vocal imitations of the trombone and clarinet. Reviewing the act at New York's Fifth Avenue Theatre, *Variety* commented, ''In appearance the girls are pleasing and their work indicates painstaking rehearsing.''

As a result of her work in vaudeville, Pert Kelton was signed to appear, in a four-minute cameo performance, in the 1925 production of *Sunny*, starring Marilyn Miller. Herman Shumlin, who worked with her on Broadway in the 1967 production of *Spofford*, commented, '' 'Pert' she was called as a child, and her pertness, her vivacity, won all of us when we saw her in her teens in *Sunny*.'' Pert Kelton made her film debut with Marilyn Miller, playing Rosie the maid, in the 1929 screen version of *Sally*. She worked both onstage and -screen in the 1930s, but the roles dwindled, and in February 1940, she filed a voluntary petition of bankruptcy.

In the 1940s, Pert Kelton was active in radio (often working with Milton Berle), and on television she was the original Alice Kramden, playing opposite Jackie Gleason in *The Honeymooners* when it was first seen as a 1951 sketch on DuMont's *Cavalcade of Stars*. (When the show became a series, Kelton was replaced by Audrey Meadows.) The 1950s was not a good decade for the comedienne in that she was branded a Communist by *Red Channels* magazine and blacklisted by the entertainment industry; she sued but later withdrew the suit.

Pert Kelton returned to Broadway in 1957, playing the feisty Irish mother Mrs. Paroo in *The Music Man*. She re-created the role in the film version of the musical, and both her stage and screen careers were reactivated for the last few years of her life.

BIBLIOGRAPHY

Shumlin, Herman. "Pert Kelton 1907–1968." *The New York Times*, November 10, 1968, p. D3.

HETTY KING (Wimbledon, England, 1883—London, September 28, 1972)

Hetty King was one of a handful of British male impersonators, who gained considerable popularity in American vaudeville with her songs "All the Nice Girls Love a Sailor" and "Piccadily." She began entertaining in 1897 and took to male impersonation in 1905. King made her American vaudeville debut at the New York Theatre in October 1907, and *The New York Dramatic Mirror* (October 19, 1907) commented, "She makes an attractive picture in her various costumes and does not waste much time in making her changes." She was back in vaudeville again in 1909, at which time *Variety* (December 18, 1909) opined, "Hetty King will linger in memory as the acme of the art of male impersonations."

A 1970 British documentary, *Hetty King: Performer*, directed by film critic David Robinson and narrated by Lindsay Anderson, shows the impersonator reminiscing about her career, applying her makeup, and performing on stage at the Royal Hippodrome, Eastbourne.

KOHL AND CASTLE

Kohl and Castle was the dominant company in early vaudeville in Chicago. The first acknowledged vaudeville entertainment in the city took place at Kohl and Middleton's West Side Museum, a dime museum founded in 1882 by C. E. Kohl and George Middleton. The following year, the two men opened the Clark Street Museum, which featured a one-hour vaudeville show. In 1884, Kohl and Middleton leased the Olympic Theatre and converted it into a vaudeville house, of which George Castle was the manager and booking agent. In 1895, Kohl and Middleton leased the Chicago Opera House, and three years later acquired the Haymarket Theatre. In 1900, Kohl bought out Middleton's interest in the partnership and formed a new one with George Castle. Kohl and Castle built the Majestic Theatre in 1906, acquired the Academy of Music in 1910 and the Star Theatre in 1911, and opened the Palace Music Hall in 1912. C. E. Kohl died in 1910, and the theatres were subsequently under the control of his widow, Caroline L. Kohl, until 1919, when they became part of the Orpheum circuit, of which Mrs. Kohl was a vice president and major stockholder.

(CLARENCE) KOLB (Cleveland, July 31, 1874—Hollywood, Ca., November 25, 1964) and **(MAX) DILL** (Cleveland, 1877—San Francisco, November 21, 1949)

Dutch-dialect, knockabout comedians Kolb and Dill were generally regarded as West Coast versions of Weber and Fields in that their shows usually originated out of San Francisco and the couple substituted for Weber and Fields in the 1901 touring production of *Fiddle-Dee-Dee*. Clarence Kolb and Max Dill met in their hometown of Cleveland while still children and entered vaudeville in 1906. Three years later, the pair were touring on the burlesque circuit. They first came to San Francisco with *Fiddle-Dee-Dee* and decided to make that their base. In 1904, they left San Francisco for a successful fourteen-month tour of Australia. Kolb and Dill made a few films together in the mid teens.

They split up in 1935, when Kolb decided to become a character actor on-screen; his credits include *His Girl Friday* (1940), *Hellzapoppin* (1941), *The Kid from Brooklyn* (1946), and *Adam's Rib* (1949). He was also active on television and a regular on *My Little Margie* (CBS and NBC, 1952–1955). Kolb and Dill reunited briefly in 1947 for *The High Cost of Living*, which played four weeks in San Francisco and a week in Los Angeles.

KOSTER AND BIAL'S MUSIC HALL

One of the first vaudeville theatres in New York, Koster and Bial's Music Hall was located at West 23rd Street and Sixth Avenue. It opened in 1870 as Bryant's Opera House, and from 1875 until 1879, when it was leased to Koster and Bial, it was used by various groups. John Koster and Adam Bial were brewers, who operated the establishment as much as a saloon as a theatre. They replaced the original stage with a platform, and in place of a curtain utilized a gigantic fan that parted in the middle and folded to each side of the stage. In 1896, after Koster and Bial had moved uptown, the 23rd Street Theatre was renamed the Bon Ton; it continued to present vaudeville until it was demolished in 1924.

KOSTER AND BIAL'S (NEW) MUSIC HALL

In 1892, Oscar Hammerstein built the Manhattan Opera House on 34th Street between Broadway and Seventh Avenue, on the site of what is now R. H. Macy's. When the theatre proved relatively unsuccessful, Hammerstein went into partnership with Koster and Bial, and on August 28, 1893, the Manhattan Opera House reopened as Koster and Bial's (New) Music Hall. The partnership was not a happy one, and the following spring, it was severed by Hammerstein. In large part because of its size, the operation was never a prosperous one, and in July 1901, the theatre closed. Motion picture history was made at Koster and Bial's (New) Music Hall on April 23, 1896, when the first films of Thomas Alva Edison were projected there under the name "Vitascope." Also on the same bill was the British music hall comedian-singer Albert Chevalier.

Fred Allen

James Barton

Nora Bayes

Kitty Doner

The Duncan Sisters

Jimmy Durante

Julian Eltinge

W. C. Fields

Trixie Friganza

Anna Held

Violet and Daisy Hilton

Elsie Janis

Harry Lauder

Eddie Leonard

Cissie Loftus

Moran and Mack

Bill Robinson

Lillian Russell

Savoy and Brennan

Singer's Midgets

Eva Tanguay

Señor Wences

Bert Williams

Ed Wynn

L

WILTON LACKAYE (Loudon County, Va., September 30, 1862—New York, August 22, 1932)

Wilton Lackaye was a major star of the legitimate stage who made his debut at New York's Star Theatre in *Francesca da Rimini* on August 27, 1883. Although primarily a romantic actor, Lackaye's greatest stage success was as Svengali in the original theatrical production of *Trilby*, which opened at the Garden Theatre, New York, on April 15, 1895. He frequently appeared on the vaudeville stage, touring in 1912, 1917, and 1918 in the playlet *Quits*, and in 1915 in the playlet *The Bomb*. He first appeared at the Palace in the summer of 1914. Lackaye appeared in three features in 1914 and 1915, including a 1915 version of *Trilby*, and in five feature films between 1921 and 1925.

BERT LAHR (New York, August 13, 1895—New York, December 4, 1967)

"His face appears to be composed of pouches, crevasses, and hummocks between two vast outcroppings of ear—a veritable terminal moraine of a face—and his pale blue eyes obviously mean a great deal to each other, since they are set close together," wrote Gilbert Millstein in a brilliant description of comic Bert Lahr. A major comedian of burlesque and vaudeville, Lahr went on to prove himself a more than capable character actor in films and on the legitimate stage. He never retired and always gave his all (and often a little too much more) to a performance. As early as September 8, 1922, *Variety* noted, "Lahr is a laugh-maker with the accent on the 'maker'. . . . Working single-handed, he mugs and gags and exhumes and originates until he reaches the point of exhaustion."

The son of German immigrants, Bert Lahr ignored the efforts of his German-born interior decorator father to persuade him to work hard in mundane tasks, and instead entered show business in 1910 as a member of a child act called The Seven Frolics. He might have sunk into obscurity had it not been for Billy K. Wells, who wrote sketches for the major Columbia Burlesque circuit, and who spotted Lahr's act in 1915 and hired him. After the First World War, Bert Lahr developed a vaudeville routine with his first wife, Mercedes Delpino, and the act of Lahr and Delpino prospered. In their most famous sketch, Lahr was a drunken cop trying to arrest hootchy-kootchy dancer Mercedes. The latter would ask, "Are you speaking to me?" To which Lahr would respond, "Yeah to you and (looking at her breasts) to you too." In 1939, Lahr and Delpino were divorced, and the comedian married Mildred Schroeder Robinson; one of the children from the first marriage is theatre critic and scholar John Lahr.

On November 28, 1927, Bert Lahr made his Broadway debut in *Harry Delmar's Revels*, but it was not until 1928 and *Hold Everything!* that Lahr established himself as a major musical comedy star. Interestingly, Lou Holtz claimed that Lahr was nothing as a single comedy act in burlesque and vaudeville, but once he was playing a scene, with the aid of a good scriptwriter, he was unbeatable. This is confirmed by Lahr, who once commented, "My kind of comedian is more like an actor. I'm just playing situations and characters." Certainly, from all accounts, Bert Lahr was not funny offstage, constantly worrying about his act and the future. "I am a sad man. A plumber doesn't go out without his tools. Does a comedian have to be funny on the street?" Lahr once asked.

Bert Lahr's fear of failure and determination always to entertain is vividly documented in his son's biography of him. In reviewing that book, Walter Kerr noted, "The throb outward was a quiver within. The bull bellowed and turned into a cowardly beastie. The Cowardly Lion in *The Wizard of Oz* was more than a piece of happy casting. Although *The Wizard of Oz* was never a very good film, it was not surprising that Lahr should have been its immediate hit, or that such children as now remember him will remember him just that way. He was just that way; it was a happy piece of what made him unhappy. A coward determined to be a lion was the sum of it."

The Wizard of Oz (1939) is the best known of Bert Lahr's films. He began his screen career in 1929 with a Warner Bros./Vitaphone short titled *Faint Heart*, in which he plays "a timid pajama designer who captures 'Dynamite Dan,' the tougher than tough criminal." Between 1931 and 1967, Lahr was featured in sixteen productions, including *Flying High* (1931), *DuBarry Was a Lady* (1939), *Ship Ahoy* (1942), and *Rose Marie* (1954).

Thanks to *Hold Everything!*, Lahr was booked to headline at the Palace in April and October 1931. It also led to many other Broadway shows, including *Flying High* (1930), *Hot-Cha!* (1932), *Life Begins at 8:40* (1934), *George White's Scandals* (1935), *The Show Is On* (1936), *DuBarry Was a Lady* (1939), *Seven Lively Arts* (1944), *Burlesque* (1946 revival), *Two on the Aisle* (1951), *The Beauty Part* (1962), and *Foxy* (1964). Reviewing Lahr's nineteen costume changes and characters in *Seven Lively Arts*, *Time* (October 1, 1951), wrote, "It is a wonderful demonstration of the art of a vanishing breed—that noisy band of U.S. comedians who were blooded in the dingy halls of burlesque, rose to astrakhan-collared eminence on the Keith-Orpheum circuits, and reached their fullest flower on Broadway in the days of Ziegfeld, prohibition and the Big Bull Market."

In 1956, Bert Lahr played Estragon in Samuel Beckett's *Waiting for Godot*, which introduced him to a new audience that may have been totally unaware of his early years in burlesque and vaudeville. The comedian's performance in *Waiting for Godot* proved the truth of Brooks Atkinson's remark that "on many occasions he proved that he was not merely a hired fool but a gifted actor."

Bert Lahr died during the shooting of *The Night They Raided Minsky's*, a film that pays generous and warm tribute to burlesque. He had not filmed enough footage to make the film a fitting tribute to his art and craft, but enough of Lahr's performance remains for the production to provide us with a glimpse of the comedian who helped make burlesque great.

BIBLIOGRAPHY

"Bert Lahr." *Current Biography*, January 1952, pp. 324–26.

"Bert Lahr." *The New Yorker*, December 16, 1967, p. 37.

"Bert Lahr and the Wit Business." *Newsweek*, April 22, 1957, p. 69.

Green, Stanley. "Bert Lahr." In *The Great Clowns of Broadway*. New York: Oxford University Press, 1984, pp. 102–27.

Kerr, Walter. "Close to the Dark Heart of Comedy." *Saturday Review*, November 15, 1969, pp. 31–33.

Lahr, Bert. "The Art of Telling a Joke." *Pageant*, February 1945, pp. 139–41.

Lahr, John. *Notes on a Cowardly Lion*. New York: Alfred A. Knopf, 1969.

Millstein, Gilbert. "A Comic Discourses on Comedy." *The New York Times Magazine*, March 31, 1957, pp. 27, 62.

Morton, Frederic. "Bert Lahr: Clown." *Holiday*, March 1958, pp. 123, 125–26, 128.

Perelman, S. J. "LAHRge World." *Theatre Arts* 47, no. 2 (February 1963), pp. 20–21.

"Pisthetairosin Ypsi." *Newsweek*, July 11, 1968, p. 85.

"$6.60 Comedian." *Time*, October 1, 1951, pp. 46–48, 51–52.

"Talk with a Star." *Newsweek*, November 16, 1959, p. 108.

Whitman, Alden. "Bert Lahr, Comic Actor, Dies." *The New York Times*, December 5, 1967, pp. 1, 51.

Zolotow, Maurice. "Broadway's Saddest Clown." *Saturday Evening Post*, May 31, 1952, pp. 34, 81–84.

BESSIE LAMB (circa 1878—Cincinnati, October 30, 1907)

Noted for both her singing and mimicry, Bessie Lamb is often credited with having introduced ragtime music to vaudeville.

PROFESSOR (MICHAEL) LAMBERTI (1891—Hollywood, Ca., March 13, 1950)

Professor Lamberti was one of vaudeville's great comic musicians. While he was playing the xylophone onstage, unbeknown to him, a woman would appear and begin performing a striptease. As the audience's response to the stripper became more enthusiastic, Lamberti would play with greater energy, and, believing the audience's applause was for him, he would perform successive encores. At the close, Lamberti would become aware of the stripper and chase her offstage, spraying her with a seltzer bottle. Lamberti was a far better musician than his act might suggest; he had trained as a classical musician and played with the Cleveland Symphony Orchestra. Producer Mike Todd featured Lamberti in his 1942 Broadway revue *Star and Garter*, and Lamberti also performed his act on film in 1943 in *Tonight and Every Night*, with Rita Hayworth playing the stripper. Lamberti also appeared in the 1947 feature film *Linda Be Good*.

HARRY LANGDON (Council Bluffs, Ia., June 15, 1884—Los Angeles, December 8, 1944)

A legendary silent film comedian noted for his innocent and naive, baby-face characterizations, Harry Langdon made his stage debut in an amateur night program in Council Bluffs, Iowa, in 1896. Subsequently, he worked in various medicine shows and also performed as a circus clown and tumbler. He entered vaudeville in 1899, initially with another young man, specializing in a chair-balancing act. In 1903, he met and married Rose Frances Mensolf, and with her developed a vaudeville routine titled "Johnny's New Car." The couple would appear to be driving a breakaway car, parts of which would collapse in sequence as Langdon (playing the meek and hen-pecked husband) would try ongoing repairs.

It was while headlining with this routine at the Orpheum Theatre, Los Angeles, in March 1923 that Langdon was invited to put his act on film by producer Sol Lesser. Mack Sennett saw the film and signed Langdon to a contract, with the comedian's first Sennett production being *Picking Peaches* (1924). In 1926, Langdon starred in two feature films now considered classics, *Tramp, Tramp, Tramp* and *The Strong Man*. He was to continue to make films until his death, but his ego undermined the quality of his productions in the late 1920s, and he failed to maintain a position of prominence in the industry.

BIBLIOGRAPHY

Langdon, Harry. "The Serious Side of Comedy Making." *Theatre*, 46, no. 12 (December 1927), pp. 22, 78.

Rheuban, Joyce. *Harry Langdon: The Comedian as Metteur-en-Scène*. Rutherford, N.J.: Fairleigh Dickinson University Press, 1983.

Schelly, William. *Harry Langdon*. Metuchen, N.J.: Scarecrow Press, 1982.

LILLIE LANGTRY (Jersey, Channel Islands, October 13, 1853—Monte Carlo, February 12, 1929)

"Vaudeville," wrote critic Acton Davies in 1905, was "a place where a great many bad actors go before they die. A good variety show is one of the finest tonics in the world, but vaudeville when for the most part it consists of fallen stars in mediocre wishy washy one-act plays is one of the finest producers of mental dyspepsia that I know of." It might well seem that Davies's remarks applied to Lillie Langtry who was, by all accounts, not a great actress, relying more on her fame, or infamy, as the mistress of King Edward VII when he was Prince of Wales than on histrionic ability. And she did embark on a vaudeville career after just about exhausting the possibilities held for her by the legitimate stage. Yet Langtry, by the sheer magnetism of her personality, completely overwhelmed critics and public alike. William Winter wrote in *The Wallet of Time* (Moffat, 1913), "While victory for Mrs. Langtry was at first gained by the beauty of the woman, it was soon ratified by the achievement of the actress."

Born Emilie Charlotte Le Breton, the daughter of a dean, on the largest of the Channel Islands, situated midway between Britain and France, the actress married Edward Langtry in 1874. He died in 1897, and two years later, she became the wife of Sir Hugo de Bathe. Langtry made her first London stage appearance at the Theatre Royal, Haymarket, on December 15, 1881, in the role of Miss Harcastle in *She Stoops to Conquer*; "it was a great social event," reported one observer. She made her American debut as Hester Grazebrook in *The Unequal Match* at Wallack's Theatre, New York, on November 6, 1882. It was the distinguished manager H. B. Marinelli who persuaded Langtry to make her vaudeville debut at the Fifth Avenue Theatre, New York, in October 1906. The vehicle was a playlet titled *Between the Nightfall and the Light* by Graham Hill, in which she was supported by Arthur Holmes-Gore and Hubert Carter. "Rush" in *Variety* (October 6, 1906) thought that Langtry was "a finished artist," but found that although she "moved gracefully through the playlet," she "hardly reached the requirements of the strongly emotional scenes."

In 1912, Lillie Langtry toured the English music halls in a twenty-two-minute comedy sketch titled "Helping the Cause," which she brought to the New York Hippodrome in October of the same year. "Mrs. Langtry is sixty-three years old according to report. She's a wonder and didn't even begin to look old alongside the Doctor who appeared about twenty-two," wrote "Dash" in *Variety* (October 4, 1912).

In 1915, Langtry toured the United States and Canada for twenty-six weeks in a one-act playlet titled *Ashes*. Her leading man was Alfred Lunt, then unknown, and he wrote of the experience in the December 26, 1936, issue of *The Billboard*:

I played the role of the man with whom Mrs. Langtry was in love. Inasmuch as Mrs. Langtry, at that time, was 63 and I was 21, audiences were inclined to be somewhat bewildered. Usually they began by thinking that I was her son, so it must have seemed a little odd to them when I suddenly began to make violent love to her. But they were really very nice about it all. . . .

I remember one week in Winnipeg when Lady de Bathe . . . shared honors with Fink's Mules. Mrs. Langtry thought the combination entirely irreconcilable. She told the booking office so in notes that probably should have been written on asbestos rather than hotel stationery. I never could understand why. The mules, it seemed to me, were unusually talented. They behaved admirably about the whole business. They made no objection at all to her sharing their billing.

Following the closure of *Ashes* in Richmond, Virginia, Langtry embarked on a new vaudeville tour, for which her leading man was Lionel Atwill. E. F. Albee's booker Edward Darling had some misgivings about the tour, but Langtry completely disarmed him with her charm, and later Darling commented that he would have paid her $2,500 a week had she been one of the Cherry Sisters.

Leading man Atwill did not fare so well; he almost lost his job for refusing to take care of Langtry's luggage.

Langtry was not kindly disposed to all of the theatre managers with whom she had to deal. When one asked her what she did, she replied, "I ride a bicycle on a tightrope." "Aren't you afraid?" he asked. "Oh no," came the reply, "I have fallen so many times."

The dramatic sketch was fast disappearing from the vaudeville stage by 1919, and by that year, Langtry's career had also ended. "The Jersey Lillie," as she had come to be known, retired with her reputation, at least on the stage, relatively intact.

BIBLIOGRAPHY

Bell, Archie. "Mrs. Langtry's Own Story." *The Green Book Magazine* 9, no. 3 (March 1913), pp. 419–27.

Birkett, Jeremy and John Richardson. *Lillie Langtry: Her Life in Words and Pictures.* Poole, England: Blandford Press, 1979.

Brough, James. *The Prince and the Lily.* New York: Coward, McCann & Geoghegan, 1975.

Dudley, Ernest. *The Gilded Lily: The Life and Loves of the Fabulous Little Langtry.* London: Odhams Press, 1958.

Gerson, Noel B. *Because I Loved Him: The Life and Loves of Lillie Langtry.* New York: William Morrow, 1971.

Langtry, Lillie. *The Days I Knew.* New York: Doran, 1925. [reprinted New York: AMS Press, 1982]

Sichel, Pierre. *The Jersey Lily: The Story of the Fabulous Mrs. Langtry.* Englewood Cliffs, N.J.: Prentice-Hall, 1958.

GRACE La RUE (Kansas City, Mo., 1882—San Francisco, March 12, 1956)

Grace La Rue was a dancer and singer of the prima donna variety in musical comedy and vaudeville who was a frequent object of parody. She entered show business at the age of twelve with a tent show in Kansas City; two years later, she joined with Josie Collins in a singing and dancing sister act, and at the age of fifteen arrived in New York, where she appeared in a burlesque show titled *Parisan Widows*. From that, she graduated to vaudeville, working with her first husband, Charles Burke. Grace La Rue's first big break came in 1906, when she was signed for a featured part in the musical comedy *The Tourists*. She appeared in the 1907, and first, edition of the Ziegfeld *Follies*, singing "Miss Ginger from Jamaica," and was also in the 1908 edition.

After costarring with Sam Bernard in a 1908 tour of the musical farce *Nearly a Hero*, La Rue appeared in *Molly May* (1910), *The Troubadour* (1910), and *Betsy* (1911), and also made a number of trips to Europe. Her big-time vaudeville debut as a single (with three supporting players) was in a fifteen-minute sketch, "The Record Breaker," by Hassard Short at Poli's Theatre in Springfield, Massachusetts, in November 1912. As part of the sketch, she sang an aria from *Madame Butterfly* and a duet with a phonograph recording by Caruso. *Variety*

(November 29, 1912) thought it gave La Rue "opportunity to display her Parisian cultivated voice, and her few nimble steps."

Grace La Rue was a hit on her debut at the Palace in 1913, when she sang "You Made Me Love You." Her singing was above reproach, but her dancing sometimes seemed uninspired; *The New York Dramatic Mirror* (September 23, 1914) described her as "a lively dancer, but of almost chorus-like personality." Of vaudeville, the entertainer recalled:

"Vaudeville was quite different from the variety in which I had worked with Charles; the salaries were far greater than any we had known, and most of the acts, even the headliners, were unknown to me. The clause in the contract whereby I was to be the sole headliner on the bill contributed to my peace of mind, however. Often there were other acts on the same bill which received more salary than I did (one of the things I was to learn about vaudeville was that the headliner is not always the highest paid), but by being the headliner, I was assured of the star dressing-room, of the best position on the program, and of first consideration from the stage-manager, house-manager, pressmen, and even from the stage hands. All of this was worth more than money to me."

Grace La Rue remained active through the 1930s. She appeared on Broadway in *Dear Me* (1921), the 1928 edition of *The Greenwich Village Follies*, and *Stepping Out* (1929). In the 1922 edition of the *Music Box Revue*, her costumes literally enveloped the stage. As Thaïs, she mounted the steps slowly until the entire stage was covered with her train; while singing "Crinoline Days," her hoop skirt got wider and wider as she rose slowly on an elevator until, yet again, it covered the stage. Grace La Rue still had time for vaudeville, headlining at the Palace in January and October 1924 and August 1927. She also worked with her third husband, actor Hale Hamilton.

BIBLIOGRAPHY

La Rue, Grace. "My Vaudeville Years." In *Selected Vaudeville Criticism*, ed. Anthony Slide. Metuchen, N.J.: Scarecrow Press, 1988, pp. 254–301.

"The Singing of a Song." *The New York Dramatic Mirror*, December 16, 1914, p. 18.

JESSE L. LASKY (San Francisco, September 13, 1880–Beverly Hills, Ca., January 13, 1958)

A motion picture pioneer and movie mogul, Jessey L. Lasky began his career in vaudeville as both a performer and a producer. As a child, he had learned to play the cornet, and he performed in the San Jose High School Orchestra before playing professionally in a San Francisco theatre. In 1900, he was lured by the Alaskan gold rush, but instead of finding gold found himself playing the cornet in a bar. On his return to San Francisco, Lasky teamed up with his sister Blanche as duo-cornetists and quick-change artists, and in this capacity, they were hired for a 1902 vaudeville tour by the magician Herrmann the Great. Lasky expanded his act, and it became Lasky's Military Octet; in 1903, he sold half-ownership in the group to B. A. Rolfe, a fellow cornetist. From 1903 through 1911, Lasky and Rolfe worked together managing and producing vaudeville acts. With his sister Blanche, he organized one-act musical comedies, complete with casts, costumes. songs, and scenery, and they were presented on the vaudeville circuits in much the same manner as would be tab shows a few years later. Blanche recalled:

"At that time it was very unusual for a vaudeville act to carry its own scenery. That was what we did with our act—designed a special set for it and carried it with us. We did the same thing with every act we staged, and it paid."

In 1911, Lasky invested his savings in a new form of entertainment, a cabaret, which was called the Folies Bergere and housed at New York's Fulton Theatre. "We brought the word 'cabaret' to America," claimed Lasky. The star of the show was Olga Petrova, who was not a success, and neither was the Folies Bergere. Despite considerable losses, Lasky continued as a producer, presenting the operetta *California* in 1912, and early in 1914 presenting the revue "Jesse Lasky's Redheads" at the Palace.

In 1913, Lasky organized the Jesse L. Lasky Feature Play Company and produced *The Squaw Man* (1914), directed by Cecil B. DeMille and Oscar Apfel, which was the first major feature film to be made in Hollywood. In 1916, Lasky's company was merged with Famous Players, and together the two became known as Paramount. Lasky remained as production head of Paramount until 1932, when he resigned and became an independent producer, initially for William Fox. He originated the radio show *Gateway to Hollywood* (CBS, 1938–1940).

BIBLIOGRAPHY

Cary, Augusta. "An Interview with Miss Blanche Lasky." *Photoplay* 7, no. 1 (December 1914), pp. 139–40.
"Jesse L. Lasky." *Current Biography*, April 1947, pp. 374–75.
Lasky, Jesse L. "Vaudeville Production." *The New York Dramatic Mirror*, January 30, 1909, p. 10.
————, with Don Weldon. *I Blow My Own Horn*. Garden City, N.Y.: Doubleday, 1957.

ALFRED LATELL

Alfred Latell was one of the more curious acts in vaudeville's early years. He specialized in the impersonation of animals, not only dressing in various guises but also providing the appropriate noises. He began his career in 1902, and by 1909 had gained considerable notoriety for his impersonations of monkeys, billy goats, bears, and dogs. It was the last animal that Latell found the most difficult to imitate, for as he explained in an article in *The New York Dramatic Mirror*, "To play the part of a dog and not to buffoon him, one is obliged to make a close study of his every action. The dog is so close to mankind that he is known more intimately than any other of the domestic beasts, with the exception possibly of the horse. . . . The cat is a difficult animal to impersonate, though not so much so as the dog, because of the fact of its slower movements. I have gone out at night with my cat suit on and have sat for hours watching the smaller back yard cats as they stalked along the fence or sat watching the moon rise o'er some neighboring buildings." Latell was a slave to his career, creating a joint for his hind leg, enabling him to move as a dog, and a tube for his mouth, permitting him to lap up milk. With the aid of a string, he could raise the fur on the back of his cat suit in impersonation of the real thing.

He also impersonated birds, including parrots and ostriches: "The parrot was one of my first bird impersonations, and I found it one of the most difficult of all, because of its crouching posture and the consequent tendency to fall over while walking. There are nine strings which have to be operated in working the head, bill and wings, and the work is laborious in every sense of the word."
BIBLIOGRAPHY
"The Art of Animal Acting." *The New York Dramatic Mirror*, May 1, 1909, p. 25.

HARRY LAUDER (Edinburgh, Scotland, August 4, 1870—Lanarkshire, Scotland, February 26, 1950)

Harry Lauder's songs are as well known and as much a part of Scottish popular culture as when he sang them seventy years or more ago. Also recognized on a worldwide basis are such Harry Lauder melodies as "I Love a Lassie," "She Is Ma Daisy," "Stop Yer Tickling, Jock," "Just a Wee Deoch-an'-Doris," "Roamin' in the Gloamin'," "She Is My Rose," and "The End of the Road." Listeners may not know what a "deoch-an'-doris" is but it makes (and made) little difference. Curiously, while the songs may remain popular, Harry Lauder's appeal is difficult to comprehend. Viewing him on film today, one is aware only of a small, grouchy-looking Scotsman putting a lot of energy but little personality into his songs and telling jokes that must have been old when he first used them. That estimation is to some extent backed up by *Variety*, which, reviewing his act at the Garrick Theatre, Chicago, in February 1930, noted that he was still a great entertainer for the Scots "but today a little slow for the young folks."

As Joe Laurie, Jr., explained it, Lauder took Scottish wisdom and humor, threw in a few songs and homemade jokes, and combined it all with a good clean monolog. Lauder worked in a flax mill and a coal mine before making his first public appearance in Arbroath, Scotland, on August 24, 1882. After years of touring in both professional and amateur engagements, he made his London debut at Gatti's Westminster Music Hall on March 19, 1900, singing, with great success, "Tobermory," "Callahan—Call Again," and "The Lass of Killiecrankie." He soon became one of the most popular and highest paid British music hall artists, touring the United Kingdom, as well as South Africa and Australia.

Harry Lauder became an international star in 1907 when he made his initial American appearance. Audiences simply would not let him leave the stage; at his first New York appearance at the New York Theatre, he was held by the audience for more than an hour. After that, Joe Laurie, Jr., wrote in *Variety* (March 1, 1950), "He remained all through the years as one of the greatest, if not the greatest, one-man show that graced our shores and theatres." William Morris, at that time with Klaw and Erlanger, handled that first and all subsequent American engagements by Lauder until his twenty-fifth, and last, tour of the

United States in 1934. The entertainer was extraordinarily loyal to Morris and to others with whom he worked. Martin Wagner was always the company manager, and Jack Lait was always the publicist.

Just as Lauder was always loyal to those who helped him, audiences were loyal to Lauder. In 1911, he was booked into the Manhattan Opera House (the first vaudevillian to play there), but because of fog and quarantine problems, he did not reach the theatre on opening night until 12:45 A.M. The audience had waited patiently for him since 8:15 P.M. and Lauder's opening remark was, "Ha' ye no hame to go to?"

A typical Lauder vaudeville stage appearance would last for an hour and fifteen minutes. When he appeared at New York's Lincoln Theatre in 1908, audiences refused again to let him leave the stage, becoming unruly in their demands of "Give us another song, Harry." He sang everything from a drunken toastmaster's wedding song, "The Wedding Bells were Ringing," to "Rocked in the Cradle of the Deep." "It is impossible to catch and analyze the peculiarly elusive charm of this great artist," wrote *Variety*. "It is a thing so subtle and indefinable it has not a name, and yet it exerts a force that cannot be escaped. . . . His every word and gesture gives a line or faithful touch of color to the picture he seeks to draw, and the whole is a vivid, forceful characterization."

During the First World War, Harry Lauder was tireless in entertaining the troops, for which he was knighted in 1919. Winston Churchill said of him, "By his songs and valiant life he rendered measureless service to the Scottish race and to the British Empire." Lauder also appeared in the United States selling Liberty Bonds. A reputation for stinginess was, apparently, without foundation, for Lauder was in reality generous, even returning $3,000 of his usual $5,000 weekly salary to William Morris for performances he had missed. His only foible was that he would never play a Sunday performance, maintaining that, like him, his audience was deeply religious. Harry Lauder's philosophy was basically to be honest, to pay one's debts, to work hard, and to save. He never strayed from those simple beliefs.

After the death of his son, Captain John Lauder, on the battlefront, Lauder returned to New York in December 1918, opening at the Lexington Theatre. There were tears in his eyes as he sang his son's favorite song, "Wee Hoose 'mang the Heather," and the keynote of this performance was a plea titled "Victory with Mercy," in which he asked, "Don't let us sing anymore about war; just let us sing of love." Lauder made a similar tour in 1928 after the death the previous year of his wife, Nancy. Beginning January 30, 1928, he played four weeks at New York's Knickerbocker Theatre. He sang all the old favorites, including the morale-boosting "The End of the Road." "Monday night, to a sold-out theatre, he was the rollicking comic, the comedian extraordinary," wrote *Variety* (February 1, 1928). "The Pagliacci in the flesh. He made them laugh; he wrung them dry after he had doused them with laughter. Then he drenched them again—with tears. A few well-chosen words, no reference by name or direct implication to his loss, and a song of courage—and he had a thousand people weeping.''

Harry Lauder made his first phonograph recording, ''To Jericho,'' in London in February 1902, and his last, ''Always Take Care of Your Pennies'' and ''It's a' Roon th' Toon'' in London in May 1933. (Some later recordings were made but not issued.) He made his first film, an experimental talkie for the British Gaumont Company, in 1904. It was titled *Inverary*. Among his feature films are *Huntingtower* (1928), *I Love a Lassie* (1932), and *End of the Road* (1936). In 1914, he made fourteen experimental sound-on-disc films for Cort-Kitsee Talking Pictures and the Selig Polyscope Company. While Lauder never played the Palace, curiously, these early films of his did. Each featured Lauder singing one of his best known songs, but, sadly, none are known to survive. Harry Lauder took credit as coauthor of virtually all the songs he performed, but as to whether he actually composed these numbers or whether his ego as performer required such credit remains unknown.

Lauder's last radio broadcast was for the BBC on Christmas Day, 1942. Officially, he retired in 1949 at the age of seventy-eight. ''Retirement is a word I've simply been far too busy to use, a word that I've avoided,'' he commented. ''I've worked hard all my life and enjoyed every minute of it. Still, I suppose a man can't go on forever, although I'd be perfectly willing to. I daresay it's time I took a breather.'' At the time of his death, *The Los Angeles Times* published an editorial tribute:

To a generation which never heard him, Harry Lauder was no more than a tradition. To their oldsters, however, Harry Lauder was the grandest of entertainers, a minstrel with a personality that won audiences wherever he appeared. There was nobody like him; nor is another such likely to appear soon.

BIBLIOGRAPHY

Baker, Darrell and Larry F. Kiner. *The Sir Harry Lauder Discography*. Metuchen, N.J.: Scarecrow Press, 1990.

Gordon, Irving. *Great Scot!: The Life Story of Sir Harry Lauder*. London: Leslie Frewin, 1968.

''Harry Lauder Used to Mine Coal, and Could Do It Now.'' *Literary Digest*, January 10, 1920, pp. 66–68.

''King of the Vaudeville Stage: Harry Lauder.'' *Current Literature*, January 1909, pp. 84–86.

Lauder, Harry. *Harry Lauder at Home and on Tour*. London: Greening, 1907.

_____. *My American Travels*. London: Newnes, 1910.

_____. *Harry Lauder's Logic*. London: Palmer & Hayward, 1917.

_____. *A Minstrel in France*. New York: Hearst's International Library Company, 1918.

_____. *Between You and Me*. New York: James A. McCann, 1919.

_____. *Roamin' in the Gloamin'*. Philadelphia: J. B. Lippincott, 1928.

_____. *My Best Scotch Stories*. London: Dundee & Valentine, 1929.

_____. *Wee Drappies*. New York: Robert McBride, 1932.

_____. *Ticklin' Tales*. London: D. C. Thomson, 1934.

Malvern, Gladys. *Valiant Minstrel: The Story of Sir Harry Lauder*. New York: Julian Messner, 1943.

Wallace, William. *Harry Lauder in the Limelight*. Lewes, England: The Book Guild, 1988.

JOE LAURIE, JR. (New York, 1892—New York, April 29, 1954)

Joe Laurie, Jr.'s, vaudeville career as a comedian was a lengthy one, but it was relatively unimportant—"Laurie has been a standard comic for years" commented *Variety* in 1931—and if the entertainer has a place in the history books, it is more as the first vaudevillian to attempt to document the history of his profession, in *Vaudeville: From the Honky-Tonks to the Palace* (Henry Holt, 1953). The volume is a primary reference source as an anecdotal history of the medium, but written, as it obviously was, without recourse to contemporary printed sources, it is annoyingly lacking in dates, and the names of many vaudeville acts are given as Laurie remembered them, rather than as they are spelled in contemporary trade papers.

His first professional appearance—in the early teens—was in partnership with Aleen Bronson, whom he married, and with whom he worked in a double act until at least 1917. In 1919, he played the Palace for the first time in a sketch "Whatika," described as a New York version of the phrase "What do I care?" "It is a good act, as Laurie puts it out, and, in fact, it could hardly be done by any one else," commented *The New York Dramatic Mirror* (October 23, 1919). "In the first place, Laurie is one of the most likable chaps on the vaudeville stage, and he invites the entire audience to visit him at his home, and then introduces them to his father and mother, and makes everyone feel comfortable and top hole by his sheer good spirits."

By 1922, Laurie was divorced, and he married Nellie Butcher (who was professionally known as June Tempest and who had worked in vaudeville with Harry Carroll). She did not join his act, and Laurie continued as a solo monologist. On Broadway, he appeared in *Over the Top* (1918), *Plain Jane* (1924), *If I Was Rich* (1926), *Weather Clear, Track Fast* (1927), and *Swing Your Lady* (1936). He claimed to have played the Palace more than twenty times, but in all probability his appearances were no more than a handful, including January 1927, March 1928, and May 1932.

For more than twenty years, the entertainer contributed a "Letters to Lefty" column to *Variety*. He also was involved in writing for the screen and for his fellow vaudevillians. Billed as "the pint-size comedian," Joe Laurie, Jr., overflowed with energy and an enthusiasm for his profession. From 1950 to 1951, he was one of the four regular panelists on the ABC television series *Can You Top This?* He was much in demand as an after-dinner speaker, and with Abel Green wrote *Show Biz: From Vaude to Video* (Henry Holt, 1951). In his will, Joe Laurie, Jr., asked that his ashes be thrown in the fireplace of the New York Lambs Club "on some winter's night when the fire is roaring" or "put in a rosin box at the Palace Theater . . . if they still have vaudeville there" or strewn around 44th Street in front of the Lambs Club. The instructions smack somewhat of self-importance, and, unfortunately, that is an image created on the printed page by Joe Laurie, Jr., and his colleague at *Variety*, Abel Green.

BIBLIOGRAPHY

Green. "Little Joe Laurie, Giant of Show Biz, Theatre's Historian, Makes Final Bow." *Variety*, May 5, 1954, pp. 2, 16.

"Joe Laurie, Jr. Dies at 61." *Daily Variety*, April 3, 1954, pp. 1, 4.

"Laurie's Will a Saga of His Great Heart." *Daily Variety*, May 7, 1954, pp. 1, 5.

GYPSY ROSE LEE (Seattle, Wa., January 9, 1914—Los Angeles, April 26, 1970)

Gypsy Rose Lee is probably the best known stripper in the history of American entertainment. At the same time, she was also a personality of intelligence and grace. She came to fame as a star of striptease, but she transformed that medium of entertainment into an art form. As she told columnist Walter Winchell, "It isn't that I shed my clothes, it's the way I do it. I've made it a rule never to be objectionable—just objective."

Born Rose Louise Hovick, Gypsy Rose Lee entered vaudeville at the age of thirteen, appearing under the guidance of her domineering mother in an act with her sister, Baby June (who later gained fame as actress June Havoc). The act was first called "Daisy Jane and Her Newsboy Songsters," but when June eloped and left the act, the name was changed to "Rose Louise and Her Newsboy Songsters." Glamour was added to the act, and a further name change took place, to "Rose Louise and Her Hollywood Blondes." At the age of fifteen, Lee decided to try her luck in burlesque, and two years later, she was working for the Minsky Brothers as a headliner.

In 1936, she was featured in the new edition of the *Ziegfeld Follies*. Writing in the *New York Post* (September 15, 1936), John Mason Brown commented, "Gypsy Rose Lee is at once the Bernhardt, the Duse and the Joan Crawford of Strip-Tease girls. . . . She has beauty and manner, a walk of which both goddesses and peacocks should be envious, and a philanthropic spirit." Three years later, Lee was the headline attraction at the New York World's Fair.

From being merely a stripper, Gypsy Rose Lee became the darling of the intellectuals in the 1940s. In 1942, she published her first novel, a mystery titled *The G-String Murders* (Simon & Schuster), which became the basis for the film *Lady of Burlesque*. A second novel (also from Simon & Schuster), *Mother Finds a Body*, followed the next year. Mike Todd starred her in his 1942 production of *Star and Garter*, and in 1943, *The Naked Genius*, a play written by Lee, was produced. At the same time, Gypsy Rose Lee never ceased to practice her "art." In May 1949, she began a six-month tour with the world's largest carnival, the Royal American Shows, at a reported salary of $10,000 a week.

In the 1950s, Gypsy Rose Lee became a television personality. In 1950, she was moderator of the quiz program *Think Fast* on ABC, and was also featured on a number of local programs. She costarred with Phyllis Diller on *The Pruitts of Southampton* (ABC, 1966 to 1967). In 1957, Lee published her memoirs, *Gypsy*, which became the basis for the 1959 Jule Styne musical, which starred Ethel Merman (as Gypsy's mother) on Broadway and Rosalind Russell in the 1962 movie version. Gypsy Rose Lee appeared in a number of films, including *Ali Baba Goes to Town* (1937), *My Lucky Star* (1938), *Wind across the Everglades* (1958), *The Stripper* (1963), and *The Trouble with Angels* (1966), but because of her reputation as a stripper, she had to appear in her 1930s films under the name Louise Hovick.

Gypsy Rose Lee never retired. Only days before her death, in April 1970, she appeared with Lily St. Cyr, Ann Corio, and others at Cincinnati's Shubert Theatre in a tribute to the city's Gayety Burlesk, which had just closed.

BIBLIOGRAPHY

Alverson, Charles E. " 'Take It Off' to 'Keep Them Talking.' " *TV Guide*, December 11, 1965, pp. 14–16.

"Gypsy." *Newsweek*, May 11, 1970, p. 44.

"Gypsy Joins the Carny." *Life*, June 6, 1949, pp. 141–45.

"Gypsy Rose Lee." *Current Biography*, December 1943, pp. 434–36.

"Gypsy Rose Lee: Dowager." *Look*, February 22, 1966, pp. 56–64.

Herndon, Booton. "Gypsy Rose Lee's New Role." *The American Weekly*, May 23, 1948, p. 4.

"Hovick-Kirkland." *Life*, September 14, 1942, pp. 41–42, 44.

Lee, Gypsy Rose. "I Was With It." *Flair*, July 1950, pp. 72–86.

———. *Gypsy: A Memoir*. New York: Harper, 1957.

McLain, Louis. "The Lady behind the Gypsy." *The American Weekly*, January 17, 1960, pp. 14–15.

McNeil, Donald G., Jr. "Gypsy Rose Lee's Love Child, Now 39, Bares His Soul in a Book about Their Lives." *People*, October 8, 1984, unpaged.

P.M. "TV Guest Star." *Cue*, October 14, 1950, pp. 15, 30.

Preminger, Erik Lee. *Gypsy and Me: At Home and on the Road with Gypsy Rose Lee*. Boston: Little, Brown, 1984.

Wilson, Elizabeth. "Triumphs with Torso and Typewriter." *Liberty*, March 24, 1945, pp. 30–31, 60–61, 73.

JANE LEE (Glasgow, Scotland, 1912—New York, March 17, 1957) and **KATHERINE LEE** (1909–   )

Jane and Katherine Lee were child actresses who first came to prominence in 1914 when they successfully supported Annette Kellermann in the film *Neptune's Daughter*. They were cute and winsome, and movie audiences liked them in films such as *Soul of Broadway* (1915) and *Swat the Spy* (1918). Between 1914 and 1919, the sisters were featured in a number of popular films, chiefly for the William Fox Company, and *Photoplay* (May 1916) went so far as to describe Jane as "one of the really great personalities of the screen."

It was natural that the girls should try vaudeville, which they did very successfully in the spring of 1920. They appeared in a skit written by Tommy Gray, set in a movie studio, which had them exchanging comic patter, impersonating a couple of old maids, and engaging in a little tragedy as Jane cried beside the bed of a dying Katherine. "The act was a riot at the Riverside [Theatre] Monday night, stopping the show cold for three or four minutes," reported *Variety* (April 2, 1920). "It's ready for the biggest and best of the big-time houses and should clean up everywhere."

In the 1920s, Jane and Katherine Lee toured in a version of the Duncan Sisters's *Topsy and Eva* and also played presentation houses. They returned to New York vaudeville in May 1926 with a fifteen-minute act at Loew's State, which proved their continued appeal despite advancing years. The sisters engaged in comic dialogue and then sat on the stage with their feet in the footlights and sang "Tie Me to Your Apron Strings Again" and "When It's Onion Time in Bermuda." As *Variety* (May 26, 1926) reported, "The result was the girls winning the hit of the show."

In June 1932, the sisters headlined at the Palace, and they were also seen on Broadway in *The Laugh Parade* (1931) and *The Dance of Death* (1932). They split up in 1932, and Jane soloed in the Fanchon and Marco touring version of *Whoopee!* A year later, they were reunited for a return to vaudeville at the RKO Theatre in Patterson, New Jersey, on November 21, 1933.

Jane and Katherine Lee would appear to have retired in the mid 1930s. At the time of Jane's death, it was believed that Katherine was still alive. There is a strong suspicion that the two may not have been sisters or even blood relatives, but two girls teamed as a sister act by Jane's ambitious mother.

RUFUS LeMAIRE
(Fort Worth, Tx., 1895—Los Angeles, December 2, 1950)

A minor entrepreneur and booker in vaudeville, Rufus LeMaire began his career in New York as an office boy in 1913. Later, he worked for the Shubert Brothers and was responsible for booking the acts for the Sunday night concerts at the Winter Garden Theatre. In the 1920s, he produced a touring show titled *LeMaire's Affairs*, featuring a number of vaudeville headliners. He came to Hollywood in 1929 as a casting director for Columbia Pictures, and soon gained a reputation for switching jobs. Damon Runyan wrote, "Why, Rufus has had as many as five jobs at five different studios just between suns. He quit three of them when superiors said boo to him and resigned the other two because he was displeased by the way the president and first vice president combed their hair. Rufus really used to be hard to please in the matter of bosses. . . . He brought 187 new people to Hollywood in his first 18 months there. . . . Oh yes, he also found time to manage George Arliss and got the old gentleman more money in pictures than he ever dreamed of."

The family name was Goldstick, and the name LeMaire was first adopted by Rufus's brother George, who was considered one of the greatest straight men in vaudeville. His act was called Conroy and LeMaire, and George LeMaire also worked as a straight man with Eddie Cantor and Joe Phillips.

BIBLIOGRAPHY
"Closed Season on Player and Pheasant: Interview with Rufus LeMaire." *Commentator*
    1, no. 5 (June 22, 1935), p. 2.
Runyon, Damon. "The Brighter Side: That Man of Many Jobs." Syndicated column,
    September 12, 1944.

DAN LENO (London, December 20, 1860—London, October 31, 1904)

The greatest of all British music hall comics, Dan Leno made only one appearance in American vaudeville. Born George Galvin on the site of what is now St. Pancras Station in London, Leno made his first stage appearance at the age of four and never stopped working. His first appearance as a pantomime dame was in the 1886 production of *Jack and the Beanstalk* at London's Surrey Theatre, and as a result of that performance, he was signed to appear in *Babes in the Wood* at the Theatre Royal, Drury Lane, for the Christmas season of 1888. He was the star, the dame, in pantomime at Drury Lane for the next fourteen years. On November 26, 1901, he appeared before King Edward VII at Sandringham, and thereafter began billing himself as "The King's Jester." Sadly, the honor and the fame went, literally, to Leno's head, and he became mentally unbalanced. In 1903, he entered a mental institution, where he supposedly remarked upon seeing a clock, "Is that clock right?" Told it was, he replied, "Well, what's it doing here then?"

Dan Leno came to the United States in March 1897, billed as "The Funniest Man on Earth." He made his vaudeville debut at the Olympia Music Hall, and while audiences were friendly, there was no way he could live up to expectations. Leno's opening night performance was reviewed in *The New York Dramatic Mirror* (April 24, 1897):

"When Leno's name was hung out there was a lot of applause, and when he made his appearance he was greeted with a roar of welcome that almost took him off his feet. When quiet was restored he began his first song, which was 'The Lucky Horseshoe.' It was not very amusing. Then came 'Wait 'til I'm His Father!' which told the story of a man who was courting a widow who had a boy who was fond of playing jokes, and Mr. Leno, with sundry expressive gestures and grimaces, told how he would settle the boy's hash as soon as he obtained parental control. The third song was called 'The North Pole.' Mr. Leno sang it dressed in a suit of grayish fur. He carried a stuffed seal about with him, and cracked icy jokes about the custom of the Esquimaux, one of which was to the effect that in Iceland nobody ever shaves; they simply let their whiskers sprout, and then break them off. This song ought to be cut out. With his fourth effort Mr. Leno caught the fancy of the audience and succeeded in getting his first genuine laughs. It was all about the feelings of a man whose wife has been ordered out of town for a week by the doctor, and the consequent joy at her departure. Mr. Leno worked in his famous squeaky laugh, and as the song progressed he got into such an ecstasy of mirth that he had to lie down and kick his heels in the air. It was all very funny and the performer was heartily applauded as he finished. In his fifth song, 'The Shop-Walker,' Mr. Leno was made up as an exaggerated type of the dry goods man who waits on every department and tries to sell people what they don't want. His pantomime and patter in this song kept the audience laughing continuously. He was on the jump the whole time, and climbed imaginary ladders and unrolled imaginary pieces of dry goods with telling effect. The same tricks have been done here by James T. Powers in *A Straight Tip*, and Henry E. Dixey, who went through them in *Gayest Manhattan* a few weeks ago. It is evident that both these comedians had seen Leno, and had appropriated his business. It made little difference to the audience, however, as they were looking for the original 'shopwalker,' and the recollection of his imitators did not interfere with their enjoyment in the least.

"As he went off after the song, Mr. Leno removed his wig and bowed. There was a great deal of applause, and he returned in his shirt sleeves to bow again, when an enthusiastic friend in one of the boxes began to shout, 'Give us the Red Red Poppies, Dan!' Everybody in the house looked at the box from which the sound came, and recognized pretty little golden-haired Julie Mackey, the American singer, who had just returned after a long stay in England. Of course Dan gave the signal to the leader and retired to fix his wardrobe for the 'Poppies' song, which he announced a dozen times in burlesque fashion as 'A little thing of me own.' It was an amusing parody on the plantation song and dance which is so popular in London, and made a hit. There was a dance at the end of it and Mr. Leno pretended that his baggy trousers were loose amidships and his struggles to make the gestures and do the steps while trying to keep the garments from falling were ludicrous in the extreme. He finally had to crawl off the stage on his hands and knees. He was enthusiastically recalled and smilingly bowed his acknowledgments as several floral horseshoes were handed over the footlights. In response to calls for a speech, he made a few remarks thanking the audience for their hearty welcome and assuring them that he would try to improve his performance every night, as he had been extremely nervous and could scarcely do himself justice. 'In regard to the flowers,' he said, 'it is beyond my powers to express my thanks to the kind friends who have sent them. In my country flowers are given only to the beautiful, and I presume (making a funny 'mug') that is why they have been handed up to me.' The applause continued after the speech, and Mr. Leno 'obliged' again, with a little monologue winding up with a well-executed jig.

"Mr. Leno's songs simply serve as an excuse for the introduction of a lot of 'patter,' or what is known on this side as 'gagging.' A great deal of it was decidedly English, but the manner in which it was rattled off by Mr. Leno made it seem really funny. He is a very lively little man, and never remains in one position for more than a second. His arms, legs and body each have a continuous performance going on while he is on the stage, and as for his face, it works overtime from the beginning to the end of his performance."

Dan Leno spent four weeks in vaudeville. He did not return again to the United States; indeed he made no other non-British appearances.

BIBLIOGRAPHY
Brandreth, Gyles. *The Funniest Man on Earth: The Story of Dan Leno*. London: Hamish
     Hamilton, 1977.
"Dan Leno's Debut." *The New York Dramatic Mirror*, April 24, 1897, p. 16.
Wood, J. Hickory. *Dan Leno*. London: Methuen, 1905.

EDDIE LEONARD (Richmond, Va., October 18, 1883—New York, July 29, 1941)

The phrase "blackface minstrel" generally brings to mind images of Al Jolson or Eddie Cantor, but the greatest of all minstrel men in vaudeville was neither of these performers but Eddie Leonard, whose career spanned the years from the 1890s through the mid 1930s. In 1927, *The Billboard* wrote of him, "Eddie Leonard is a great showman; he knows minstrelsy to the last lilt; his graceful stepping equals any of the former masters of the art, and he deserves every favor extended to him by his audience. He is indeed the minstrel of the hour." Leonard's showmanship extended beyond the vaudeville stage. He was one entertainer who understood the value of publicity. He would purchase several thousand dollars' worth of advertising in *Variety*, he knew exactly how the copy should read, even though he could not spell the word "thousand." At one point, he tried to purchase an eight-page insert in the trade paper, but had to settle for a mere four.

"The Minstrel of the Hour," as he was always billed, had no time for a formal education. He had to support his mother, and so became an apprentice at a Richmond, Virginia, rolling mill. James Decker, an agent for Lew Dockstader, heard of Leonard's rich singing voice, with which he used to entertain his fellow workers, and invited the boy to join the Lew Dockstader Minstrels in the early 1890s. From Dockstader's Minstrels, Eddie Leonard joined the Haverly Minstrel Troupe, and by 1902 was one of the stars of the company.

With his wife, Mabel Russell, Eddie Leonard became one of the favorites of the vaudeville stage. In 1909, *Variety* hailed him as "easily up with the leaders in modern minstrelsy." His song-and-dance act would usually include "coon" songs such as "Wha, Wha Coon" (performed by Mrs. Leonard) and a number of songs composed by Leonard, including "Ida, Sweet as Apple Cider," "Roly Boly Eyes" and "Just Because She Made Them Goo-Goo Eyes."

Leonard's popularity did not diminish in the next two decades. Reviewing his act on December 21, 1918, *The New York Dramatic Mirror* noted that "Eddie is looking younger than ever and has never been in better dancing form." Two years later, *The New York Dramatic Mirror* (November 6, 1920) caught Leonard at the Colonial Theatre and commented, "Eddie is a master minstrel. He takes us back to the great days of a cruder and more sentimental America. . . . Leonard is one of the most charming entertainers in America, and his presence on any bill is an occasion for genuine enthusiasm." The minstrel was a frequent headliner at the Palace, playing there in March 1924, November 1926, October 1927, and (for the last time) in April 1932. In 1928, Leonard took three pages of advertising in *Variety*, pointing out that he was as good as, if not better than, Jolson, and few would have disagreed. He was the last of a line of minstrels that could be traced back to the Southern plantations.

Eddie Leonard made very few screen appearances. His only two feature films are *Melody Lane* (1929) and *If I Had My Way* (1940).

As minstrelsy died out in the 1930s, so did Eddie Leonard's fame and career disappear. He died under mysterious circumstances. He left the hotel where he was staying with his wife and checked into the Imperial Hotel in the Herald Square section of New York, close to the sites of many of his successes. A few hours later, he was found dead in his room—apparently of natural causes. No one knew why he had checked into the hotel, but it was reported that he was virtually penniless at the time of his death and that ASCAP had to pay for his funeral (a report subsequently denied by that organization).

Critics considered Eddie Leonard a gentle minstrel performer with an appealing voice that did not hide a slight Irish brogue. He was equally at home with both Negro spirituals and comedy songs. His act was never racially insulting, but rather, as one critic has remarked, he transformed burnt cork into a thing of beauty. He was tender and he was graceful. A critic wrote, "Here is a rare performer, one with the discernment to see the vast wealth that is the heritage of the millions of Negroes in America. Much great art is naive, simple and unaffected—and this is the quality of Negro art. Leonard is a Southerner, is deeply in sympathy with the Negro, and as faithful as [Stephen] Foster in his depiction of the spiritual qualities of the race."

BIBLIOGRAPHY

Leonard, Eddie. *What a Life: I'm Telling You*. New York: The Author, 1934.

HARRY LESTER. See THE GREAT LESTER

ETHEL LEVEY (San Francisco, November 22, 1881—New York, February 27, 1955)

Variety's Sime Silverman described Ethel Levey as "always the perfect song deliverer," but she was far more than a good singer, being an accomplished dancer and a comedienne with a vibrant and exuberant personality. Ethel Levey was born Ethelia Fowler, and she took the name Levey from her Jewish step-father. As a child she appeared in amateur theatricals and at the age of eight was recognized as an accomplished pianist and elocutionist. The performer made her professional debut with a "coon" song specialty at San Francisco's Columbia Theatre on December 31, 1897, in *A Milk White Flag*. Her New York debut came at Weber and Fields's Music Hall, and this led to a twenty-two week engagement at Koster and Bial's Music Hall.

In 1898, Ethel Levey met George M. Cohan, and they were married the following year. For the next seven years, Levey was to appear in all of her husband's productions, including *The Governor's Son* (1901), *Running for Office* (1903), *Little Johnny Jones* (1904), and *George Washington, Jr.* (1906). However, Cohan and Levey were strong-willed, individual personalities, too much so to coexist for any length of time, and they were divorced on February 18, 1907.

After the divorce, Ethel Levey returned to vaudeville, with an initial engagement at the Harlem Opera House. There was no question as to her popularity; every seat in the house was sold, and standing patrons were lined up four deep behind the orchestra rail. Levey sang four songs, including her big hit from *George Washington, Jr.*, "I Was Born in Virginia." *Variety* (January 19, 1907) commented, "In a handsome gray gown, Miss Levey sang three songs and would have stopped there but the audience insisted upon one more. . . . With her reappearance in vaudeville as a single entertainer Ethel Levey scored a great big solid hit."

In 1909, Ethel Levey was in London, where she had first appeared in 1900. She returned again to London in 1912 to appear in *Hullo, Ragtime!*, followed in 1913 by *Hullo, Tango*. In the teens, Ethel Levey's biggest successes were in London, with shows such as *Follow the Crowd* (1916), *Three Cheers* (1917), and *Oh! Julie* (1920). However, there was no question that she remained a favorite also with New York audiences. In 1911, she followed an appearance at New York's Folies Bergere with a cabaret performance in Hammerstein's Roof in July of the same year. She delighted the audience with her four songs, four dances, and four costume changes. They cheered her singing of "Pride of the Prairie" and "Dear Old Broadway," but above all they applauded her dancing, which was always the high spot of any vaudeville appearance.

In January 1921, Ethel Levey returned to New York, and to the Palace, where she had first appeared in 1913. She continued to make stage appearances— including *Go Easy Mabel* (1922), *Sunny River* (1941), and *Marinka* (1945)— through the 1950s. She also filed suit against Warner Bros. when it filmed George M. Cohan's life story in 1942 as *Yankee Doodle Dandy*, despite the fact that her name was not used in the production.

BIBLIOGRAPHY

Parsons, Chauncey L. "Ethel Levey of New York and Paris." *The New York Dramatic Mirror*, May 17, 1911, pp. 10–11.

TED LEWIS (Circleville, Oh., June 6, 1890—New York, August 25, 1971)

With his battered top hat, his clarinet, and his greeting, "Is *ev'*rybody happy?," Ted Lewis became an American institution, billed as "The Jazz King," quite erroneously, because he did not play jazz as we know it today. That croaky voice of his introduced such songs as "When My Baby Smiles at Me" and "Me and My Shadow," from which he extracted an element of drama as well as a hint of jazz. Ted Lewis was first and foremost a showman, more than he was a musician; he came on stage twirling a cane and let his hat roll down his arm before catching it—a gag he claimed to have learned from W. C. Fields.

Born Theodore Leopold Friedman, Lewis's first professional engagement was singing at a nickelodeon in his hometown of Circleville, Ohio. He learned to play the clarinet in the public school band. A few years later, in New York, he changed his name to one that would fit a theatre marquee and formed the Ted Lewis Nut Band. He acquired the battered top hat from a hack driver called Mississippi in a dice game at Rector's Restaurant in 1917, and it was at Rector's that Lewis first gave his famous introduction. In 1918, Ted Lewis opened his own cabaret in New York, the Bal Tabarin, which was to be followed later by the Montmartre Club and the Ted Lewis Club.

Ted Lewis had, of course, played small-time vaudeville prior to his coming to New York in the early teens, but his first major New York vaudeville appearance was at the Palace in September 1919. *The New York Dramatic Mirror* (September 4, 1919) reported:

"He made his entry at the Palace with a bang and kept on banging clean through his exit to a curtain speech. There are few who would dare dispute his title of 'Jazz King.' His middle name is rhythm and he fingers a wicked clarinet not to mention a mean shimmy. His four abettors, togged out like the clown dog in an animal act, give valuable assistance. The laughing trombone is a wonder. Altogether, Ted and the boys make a prize bunch of Jazz banditti."

The entertainer returned to the Palace on many other occasions; in the late 1920s, he was there in November 1927, July, November and, December 1928, and December 1929. In May 1922, he played the Palace with much the same routine as earlier, except that now the members of his band (five brasses, a drummer, and a pianist) were dressed in tuxedos rather than clown costumes. The big number was "You've Made a Dr. Jekyll and Mr. Hyde Out of Me." Later in 1922, Ted Lewis was to introduce "Me and My Shadow," with Eddie Chester as the first and most famous shadow. In 1924, Lewis was back at the Palace with an act that included comedy sketches and a far larger band. His showmanship paid off as he played a jazz preacher uniting the trombonist and the cornet player, and the baton-twirling leader of a small-town band, using an effect that appears to have been similar to the flickering lights so popular in discos. "Lewis is in a class by himself as an entertainer," wrote *Variety* (September 10, 1924). "He is the John Henry of the band leaders."

Aside from vaudeville, Ted Lewis was featured in a number of revues, including the 1919 edition of Ziegfeld's *Midnight Frolic*, the 1921 edition of *The Greenwich Village Follies*, and *Artists and Models* (1927). In the summer of 1925, he and the Dolly Sisters were a big hit at London's Kit Kat Klub.

"My shows were always clean and always entertaining to the masses," recalled Lewis in 1970. "What most people want are lyrics that come straight from the heart." Rock and roll put an end both to lyrics straight from the heart and to Ted Lewis's career. He retired at the age of seventy-seven, declaring, "They think Ted Lewis is too corny." He died with his wife, Adah Becker, at his side. They had been married fifty-six years, and she had appeared in burlesque prior to their marriage, at which point she became Lewis's secretary and business

manager. She worked to create a museum to her husband's memory, and on
June 5, 1977, the Ted Lewis Museum opened at 133 West Main Street, Circleville, Ohio 43113. Adah Lewis died on May 30, 1981, at the age of 83.

BIBLIOGRAPHY
Brown, David, and Ernest Lehman. "Is Everybody Happy?" *Collier's* 103, no. 21 (May
       27, 1939), pp. 19, 62, 64.
Cantor, Eddie. "Ted Lewis." In *As I Remember Them*. New York: Duell, Sloan and
       Pearce, 1963, pp. 71–73.

WINNIE LIGHTNER (Greenport, N.Y., September 17, 1900—Sherman Oaks,
Ca., March 5, 1971)

A flaming redhead with a vivacious personality combining a hard-boiled outlook on life with a warmhearted inner quality, Winnie Lightner was the perky
star of a number of early Warner Bros. sound features, including *The Gold
Diggers of Broadway* (1929), *The Life of the Party* (1930), *Gold Dust Gertie*
(1932), and *She Had to Say Yes* (1933). One has only to see and hear her in the
Warner Bros. 1929 all-star musical *Show of Shows* performing "Singin' in the
Bath Tub" (supported by a male chorus in female attire) to recognize the qualities
that made Lightner so popular. In vaudeville, she sang many of her numbers so
quickly and performed with such zest—preferring a hasty exit without an encore,
to leave the audience wanting more—that she became known as "The Song-a-
Minute Girl."

Born Winnifred Hanson, Lightner entered vaudeville as a singer and comedienne in the late teens. In 1920, she teamed with two other vaudevillians to
form the Lightner Sisters and Newton Alexander (1884–1949). The other woman
was not her sister but Alexander's wife. *The New York Dramatic Mirror* saw
the trio perform at New York's Alhambra Theatre in August 1920 and commented, "The Lightner Girls and Newton Alexander, featuring that inimitable
facial contortionist, Winnie Lightner, dispensed patter, ditties and puns that
would have died an early death had it not been for Winnie's face comedy." In
October 1920, the act played the Palace. For the first time, besides the zippy
comedy numbers of "Since the Jazz Has Gone to China Town" and "Tric-Tric-
Tricoline," Winnie Lightner displayed a serious side by performing a ballad,
"Wonderful Eyes," with great success. "A bright shining star is little Winnie
Lightner," reported *The New York Dramatic Mirror* (October 16, 1920). "She
is a whole show in herself. She is peppery, vivacious, clowning one minute and
singing a straight ballad the next."

The trio were featured in the 1922 edition of George White's *Scandals*, and
Lightner was featured solo in the 1923 edition, singing George Gershwin's "I'll
Build a Stairway to Paradise," backed by Paul Whiteman and His Orchestra.
The following year, she scored another success with Gershwin's "Somebody
Loves Me." In many ways, it was remarkable how this rough and rowdy woman
could put across a gentle ballad with such feeling. Winnie Lightner also appeared
on Broadway in *Gay Paree* (1925) and Harry Delmar's *Revels* (1927), alternating

with headlining on the vaudeville stage. In June 1927, she headlined at the Palace, and after describing her act as "fast, furious and always to the point," *Variety* (June 15, 1927) commented, "Miss Lightner turns loose some lyrics that may have had a couple of blushes in them for the unwary. Regardless of that they were very much in the Lightner style and what this girl can do with such a number is well known. . . . This girl can stay in vaudeville for so long as she wills."

Variety's opinion notwithstanding, Winnie Lightner decided to enter films in 1928 at the suggestion of director Roy Del Ruth. She devoted her time to motion pictures until 1934, when she retired and married Del Ruth. It was her third or fourth marriage, but a lasting one. Brother Fred Lightner was a popular comedian on the vaudeville stage.

BIBLIOGRAPHY

Earle, Eugene. "Winnie Wows 'Em!" *Photoplay* 37, no. 4 (March 1930), pp. 71, 92.
"The Tomboy of the Talkies," *Photoplay* 39, no. 3, February 1931, pp. 57, 130–31.

BEATRICE LILLY (Toronto, Canada, May 29, 1894—Henley-on-Thames, England, January 20, 1989)

When *Life* (July 10, 1931) hailed Beatrice Lillie as "champion lady clown of the world," the title was perhaps something of a misnomer in that the entertainer was anything but a clown in the old-fashioned sense. There was a sophistication to her performance that could be appreciated only by an intellectual audience. There was never anything clown-like about her costumes onstage; she was always impeccably dressed and elegantly coiffed. In fact, critic John Mason Brown pointed out that the elegant facade was as much her "clown's costume" as Charlie Chaplin's hat and cane were his.

Born Beatrice Gladys Lillie, the daughter of a British civil servant, the entertainer, along with her older sister, Muriel, took piano and acting lessons as a child. She learned quickly that she was capable of getting laughs by making grotesque faces and began appearing at local theatres. In 1913, with her mother and sister, she came to England, and the following year made her British stage debut at the Chatham Music Hall, singing "Pretty Kickapoo." She auditioned for André Charlot, one of the great European producers of revues, and in October 1914, she opened at London's Alhambra Theatre in his show *Not Likely*. A series of Charlot revues followed, in each of which Beatrice Lillie began gaining more attention: *5064 Gerrard* (1915), *Now's the Time* (1915), *Samples* (1916), *Some* (1916), *Cheep* (1917), *Tabs* (1918), *Oh, Joy* (1918), *Bran-Pie* (1919), *Now and Then* (1921), *Pot Luck* (1921), and *A to Z* (1922).

In January 1920, she married the Honourable Robert Peel, an ancestor of the man who created the British police force. (He died in 1934, and their only son Robert died in 1942.) On January 9, 1924, Beatrice Lillie made her New York debut at the Times Square Theatre in *Charlot's Revue of 1924*, in which she costarred with Jack Buchanan and Gertrude Lawrence. She returned the following year for *Charlot's Revue of 1925* and also appeared in *Oh, Please!* (1926). In

1927, Lillie made her Hollywood screen debut in M-G-M's *Exit Smiling*, which despite being a silent film works well as a Beatrice Lillie vehicle, thanks to her grimacing and mugging. She made a handful of sound films, including *The Show of Shows* (1929) and *Thoroughly Modern Millie* (1967), and the best is the 1944 British feature *On Approval*, in which she proves a perfect foil for actor Clive Brook.

Lillie made her New York vaudeville debut at the Palace in November 1928; she returned there, always as the headliner, in April, September, and November 1929 and February 1931. In 1929, she shocked the Palace management by using the word "goddam" on stage, but as Lady Peel (a title of which she never ceased to remind her critics), she could get away with it. A 1927 tour on the Orpheum circuit was less successful, perhaps because audiences outside of New York lacked an understanding of her peculiar humor. Strangely enough, she also did badly the following year when she starred at the London Palladium. "Bea Lillie Dies at the Palladium" was *Variety*'s summation. Palace audiences were always appreciative, and Lillie easily lived up to her billing as "The Great International Stellar Comedienne."

In 1928, an association with Noël Coward began when Beatrice Lillie starred in his show *This Year of Grace*, and in 1931, she introduced Coward's "Mad Dogs and Englishmen" in *The Third Little Show*. Throughout the 1930s and 1940s, Lillie divided her time between New York and London, in the former city seen with Bert Lahr in *The Show Is On* (1936), in London teamed with Bobby Clark in *Walk a Little Faster* (1932).

From 1952 onward, Beatrice Lillie toured the United States, in company with Reginald Gardiner, in *An Evening with Beatrice Lillie*. In 1957, the entertainer starred in what was billed as the golden jubilee edition of the *Ziegfeld Follies*; she appeared as a Charles Addams cartoon character singing "Milady Dines Alone," together with "Kabuki Lil" and "Song of India." The following year, she returned to London to star in *Auntie Mame*, and in 1964 was back in New York in a musical version of Coward's *Blithe Spirit*. Titled *High Spirits*, the show was to be Beatrice Lillie's last New York stage appearance. At that time, Coward, in an interview with *Life* (May 15, 1964), pointed out that there was no absolute proof that Beatrice Lillie was "the funniest woman in the world," but he continued, "I think we can state with reasonably assurance that Beattie has been for years and still is the funniest woman of our civilization."

With the passing years, Beatrice Lillie's mental health deteriorated, and more and more she began to rely on the judgment of a young male companion named John Philip Huck, whom most of her friends viewed with suspicion. Lillie's mental instability became evident in August 1971, when at a screening of her 1930 film *Are You There?* at the Museum of Modern Art, she exposed her breast, asking the audience, "How do you like that?" In 1977, a conservator was appointed to oversee and protect her property, and in September of that year, she left the United States for good, returning to her home in England. The day after she died, John Philip Huck also died, and the two were buried side by side at Harpsden, near Henley-on-Thames in the south of England.

The final word on her talent should be left to Beatrice Lillie. When asked, "What lies at the bottom of your art?," she replied, "There are fairies at the bottom of my art."

BIBLIOGRAPHY

"Backstage with Bea Lillie," *PM*, January 28, 1945, pp. M3–M4.

"Beatrice Lillie." *Current Biography*, February 1945, pp. 347–50.

Heggie, Barbara. "Hit on the Head with a Wand." *Saturday Evening Post*, May 26, 1945, pp. 22–23, 34, 37, 39.

Laffey, Bruce. *Beatrice Lillie: The Funniest Woman in the World*. New York: Wynwood Press, 1989.

Lillie, Beatrice. "Don't Be Silly!" *Collier's*, June 12, 1926, pp. 10+.

———, with John Philip Huck and James Brough. *Every Other Inch a Lady*. Garden City, N.Y.: Doubleday, 1972.

"Miss Lillie." *The New Yorker*, November 15, 1952, pp. 34–36.

"Miss Lillie," *The New Yorker*, February 13, 1960, pp. 26–28.

Tynan, Kenneth. "The Lady Is a Clown." *Holiday*, September 1956, pp. 96, 116–18.

Woolf, S. J. "Beatrice Lillie's Recipe for Laughter." *The New York Times Magazine*, November 26, 1944, pp. 13–14.

Young, Stark. "Beatrice Lillie." *The New Republic*, March 30, 1927, pp. 169–70.

LITTLE JACK LITTLE (London, May 28, 1900—Hollywood, Fl., April 9, 1956)

As his name suggests, Little Jack Little was a diminutive bandleader and composer whose primary fame was on radio in the 1930s, but who also appeared on the vaudeville stage. He played the Palace in May 1932. Little came to the United States with his father at the age of nine, and put together his first band while a medical student at the University of Iowa. After working as a song plugger, he became a composer in his own right, with his best known songs being "Jealous," "I've Always Called You Sweetheart," and "A Shanty in Old Shanty Town." In the 1930s, Little Jack Little and his band were featured at such popular night spots as the Ambassador Hotel in Atlantic City and the Palmer House in Chicago. He was one of radio's first crooners, signed to a long-term CBS contract in the 1930s, but his popularity diminished after the Second World War. Little continued to work as a single performer and a disc jockey, but a serious bout with hepatitis led to his committing suicide.

ALICE LLOYD (London, October 20, 1873—Banstead, England, November 16, 1949)

Marie Lloyd might have been the best known and most popular member of the Lloyd family as far as English audiences were concerned, but it was her sister Alice who was far better known and liked in the United States. Her career in America spanned the years 1906 through 1927 with one of her last popular songs from the 1920s, "Good Old Iron—Never Been Known to Rust," providing an imperfect metaphor of her appeal. She was billed as "The Ideal Daintee Chanteuse," and she was a pleasant-faced, rather than pretty, buxom entertainer. Writing in *American Vaudeville*, Douglas Gilbert suggested that she was nothing more than a pretty face, helped along by a good press agent, but it was obviously more than looks that attracted vaudeville audiences.

Alice Lloyd made her first stage appearance with her sister Grace as The Sisters Lloyd at the Forester's Music Hall, London, on February 20, 1888. She continued to appear with her sister until the latter married, at which time Alice embarked on a solo career. She made her American debut at New York's Colonial Theatre in February 1907, and proved so popular she was selected to headline the bill for the second week of her engagement. On March 23, 1907, she was featured for the first time on the cover of *Variety*, and something of her popularity in the United States may be gauged from her reappearance on *Variety*'s cover for its fourteenth anniversary issue on December 26, 1919. On her first American engagement, Lloyd sang "May," "Stockings on the Line," "The Tourist and the Maid," "Never Introduce Your Bloke to Your Lady Friend," and "Who Are You Looking At?" It was the last song that the audience loved, and *Variety* (March 2, 1907) reported, "No more dainty, artistic bit of song acting has been given on the American stage and there is not an American actress who could not benefit by listening to this number."

The singer quickly became virtually a resident of the American vaudeville stage. At the Majestic Theatre, Chicago, in June 1908, she provided the proverbial knockout, reported *Vanity*, and was retained, yet again, to headline for a second week. In 1913, she had a new hit song with "Who Are You Getting at, Eh?" Sime Silverman wrote in *Variety* (October 31, 1913), "There's only one Alice Lloyd. There's something about that English girl, and she's a great little girl, Alice, on or off the stage." The following year, she and Marie Lloyd were playing on opposite sides of Times Square, Alice at the Palace and Marie at Hammerstein's. There was little question among critics and audiences as to which was the bigger draw. At that time, Alice Lloyd sang six songs with as many costume changes. The hit of the tour was "Mother, Mother, Mother," in which Lucy explains that because she was afraid of the dark she did not come back from the party at eleven but waited for the break of day. As *The New York Dramatic Mirror* (April 29, 1914) noted, "Most of Miss Lloyd's numbers come under the category of 'blue'—but the broad English humor somehow strikes home. We can't help laughing at Marie Lloyd's melodic innuendos or smiling at Alice Lloyd's touch of risqué suggestion."

After a three-year absence, Alice Lloyd was back in vaudeville in 1919, again headlining at the Palace. It was back to the Palace yet again in September 1925, after a three-year tour of the world. She was considerably plumper than she had been ten years before, but audiences were just as enthusiastic about her songs, which included "Naughty but Nice," "Have a Little Dip with Me," and "The Older the Fiddle the Sweeter the Tune." In 1927, Lloyd toured the Pantages western circuit at a salary of $1,250 a week—"the cheapest act for drawing power Pan had had in months," according to *Variety* (January 18, 1928). She turned down an offer to appear on an all-English bill at the Palace for the week of January 23, 1928, but instead returned to England on January 14, 1928, thus ending her years on the American vaudeville stage. Curiously, she was not hailed as a legitimate successor to her sister until January 1927, but, of course, her act was not imitative of Marie Lloyd's, and she was a star performer in her own right.

BIBLIOGRAPHY

Lloyd, Alice. "Why I Am So Grateful." *Variety*, December 11, 1909, p. 32.

MARIE LLOYD (London, February 12, 1870—London, October 7, 1922)

"Marie Lloyd is more than a dissipation," said one wit. "She's a beloved 'abit, which grows on you just like your mustache." She was the most famous performer in British music hall—a national institution—and yet she was eclipsed in American vaudeville by her sister Alice, and never achieved lasting popularity here, making only two visits to these shores. Perhaps her songs were simply too English for American tastes and audiences failed to understand the nuances of the risqué lyrics.

Born Matilda Alice Victoria Wood in the London slum neighborhood of Hoxton, Marie Lloyd made her first stage appearance as Bella Delmere at London's Eagle Assembly Rooms on May 9, 1870; six months later, she had become Marie Lloyd, taking her name from the popular newspaper *Lloyd's News*. Shortly thereafter, the entertainer had her first big success at the Middlesex Theatre on Drury Lane, singing the song "The Boy I Love Sits up in the Balcony." Quickly she became known for her raunchy songs, such as "She'd Never Had the Ticket Punched Before" and "Johnny Jones," with its suggestive lyric:

> What's that for, eh! Oh tell me Ma.
> If you won't tell me, I'll ask Pa.
> But Ma said, Oh it's nothing, hold your row.
> Well, I've asked Johnny Jones see,
> So I know now!

The earliest of the great British music hall songs identified with Marie Lloyd was "Oh, Mr. Porter," the tale of a girl who took the wrong train, which she first sang at the Royal Theatre, Holborn, in 1893. British audiences loved the plump little girl with her cheeky songs, many of which have become classics in England, including "A Little of What You Fancy Does You Good" and "My Old Man Said Follow the Van." She had a unique knack for dealing with her audience. When a galleryite shouted, "Marie, give us a dirty look!" she retorted, "No need, you've got one."

Marie Lloyd gave of herself wholeheartedly, both physically and financially. However tired she might be, she would always appear before her audience full of energy. Her generosity was boundless. She once took over a shop in London's

East End and handed out its stock to the poor; when nothing was left, she proceeded to give money to latecomers.

In October 1907, Marie Lloyd made her first New York appearance but failed to appeal. She returned to America in the fall of 1913, and her arrival created a considerable stir when immigration officials refused to permit her to leave the S.S. *Olympic* on which she had been traveling, because Bernard Dillon, the man with whom she had been sharing a cabin, was not her husband—they were subsequently married in February 1914—and because Lloyd used a few too many four-letter words to the immigration officers. Eventually, E. F. Albee and various vaudeville performers intervened on her behalf, and Lloyd was permitted to enter the country. She appeared at the Palace in early October singing "Something on His Mind," "Woman Knows How Far She Can Go," and "A Little of What You Fancy Does You Good," among others. Writing in *Variety* (October 17, 1913), Sime Silverman thought her songs and jokes too mild for her reputation, but continued, "She held the house and it was a nice audience that seemed to have all good feeling for the English woman. Marie Lloyd will draw business this trip." In reality, Marie Lloyd drew the biggest crowd seen at the Palace on opening night since Sarah Bernhardt played there.

The distinguished drama critic Acton Davies reviewed her performance in the *New York Evening Sun* (October 16, 1913): "Marie Lloyd is a wonder. More than that, she is a consummate artist. . . . This woman with a few notes of music to help her out could make the City Directory sound like the bluest of Blue Books, and she would achieve her purpose not with her voice, which may be regarded as a strictly limited asset, but by a mere glance of her eye."

Marie Lloyd once remarked, "I seem to have had a busy life, eh? Wonderful constitution they must think I have." The life she led gradually took its toll. Early in October 1922, she appeared at the Edmonton Empire, London, closing her act with another of her famous cockney songs, "One of the Ruins That Cromwell Knocked about a Bit." The audience roared at her imitation of a drunken woman, little realizing they were watching an actress so sick she could hardly stand. Three days after her performance, Marie Lloyd died at her Golders Green, London, home. Ten thousand people attended the funeral, and another 100,000 visited the graveside that first weekend. She was indeed, as Sarah Bernhardt said, "the most artistic comedienne of the English stage," for, as T. S. Elliot wrote, she expressed the soul of the people.

As early as September 21, 1908, *Variety* commented, "The record of the Lloyds to date in point of merit and public appreciation now stands Alice, Marie, Daisy, and Rosie." The trade paper was referring to Daisy Wood, a sister, who played vaudeville, and Rose Lloyd, who appeared with Alice as The Sisters Lloyd. Additionally, Marie Lloyd's daughter worked in music hall and vaudeville, initially as Marie Courtney and later as Marie Lloyd, Jr.

BIBLIOGRAPHY

Farson, Daniel. *Marie Lloyd and Music Hall*. London: Tom Staceau, 1972.

Jacob, Naomi. *Our Marie*. London: Hutchinson, 1936.

LOCUST SISTERS

The Locust Sisters were a singing quintet of five sisters, with the youngest, Hilda, performing blues singles and Mathilda at the piano. Discovered by Gus Edwards, they appeared in vaudeville, primarily on the East Coast, in the late 1920s and were also in the original Broadway production of *Hit the Deck!* (1927). This somewhat unattractive group of ladies recorded for Columbia and also appeared in at least one film short, *Metro Movietone Revue No. 2* (1929).

MARCUS LOEW (New York, May 8, 1870—Glen Cove, N.Y., September 5, 1927)

Marcus Loew was the first of the great movie moguls who created Metro-Goldwyn-Mayer and also had an impact on vaudeville. He started work at the age of six, selling newspapers on the streets of New York, and in 1905 opened his first nickelodeon theatre in Convington, Kentucky. It was not successful, but Loew persevered, determined to become influential in show business while continuing as a Manhattan furrier. In 1908, he leased four unprofitable theatres from the Shubert Brothers and converted them into movie theatres. As well as presenting films, Loew introduced vaudeville on his programs, offering employment not to the headliners who would play the Palace but rather the second-string vaudeville acts willing to work for lesser salaries.

In 1910, Marcus Loew formed Loew's Consolidated Enterprises, in association with Adolph Zukor and Nicholas Schenck. The organization operated nickelodeons which continued to offer vaudeville entertainment. The company was reorganized in 1911 as Loew's Theatrical Enterprises, with a capital of $5 million. To assure a steady flow of films for his theatres, Loew acquired the Metro Pictures Corporation in 1919, and in 1924, he merged the company with Goldwyn Pictures Corporation and Louis B. Mayer's independent production organization, forming Metro-Goldwyn-Mayer.

When he died, Marcus Loew left an estate of $30 million. On the day of his burial, September 8, 1927, virtually every theatre in the United States and Canada remained closed until 2:30 P.M. A statement from the board of directors of the Motion Picture Producers and Distributors of America read, "His death eclipsed the gaiety of nations and impoverished the public stock of harmless pleasure."

BIBLIOGRAPHY

Loew, Marcus. "My Story." *American Weekly*, June 1918, pp. 33–34.
"Marcus Loew's Long Leap from Penny Arcades." *Literary Digest*, September 24, 1927, pp. 38–45.
"The Men Who Made the Movies." *News Front*, April 1961, pp. 34–37.
"The Rise of Marcus Loew." *The New York Dramatic Mirror*, May 7, 1910, p. 23.

LOEW CIRCUIT

At the height of its power in the mid 1920s, the Loew circuit consisted of the following vaudeville theatres:

New York City

American

Avenue B

Boulevard

Delancey Street

Greeley Square

Lincoln Square

National

Orpheum

State

Victoria

Brooklyn

Bay Ridge

Gates

Loew's Bedford

Loew's Hillside

Loew's Melba

Metropolitan

Palace

Premier

Willard

Out of Town

Grand Theatre (Atlanta)

Temple Theatre (Birmingham, Al.)

Orpheum (Boston)

State (Buffalo, N.Y.)

Rialto (Chicago)

State (Cleveland)

Melba (Dallas)

Victory (Evansville, In.)

Loew's (Hoboken, N.J.)

Loew's (Washington, D.C.)

Loew's (London, Canada)

State (Memphis, Tn.)

Miller's (Milwaukee)

Loew's (Montreal, Canada)

State (Newark, N.J.)

Crescent (New Orleans)

State (Norfolk, Va.)

Emery (Providence, R.I.)

Broadway (Springfield, Ma.)

State (White Plains, N.Y.)

Yonge Street (Toronto, Canada)

CISSIE (CECELIA) LOFTUS (Glasgow, Scotland, October 22, 1876—New York, July 12, 1943)

"The Queen of Mimics" and "That Incomparable Mimic" are just two of the titles bestowed upon Cissie Loftus, one of vaudeville's greatest impressionists, whom *Variety* labeled "one of the most versatile women on the stage." Loftus carried on the show business tradition set by her mother Marie Loftus (1857–1940), who had been a popular performer in American burlesque. (Her songs included "And She Lisped When She Said 'Yes,' " "One Touch of Nature Makes the Whole World Kin," "Don't You Believe It, Dear Boys," "She Wore a Little Safety Pin Behind," and "To Err Is Human, To Forgive Divine.") Cissie Loftus made her first stage appearance at the Alhambra Theatre, Belfast, Northern Ireland, in October 1892, singing a ballad titled "Molly Darling." Less than a year later, she made her London debut at the Oxford Music Hall, on July 15, 1893.

Loftus made her American debut at Koster and Bial's Music Hall on January 21, 1895, and for the rest of her life traveled constantly between London and New York. Aside from vaudeville, she was in great demand for the legitimate stage. In 1900, she appeared with Madame Modjeska's Company; in 1901, she became E. H. Sothern's leading lady; in 1903, she played Marguerite opposite Sir Henry Irving in *Faust*; in 1905, she played *Peter Pan* in a revival of the J. M. Barrie play at London's Duke of York's Theatre; during 1913 and 1914, she toured with William Faversham in *Romeo and Juliet* and *Othello*. Cissie Loftus was a uniquely talented lady.

Her impersonations in vaudeville were highly regarded and included Bert Williams, Nazimova, Caruso, Sir Harry Lauder, Nora Bayes, and Irene Franklin. Her vaudeville tours across America, whether with her impressions or in one-act plays such as *The Diamond Express* (1906), were immensely successful. In September 1909, she broke the attendance record at the Masonic Temple in Chicago. In 1915, Loftus appeared with Marie Dressler at the Palace and did a "sister" act, with gags like "She never married, did she?" "No, her children wouldn't let her." After several years of absence from the American vaudeville stage, Cissie Loftus came back to the Palace to top the bill in November 1923. She was scheduled to appear onstage for twenty minutes, but the audience simply would not let her go; she remained and performed for over one hour. At that time, *Variety* noted she could entertain both the masses and the classes with her impersonations of Lauder, Ethel Barrymore, and Alice Delysia. In April 1925,

Loftus was one of the stars appearing in the old-timers week at the Palace, and despite the presence of Weber and Fields and Marie Cahill, there was no question that she was the star old-timer.

Cissie Loftus made one silent feature film, *A Lady of Quality*, in 1914, but made frequent screen appearances in the 1930s. She also continued performing onstage and never missed a performance, despite alcoholism's becoming more and more of a problem for her. In addition, she was hauled into a London court on charges of possession of narcotics. Despite such setbacks, Cissie Loftus continued with her impersonations in a series of summer concerts and Sunday night performances at New York's Vanderbilt Theatre during 1938, and that same year, she also appeared in Noël Coward's *Tonight at 8:30* at the Vanderbilt. A year before she died in her room at New York's Lincoln Hotel, Cissie Loftus toured in *Arsenic and Old Lace*.

BIBLIOGRAPHY

"Cissie Loftus." *Current Biography*, September 1940, pp. 515–16.

LOOKERS

The Lookers was a social club organized in 1918 by Jimmy Hussey and George Whiting. It was quickly disbanded when E. F. Albee became concerned it might develop into a union for vaudevillians.

VINCENT LOPEZ (Brooklyn, N.Y., December 10, 1894—Miami Beach, September 20, 1975)

Vincent Lopez and His Orchestra was one of the first major bands to appear on the vaudeville stage, featured at the Palace in January 1923 and at the New York Hippodrome in January and February of the following year. Writing in her book *The Palace*, Marian Spitzer commented:

"Probably the one big band that made the highest Palace score was that of Vincent Lopez. Lopez didn't hold the record for consecutive appearances, but, looking back, it seems that he and his band played the Palace every two or three weeks for several years. Once in the middle twenties he was there four weeks in a row, away for two or three, and then back for five more consecutive weeks.

"Lopez not only had a good band; he was a real showman. When he and his men were on stage you not only heard music, you saw it dramatized, whether it was 'Waiting for the Robert E. Lee' with miniature side-wheelers racing along the Mississippi on the cyclorama, or Tchaikowsky's '1812 Overture' with realistic-looking flames billowing to the sky as Napoleon's troops made their celebrated retreat from Moscow."

Vincent Lopez's father wanted him to be a priest, but the abbot of a local monastery, in Dunkirk, New York, thought the boy was better qualified for a musical career as a pianist. He first began playing at the Pennsylvania Hotel Grill in 1921, with his initial group known as the Hotel Pennsylvania Orchestra, and in the late 1920s became a fixture at the St. Regis Roof. In 1925, Lopez opened his own nightclub, the Casa Lopez, in New York. His longest engagement was from 1941 to 1966 at the Grill Room of New York's Hotel Taft.

The orchestra leader gained a far wider audience thanks to radio, whose listeners heard his familiar greeting of "Hello, everybody, Lopez speaking" for the first time on WJZ–New York on November 27, 1921. The introduction became as well known as Lopez's theme song, "Nola" (written in 1915 by Felix Arndt). Among the orchestra members through the years were Glenn Miller, Artie Shaw, Charlie Spivak, and Xavier Cugat, and Lopez's singer discoveries included Abbe Lane and Betty Hutton. As late as 1939, Vincent Lopez toured the vaudeville circuit with Hutton and Abbott and Costello.

In the 1940s, Vincent Lopez became interested in numerology, and in 1961 published a book on the subject. He made his last public appearance in May 1975 at the River Boat in New York's Empire State Building.

LOS ANGELES
The first vaudeville theatre in the city was Mott's Hall, opened in 1895 under the management of Jake Gottloeb, Martin Lehman, and Alfred Ellinghouse. The following year, the Grand Opera House became the Orpheum. Later, the Los Angeles Theatre, which had opened in 1905, became a vaudeville house controlled by the Sullivan and Considine circuit. As of 1906, there were eight vaudeville houses in the city: the Empire, the Novelty, the Star, the Orpheum, the Garnet, Chutes, Fischer's, and the Unique. By 1921, there was only one remaining, the Orpheum. A new Orpheum Theatre opened in Los Angeles on February 15, 1926, at which time the old Orpheum was renamed the Palace. The Hillstreet Theatre, on the street of the same name in downtown Los Angeles is often described as a vaudeville theatre, but it was a presentation house, which opened in 1922 with the film *Announce Your Marriage* and eight acts of Orpheum vaudeville.

LOUISVILLE
In 1906, the Buckingham and the Hopkins were the city's only vaudeville theatres. By 1921, with Louisville's population at 234,891, there were still only two vaudeville houses: B. F. Keith's Mary Anderson and B. F. Keith's National.

ED LOWRY (New York, February 1, 1896—Beverly Hills, Ca., August 17, 1983)
A comedian who also played the saxophone, Ed Lowry began in vaudeville while still in his teens, and in 1913 met and married Teddy Prince, with whom he formed a vaudeville act. He was prominent in the 1930s, in the waning years of vaudeville, acting as an in-house master of ceremonies at various theatres which featured both vaudeville and film presentations. He was most associated with the Ambassador Theatre, St. Louis, but also worked at the Mastbaum Theatre, Philadelphia; the Stanley Theatre, Pittsburgh; Loew's State, Los Angeles; and Loew's State, Chicago. He retired from performing in the early 1940s.

NICK LUCAS (Newark, N.J., August 22, 1897—Colorado Springs, Co., July 28, 1982)

The Billboard (May 27, 1939) grasped the essential appeal of Nick Lucas when reviewing a typical performance it noted that his "voice is very soothing to the ears." The secret of Lucas's success was that he always gave a relaxed and relaxing performance, singing his melodies in a gentle manner, entirely devoid of gimmickry. The songs and the way in which he put them over were his act. He never told jokes or conversed with the audience, and his act did not fundamentally change in more than fifty years—except that toward the end of his life, he would offer a mild wisecrack about his age. "I had to create a style that was accepted by the general public," said Lucas. "When you play the theatre, you play to all age brackets and all different types of people who like simple music that they can understand. I adopted a style of singing and playing my guitar that became successful, and that's all that matters."

Born Dominic Lucanese, the son of poor Italian immigrants, the singer learned to play the mandolin and guitar from his brother, an accordionist, and together the two would perform at local saloons. "It was practically a necessity that I got started in the music business," recalled Lucas. Around 1915, he began to work as a solo performer in cabarets, singing and playing the banjo. As he remembered, "I was working as a musician at the Edgewater Beach Hotel in Chicago with Ted Fio Rito's Orchestra, and I was on the radio a lot, when radio was practically in its infancy. I gained popularity unbeknownst to me, and then Brunswick asked me to do a recording—the band used to record for Brunswick. And the record was so big that immediately I left the band and went on my own."

In fact, Lucas had made a recording by himself, playing the guitar, as early as 1922, but it was with his 1924 recording of "My Best Girl" and "Dreamer of Dreams" that he was able to establish himself as a major vaudeville entertainer, often appearing in the guise of a Venetian troubadour and accompanying himself on the mandolin. Lucas's big vaudeville break came in December 1924, when he appeared as one of the acts prior to the feature film at a major presentation house, the Chicago Theatre. *Variety* (December 17, 1924) reported, "Lucas has a soft sweet tenor, particularly suited to such songs as he uses in this appearance. His voice and the remarkably fine setting made the picture a memorable one."

When he first started in vaudeville, Lucas did not use a microphone; they were unnecessary because the acoustics of theatres such as the Palace were superb. He recalled, "I think the first time I had a microphone was when I played the Roxy Theatre in New York. They had them in the footlights. They wouldn't dare put them on the stage—the audience wouldn't accept them. But then eventually they put the microphone on the stage. Sometimes I wonder how I did it, singing to three thousand people without a microphone, but then, of course, I studied voice for two years in Chicago while I was appearing at the Edgewater Beach Hotel."

Between 1924 and 1934, Nick Lucas recorded more than one hundred songs, but there is no question that the best known and the one most closely associated with him was "Tip-Toe thru the Tulips." " 'Tip-Toe thru the Tulips' found me," commented Lucas.

Back here in Los Angeles in 1929 I was appearing at the Orpheum Theatre on Broadway and Ninth Street, and one night there was a talent scout there from Warner Bros., that was making a picture called *Gold Diggers of Broadway*. And after the show, this chap came backstage and asked me if I would be interested in making a picture. I said, "Why not?" So the next day I went up to the studio and Mr. Zanuck heard me and said, "Hire him." They had only one song written for me in the film, "Painting the Clouds with Sunshine," and so the writers, Joe Burke and Al Dubin, were requested to write some more songs for me. And they wrote this song "Tip-Toe thru the Tulips," and when Zanuck heard this song he turned it into a big production number. That's how I latched onto "Tip-Toe thru the Tulips," which became synonymous with me.

Although Lucas was also featured in Warner Bros. all-star revue *Show of Shows* (1929), in which he appeared in a somewhat turgid and overlong number with Myrna Loy, he turned down a career in films for one onstage and in the recording studio. Curiously, motion pictures came back into his life in 1974, when his voice was heard on the soundtrack and record album for *The Great Gatsby*, singing "When You and I Were Seventeen," "Five Foot Two, Eyes of Blue," and "I'm Gonna Charleston Back to Charleston." He received no credit for his work on either the film or the album.

Nick Lucas was the headliner on the last all-vaudeville bill at the Palace Theatre, the week of November 12, 1932. (Others on that bill were Hal Le Roy, Giovanni, the Honey Family, Ross and Edwards, Ola Lilith, and Sid Marion, whom Lucas remembers as a particularly fine comedian.) He was not particularly aware that he was participating in the end of an era: "The wane was coming, I could see it, but I was surprised to find that was the last big-time vaudeville show."

From 1937 until the end of his performing years in the late 1970s, Nick Lucas was based in Los Angeles, and from there he made an extensive tour of Australia on the Tivoli circuit (also in 1937) and, of course, worked for the U.S.O. during the Second World War. In an interview in 1980, he commented, "I don't seek work, but if it comes I grab it. I would like to work three days a week for the rest of my life." He joked that once thousands of women came to hear him in theatres, but now he would be happy to go door to door, performing for lonely housewives on an individual basis. As a vaudevillian, Nick Lucas was a curiosity in that his style of singing was an intimate one, and yet he was able to project that intimacy to an audience of thousands. It was a successful style and one that still appeals. As he noted, "Every song tells a story, and if you get them to listen to you from the beginning to the end, then you're a hit."

AUBREY L. LYLES.   See MILLER AND LYLES

M _____

CHARLES MACK. See MORAN AND MACK

MADISON'S BUDGET

Self-described as "a cyclopedia of comedy material for vaudeville artists, radio stars, masters of ceremony, etc., containing original monologues, sketches, minstrel first-parts, sidewalk patter, wise cracks, revue and burlesque bits, etc. etc.," *Madison's Budget* was first published, on a twice-yearly basis, in 1898, and was still being published as late as 1928. All the material in the periodical was written by James Madison, and for the purchase price of $1, vaudevillians had free use of anything therein. Most of the humor was racial in content:

"A Chinese laundryman had an addition to the family the day Lindbergh landed in Paris. One of his friends wanted him to name the boy Charlie Fly after Lindbergh. But the proud father replied, 'That no good Chinese name. I callee him 'One Long Hop.' "

or:

"A little dialogue heard in the Black Belt: 'Ah hear you-all's left yo' husband, Mandy. Is it true?' 'It sure is, Eliza. Dat nigger was so shiftless, he couldn't find enough washin' to keep me busy.' "

or:

"In the good old days, an Irishman was running a saloon with a fine free lunch counter attached, when in walked Cohen. He ordered a glass of beer for a nickel and then ate up all the cheese in sight. The Irishman protested and said, 'Look here, that cheese cost thirty cents a pound.' 'Vell,' replied Cohen, 'it's worth it.' "

After the demise of vaudeville, Madison sold complete sets of his *Budget* to Fred Allen, Eddie Cantor, and others to use on their radio programs.

MAGICIANS

Magic acts in vaudeville covered the spectrum from illusion to "con" tricks, from levitation and escapology to card manipulation and the palming of cigarettes. There was, and is, nothing new in magic, although the props may change through the decades. It has all been done before, with magic acts first gaining public acceptance in Europe in the 1700s. "Burmain" first produced a rabbit from a hat circa 1830, although it is doubtful he used the classic vaudeville repartee: "I always use a rabbit, because you know rabbits are smart, they can multiply."

Jean-Eugene Robert-Houdin (1805–1874) in France and John Nevil Maskelyne (1839–1917) in England are generally considered the fathers of modern magic. Some of the greatest magicians, such as Harry Houdini, Harry Blackstone, and Harry Kellar, were not merely players on a vaudeville bill, but hosted their own complete shows, running two hours or more and in constant demand throughout the world. They took themselves very seriously, unlike, say, "Think-a-Drink" Hoffman or Frank Van Hoven.

There were a few female magicians, including Mrs. Adele Herrmann, the Great Lala Selbini, and Mlle Talma, but the profession was primarily male dominated. Somehow audiences equated magic with the Chinese, and a number of pseudo-Chinese performers flourished, including the Great LaFollette (George Reuschling), Chang (Juan Pablo), and the best known, Chung Ling Soo (William Ellsworth Robinson).

One of the few genuine Orientals on the vaudeville stage was Ching Ling Foo (1854–1918), who earned a reported $2,000 a week while touring the Loew's circuit in 1913. He even had an imitator, Houang Yuen (who was, in reality, a Caucasian American). From under his flowing mandarine robe, Ching Ling Foo would produce goldfish bowls, a garbage can filled with milk, and a tub of live ducks. In 1933, an acrobatic act titled Ching Ling Foo, Jr. toured the vaudeville circuits, but it appears to have had no connection to the famed magician.

Among the American magicians who began appearing on the vaudeville stage in the 1800s were mentalists John Randall Brown and Washington Irving Bishop. French-born Buatier de Kolta (1847–1903) appeared in New York in 1891 and 1903, making first a bird cage and canary disappear and later a young girl. English magician Charles Bertram (1855–1907) also appeared in American vaudeville, ending each trick with the words, "Isn't it wonderful?" American Frederick Bancroft was billed initially as "Decastro, the boy magician" and later elevated himself to "Prince of Magicians." Frenchman Felicien Trewey toured for years as a magician, but gained later fame in the late 1890s as the representative of the Lumière brothers, presenting their new magic invention, the motion picture, to audiences throughout the world.

Some magicians combined magic with ventriloquism. Many used guns as part of the act. Will B. Wood would fire a pistol and make his daughter disappear; in February 1908, both of them vanished under mysterious circumstances while at sea off the Mexican coast. The specialty of Servais Le Roy (1865–1953) was to levitate his assistant and then have her disappear into thin air. Dr. Walford Bodie (1870–1939) was a flamboyant con artist who began in his native England and soon gained an audience in the United States with an act similar to faith healing, in which he could cure physical paralysis. Nightly, he claimed to demonstrate "hypnotism, Bodie force and wonders of bloodless surgery."

James William Elliott (1874–1920) billed himself as "The World's Champion Card Manipulator," a title that later belonged to Cardini. P. T. Selbit, an English magician, introduced the trick of sawing a woman in half in 1920, but Horace Goldin perfected and popularized the act in American vaudeville. Other major magicians in vaudeville included Charles J. Carter (1874–1936), Lafayette (1872–1911), Eugene Laurant (1875–1944), John Mulholland (1898–1970), Nicola the Great (1880–1946), and Frederick Eugene Powell (1857–1938), who was known as the "Dean of American Magicians."

See also HARRY BLACKSTONE, CARDINI, ANNA EVA FAY, HORACE GOLDIN, ALEXANDER HERRMANN, HARRY HOUDINI, HARRY KELLAR, PAULINE, CHUNG LING SOO, "THINK-A-DRINK" HOFFMAN, THURSTON, FRANK VAN HOVEN.

BIBLIOGRAPHY
Christopher, Melbourne. *Panorama of Magic*. New York: Dover, 1962.
Gilbert, Douglas. "Magic, Mental Acts." In *American Vaudeville: Its Life and Times*. New York: Whittlesey House, 1940, pp. 306–320.
Hay, Henry, ed. *Cyclopedia of Magic*. New York: David McKay, 1949.
Laurie, Joe, Jr. "Abracadabra." In *Vaudeville: From the Honky-Tonks to the Palace*. New York: Henry Holt, 1953, pp. 104–117.
Maskelyne, Nevil. *Maskelyne on the Performance of Magic*. New York: E. P. Dutton, 1911.

WILL MAHONEY (Helena, Mt., February 5, 1894—Melbourne, Australia, February 8, 1967)

No one better exemplified the originality and talent of comedians on the vaudeville stage than Will Mahoney. He was a "nut" comedian whose biggest claim to fame was that he played the xylophone, but while others played the instrument with their hands, he used hammers attached to his feet. Prior to the xylophone act, he performed with a live duck and executed various comic dance routines. "It's not how old the joke is. It's the confidence you put into it," was how Mahoney summed up the secret of his success.

Although he is often described as an Australian comedian, Will Mahoney was born William James Fitzpatrick Mahoney in Montana, and made his first public appearance as a dancer at the age of eight in Spokane, Washington. He toured the western vaudeville circuits before coming to New York in the early 1920s, when *Variety* (October 28, 1921) called him "another 'nut' single from the West that impresses as being not above the ordinary." By the middle of the decade, *Variety* had improved its opinion of Mahoney, just as the comedian had improved his act. Mahoney appeared in the 1924 edition of George White's *Scandals* and was a frequent performer at the Palace: in December 1925, August 1926, May 1927, May 1928, April 1929, April 1932, and January 1933. When he headlined there in 1927, the critic for *The New York Times* (January 11, 1927) commented, "Mahoney employs a disarmingly joyous insouciance and gusto in putting over his songs and does his tap-and-clog dances with the tireless precision of an automaton."

Will Mahoney introduced his xylophone dance in the spring of 1930 in *Earl Carroll's Sketch Book*. Sime Silverman reviewed the dance in *Variety* (April 2, 1930) as a favor to Mahoney, who wished to ensure his claim to the creation of the routine. Silverman wrote, "The specially built xylophone is of the usual style but quite long. Mahoney, with a hammer attached to each shoe, steps upon the instrument without his shoes causing a sound. He had just finished his 'Mammy' song on the stage, and went upon the instrument when urged back to finish his act after he had sobbingly said he couldn't do any more [business]. With the music starting Mahoney commences to dance, the hammers hitting the keys to perfect rhythm. It's a complete surprise, and when the dancer did his third and last number, Sousa's 'Stars and Stripes,' the house burst into heavy plaudits. The idea is magnificent in its originality, and Mahoney is splendid in the execution." The comedian brought his new specialty to vaudeville and the Palace in 1930, under the title "Glorifying Feet, Falls, and Foolishness."

In addition to the 1930 edition of *Earl Carroll's Sketch Book*, Mahoney appeared in the 1931 edition and was also seen in *Take the Air* (1927). He was popular in England and in 1935 starred in *Radio New York* at London's Holborn Empire. The critic for the *Daily Telegraph* wrote, "He is perhaps the most good-humored comedian in variety and the secret of his success is that he infects the whole audience with his own sense of the ridiculous. It is impossible not to laugh at him."

Will Mahoney remained popular until his death. In 1955, he starred as Finian McLanergan in the New York revival of *Finian's Rainbow*, and three years later made his last Broadway appearance in *The Man Who Never Died*.

MALE IMPERSONATORS

While never as popular or as many in number as female impersonators, male impersonators enjoyed a vogue on the vaudeville stage from the turn of the century through the early 1920s. Their appeal was primarily to the men in the audience. Victorian and Edwardian gentlemen enjoyed watching male impersonators perform because of their boyish figures and attire. An entire generation of sexually repressed men could live out their homosexual fantasies through attending vaudeville programs featuring male impersonators, such as Vesta Tilley or Ella Shields. The natty clothes and the tight trousers, the bobbed hair and the masculine swagger were what males in the audience desired, and what they could watch and enjoy in a darkened theatre without fear of retribution and often in the company of their wives.

Four performers were preeminent in British music hall, Vesta Tilley, Ella

Shields, Hetty King, and Bessie Bonehill, and all enjoyed popularity in the United States, where their closest rivals were Kathleen Clifford and Kitty Doner. Bessie Bonehill first came to the United States in 1891, and subsequently made her home here after appearing as a principal boy in British pantomime. She died at the age of forty-five in August 1902 while on a visit to England, and *The New York Dramatic Mirror* commented at this time:

> It has been said of her as of the hero of Paul Jones that she was "divinely tall, still more divinely fair." The intonation of this magnetic woman's voice is such as to cause question of its particular calibre. In rich and powerful mezzo strains she pours forth melody in an enchanting way. Her critics have differed as to what quality her tones really were, and instead of calling her's a mezzo voice, they all agreed it was a Bessie Bonehill voice.

Also from England in the 1890s came Florence Bindley, who appeared both there and in American vaudeville with success. Tillie Santoy was first seen on the vaudeville stage in 1907, billed as "England's Male Impersonator."

American male impersonator Ella Wesner was popular in the 1880s, playing a drunken dandy who falls asleep in the barber's chair. She would also appear in military attire, singing "Captain Cuff":

> Captain Cuff, Captain Cuff,
> You can tell me by my collar.
> Captain Cuff, Captain Cuff,
> Not worth half-a-dollar.
> With my military style,
> My cigarette I puff,
> While they all cry clear the way,
> Here comes Captain Cuff.

Male impersonation was very much a British tradition, and so American Louise Elliott, who played vaudeville and was the star of Pepple and Greenwald's *All Girl Revue of 1917*, billed herself as "The Vesta Tilley of America." Grace Leonard was praised by *Variety* in 1909 for the manner in which she wore her male clothing. She was probably American, as were Toma Hanlon and Renée Graham. Helene Mora was billed as "The Great Female Baritone," and in 1898 played Hamlet in a vaudeville sketch.

Evelyn Wilson attempted male impersonation in vaudeville as late as 1929. Gypsy Byrne played New York nightclubs and vaudeville houses in 1927 and 1928. "She makes a 'cute' boy and while not actually attempting to fool the customers is pleasantly boyish in her brown business suit and mannish slouch hat," commented *Variety* (January 28, 1928).

See also KATHLEEN CLIFFORD, KITTY DONER, HETTY KING, ELLA SHIELDS, VESTA TILLEY.

BIBLIOGRAPHY
"The Gentle Art of Being a Man." *The New York Dramatic Mirror*, March 4, 1914,
    p. 23.
Slide, Anthony. *Great Pretenders: A History of Female and Male Impersonation in the
    Performing Arts*. Lombard, Ill.: Wallace-Homestead, 1986.
"Women in Masculine Roles." *The New York Dramatic Mirror*, July 2, 1910, p. 3.

FAY MARBE

An accomplished singer and dancer, Fay Marbe made her vaudeville debut
in the late teens. She appeared at the Palace Theatre in September 1920, accompanied by Jerry White at the piano, singing "The Kiss," "Tra Tra La,"
"The Jazz Vampire," "Sweet Daddies," and "Mexico." *The New York Dramatic Mirror* (September 18, 1920) reported, "She got along swimmingly with
the vocal numbers assigned and then cavorted in the style of pep and animation
that established her in big favor."

A New York society woman with Spanish-looking features, Fay Marbe became
bored with her life and entered show business in 1917 as a dancer in Jerome
Kern's *Oh Boy*. She had apparently been seen by a theatrical producer while
dancing at a charity carnival. She also danced in Victor Herbert's *The Velvet
Lady* (1920). Marbe claims to have worked at the Vitagraph Studios circa 1918
or 1919, but her first credited role in a feature film is as a dancer in the 1920
Metro release *The Very Idea*. She also claimed to have danced in D. W. Griffith's
Orphans of the Storm (1921).

In the early 1920s, the entertainer was seen on Broadway in *The Hotel Mouse*
(1922) and *Topics of 1923*, but then she went to Europe, appearing on the
London stage and starring in eight films for Ufa in Germany. Returning to the
States later in the decade, Marbe was billed as "The Magnetic International
Star," and toured in a one-woman show, *A Continental Revue*, featuring songs
and dances from Europe sung in the languages of the various countries. Critics
compared her to London's Beatrice Lillie, Madrid's Raquel Meller, Paris's
Yvette Guilbert, and Vienna's Fritzi Scheff. She starred in the 1929 "Poverty
Row" film production *The Talk of Hollywood*, which also featured her brother
Gilbert (with whom she had performed "The Blue Danube Waltz" on the vaudeville stage). Fay Marbe disappeared from show business in the early 1930s, and
may have moved to Australia.

While virtually unknown today, Marbe was the subject of a massive publicity
campaign in 1920. A critic in *The New York Dramatic Mirror* wrote of her,
"Miss Marbe has youth—is fairly alive with it and as she has a comely face
and an attractive figure and knows just the kind of stage outfits to wear to catch
both the masculine and feminine eyes, the answer is all in her favor. And how
she works! A butterfly of kaleidoscopic colors one minute and a whirling, graceful
exponent of the art of terpsichore the next. It is a treat."

BIBLIOGRAPHY
"Fay Marbe Is Ambitious." *The New York Dramatic Mirror*, November 20, 1920, p. 955.
Stevens, Ashton. "Twenty-Thousand Dollar Legs." In *Actorviews*. Chicago: Covici-
    McGee, 1923, pp. 209–14.

Talley, Alma. "She Gave Up Society for a Career." *Movie Weekly*, October 27, 1923, pp. 3, 28.

MARCELLE AND SEA LION

An English importation into American vaudeville in the mid 1920s, Marcelle and Sea Lion was considered one of the better sea acts because the animal (whose name in 1924 was Jackie) did not appear to be getting any visual cues from Marcelle. It performed tricks, such as picking up objects to juggle and balance, singing, laughing, mimicking a cat, applauding, and shaking hands. While the sea lion performed, Marcelle would chat with the animal and with the audience, which was invited to shout instructions to the sea lion, all of which he obeyed. On a January 1925 bill at the Hippodrome, *Variety* thought the sea lion shared top honors with Vincent Lopez and His Orchestra.

The only other prominent sea lion act in vaudeville was Hughling's Seals, which featured Sharkey, who was supposedly the first sea lion to applaud himself.

H.B. MARINELLI (Thuringe, Germany, 1864—Paterson, N.J., January 7, 1924)

H. B. Marinelli was one of America's great theatrical agents in the early twentieth century, responsible for bringing over many European stars for vaudeville, including Gaby Deslys and Harry Lauder, whose first U.S. appearance was arranged by Marinelli in 1907. Marinelli also reversed the process, taking American vaudeville stars, such as Evelyn Nesbit Thaw, to Europe. Born into a well-known theatrical family, Marinelli made his stage debut at the age of seven and his U.S. debut, as a contortionist billed as "The Boneless Wonder," in San Francisco in 1885. He became a theatrical agent in 1898.

FALLY MARKUS (circa 1887—New York, October 20, 1955)

Fally Markus is something of a legend in vaudeville history, but one of whom little is known. He specialized in booking small-time acts for small-time vaudeville houses, and always claimed he could book any act if the price was low enough. Sometimes headliners would work for him under assumed names during hard times or when they were trying to break in new material. *Equity* magazine (November 1923) described Markus as "a refuge for broken down, unsuccessful acts which cannot get employment elsewhere. This applies in particular to the one night stands, in which salaries are scarcely large enough to cover the most meager sort of living while on the route." It was a description to which Markus took great exception, and one of the few occasions when he lost his temper. Whatever his failings, Fally Markus was remembered by vaudevillians as the most polite of theatrical booking agents. After the demise of vaudeville, he became a ticket agent in New York.

MARX BROTHERS

Audiences that have enjoyed the antics of the Marx Brothers on-screen for the past sixty years in classic comedies such as *Animal Crackers* (1930), *Monkey Business* (1931), *Duck Soup* (1933), and *A Night at the Opera* (1935) should not forget that the clowning and, above all, the superlative timing of the gags had been worked out in vaudeville and on the revue stage long before they made their motion picture debut. The Marx Brothers themselves recognized the value of vaudeville, and would even try out some of the routines for their films before live audiences prior to including them in their productions.

Groucho Marx was the first of the brothers to enter vaudeville, in 1905, as a member of the Leroy Trio. Groucho recalled that the trio sang a song titled "I Wonder What's the Matter with the Mail," a question that continues to be raised. Later, Groucho, Gummo, Lou Levy, and Mabel O'Donnell formed the Four Nightingales, which Harpo joined after Mabel O'Donnell's departure in 1910.

Harpo/Arthur (New York, November 23, 1893—Hollywood, Ca., September 28, 1964), Groucho/Julius (New York, October 2, 1895—Los Angeles, August 19, 1977), Chico/Leonard (New York, March 22, 1891—Beverly Hills, Ca., October 11, 1961), and Gummo/Milton (New York, October 3, 1892—Palm Springs, Ca., April 21, 1977) came together as an act when their uncle Al Shean, later of Gallagher and Shean, wrote a sketch for them titled "Fun in Hi Skool." The act, which also included three others, was favorably reviewed by Sime Silverman in *Variety* when it first came to New York in February 1912. The sketch was obviously based on Gus Edwards's "School Boys and Girls" routine, but Silverman was quick to point out that the Marx Brothers' sketch was superior. Groucho played the schoolteacher in the then-popular style of a Dutch comedian, while Harpo had the opportunity to play his harp halfway through the twenty-seven-minute routine. The dialogue went something like this:

Groucho: What is the shape of the world?

Harpo: I don't know.

Groucho: Well, what shape are my cuff links?

Harpo: Square.

Groucho: Not my weekday cuff links, the ones I wear on Sundays.

Harpo: Oh, round.

Groucho: All right, what is the shape of the world?

Harpo: Square on weekdays, round on Sundays.

Al Shean helped the Marx Brothers again in 1914, when he provided them with a second sketch, "Home Again," which their mother, Minnie Palmer, directed. Harpo was featured in another harp solo, while Chico performed a piano solo. The sketch kept the brothers busy during the First World War, with Zeppo/Herbert (New York, February 25, 1901—Palm Springs, Ca., November 29, 1979) replacing Gummo when the latter was drafted. Amusingly, the Marx Brothers' dealings with the draft board sounds rather like one of their routines.

In September 1917, they appeared en masse at a Chicago recruiting station and were promptly rejected, one for defective eyes, one for flat feet, one because of physical disability due to an operation, and one for general reasons.

The Groucho Marx style of behavior, familiar to viewers of his films, together with his television series *You Bet Your Life* (NBC, 1950–1961), was already apparent this early in his career. Songwriter Gus Kahn's widow, Grace, recalled their first meeting:

Gus had a song that he wrote with a man called Van Alstyne. I was working for Remick and Company, that was a big music publisher, and they sent me as a song plugger to Grand Rapids to get Groucho to sing this song when he came to Chicago. You see, they always tried to get 'em out of town so they would know the song when they got to Chicago. That was the funniest meeting you ever heard of. I rapped at the door, and Groucho said, "Come in." He said, "Sit down." I said, "I'm from a publisher and I'm here about a song." He said, "Have a cigar." I said, "No, thank you." We started to talk about the song, and he said, "You want to take a shower?" After that we became close friends. In fact, my daughter Irene married his son. Anyway, he put the song in the act, and I think we paid him twenty-five dollars a week to sing it.

The Marx Brothers appeared at the Palace in January 1917 with "Home Again," and *Variety* (February 2, 1917) thought it was "the best tabloid for value in the vaudeville." The trade paper continued, "Mrs. Minnie Palmer, their mother, can feel that mother's pride that she brought up four good boys who have made good as well." In 1919, the brothers were appearing in a sketch titled " 'N Everything," again written by Al Shean. *The New York Dramatic Mirror* (October 23, 1919) reported that the part that seemed to please the most was Arthur Marx's harp playing, and then embarked on a discourse on harp playing in vaudeville: "As we have said many times before there is not enough harping on the vaudeville stage. About the only harping we get is the harping some acts do on old jokes. The harp is especially suited for syncopated ballads, and although good harpists are hard to get, it can be done. The trouble it takes would be amply rewarded by the way the act is built up which has an harpist."

When the Marx Brothers again headlined at the Palace in August 1920, *The New York Dramatic Mirror* (August 21, 1920) wrote of "the Marx family using its familiar roughhouse antics and coarse idioms of speech, with the musical specialties by the comedy of the troupe proving the big feature." Incidentally, the Marx Bros. (as they were usually billed in vaudeville) made their first appearance at the Palace in Christmas Week 1915. They continued to headline there in the 1920s, in April 1929, October 1930, and January 1932. They also found time to headline at London's Palace Theatre in January 1931.

However, by the 1920s, the Marx Brothers' vaudeville career was drawing to a close. As Groucho recalled in his autobiography, the brothers were discontented. There were new worlds to conquer. There was a prestige attached to being a Broadway star that they never could attain in vaudeville. They had already appeared in a 1919 musical comedy, *The Cinderella Girl*, with lyrics by Gus Kahn, and in 1924 they were to star in a revue that would assure them a permanent place on the legitimate stage. Titled *I'll Say She Is*, the revue was almost universally panned by the critics as one of the worst ever produced, but, thanks to the ad-libbing antics of the Marx Brothers, it was also one of the funniest. Robert Benchley's comment in the humor magazine *Life* was to be echoed by critics and public alike in the years ahead: "Not since sin laid its heavy hand on our spirit have we laughed so loud and so offensively."

BIBLIOGRAPHY

Adamson, Joe. *Groucho, Harpo, Chico and Sometimes Zeppo: A History of the Marx Brothers and a Satire on the Rest of the World.* New York: Simon & Schuster, 1973.

Beranger, Clara. "The Woman Who Taught Her Children to Be Fools." *Liberty* 10, no. 22 (June 3, 1933), pp. 22–25.

Chandler, Charlotte. "Playboy Interviews Groucho Marx." *Playboy*, March 1974, pp. 59–60, 62, 66, 69, 72, 74, 185–86.

————. *Hello, I Must Be Going: Groucho & His Friends.* Garden City, N.Y.: Doubleday, 1978.

Crichton, Kyle. *The Marx Brothers.* Garden City, N.Y.: Doubleday, 1950.

Dali, Salvador. "Surrealism in Hollywood." *Harper's Bazaar*, June 1937, pp. 68–69, 132.

Donnelly, William. "A Theory of the Comedy of the Marx Brothers." *The Velvet Light Trap* no. 3 (Winter 1971/72), pp. 8–15.

Eyles, Allen. *The Marx Brothers: Their World of Comedy.* New York: A. S. Barnes, 1969.

Gehring, Wes D. *The Marx Brothers: A Bio-Bibliography.* Westport, Ct.: Greenwood Press, 1987.

Martin, Pete. "I Call on Groucho." *Saturday Evening Post*, May 25, 1957, pp. 31, 85–86, 89.

Marx, Arthur. *Life with Groucho.* New York: Simon & Schuster, 1954.

————. *Son of Groucho.* New York: David McKay, 1972.

Marx, Groucho. "Vaudeville Talk." *The New Yorker*, June 20, 1925, p. 14.

————. *Many Happy Returns: An Unofficial Guide to Your Income-Tax Problems.* New York: Simon & Schuster, 1942.

————. *Groucho and Me.* New York: Random House, 1959.

————. *Memoirs of a Mangy Lover.* New York: Bernard Geis Associates, 1963.

————. *The Groucho Letters: Letters from and to Groucho Marx.* New York: Simon & Schuster, 1967.

————, and Richard J. Anobile. *The Marx Bros. Scrapbook.* New York: Darien House, 1973.

————. *The Groucho File: An Illustrated Life.* New York: Bobbs-Merrill, 1976.

————, with Hector Arce. *The Secret Word Is Groucho.* New York: G. P. Putnam's Sons, 1976.

Marx, Harpo, with Rowland Barber. *Harpo Speaks!* New York: Bernard Geis Associates, 1961.

Marx, Maxine. *Growing Up with Chico.* Englewood Cliffs, N.J.: Prentice-Hall, 1980.

"Marx Bros." *Current Biography*, May 1948, pp. 425–30.

Seton, Marie. "S. Dali + 3 Marxes = " *Theatre Arts*, October 1939, pp. 734–40.

Stone, Edward. "Groucho and Adolf; or, the Summer of 1941." *Journal of Popular Film* 2, no. 3 (Summer 1973), pp. 219–29.

Wolf, William. *The Marx Brothers*. New York: Pyramid Publications, 1975.
Zimmerman, Paul D., and Burt Goldblatt. *The Marx Brothers at the Movies*. New York:
    G. P. Putnam's Sons, 1968.

MASQUERS CLUB

The Masquers Club was founded in Hollywood on May 12, 1925, as a fraternal
organization for those in all areas of show business. The founding members were
Fred Esmelton, Ned A. Sparks, John Sainpolis, Robert Schable, George E. Read,
Warner Baxter, Alphonz Ethier, and Robert Edeson, who was elected the first
president, or harlequin. The club's motto was "We Laugh to Win." The original
clubhouse was located at 6735 Yucca Street, but in 1926, Antonio Moreno purchased a new clubhouse at 1765 North Sycamore Street in Hollywood, which the
Masquers was able to acquire from him at cost, the residence becoming the club's
property in 1932. The Masquers produced a series of annual *Revels* in Hollywood
and also produced a series of two-reel comedies for RKO in the early 1930s.
Through the years, it also produced a number of plays, the most famous of which
was a Hollywood production of *What Price Glory*, directed in 1950 by John Ford,
and featuring John Wayne, Gregory Peck, Maureen O'Hara, Pat O'Brien, Ward
Bond, George O'Brien, Oliver Hardy, and Ed Begley.

In October 1965, a women's auxiliary was formed, the Masquerettes, with
Jane Withers as the first harlequeen. In March 1984, the organization was forced
to sell its clubhouse to pay off a substantial debt, and since then the Masquers
Club has occupied various temporary quarters.

Address: 11110 Victory Boulevard, North Hollywood, Ca. 91606.

BIBLIOGRAPHY

Charlesworth, Geri. "Masquers 45 Years Young." *Hollywood Studio Magazine*, De-
    cember 1960, pp. 7–9.
Scott, Tony. "Founded on Laughter and Love, Masquers Keeps Young in Spirit and
    Enthusiastic in Outlook." *Daily Variety*, October 31, 1972, pp. 46–47, 54, 150.
————. "Readying for 50th Anni, Masquers Have Happy Memories of the Past,
    Apprehensive Hope for the Future." *Daily Variety*, April 25, 1975, pp. 3, 10.

BESSIE McCOY (1888—Bayonne, France, August 16, 1931)

On June 3, 1908, *Three Twins* opened at New York's Herald Square Theatre.
The musical comedy made a star of Bessie McCoy, and introduced the song that
will always be associated with her, "The Yama-Yama Man" (written by Carl
Hoschna). It was not merely McCoy's vocal rendition of this song of a bogeyman
lurking in dark corners that put the number over, but equally the wild, demonic
dance that accompanied her performance. "There is no very deep appeal in the
expressional motive but plenty of simple, naive charm, used with unabashed
consciousness, frankly alluring and not a little saucy," commented Caroline
Caffin in *Vaudeville* (1914).

Born Elizabeth Genevieve McEvoy, Bessie McCoy had earlier worked in
vaudeville with her sister Nellie. Richard Harding Davis, the distinguished newspaper correspondent and novelist, was besotted with Bessie McCoy's perfor-

mance as "*The Yama-Yama Girl*," and the couple were married on July 8, 1910. At Davis's insistence, she retired from the stage. However, following his 1916 death, she returned to the theatre in 1917, starring in *Miss 1917*, and was also featured in the 1919 and 1920 editions of *The Greenwich Village Follies*. In March 1918, she returned to vaudeville, headlining at the Palace as Bessie McCoy-Davis. "Trim in figure and with a personality that stood out, she had them applauding before 20 seconds had passed," reported "Wynn" in *Variety* (March 28, 1918). Injured in the early 1920s, McCoy retired again, finally, moving with her daughter to France.

PAUL McCULLOUGH. See CLARK AND McCULLOUGH

OWEN McGIVENEY (Preston, England, May 4, 1884—Woodland Hills, Ca., July 31, 1967)

Owen McGiveney was the best known fast-change artist in vaudeville, often playing as many as five different roles in a ten-minute act. His success lay in both the speed of his changes and the variety of his characterizations, created also through makeup and the adoption of various voices. He was not, however, a great actor; audiences frequently complained that it was difficult to understand what he was saying, and *Variety* once commented that watching McGiveney was tantamount to seeing a play in a foreign tongue after having read the book in English.

The actor began his career in his native England in 1904, initially as a legitimate performer before making an early transition to the music hall stage. He came to the United States circa 1910. In May 1913, he was one of the supporting acts to Sarah Bernhardt at the Palace Theatre, and *Variety* (May 23, 1913) wrote of him, "The changes may be analyzed to account for the swiftness of execution and the almost immediate reappearance of the lone player each time, but the effect is very big. McGiveney, for changes in protean work, excels anyone who has appeared over here. He has a setting which helps the results obtained, and while Mr. McGiveney is not a great dramatic player nor reader, this does not lose him anything in vaudeville." (McGiveney was billed as a protean player, indicating versatility, rather than as a quick-change artist.) The performance at the Palace consisted of what was to be McGiveney's greatest success, an excerpt from Charles Dickens's *Oliver Twist*, in which he appeared as both Bill and Nancy Sikes.

With the demise of vaudeville in the 1930s, McGiveney returned to England, but Ken Murray (who had appeared with him at the Palace in 1927) brought him back to America in 1946 to appear in his *Blackouts* in Los Angeles. Audiences at *Blackouts* had the opportunity to discover how the quick changes were made; following his *Oliver Twist* sketch, McGiveney would have the stage lights come up, and it was seen that he had two or three dressers who slipped him false-fronted costumes. McGiveney came back to the United States with his family, settled in Los Angeles, and encouraged his son Owen McGiveney, Jr., to continue the act. McGiveney also embarked on a new career as a character actor on screen, appearing in, among others, *If Winter Comes* (1948), *Showboat* (1951), *Pat and Mike* (1952), *Brigadoon* (1954), *Snow White and the Three Stooges* (1961), and *My Fair Lady* (1964).

The only American fast-change artist who came close to McGiveney in popularity was Mark Linder, who appeared in a sketch playing four types of prisoners about to be released from jail, ending with a ''Hebrew'' and a Chinaman. Another exponent of the quick-change was Edgar Atchison-Ely who, in 1901, appeared in a sketch titled ''The Future Dude,'' in which he made his first costume change in five seconds and his second in seven seconds.

(JAMES) McINTYRE (Kenosha, Wi., August 8, 1857—Noyack, N.Y., August 18, 1937) and **(THOMAS) HEATH** (Philadelphia, August 11, 1853— Setauket, N.Y., August 18, 1938)

The most famous partnership in the annals of blackface minstrelsy was that of McIntyre and Heath, dating from 1874 through 1924. Both men grew up in the South, and as a 1908 biographer noted, ''As children living in the South, the boys studied the language and characteristics of the Negro 'befo' de war.' '' They joined forces in San Antonio, Texas, in 1874, and became headliners at the Theatre Comique in St. Louis two years later. Prior to the partnership, McIntyre had toured the South with Kate Pullman, performing clog dances and playing Little Willie in *East Lynne*; in 1869, he joined a circus and sang and danced his way through the mountains of Alabama.

Heath was the straight man of the team, and, as *Variety* noted, he was the perfect feed for McIntyre. The couple became famous for a number of classic minstrel sketches, including ''The Georgia Minstrels.'' ''The Man from Montana,'' ''The Ham Tree'' (which was adapted into play form, and in which they toured for a number of years for Klaw and Erlanger), ''Chickens'' (in which McIntyre appeared in drag), and ''Back to the Stable'' (a sequel to ''Georgia Minstrels'' which McIntyre and Heath introduced in 1918). A fairly good description of this sketch survives. It opened with Otto T. Johnston's pasting up a three-sheet poster announcing the coming of a minstrel show, at which point Alexander (McIntyre) sauntered onstage, leading a small white donkey. Alexander sells the donkey to Johnston for $25 and an I.O.U., which McIntyre insists on calling an U.O.I. Heath then enters in the guise of the owner of the minstrel show, and separates Alexander from the $25. It may not sound very funny, and perhaps it was not, for by 1916, Frederick James Smith was complaining in *The New York Dramatic Mirror* that 90 percent of the McIntyre and Heath act was tedium with only 10 percent laughs.

In *American Vaudeville*, Douglas Gilbert recalls a typical slice of McIntyre and Heath dialogue:

Heath: Well, didn't that train stop?

McIntyre: No, it didn't stop. It didn't even hesitate.

Heath: You got egg on your chin.

McIntyre: Thas jes clay from the ditch where I slep' last night.

Heath: Well, didn't that woman at the house where I sent you up give you something to eat?

McIntyre: No, she didn't. I saw she looked kinda hard and I thought of the old minstrel joke so I got down and started to eat the grass thinkin' that might touch her. An' she said to me, "You poor man, you must be starvin', come around to the back yard an' I'll show you where the grass is longer."

McIntyre claimed that the team originated ragtime, in the form of a buck-and-wing dance accompanied by clapping hands to the tune of an old "Rabbit" song McIntyre had learned from Southern Negroes, and introduced to New York at Tony Pastor's in 1879. This claim was disputed by Ben Harney, who said he originated ragtime with two of his songs, "Mr. Johnson Turn Me Loose" and "You've Been a Good Old Wagon, but You've Done Broken Down."

After an enthusiastic farewell tour in 1924, McIntyre and Heath retired. They did make one final, farewell appearance together in 1929, on radio with Rudy Vallee. The pair remained friends and lived close to each other, denying rumors that they had not spoken in twenty-five years. Heath died exactly a year to the day after McIntyre; he had not been told of his partner's death.

LEILA McINTYRE. See JOHN HYMANS AND LEILA McINTYRE

McNALLY'S BULLETIN

Published (as far as can be ascertained) between 1916 and 1940, *McNally's Bulletin* was self-described as "A Book of Comedy for Vaudeville and Dramatic Entertainers containing Monologues, Sketches, Acts, Parodies, Farces, Minstrel First-Parts, Afterpieces, and numerous other Stage Material" For the purchase price of $1 an issue, vaudevillians might use any of the *Bulletin*'s contents. The primary focus was on lengthy sketches, but also included were "sidewalk conversations" for male and female comedy teams, such as:

She: I've just become engaged to an Irishman.

He: Oh! Really?

She: No, O'Reilly!

and parodies of popular songs, such as the following number by a Peeping Tom, sung to the music of "I'm a Dreamer—Aren't We All?":

> I'm a peeper—Aren't we all?
> Just a peeper—Aren't we all?
> There's a maid, forgets the shade,
> On the windows 'cross the hall.
> And when she's home for the night,
> Shades of Salome, what a sight,
> It's not right, for she turns out the light,
> And I am fooled, but aren't we all?

McNally's Bulletin was written and published in New York by William McNally, who also published *Casper's Encore, Mack's Vaudeville Guide*, and *Mack's Recitations*.

RAQUEL MELLER (Madrid, March 10, 1888—Barcelona, July 26, 1962)

Just as Raquel Meller's name has not weathered the passing of time, so the intervening years have not helped an appreciation of her own peculiar talent. On viewing a film of Meller performing one of her celebrated *chansons*, one is aware only of a somewhat overweight, dowdy woman singing a monotonous air in an unmelodious manner. Yet in the 1920s, Raquel Meller was the darling of the intelligentsia. Of her, Sarah Bernhardt said, "If there is one woman in the world who possesses genius, it is Raquel Meller." Chaplin adored her and planned to costar with her in a film on the life of Napoléon and Josephine. In "An Appreciation of Raquel Meller," Arthur Hopkins wrote, "To the question 'Is acting an art?' the best answer I know is Raquel Meller." After watching her perform, critic George Jean Nathan commented, "She creeps over the footlights like an odourless incense, hypnotically, alluringly. She is like a convent on fire."

Born Francesca Marques, Raquel Meller became a Spanish music hall star in the early years of this century. From her native country, she went on to conquer the world, starring at the Olympia Music Hall in Paris in 1919, taking top billing in Alfred de Courville's *Joy Bells* at the London Hippodrome in 1920, appearing in several European films (the most famous of which was a 1926 production of *Carmen*), and embarking on a successful year-long tour of South America. She continued to appear onstage through 1946.

Meller first came to the United States in the spring of 1926 for a four-week engagement at New York's Empire Theatre. Her New York appearance, which began on April 14, 1926, and in which she was assisted by an orchestra selected from the Philharmonic Society of New York under the direction of Victor Baravelle, was cosponsored by a committee of patrons and a committee of the theatre, including Otto Kahn, Mrs. Anthony J. Drexel Biddle, Sr., Howard Chandler Christy, Charles Dana Gibson, Ethel Barrymore, Irving Berlin, Lynn Fontanne, Otis Skinner, Eva Le Gallienne, and David Belasco. In connection with her appearance, a lavish souvenir program was published, featuring a poem to her art by Robert Underwood Johnson and a critical appraisal by Randolph Bartlett which described Meller as "El Alma Que Canta—The Soul That Sings."

The diseuse sang from twelve to fifteen songs at each performance. Many were featured on the twenty-three phonograph records by Raquel Meller available in the United States in the 1920s, including "El Relicario" (The Charm), "El Peligro de las Rosas" (The Treachery of the Roses), "Besos Frios" (Kisses of Marble), and "Diguili que Vingui" (Tell Him to Come). A description of each song was published in the program. For example, one of her songs, "Mariana," was described thusly: "Mariana is the loveliest girl in all Andalusia. She is carrying on a flirtation with a village boy and her cousin. Her friends all warn her not to whisper, by mistake, the name of her cousin in the ear of his rival.''

There were, of course, those who were not transported into ecstasy by Meller's performance. One such individual was humorist Robert Benchley, who published his own versions of the songs, complete with synopses. A typical Benchley parody was "Camisetas de Flanela" (Flannel Vests): "Princess Rosamonda goes nightly to the Puerto del Sol to see if the early morning edition of the papers is out yet. If it isn't, she hangs around humming just the same. One night she encounters a young matador who is returning from dancing school. The finches are singing and there is Love in the air. Princess Rosamonda ends up in the police station.''

Benchley was the exception among New York critics, for most agreed with Arthur Hopkins's description of a Meller song:

In Raquel Meller we find the artist freed. Her every song seems a fine flight away from mundane reality into a new and blazing reality which somehow seems a part of all time and place. The beautiful, graceful woman fades away and one feels only the embodiment of gay, poignant, sullen, grieving, tragic emotions. And the body thus abandoned finds a new and glorious grace. Its motions are effortless. The face looks far, far away. The hands are like faces. And Raquel Meller finally drifts back to her body. The song is over, but you feel you never again will quite get back to the same place you were when the flight began.

Raquel Meller returned to New York, this time to the Henry Miller Theatre, for thirteen more performances beginning on October 25, 1926. Subsequently, she embarked on a reasonably successful U.S. vaudeville tour. She also appeared in two of the first Fox Movietone sound shorts to be released.

As a performer, Meller belonged to another time and another place; her songs of tragedy and joy seemed somewhat out of style in a contemporary Spain trying to shed the image created by General Franco. Her place in an encyclopedia of vaudeville is, however, assured, not simply because of her American appearances, but because of her unique place in European music hall.

BIBLIOGRAPHY

Benchley, Robert. "More Songs for Meller." In A Subtreasury of American Humor, ed. E. B. White and Katharine S. White. New York: Coward-McCann, 1941, pp. 258–59.

O'Leary, Liam. "Raquel Meller." Cinema Studies 2, no. 4, June 1967, pp. 61–64.

ROSE MELVILLE (Terre Haute, In., January 30, 1873—Lake George, N.Y., October 8, 1946)

Rose Melville was a singing comedienne known solely for the character of "Sis Hopkins" that she played more than five thousand times between 1900 and 1918. She had first appeared as "Sis Hopkins" in the 1899 play By the Sad Sea Waves. In 1910, Melville married Frank Minzey, who played opposite her. She retired after the final performance of "Sis Hopkins" in Kansas City in 1918.

(FLOURNEY E.) MILLER (Columbia, Tn., April 14, 1887—Hollywood, Ca., June 6, 1971) and **(AUBREY L.) LYLES** (Jackson, Tn., 1884—New York, July 28, 1932)

Miller and Lyles were a black American team equally adept at writing comedy as they were at performing it. "Miller and Lyles were remarkable for the fact that they were not an actor and a stooge but two expert comedians neither of whom played the other into the shadow," commented *Theatre Arts* in 1942. Their routines were later copied by blackface comedians depicting black Americans who "tore up" (as Miller described it) the English language and used phrases such as "I'se regusted" and "Is you or is you ain't?"

The two men met while attending Fisk University. In 1907, they came to Chicago and began writing for Robert Motts's Pekin Theatre, an all-black stock company which attracted not only the leading black players of the day but also vacationing black tourists. The first Miller and Lyles production there was probably *The Husbands* in April 1907. Interestingly, the show they wrote but in which they did not appear featured a song titled "I'm Runnin' Wild." In later years, Miller claimed to have written the musical play *The Oyster Man*, featuring the distinguished black entertainer Ernest Hogan and first produced in 1907, but Miller's name does not appear in contemporary publicity for the show.

In 1908, Miller and Lyles worked briefly in vaudeville, and then in August 1909 returned to the Pekin Theatre to make their stage debut there in *The Colored Aristocrats*. The following year, they appeared in New York for the first time, and in 1911 played Hammerstein's Victoria Theatre. The first major black musical in which the couple appeared was *Darkydom*, which opened at the Howard Theatre in Washington, D.C., in 1915. After a return to vaudeville, in 1918, Miller and Lyles opened in Chicago in *Who's Stealing?* From that show developed *Shuffle Along*, for which Miller and Lyles provided the book and Noble Sissle and Eubie Blake provided the music and lyrics. *Shuffle Along* opened in New York in 1921 and was the first important all-black musical show to attract a white audience, introducing such classic songs as "I'm Just Wild about Harry" and "Love Will Find a Way."

After writing and appearing in a couple of minor dramas, Miller and Lyles produced, wrote, and starred in *Runnin' Wild*, which opened on Broadway on October 29, 1924, and introduced the Charleston. Three other, lesser shows followed, and then in 1928, the team split after a tour on the Keith circuit, for which they were paid $1,250 a week, with Lyles deciding to go to Africa. He returned to New York the following year, but the two men worked separately— Miller wrote and starred in Lew Leslie's *Blackbirds of 1930* until the close of 1930, at which time they were reunited. Their last show together was *Sugar Hill*, which opened at New York's Forrest Theatre on December 25, 1931, and ran a mere eleven performances. Following Lyles's death in 1932 following an operation for gastric ulcers, Flourney E. Miller teamed in vaudeville with Mantan Moreland. He tried unsuccessfully to prove that the CBS radio series *Amos 'n' Andy* was based on the act of Miller and Lyles. He began a film career in 1932, which lasted through 1951 and included appearances in a number of all-black productions, among which was the first all-black Western, *Harlem Rides the Range* (1938).

While it might be politically correct to denigrate Miller and Lyles for presenting a stereotypical, negative black image onstage, it is important to note that the two men were possibly the first black Americans to appear successfully in mainstream vaudeville, touring the B. F. Keith circuit as early as the summer of 1910. They were also the first black American entertainers to find an audience in Europe, going to London in 1915 and spending much of the First World War there. They were educated, intelligent men—Miller had a bachelor of arts degree—and had the business acumen to raise the financing for *Shuffle Along* from the black community.

BIBLIOGRAPHY

Govern, Peggy. "He Never Wrote an Off-Color Joke." *The Afro-American*, March 5, 1938, p. 11.

"Miller and Lyles." *Theatre Arts* 26, no. 8 (August 1942), p. 500.

Sampson, Henry T. *Blacks in Blackface: A Source Book on Early Black Musical Shows*. Metuchen, N.J.: Scarecrow Press, 1980.

———. *The Ghost Walks: A Chronological History of Blacks in Show Business, 1895–1910*. Metuchen, N.J.: Scarecrow Press, 1988.

FLORENCE MILLS (Washington, D.C., January 29, 1895—New York, November 1, 1927)

"The Pride of Harlem," as Florence Mills was often described (despite being born in Washington, D.C., and some years earlier than she claimed), was a dainty, elfin-like black girl with a sweet voice and vivacious personality. Her forte was the revue stage, and she delighted audiences with her performances in *Shuffle Along* (1921), *The Plantation Revue* (1922), *The Greenwich Village Follies* (1923), *Dixie to Broadway* (1924), and *Blackbirds* (1926). *The Billboard* on December 13, 1924, featured a photograph of Mills and her supporting players in *Dixie to Broadway* and noted the show "is the first colored attraction ever to command a $3 top price of admission."

Following her success in America, Florence Mills became the first Negro performer also to become a star in Paris, paving the way for Josephine Baker and others. Mills was the antithesis of Baker, as delicately beautiful as Baker was grotesque in her body movements and facial expressions.

Mills began her vaudeville career appearing with an act called the Tennessee Ten, whose members included a dancing trap drummer named U. S. Thompson, whom she later married. In the teens, she played the Pantages circuit as a member of a trio called The Panama Girls. After *Dixie to Broadway* closed, she returned to vaudeville, headlining the act Florence Mills and Company, which opened at New York's Hippodrome in late April 1925. The act, which was described as one of the first "colored productions" to play big-time vaudeville, featured Will Vodery and His Orchestra (also from *Dixie to Broadway*), blues trumpeter Johnny

Dunn, and Johnny Nit, "the brown skin dancer with the pearly teeth." Mills sang two numbers from *Dixie to Broadway*, "Bamboula" and "Back to Dixie," together with the number that will always be associated with her, "I'm a Little Blackbird Looking for a Bluebird, Too."

The act was reviewed somewhat patronizingly by "Ibee" in *Variety* (April 29, 1925). He commented, "Florence Mills has been a name along Broadway and in Broadway's night places for seasons. There is no reason why the Mills turn should not get the best of the big-time bookings for it is understood the salary is not exorbitant."

Florence Mills died young, adding to her legend, following an operation for appendicitis.

BIBLIOGRAPHY

"Florence Mills's Last Curtain Call." *Literary Digest*, December 3, 1927, pp. 29–30.
MacDonald, W. A. "Harlem Says Bye Bye Honey to Florence Mills." *The Bookman*, February 1928, p. 646.
Newman, Richard. "Florence Mills." In *Notable Black American Women*, ed. Jessie Carney Smith. Detroit: Gale Research, 1992, pp. 752–56.

MILLS BROTHERS

Noted for their relaxed singing style and harmonic blend, the black American group the Mills Brothers consisted of John, Jr. (bass), Harry (baritone), Herbert (first tenor), and Donald (second tenor). They began singing in the mid 1920s on radio station WLW in Cincinnati, and in 1930 were brought to New York, where they signed a contract with CBS. Billed as "Radio's New Sensations," the brothers came to fame in vaudeville after playing the Palace the week of January 23, 1931. In 1933 and 1934, the Mills Brothers performed regularly at the Paramount Theatre, Los Angeles, and as of January 1934 held the attendance record there with 82,467. Although they refused to tour the South after experiencing racial prejudice there in 1936, they were often featured as members of a minstrel troupe in vaudeville. For example, in January 1934, they played the Los Angeles Paramount with the Georgia Minstrels.

John Jr., died in 1936, and he was replaced by his father, a former opera singer. When he retired in 1957, a year before his death, the group became a trio. The trio continued to perform, with songs such as "Glow Worm," "Lazy River," "Paper Doll," and "Yellow Bird," until Harry died in June 1982.

MILWAUKEE

In 1906, four vaudeville houses were in operation in the city: the Crystal, the Forst-Keller, the Grand, and the Star. By 1921, at which time Milwaukee had a population of 485,000, it had three: the Majestic, the Miller, and the Palace.

HENRY CLAY MINER (New York, March 23, 1842—New York, February 22, 1900)

Henry Clay Miner operated what might be considered the first circuit of vaudeville theatres in the United States. He began his show business career in 1863, opening a museum and variety hall in Baltimore, in collaboration with

Charles A. Miles. In 1864, he worked as an advance man for Signor Blitz, a bird trainer and magician, and three years later became manager of Falk's Volks Garden on New York's Bowery. In 1875, Miner built and opened his first vaudeville house, the London Theatre, on the Bowery. Later, he sold the London and built the American Theatre on 13th Street, Miner's Bowery Theatre, the People's Theatre, and the Eighth Avenue Theatre. Miner also leased and managed the Brooklyn Theatre and opened the Newark Theatre in New Jersey. In 1890, he leased the Fifth Avenue Theatre, New York, and when it was destroyed by fire, rebuilt it as the Imperial Music Hall.

In 1894, Henry Clay Miner was elected to Congress on the Democratic ticket, representing New York's Ninth District, at which time his son Edwin D. Miner took over management of the theatrical empire. Edwin and his three brothers—Clay, Thomas, and George—continued to run the business after Miner's death. Aside from the theatres, the family also owned the Henry C. Miner Lithography Company, which printed most of the theatrical posters of the period.

BIBLIOGRAPHY

"The Death of Henry Clay Miner." *The New York Dramatic Mirror*, March 3, 1900, p. 17.

BORRAH MINEVITCH (Kiev, Russia, 1903—Paris, June 15, 1955)

As Borrah Minevitch proved, there were few acts in vaudeville more irritating and tiresome than a group of semi-midgets playing the harmonica. *Variety*'s Abel Green might have described him as "a Continental personality of stature," but in hindsight it is difficult to understand the appeal of Borrah Minevitch and His Harmonica Rascals, who from the late 1920s through the 1950s romped around the world's vaudeville stages, playing mouth organs of varying sizes. At the same time, one must admit that Minevitch had his many fans, and he was popular not only in vaudeville but also on radio; he popularized the harmonica and even created the Harmonica Institute of America.

Borrah Minevitch became interested in the harmonica as a youth and played his first solo number with the orchestra of Hugo Riesenfeld at the Tivoli Theatre. *Variety* (May 13, 1925) caught his act at the Palace and commented:

Coincident with what seems to be a growing fad for mouth organs comes this youthful harmonica soloist who seemingly floored the house with his appearance and then went on to render four selections to much approval. Minevitch, as to the front he presents dressed in a dinner jacket, begins where most of the dance orchestra boys proverbially end. For that reason he's a cinch with the feminine patrons before starting. His playing sounds intricate and smacks of expert technique during the manifold variations of the theme melody, whatever it may be. The repertoire is away from "blues," and mainly confines itself to popular dance selections of the semi-classical type. Minevitch seemingly depends upon his manipulation for effects to get the numbers across.

Borrah Minevitch was featured in a number of Broadway shows: *Puzzles of 1925* (1925), *Betsy* (1926), *Good Boy* (1928), and *Sweet and Low* (1930). He headlined at the Palace in December 1930 and July and October 1931.

According to another harmonica-playing vaudevillian, Ted Waldman, Minevitch was temperamental and unpopular with his colleagues. Waldman recalled one theatre manager who did not understand why Minevitch was screaming at him when his name was at the top of the bill on the theatre marquee. Minevitch yelled, "You've got too many M's and no V," to which the manager replied, "I know how to spell it—it rhymes with son-of-a-bitch."

Minevitch conceived the idea of a harmonica orchestra, which became his Rascals, a group he owned but which did not always appear with him. In addition to touring in vaudeville and playing nightclubs, Borrah Minevitch operated a bistro in Paris, was involved in film and television productions, and also owned a harmonica factory. He died while honeymooning with his second wife.

The most famous member of the Rascals was Johnny Puleo. His role in the group was that of the silent, put-upon member, who was ignored but would run around trying to gain the limelight. When the Rascals played the Palace in April 1952, supporting Betty Hutton, the group was led by Johnny Puleo, and when Minevitch died he formed a new group, Johnny Puleo and His Harmonica Gang. Both Minevitch and Puleo appeared in a number of films; the latter's last was *Trapeze* in 1957. Johnny Puleo died in Washington, D.C., in May 1983 at the age of seventy-four.

MINNEAPOLIS/ST. PAUL

In 1906, the combined cities of Minneapolis/St. Paul had six vaudeville houses: The Orpheum (Minneapolis), the Unique (Minneapolis), the Dewey (Minneapolis), the Orpheum (St. Paul), the Empire (St. Paul), and the Unique (St. Paul). By 1921, at which time the cities had a combined population of 619,000, there were still six vaudeville theatres: the Orpheum (Minneapolis), the Palace (Minneapolis), the Pantages (Minneapolis), the Orpheum (St. Paul), the Palace (St. Paul), and the Grand (St. Paul).

MINSKY BROTHERS

The Minsky Brothers were synonymous with burlesque entertainment in New York, with the leader of the clan being Michael William (Bill) Minsky (1890–1932). The Minskys' father, Louis, had come from Russia to New York's Lower East Side in 1883, adopting the name of Minsky from the city of Minsk, which was the closest to where the family had originally lived. In 1912, "Pop" Minsky built the National Theatre on East Houston Street as a home for Jewish theatre. A second auditorium on the building's roof was operated by Billy and his brother Abe as a movie theatre until 1914, when, joined by a third brother, Herbert, they converted it to a burlesque house. Initially, burlesque shows there were booked on the American Wheel circuit, but in the summer of 1916, the brothers decided to present their own in-house productions, and claimed to have the first burlesque theatre with a runway on which the showgirls could strut from the orchestra pit to the center of the audience.

On April 20, 1925, Minsky's National Winter Garden Theatre was raided by the police at the instigation of John Sumner, secretary of the New York Society for the Suppression of Vice. The raid formed the basis for the 1966 book *The Night They Raided Minsky's* and the 1968 film of the same name. The complaint against the Minsky Brothers was dismissed in court.

Meanwhile, in 1922, the brothers had taken over operation of the Park Theatre on Columbus Circle, but gave up the lease a year later. In 1923, they purchased the Apollo Theatre on 125th Street, and ran it until 1928, when it was taken over by the Hurtig & Seamon burlesque circuit. When *Abie's Irish Rose* closed in 1928 after a six-year run at the Republic Theatre, the Minskys took over the theatre and converted it to a burlesque house, the first such establishment on 42nd Street. The Republic reopened on February 12, 1931, with the Minskys' production of *Fanny Fortsin from France*, starring Gypsy Rose Lee, supported by comics Hay Hyatt, Harry Clexx, Burt Carr, and Harry Seymour. While *Variety* was always opposed to the Minsky Brothers, Brooks Atkinson in the *New York Times* and *The New Yorker* were supportive, and the last dubbed that section of 42nd Street Minskyville. Among the comedians who played the Republic were Abbott and Costello, Pigmeat Markham, Rags Ragland, and Phil Silvers. The three strippers most closely associated with the theatre were Ann Corio, Margie Hart, and Gypsy Rose Lee.

Also in 1931, the Minskys leased the Central Theatre at 48th Street and Broadway, operating it in association with Izzy Herk. That same year, Abe Minsky split with his brothers and opened the Gaiety Theatre on 45th Street and the New Gotham on 125th Street.

In September 1935, the city of New York, in answer to many complaints from merchants and civic groups, was successful in closing down the Republic Theatre. The Minsky Brothers subsequently acquired a theatre at Broadway and 51st Street, and opened it in November 1936 as Minsky's Oriental Theatre. However, on April 30, 1937, working with the Commissioner of Licenses, New York Mayor Fiorello La Guardia was able to close all burlesque theatres in New York, and at the same time banned the use of the Minsky name and the word "burlesque."

Morton Minsky (1902–1985), who had taken over operation of the family business following Billy's death in 1932—he had first worked with his brothers in 1929—converted the burlesque houses into movie theatres and in 1939 presented a Minsky show at the Canadian World Exposition in Toronto, starring Phil Silvers, but it failed to attract an audience. Abe's adopted son Harold Minsky (1915–1977) brought *Minsky's Follies* to the Desert Inn, Las Vegas, in 1950, and began a long-term relationship with the desert entertainment center. He relocated to Las Vegas in 1957 and presented shows at the Dunes, the Silver Slipper, the Thunderbird, the Aladdin, and the Fremont (where his last show was staged in 1975).

BIBLIOGRAPHY

Barber, Rowland. *The Night They Raided Minsky's: A Fanciful Expedition to the Lost Atlantis of Show Business*. New York: Simon & Schuster, 1966.

Minsky, Morton, and Milt Machlin. *Minsky's Burlesque: A Fast and Funny Look at America's Bawdiest Era*. New York: Arbor House, 1986.

"The Minsky Brothers Run N.Y. Burlesque." *Life* 2, no. 22 (May 31, 1937), p. 21.

Pringle, Henry F. "The Minsky Kids." *Collier's* 99, no. 10 (March 6, 1937), pp. 15, 60.

MINSTREL SHOWS

A forerunner to vaudeville, minstrel shows developed in the 1820s, with white Americans appearing in blackface and singing what were purported to be Negro songs. The most famous of these songs and dances was "Jim Crow," introduced by Thomas D. Rice, who on a tour in 1828 had witnessed an elderly Negro performing an odd-looking dance while singing:

> Weel about and turn about and do jus so,
> Ebery time I weel about, I jump Jim Crow.

While minstrel shows originated in the South, they quickly became popular in the northern states. Supposedly the first minstrel act seen in New York was the Virginia Minstrels, who performed at the Bowery Amphitheater on February 6, 1843. That same year, the Kentucky Minstrels appeared at the Vauxhall Gardens. Christy's Minstrels made their New York debut at Palmer's Opera House on October 22, 1846, while Bryant's Minstrels were in residence at the Mechanic's Hall from 1847 to 1857. Wood's Minstrel Hall, a former Jewish synagogue, opened at 514 Broadway in 1862.

By the middle of the nineteenth century, a format had been established for the minstrel show, which would open with the performers entering on a song, forming a semicircle, and being told "Gentlemen, be seated!" by the interlocutor who served as master of ceremonies. At each end of the semicircle sat the comedians, known as "Bruder Tambo" and "Bruder Bones," who would joke with the interlocutor. These comedians were identified as the "endmen." The first part of the show consisted of comedy, dances, and songs. The second part featured individual variety or vaudeville turns performed in front of the oleo/olio curtain. While the second act took place, the scenery was changed for the third and final act, which featured the entire company, often in a plantation setting.

Following the Civil War, minstrel shows increased in size and popularity. The shows remained all-white male, with the men appearing in blackface and also playing female or "wench" characterizations, but also a number of black minstrel troupes began to be formed, including Hicks and Height's Georgia Minstrels and Callender's Minstrels.

With the rise of vaudeville, minstrel shows lost their popularity in the 1890s, with many of the best known minstrels turning to the vaudeville stage. Blackface entertainment continued in vaudeville into the 1930s, and Al Jolson continued the tradition of minstrelsy into the motion picture.

See also LEW DOCKSTADER, GEORGE "HONEY BOY" EVANS, AL JOLSON, McINTYRE AND HEATH, GEORGE H. PRIMROSE, AL REEVES.

BIBLIOGRAPHY

Nathan, Hans. *Dan Emmett and the Rise of Early Minstrelsy*. Norman: University of Oklahoma Press, 1962.

Paskman, Dailey, and Sigmund Spaeth. *Gentlemen Be Seated!: A Parade of the Old Time Minstrels*. Garden City, N.Y.: Doubleday, 1928.

Rice, Edw. Le Roy. *Monarchs of Minstrelsy: From "Daddy" Rice to Date*. New York: Kenny Publishing Company, 1911.

Toll, Robert C. *Blacking Up: The Minstrel Show in Nineteenth Century America*. New York: Oxford University Press, 1974.

————. "The Minstrel Show: Show Biz in Blackface." In *On with the Show: The First Century of Show Business in America*. New York: Oxford University Press, 1976, pp. 81–109.

Witke, Carl. *Tambo and Bones: A History of the Minstrel Show*. Durham, N.C.: Duke University Press, 1930.

MONOLOGISTS

Monologists were the mainstay of vaudeville, presenting acts entirely reliant upon talk without the use of stooges, straight men, songs, dances, or props. Occasionally, in early years, a monologist might appear in blackface or in ethnic characterization, but generally makeup and costuming was irrelevant. "The monologist was the King of the Varieties," wrote Joe Laurie, Jr., in 1931. "He would go on without the use of make-up, scenery or music. Their motto was to walk off on a big laugh. Use enough music to play them on and off. 'Auld Lang Syne' was the standby while Irish comedians would use 'The Wearing of the Green,' the Hebrew comics would use 'Chosen Kallah Mazeltough.' The great monologists of the past have never been equalled for their wit, humor and story telling."

Among the great monologists of vaudeville's golden age were Walter C. Kelly, James J. Morton, Joe Welch, and, of course, Will Rogers. Sometimes, the monolog might consist of an observation on politics, on life, or on the comedian's family. Blackface monologist Bert Swor, who was the original partner of Charles Mack of Moran and Mack, would take out and read a letter from home, ending with the phrase, "God bless and keep you—from your loving Ma and Pa." While less in evidence and less successful, there were female monologists. In 1915, Beatrice Herford was popular with her stories of two women and a little girl visiting a restaurant while on a shopping trip, a lady from the suburbs visiting an employment agency in search of a maid, and a ten-cent-store clerk.

Arguably the greatest of all monologists was Julius Tannen, who discussed his "art" in a 1919 article in *Variety*:

The current monologist . . . must . . . study the public mind through the press, that he may humorously discuss the subjects in which people are interested. He must be possessed of tact and have respect for views that, while foreign to him, are sacred to his audiences. To make an allusion, south of the Mason and Dixon line, extolling elements to which they are permanently opposed, is stupid and must prove suicidal. To try and convert into humor, racial characteristics or to play upon unwarranted impressions of an individual or creed, is rank bad taste besides being commercially unsound. . . . Then too, the monologist must be colloquial. He must speak the language of the man in the street and some men, remember, go through the streets in their limousines.

As to where material may be had—anywhere, everywhere. In observation of what occurs daily. In innumerable libraries. In current magazines and newspapers and of all sources, the latter is inexhaustable. We have the finest column conductors in the world, our news reporters are not only impressive, but the baseball experts among them can make English bend double, do triples and perform acrobatic stunts that amuse while they terrify.

BIBLIOGRAPHY

Gordon, Cliff. "The Monologue Man." *Variety*, December 14, 1907, p. 17.

Laurie, Joe, Jr. "The Monologists." *Variety*, December 29, 1931, p. 22.

_____. "Monologists and Entertainers." In *Vaudeville: From the Honky-Tonks to the Palace*. New York: Henry Holt, 1953, pp. 170–200.

Tannen, Julius. "The Monologist—And Why." *Variety*, December 26, 1919, p. 19.

DAVID MONTGOMERY. See FRED STONE

MARSHALL MONTGOMERY (Brooklyn, N.Y., 1886—Brooklyn, N.Y., September 30, 1942)

Marshall Montgomery was a vaudeville ventriloquist with an international reputation who began his career with a comic musical act, impersonating George M. Cohan at the piano and playing the harmonica. He claimed to be the first ventriloquist to use a girl (Edna Courtney) in his act. In the last few years of his life, Montgomery worked as a nightclub entertainer at $50 per week.

FLORENCE MOORE (Philadelphia, November 13, 1886—Darby, Pa., March 23, 1935)

Florence Moore was a popular comedienne and singer on the vaudeville stage and in revue. She was also adept at mimicry, and Joe Laurie, Jr., recalled her excellent impersonation of Eddie Leonard. She began performing around the turn of the century teamed with her brother Frank as Florence Moore & Brother, but gained greater prominence in an act called Montgomery and Moore, working with her second husband, William Montgomery. Florence Moore's first Broadway success came in 1912 with *Hanky Panky*, "a jumble of jollification," which opened at the Broadway Theatre on August 5, 1912. She was also seen in *The Passing Show of 1916, Breakfast in Bed* (1920), the 1921 and 1923 editions of the *Music Box Revue*, the 1925 edition of the *Greenwich Village Follies, She Couldn't Say No!* (1926), *Artists and Models* (1927), and *International Revue* (1930). In the late 1920s, the Palace Theatre introduced the idea of masters of ceremony, and in March 1927, Florence Moore became its first mistress of ceremonies. She returned to the Palace again in July and December 1928, appeared in a few short subjects, and made her last Broadway appearance in a 1932 revival of *Cradle Snatchers*.

VICTOR MOORE (Hammonton, N.J., February 24, 1876—East Islip, N.Y., July 23, 1962)

With his owl-like features, diffidence, and solemnity, Victor Moore was the quintessential timid man, who behaved as if he should apologize for his existence. Short, pudgy, and balding, he played the role of the forgotten man and made him unforgettable.

Victor Moore began his stage career as a "super" in a June 1893 production of *Babes in the Wood* at a Boston theatre. The following year, he joined the Ideal Repertory Company, touring Massachusetts, and subsequently worked with other stock companies. In the late 1890s, Moore turned to vaudeville and came to fame in 1902 with a sketch titled "Change Your Act, or Back to the Woods," for which he paid a fellow actor $125. The sketch had a theatrical background and concerned a vaudeville team that is given notice and heckled by one of the stagehands. While appearing in the sketch at New York's Brighton Beach Music Hall in 1903, Moore met Emma Littlefield; they married and she joined the act. (Littlefield died in 1933.)

George M. Cohan saw Victor Moore in "Change Your Act" at Hammerstein's in 1905, and he wrote the part of Kid Burns, the prizefighter, in *45 Min-utes from Broadway* (1906) for him. The show made Moore a star, and he was featured the following year in another Cohan production, *The Talk of New York*. Moore entered films in 1915 and returned to the screen intermittently through 1955, when he appeared as a plumber discovering Marilyn Monroe in the bathtub in *The Seven Year Itch*. His finest screen role is undoubtedly as Barkley Cooper, playing opposite Beulah Bondi in *Make Way for Tomorrow* (1937).

Appearances on stage and screen were little more than interruptions to the actor, for, as *Theatre Arts* (March 1942) commented, "legitimate and film roles were merely intermissions between vaudeville tours, and when he finally did desert his first love, it was only to move over to its polished offshoot, musical comedy."

As late as May 1931, Victor Moore headlined at the Palace, but in December of that same year, he played what was to become his favorite stage role, that of U.S. vice president Alexander Throttlebottom in *Of Thee I Sing*. With the role of Senator Oliver P. Loganberry in *Louisiana Purchase*, which Moore played onstage in 1940 and on-screen in 1941, it remains his finest achievement. Other Broadway shows in which Moore appeared include *Let 'em Eat Cake* (1933), *Anything Goes* (1934), *Leave It to Me!* (1938), and *Nellie Bly* (1946). He also starred in a successful 1953 revival of *On Borrowed Time*.

BIBLIOGRAPHY

Coffin, Patricia. "Victor Moore." *Look*, August 5, 1942, pp. 46–49.

Funke, Lewis B. "Victor Moore, or Forty Years a Timid Man." *The New York Times Magazine*, January 6, 1946, pp. 12, 38–39.

Lincks, Peggy. "It's a Gay Life—If You Don't Weaken!" *Motion Picture Magazine*, August 1918, pp. 41–42.

Smith, Cecil. "Critic Describes Victor Moore's Acting as True Genius." *Chicago Tribune*, December 7,1941, part 6, p. 2.
Smith, Frederick James. "Lonely Comic: The Private Life of Victor Moore." *Liberty* 14, no. 46 (November 13, 1937), pp. 37–38.
"Victor Moore." *Time*, May 27, 1946, p. 43.
"Where Are They Now?" *Newsweek*, November 12, 1956, p. 24.

(GEORGE) MORAN (Elmwood, Ks., 1882—Oakland, Ca., August 1, 1949) and **(CHARLES) MACK** (White Cloud, Ks., November 22, 1887—Mesa, Az., January 11, 1934)

After the demise of McIntyre and Heath, one blackface comedy team was left to continue the tradition established by those preeminent minstrels, and that was Moran and Mack. Also known as the Two Black Crows, Moran and Mack had become partners in the late teens, but it was not until 1927 that they became major stars, thanks largely to their recording of the sketch "The Early Bird Catches the Worm." It was, and remains, a classic routine, with Mack as the stereotypical lazy Negro, shuffling around the stage and speaking his lines slowly, very much as Stepin' Fetchit was to do on-screen a few years later. Mack would explain to Moran, "I would go to work, if I could find any pleasure in it." When asked to spell Ohio, he replied, "Capital O-h-ten." When Moran asked Mack to explain why the white horses on the farm ate more than the black horses, Mack responded, "We never could find out, unless it was because we had more of the white horses than black horses." It may not read well in print, but as recorded on film, the dialogue was hilarious, aided by Moran and Mack's immaculate timing.

Charles Mack entered show business as a stage electrician after serving as a catcher on the Olympia (Washington) baseball team. Because his jokes and stories went over so well with vaudevillians, Alexander Pantages suggested that Mack go onstage as a single act. As a solo performer, he was on the same bill as a blackface act called Garvin and Moran, and at Mack's suggestion, the latter teamed with him in a blackface double act. One of the pair's first major appearances was in the Sigmund Romberg revue *Over the Top*, which opened at the 44th Street Roof Theatre on November 28, 1917, with a cast that also included Fred and Adele Astaire, Justine Johnstone, and Mary Eaton. In the 1920s, Moran and Mack were possibly more popular on the revue stage than in vaudeville, although they did headline at the Hippodrome in September 1925 and at the Palace in May 1927. They were seen in the 1920 edition of the Ziegfeld *Follies*, the 1924 edition of *The Greenwich Village Follies*, and the 1927 edition of Earl Carroll's *Vanities*. In the last, Moran and Mack introduced another classic routine, "The Rock Pile," in which they appeared as two convicts and engaged in the following dialogue:

Moran: Man, is it hot.

Mack: Sho, nuff. Wish I had an ice-cold watermelon.

Moran: Oh, lawdy. Me, too.

Mack: Wish I had a hundred ice-cold watermelons.

Moran: Hm, huh.

Mack: Wish I had a thousand ice-cold watermelons.

Moran: Glory be. I bet if you had a thousand ice-cold watermelons you'd give me one.

Mack: Oh, naw! No siree. If you are too lazy to wish for your own watermelons, you ain't gonna get none of mine.

In 1927, Moran and Mack recorded "The Early Bird Catches the Worm" for Columbia, and it became an immediate best-seller. So popular were the pair that, in 1928, another act, Moss and Frye, tried to bill themselves as the Two Black Crows.

With their popularity in revue and vaudeville, it was natural that Moran and Mack should enter motion pictures, which they did in 1929 with the Paramount feature *Why Bring That Up?*, written by the popular Jewish writer of Negro stories Octavus Roy Cohen and directed by Broadway producer George Abbott. Moran and Mack was an unusual act offstage in that it was owned exclusively by Charles Mack—he controlled Moran and Mack as a registered, copyrighted trademark. Mack wrote most of the material and took the lion's share of the team's salary. When Moran demanded an equal portion of the pair's earnings, Mack refused, and Moran walked out on the act.

One supporter of Moran was Robert Benchley, who wrote in *Life* (December 16, 1926), "It always seemed to us that of all semi-straight-men Mr. Moran possessed the most individuality and skill. In our enthusiasm for the lethargic Mr. Mack we are apt to neglect Mr. Moran's contribution to the philosophical discussion. He was always so cross and scowling and so thoroughly impatient with his companion's phlegmatic search after Truth and he built up quite a character of his own."

It is possible that there was more than one replacement for the original Moran, but the most important was Bert Swor, who had been half of the blackface act of the Swor Bros., and who had appeared in *Why Bring That Up?* With Swor, Mack starred in a second Paramount feature *Anybody's War*, released in the summer of 1930. Despite the change in personnel, the film's stars were billed as Moran and Mack. The two appeared in blackface throughout, but the production was not a success, with Sime Silverman writing in *Variety* (July 16, 1930), "Story itself is silly without being laughable." After the release of *Anybody's War*, George Moran returned to the act in time to play the RKO circuit in September 1930 at a salary of $5,000.

While driving to New York with George Moran and Mack Sennett, and with plans to appear in a series of comedy shorts for the producer, Charles Mack was killed in an automobile accident near Mesa, Arizona. After Mack's death, Moran continued with the act for a few years, but the popularity of blackface acts declined rapidly in the 1930s. During the Second World War, Moran toured with the U.S.O. He died in the charity ward of an Oakland, California, hospital.

There might appear to have been much that was racist in Moran and Mack's performance, but no contemporary criticism was ever leveled at them on this point. Indeed, *Variety* noted that Moran and Mack probably had as many fans among black Americans as white audiences.

BIBLIOGRAPHY
Carle, Teet. "Moran and Mack: The Two Black Crows." *Hollywood Studio Magazine*, July 1972, pp. 14–18.
Lewis, Lloyd. "Two Black Crows." *The New Republic*, March 14, 1928, pp. 124–25.
Mack, Charles. *Two Black Crows in the A.E.F.* Indianapolis: Bobbs-Merrill, 1928.
Maltin, Leonard. "Moran and Mack." In *Movie Comedy Teams*. New York: New American Library, 1970, pp. 318–22.

HELEN MORGAN (Danville, Il., August 2, 1900—Chicago, October 8, 1941)

The name Helen Morgan immediately brings to mind the vision of a small woman with a hauntingly beautiful face perched on top of a grand piano and singing a lament about her lost man. The artist James Montgomery Flagg thought her singing "a composite of all the ruined women in the world," while one critic described her as "Camille on a piano." The songs that she sang—"Bill," "Can't Help Lovin' Dat Man," "Why Was I Born?," "What Wouldn't I Do for that Man," and "Body and Soul"—were exclusively her property. No other performer could sing them, before or since, with the same feeling and the same emotional tug at the heartstrings.

Born of French-Canadian parents, Helen Morgan began her working life in the Chicago area as a lingerie model, a clerk at Marshall Field's, and a packer with the National Biscuit Company. She once claimed that she always perched on a piano during her act because "I had to stand up twelve hours a day for years, boxing crackers, and I made a vow to sit down forever if I got the chance." Helen Morgan came to New York in 1918 after winning a couple of beauty contests and was eventually hired by Florenz Ziegfeld to appear in the chorus of *Sally*, which opened at the New Amsterdam Theatre on December 21, 1920. It ran for two years, and when it closed, Morgan went to Chicago for an engagement at the Café Montmartre.

She returned to New York and accepted various nightclub engagements and performed in extremely minor roles in several shows, although it seems impossible to identify which. She was definitely in the 1925 edition of George White's *Scandals* and, despite having no billing, was also in the 1926 show *Americana*, singing "Nobody Wants Me." By the mid to late 1920s, Helen Morgan was also appearing in various nightclubs that bore her name: Helen Morgan's 54th Street Club, Chez Helen Morgan, Helen Morgan's Summer House, and The House of Morgan. (In 1928, she was arrested for violation of the prohibition laws.) In these clubs, Morgan developed the technique of delivering her songs perched on a grand piano; one story, probably apocryphal, is that there was so little room for Morgan to stand and perform that Ring Lardner picked her up and placed her on the piano. It's a nice story, even if untrue, and there is no doubt that by late 1926, that style of delivery had become Morgan's trademark.

Variety mentions it in reviewing Helen Morgan's first appearance in vaudeville at the Palace in January 1927. With Joe Santley at the piano, she sang four numbers, and the trade paper described her as "an exotic brunette [who] would be a find for vaudeville ordinarily. She is a treat optically and a talented entertainer." Helen Morgan returned to headline at the Palace in March 1930 and February 1931.

The one role with which Helen Morgan will always be associated is that of Julie in *Show Boat*, which opened at the Ziegfeld Theatre on December 26, 1927, after tryouts in Washington, D.C., Philadelphia, Pittsburgh, and Cleveland. Legend has it that the show's composer, Jerome Kern, saw Morgan sing "Nobody Wants Me" in *Americana* and declared that he had found his Julie. Certainly, she *was* Julie, and no one could sing "Bill" and "Can't Help Lovin' Dat Man" as she did. Fortunately, a record of her performance exists in the 1936 screen version of *Show Boat*, one of a half-dozen feature films in which she appeared in the 1930s. She had entered films in 1929 in Rouben Mamoulian's *Applause*, in which she gives an extraordinary performance as the boozy burlesque queen Kitty Darling. Incidentally, this motion picture provides a perfect re-creation of a small-town 1910 burlesque show.

But by 1929, the boozy Kitty Darling was beginning to resemble the real-life Helen Morgan a little too closely. Liquor was taking its toll on the singer, as her face clearly indicated. She continued to appear in vaudeville, nightclubs, and musical comedies—including the 1929 edition of Ziegfeld's *Midnight Frolic* and the 1931 edition of the *Follies*—but not always in front of enthusiastic audiences. On April 5, 1930, *The Billboard* complained that all Helen Morgan's songs were the same; she was always crooning about her man and plaintively melodizing about her "chronic melancholy." In September 1941, she came to Chicago to appear in a version of *George White's Scandals* at the State Lake Theatre. She became seriously ill with a liver complaint brought on by her drinking and died there in the city where her career had begun.

Since her death, there have been at least two versions of Helen Morgan's life story, the first on CBS's *Playhouse 90* in 1957, starring Polly Bergen. The second, filmed by M-G-M, featured Ann Blyth, with songs dubbed by Gogi Grant, in *The Helen Morgan Story*, also from 1957. Neither did justice to this unique show business personality.

BIBLIOGRAPHY

Bolitho, William. "Two Stars." *The Delineator*, January 1931, p. 15.
Hoffman, Irving. "Helen Morgan the Magnificent." *Life* 99, no 2563 (February 1932), pp. 34–35, 53.
Maxwell, Gilbert. *Helen Morgan: Her Life and Legend*. New York: Hawthorn Books, 1974.
Taylor, Tim. "The Girl on the Piano." *Cue*, May 4, 1957, pp. 17, 55.
"Torchbearer's End." *Time*, October 20, 1941, p. 79.
"Voice of an Era." *Newsweek*, October 20, 1941, p. 70.

LILY MORRIS (London, 1884—London, October 3, 1952)

One of the great singing comediennes of British music hall, Lily Morris was a buxom entertainer who would appear onstage wearing an outrageous hat and a loose-fitting, unattractive dress. Often ending her numbers with an eccentric dance involving high kicks, Morris immortalized two comic songs, "Why Am I Always the Bridesmaid?" and "Don't Have Any More Mrs. Moore," with its plaintive line, "Too many double gins, gives the ladies double chins." Happily, both songs are preserved on film in the 1930 British production *Elstree Calling*.

Lily Morris began her show business career in pantomime in London at the age of ten, and within a dozen years was a major star. She made her U.S. vaudeville debut at the New York Hippodrome in January 1925 and was an immediate hit with the audience, being brought back for an encore and a brief speech of thanks. Writing in *Variety* (January 7, 1925), "Skig" commented, "Miss Morris earned the major share of applause allotted and deserved it.... Her clear-cut enunciation was especially noteworthy. In fact, Miss Morris' entire performance smacked of experienced showmanship.... She impresses as an English comedienne capable of taking care of herself anywhere." The entertainer returned to the United States in 1928 and was the headliner on the bill at the Palace Theatre for the week of January 23, singing the aforementioned songs together with "I Don't Wanna Get Old," "What You Gonna Do about Salena," and "In the Shade of the Old Apple Tree" (which proved an immediate favorite with the audience). The critic for *The Billboard* (February 4, 1928) suggested Morris could have stayed onstage for an hour, noting, "Here is a great artiste, it is undeniable. Standing alone as an entertainer, she alone of contemporary entertainers affects the senses in a new way, offering from her kit-bag of songs new things that thrill one with new thrills. Miss Morris gets under the skin, rivets the attention, soothes jaded amusement appetites and quickens the interest."

WILLIAM MORRIS (Schwartzenau, Germany, May 1, 1873—New York, November 1, 1932)

The founder of the agency that bears his name and which now covers all aspects of show business representation, William Morris was the leading independent vaudeville agent and booker. Noted for his showmanship and the publicity he could generate for his clients, Morris brought Harry Lauder to American vaudeville, and Lauder always remained loyal to him as did the agent's many other clients.

Morris began his career in the United States soliciting advertising for a tobacco trade paper before becoming assistant to agent George Liman. When the latter died, at the suggestion of William Hammerstein and Percy G. Williams, Morris founded his own agency. When the United Booking Office was formed in 1906, Morris was offered a managerial position with the B. F. Keith organization, but he turned it down, preferring to remain an independent, booking acts for smaller circuits and independent theatres outside of the Keith control, such as the United States Amusement Co., Poli, Tony Pastor, Hyde and Behman in Chicago, and Kohl and Castle in Chicago. At one point, he operated the Boston Music Hall in opposition to B. F. Keith, and became an ardent foe of Keith executive E. F. Albee.

William Morris died at the Friars Club while playing pinochle. He was succeeded as president of the agency by his son William Morris, Jr. When Jr. retired in 1952, he was succeeded by Abe Lastfogel (who had worked with William Morris, Sr.), and when Lastfogel became board chairman in 1969, he was succeeded as president by Nat Lefkowitz.

LEE MORSE (Tennessee, 1904—Rochester, N.Y., December 16, 1954)

A contralto with a low register, Lee Morse was a blues singer who enjoyed considerable popularity in the 1920s and 1930s as a Columbia recording artist. She made her vaudeville debut in 1920, and with Frank Fay was one of the stars of the revue *Artists and Models*, which opened at New York's Shubert Theatre on August 20, 1923. Lee Morse was often heard on radio with her Blue Grass Boys, and her best known song, which typifies the numbers she performed, is "Moanin' Low." A comeback attempt in the 1940s was unsuccessful.

Lee Morse's brother was Glenn Taylor, a former Democratic senator from Idaho and nominee for vice president on the Progressive Party ticket in 1948.

JAMES J. MORTON (Boston, December 25, 1861—Islip, N.Y., April 10, 1938)

Billed as "The Boy Comic," James J. Morton weighed more than 250 pounds and gave the impression of an overgrown child desperate to please the audience. He would sing songs without music and without a rhyme, and would tell jokes that were pointless. Sometimes, as an encore, he would return to the stage announcing that he had left out a couple of lines from one of his songs, then proceed to sing lyrics that made absolutely no sense. In the 1890s, he appeared in vaudeville with his wife, Maude Revel, but then developed a single act. In 1906, at New York's American Theatre, he appeared for the first time as a master of ceremonies, and in the years before professional masters of ceremonies were utilized in vaudeville, became the medium's first. He would stand at the side of the stage and ad-lib comments on the various acts that were about to appear. For many years, he feuded with another vaudeville act, James C. Morton, who also worked as Morton and Moore, and spent large sums of money advertising in the trade papers that he was James *J.* Morton. He died penniless, a resident of the Percy Williams Home for Actors.

MOSCONI BROTHERS

Louis and Charles Mosconi presented a fast-moving dance act, involving their seemingly walking up the side of the set, often with the latter dressed as a girl. They learned to dance at a school founded by their father, Charles Mosconi, Sr., in Philadelphia circa 1908, and began appearing professionally while still children in the Philadelphia area. As early as June 1915, the brothers played the Palace, with Louis impersonating Charlie Chaplan and Charles impersonating a woman. They were subsequently to appear at the Palace on many occasions, including 1919, 1923, and 1924, and claimed to hold the record for the number of weeks at the theatre—fifty-two over a seven-year period. The brothers also appeared in *A World of Pleasure* (1915), *All Star Jamboree* (1921), and the 1925 edition of the Ziegfeld *Follies*.

In 1923, Louis and Charles Mosconi with sister Verna and brother Willie played the London Palladium, billed as "The Eighth Wonder of the World." Willie and Verna would occasionally join the act, as would Charles, Sr., at which point the Mosconi Brothers became the Mosconi Family. Louis and Charles last played vaudeville at New York's Orpheum Theatre on 86th Street in 1934. Charles, Sr., died in Philadelphia on February 27, 1942, at the age of seventy-four. After retiring from vaudeville, Louis Mosconi operated a dance school in Los Angeles, which remained open through 1967. He died in Hollywood, California, on August 1, 1969, at the age of seventy-four. Charles, Jr., became a ticket broker; he died in New York on March 1, 1975, at the age of eighty-four. A cousin, Willie Mosconi, was a noted world billiards champion.

BIBLIOGRAPHY

Smith, Bill. "Charles Mosconi." In *The Vaudevillians*. New York: Macmillan, 1976, pp. 140–44.

JOHN J. MURDOCK (Scotland, 1865—Los Angeles, December 8, 1948)

The second-in-command at the B. F. Keith circuit, under E. F. Albee, was John J. Murdock, who remained in the background at the organization but was, when needed, as ruthless as his boss. Murdock was a small, innocent-looking man with considerable guile and a strong sense of the value of money. Surprisingly, unlike Albee, he was generally well liked by vaudevillians, perhaps because he kept aloof from most public disputes and arguments and was fervently loyal to friends and former colleagues. When Albee had a bitter dispute with Sime Silverman and *Variety*, Murdock retained his friendship with the publisher and provided him with inside information on the Keith organization. Murdock also had his own stool pigeons, vaudevillians who were paid by him to listen to backstage gossip and report on the remarks of their fellow performers, some of whom were blacklisted as a result of what Murdock learned.

Murdock began his working life as an electrician, but by 1900 had his own theatrical stock company in Cincinnati. At the turn of the century, he managed the Masonic Temple Roof in Chicago, which was often referred to as Murdock's

Roof, and made it a major vaudeville venue. While managing the Roof, Murdock advertised a forthcoming vaudeville act as "The Girl with the Auburn Hair." There was no such performer, but he had a minor entertainer named Grace Akis appear onstage in the role, posed with a group of choir boys singing semireligious numbers. Subsequently, Murdock married her.

From Chicago, "J.J.," as he was generally known, came to New York to join Keith and Albee and remained with the organization throughout its existence. Murdock tried unsuccessfully to persuade Albee to alternate vaudeville acts with motion pictures in the Keith theatres in the early 1920s. It was possibly Albee's intransigence that led Murdock to sell his shares in the B. F. Keith organization to Joseph P. Kennedy and thus set in motion the takeover of the company. Murdock was responsible for the purchase of the Producers Distributing Corporation by Keith-Albee, and when the company's name was changed to Pathé, he became chairman of the board, a position he held until his retirement in 1929.

BIBLIOGRAPHY

Laurie, Joe, Jr. "John J. Murdock (The Last of a Great Tradition)." *Variety*, December 15, 1948, pp. 2, 18.

J. HAROLD MURRAY (South Berwick, Me., February 17, 1891—Killingworth, Ct., December 11, 1940)

Best known for his role as Jim in the original stage production of *Rio Rita*, which he played for two years from 1927 through 1929, J. Harold Murray had an attractive, virile voice and a pleasing personality. It is unfortunate that John Boles and not he was asked to star in RKO's 1929 film version, for Murray's rendition of "The Ranger's Song" has far more bite to it than Boles's.

J. Harold Murray was born Harry Roulon and began his career as a song plugger for publisher Leo Feist. He entered vaudeville in 1918 and was kept busy in that medium until 1920, when he made his Broadway debut in *The Passing Show of 1921* at the Winter Garden Theatre. For the remainder of the 1920s, Murray was active on the Broadway stage, starring in *Vogues of 1924*, *China Rose* (1925), *Captain Jinks* (1925), and *Castles in the Air* (1926), among others.

He also found time for the occasional vaudeville appearance; in November 1924, Murray appeared in the number four position on the bill at the Palace in a fourteen-minute act with Leo Feiner at the piano. He sang "On the Road to Mandalay," "Dear One," and "Falling in Love with Someone." "Con" in *Variety* hailed him as "the singing find of the season for vaudeville. . . . He has everything—appearance, good rangey singing voice, and more personality than any other singer of this type usually allows himself." A few years later, on March 27, 1929, *Variety* dubbed Murray "a natural for vaudeville or the picture palaces." The singer chose the latter, signed a contract with William Fox, and starred in *Happy Days* (1929), *Married in Hollywood* (1929), *Cameo Kirby* (1930), *Women Everywhere* (1930), and *Under Suspicion* (1931), among others.

Reviewing *Women Everywhere, Photoplay* (July 1930) noted that "J. Harold Murray has a voice that can't fail to charm you."

Murray returned to the Broadway stage for *East Wind* (1931) and *Face the Music* (1932). His last major stage role was in *Venus in Silk*, which closed in Pittsburgh before reaching Broadway. Gradually, Murray drifted away from show business (although he did star in the late 1930s on a radio program emanating out of Hartford, Connecticut) and devoted his time to the New England Brewing Company of which he was president and whose product was labeled Murray's Beer. The genial baritone died a wealthy man.

KEN MURRAY (New York, July 14, 1903—Burbank, Ca., October 12, 1988)

Ken Murray personified show business. He was a vaudeville star of the 1920s and 1930s who once boasted Bob Hope as his understudy. He became a leading man on-screen in 1929. He had his own radio program in the 1930s and his own television series in the 1950s. He headlined for an unprecedented twenty-five straight weeks in Las Vegas. His was the author of several books. He received a Special Academy Award in 1947 for his extraordinary feature *Bill and Coo*. Then, of course, there was Ken Murray's *Blackouts*, which ran for seven and one-half years from 1942 to 1949, played to five million paying customers, and was renowned as Hollywood's most popular show. If all that was not enough, Ken Murray had been taking home movies of the stars for many years, and he edited these into a number of compilation films, including *Hollywood—My Home Town* (1962), *Ken Murray's Hometown Hollywood* (1973), and *Ken Murray Shooting Stars* (1978).

Born Kenneth Abner Doncourt, Murray made his stage debut with the Pete Curly Trio in vaudeville, in Huntington, Long Island, in 1922. That same year he changed his name to Murray, when a fellow named Morey left the act of Morey, Senna, and Dean, and Charles Senna invited Ken to join the act. The name change to Murray, Senna, and Dean was close enough to the original for bookers to be unaware of a change in personnel.

With his first wife, Charlotte, Murray developed a reasonably successful vaudeville routine. *Variety* (April 14, 1926) reviewed the act at New York's Broadway Theatre and commented, "Ken Murray is one of those swift-talking nut comics who runs from one gag into another with lightning rapidity. . . . He has a good sense of pacing the act and when he comes to the end, he gives a climax and gets off—commendable." *Variety* liked Murray's clarinet playing, which he did very well and which became a staple of his act through the years, but found Charlotte meant nothing to the routine, a comment with which Murray obviously agreed, because he divorced her shortly thereafter.

Variety also questioned the risqué nature of some of Murray's jokes, but these were the performer's stock-in-trade during his vaudeville years. A typical one-liner was, "Two old maids took a tramp in the woods—the tramp died." It was because of such jokes that Ken Murray acquired his most famous prop, a cigar. As he recalled, he was playing Proctor's Newark and read a write-up of his act the next day in which the reviewer complained that Ken's countenance, his cherubic face, belied the type of risqué material that he performed. "So what I did," said Murray, "was take the cigar merely to put some miles on my countenance. There were many comedians in those days who had a cigar, and while George Burns gets credit for the cigar today, he didn't even start in as early as I did." Ken Murray's other trademark, the crewcut, dates not from his vaudeville years but from the 1940s, when he was in *Blackouts*. Taking a vacation in the Canadian backwoods one year, he asked his barber to give him a crewcut so he would not have to worry about his long hair. Murray liked the convenience of the crewcut so much that he decided to retain it.

By April 1928, Murray was headlining at the Palace—he was back there in October 1928 and December 1928, September and December 1929, November and December 1930, and April 1932—and according to *Variety*, he was carrying the show. Ken Murray had reached the top of one profession, and, unlike many of his fellow vaudevillians, he decided to try something new. He became a movie star, playing lead roles in *Half Marriage* and *Leathernecking* for RKO in 1929 and 1930 respectively. Next, it was radio, on which he made his debut in 1932 as a guest of Rudy Vallee's on *The Fleischmann Hour*, followed in the same year by his own short-lived *The Ken Murray Show*. In 1935, Murray starred in *Earl Carroll's Sketch Book*, his debut in a Broadway musical. Television was an obvious challenge for Ken Murray, one that he readily accepted with *The Ken Murray Show*, a comedy variety series featuring Darla Hood (of the "Our Gang" series), Jack Mulhall (a former silent screen leading man), and Tony Labriola (who had been with Murray on radio, in the character of "Oswald"). The series ran on CBS from January 7, 1950, through June 21, 1953. Murray also found time to produce a sixty-minute color feature for Republic Pictures, *Bill and Coo*, with a cast comprised entirely of birds whose story is narrated by him. For his work, he received a Special Academy Award, "for a novel and entertaining use of the medium of motion pictures."

Bill and Coo developed from one of the acts—George Burton's Birds—featured in Murray's long-running variety show *Blackouts*. Nothing more than a glorified vaudeville show, *Blackouts* opened at Hollywood's El Capitan Theatre on June 24, 1942, and finally closed some seven years later on April 28, 1949. *Blackouts* featured Marie Wilson (into whose cleavage Ken Murray was forever leering), along with Daisy the Dog, Jack Mulhall, and the Hollywood Elder-lovelies, nine senior citizens who proved as talented and vivacious as the showgirls called the Glamourlovelies in *Blackouts*. The show was very much in the vaudeville tradition with its ongoing comedy poker game—a standout feature in which many famous Hollywood personalities participated—and its gags along the same risqué lines as Murray's act from the 1920s. A typical routine might open with Murray's asking Marie Wilson, "Do you have a fairy Godmother?," to which she would respond, "No, but I have an uncle in Philadelphia we're not too sure about." *Blackouts* had a brief New York run, opening at the Ziegfeld

Theatre on September 6, 1949, and closing fifty-one performances later on October 15 of the same year.

The key to Ken Murray's success through the years is not hard to discover. Of course, talent and old-fashioned showmanship had a lot to do with it, but it was also his willingness to get involved. He did not merely introduce other acts in vaudeville, television, or *Blackouts*; he participated in those acts, whether doing acrobatics, playing his clarinet with Louis Armstrong, or performing a buck and wing with Pat Rooney, Jr. Ken Murray was an all-around entertainer in an age of one-dimensional performers.

BIBLIOGRAPHY

Murray, Ken. "How I Broke into Society." *Liberty* 18, no. 13, March 29, 1941, pp. 55–56.

―――――. *Life on a Pogo Stick: Autobiography of a Comedian*. Philadelphia: Winston, 1960.

―――――. *The Golden Days of San Simeon*. Garden City, N.Y.: Doubleday, 1971.

―――――. *The Body Merchant: The Story of Earl Carroll*. Pasadena, Ca.: Ward Ritchie Press, 1976.

―――――. "Introduction: Happiness *Was* Being a Vaudevillian." In *The Vaudevillians: A Dictionary of Vaudeville Performers* by Anthony Slide. Westport, Ct.: Arlington House, 1981, p. ix.

Smith, Bill. "Ken Murray." In *The Vaudevillians*. New York: Macmillan, 1976, pp. 195–202.

N _____

CARRY AMELIA MOORE NATION (Garrard County, Ky., November 25, 1846—Leavenworth, Mo., June 9, 1911)

Carry (also known as Carrie) Nation was a woman of commanding appearance and fierce belief in the rightness of her cause, which was the abolition of alcohol. She began her campaign in the 1890s when she founded a local branch of the Woman's Christian Temperance Union, and by the turn of the century, she had become a well-known figure throughout the country, swinging her axe and destroying any saloon unfortunate enough to be in her path. Her 1904 autobiography, *The Use and Need of the Life of Carry A. Nation*, was a best-seller.

Such was Nation's popularity that she engaged a personal manager, Harry C. Turner, and accepted bookings through the Furlong Lyceum Bureau. It was no surprise that she should have found an audience in vaudeville. In December 1903, she was starred in a playlet titled *Ten Nights in a Bar Room* at New York's Third Avenue Theatre. Mrs. Nation provided her own dialogue, wrecked the bar scene at every performance, passed through the audience selling miniature hatchets, and also talked back to the hecklers in the crowd. "She is the most daring star we have even seen, for she talks back to her audience, and Third Avenue is delighted," reported *The Billboard* (December 26, 1903).

Her reception was less than friendly when Carry Nation played the London music halls in February 1909. Eggs were thrown at her, there were shouts of "Get off," and a voice from the gallery suggested, "'ave a drop o' gin, old dear." Nation labored bravely on, even telling a few members of the audience in the front rows what she thought of them, but the management of London's Canterbury Music Hall decided it was safer to cancel her contract. "She simply wasn't popular," commented *Variety* (February 13, 1909), somewhat understating the situation.

BIBLIOGRAPHY

Ashbury, Hebert. *Carry Nation*. New York: Alfred A. Knopf, 1929.

Beals, Carleton. *Cyclone Carry: The Story of Carry Nation*. Philadelphia: Chilton, 1962.

Madison, Arnold. *Carry Nation*. Nashville, Tn.: Thomas Nelson, 1977.

Taylor, Robert Lewis. *Vessel of Wrath: The Life and Times of Carry Nation*. New York: New American Library, 1966.

NATIONAL AMUSEMENT MANAGERS' ASSOCIATION

A successor to the National Vaudeville Managers' Association, founded in 1907, the National Amusement Managers' Association was an alliance of small-time vaudeville houses, amusement parks, and similar institutions for which acts were furnished by Gus Sun. It was inactive by the early 1920s.

NATIONAL VAUDEVILLE ARTISTS, INC.

The National Vaudeville Artists, Inc., was created in 1916 by E. F. Albee as a "company union." As *Equity* magazine commented in March 1924, "It was formed so that the vaudeville artists could be herded into an organization under the control of the vaudeville managers. The N.V.A. is a lightning rod down which the collective strength of the vaudeville actor runs harmlessly into the ground." The National Vaudeville Artists was a successful attempt by Albee to dissipate the strength of the White Rats (q.v.), and when the latter organization struck, with disastrous results to itself, in 1917, Albee was able to acquire its clubhouse in 1919 as the headquarters for the N.V.A. Located at 229 West 49th Street in New York, the clubhouse was an elegant establishment, providing bedrooms, a cafeteria, and a swimming pool for members, who paid an annual fee of $10. Eddie Leonard was the organization's first president, succeeded tin June 1917 by Willard Mack. The secretary was a former vaudevillian named Henry Chesterfield, who answered directly to Albee.

In order to obtain a booking on the B. F. Keith or Orpheum circuits, vaude-villians were required to warrant their membership in the N.V.A. If needed, they were expected to perform without pay at the N.V.A. Sunday concerts, and were also expected to take paid advertising in the handsome souvenir books put out annually by the association. There was no choice as to the size or price of the advertisement; that was determined by Albee and his colleagues. In return for their membership dues, vaudevillians were promised a $1,000 death benefit, and the story is told of Duffy and Sweeney's sending a telegram to the N.V.A., reading, "We died here at the matinee, please send $1,000."

In 1925, E. F. Albee opened the N.V.A. Lodge at Saranac Lake, New York, for those vaudevillians suffering from tuberculosis. In 1936, the lodge was turned over to the Will Rogers Memorial Commission, and continues through the present as the Will Rogers Institute, funded by the motion picture industry.

In the late 1920s, as vaudeville went into decline, E. F. Albee lost interest in the N.V.A. At his death, he left no money toward the upkeep of the clubhouse, and in 1937 it was sold, although the National Vaudeville Artists continued in existence through the 1950s.

ALLA NAZIMOVA (Yalta, Russia, May 22 or June 4, 1879—Los Angeles, July 13, 1945)

Alla Nazimova was one of the leading stage actresses of the early twentieth century, who brought a new realism and naturalistic performance to the medium. As she explained in 1937, "The actor should not play a part like the Aeolian harps that used to hang in the trees to be played only by the breeze, the actor should be an instrument *played upon* by the character he depicts.'' Born Alla Leventon, Nazimova made her U.S. debut, speaking in Russian, as Lia in *The Chosen People* at New York's Herald Square Theatre on March 23, 1905. She made her English-language debut at New York's Princess Theatre on November 13, 1906, as the title character in *Hedda Gabler*. It was the first in a long line of definitive portrayals that were to include Nora in *A Doll's House*, Hilda in *The Master Builder*, Christine Mannon in *Mourning Becomes Electra*, O-Lan in *The Good Earth*, and Mrs. Alving in *Ghosts*.

Nazimova made her vaudeville debut at the Palace Theatre in 1914 in a one-act play by George Middleton titled *The Unknown Woman*. The production was a comment on the hypocrisy of New York's divorce laws and concerned a fallen woman (Nazimova) hired by a rich man to provide fake evidence in a divorce action. At the first Monday afternoon performance, the play was seen by a representative of the New York Roman Catholic diocese, a complaint was immediately lodged with E. F. Albee, and Nazimova's performance was cancelled. However, because she was under contract to appear for five weeks, the actress received payment of $15,000 in full.

No grudge was held between Nazimova and Albee, and she returned to the Palace in 1915 in a one-act play by Marion Craig Wentworth titled *War Brides*. The pacifist drama was well received, and Nazimova took it on a tour of the Orpheum circuit. The success of that vaudeville tour led to Nazimova's being signed by Lewis J. Selznick to make a film version of the play. Herbert Brenon directed the 1916 film which marked the screen debut of Richard Barthelmess, whose mother had taught Nazimova English. In all, Nazimova made some twenty-two feature films, including *Revelation* (1918), The Red Lantern (1919), *Camille* (1921), *Salome* (1923), *Blood and Sand* (1941), and *Since You Went Away* (1944, and last). Her Hollywood home at 8150 Sunset Boulevard was later turned into a popular hotel/apartment complex known as the Garden of Allah (demolished in 1959).

Despite her stage and film work, Nazimova found time to return to the Palace in October 1923, April 1926, September 1927, and January 1928. On that last occasion, she starred in a twenty-five-minute drama titled *India*, written by Edgar Allen Woolf and Fanny Hartz Friend, and supported by H. Paul Doucet and Isabelle Hill. She played one of the wives of a wealthy Indian, with a strong feminist viewpoint. As *Variety* (January 18, 1928) reported the plotline, ''When her baby is trampled during a parade in honor of an English prince the wife's emotions are crystallized. Hysterically she cries she is glad her baby is dead rather than have it live the life she has lived, and in a frenzied voice, exhorts the women of India to unshackle their bonds of ancient traditions.'' The unidentified reporter continued, ''Nazimova wears a scant costume and looks very attractive in it. Also the dialog is rather sexy in an adroit style.''

Because Nazimova's acting style in her few extant films seems rather outmoded, it is difficult for modern audiences to appreciate the immense respect in which she was held by the acting fraternity and by contemporary critics. Writing in 1949, Alexander Kirkland provided evidence of her attraction: ''As she talked her eyes changed color and mood like March sky. Cumulus of tears and sunspots of humor swept across the pupils without regard to the content of the outward conversation—as if her subconscious experience was so close to the surface of her consciousness that its contrapuntal functioning was mysteriously visible. When she stepped upon the stage the two forces joined to sweep all before them.''

BIBLIOGRAPHY

Bodeen, DeWitt, ''Nazimova.'' *Films in Review* 23, no. 10 (December 1972), pp. 577–604.

Eustis, Morton. ''The Actor Attacks His Part: IV, Nazimova.'' *Theatre Arts* 20, no. 12 (December 1936), pp. 950–60.

''Exit Alla, with Flowers.'' *Newsweek*, July 23, 1945, p. 83.

Kirkland, Alexander. ''The Woman from Yalta.'' *Theatre Arts* 33, no. 11 (December 1949), pp. 28–29, 48, 94–95.

Lewton, Lucy Olga. *Alla Nazimova, My Aunt: A Personal Memoir*. Ventura, Ca.: Minutemen Press, 1988.

West, Magda Frances. ''Nazimova's Views on Love, Husbands and Wicked Women.'' *The Green Book Magazine*, March 1913, pp. 414–18.

NEW BRIGHTON MUSIC HALL

Located at Sea Breeze Avenue and Ocean Boulevard, Brighton, Coney Island, the New Brighton Music Hall opened in June 1909 as a summer home for New York vaudeville. Seating eighteen hundred and costing $350,000 to build, it also featured an attached restaurant.

NEW ORLEANS

As of 1906, there were only two vaudeville houses in New Orleans, the Greenwald and the Orpheum. In 1921, at which time the city's population was 387,408, there were four: Loew's Crescent, the Louisiana, the Orpheum, and the Palace.

NEW YORK CLIPPER

An important primary source of vaudeville information, the *New York Clipper* was founded by a Philadelphia oculist named Frank Queen as a sports paper. The first issue was published on May 14, 1853. Gradually, it began to cover all aspects of theatrical entertainment, even publishing a column on cockfighting, and in 1859 became a trade paper, announcing it would be of use in the future both to the profession as well as a general readership. Between 1865 and 1875, the *New York Clipper* was probably the only American theatrical newspaper. As well as its weekly issues, the *New York Clipper* published an *Almanac* in the 1870s and an *Annual* from, as far as can be ascertained, 1880 to 1900. The last issue as the *New York Clipper* was published on July 11, 1923. From July 1923, through July 12, 1924, it was titled simply the *Clipper*. The publication was taken over by Sime Silverman, owner of Variety, in 1924, and he allowed it to cease publication.

The *New York Clipper* is available on microfilm from the Kraus-Thompson Organization Ltd.

BIBLIOGRAPHY

Christ-Janer, Virginia. "The 'Cyclopedic Dimensions' of the *New York Clipper.*" *Bulletin of the New York Public Library*, June 1966, pp. 347–55.

Vallillo, Stephen M., "Popular Entertainment in the Trades: A Case Study of the *New York Clipper* and the *New York Dramatic Mirror.*" In *Performing Arts Resources* 14, ed. Barbara Naomi Cohen-Stratyner. New York: Theatre Library Association, 1989, pp. 59–68.

THE NEW YORK DRAMATIC MIRROR

A major source of contemporary information on vaudeville, *The New York Dramatic Mirror* began publication on January 4, 1879. The cover of the first issue featured an engraving of Tony Pastor, evidence of the paper's determination to cover all aspects of popular theatrical entertainment, including vaudeville. It was subtitled "The Organ of the American Theatrical Profession," and was also the official organ of the Vaudeville Comedy Club. Published on a weekly basis, *The New York Dramatic Mirror* took a more intelligent approach to theatrical entertainment than its competitor, *Variety*, and its articles and reviews were far better written.

Between the summer of 1910 and the summer of 1913, the paper published almost no vaudeville-related news. Its coverage of vaudeville reappeared in the fall of 1913, with Frederick James Smith apparently doing the bulk, if not all, of the reporting and criticism. A young writer who was also associated with a number of film-oriented fan magazines, Smith's comments have an intellectual quality missing from those of the reviewers in *Variety*, but Smith is also brash and often displays a questionable bias. No vaudeville section was published in *The New York Dramatic Mirror* after the summer of 1916 until 1919, when Walter J. Kingsley began providing editorial commentary and reviews of new acts.

Interestingly, in its early years, the paper was known simply as *The New York Mirror*, and in its final years, it dropped the reference to New York and was titled simply *Dramatic Mirror*. The paper continued as a weekly until January 7, 1922, and then published two final monthly issues in March and April of that year. The caliber of the writing in *The New York Dramatic Mirror* may be gauged from the last two major articles that it published. In March 1922, Heywood Broun wrote on "Why I Stopped Criticizing Plays," and in April 1922, Alexander Woolcott wrote of "The Maligned First Nighters."

BIBLIOGRAPHY

Vallillo, Stephen M. "Popular Entertainment in the Trades: A Study of the *New York Clipper* and the *New York Dramatic Mirror.*" In *Performing Arts Resources* 14, ed. Barbara Naomi Cohen-Stratyner. New York: Theatre Library Association, 1989, pp. 59–68.

FRED NIBLO (York, Ne., January 6, 1874—New Orleans, November 11, 1948)

Primarily known as a Hollywood director of pretentious and stolid feature films such as *The Three Musketeers* (1921) and *Ben-Hur* (1926), Fred Niblo had enjoyed a lengthy and prosperous career as a monologist in vaudeville. Writing in *Vaudeville*, Joe Laurie, Jr., describes Niblo as "a cultured and original monologist," and continues:

It was Fred who originated a gag that's been used by many comics and "unquoted" in many a joke book. "I asked my girl to marry me. And she told me to go to Father. Now she knew that I knew her father was dead, and she knew that I knew the life he had led, and she knew what she meant when she said, 'Go to Father!' Well, we weren't married!"

Born Federico Nobile, Fred Niblo worked on the East Coast in the early 1890s as a small-time entertainer, billed as "Frederick Niblo, Refined Entertainment, An Entire Evening of Mirth, Education and Magic." From there, he went into minstrel shows, and at the turn of the century developed a successful vaudeville act as a blackface monologuist. In 1907, he filmed a number of travelogues with which he lectured.

In 1903, Niblo produced *Running for Office*, written by George M. Cohan and starring the Four Cohans, and that same year he married Cohan's sister, Josephine. Seven years later, Niblo became associated with Cohan as his manager and as an actor with the company. In 1915, Cohan wrote the farce *Hit-the-Trail Holliday* for his brother-in-law, and it was highly successful, running for 336 performances at New York's Astor Theatre. Josephine Cohan Niblo died in 1916, and for reasons that remain unclear, her death led to a bitter feud between Niblo and Cohan which continued until the latter's death.

Between 1912 and 1915, Fred Niblo was working primarily in Australia, and there he became involved in film production with the J. C. Williamson theatrical concern. In Australia, he met an actress named Enid Bennett, and when Niblo came to Hollywood as a writer for producer Thomas H. Ince in 1918, he renewed his acquaintance with Bennett (who was also under contract to Ince) and the couple married. Niblo became a major Hollywood director in the 1920s, handling many of the prominent stars of the day, including Douglas Fairbanks in *The Mark of Zorro* (1920) and *The Three Musketeers* (1921); Rudolph Valentino in *Blood and Sand* (1922); Greta Garbo in *The Temptress* (1926); and Norma Talmadge in *Camille* (1927). Niblo's film career ended somewhat abruptly in 1932.

BIBLIOGRAPHY

"The Alert Comedian." *The New York Dramatic Mirror*, February 24, 1900, p. 18.
Cheatham, Maude S. "Bennett & Co., Inc." *Motion Picture Classic* 10, no. 5 (July 1920), pp. 32–33, 67.
"Fred Niblo." *Film Dope* no. 47 (December 1991), pp. 31–33.
McGaffey, Kenneth. "Doug's Director." *Motion Picture Classic* 13, no. 2 (October 1921), pp. 60–61, 88.

NIBLO'S GARDEN

Located in lower Manhattan at the corner of Broadway and Prince Street, Niblo's Garden was the most popular venue for al fresco vaudeville entertainment in the summer months during the nineteenth century. The facility was opened by William Niblo on July 4, 1828, as the Sans Souci, and renamed Niblo's Garden and Theatre the following year. A fire destroyed the enterprise in 1846, but it reopened in 1949. In 1852, the Metropolitan Hotel was built on the site of the garden, but the theatre remained operative at the hotel's rear and accessible through its lobby. A second fire in 1872 failed to close down Niblo's Garden, but eventually, in 1895, both the hotel and the theatre were demolished.

The most important production to play at Niblo's Garden was *The Black Crook*, which opened there in 1866 and ran for sixteen months. It introduced the chorus girl to American theatre and also demonstrated the appeal of an attractive woman to American audiences.

NICHOLAS BROTHERS

Fayard (New York, October 20, 1914–   ) and Harold (Philadelphia, March 17, 1921–   ) Nicholas were the most explosive black tap dancers on the vaudeville stage, performing acrobatic leaps and splits so astounding in their vigor that they were painful to watch. The brothers grew up in Philadelphia, where their parents had a pit orchestra, Nicholas' Collegians, at the Standard Theatre in the 1920s. After seeing Bill Robinson, they determined to be dancers, and they learned their craft not at school but by watching other performers. With sister Dorothy, the Nicholas Brothers developed a dance act and began performing professionally in 1930 at the Standard Theatre, Philadelphia. In 1932, minus Dorothy, they came to New York and became regulars at the Cotton Club.

The Nicholas Brothers made their first film appearance in a 1932 short, *Pie, Pie Blackbird*. They first came to Hollywood in 1934 to appear in the Eddie Cantor vehicle *Kid Millions*. Other feature films in which they appeared are *The Big Broadcast of 1936* (1935), *Down Argentine Way* (1940), *Tin Pan Alley* (1940), *Sun Valley Serenade* (1941), and *The Pirate* (1948). Their most memorable screen appearance is in *Stormy Weather* (1943), with the two jumping one over the other in full splits. They first appeared in Europe in *Lew Leslie's Blackbirds of 1936*, produced on the London stage. Also in 1936, they were featured in *The Ziegfeld Follies*, which opened at the Winter Garden Theatre on January 30 of that year. *Variety* (February 5, 1936) described them, patronizingly, as simply "two colored lads," but did admit that they delivered "exceptional tap dancing." As Ivor and Irving DeQuincy, the Nicholas Brothers were highlighted in the Rodgers and Hart musical *Babes in Arms*, which opened at the Shubert Theatre on April 14, 1937.

The dancers continued to appear on the vaudeville stage, and they were on the bill of the last show at the Riviera Theatre, Brooklyn, in April 1939. "Style is fast, showy, with eccentric and acro interspersed throughout the tap routines," reported *The Billboard* (April 22, 1939). The popularity of the two men peaked in the 1940s, although they remained active. Between 1958 and 1964, Harold worked in Europe, while Fayard toured the United States. Fayard was seen in a dramatic role in the film *The Liberation of L. B. Jones* (1970), as was Harold in *Uptown Saturday Night* (1975). With the passing years, audiences have come to respect and admire the Nicholas Brothers anew, and in 1991 they were recipients of the Kennedy Center Honors.

In conversation with Rusty Frank, Fayard Nicholas described his and Harold's dance routines:

"Our type of dancing we called 'classical tap.' I'll try to explain that. When we tapped, we added a little ballet to it, plus a little eccentric, a little flash, and we used our hands a great deal. With style and grace we used the whole body from our heads down to our toes. And that's why we called our type of dancing classical tap. That's what it is—the lacing together of tap, balletic leaps and turns, and dazzling acrobatics. You put it all together and it's the Nicholas Brothers! It's not a 'white style' and it's not a 'black style.' When you look at the Nicholas Brothers, you're looking at classical tap."

BIBLIOGRAPHY
Collier, Aldore. "Whatever Happened to the Nicholas Brothers?" *Ebony*, May 1983, pp. 103–104, 106.
"Flash Act." *The New Yorker*, February 15, 1988, pp. 25–27.
Frank, Rusty. "The Nicholas Brothers." In *Tap!: The Greatest Tap Dance Stars and Their Stories, 1900–1955*. New York: William Morrow, 1990, pp. 64–74.

KARYL NORMAN (1896—Hollywood, Fl., July 23, 1947)

A highly successful female impersonator, Karyl Norman billed himself as "The Creole Fashion Plate," and behind his back was known to his fellow vaudevillians as "The Queer Old Fashion Plate." Born George Paduzzi, Karyl Norman chose his first name because it was sexless, while Norman was his father's name. He ran away from home at the age of sixteen and joined Neil O'Brien's Minstrels. Norman entered vaudeville on the West Coast and did not make his New York debut until May 1919, when he was the surprise hit on the bill at the Riverside Theatre. *The New York Dramatic Mirror* (May 27, 1919) commented:

Not only does this impersonator wear his feminine toggery in tiptop shape but has a voice that fools 'em at the start. Then to a lower register he descends—a lusty masculine voice that could be attuned to a straight "single" and put over. He's the worthy vaudeville substitute to Julian Eltinge. And he doesn't appear a bit effeminate on the change for the finale.

The same year, 1919, a second female impersonator, Francis Ryan, appeared, billed in similar fashion to Norman, this time as "The Vaudeville Fashion Plate." It did not take the audience long to realize he was a man, his being a little too husky to pass as a woman, and Ryan quickly disappeared from the scene.

Norman appeared at the Palace in May 1923, September 1924, and as late as

March 1931. He was also featured in *Lady Do* (1927). In the 1930s, Norman's act was billed as "Glorifying the American Boy-Girl."

Karyl Norman was well remembered by his fellow vaudevillians. Milton Berle recalled Norman's act in the 1920s, half-way through which he would appear in a Huckleberry Finn outfit with no wig and barefoot: "He was so used to walking in high heels, he couldn't walk in men's shoes!" Fifi D'Orsay met him when he was in the 1924 edition of the *Greenwich Village Follies*:

He was marvelous. He was a great performer and I loved him. Karyl Norman was a wonderful guy, beloved and respected by everybody, although he was a gay boy, and the gay boys in those days it was harder for them than it is today. He did an act with two pianos and those gorgeous clothes. He had such class and he was so divine.

The story is told of Norman's applying for membership in the Friars Club, when Joe Frisco and Jay C. Flippen were on the admissions committee. Frisco said, "The Creole Fashion Plate, he's a homosexual. Who needs him? We don't need him. We've got one homosexual—Jay Brennan [of Savoy and Brennan]." To which Flippen replied, "Yes, but supposing he dies?"

Little is known of Karyl Norman's background or his later life, although Milton Berle believes he worked at San Francisco's famed drag club Finocchio's. He does not appear to have been born in the United States. A former FBI agent recalls that in the 1930s, Norman was arrested in Detroit on a morals charge: "He would have been deported, but for the intervention of Eleanor Roosevelt. Seems he had done a benefit for some charity she was interested in, and she 'owed him one.'"

BOBBY NORTH (New York, February 2, 1884—Los Angeles, August 13, 1976)

Robert (Bobby) North was a highly talented individual, rising from the ranks of vaudeville and the legitimate stage to be one of the film industry's leading producers in the 1930s, responsible for many major feature films at First National and Warner Bros., including *The Dawn Patrol* (1930). "I started in show business when I was twelve-and-a-half years old," North recalled:

"I left New York and joined a company, and at that time there was a vogue of a soubrette, as we called her, singing on the stage, and a kid would get up from the gallery and sing the chorus. The Gallery Gods, of course, thought he was one of them and applauded loudly, and she made a hit. I was the kid in the gallery. I had the voice and I could sing. From that I graduated into little shows, one-night stands, and so on. In those days you had a lot of companies which traveled all over the country, playing little towns with ten and fifteen thousand populations. Every little town had an opera house or a theatre, and they might be open one or two days a week. What we called number two or number three shows of a New York success would play through the country in these one- and two-night stands. I did a lot of that. In these theatres, you *did* learn your trade because you were an amateur; you learned to communicate with an audience;

you learned to feel what an audience wanted; and it gave you a great education in how to play a part.''

While in his early twenties, Bobby North was involved in many aspects of entertainment. He appeared in the 1909 Emerich Kalman operetta *The Gay Hussars*. He was a straight actor in the 1910 play *Just a Wife* and a comedian in the 1912 "jumble of jollification" *Hanky Panky*. In 1910, North and Cliff Gordon coproduced *The Merry Whirl*, which ran a mere twenty-four performances. North, along with Fanny Brice and Bert Williams, was one of the stars of the 1910 edition of the Ziegfeld *Follies*. According to *Variety* (June 18, 1910), he "sang parodies to big applause." However, it was as a monologist telling Jewish stories that North headlined at the Palace in 1914, having appeared in vaudeville in a similar capacity since 1909.

It was in January 1909 that North dropped his song-and-dance act to play New York's Colonial Theatre as a "Hebrew impersonator," a strange title for an act that involved telling gently humorous stories with a Jewish accent. His delivery was similar in style to that of another vaudevillian of the period, Julian Rose, and included parodies of popular songs and typical Yiddish patter. Sime Silverman reviewed the act in *Variety* (January 23, 1909), found it too long—it ran eighteen minutes—and thought North was a better singer than monologist.

Robert North entered films because he found touring the halls with a pregnant wife and young son (who grew up to be the distinguished screenwriter Edmund H. North) too exhausting. His film career began in 1915 with Popular Plays and Players, for whom he produced the films of vaudeville star Olga Petrova. North devoted the remainder of his life to motion pictures.

RUBY NORTON

A minor recording star and vaudeville headliner of the teens and 1920s, Ruby Norton was billed as "The Little Big Star of Song," and usually appeared accompanied by Clarence Senna at the piano. She was featured in the original 1912 production of Rudolph Friml's *The Firefly*, along with Sammy Lee, with whom she also appeared on the last program at Hammerstein's Victoria Theatre, New York, in 1915. In 1921, Norton appeared in an experimental sound short produced by Orlando E. Kellum, one of a group presented as a supporting program to D. W. Griffith's *Dream Street*; the Norton short is preserved at the UCLA Film and Television Archive. The following year, Ruby Norton made a tour of British music halls. She made her last major appearance at the Palace Theatre in December 1927.

JACK NORWORTH. See NORA BAYES

O ―――――――――――――――――――――――

OLIO/OLEO CURTAIN   The olio or oleo curtain is the name of the drop in front of which an act, usually a singer or comic, could perform while the scenery was being changed behind for the next performer(s).

(OLE) OLSEN (Peru, In., November 6, 1892—Albuquerque, N.M., January 26, 1963) and **(CHIC) JOHNSON** (Chicago, March 5, 1891—Las Vegas, February 26, 1962)

Ole Olsen and Chic Johnson were unlike other comedy teams in that there was no sharp dividing line between the straight man/stooge and the funny man. Each was equally funny in his own right, although perhaps Johnson with his shrill, high-pitched laughter was the more outrageous of the two. As early as 1918, when they were playing New York's Royal Theatre with a ten-minute act of comedy and songs, accompanying themselves on the piano and violin, *Variety* (September 13, 1918) commented, "It's the way they do their act that counts." And the manner in which they pursued their act was sheer lunacy, which reached its climax with the greatest vaudeville revue of all time, *Hellzapoppin*. Just as *Billy Rose's Jumbo* was the ultimate in sophisticated, vaudeville-style revues, *Hellzapoppin* was the ultimate in comic, low-brow vaudeville revues, taking the best, and sometimes the worst, from vaudeville and burlesque routines of the past and adding more than a touch of Olsen and Johnson mayhem.

The couple met in 1914, when the pianist in Olsen's quartet, The College Four, quit the group and Johnson became his replacement. The two began to throw in comedy ad-libs to help the vaudeville routine, and from this developed their comedic style. *Variety* critic "Mark" reviewed them (September 13, 1918) at New York's Royal Theatre:

> At first this pair start out like the skeenteenth and one "two man" duos, but before they are well under the fire of the calcium swing into versatile melange of musical "bits" that had the Royal audience voting them one of the hits of the night. On the opening one boy, the stouter of the two, tickles the ivories and occasionally breaks into "barber shop chords" with his partner, who seems to be a combination of some of our character

comedians of vaudeville fame, his voice having sort of two registers, at times running into a nasal falsetto that enables him to use it to good advantage. This chap goes after a topical song hammer and tongs, puts his idea of it into expression and mannerism that never failed to register. Later he handled a violin, first awkwardly and playing off key with the piano, but all for fun, and good fun at that. Then they swing into harmonious chords that send them off to rousing returns. An idea of the gag-and-bit stuff employed may best be deduced by the imitation of the college boys at the bar, tipsy and just chockful of song, when Olsen and Johnson, using a miniature bar rail, stand with one foot on it and assisted by a stage hand who worked in most acceptably, sang ''Sweet Adeline'' a la barroom exuberance. The piano boy held his own, both in handling the keyboard and in rendering first aid on the ''bits'' requiring two voices. Olsen and Johnson will have no trouble in getting Eastern bookings. It's the way they do their act that counts.

By 1926, the pair was billed as ''The Mad Monarchs of Monkey Business,'' appearing at the Palace on a fairly regular basis: May 1923, November 1928, and October 1929. (They made their last appearance at the theatre the week of March 11, 1952.) Olsen and Johnson appeared in the wonderfully named *Atrocities of 1932* and also made a few film appearances, none of which do them justice: *Oh, Sailor Behave!* (1931), *Gold Dust Gertie* (1931), *Country Gentleman* (1936), and *All over the Town* (1937).

However, it is for *Hellzapoppin* that Olsen and Johnson will always be remembered, and which was their greatest single achievement. ''Assembled and produced'' by Ole Olsen and Chic Johnson, *Hellzapoppin* opened at the 46th Street Theatre on September 22, 1938, and closed 1,404 performances later (after transferring to the Winter Garden) on December 17, 1941. It was comedy of the lowest type, totally devoid of intellect, and it was hated by all the New York critics with the exception of Walter Winchell, who continually plugged it in his column. ''We try to devise situations which are so sure fire that you or Bill Jones or John Smith could step into them and get laughs,'' explained Olsen. Those situations might include throwing plastic or rubber snakes and spiders into the audience, someone walking up and down the aisles selling tickets to rival shows, or a gift night sketch in which the duo gave away everything from a washtub to a live chicken. A fruit-laden girl would be asked where she was going and respond, ''Orange, New Jersey.'' A famous running gag in *Hellzapoppin* was to have a stooge in the audience shout out, ''Hey . . . which of you mugs is Johnson?'' At the conclusion of each performance, Olsen would turn to Johnson and say, ''May you live as long as you want,'' to which Johnson would reply, ''And may you laugh as long as you live.''

Two comments sum up *Hellzapoppin*. The first is from *Variety*'s review: ''It's an object lesson in how entertaining vaude can be.'' The second is by newspaper columnist H. I. Phillips: ''Good old Olsen and Johnson. They are to be congratulated for one thing if for no other, and that is, they gave the boys of this war an opportunity to laugh at the same jokes their fathers did in World War One.'' As Olsen and Johnson proved, there is no joke like an old joke.

Unfortunately, after *Hellzapoppin*, there was nothing left for Olsen and Johnson to do except re-create it, fairly successfully, in a film version for Universal in 1941 and in such Broadway shows as *Laffing Room Only* (1945), *Funzapoppin* (1949) and *Pardon My French* (1950).

Eventually, the team split up, with Johnson touring in *The Chic Johnson Revue* and Olsen entertaining the troops abroad. Johnson died in Las Vegas while checking out the possibility of opening a restaurant there. Olsen died a year later. Just as they had been inseparable in life, so it was in death. Late in 1963, Olsen's body was shipped from Kansas, where it had been initially interred, to be buried alongside Johnson's in Las Vegas. That unique blend of Olsen and Johnson slapstick, which they described as "gonk," meaning "hokum with raisins," has never since been satisfactorily re-created—and probably never will be.

BIBLIOGRAPHY

Maltin, Leonard. "Olsen and Johnson." In *Movie Comedy Teams*. New York: New American Library, 1970, pp. 238–63.

"Olsen, John Sigvard, and Johnson, Harold Ogden." *Current Biography*, September 1940, pp. 623–24.

Reynolds, Quentin. "Broadway Madhouse." *Collier's* 102, no. 24 (December 10, 1938), pp. 17, 46.

OLYMPIA THEATRE

Covering an entire New York city block on Broadway between 44th and 45th streets, the Olympia Theatre was actually two theatres, and its opening in 1895 signaled the uptown move of the theatrical district to Times Square. Developed by Oscar Hammerstein, the Olympia was to have included three theatres, a roof garden, a bowling alley, billiard rooms, a Turkish bath, and restaurants, with one admission charge to cover access to all the amenities. The first theatre in the complex, the Lyric, opened on November 25, 1895, with *Excelsior, Jr.* The second theatre, the Music Hall, opened on December 17, 1895, with a show starring Yvette Guilbert. Hammerstein had taken out a mortgage of $900,000 with the New York Life Insurance Company to finance the building of the Olympia, and four years after its opening, the insurance company foreclosed. The Olympia was sold on June 20, 1898.

The Lyric was renamed the Criterion Theatre, and the Music Hall was renamed the New York. The latter continued as a vaudeville theatre. Its roof garden was named the Jardin de Paris, and it was here in 1907 that Florenz Ziegfeld presented his first *Follies*. Both theatres were demolished in 1935.

OPERA SINGERS.   See SISSIERETTA JONES, ROSA PONSELLE, YVETTE RUGEL, FRITZI SCHEFF

ORCHESTRAS

It was not until the mid 1920s that orchestras and dance bands began to move from hotels and nightclubs to vaudeville stages. Once they arrived, they discovered that vaudeville offered a perfect winter booking for orchestras that had been kept busy all summer long at resorts such as Atlantic City's Million Dollar Pier and New York's Coney Island. By the mid 1930s, there was hardly a vaudeville bill in the country that did not feature a popular orchestra.

Early groups of musicians on the vaudeville stage usually numbered between four and six or were of a specialized nature, such as the Russian Balalaika Orchestra. One early orchestra mentioned in Caroline Caffin's 1914 study of *Vaudeville* is that of Franceso Creatore, who held the audience spellbound with his conducting:

The wild flap of his hair over his forehead, which, as he waves his head in crazy excitement, threatens to blind him—the crouching grasp with which he seems to be plucking a melody from the atmosphere, or the defiant rage with which he flings it at the performers—the beckoning, the nodding and all the capers in which he indulges, become so engrossing that the actual music passes unheeded. It is true that he can stimulate his audience to a thrilled enthusiasm; yet the spell is not that of music but of his own excitable, effervescent personality.

Francesco Creatore set the style for the future, in which audiences came because of the personality of an orchestra's leader as much if not more so than for the music. In 1923, dance bands appearing on the vaudeville circuits included Al Tucker and Band, Carl Shaw and Band, and Verne Buck and His Merry Garden Orchestra. The last was "void of all personality," according to *Variety*. Al Tucker was a trick fiddler who appeared in a tramp costume, and his band played jazz with a measure of opera and a Sousa march thrown in. Carl Shaw's band was a small, five-piece affair, and the highlight of its March 1923 appearance at the 23rd Street Theatre was a Gallagher and Shean routine between cornet and clarinet. Like most bands in vaudeville at this time, Carl Shaw was the closing act on the bill.

In the mid 1920s, the Ray Miller Band was popular in vaudeville; noted, but less popular, was the minor act of Tom Kerr and His Musical Kerriers. The California Collegiates, who began their career in Laguna Beach, California, in 1923, are of interest in that the group's saxophonist at that time was actor-to-be Fred MacMurray. Horace Heidt and His Orchestra successfully toured in Fanchon and Marco productions, primarily on the West Coast. Jan Garber and His Band featured a dance team, and most orchestras and dance bands found it necessary to include vocalists and dancers as part of their vaudeville acts.

John Philip Sousa, the march king, had a band that was frequently heard on the vaudeville stage. In April 1927, he began a ten-week engagement at New York's Paramount Theatre at a weekly salary of $10,000. Joe Laurie, Jr., claims there were sixty well-known bands in vaudeville by 1925. Many had financial problems in view of the size of their operation, but one that did not was the orchestra of Roger Wolfe Kahn, not only because it was successful, but also because Kahn was the son of millionaire steel magnate and art collector Otto Kahn. He headlined in a twenty-three-minute act at the Palace in February 1929, with a program that also included the two William Sisters. Kahn played dance music, and *Variety* complained they did not dance in vaudeville theatres. Al Rinker of the Rhythm Boys said there was no comparison between Kahn and Paul Whiteman, either in their approach to music or in personality: "Roger Wolfe Kahn played the piano, and he played well. I remember we used to go down to hear him at the Pennsylvania Hotel, and we all thought he had a hell of a band."

After making a name for himself at the Cotton Club, Duke Ellington played the Palace in May 1930 with a thirty-four-minute act. Sime Silverman wrote in *Variety* (May 21, 1930) that "In appearance and also in deportment on stage, Ellington is remindful of Horace Heidt.... They can play anything and seem to play everywhere.... Won't be surprised if the Palace holds over Ellington. I should. That band will grow and draw in any house."

Orchestras came into their own in the 1930s with the development of the presentation houses. Among the most notable were those of Ben Bernie, Mike Riley, Joe Venuti, Teddy King, Abe Lyman, Tommy Dorsey, Henry Busse, Isham Jones, Lou Breese, Anson Weeks, Glenn Miller, Frankie Masters, Al Donahue, and Eddie Delange. Eventually, the stage was swamped with orchestras and dance bands, and audiences tired of them, and as Joe Laurie, Jr., reported, "About 1945 there were a lot of bands, but no dates for them."

See also ALL-GIRL ORCHESTRAS, VINCENT LOPEZ, PAUL WHITE-MAN.

ORPHEUM CIRCUIT

The Orpheum circuit was the major vaudeville circuit for the West Coast and parts of the midwest, as important and as powerful as the B. F. Keith circuit. Its origins date back to June 30, 1887, when Gustav Walters opened the first Orpheum Theatre in San Francisco. Heavily in debt, Walters disposed of the theatre to Morris Meyerfeld and Dan Mitchell. Martin Beck became associated with Meyerfeld and Mitchell in 1899, and by 1905 was in command of the company, which had expanded with the acquisition of theatres in Los Angeles, Kansas City, and Omaha, and by 1905 was operating seventeen houses as far east as Chicago.

The Orpheum Circuit, Inc., was incorporated in Delaware in 1919, and in 1923, Martin Beck was voted out of the presidency of the corporation. A subsidiary company, Excelsior Collection Agency, was operated by the Orpheum to collect a 5 percent commission from all performers who played its theatres. Among the major Orpheum theatres were the Palace, New Orleans (opened January 20, 1902), the Orpheum, Oakland, California (opened September 30, 1907), the Heilig, Portland, Oregon (opened August 17, 1908), the State-Lake, Chicago (opened March 17, 1919), and the Hillstreet Theatre, Los Angeles (opened March 20, 1922). The first Eastern theatre opened—on February 8,

1898—by the circuit was the Orpheum, Kansas City, Missouri. The last Orpheum Theatre to be opened was in Los Angeles on February 15, 1926. At that time, the original Orpheum, which had opened in 1894, was renamed the Palace.

At the height of its power in the 1920s, the Orpheum circuit consisted of the following theatres; seating capacity is given after the name of the city:

California

White (Fresno; 1,293)

Orpheum (Los Angeles; 2,011)

Orpheum (Oakland; 1,621)

Clunie (Sacramento; 1,124)

Orpheum (San Francisco; 1,579)

Canada

Grand (Calgary; 1,499)

Orpheum (Vancouver; 1,700)

Royal Victoria (Victoria; 1,507)

Orpheum (Winnipeg; 1,926)

Colorado

Orpheum (Denver; 1,400)

Illinois

Orpheum (Champaign; 916)

American (Chicago; 1,228)

Lincoln (Chicago; 1,540)

Majestic (Chicago; 1,965)

Palace (Chicago; 1,346)

State-Lake (Chicago; 2,774)

Empress (Decatur; 947)

Palace (Moline; 954)

Palace (Rockford; 1,370)

Majestic (Springfield; 989)

Indiana

New Grand (Evansville; 1,149)

Orpheum (South Bend; 1,102)

Hippodrome (Terre Haute; 1,441)

Iowa

Columbia (Davenport; 1,350)

Orpheum (Des Moines; 1,434)

Orpheum (Sioux City; 1,456)

Louisiana

Orpheum (New Orleans; 2,260)

Palace (New Orleans; 1,823)

Minnesota

Orpheum (Duluth; 1,037)

Orpheum (Minneapolis; 1,850)

Orpheum (St. Paul; 2,035)

Missouri

Orpheum (Kansas City; 1,834)

Grand Opera House (St. Louis; 2,264)

Rialto (St. Louis; 1,851)

Orpheum (St. Louis; 2,128)

Nebraska

Orpheum (Lincoln; 1,259)

Orpheum (Omaha; 1,398)

Oregon

Heilig (Portland; 1,484)

Tennessee

Orpheum (Memphis; 1,393)

Utah

Orpheum (Salt Lake City; 1,823)

Washington

Moore (Seattle; 1,521)

Wisconsin

Orpheum (Madison; 1,052)

Majestic (Milwaukee; 1,902)

Palace (Milwaukee; 1,965)

JACK OSTERMAN (Toledo, Oh., ?—Atlantic City, June 8, 1939)

A popular comedian of his day with both audiences and the vaudeville fraternity, Jack Osterman was described by *Variety* as "A Merry Andrew and a Broadway Playboy," but he was also known as "The Bad Boy of Broadway" because of his quick and flippant wit and heavy drinking. The son of operetta star Kathryn Osterman and road show manager and publicist J. J. (Jake) Rosenthal, Jack Osterman made his stage debut as a bellboy in the 1917 Jerome Kern musical *Oh, Boy*. In the 1920s, he was earning $1,750 a week as a vaudeville headliner and revue star; he appeared at the Palace in March 1924 and April 1932, and was also seen on Broadway in *All Star Jamboree* (1921), *A Night in Paris* (1926), and *Artists and Models* (1927, to which show he also contributed lyrics).

Jack Osterman contributed occasional columns to *Variety*, and in reference to his hometown always complained that the three worst weeks in vaudeville were Christmas, Holy Week, and Toledo. A doting mother generally bailed him out financially, and in the mid 1930s, she financed a club for her son, the Osterman, on New York's 52nd Street. Osterman died of pneunomia at the reported age of 37.

P ─────────────────────────

PALACE THEATRE

Located at Broadway and 47th Street, New York City, the Palace Theatre was both the flagship of vaudeville and of the B. F. Keith vaudeville circuit. When it was first built it was neither, and the general feeling in the vaudeville fraternity was that it would close before the year was out. It was the dream child of Martin Beck (q.v.), who wanted to expand his Orpheum circuit by opening a theatre in New York. Beck leased the site for the theatre on October 21, 1911, from George J. Earle, Jr., of Philadelphia, and on January 1, 1912, building commenced. By the time it opened on Easter Monday, March 24, 1913, Beck had become a minority owner, with 51 percent of the stock controlled by the B. F. Keith vaudeville interests led by E. F. Albee.

The opening program consisted of the Eight Palace Girls, caricaturist Hy Mayer, Ed Wynn, a one-act musical comedy titled *The Eternal Waltz*, featuring Cyril Chadwick and Mabel Berra, monologist Taylor Holmes, Milton Pollock and Company in a one-act playlet by George Ade titled *Speaking to Father*, a wire walking act called the Four Vannis, Ota Gygi, billed as "Violinist of the Spanish Court," and pantomimist and dancer La Napierkowska. "The show can be called nothing else but a vaudeville show, altho if a regular vaudeville theater were to offer it as a regular bill patronage would undoubtedly be small after the Monday matinee," commented *The Billboard* (April 5, 1913). The *New York World* opined, "The opening bill did not lend much enthusiasm to the occasion," while *Variety* was outright scathing, attacking the theatre for offering seats at as high as $2 apiece and declaring the fate of $2 vaudeville was sealed even before the theatre opened its doors.

It was not until May 1913 that the Palace began attracting major audiences, and that was because the headliner that month was Sarah Bernhardt, whom Martin Beck had signed on a trip to Paris. On May 16, the Palace closed because of the heat and lack of air conditioning. Fritzi Scheff was the headliner on the opening bill, September 1, 1914, supported by monologist Julius Tannen and British dancer and singer Laddie Cliff. It took time, but by December 1914,

Variety was describing the Palace as ''the greatest vaudeville theatre in America, if not the world.'' It was the desire of every vaudevillian to play there, and E. F. Albee traded on the theatre's importance by forcing acts to take a pay cut for the privilege of playing the Palace. Nevertheless, to open at the Palace was an indication that one had reached the pinnacle of success. Male impersonator Kitty Doner recalled:

It was every actor's ambition to play the Palace in New York. Monday afternoon was the first show, and the house would be filled with performers from the shows around town. They'd come in for the matinee. And all the Broadway talent scouts and agents would come down to catch the first show Monday afternoon at the Palace, because how you went over determined what your future bookings would be. That was the biggest excitement in your life, I guess, playing a Monday afternoon at the Palace. It was just thrilling.

Carlton Hoagland was the first booker for the Palace, but its best known and most important booker was Edward ''Eddie'' Darling. Frank Thompson was the first manager, followed by Doc Breed, William Wood, and Elmer Rogers. The theatre's first musical director was Paul Shindler. The B. F. Keith organization maintained its offices on the fifth floor of the Palace building. While most vaudevillians played the Palace at least once, among the big names who did not were George M. Cohan, Al Jolson, and Will Rogers.

The theatre cost a reported $1 million to build. An average bill during its heyday cost $12,000 in salaries, and the Palace made an average profit of $500,000 a year.

The headliner with the longest run at the Palace was Kate Smith, for ten weeks from August 1 through October 3, 1931. Eddie Cantor, George Jessel and Burns and Allen played the Palace for nine weeks from October 31 to December 26, 1931. Frank Fay had an eight-week run from May 24 through July 12, 1926, as did Lou Holtz, Lyda Roberti, and William Gaxton from July 11 to August 29, 1931.

The last two-a-day vaudeville bill at the Palace was the week of May 7, 1932. The program consisted of Allan Mann and Dorothy Dell in a song-and-dance routine, black singer Ada Brown, Henry Santrey and His Band, Rosetta Duncan, William Demarest and Estelle Collette, radio commentator Floyd Gibbons, comedians Frank Mitchell and Jack Durant, Charlie Jordan and Johnny Woods, who burlesqued radio personalities, and Dave Apollon. The last week of straight vaudeville at the Palace was July 9, 1932, with a bill headlined by columnist Louis Sobol, supported by The Ingenues, the Diamond Boys, Fred Keating, Leon Janney, Ross Wyse, Jr., Richy Craig, Jr., Seiler and Wills, and Pepito. The following week, the Palace began screening films with vaudeville acts, with the first motion picture entertainment being Frank Buck's animal film *Bring 'em Back Alive*.

From then on, it appeared that the management of the Palace was not certain what to do. From November 12, 1932 to January 7, 1933, the Palace presented all-film programs. From January 7 to February 4, 1933, it reverted to a two-a-day house, but with vaudeville acts and a motion picture. From February 11 to April 29, 1933, it presented only films. Then it switched to a combination of vaudeville and films until September 20, 1934, when it became a motion picture theatre. On May 19, 1949, Sol A. Schwartz, president of RKO Theatres, owners of the Palace as successors to B. F. Keith, decided to reinstitute a vaudeville and film policy, featuring eight acts and a first-run feature.

On October 16, 1951, Judy Garland made a "comeback" at the Palace in a four-week engagement that was extended for an additional fifteen weeks. She was supported by Smith and Dale, English comedian-singer Max Bygraves, and others. Garland returned to the Palace for an eight-week engagement beginning September 27, 1956. Lauritz Melchior headlined at the Palace beginning February 26, 1952; José Greco was there beginning March 11, 1952; Betty Hutton headlined at the Palace for four weeks beginning April 12, 1952, and was back again on October 14, 1953; Danny Kaye headlined at the Palace for fourteen weeks beginning January 9, 1953.

When not featuring major stars, the Palace reverted to film presentation, supported by vaudeville acts, but it soon became apparent that audiences expected more. Jerry Lewis and Liberace proved major attractions in 1957, but on August 13, 1957, the vaudeville acts were dropped and the Palace became a regular movie theatre, except for a September 1959 engagement by Harry Belafonte. In August 1965, the theatre was acquired by James Nederlander for a reported $1,600,000. The last feature film played there that same month (*Harlow*), the building was remodeled, and on January 29, 1966, it reopened as a legitimate Broadway theatre with *Sweet Charity*. It has continued ever since as a major Broadway house.

BIBLIOGRAPHY

Green, Abel. "Toujours the Palace." *Variety*, January 9, 1957, pp. 274, 277.
Laurie, Joe, Jr. "Show Biz Made, Big Biz Unmade, Keith's Palace." *Variety*, January 4, 1956, p. 424.
Rubin, Benny. "Gave Her All for Date at Palace." *Variety*, January 4, 1956, p. 424.
Spitzer, Marian. *The Palace*. New York: Atheneum, 1969.

ALEXANDER PANTAGES (Greece, 1864—Los Angeles, February 17, 1936)

A vaudeville entrepreneur whose empire was primarily located on the West Coast, Alexander Pantages was a colorful and eccentric character who amassed a considerable fortune but could neither read nor write. Employees would read telegrams and letters that he received, and his wife would take care of his personal correspondence. He did not know where or when he was born, only that it was on an island off the coast of Greece. At the age of nine, he went with his father to Cairo, where he ran away, eventually making his way some nine years later to the Klondike in search of gold.

From the Klondike, Pantages came to Seattle in 1902, operating a ten-cent theatre, which became the basis for his theatrical empire. He soon came up against the powerful Sullivan and Considine chain, controlled by John Considine, and a feud developed between Pantages and Considine which ended only with the marriage of Pantages's daughter Carmen to John W. Considine, Jr. Pantages created a West Coast circuit of vaudeville theatres that eventually stretched as far as Birmingham, Alabama, and Niagara Falls, New York. As of 1926, the Pantages circuit consisted of the following theatres:

Bellingham, Wa.: Pantages

Brandon, Moose Jaw, Canada: Regina

Calgary, Canada: Pantages

Chicago: Chateau

Cleveland: Circle

Colorado Springs, Co.: Burns

Columbus, Oh.: James

Dallas: Pantages

Denver: Empress

Detroit: Miles

Detroit: Regent

Edmonton, Canada: Pantages

Fort Worth, Tx.: Pantages

Hamilton, Canada: Pantages

Indianapolis: Chateau

Kansas City, Mo.: Pantages

Long Beach, Ca.: Hoyt

Los Angeles: Pantages

Memphis, Tn.: Pantages

Minneapolis: Pantages

Newark, N.J.: Newark

Niagara Falls, N.Y.: Strand

Oakland, Ca.: Pantages

Ogden, Ut.: Orpheum

Omaha, Nb.: World

Pasadena, Ca.: Pantages

Portland, Or.: Pantages

Regina, Canada: Pantages

Sacramento, Ca.: Pantages

Salt Lake City: Pantages

San Diego, Ca.: Pantages

San Francisco: Pantages

Saskatoon, Canada: Pantages

Seattle: Pantages

Spokane, Wa.: Pantages

Tacoma, Wa.: Pantages

Toledo, Oh.: Rivoli

Toronto, Canada: Pantages

Vancouver, Canada: Pantages

Winnipeg, Canada: Pantages

Writing in *Variety*, Joe Bigelow commented:

The Pantages at one period was the most important independent vaudeville circuit in the country in amount of weeks offered and territory covered. It was booked out of New York and Chicago on a circuit basis, with acts traveling in roadshow fashion. Bookings extended as high as 32 weeks at various times, but the standard and famous Pantages contract always read, "14 weeks or more," and the acts knew that six of the weeks would be played at a 25% cut. The cuts were usually enforced when the acts reached the coast. . . .

Personally, Pantages favored the acrobatic type of act and played at least one on all his shows. He was noted among agents and producers for breaking up big acts in order to obtain certain parts that happened to catch his fancy. For instance, if he liked a dance act in a flash act, but didn't care for the rest of the turn he would route the whole act out to the Coast and then lift the teams and book it alone when it got there.

In 1929, Alexander Pantages sold the majority of his theatre holdings to RKO for a figure reported as low as $3.5 million and as high as $24 million. In March 1932, Pantages announced plans for a nationwide theatre circuit of between two hundred and five hundred houses, but it failed to materialize. In 1933, he did try a comeback, leasing theatres in Hollywood, California, Seattle, and Salt Lake City. At the time of his death, his only theatre holding was the Pentages in Hollywood, run by his son Rodney. Another son, Lloyd, was a gossip columnist for the Hearst newspapers.

Alexander Pantages was the center of a major scandal in 1929, when he was accused of having lured a seventeen-year-old chorus girl named Evelyn Pringle into a room in his theatre and raped her on August 9, 1929. Pantages was charged with statutory rape, and his first trial ended with his being convicted and sentenced to fifty years in state prison. A second trial was held on appeal in the fall of 1931, and the day before Thanksgiving, Pantages was found not guilty. Evelyn Pringle and her mother filed a civil suit seeking $1 million in damages, but the suit was settled in December 1931 for $3,000.

BIBLIOGRAPHY

"Alex. Pantages, Vaudeville's Best Friend, Is Dead." *Motion Picture Herald*, February 22, 1936, p. 28.

Bigelow, Joe. "Pantages, Vet Vaudeville Showman, Dies at 65; Had a Colorful Career." *Variety*, February 19, 1936.

Crane, Warren E. "Alexander Pantages." *System*, March 1920, pp. 501–503.

Giesler, Jerry, as told to Peter Martin. "Alexander Pantages." In *The Jerry Giesler Story*. New York: Simon and Schuster, 1960, pp. 14–39.

Laurie, Joe, Jr. "Alexander Pantages." In *Vaudeville: From the Honky-Tonks to the Palace*. New York: Henry Holt, 1953, pp. 401–403.

EDDIE PARKES (New York, February 1893—Hollywood, Ca., July 24, 1985)

A song-and-dance man, Eddie Parkes played the Union Square Theatre as a member of a blackface pickaninny troupe in 1902 and also sang for pennies at Nigger Mike's saloon on New York's Pell Street. As half of Lyons and Parkes, he appeared at Hammerstein's Victoria Theatre while still a teenager, and Oscar Hammerstein was so impressed by his voice that he offered to send Parkes to Italy to study opera. The boy refused, and instead teamed with John Coogan, the father of child star Jackie Coogan. He appeared in the last (1943) edition of the *Ziegfeld Follies* and also made a number of film appearances as a bit player. Parkes's last appearance was in Los Angeles in June 1985 with his last partner, Patrick Sullivan Burke, at the Hollywood Comedy Club.

BIBLIOGRAPHY

Dwan, Robert. "Eddie Parkes—84 Years in Show Biz." *Los Angeles Times Calendar*, December 6, 1981, pp. 6–7.

TONY PASTOR (New York, May 28, 1832—New York, August 26, 1908)

"The Father of Vaudeville," Tony Pastor transformed vaudeville from a cheap form of entertainment relegated to the saloons of New York into an American institution, popular with and suitable for the entire family. For the first time, he presented vaudeville bills with a diversity of performers, recognizing the talents of Maggie Cline, Lillian Russell, Nat C. Goodwin, Weber and Fields, and many others, and for the first time, brought to the American stage a new breed of entertainer from England, including Little Tich, Bessie Bonehill, Vesta Tilley, and Vesta Victoria. He widened the scope of American popular entertainment, embracing the notion of burlesquing popular musical comedies of the day, notably the operettas of Gilbert and Sullivan. He began as an entertainer but became an entrepreneur.

Tony Pastor made his first public appearance singing at a temperance meeting at the age of six, and doubtless that experience and his family background was influential in his desire to "clean up" the vaudeville stage. Pastor's first professional engagement was at P. T. Barnum's Museum at Broadway and Anne Street, New York, in the fall of 1846. In April 1847, he became a blackface minstrel with the Raymond and Waring Menagerie. That same year, he joined Welch, Delevan and Nathan's Circus, with which he remained until 1853. After a number of engagements in various capacities with other circus troupes, Pastor made his debut in variety, as it was then known, in 1860 at Frank Rivers's Melodeon in Philadelphia as a comic singer. On April 17, 1861, he came to New York to appear at the American Concert Hall, generally known as "444" (its address on Broadway), billed as "the greatest clown and comic singer of the age." Coincidental with Pastor's engagement at the "444," the hostilities signaling the start of the Civil War broke out, and, in a patriotic gesture, Pastor sang "The Star Spangled Banner" at the close of his act. According to Pastor's biographer Parker Zellers, that was the first time the anthem had been sung on a vaudeville stage; Pastor continued to use it to conclude his performance throughout the Civil War period, and also added other patriotic songs to his repertoire.

Onstage, Tony Pastor was not a prepossessing figure. He was short and stout with a Napoleonic moustache, and might well have been mistaken for an Italian opera singer rather than a hero of the vaudevillian stage.

The entertainer first entered management in 1865 with the formation of a minstrel troupe, Tony Pastor's Variety Show, the first of many companies that he sent out on the road under his name through the 1890s. Also in 1865, Pastor began a partnership with Sam Sharpley, and the two men opened Tony Pastor's Opera House (formerly the Bowery Music Hall) on July 31 of that year. In 1866, Sharpley quit the partnership, but the Opera House remained in operation under Pastor's management until March 1875, with Tony Pastor appearing at every performance. Pastor sublet the theatre, and on October 4, 1875, took over the Metropolitan Theatre at 585 Broadway. The following year, for the first time, he used the term "vaudeville" to describe the entertainment there, which did not merely cater to gentlemen needing to drink and smoke while watching a variety show, but which also featured popular matinees for women and children. The Metropolitan Theatre was, arguably, the first vaudeville theatre, as opposed to variety theatre, operational in New York.

By then the most prominent figure in the vaudeville field, Tony Pastor decided to lease the Germania Theatre. Located on 14th Street between Irving Place and Third Avenue, the Germania was formerly Bryant's Minstrels Hall, and located in the Tammany Society Building (opened in 1868). The theatre was renamed Tony Pastor's New Fourteenth Street Theatre and opened in the summer of 1881. He announced that it would be "catering to the ladies, and presenting for the amusement of the cultivated and aesthetic Pure Music and Comedy, Burlesque, and Farce." Special matinees for women and children were presented every Tuesday and Friday. The first major success at the new theatre was not a vaudeville bill but a burlesque of the Gilbert and Sullivan operetta *Patience*, titled *Patience; or, the Stage Struck Maidens*, which opened on January 23, 1882, with a cast including Lillian Russell and May Irwin.

Tony Pastor's New Fourteenth Street Theatre was the most popular New York theatrical establishment of the 1880s—earning Pastor the title of "The Impresario of 14th Street"—and it paved the way for the theatrical ventures of B. F. Keith, F. F. Proctor, and Oscar Hammerstein. The theatre continued in operation into the twentieth century, but it suffered in attendance with the move northward of New York theatres and their audiences from 14th Street to Times Square. In the spring of 1908, the Fourteenth Street Theatre became a motion picture theatre, still under Pastor's management, but in September of that same year, Pastor's lease expired and he decided not to renew it. (The theatre was renamed the Olympic and closed finally in 1928.)

In many respects, Tony Pastor was a nineteenth-century figure, unable to adjust to twentieth-century business. At his death, the trade papers noted his generosity through the years, suggesting that his estate was valued at so little—$72,500—because he had given away more than $1 million in his lifetime. Pastor created American vaudeville, but those who came later profited from it.

BIBLIOGRAPHY

(Eleven Tony Pastor songbooks were published between 1862 and 1891; information on these can be found in the Parker Zellers biography.)

"Dean of Vaudeville Celebrities." *Variety*, March 24, 1906, p. 5.

Goewey, Edwin A. "Tony Pastor, the Starmaker." *Dance Magazine*, August 1928, pp. 12–13, 57–58.

"The Passing of Tony Pastor." *Green Book Album*, January 1909, pp. 190–92.

Pastor, Tony. "Tony Pastor Recounts the Origin of American 'Vaudeville.' " *Variety*, December 15, 1906, pp. 17, 49.

Sargent, Epes W. "Tony Pastor and Vaude." *Variety*, December 27, 1931, pp. 21, 148.

"Tony Pastor." *New York Clipper*, December 26, 1903, p. 11.

"Tony Pastor, Father of Vaudeville." *Harper's Weekly*, September 5, 1908, p. 10.

Traber, J. Milton. "Pen Sketch of Tony Pastor, the Father of Modern Vaudeville." *The Billboard*, February 18, 1911, p. 5.

Zellers, Parker. *Tony Pastor: Dean of the Vaudeville Stage.* Ypsilanti, Mi.: Eastern University Press, 1971.

MISS PATRICOLA (1886—Manhasset, N.Y., May 23, 1965)

In much the same manner as Giselle MacKenzie delighted television audiences in the 1905s on *Your Hit Parade* with both her pleasant personality and her violin playing, Miss Patricola entertained vaudeville audiences in the late teens and 1920s. At an early vaudeville performance, she won over the audience with her first number, "Sweet Adeline," and by the second chorus, even the orchestra was joining in with enthusiasm. "Opening in a spot is rather a superficial business for Patricola," wrote *The New York Dramatic Mirror* (March 1, 1919), "for she possesses enough natural personality not to have to emphasize what many artists haven't when they enter the stage door. . . . Her violin playing showed skill . . . Patricola is such a personable young woman that she could entertain almost any audience."

In 1919, she was the opening act on a typical vaudeville bill, but by October 1923, Miss Patricola was headlining at the Palace, where she returned in July 1926, May 1927, and July 1928. Billed always as Miss Patricola, her first name was Isabella. A brother, Tom Patricola (died Pasadena, Ca., January 1, 1950, age 59), was an eccentric dancer and comedian in vaudeville, and a feature in *George White's Scandals* from 1923 to 1928.

PAULINE (1874—Rochester, N.Y., November 11, 1942)

The most successful hypnotist in vaudeville, Dr. J. Robert Pauline (the title was probably self-assumed) billed himself as "Pauline." He would travel the vaudeville stages with as many as fourteen stooges planted in the audience and called to the stage to act as volunteers. They would be hypnotized and ordered to perform various stunts, such as barking like a dog or assuming grotesque postures. His favorite stunt was to put his hands in front of the eyes of a victim, utter the word "rigid," and have the subject stiffen and then be laid across the tops of two chairs. "Rigid" became a popular catchphrase of the day, as famous as Pauline's remark to the audience, "If it's a fake, it's a good one, isn't it?"

Pauline performed two memorable stunts. The first was to hypnotize a 110-pound girl, suspend her with her ankles and neck resting on bars, and then break a 400-pound rock on her torso. The other trick involved taking blood from the arm or hand of a volunteer without piercing the skin. Surprisingly, because he was always so well dressed and presented such a suave exterior, audiences accepted Pauline as a legitimate hypnotist.

He spent more than a dozen years on the stage before gaining fame at Hammerstein's Victoria Theatre in 1909. He retired in 1937.

EDDIE PEABODY (Reading, Ma., February 19, 1902—Covington, Ky., November 7, 1970)

A master exponent of the banjo, Eddie Peabody would often play instruments sufficiently large to emphasize his diminutive stature. He polished his technique in the dying days of vaudeville, and gained a wider audience in the early 1940s thanks to his appearances on the popular NBC radio series *The National Barn Dance*. Because of his commission in the navy during the Second World War, Peabody was billed on the show as Lieutenant Commander Eddie Peabody. The banjoist's audiences ranged from King Gustav of Sweden, President Franklin D. Roosevelt, and King George VI of Great Britain to U.S. soldiers in a foxhole on Guam during the War. Literally, Eddie Peabody played the banjo until the day he died, suffering a stroke while performing at a nightclub in Covington, Kentucky.

JACK PEARL (New York, October 29, 1895—New York, December 25, 1982)

Jack Pearl enjoyed his greatest fame on radio as the character Baron von Munchhausen in the 1930s, but he had served a long apprenticeship as a vaudeville comedian. Born Jack Pearlman, he entered show business in one of Gus Edwards's shows and worked as a comic in burlesque before teaming with straight man Ben Bard in vaudeville. In the 1920s, Pearl appeared in a number of Broadway shows—*The Dancing Girl* (1923), *A Night in Paris* (1926), *Artists and Models* (1927), and *Pleasure Bound* (1929)—and was also a frequent headliner at the Palace in 1928. Pearl became popular on radio in 1932, when he was heard on CBS's *Ziegfeld Follies of the Air*, and as a result, he was signed to a contract by Lucky Strike for *The Jack Pearl Show*, first heard on NBC in September 1932.

On radio, Jack Pearl perfected the character of Baron von Munchhausen, who would tell stories of his wild exploits. Whenever straight man Cliff Hall, as the character Sharlie, questioned the veracity of the baron's tales, Pearl would respond, "Vas you dere, Sharlie?" His jokes were always on the silly side. He announced, "I have the smallest radio in the world. My radio is so small that when *Amos 'n' Andy* is on, all I get is Amos." He told Hall, "I never forgot the time I was fighting a lion single-handed." "How did you come out?" asked Hall. Back came the reply, "Single-handed."

Pearl's character was featured in a 1933 M-G-M film, *Meet the Baron*, and the comedian appeared the following year in another M-G-M production, *Hollywood Party*. Aside from his radio work in the 1930s, Pearl also found time to appear on the New York stage in *International Revue* (1930), the 1931 edition of the Ziegfeld *Follies*, *Pardon My English* (1932), and *One Flight Down* (1937). His last Broadway appearance was in *All for All* in 1945.

JOE PENNER (Nagechkerek, Hungary, November 11, 1904—Philadelphia, January 10, 1941)

Born Josef Pinter, Joe Penner emigrated to the United States at the age of ten and grew up in Detroit. At the age of sixteen, he entered show business in various menial capacities, before becoming a burlesque comedian. Initially, there was little finesse to his act; he would imitate various ethnic characters and even appear as a female impersonator. Gradually, he developed a comedic style, always appearing in a derby hat and smoking a cigar, and asking the audiences questions such as, "Wanna buy an ash can?" In 1931, while appearing in a revue in Birmingham, Alabama, he discovered that he always got a laugh when he asked the audience, "Wanna buy a duck?" It became his catchphrase.

In 1933, Penner made his radio debut with Rudy Vallee on *The Fleischmann Hour*. He asked Vallee, "Wanna buy a duck?" Vallee said no, and Penner responded, "You nah-h-sty man." Suddenly, Joe Penner was a major radio personality, and later in 1933, he was signed to host *The Bakers' Broadcast* on CBS, where he introduced another catchphrase, "Iz dat so?" Unfortunately, audiences tired rather quickly of Penner's style, and in 1940, he quit radio. He died while appearing in a show titled *Yokel Boy*.

BIBLIOGRAPHY
Ulman, William A., Jr. "Now You Will See Joe Penner." *Silver Screen* 5, no. 2 (December 1934), pp. 47, 57.

ANN PENNINGTON (Camden, N.J., December 23, 1892—New York, November 4, 1971)

A petite dancer who lit up the stage in both the Ziegfeld *Follies* and George White's *Scandals*, Ann Pennington introduced the Black Bottom in the 1920s. Known as "The Girl with the Dimpled Knees," she proudly admitted not only to rouging her cheeks but also her knees. Pennington studied dance in Philadelphia, and at the age of fourteen or fifteen joined a vaudeville act called the De Haven Sextet. In 1911, she appeared in the chorus of the Raymond Hitchcock musical *The Red Widow*. At some point, Florenz Ziegfeld recognized her talent, and in 1915, she was teamed with dancer George White in the *Follies*.

Ann Pennington became the mistress of George White, and in 1919, when the first edition of his *Scandals* opened, she was its star. Florenz Ziegfeld offered Pennington and White $2,000 a week to return to the *Follies*, but the offer was rejected. However, Ann Pennington did appear in the 1923, 1924, and 1925 editions of the *Follies*. She starred in George White's *Scandals* in 1920, 1921, 1926, and 1928. She introduced the Black Bottom in the 1926 edition. Pennington also appeared on Broadway in *Jack and Jill* (1923), *The New Yorkers* (1930), and *Everybody's Welcome* (1931).

The dancer had a brief film career in the teens: *The Rainbow Princess* (1916), *Susie Snowflake* (1916), *The Antics of Ann* (1917), *The Little Boy Scout* (1917), and *Sunshine Nan* (1918). During 1924 and 1925, she made a further seven feature films, then returned to the screen in 1929, with the coming of sound, in an attempt to bolster a flagging career. She appeared in the 1929 Warner Bros. feature *Gold Diggers of Broadway*, supporting Nancy Welford, a young singer and dancer who had been hired for the chorus of the 1919 edition of George White's *Scandals*. "I played the lead and Ann Pennington was a dancer," recalled Welford. "And it was quite nice! I was never nasty or anything, but it was nice to think I was meeting her as the lead in the film."

In 1930, Ann Pennington returned to vaudeville. In February of that year, she headlined at the Palace. In August, she was featured at New York's Paramount Theatre, but there were complaints that she was not audible to audiences in the rear of the auditorium. *Variety* (August 27, 1930) commented, "Ann Pennington did not seem at home in this large picture house. Her very attractive personality, usually a clincher before she starts to sing or dance in the smaller vaude and legit theatres, was but slightly evident three-quarters back here."

In 1943, Pennington tried unsuccessfully for a comeback in a Broadway revival of *The Student Prince*. Her last public appearance was in a 1946 vaudeville tour. Never married, she ended her days, as *Newsweek* (November 15, 1971) put it, "a poignant obscurity living in side-street hotels off Broadway and shuffling along the Great White Way." When asked where all the money had gone, Pennington responded, "In living, honey."

BIBLIOGRAPHY

Adams, Cindy. "How to Get Rid of a Million Bucks without Hardly Trying." *Pageant*, March 1964, pp. 142–48.

Lamb, Grace. "Penny." *Motion Picture Classic* 6, no. 6 (August 1918), pp. 45–46, 79.

Oderman, Stuart. "Ann Pennington." *Films in Review* 37, no. 5 (May 1986) pp. 271–281.

Seitz, Carl W. "A Moment or Two with 'Petite Ann' Pennington." *Motion Picture Magazine* 14, no. 12 (January 1918), pp. 132–34.

JACK PEPPER (Palestine, Tx., June 14, 1902—Los Angeles, March 31, 1979)

Jack Pepper was a juvenile comedian with a fresh-faced, college boy demeanor who could perform a startling falsetto rendition of "St. Louis Blues." Unfortunately, his humor was as juvenile as his appearance. Pepper worked in vaudeville in the 1920s with his sisters Helen and Winnie Mae, and with Frank Salt in an act titled Salt and Pepper. He made his screen debut in the 1929 M-G-M short *Metro Movietone Revue No. 4*, and was active on-screen in minor roles through the 1970s. He had bit parts in seven of the "Road" pictures starring Bob Hope, Bing Crosby, and Dorothy Lamour, and also went with Hope on a number of the comedian's U.S.O. tours.

OLGA PETROVA (Brook, England, 1885—Clearwater, Fl., November 30, 1977)

To attempt to classify Olga Petrova's vaudeville act is not an easy task, in large part because Madame Petrova was in a class all her own. She was a patrician of the stage in the manner of Ethel Barrymore or Mrs. Patrick Campbell. She gave recitations and she sang, and sometimes she merely stood there and cried— and audiences knew they were in the presence of someone unique. She was exceptional, and as *The New York Dramatic Mirror* (March 1, 1919) described her, "a rare trinity of emotional actress, screen star, and vaudeville artist."

Madame Petrova's entire life was an act, carefully stage-managed and never underrehearsed. The compiler of this encyclopedia had the good fortune to know her well in her last years, and the closest she came to intimacy was to permit him to address her as Petrova rather than Madame Petrova. Although born in England and a resident of the United States for more than sixty years, she insisted on speaking with a Russian accent, that occasionally would be forgotten— obviously due only to advancing years. Robert North, who was an associate of Petrova's during her screen career, recalled:

> She had a Russian accent. Always. She never, never forgot that. Of course, we all knew she was an English girl, but she never lost that Russian accent. Day or night, the accent was there—offstage or onstage. I don't think she ever spoke without that accent, even to her husband at home. That was part of her personality, and, of course, she capitalized on it.

Aside from being a star, and a major one, of vaudeville and motion pictures, Petrova was also an ardent feminist. "She wouldn't listen to any talk about women being inferior at all. She raised hell about it," said North. In stage plays and on-screen, Petrova always portrayed women with strong personalities and minds of their own. In a 1918 production, *The Light Within*, for example, she played a doctor of bacteriology who discovers a cure for meningitis and anthrax. She told *Motion Picture Classic* (September 1918), "I do want to bring a message to women—a message of encouragement. The only women I want to play are women who do things. I want to encourage women to do things—to take their rightful place in life.'' She even wrote poetry on women's rights, such as ''Thus Speaks Woman,'' first published in 1919.

Petrova's life was a struggle for independence, for herself and for her sex, and much of that struggle is documented in her autobiography, *Butter with My Bread*, which tells of her early life in England and of her fight to gain freedom from a tyrannical father. As she commented, her autobiography is ''a tale of my struggle as a female child to break away from that life, a struggle to obtain by devious means—the screen happening to be one of them—a home, bread, and butter of my own.'' After amateur theatricals and minor stage roles, Petrova came to London at the age of twenty, and within four years, through a combination of hard work and talent, she had become a prominent stage actress.

Although she vehemently denied it, Olga Petrova was apparently born Muriel Harding, and under that name, she began her stage career. A London theatrical booker named Leon Zeitlin suggested she change her name because it did not suit her red-haired, regal looks or her temperament. Thinking of her one-time husband Boris Petrov, the actress suggested Olga Petrova. Zeitlin added the ''Madame,'' liking the name because it reminded him of Anna Pavlova. The latter was starring at London's Palace Theatre, and Petrova was about to become a star at the London Pavilion—on April 5, 1911, to be precise.

As a result of her successful appearance at the Pavilion and other British music halls, Petrova was signed by Jesse L. Lasky and Henry B. Harris for their Follies Bergere cabaret in New York. Despite the assistance of comedian and master of ceremonies James J. Morton, Petrova was not a success with her songs and impersonations. Writing in *Variety* (August 5, 1911), Sime Silverman described Petrova's act as ''very light, in texture and execution,'' and ended his review with the comment, ''Petrova should go in for the dramatic matter or employ other numbers, and change her name back to where it was.'' Petrova did neither, but instead accepted the role of Diane in Henry B. Harris's production of the Lionel Monckton musical comedy *The Quaker Girl*, which opened at New York's Park Theatre on October 23, 1911, and which was to run for 240 performances.

From *The Quaker Girl*, Petrova went into vaudeville. She refined and perfected her act, adding an impersonation of Lena Ashwell in her 1906 success *The Shulamite* and singing a French translation of ''Oh, You Beautiful Doll.'' Eddie Darling wanted to book her into the Fifth Avenue Theatre, and Petrova agreed under certain conditions: she wanted no money and no billing for the first week. Darling agreed, of course, and Petrova was an immediate hit; the theatre was flooded with inquiries about the unbilled performer who cried real tears during the scene from *The Shulamite*. Petrova played a second successful week, but the third week, she demanded billing as the headliner. Darling consented, and the English actor R. A. Roberts (noted on the American vaudeville stage for his characterizations from the novels of Charles Dickens), who was supposed to be the headliner, agreed to second billing. What happened next is unclear, except that when Roberts discovered who had preempted his status, he walked out of the show. Some claim that Petrova had sought revenge against Roberts, who had treated her badly when, as Muriel Harding, she toured with his company in South Africa. Petrova denied this was so, claiming she did not know that Roberts, whom she described as "a very clever protean performer," was the headliner. One thing is certain, and that is that Petrova was tremendously successful. Seeing her performance at the Fifth Avenue Theatre, *Variety* (April 6, 1912) described her as "one of the cleverest, classiest, and most attractive of turns." Edward Darling wrote to her, "I am quite sure that anything I was able to do for you has been warranted by your own talent. It is so seldom one meets with originality that to have given you the opportunity at a New York theatre was as much a pleasure to me as it was to you."

Petrova returned to the legitimate stage in Monckton Hoffe's *Panthea*, which opened at New York's Booth Theatre on March 23, 1914, with Milton Sills in the male lead. *Variety* (April 3, 1914) did not care for the play, but its critic, "Jolo," was bemused by Petrova: "Zat Madame Petrova is ze most exotic figure on ze New York stage zere can be little doubt. Her full white zroat has ze lines zat Praxicles molded in Aphrodite—her ruby lips retain zere poster redness even though Pantzea (as she pronounces it) makes her entrance rescued from the sea, and her Burne-Jones hair is given an extra marcel or two by the waves of the Northumberland coast."

While appearing on tour in *Panthea* in Chicago, Petrova was offered a film contract. Her first feature, *The Tigress*, released in December 1914, proved popular, and subsequently she signed a two-year contract with Popular Plays and Players, for whom she starred in *The Heart of a Painted Woman* (1915) and *The Black Butterfly* (1916), among others. Petrova later signed with Famous Players–Lasky for *the Undying Flame*, *The Exile*, and *The Law of the Land*, all released in 1917; she then formed her own Petrova Picture Company, which released five features through First National. Besides starring in films, Petrova later found time to write articles and interviews for a number of film periodicals, including *Shadowland*, *Motion Picture Magazine*, and *Photoplay Journal*.

In 1919, Petrova returned to vaudeville, making her first appearance at the Orpheum in New York in February. She recited an original verse titled "There, Little Girl, Don't Cry," sang songs in four different voices, gave an excerpt again from *The Shulamite*, and performed "My Hero." *The New York Dramatic Mirror* (March 1, 1919) commented, "Few actresses have caused editorial pens so much perplexity as to the proper classifying of her particular style of work. Some of the scribes have got real mad about the difficulty and others have used excessive flattery as the easiest way to untie the knot. Such a state of editorial indecision makes her a distinct novelty." After six weeks at the Orpheum, Petrova set out on an extended tour which included twenty-two different theatres in as many cities. In eighteen of these, she broke the records for attendance— a feat previously accomplished only by Sarah Bernhardt. As Petrova's act would often include an impersonation of Bernhardt fainting, the performer must have gained considerable satisfaction in seeing her success compared to that of the great French actress.

Petrova's debut at the Palace came in 1919, at which time she performed a recitation of her own authorship, titled "To a Child That Enquires." The full dramatic impact is somewhat lacking without Petrova's voice and inflections:

> How did you come to me, my sweet?
> From the land that no man knows?
> Did Mr. Stork bring you here on his wings?
> Were you born in the heart of a rose?
> Did an angel fly with you down from the sky?
> Were you found in a gooseberry patch?
> Did a fairy bring you from fairyland?
> To my door—that was left on the latch?
> No—my darling was born of a wonderful love,
> A Love that was Daddy's and mine.
> A love that was human, but deep and profound,
> A love that was almost divine.
> Do you remember, sweetheart, when we went to the zoo?
> And we saw that big bear, with a grouch?
> And the tigers and lions, and that tall kangaroo
> That carried her babes in a pouch?
> Do you remember I told you she kept them there safe
> From the cold and wind, till they grew
> Big enough to take care of themselves,
> Well, dear heart, that's just how I first cared for you.
> I carried you under my heart, my sweet,
> And I sheltered you, safe from alarms,
> Till one wonderful day the dear God looked down—
> And I cuddled you tight in my arms.

E. F. Albee apparently found the verse to be indecent.

In the 1920s, Petrova was primarily occupied with three plays: *The White Peacock* (1921), *Hurricane* (1923), and *What Do We Know?* (1927), all of which she wrote and starred in. The last two dealt with birth control and spiritualism respectively, and like many of Petrova's activities were controversial. After a three-year absence, she returned to the vaudeville stage at the Palace Theatre in Chicago, in May 1923, with a thirty-four-minute act which included all her earlier songs and recitations. She even moved the piano when she found it was not in exactly the right position onstage, telling the audience, "If you want anything done right . . ." *Variety* (May 24, 1923) reported that, as usual, she was dramatic in all that she did, and, as usual, she was a great success with the audience. In 1925, Petrova headlined at the New York Hippodrome, singing a French and Spanish number and closing her act with "Carry Me Back to Old Virginny" sung in three different voices: baritone, soprano, and very high falsetto. "With Petrova," commented *Variety* (October 21, 1925), "the secret is charm, showmanship, dry European wit, and a startlingly different way of doing things."

Petrova invested her money wisely and retired to the south of France in the late 1920s. At the outbreak of the Second World War, she returned to the United States and settled in Clearwater, Florida, where she died. Asked to define greatness, she replied, "What is little? What is great? Let me put it this way. I did achieve what I set out as a child to get, my own bread, my own butter, my own house in which to enjoy it. That—to me—is the height of what I will accept and acknowledge as greatness."

BIBLIOGRAPHY

Petrova, Olga. *Butter with My Bread*. Indianapolis: Bobbs-Merrill, 1942.

Slide, Anthony. "Olga Petrova." In *The Idols of Silence*. New York: A. S. Barnes, 1976, pp. 47–55.

PHILADELPHIA

In 1906, there were five vaudeville houses in Philadelphia: the Ninth and Arch Street Museum and Theatre, the Bijou, the Lyceum, the Trocadero, and B. F. Keith's. By 1921, with Philadelphia's population at 1,823,158, there were still five: the Grand Opera House, B. F. Keith's, the People's, the Broadway, and the William Penn.

MOLLY PICON (New York, February 28, 1898—Lancaster, Pa., April 5, 1992)

A great star of the Yiddish theatre—"I'm the last of the Yiddish theatre, they hang onto me," she once said—Molly Picon was born Margaret Pyckoon. She began her career at the age of five in vaudeville and burlesque, introducing herself to theatrical producers with the words, "I sing, dance, play the piano and ukelele, and do somersaults." Between 1915 and 1918, she toured with an act called The Four Seasons, singing and dancing on the Gus Sun and other small-time vaudeville circuits.

Following her early vaudeville career, Molly Picon became a leading lady in the Yiddish theatre, which was centered on New York's Second Avenue. In 1919, she married Joseph Kalich, who wrote many Yiddish operettas for her until his death in 1975. Songs with which she is associated include "Temperamental Tilly" and "Yiddishe Blues." As a result of her success in Yiddish theatre, the actress was invited to headline at the Palace in the spring of 1929 at a salary of $2,500 a week. She took some of the Yiddish numbers she had performed on Second Avenue with her and translated them into English for her big-time vaudeville debut. Sophie Tucker, who was on the same bill, did the reverse and performed half of her act in Yiddish, causing *Variety* to comment, "The Broadway actress did a Second Avenue show and the Second Avenue actress did a Broadway show."

Her success at the Palace led Molly Picon to appear in vaudeville elsewhere, including a 1932 stint at the London Palladium. She became a regular at the Palace, with her salary rising to $3,000 a week. In July 1930, Picon's Palace act included an interview with "Mister Ziegenfeld," in which she tried to put Fatima Goldberg in the glorifying business, together with such songs as "The

Immigrant Boy," "Kiss Me Again," and "Temperamental Tillie," composed by Joseph Rumshinsky, known as the Second Avenue Irving Berlin. *Variety* (July 16, 1930) noted, "A clever artiste, that Picon girl. The favorite Yiddish soubrette on the East Side, her transition to Broadway and Forty-seventh is heightened, if anything, by her Broadway material and further presented in cameo relief by her own charming personality and style."

Vaudeville was, however, nothing more than a side venture for the petite and effervescent Molly Picon. It was on a par with her occasional film appearances—notably *Come Blow Your Horn* (1963)—and her forays into mainstream Broadway plays, such as *A Majority of One* (1960). In 1938, she appeared in *Vaudeville Marches On*, and in 1979, she wrote and performed in the revue *Those Were the Days*, which played New York in Yiddish and Philadelphia in English.

BIBLIOGRAPHY

"Molly Picon." *Current Biography*, June 1951, pp. 488–90.
Picon, Molly, with Jean Grillo. *Molly!* New York: Simon & Schuster, 1980.

"POISON IVY"

"Poison Ivy" was the name given to any theatre blacklisted by the B. F. Keith and Orpheum circuits. No act wishing to play those circuits would accept a booking at a "poison ivy" house.

POLAIRE (Agha, Algeria, May 13, 1879—Champigny-sur-Marne, France, October 14, 1939)

Polaire had a strange, and short, career in American vaudeville. She was one of the darlings of Parisian music halls in the early years of this century, famed for her beauty (although she did have a rather sharp, pointed nose, which was often caricatured) and for her extraordinary fifteen-inch waist. She had neither a great voice nor great acting ability, but she was a passionate and intense performer, who, one critic noted, "shook like an infuriated wasp" while she was onstage. Polaire portrayed Claudine when Colette's books featuring that character were transferred to the stage, and the latter described Polaire as "a strange young woman who had no need of true beauty to put all other women in the shade, an inspired actress to whom training and study were equally unnecessary." She was a temperamental star, concerned only with her performance. When Colette told her to sleep well, the actress replied, "Oh, I don't sleep much, you know. I lie and wait." When Colette asked for whom, her star replied, "Nobody! I wait and wait for tomorrow's performance."

Algerian by birth, Polaire was born Emile Bouchard but was renamed by her brother, who brought her to Paris and first obtained work for her, singing in boulevard cafés. Willie Hammerstein brought Polaire to America in June 1910 as a freak act at his Victoria Theatre, paying her the staggering sum of $2,800 a week. Very unfairly and inaccurately, Hammerstein billed Polaire as "The Ugliest Woman in the World," and offered prizes to women who, with the aid of corsets, could beat Polaire's fifteen-inch waist. In hindsight, it is difficult to comprehend how an actress who was noted in France for her beauty could be billed as ugly in the United States, but the description appears to have been based in large part on Polaire's wearing a ring in her nose, a novelty with which American audiences were unfamiliar.

Polaire was featured in a twenty-minute, French-language playlet titled *Le Visiteur*. She appeared as an actress who returns to her bedroom after a meeting with her lover. Hearing a noise in the garden, she assumes it is her lover returning, but in reality it is a burglar, "an Apache of the worst sort," who demands she hand over her jewelry. The actress dances with the Apache, toying with him and not realizing the situation she is in. "Go to the window and look in the garden," says the burglar. She does, and sees the dead body of her lover, knifed by the Apache. Violently, the actress dances with the Apache until she is able to grab hold of his knife, which she plunges into his neck. As the burglar collapses and dies, the actress also falls exhausted at his side. The maid enters, sees the two, and believes the burglar is her mistress's lover. As the curtain falls, she comments, "Ah, these young lovers—like puppies—always playing."

Audiences were thrilled by the Apache dance that was new to America, and were intrigued by the sight of a woman being knocked around onstage. However, after a couple of weeks, attendance dropped, and, apparently, there was more applause for Bedini and Arthur's burlesque of Polaire's act on the same bill than there was for the French star herself. Out-of-town managers were unwilling to meet Polaire's high salary demands, and so in July 1910, the star returned to France.

Much of the credit for Polaire's initial American success must go to Hammerstein's press agent Nellie Revel, who thought up "The Ugliest Woman in the World" title, which, incidentally, Polaire demanded be removed from outside the theatre, along with photographs of herself that she claimed were not good likenesses. Nellie Revel had the idea of photographing Lillian Russell with Polaire, captioning the result as "The Ugliest and Handsomest Women in the World," but she was beaten out by Morris Gest. In anger, Revel punched Gest in the nose and quit her job with Hammerstein.

American audiences had one further opportunity to see Polaire, when she was featured in the three-reel film *The Sparrow*, produced by Eclair and released in the United States on April 10, 1914.

In many respects, Polaire was little more than a freak attraction, and by the 1920s, she had disappeared from the stage. She relied for financial support on old friends such as Colette, for, as one writer noted, Polaire had become as outdated as the corset that had made her fifteen-inch waist famous.

BIBLIOGRAPHY

Bell, Archie. "The Ugliest Actress." *The Green Book Magazine*, June 1914, pp. 833–
     40.

SYLVESTER Z. POLI (Lucca, Italy, 1860—Woodmont, Ct., May 31, 1937)

Sylvester Z. Poli operated a small circuit of vaudeville houses in New England, and although very much liked within the community, he was well-known for his parsimony toward performers. A sculptor by trade, Poli was brought over to the United States to make faces and remodel the exhibits at the Eden Musée, when it opened in New York in 1881. While working on wax figures for the exhibit, he was also making a few for himself on the side, and when he had a sufficient number, he quit the Eden Musée and opened a sideshow attraction at Ontario Beach, a resort near Rochester, New York. From there, he moved to New Haven, Connecticut, and opened a waxworks museum which offered variety turns as a side attraction.

As the variety acts gained in popularity, Poli began opening small vaudeville houses, relying on acts agreeing with his small salaries because they had no better offer. All week, a vaudeville act would wait in hope of a booking, and when none materialized would agree to play Poli's. Often he was unable to announce his next week's bill, but local audiences did not mind, because they knew that the Poli theatres would offer major headliners in need of bookings. By all accounts, Poli was a thoroughly likeable individual, whom vaudevillians found amusing.

He relied very much on agent William Morris to find him talent, but eventually was forced to book his acts through the United Booking Office. In 1928, Poli retired and sold his theatres to William Fox for a reported $30 million.

The Poli circuit consisted of the Poli and Palace theatres in Bridgeport, Connecticut, the Palace and Capitol theaters in Hartford, Connecticut, the Poli Theatre in Meriden, Connecticut, the Palace Theatre in New Haven, Connecticut, the Poli Theatre in Scranton, Pennsylvania, the Palace Theatre in Springfield, Massachusetts, the Palace Theatre in Waterbury, Connecticut, the Poli Theatre in Wilkes Barre, Pennsylvania, and the Poli Theatre in Worcester, Massachusetts.

BIBLIOGRAPHY

Laurie, Joe, Jr. "Sylvester Z. Poli." In *Vaudeville: From the Honky-Tonks to the Palace.* New York: Henry Holt, 1953, pp. 397–400.

ROSA PONSELLE (Meriden, Ct., January 22, 1897—Green Spring Valley, Md., May 25, 1981)

Born Rosa Ponzillo and one of America's greatest sopranos, Rosa Ponselle was a frequent performer on the vaudeville stage, usually singing duets with her elder sister, mezzo-soprano Carmela (1892–1977), before coming to the attention of Enrico Caruso in 1918 and making her debut that same year opposite him in *La Forza del Destino* at the Metropolitan Opera. Ponselle appeared for nineteen seasons at the Metropolitan before retiring in 1937.

BIBLIOGRAPHY

Ponselle, Rosa, and James A. Drake. *Ponselle: A Singer's Life.* Garden City, N.Y.: Doubleday, 1982.

POSTAGE STAMPS

Commemorative postage stamps have been issued by the U.S. Postal Service to commemorate the one-hundredth anniversaries of the births of Will Rogers and W. C. Fields. Additionally, a series of postage stamps featuring caricatures by Al Hirschfeld were issued in 1991; included on the stamps were the following vaudevillians: Abbott and Costello, Edgar Bergen, Jack Benny, and Fanny Brice.

POWER'S DANCING ELEPHANTS

A long-running attraction at the New York Hippodrome in the late teens and early 1920s was Power's Dancing Elephants, which not only danced but also played baseball and fenced with the trainer. In May 1923, Power's Dancing Elephants had the distinction of being the first elephant act to play the Palace.

Because of their size, it was difficult not only to present elephant acts on the vaudeville stage, but also to move them from theatre to theatre. For this reason, Power's tended to stay in the New York area, where its only competitors were Lockhart's Elephants and Gruber's Elephants. In 1924, a fourth elephant act was announced: John Robinson's Military Elephants. That act consisted of "4 Talking, Singing, Dancing and Play Acting Elephants" and featured Tillie, "108 Years Old, Only Talking Elephant in the World—20 Tons of Animal Intelligence."

PRESENTATION HOUSES

Theatres that presented vaudeville acts in support of films were called presentation houses. The term came into common usage in the late 1920s, with two of the best known being the Paramount Theatre in New York and the Chicago Theatre in Chicago. On July 16, 1932, the Palace became a presentation house, offering a combination of vaudeville acts and the feature film *Bring 'em Back Alive*.

GEORGE E. PRICE (New York, January 5, 1900—New York, May 10, 1964)

Georgie Price (as he was generally known) was a popular song-and-dance man and impressionist in vaudeville, noted for his large, jug-like ears and his performance of "Bye, Bye, Blackbird." He began in show business in his preteens as one of Gus Edwards's child performers, and made his first appearance at the Palace in 1913 with "Gus Edwards Revue." In 1919, he signed a long-term contract with the Shubert Brothers. It was not a happy relationship, one that the Shuberts tried, unsuccessfully, to break. When the contract expired in 1926, Price starred on Broadway in *The Song Writer*, for which he also wrote the music and lyrics.

The performer was a frequent headliner at the Palace, and in 1925 was the only entertainer to receive double billing, because he was presenting two acts. There was a warmth to his song delivery, reminiscent of Al Jolson, and perhaps it is not coincidental that in the early 1930s, he and Willie Howard would appear onstage, impersonating Jolson rival George Jessel singing "My Mother's Eyes."

In 1934, Price retired from vaudeville and purchased a seat on the New York Stock Exchange. He did return for a number of charity performances and agreed to become president of the American Guild of Variety Artists, of which he was a founder.

GEORGE H. PRIMROSE (London, Canada, November 12, 1852—San Diego, Ca., July 23, 1919)

One of America's great blackface minstrels and a popular favorite on the vaudeville stage, George H. Primrose began his career in Detroit in 1867 with McFarland's Minstrels, billed as Master Georgie, "the infant clog dancer." In 1871, he formed a partnership with Bobby McGown, performing a double clog dance, but the partnership was dissolved before the year was over, and Primrose formed a new alliance with William H. West. The couple worked in various minstrel shows until the summer of 1882, when, in partnership with George Thatcher, they formed Thatcher, Primrose and West's Minstrels at Elmira, New York. In the summer of 1889, Primrose and West's Minstrels gave its first performance, continuing until April 1898. From 1898 to 1903, Primrose worked in association with Lew Dockstader, and Primrose and Dockstader became America's preeminent minstrel company. From 1903 onward, Primrose headed his own minstrel company and also worked extensively in vaudeville.

The vaudeville presentations were similar to his work in minstrels. He did not appear alone; for example, in April 1909 at New York's Lincoln Square Theatre, he performed a singing and dancing act backed by four blackfaced men. In 1918, he had a support group of seven men in blackface at the Fifth Avenue Theatre in a twenty-five-minute act. The act was little more than a minstrel show in miniature, with songs, dances, and comedy from the supporting group and Primrose appearing at the finale. Sime Silverman wrote in *Variety* (September 13, 1918):

> He appears in whiteface, closing the act with his soft shoe dance, announced by the interlocutor as the greatest soft shoe dancer in the world. If anyone has ever disputed that just title applied to Mr. Primrose, his protest has never been heard around these parts. He still dances, that veteran, and "show business" must have grown to be a set habit with him. He's been at it a long while, so long he is beyond criticism, if there was any to be directed at him or his act.

The performance at the Fifth Avenue Theatre marked the end of George Primrose's career. He died less than a year later.

F. (FREDERICK) F. (FREEMAN) PROCTOR (Dexter, Me., March 17, 1851—Larchmont, N.Y., September 4, 1929)

F. F. Proctor was one of the legendary showmen in the annals of vaudeville, founder of the Proctor chain of theatres and originator of continuous vaudeville. Despite being a born showman, Proctor did not come from a theatrical family. His father was the local doctor, and when he died in 1860, Proctor had to leave school and earn a living, initially with a dry goods company in Boston. In his spare time, the young man practiced acrobatics and gymnastics, and teamed up with a twenty-two-year-old named George E. Mansfield to form a vaudeville act called the Levantine Brothers. They purchased the name from a retired act. As early as 1866, the Levantine Brothers appeared in New York, and in 1872 made their first trip to Europe, followed by a second European tour in 1876. By then, Proctor was either working as a solo act or teamed with other partners, but still using the name Fred Levantine, under which he was billed as the "World's Champion Equilibrist."

In the late 1870s, Proctor settled in Albany, New York, and there, in 1880, he acquired his first theatre, the Green Street, which he renamed Levantine's Theatre. Four years later, Proctor leased the Theatorium in Rochester, New York, and the Martin Opera House in Albany. In 1886, he opened Proctor's Novelty Theatre in the Williamsburg section of Brooklyn, followed the next year by Proctor's Criterion Theatre, also in Brooklyn. In 1889, Proctor purchased a site at 141 West 23rd Street, between Sixth and Seventh Avenues, where he built the 23rd Street Theatre, which, for the first two years of its life, was the home of Charles Frohman's stock company. There, in 1892, Proctor introduced continuous vaudeville, with programs running without interruption from 11 A.M. to 11 P.M.

The 23rd Street Theatre paled in comparison to Proctor's Pleasure Palace on 58th Street between Lexington and Third avenues, which opened on Labor Day 1895, with a bill that included Weber and Fields, Sam Bernard, Lew Dockstader, and Lottie Gilson. In part because the facility included not only a theatre, but also a roof garden, a nightclub, and a palm garden, Proctor's Pleasure Palace was not successful. It was followed by the opening of Proctor's first theatre in New Jersey, the Newark Theatre, in 1898. By this time, Proctor's empire included some twenty-nine theatres in New York, Connecticut, Pennsylvania, Massachusetts, and Delaware. Beginning in 1900 with the Fifth Avenue Theatre, New York, Proctor opened a further twenty-four theatres, including the 125th Street Theatre (opened in 1900), the Lyric Theatre, Newark (1905), the Lyceum, Troy, New York (1912), the Grand Theatre, Albany (1913), and the 86th Street Theatre (1927, and his last). From heavy competition with B. F. Keith, Proctor became his partner in May 1906, when the creation of the Keith and Proctor Theatres was announced.

In 1928, Proctor began selling off his assets, and in May 1929, the remaining eleven theatres under his control were sold to the Radio-Keith-Orpheum Corporation. In 1904, he had married a vaudevillian named Georgie Lingard, whose act consisted of dancing and rope-skipping.

BIBLIOGRAPHY

Grau, Robert. "Frederick F. Proctor and His Theatres." *American Magazine*, November 1916, pp. 84–85.

Marston, William Moulton, and John Henry Feller. *F. F. Proctor: Vaudeville Pioneer*. New York: Richard R. Smith, 1943.

PROTEAN ACTS

Protean acts were similar to, but not the same as, quick-change routines. Unlike the latter, which had little dialogue or plot lines, protean acts were usually presented by legitimate stage performers who made multiple costume changes but also built characterizations and presented complete dramatic scenes. According to Joe Laurie, Jr., in *Vaudeville: From the Honky-Tonks to the Palace*, the first protean act was presented in 1873 by a former minstrel named G. Dwayne Buckley. The act was titled "On the Track" and involved eight costume changes, the playing of ten musical instruments, the singing of twelve songs, and the performance of six dances. In the 1890s, Leopoldo Fregoli in France presented the entire opera *Faust* as a protean act; he came to the United States in 1906, and when he died, the act was taken over by his wife.

British actor R. A. Roberts was noted for his protean act "Dick Turpin." Other protean acts mentioned by Laurie were those of Charles T. Aldrich and Roland West (who later became a prominent Hollywood director). West introduced his act "The Criminal" in 1906; it concerned an elderly professor arrested for the murder of a girl, with the chief accusation against him coming from his son. The setting of a police inquisition allowed West to adopt seven characterizations, three of a comic nature, ranging from an old man to a newsboy. "The Criminal" was possibly the first protean act to mix comedy and drama.

Protean acts were not always male. In 1909, Charlotte Parry presented "Into the Light," in which she played a woman on trial for murder, as well as the witnesses testifying against her. Subsequently, she married Joshua Lowe, who wrote for *Variety* under the name "Jolo." In 1906, Margaret Wycherly presented a protean act titled "In Self-Defense" (her vaudeville debut), in which she portrayed six characters.

BIBLIOGRAPHY

Laurie, Joe, Jr. "Transfigurators!" In *Vaudeville: From the Honky-Tonks to the Palace*. New York: Henry Holt, 1953, pp. 96–98.

EVA PUCK (Brooklyn, N.Y., November 27, 1892—Granada Hills, Ca., October 25, 1979)

Eva Puck was a bright dancing and singing comedienne, who, with her husband, Sammy White (1894–1960), played the comic leads in Rodgers and Hart's *The Girl Friend* (which opened at New York's Vanderbilt Theatre on March 17, 1926) and Jerome Kern and Oscar Hammerstein II's *Show Boat* (which opened at New York's Ziegfeld Theatre on December 27, 1927).

Prior to Puck and White's becoming a team, Eva Puck had worked in vaudeville with her brother Harry in an act titled Puck and Puck, while White was half of the team of Clayton and White. Puck and White's vaudeville routine was titled "Opera versus Jazz." It began with White portraying a dancing teacher trying to instruct a stupid Puck, followed by a burlesque of grand opera and classical dancing. Reviewing the act at the Palace, Abel Green wrote in *Variety* (December 27, 1923), "Both go in for comedy in a broad vein, but it is judiciously counterbalanced by the other when each is featuring a specialty." *Variety*'s Chicago critic "Loop" caught the couple's act at the Chicago Theatre and declared them "ideal entertainers whether in revue, vaudeville, or picture houses."

If Puck and White are remembered at all, it is for introducing "Life Upon the Wicked Stage" in *Show Boat*, a number that showcased their talents as both singers and dancers. Eva Puck and Sammy White headlined at the Palace in August 1929 and October 1931. Her brother Harry was one of the last vaudevillians to play there, in May 1932.

ISMA BERLINGER (JACK) PULASKI (Cuthbert, Ga., 1883—New York, July 16, 1948)

Jack Pulaski was one of *Variety*'s best known theatrical reporters and critics, writing under the pen name of "Ibee." Educated in Philadelphia, he began writing for *Variety* in Atlantic City in 1910. Four years later, he moved to New York and wrote sports commentary for the *Evening Mail* under the name of "Left Jab." In 1915, he joined the permanent staff of *Variety*, where he remained until his death in 1948. In 1917, he briefly took charge of *Variety*'s Chicago office, but departed in October of the same year, replaced by Jack Lait. Pulaski was, supposedly, the only member of *Variety*'s editorial staff never fired by Sime Silverman. His funeral was attended by more than 750, and included tributes by Bert Lytell, as president of the Lambs and ex-president of Actors Equity, and producer Brock Pemberton.

R _____

RADIO

Eventually radio was to supplant vaudeville as America's preeminent form of popular entertainment, but in the 1920s and even as late as the early 1930s, the two mediums interacted, with vaudevillians finding employment in radio, and radio personalities using the vaudeville stage to expand or consolidate their popularity. According to Morris Markey, writing on "The Salaries of Radio Stars" in *Liberty* (June 9, 1934), the highest paid radio personalities were all former vaudevillians, with Ed Wynn, Al Jolson, George M. Cohan, Eddie Cantor, and Will Rogers all earning a minimum of $5,000 a week. Thanks to radio, and to a lesser extent the motion picture, Jack Benny, Edgar Bergen, and George Burns and Gracie Allen considerably advanced their careers—and without radio, there would have been no lucrative television contracts in the 1950s. Kate Smith found an audience on radio far greater than she would have played to had she continued working in vaudeville and musical comedy. Fred Allen was a great vaudevillian, but he was an even greater radio personality.

Vaughn DeLeath (1896–1943) was the first lady of radio, the medium's first crooner whose voice was selected by Dr. Lee De Forest as best suited to the radio microphone. Yet she also enjoyed a career in vaudeville in the 1920s and 1930s, with her warm, engaging personality making her an audience favorite.

After initial fame on radio, Arthur Tracy and Rudy Vallee came to vaudeville to prove they were talented, that they had faces and personalities—and could sing just as well without the aid of a radio microphone. Typical of the radio-made personalities who were welcomed by vaudeville was Tito Guizar, who was a favorite on CBS. In 1934, he toured vaudeville, and "Cher" in *Variety* (July 3, 1934) commented, "With a guitar, a little stool for one of his feet, a microphone and a pleasing personality as his supplemental aids, Tito Guizar, of radio, makes a strong voice mean something."

The situation changed in the mid 1930s, as radio became all-powerful and all-popular, and there was no longer a need for radio personalities to venture onto the dying vaudeville stage.

BIBLIOGRAPHY

Buxton, Frank, and Bill Owen. *The Big Broadcast, 1920–1950*. New York: Viking Press, 1972.

Dunning, John. *Tune in Yesterday: The Ultimate Encyclopedia of Old-Time Radio, 1925–1976*. Englewood Cliffs, N.J.: Prentice-Hall, 1976.

Henderson, Amy. *On the Air: Pioneers of American Broadcasting*. Washington, D.C.: Smithsonian Institution Press, 1988.

Settel, Irving. *A Pictorial History of Radio*. New York: Bonanza Books, 1960.

Slide, Anthony. *Great Radio Personalities in Historic Photographs*. New York: Dover, 1982.

RADIO CITY MUSIC HALL

The foremost film showplace in the United States, designed by Donald Deskey and with seating for sixty-two-hundred, Radio City Music Hall opened at New York's Rockefeller Center on December 27, 1932. The opening night presentation was strictly a vaudeville show, and through the years, the theatre was noted as much for its live entertainment as for its film presentations. Among those participating in the opening night bill were the aerialists the Wallenda Family, Ray Bolger ("Outstanding Young American Dancing Comedian"), Doc Rockwell, Taylor Holmes, and John Pierce (who later enjoyed fame on the operatic stage as Jan Peerce). The very long evening ended with a nostalgic performance by Weber and Fields. The program was presented by Radio City Music Hall's first director general, S. L. Rothafel (who remained there until 1934). Reviewing the program, Brooks Atkinson wrote in *The New York Times* (December 28, 1932), "High jinks and buffoonery flourish in more intimate surroundings; and, for that matter, princes of display and promotion are seldom cursed with a sense of humor. Although the opening bill is dull, it is likely that Roxy [S. L. Rothafel] will develop an ornate type of music hall diversion better suited to his tremendous palace."

The opening night program also included precision dancing by the Roxyettes Ballet Corps. Formed by dancer Russell Markert in St. Louis in 1925 as the Missouri Rockets, this group had earlier been featured by Rothafel at his Roxy Theatre, and the name was changed to the Rockettes to avoid an implied connection with the latter theatre. The best known routine of the Rockettes is the specialty "Parade of the Wooden Soldiers," danced at the annual Christmas show to the music of Victor Herbert.

The first feature film to be screened at Radio City Music Hall was Frank Capra's production of *The Bitter Tea of General Yen*. Increasing financial problems forced the closure of the facility on April 12, 1978, but it was saved from demolition thanks to the concerted efforts of various groups, and it reopened on May 31, 1979, as an entertainment center, offering live shows and film presentations.

Radio City Music Hall is located at 50th Street and Avenue of the Americas, New York, N.Y. 10020. It maintains a Radio City Music Hall Archives (de-

scribed in the Summer 1982 issue of *Broadside*, the newsletter of the Theatre
Library Association).

BIBLIOGRAPHY

Ansen, David, "Radio City Redux." *Time*, June 11, 1979, p. 60.
Francisco, Charles. *The Radio City Music Hall: An Affectionate History of the World's
    Greatest Theater*. New York: E. P. Dutton, 1979.
Morris, Joe Alex. "The Music Hall." *Saturday Evening Post*, January 11, 1959, pp. 35,
    90–92.
Shepard, Richard F. "Radio City Music Hall Returns." *The New York Times*, June 1,
    1979, pp. C1, C6.

SALLY RAND (Hickory County, Mo., April 3, 1904—Glendora, Ca., August
31, 1979)

The woman whose name is synonymous with fan dancing was born Helen
Gould Beck in the heartland of America. She refused to be billed as an exotic
dancer, claiming, "The dictionary defines 'exotic' as that which is strange and
foreign. I'm not 'strange'; I like boys. I am not foreign; I was born in Hickory
County, Missouri." Sometimes she would use a large, balloon-like ball in her
act, but generally she danced in the nude, using two ostrich feathers, which she
would move with perfect precision, covering and uncovering various parts of
her body. Her favorite musical accompaniment was Debussy's "Claire de Lune."
The audiences got no glimpse of pubic hair or a naked breast as Sally Rand
danced. Indeed, photographs of her reveal far more than she was willing to
expose onstage; for example, readers of the *Police Gazette* for December 12,
1933, with a cover shot of Rand and Max Baer, saw a great deal more of her
shapely body than had ever been seen in vaudeville and burlesque houses.

Sally Rand "lifted" her stage name from the Rand McNally atlas. Why she
picked Rand rather than McNally has never been explained, but perhaps it was
because it provided her with the pun line, "The Rand is quicker than the eye."
She worked as an acrobat in circuses and carnivals, and at the age of thirteen,
she became a cigarette girl at a cafe in Kansas City. The following year, the
performer became a member of the Empress Theater Stock Company, and shortly
thereafter joined the Gus Edwards troupe.

In the mid 1920s, she came to Los Angeles, seeking film work, and was hired
to appear in a number of Hal Roach comedies. Subsequently, she was signed
to a contract by Cecil B. DeMille, and he featured her in a number of his own
productions and also loaned her out to other companies. Sally Rand's silent films
include *Man Bait* (1926), *Night of Love* (1927), *His Dog* (1927), *Getting Gertie's
Garter* (1927), *Galloping Fury* (1927), *Heroes in Blue* (1927), *Crashing Through*
(1928), *A Girl in Every Port* (1928), *Woman against the World* (1928), *Nameless
Men* (1928), *Golf Widows* (1928), and *Black Feather* (1928). She appeared in
only one film directed by DeMille, and that was *King of Kings* (1927), in which
she plays Mary Magdalene's handmaiden. A 1925 publicity handout from
DeMille's P.D.C. Studios described her as "saucy, piquant—your eye just nat-

urally goes to her. She's a cute, lithesome charmer, whether as a blonde or a brunette—and above all she radiates personality.''

Following her initial screen career (she was back at Paramount in 1934 with a featured role in *Bolero*), Sally Rand toured the vaudeville circuits, and even headlined at the Palace in September 1928 with a twenty-two minute act titled ''Sally's Boy Friends.'' With the aid of three male dancers and an octet of male singers, Rand did an adagio act plus a little tap dancing. Her reception at the Palace was ''indifferently pleasant,'' according to Abel Green in *Variety* (September 26, 1928).

Sally Rand's career faltered during the depression, and she was reduced to working in the chorus at New York's Capitol Theatre, modeling and accepting occasional nightclub jobs. It was the fan dance that brought her back to stardom. She first performed it at a Chicago nightclub in 1932, and the following year gained nationwide fame as an attraction in the ''Streets of Paris'' section at the Chicago World's Fair. On opening night, she appeared as Lady Godiva, complete with a white horse and a strategically placed long-haired wig. As a result of her performance at the fair, she was hired to play five shows a day at the Chicago Theatre. The first week, her act attracted an audience of seventy-three thousand, and by the third week, her salary had risen from $1,000 to $3,000 a week.

In 1939, Sally Rand's Nude Ranch was the biggest attraction at the San Francisco World's Fair. At the same time, she was giving three shows a night at the Music Box nightclub on O'Farrell Street. ''Only Sophie Tucker and Harry Richman rank with her as night-club draws, and no one comes close to her drawing power in the vaudeville and picture houses of our land,'' commented journalist Quentin Reynolds in *Collier's* magazine.

She worked continuously in nightclubs and on the burlesque stage, and in 1965 replaced Ann Corio as mistress of ceremonies in *This Was Burlesque* on Broadway. One of Rand's last public appearances was at a 1978 benefit at the Midland Theatre in Kansas City, where her career began.

BIBLIOGRAPHY

Hempstead, Susan. ''Sally, Wave Those Fans!'' *Shadowplay* 2, no. 6 (February 1934), pp. 42–43, 72–74.
Reynolds, Quentin. ''Business Woman.'' *Collier's* 104, no. 9 (August 26, 1939), pp. 23, 56–57.

ALBERTINA RASCH (Vienna—Woodland Hills, Ca., October 2, 1967)

Albertina Rasch was one of the leading presenters of semiclassical dancing on vaudeville bills, usually choreographing or directing the turns but also sometimes appearing as a soloist. She arrived in the United States from her native Vienna in time to appear at the New York Hippodrome in September 1909. At the request of Otto Kahn, she began dancing at the Metropolitan Opera House, but she left to devote her energies to the vaudeville stage. In July 1916, she performed what was termed ''new classic dancing'' at New York's Colonial Theatre. In the 1920s, she and her ballet troupe were almost a permanent fixture in New York's vaudeville houses, playing the Hippodrome in April 1924 and May 1926 and the Palace in December 1925, July 1926, October 1928, December 1929, and December 1930.

As a director and choreographer, Rasch first came to notice in 1925, when she staged a ballet to George Gershwin's "Rhapsody in Blue" at the Hippodrome. She began providing ballet units to musical comedies in 1927 with *Rio Rita*, which was the start of a long-term relationship with Florenz Ziegfeld. Other Broadway shows choreographed by Rasch include *The Band Wagon* (1931), *The Cat and the Fiddle* (1931), *The Great Waltz* (1934), and *Lady in the Dark* (1941). Her last Broadway show was *Marinka* in 1945.

Albertina Rasch began her long association with Hollywood in 1934, when she choreographed the Maurice Chevalier–Jeanette MacDonald musical *The Merry Widow*. At the same time, she started a corps de ballet, which she maintained at the M-G-M studios. In 1938, Rasch boasted that she directed some eight-hundred dancers in a single week in three M-G-M features: *Marie Antoinette*, *The Great Waltz*, and *Sweethearts*.

She retired because of ill health shortly after the conclusion of the Second World War. In 1925, Albertina Rasch married composer Dimitri Tiomkin (1899–1979).

MARTHA RAYE (Butte, Mt., August 27, 1916—)

A raucous singing comedienne, Martha Raye was born Margaret Teresa Yvonne O'Reed and began appearing in her parents' vaudeville act at the age of three. As early as 1932, she was a featured vaudeville player in New York, appearing at the Hollywood and Loew's State. Her first major attempt at the comedy style for which she is best known was in the 1934 revue *Calling All Stars*. Later she toured in vaudeville with, and was fired by, comedian Ben Blue. Concurrent with her vaudeville appearances in the 1930s, Raye was also appearing in nightclubs, and while performing at the Trocadero in Los Angeles in 1936, she was seen by Bing Crosby and director Norman Taurog and signed to appear in the Paramount feature film *Rhythm on the Range*, in which the Sam Coslow song "Mr. Paganini" showcased both her singing and her comedy. Of her performance, Frank Nugent wrote in *The New York Times* (July 30, 1936):

She is a stridently funny comedienne with a mammoth cave, or an early Joe E. Brown mouth, with a dental supply vaguely reminiscent of those frightening uppers and lowers that used to hang over the portals of painless extraction emporia, and a chest which—in moments of burlesque aggressiveness—appears to expand fully 10 inches.

None of Raye's Paramount feature films particularly added to her stature, and it was not until the 1947 Charlie Chaplin feature *Monsieur Verdoux* that she came into her own as a screen comedienne. Unfortunately, that film also marked the end of Raye's film career, aside from a handful of cameo performances. She fared much better on television, as one of the stars of NBC's *All Star Revue* in 1951, with a series of specials, and eventually with a weekly program, *The*

Martha Raye Show, seen on NBC between 1953 and 1956. In later years, she was a regular on *McMillan and Wife* (NBC, 1976–1977), and beginning in 1980, Raye was the television spokesperson for Polident.

Martha Raye was seen on Broadway in 1967 in *Hello, Dolly!* and, in 1972, in *No, No, Nanette*. After a twenty-five-year absence from New York cabaret, she returned in November 1985, appearing at the Ballroom. Two years later, Raye replaced Rose Marie in *4 Girls 4*, touring with Margaret Whiting, Helen O'Connell, and Rosemary Clooney. An energetic entertainer of the troops during the Second World War, Raye's work in that and for other charitable causes resulted in her receiving the 1969 Jean Hersholt Humanitarian Award from the Academy of Motion Picture Arts and Sciences.

The entertainer was the subject of considerable publicity in 1991 as a result of her September 25, Las Vegas marriage to forty-two-year-old promoter Mark Harris. Raye was seventy-five and had been married six times previously between 1937 and 1958. As a result of that marriage, Raye's only child, Melodye Condos (the daughter of dancer Nick Condos), received permission for a conservator to be appointed to oversee her mother's financial affairs.

BIBLIOGRAPHY

"At Home, She's Quieter." *Look*, February 9, 1954, pp. 81, 83.
Churchill, Edward. "Behind Martha Raye's Divorce." *Photoplay* 51, no. 11 (November 1937), pp. 23, 72.
Hartley, Katharine. "Ultra Violent Raye." *Photoplay* 51, no. 1 (January 1937), pp. 41–45, 96–97.
"Martha Raye." *Current Biography*, July 1963, pp. 356–57.
"Muggs and Cupid Put the Bite on Martha in a Busy Week." *Life*, May 3, 1954, pp. 133–39.
Park, Jeannie, and Joyce Wagner. "A Star's September Song." *People*, January 27, 1992, pp. 83–84, 87.

ADA REEVE (London, March 3, 1874—London, September 25, 1966)

Ada Reeve was a light comedienne who specialized in performing a mix of sweet and comic songs, delivered with great dignity and artistry. Her career encompassed both vaudeville and musical comedy, and she also appeared on screen and television in her native England. The performer made her British music hall debut in 1886 and her first U.S. appearance at Koster and Bial's Music Hall, New York, in 1893. The following year, Reeve made her musical comedy debut in the London production of *The Shop Girl*, but her biggest success in that genre came in 1899, when she starred in *Florodora*. During the First World War, Reeve was an ardent entertainer of the troops, introducing the popular song "The Long, Long Trail."

Her frequent visits to American vaudeville always included headlining at the Palace and the introduction of her act with the song "Beware Young Ladies." After a 1912 U.S. vaudeville tour, Reeve did not return to the States until 1925. Reviewing her appearance at the Palace, Sime Silverman commented in *Variety* (November 11, 1925), "You don't see an Ada Reeve every day, whether 13 years ago or now. . . . There's a dignity to Ada Reeve, also class. It's immensely to her vogue and reputation that she can return to American vaudeville after a lapse of 13 years to find that though time and customs over here on that stage have passed along to many changes, her impressionable singing can still stand out.'' Ada Reeve made her last appearance at the Palace in January 1928, ending her act with a character study of a cockney mother talking to her baby. ''A lot of personality and enthusiasm enters into the entertainment of Miss Reeve which, coupled with the sure-fire nature of the songs, makes the act one to be thoroughly enjoyed,'' commented *The Billboard* (February 4, 1928).

Ada Reeve remained active until the end of her life, gaining further acclaim in 1943 for her performance in J. B. Priestley's play *They Came to a City*. She was, as Britain's *Daily Telegraph* (June 8, 1912) commented, ''Without an equal.''
BIBLIOGRAPHY
Reeve, Ada. *Take It for a Fact*. London: Heinemann, 1954.

AL REEVES (New York, May 30, 1865—Brooklyn, N.Y., February 26, 1940)
Al Reeves was a singer and noted banjo player in both vaudeville and minstrel shows. His costume displayed the many medals he claimed to have won for his playing, and his banjo was supposedly gold-plated and set with precious jewels. Reeves's trick was to feature a march on the banjo with the orchestra carrying the bulk of the musical load and Reeves making a great deal of noise.

Al Reeves began performing in 1878 and in 1891 launched his own company, Al Reeves and His Beauties. After many years as a minstrel, he entered burlesque at the turn of the century, remaining there until 1922, when he became a vaude-villian, touring as Al Reeves Specialty Co. and his Big Beauty Show, billed as ''99% Girls 99%.'' Reeve's catchphrase was ''Give me credit, boys,'' and he would often bill himself as ''The King of Burlesque.''

FRANCIS RENAULT (Providence, R.I., circa 1893—New York, May 29, 1955)
Francis Renault was a female impersonator who was as good-looking a man as he was a woman. He billed himself as ''The Original Slave of Fashion.'' He claimed his costumes were valued at $35,000, and each Friday afternoon at the vaudeville theatre in which he was performing, these costumes would be displayed onstage for the admiring and envious gaze of the ladies of the audience. Aside from his clothes, Renault possessed a reasonably good singing voice.

He first came to attention in 1916, when his repertoire included ''In the Garden of Allah,'' ''Rackety Coo,'' and ''The Sunshine of Your Smile.'' *Variety* first reviewed him on September 22, 1916, and commented, ''One of the new crop of female impersonators and from appearances should hold up with the best in this division.'' Renault continued in vaudeville through the 1920s and was also in *The Passing Show of 1922*. In 1926, he was operating the Club Francis Renault in Atlantic City. He continued to work long after the demise of vaudeville, and in the last years of his life gave semiannual concerts at New York's Carnegie Hall, the last of which took place in October 1954. Fred Allen was a big fan of these events, in which Renault billed himself as "The Last of the Red Hot Papas." Francis Renault's real name was Anthony Auriemma.

LIEUTENANT GITZ RICE (New Glasgow, Canada, March 5, 1891—New York, October 16, 1947)

Whereas other vaudevillians such as Elsie Janis, Harry Lauder, and Irving Berlin enhanced their reputations as a result of their efforts at entertaining the troops during the First World War, Lieutenant Gitz Rice became a vaudevillian because of his war efforts. A Canadian, Gitz Ingraham Rice (who was always billed as Lieutenant Gitz Rice) organized entertainment for his country's soldiers during the war and also wrote a number of popular wartime songs, of which the best known are "Dear Old Pal of Mine" and "Keep Your Head Down, Fritzi Boy" (based on the British music hall song "Hold Your Hand Out, Naughty Boy").

At the close of the war, Rice found himself in demand as an entertainer, usually accompanying other vaudevillians at the piano, but popular enough to be featured on the front cover of the March 1, 1919, edition of *The New York Dramatic Mirror*. In 1919, he toured this country with Irene Bordoni in an act that had the chanteuse singing "Over There" and "Dear Old Pal of Mine" in French. *The New York Dramatic Mirror* (May 6, 1919) prophesied that they could become "the classiest song team in vaudeville." A year later, Rice was touring vaudeville with Frank Fay in an act titled "Bits of Hits of Their Own Conception." After Rice's entrance, the telephone on his piano would ring, and the soldier-composer would supposedly talk to Fay, inviting him to come down and play a little vaudeville. Fay would then appear, and between Rice's piano solos, he would provide some comic patter and songs, including an imitation of opera star John Charles Thomas singing "Darktown Strutter's Ball." While doubting Rice's ability to hold down the stage without Frank Fay, *Variety* (March 12, 1920) thought the act "a valuable addition to any bill."

Lieutenant Gitz Rice also worked as a solo act in vaudeville and with lesser known partners. In the late 1920s, he put together an act with a group of male singers billed and dressed as members of the Royal Canadian Mounted Police, and with a dancer identified only as Marie. Rice featured his own compositions, and the eighteen-minute act played the number two spot at the Palace in October 1927. *Variety* (October 12, 1927) commented, "The ensemble has trained voices, harmonize well and make a good appearance. . . . The costuming is effective and the harmony gets the act over."

In the 1930s, Rice retired from vaudeville and entered public relations. However, at the outbreak of the Second World War, he returned to the stage, entertaining Canadian troops. His other compositions include

"Mother, I Love You," "Under the Roof Where Laughter Rings," "Because You're Here," "By My Fireside," "Waiting for You," and "I Have Forgotten You Almost."

HARRY RICHMAN (Cincinnati, October 10, 1895—Hollywood, Ca., November 3, 1972)

"When the Red, Red Robin," "On the Sunny Side of the Street," "This Is My Lucky Day," "It All Depends on You," and "Puttin' on the Ritz" are just a few of the songs associated with Harry Richman, a song-and-dance man whose trademarks were a straw hat and cane or top hat and tails. He composed many of his own hits, including "Shake Hands with a Millionaire," "Singing a Vagabond Song," and "Walking My Baby Back Home." His colorful career embraced vaudeville, films, radio, nightclubs, musical comedies, and revues. It included three marriages and romantic affairs with innumerable women, including—according to his autobiography—Mae West, Clara Bow, and Nora Bayes. For his second marriage, to showgirl Hazel Forbes, Richman spent $30,000, with $5,000 going for flowers alone. He was involved with gangsters and payola in the early days of radio. Bob Hope recalled costarring with Richman in *Say When* (1934). When he asked "Who let those mugs in?," referring to Lucky Luciano and his mob, Richman replied, "They're the backers and you better be funny—or you get a concrete overcoat." He claimed to have earned and lost $13 million, although most of his colleagues put the amount at closer to $7 million. His Club Richman on Park Avenue was one of New York's top night spots in the 1920s, and he even played the Palace with an act titled "A Night at Club Richman."

Born to a German mother, he was named for his Russian father, Harry Reichman, and as early as 1907, he became an entertainer in Cincinnati, playing piano in cafes and honky-tonks. In his autobiography, Richman recalls that Sophie Tucker came to the city, heard him play, and told his mother that he had talent and a great future. At the age of fourteen, he teamed up with a violin player named Bud Remington, and they formed an act called Remington and Reichman. By the time he played San Francisco in 1914, Remington had disappeared, and Harry Reichman was now billing himself as "The English Comedian."

The first big break came in the late teens, when Harry Richman became a piano accompanist for Mae West and later the Dolly Sisters. As West recalled at a 1962 Friars Club testimonial to Richman, "I don't remember if I discovered you or if you discovered me, Harry. But I do remember you had a great touch—even with a piano." In the early 1920s, Richman started singing on WHN, one of New York's two radio stations, working with Nils T. Granlund. "I was on from noon till midnight," Richman recalled. "Nils T. Granlund would get on the air and recite something like 'Boots, Boots, Boots!' and then I would sing. We didn't get paid anything because they didn't know whether anyone was listening. Those were the early days of crystal sets, when you had to listen with earphones. I went around to song publishers and made deals where, if I sang a song on the air, they'd give me a dollar. I was the first nationally known radio performer.'' Thus was payola born!

In 1923, Richman put together a new vaudeville act in which he appeared with a midget, sang a "mammy" song, and gave impersonations of Al Jolson and legitimate actor David Warfield. Reviewing his act at the Fifth Avenue Theatre, *Variety* (March 29, 1923) commented, ''Richman made a good appearance, and his turn is made different. On second place [on the bill] he served well enough. The numbers may be new, though they did not impress for melody values. Richman's ability to put 'stuff' into their rendition counted.'' In 1925, he was appearing at the Palace with Eddie Elkins and His Band, and his way of putting over a song with a rich voice, a slight lisp, and mannerisms reminiscent of Al Jolson and Ted Lewis had been perfected. The secret of Richman's success was not his face, nor even the manner in which he held his body, but rather the simple fact that he had personality in his voice. As *Variety* (February 4, 1925) noted, ''Richman now struts himself without a blush and takes on all the mannerisms of a star.'' Harry Richman was later to headline at the Palace in August and September 1930 and January 1931.

The entertainer's career was further enhanced by appearances in the 1926 and 1928 editions of George White's *Scandals* and by an appearance as the master of ceremonies in the 1931 edition of the *Ziegfeld Follies*. He claimed to be earning between $25,000 and $30,000 a week, a staggering amount in those days of little income tax. In 1937, Richman appeared before England's King George VI and Queen Elizabeth, sang ''The Birth of the Blues,'' and ended his act by telling them, ''May God bless and keep you. I wish I could afford to!''

In 1947, Richman recalled, ''my voice was beginning to go—I was having more and more trouble hitting the big ones.'' And as his voice went, so did his career. (Of course, Richman could not resist pointing out that every other part of him was in excellent shape, and that he could still satisfy two ladies a day.) In August 1963, Richman tried a comeback at New York's Latin Quarter, where *The New York Times* (August 24, 1963) noted, ''Most of the patrons are old enough to remember the days when he was one of the biggest names in town.'' But to most people, the man whose suavity and debonair manner personified Broadway—''Beau Broadway,'' as he liked to be called—had become an unknown entity. At his funeral, George Jessel delivered the eulogy and might well have quoted the title of Richman's autobiography as the singer's epitaph, ''A hell of a life.''

BIBLIOGRAPHY

Lawrenson, Helen. ''The Richman Era.'' *Show*, June 1962, pp. 75–76, 106–107.

Richman, Harry, with Richard Gehman. *A Hell of a Life*. New York: Duell, Sloan and Pearce, 1966.

BLANCHE RING (Boston, April 24, 1877—Santa Monica, Ca., January 13, 1961)

One of the great names of musical comedy and vaudeville, Blanche Ring had an infectious way of presenting a song. As *The New York Dramatic Mirror* (May 6, 1919) commented, "Blanche Ring is one of vaudeville's heartiest smiles. She is radiant with this element. Few singing actresses know how to put a song over better than she." Ring is credited with being the first entertainer in vaudeville to get an audience to sing along with her, and the songs she made famous were definitely audience-participation numbers: "In the Good Old Summertime," which she introduced in *The Defender* (1902); "Waltz Me Around Again, Willie"; "When Ireland Comes into Her Own"; "Yip-I-Addy-I-Ay," which she had to reprise five times when she first introduced it to vaudeville in 1913, and with a "Yip" that demanded an audience yell its collective head off; and, of course, "I've Got Rings on My Fingers," from *The Midnight Sons* (1909). The last became her theme song, performed, as were all her numbers, in a jovial Irish brogue which was not so Irish as to be incomprehensible but sufficiently reminiscent of the old country to send all Irish-Americans into spasms of ecstasy.

Reviewing her act in 1919, *The New York Dramatic Mirror* commented, "Not every actress can include the audience in her cast and still retain the footlight illusion." In addition to her songs, Ring would include character studies of an Irish hotel maid, a manicurist, and a telephone operator, and she would also call on the audience to shout out topics for her to discuss. "Of course she must have had plants to shout out these parties or topics which would dovetail into her song material," wrote *The New York Dramatic Mirror*, "but what of that, it was such a merry program and she cheered the blues out of all present, so thanks to her for being the jolly comedienne she always was and is."

Her father and grandfather, both named James Ring, were actors. Early in her career, Blanche Ring appeared onstage with Nat C. Goodwin and Irish tenor Chauncey Olcott, but it was not until 1902, when she appeared in the musical comedy *The Defender*, that she came to prominence. Among her many hits were *The Jewel of Asia* (1903), *The Jersey Lily* (1903), *About Town* (1906), *The Wall Street Girl* (1911), *When Claudia Smiles* (1913), and *The Passing Show of 1919*. Ring made her London debut in a vaudeville act at the Palace Theatre on November 16, 1903. In 1908, she toured with Joe Weber in his burlesque of *The Merry Widow*, and in 1909, she made her first appearance as *The Yankee Girl*, her most famous stage role, which she filmed in 1915. That feature-length production is preserved at the UCLA Film and Television Archive but gives scant indication of Ring's dynamic personality. She also appeared in two other feature films, *It's the Old Army Game* (1926) and *If I Had My Way* (1940).

The actress was married four times. Her last husband was character actor Charles Winninger, whom she married in 1912, separated from in 1928, and eventually divorced in 1952.

Ring was always a favorite with vaudeville audiences; she was the hit of the show when she appeared on an old-timers bill at the Palace in 1925. When she performed at New York's Colonial Theatre in 1913, "Dash" wrote in *Variety* (February 6, 1913), "It has ever been a question whether a singer made a song or a song the singer. With Ring and her record of song hits, she seems entitled to any doubt." There is no question that Blanche Ring was one of the great purveyors of hearty songs, and in part because of the continued appeal of such songs, she is one of the few songstresses from this era whose personality can still be discerned on primitive phonograph recordings.

BIBLIOGRAPHY

"Blanche Ring on Vaudeville." *Variety*, December 11, 1909, p. 47.

Ring, Blanche. "How to 'Put 'em Across.' " *Green Book*, July 1912, pp. 45–49.

RITZ BROTHERS: AL (Newark, N.J., August 27, 1901—New Orleans, December 22, 1965), **HARRY** (Newark, N.J., May 28, 1907—San Diego, Ca., March 29, 1986), and **JIMMY** (Newark, N.J., October 22, 1904—Los Angeles, November 17, 1985)

The Ritz Brothers exemplify a certain type of trio or quartet act popular in vaudeville in the late 1920s and 1930s, which combined slapstick and acrobatic comedy in a rowdy and robust format. As Frank Condon wrote in 1937, "They can all three sing, dance, cavort, gambol and submit to painful physical indignities with never a grimace." Similar acts to the Ritz Brothers included The Three Jolly Tars (Eddie Mills, Joe Kirk, and Harry Martin), the Slate Brothers, and the Runaway Four. The Slate Brothers (Jack, Henry, and Syd) began as Charleston dancers in the 1920s, worked in vaudeville and films, and continued as a duo when Henry left the act in 1956; Jack was coowner of the Slate Bros. Club, a well-known comedy establishment in Los Angeles. The Runaway Four would combine their bodies to form a camel, with the lead performer spouting water from his mouth. It was all very vulgar, and very funny—and so similar in popularity that these groups could never play the same bill together.

The sons of a haberdasher named Max J. Joachim, Al was the first to enter vaudeville as a song-and-dance man. They first appeared together as a trio at a Coney Island night spot called the College Inn, billed as The Collegians. Their first vaudeville appearance together was probably at the Albee Theatre, Brooklyn, in September 1925, dressed in oversized baggy pants, red ties, and flamboyant socks, in a parody of the fashions favored by college youths. The following year, the brothers appeared in the 1926 edition of George White's *Scandals* and introduced the song "Collegiate." The act in the mid through late 1920s consisted of a little clowning, a little dancing, and the playing of the ukelele.

The Ritz Brothers headlined at the Palace in March 1929 and March 1932. They also toured in a musical called *The Florida Girl*, playing Al Socrates, Jimmy Plato, and Harry Aristotle.

Their broad humor and clowning made the Ritz Brothers at home in both vaudeville and burlesque. One might compare them to the Marx Brothers, but they lacked the subtlety of the latter's humor, for everything that the Ritz Brothers did was loud. One favorite antic of theirs was to dress in grotesque female clothing, with rolled-up trousers peeping out from under the dresses. The Marx Brothers would never have stooped that low, nor, would Ritz Brothers aficionados cry, could they have gotten away with it. In a 1937 interview, the Ritz Brothers jokingly recalled that they played the best vaudeville houses for two weeks. "Then they all closed down. We played Shubert shows, Carroll revues. Then we played for two years in revolving doors. That's where we got dizzy."

In 1934, the Ritz Brothers made their screen debut in a 1934 educational short subject titled *Hotel Anchovy*. It was the first of sixteen films in which they were featured, including *On the Avenue* (1937), *The Three Musketeers* (1939), *Argentine Nights* (1940), and *Never a Dull Moment* (1943). Those films guaranteed the Ritz Brothers an immortality denied the Slate Brothers or the Runaway Four. But a career in motion pictures did not keep the Ritz Brothers away from vaudeville. In 1939, they embarked on a well-received tour with an act that *The Billboard* (June 3, 1939) described as "zany heckling that defied classification," but included a parody of the Walt Disney film *Snow White and the Seven Dwarfs* with the brothers as the wicked witch and two of the little fellows, a hybrid Spanish song, a fair amount of climbing into the orchestra pit, confrontations with those members of the audience seated in the front of the theatre, and a general assassination of the king's English.

BIBLIOGRAPHY

Condon, Frank. "Triple Hysterics." *Collier's* 99, no. 9 (February 27, 1937), pp. 13, 46.

Maltin, Leonard. "The Ritz Brothers." In *Movie Comedy Teams*. New York: New American Library, 1970, pp. 221–37.

Robinson, Jeffrey. "Ritz Brothers." In *Teamwork*. New York: Proteus, 1982, pp. 59–69.

Smith, Bill. "Harry Ritz." In *The Vaudevillians*. New York: Macmillan, 1976, pp. 179–81.

A. ROBINS

A. Robins was a clown with a novelty act that involved his pulling every known musical instrument from out his clothing. "He was so great he could pull out a grand piano," recalled Ted Waldman, while Ken Murray remembered that Robins would also change outfits and began taking a seemingly endless number of bananas from his pockets. In the words of *The Billboard* (April 19, 1930), it was "a sure-fire act."

Variety (September 3, 1920) provides a fairly detailed account of the act A. Robins was presenting at that time at New York's Fifth Avenue Theatre. For his backdrop, Robins had cardboard representations of musicians which he worked mechanically to give the impression that they were performing. From his clothing, he took cups and saucers, and ended by pouring milk from his sleeves. "It's ready for the big-time bills as it stands," was *Variety*'s estimation.

Robins played the Palace as early as 1918; he was back there in November 1926 and May and November 1930. He was featured in *Billy Rose's Jumbo*, and made his last Broadway appearance in *Top-Notchers* in 1942. He also appeared on television in the 1950s. Little is known of the comedian's background; according to a biography in the Palace Theatre program, A. Robins was born in Vienna and had been imperial jester at the court of the czar of Russia, but that sounds suspiciously like an appointment created by an overly enthusiastic publicist.

BILL ROBINSON (Richmond, Va., May 25, 1878—New York, November 25, 1949)

The greatest tap dancer in vaudeville, Bill Robinson stepped with a relaxed assurance that film audiences were later to appreciate and admire. When he appeared in his most famous film, the 1935 20th Century—Fox production of *The Little Colonel*, he explained to star Shirley Temple, "All you gotta do is listen with your feet." There was a joyousness to Robinson's dancing style that infected not only his fellow black Americans, but white audiences as well. Even his nickname, "Bojangles"—nobody knows what it means, but it has a happy sound—was given to him by a fellow black as an expression of delight and admiration on seeing Robinson dance. Fred Astaire paid his own tribute to Bill Robinson with the "Bojangles of Harlem" number in the 1936 film *Swing Time*. Robinson invented the word "copacetic" to express his pleasure with the world in which he danced, a world far removed from that into which he was born in Richmond, Virginia.

Both of Robinson's parents died when he was still a child, and he was brought up by his grandmother, a former slave. "I had to shell peas to make a living," he once recalled. Other odd jobs followed after he ran away from home to Washington, D.C., menial tasks such as selling newspapers and shining shoes, while dancing at night for pennies in clubs and beer halls. At the age of seventeen, he formed a partnership with an older black vaudeville dancer named George Cooper. Agent Marty Forkin (who was married to Rae Samuels) saw the two and signed them; later he persuaded Robinson to go solo and remained Robinson's agent for the rest of his life. Robinson gradually made the transition from black vaudeville to mainstream vaudeville. In July 1915, he was featured at Henderson's in Coney Island, not only dancing, but also singing and imitating various musical instruments. "Bill dances," reported *Variety* (July 2, 1915), "and it will be a hard audience that will not take kindly to his work along this line. Bill Robinson is a clever entertainer who can hold down an early spot on a big-time program."

By the 1920s, Bill Robinson had become a regular at the Palace, and had taken to billing himself as "The Dark Cloud of Joy." In 1924, he was billed as "The Chocolate Nijinsky." He would usually appear in the number two spot on the bill, a spot often occupied by a song-and-dance man, but in *American Vaudeville*, Douglas Gilbert recalls that Robinson's position on the program would often have to be changed because no one would go on after him; invariably he closed the show. Robinson was at the Palace in June 1926, April and September 1927, June 1929, February and August 1930, and January and February 1931.

Because of the color of his skin, Bill Robinson did suffer racial prejudice. While appearing at the Maryland Theatre in Baltimore on August 21, 1922—in the usual number two spot—he was hissed by a group of women, "apparently refined, and certainly well-dressed, of middle-age" (according to *Variety*). However, after the women were asked to leave, Robinson's act was enthusiastically applauded. *Variety* (August 25, 1922) reported, "He said that in thirty years in show business such a thing had never happened to him before, and that he had been taught that, should it ever happen, to ignore it. He did and won his house by the neat way he turned the tide."

Eleanor Powell recalled that, in 1928, she and Bill Robinson devised a dance routine together in which they would challenge each other, and they performed at various private parties organized by the Vanderbilts, the Rockefellers, and others. They were paid $500 a night. Powell remembered:

Although he was a big star, they would not allow him to ride up in the front elevator, so I always used to ride up in the service elevator with Bill. And we would wait in the butler's pantry to go on. After we were finished, we were perspiring and waiting to dry off, and invariably they would ask me if I would like a glass of water, and I would say yes if Mr. Robinson could have one. And they would give him one. And each time he would break the glass and pay for it—crystal glass. I said to him the first time, "What did you do that for?" He said, "Well I'm just beating them to the punch. I know no one will drink out of that glass." It was sort of a revenge kind of thing. It was very difficult, because a white person was not allowed on the stage with what we called coloreds.

In time, Bill Robinson became a spokesman for blacks, but he stayed clear of ideologies, and most black militants today would have questioned his attitude. Robinson's acceptance of himself as a black in a white world was pleasing to white audiences. It was a "white" organization, the New York League of Locality Mayors, that named him Honorary Mayor of Harlem in 1934, and it was not until 1948 that a group of blacks organized an election whereby Harlem residents could select their own mayor. Their choice was not Robinson, but the owner of a chain of barbecue restaurants. However, one should not denigrate Robinson, for he was the most generous of men when it came to his own race, giving away literally millions of dollars to worthy causes and individuals. He gave much to his hometown of Richmond, Virginia, where he is honored with a life-size statue on whose base he is described as "Dancer, Actor, Humanitarian."

During the 1920s, Robinson expanded his career. He was a big hit at London's Holborn Empire in July 1926. He starred in two revues, *Blackbirds of 1928* (in which he introduced "Doin' the New Low-Down") and the 1930 production of *Brown Buddies*. In the 1930s, Bill Robinson embarked on a new career in films, including *Dixiana* (1930, and first), *The Little Colonel*, *The Littlest Rebel* (1935), *Dimples* (1936), and *Rebecca of Sunnybrook Farm* (1938). He and Shirley

Temple made an ideal team, and in *The Little Colonel*, the two of them danced the famous stair dance, which Eleanor Powell said he taught only to her and Temple; Powell danced it in *Honolulu* (1939).

Bill Robinson deserted films briefly to star in *The Hot Mikado*, which opened at the Broadhurst Theatre on March 23, 1939. Reviewing his performance in this show, *The Billboard* (April 1, 1939) commented, "One of the world's greatest living actors, he delivers a concert in taps that stand sole and heels above anything else of its type in the known world."

Despite advancing age, Bill Robinson remained active and never lost his youthful vitality. Perhaps it was because of his dancing, or perhaps because he neither smoked nor drank alcohol. Eleanor Powell recalled that his one big vice was ice cream, but it never affected his weight. On his sixty-second birthday, Robinson danced for fifty-two blocks up Broadway. He was honored by New York City on April 29, 1946, when Mayor William O'Dwyer proclaimed Bill Robinson Day.

Following his death, forty-five thousand people stood in line, waiting to file past Robinson's casket. More than one-and-a-half million lined the funeral route from Times Square to Harlem. Over the front of the Palace Theatre was hung a banner with a legend, in black letters, "So Long, Bill Robinson. His Dancing Feet Brought Joy to the World." In Times Square, a thirty-piece band played "Give My Regards to Broadway," and in a eulogy, Mayor O'Dwyer said, "Without money, just good manners and decency, you got into places no money can buy. You got into the hearts of all America." Of the man who was the "King of the Tap Dancers," Eleanor Powell said, "Bill was the first one to do intimate tap dancing, a slow, confined type of dancing."

BIBLIOGRAPHY

Austin, Mary. "Buck and Wing and Bill Robinson." *The Nation*, April 28, 1926, p. 476.
"Bill Robinson." *Current Biography*, February 1941, pp. 719–21.
Haskins, Jim, and N. R. Mitgang. *Mr. Bojangles: The Biography of Bill Robinson*. New York: William Morrow, 1988.
Robinson, Bill "Bojangles," and Roy Barclay Hodges. "How to Keep Fit." *American Magazine*, October 1946, pp. 48–49, 154–56.
Smith, Frederick James. "Bojangles of Harlem." *Liberty* 14, no. 16 (April 17, 1937), p. 60.
Strouse, Richard. "At 70, Still Head Hoofer." *The New York Times Magazine*, May 23, 1948, pp. 17, 48–51.

WILLIAM ROCK (Bowling Green, Ky., 1875—Philadelphia, June 27, 1922) and FRANCES WHITE (1898—Los Angeles, February 24, 1969)

William Rock was dubbed a character dancer in vaudeville, in that he could appear in the guise of anything from an old man to a roué, characterizations he claimed drew the audience's attention away from his feet. As *Variety* (June 30, 1922) noted, "He was a better showman and producer than dancer." After an early career in musical comedy, Rock teamed with Maude Fulton in vaudeville. He is credited with being the first vaudevillian to have a band, which accompanied his act onstage, and also one of the first to condense a Broadway play for the vaudeville circuits.

In 1916, Maude Fulton decided to go solo again and dissolved her partnership with Rock. At that time, he was appearing on the West Coast, and in San Francisco, he spotted a chorus girl named Frances White, whom he felt had talent. (She had begun her career singing "Splash Me" at the Bristol Cafe on the Santa Monica Pier on the outskirts of Los Angeles.) The couple made their New York debut at the Palace in May 1916 in an act titled "Dansant Charac-teristique," and Sime Silverman reported in *Variety* (May 5, 1916) that Frances White was "very young, of considerable personality, a pleasant singer, an ex-cellent and graceful dancer, besides good-looking and able to deliver dialogue." In *The New York Dramatic Mirror* (May 13, 1916), Frederick James Smith wrote that "Miss White is a chubby little person of a certain brash, slangy, sure-of-herself cuteness." Soon it was Frances White who was the star attraction of the act. She closed the 1916 Ziegfeld *Follies* singing "The Midnight Frolic Rag."

In March 1917, Rock and White were forced to perform a fifty-five-minute act at the Royal Theatre in the Bronx because of the audience's overenthusiasm for White, particularly when she sang in a lisping, childlike voice, "M-i-s-s-i-s-s-i-p-p-i," spelling out each of the letters. A 1928 M-G-M short featuring Frances White preserves her performance of the song, and it is a delight. Another hit song from this period had Frances White complaining, "Six times six is thirty-six and six is forty-two, and as the rabbits multiply, why can't I?"

In December 1917, William Rock and Frances White were signed at $2,000 a week to appear in the *Ziegfeld Revue* on the New Amsterdam Theatre Roof. All went well until April 1918, when Ziegfeld brought in Ann Pennington to strengthen the bill. White walked out, disliking the attention her costar was receiving from the audience. Zeigfeld made no effort to encourage Frances White to change her mind, probably because of an incident that had occurred a few days earlier, when White appeared in court for driving the wrong way down a one-way street and for calling a police officer—in the words of *Variety*—"what the officer knew he was not."

Rock and White were not husband and wife in private life. Rock was married to Helen Eby, while White was the wife of Frank Fay. The Fays were separated in June 1917, after which, *Variety* noted, Rock and White gave a noticeably smoother performance. Frank Fay's only comment was, "It cost me $3,800 to be known as Frances White's husband." It was said that after the divorce, White would purchase front row seats at Fay's shows in order to make faces at him.

In September 1919, shortly after returning from a starring engagement in *Hullo America* at London's Palace Theatre, Rock and White announced that the act was splitting up. White went into Ziegfeld's *Midnight Frolic*, and Rock was starred in *What's the Odds*. Later, Rock played vaudeville with his wife.

Frances White continued in vaudeville as a solo performer, but as the years passed by, the engagements became fewer and fewer. She appeared in a couple of Broadway shows—*Jimmie* (1920) and *The Hotel Mouse* (1922)—and as late as April 1928 headlined at the Palace. In September 1930, Frances White was arrested in New York for failure to pay a $3.50 taxicab fare. With only thirty cents to her name, she was thrown in jail until, eventually, Frank Fay came to her aid. A couple of years later, White repaid Fay by demanding thirteen years of back alimony from him. She retired in the late 1930s.

GEORGE L. "DOC" ROCKWELL (Providence, R. I., 1890—Brunswick, Me., March 2, 1978)

With the billing "Dr. Rockwell, Quack, Quack, Quack," George L. Rockwell was one of the great "nut" acts of vaudeville. Utilizing a banana stalk to illustrate his points, Rockwell would lecture on human anatomy, and he entertained audiences for three decades from the teens through the early 1940s, when he retired. Prior to developing his standard routine, Rockwell had worked as both a theatrical booker and a magician. He appeared on Broadway in the 1920 edition of George White's *Scandals*, the *Greenwich Village Follies* (1928), *Broadway Nights* (1929), *Let's Play Fair* (1938), and *Seven Lively Arts* (1944). He headlined at the Palace in April 1925, May 1926, December 1926, January 1927, February 1931, and May 1931; he was on the opening bill at the new Orpheum Theatre, Los Angeles, on February 15, 1926, and at Radio City Music Hall on November 27, 1932. In February 1939, Rockwell began his own thirty-minute radio program, every Tuesday night on NBC, on which he presented a travesty on brain trusts.

Following his retirement, Rockwell moved to a farmhouse at Southport, Maine, which he owned for more than forty years and which he called "Slipshod Manor." His son was the slain American Nazi Party leader George Lincoln Rockwell.

WILL ROGERS (Oolagah, Ok., November 4, 1879—South Barrow, Ak., August 15, 1935)

Will Rogers wore many caps—journalist, humorist, columnist, film star, trick roper, and, of course, America's homespun philosopher-hero—but it was as a vaudevillian that he first came to fame. And it was in vaudeville that he developed his technique of simply talking casually to an audience, a technique he was to use to advantage in his later careers as a newspaper columnist and easygoing star of sound films. "Will Rogers is the only living person who can get away with timely material and he changes his every day," wrote Robert Benchley in *Life* (February 15, 1923). "Furthermore, his remarks are only frosted with timeliness, for underneath most of them lies a quality which makes them good for all time, as, for example, his warning that we mustn't get into another war now because we haven't any slogan. If any wiser, more discerning satire for the ages than that has been produced in the last ten years, we haven't heard it."

The Oklahoma cowboy entered show business in Wild West shows, and it was in Chicago—at the Cleveland Theatre—that Rogers first appeared before a vaudeville audience, in 1904. On April 27, 1905, he made his New York debut with Colonel Mulhall's troupe of trick ropers and riders at Madison Square Garden.

From the Garden, Rogers went to Keith's Union Square Theatre, where he opened on June 12, 1905; vaudeville engagements followed elsewhere in New York and also in Boston and Philadelphia. At the time, Rogers was appearing with his pony and with a rider, Buck McKee, and performed various rope tricks, but he did not speak to the audience. Then a fellow performer told Rogers that one trick, in which he threw two ropes and caught the horse and rider separately, was so good that he should announce it. According to Rogers's autobiography, he had no idea what he was going to say to the audience; he simply stopped the orchestra and began to talk. At first, he was horrified when the audience began to laugh at him, but he soon realized his potential as a comedian with lines such as "A rope ain't bad to get tangled up in if it ain't around your neck." His understatement, his Oklahoma drawl, and his slow delivery of lines appealed to New York audiences, and in one year, 1905, his salary rose from $75 to $250 a week. (By 1921, Rogers was touring for the Shuberts at $3,000 a week.)

In 1906, Will Rogers visited Europe, playing vaudeville engagements in Paris, London, and Berlin. In the last city, his performances at the Winter Garden proved a huge success. Less triumphant was a Wild West act Rogers brought to London in 1907.

For the next few years, Will Rogers went from success to success in vaudeville, taking time out in 1912 to appear with Blanche Ring in the musical production of *The Wall Street Girl* and in 1914 to play with Nora Bayes in London in *The Merry-Go-Round*. Rogers developed and perfected his vaudeville routine, including chewing gum while he roped and talked. He was totally unpretentious in explaining changes in his act; in 1911, he told the audience, "I've been getting away with this junk for so long that I thought you would get wise to me sooner or later so I went out and dug up a little new stuff with which to bunk you for a few more years." The new stuff included imitations of Fred Stone performing his lariat dance and of George M. Cohan if he had to throw a rope while dancing. As time passed, the rope tricks became almost incidental to Rogers's commentary, for, as *Variety* (January 14, 1911) noted, "It is Rogers, though, who is liked. His personality, careless manner, and broad grin are worth more than the most intricate tricks that could be figured out."

Will Rogers's involvement with Florenz Ziegfeld began in 1915, when the showman hired him to appear in his *Midnight Frolic*, a revue-style entertainment which began at precisely the stroke of midnight on the roof of New York's New Amsterdam Theatre. Apparently, Ziegfeld was unimpressed by the cowboy star until he saw how popular he was with an audience. It was the time of Henry Ford's attempts on behalf of the pacifist movement to stop the First World War, and Rogers joked, "If Mr. Ford had taken this bunch of girls in this show, and let 'em wear the same costumes they wear here, and marched them down between the trenches, believe me, the boys would have been out before Christmas!" Rogers claimed that this was his first topical joke, and its success led him to bring more and more jokes about politics in general, and Congress in particular, into his act: "It takes nerve to be a Democrat, but it takes money to be a Republican." "That's just the kind of men we want in politics in this country—men who are not candidates." "My little jokes don't hurt nobody, but when Congress makes a joke, it's a law. When they make a law, it's a joke."

When Ziegfeld needed a headliner for his 1916 *Follies*, it was little wonder that he selected Rogers, still appearing in the *Midnight Frolic*, to join his cast, which included W. C. Fields, Fanny Brice, Bert Williams, and Ann Pennington. Rogers was subsequently to appear in the *Follies* of 1917, 1918, 1922, and 1924. He was always depicted as a man of the people. Someone with an opposing view was Kathryn Perry, a showgirl in the *Follies*, who later became a leading lady in silent films: "I didn't like Will Rogers. I was probably the only one in the world who didn't like him. While the other stars went out to lunch different places, he would mingle with the prop men and all those people, and he did it in such a way that you knew it was just on the surface. To me he was a phoney."

Between appearances in the *Follies*, Rogers was still to be seen on the vaudeville stage. *Variety* (November 4, 1921) reviewed his act at Washington's Belasco Theatre and noted, "His talk is right up to the minute as always, just full of honest-to-goodness laughs, and he is just as dexterous as ever with his ropes. He belittles the films as well as praising them, referring to himself as the homeliest man that ever appeared on the screen." Rogers also commented that after two and one-half years in pictures, he came out with the same wife. Rogers had entered films in 1918 and was to continue making them, on and off, through 1935. At the time of his death, along with Shirley Temple, he was the most popular star at the box office, earning $250,000 per feature. He was generally disparaging with regard to the medium. When told that film was an art form, he responded, "Everything that makes money and gives pleasure is not art. If it was, bootlegging would have been the highest form of artistic endeavor." At the 1934 Academy Awards banquet, he commented, "If the movies are an art, I kinda think it'll leak out somehow without bein' told; and if they're a science—then it's a miracle."

In 1922, Rogers started his legendary newspaper column. The commencement of the column coupled with his film career offered him audiences far wider than he could possibly have hoped to reach on the stage, and under such circumstances, it was natural that Rogers should retire from vaudeville.

Will Rogers obtained much personal satisfaction and pleasure from his years in vaudeville, for, as he wrote in his autobiography:

I did the old act with the horse for almost six years; then I tried the act without the horse, just doing tricks, and trying all the time to develop the comedy end of the act. I wasn't any headliner, but they played me steady all the time, and I kept practicing new tricks, as I loved roping better than anything else in the world. I work out lots of tricks that I never do on the stage, but I have them for my personal satisfaction. And lots of days yet I go to the theatre and rope for six or eight hours just because I like to.

Will Rogers died at the height of his popularity while flying over Alaska with Wiley Post. In his honor, a two-minute silence was observed by audiences in twelve thousand movie theatres across America, and President Roosevelt issued a simple yet direct statement: "He loved and was loved by the American people." On the centenary of his birth in 1979, the U.S. Postal Service issued a commemorative stamp; along with W. C. Fields, Will Rogers is the only vaudevillian to be so honored.

BIBLIOGRAPHY

Axtell, Margaret Shellabarger. *Will Rogers Rode the Range.* Phoenix: The Beatitudes, 1972.

Beatty, Jerome. *The Story of Will Rogers.* Akron, Oh.: Saalfield Publishing Co., 1935.

Brown, William R. *Imagemaker: Will Rogers and the American Dream.* Columbia: University of Missouri Press, 1970.

Collings, Ellsworth. *The Old Home Ranch: The Will Rogers Range in the Indian Territory.* Stillwater, Ok.: Redlands Press, 1964.

Collins, Reba Neighbours. "Will Rogers: The Story behind His First Talking Picture." *American Classic Screen* 6, no. 2 (March/April 1982), pp. 31–34.

Day, Donald. *Will Rogers: A Biography.* New York: David McKay, 1962.

De Young, Joe. *Friend Will.* Santa Barbara, Ca.: The Schauer Printing Studio, 1936.

Janis, Elsie. "What I Know about Will Rogers." *Liberty* 10, no. 10 (March 11, 1933), pp. 32–34.

Ketchum, Richard M. *Will Rogers: His Life and Times.* New York: American Heritage, 1973.

Love, Paula McSpadden, ed. *The Will Rogers Book.* Indianapolis: Bobbs-Merrill, 1961.

Maltin, Leonard. "Will Rogers on Screen." *Film Fan Monthly* no. 132 (June 1972), pp. 3–8.

McNamara, Sue. "Will the Unkissed." *Pantomime* 1, no. 13 (December 24, 1921), p. 26.

O'Brien, P. J. *Will Rogers, Ambassador of Good Will, Prince of Wit and Wisdom.* Philadelphia: Winston, 1935.

Rogers, Betty. *Will Rogers: His Wife's Story.* Indianapolis: Bobbs-Merrill, 1941.

Rogers, Will. *Letters of a Self-Made Diplomat to His President.* New York: Albert & Charles Boni, 1926.

————. *Twelve Radio Talks Delivered by Will Rogers during the Spring of 1930 through the Courtesy of E. R. Squibb & Sons.* New York: E. R. Squibb & Sons, 1930.

————. *The Autobiography of Will Rogers.* Boston: Houghton Mifflin, 1949.

Rollins, Peter C. "Will Rogers: Symbolic Man and Film Image." *Journal of Popular Film* 2, no. 4 (Fall 1973), pp. 323–52.

————. "Will Rogers: Symbolic Man, Journalist, and Film Image." *Journal of Popular Culture,* Spring 1976, pp. 851–77.

————. "Innocence Protected." *American Classic Screen* 3, no. 5 (May/June 1979), pp. 8–12.

————. *Will Rogers: A Bio-Bibliography.* Westport, Ct.: Greenwood Press, 1984.

Rowland, Lloyd W. *Will Rogers.* Tulsa, Ok.: P. E. Corrubia, 1940.

Rubin, Martin. "Mr. Ford and Mr. Rogers." *Film Comment* 10, no. 1 (January-February 1974), pp. 54–57.

Slide, Anthony. *The Films of Will Rogers*. Beverly Hills, Ca.: Academy of Motion Picture
    Arts and Sciences, 1979.
Sterling, Bryan B., ed. *The Will Rogers Scrapbook*. New York: Grosset & Dunlap, 1976.
————, ed. *The Best of Will Rogers*. New York: Crown, 1979.
Sterling, Bryan B., and Frances N. Sterling. *A Will Rogers Treasury: Reflections and
    Observations by Will Rogers*. New York: Crown, 1982.
————. *Will Rogers in Hollywood*. New York: Crown, 1984.
Traveller, Gil. *When I Met Will Rogers*. Alamosa, Co.: Traveller Horse Ranch, 1939.
Trent, Spi M. *My Cousin, Will Rogers*. New York: G. P. Putnam's Sons, 1938.
Wallenstein, Marcel H. "Ropin' a Rat." *Filmplay Journal* 1, no. 8 (February 1922),
    p. 12.
Wertheim, Arthur Frank. *Will Rogers at the Ziegfeld Follies*. Norman: University of
    Oklahoma Press, 1992.
"Will Rogers as Our Aristophanes." *Literary Digest*, December 16, 1922, p. 29.
"Will Rogers, Cowboy Comedian." *Current Opinion*, January 1923, pp. 103–104.
Wilson, Leland. *The Will Rogers Touch*. Elgin, Il.: Brethren Press, 1978.
Wortman, Art, ed. *Will Rogers: Wise and Witty Sayings of a Great American Humorist*.
    Kansas City, Mo.: Hallmark Editions, 1969.
Yagoda, Ben. *Will Rogers*. New York: Alfred A. Knopf, 1993.

ROOF GARDENS

A lack of air conditioning forced the closure of New York theatres in the
summer months, and in an effort to offset the resultant loss of profits, the owners
of several New York vaudeville theatres conceived the notion of creating alfresco
entertainment areas on the roofs. These roof gardens began to appear in the
1890s and continued in popularity through the 1920s. Writing in *The Illustrated
American* in 1896, Julian Jerrold commented:

"The roof-garden is still a novelty even in New York, where the idea was
originally developed. Its popular success insures its permanency as an institution
of our stifling summer season. . . . In the cool of the evening during dog-days
the entire population seeks pantingly, in one way or another, that refreshing
upper stratum of the atmosphere, above the clutter and dust of the oven-like
streets, and where the currents of air circulate without the stimulus of electric
fans. If there is a place where the amusement-seeker or comfort-lover can have
all this, and at the same time be entertained with soothing music, graceful
dancing, and mirth not sicklied o'er with the pale cast of thought, while absorbing
his favorite refreshment and perhaps breathing his cigarette—provided such a
place as this, I say, and it is sure to be thronged, almost regardless of the
admission tariff."

The first major roof garden was located at the Olympia Theatre complex.
Covered with glass, the area was planted with flowers and shrubs with the stage
"flanked by Swiss and Italian grottoes, with rocks and rustic bridges and pools
of real water, in which live ducks and swans disport themselves." The roof
garden that Oscar Hammerstein created at the Olympia was small in comparison
to the Paradise Roof on top of his Victoria and Republic Theatres. It featured
live ducks, a goat, and a cow that was milked nightly by a costumed dairymaid.
There was also a monkey that had been taught to put its paws up the skirts of

the females in the audience. Occasionally, the Paradise Roof Garden would feature "freak acts" that might have felt more at home in the theatre below. One was a black girl named "Sober Sue," whom audiences were offered prizes to make laugh. She did not because her face muscles were paralyzed.

Other roof gardens were at the American Theatre, where Sunday night concerts were presented; the Casino Theatre, where Elsie Janis made her New York stage debut in 1900; the Century Theatre, known as the Cocoanut Grove; and at the Grand Central Palace of Industry, covering an entire city block on Lexington Avenue from 43rd to 44th Street. Although not on the roof of a theatre, the last, opened in 1896, did offer stage entertainment. The roof garden at Madison Square Garden offered vaudeville entertainment in the summer months, and it was here, on June 25, 1906, that Harry Thaw shot and killed Stanford White. The first Ziegfeld *Follies*, in 1907, was presented on the roof of the New York Theatre, known as the Jardin de Danse. Florenz Ziegfeld obviously liked roof gardens, and from 1915 to 1922, as well as presenting his *Follies*, he also produced the *Midnight Frolic* on the roof of the New Amsterdam Theatre. He used the *Midnight Frolic* to try out potential performers for the *Follies* and also encouraged his *Follies* audience to move upstairs after the show to the *Frolic*, which, as its title suggests, started exactly at midnight.

BIBLIOGRAPHY

Jerrold, Julian. "Midsummer Nights' Dreams: The Roof-Gardens." *The Illustrated American* 20, no. 337 (July 25, 1896), p. 143.

PAT ROONEY, JR. (New York, July 4, 1880—New York, September 9, 1962) and **MARION BENT** (New York, December 23, 1879—New York, July 28, 1940)

An old vaudeville joke ran, "Just because I'm a fool, don't think I'm Irish," but that was a gag that never could be applied to the Rooneys, vaudeville's great Irish family of entertainers. They took Irish performers away from the stereotype of the lowbrow comic to a new level of artistry. In the nineteenth century, Pat Rooney, Sr., was the most famous member of the family, but in the twentieth century, it was his son Pat Rooney, Jr., and Jr.'s wife, Marion Bent, who delighted audiences for more than fifty years.

Despite his Irish name, Pat Rooney, Sr., was born in Birmingham, England, in 1844. He made famous such songs as "The Old Dinner Pail," "Katy Is a Rogue," "Pretty Peggy," and "His Old High Hat." In the December 20, 1912, issue of *Variety*, Rooney, Jr., reminisced about his father: "His characterizations had that intimate touch of human reality without which no comic presentation of a type can be more than crude burlesque." In *American Vaudeville*, Douglas Gilbert recalled that sometimes Rooney, Sr., would appear onstage in knee pants, sack coat, ballet skirt, flowing tie, and a soft hat. At other times, he would appear wearing a cutaway coat with tight sleeves, a fancy waistcoat, large plaid-check pants, and a plug hat to sing "Owen Riley," "The Day I Played Baseball," "The Sound Democratic," and "Biddy the Ballet Girl." The last has some similarity to Fanny Brice's "Becky Is Back in the Ballet," and during the chorus, Rooney, Sr., would perform a clog dance in ballet style:

On the stage she is Mamselle La Shorty,
Her right name is Bridget McCarthy.
She comes at night and from matinees,
With baskets of flowers and little bouquets . . .
She's me only daughter,
And I am the man that taught her,
To wear spangled clothes
And flip 'round on her toes,
Oh, the pride of the ballet is Biddy.

Patrick James Rooney, Sr., died of pneumonia in 1892, by which time his son Pat and daughter Mattie were already appearing on the vaudeville stage in a singing and dancing act titled "Two Chips off the Old Block." In 1900, Pat and Mattie Rooney advertised themselves as "The Premier Eccentric Dancing Act of the Business—Bar None."

Pat Rooney, Jr., was born on July 4th (like George M. Cohan), and it is interesting to note that Pat Rooney, Sr.'s, song "Is That Mr. Riley?" told of the Irishman's dream of having July 4th declared St. Patrick's Day. Rooney, Jr., began dancing professionally at the age of ten with his father and mother (Josie Granger). He once recalled, "When I was a kid in Baltimore, I'd go down to the corner grocery where they had one of those wooden cellar floors. On that I would practice tap dancing. It was fun because the floor had a nice hollow sound and, besides, I could attract a lot of attention before the grocer got fed up and chased me."

With his height of five feet, three inches, and his pixieish face, it is not difficult to liken Pat Rooney, Jr., to a leprechaun. His smile was devilish and his dancing divine. W. C. Fields once remarked, "If you didn't hear the taps you would think he was floating over the stage." Taking after his father, Rooney, Jr., became a classic clog dancer whose best known routine was "The Daughter of Rosie O'Grady" (written in 1918 by Monty C. Brice and Walter Donaldson), which he performed with his hands in his pockets, hitching up his trousers with a grin on his face. Graceful as any ballet dancer, Rooney, Jr., would waltz around, leap up in the air, click his feet together, and perform steps that dazzled in a curious mix of intricacy and simplicity. "A sort of electrified hairpin" is how Frederick James Smith described Rooney, Jr., in *The New York Dramatic Mirror* (May 20, 1916).

Marion Bent was the daughter of cornet soloist Arthur Bent. She and Pat Rooney, Jr., met when they were both children; they first appeared together professionally in *Mother Goose*, "a musical extravaganza" by J. Hickory Wood and Arthur Collins, starring Joseph Cawthorn, which opened at the New Amsterdam Theatre on December 2, 1903. Rooney and Bent were married shortly thereafter, and they quickly became vaudeville's best-loved couple. There was something about Pat Rooney and Marion Bent that made one feel they were Pa and Ma to the vaudeville family. Writing of Pat Rooney in *Variety* (November 2, 1917), Sime Silverman commented, "He and his wife are among the most popular of the big time faves."

Onstage, Rooney and Bent would both dance and sing, throwing in a little comedy repartee. Sometimes, as in the thirty-three-minute revue sketch "Dances of the Hour" at the Palace Theatre in May 1925, their act would be augmented by a chorus of seven dancing girls, but it was always, as *Variety* (May 13, 1925) noted, "crammed with superlative action." The comedy cross talk would be along the lines of:

Rooney: "What's your favorite stone?"

Bent: "Turquoise."

Rooney: "Mine's a brick."

Advancing arthritis forced Bent to retire in 1932, although she did come out of retirement on her wedding anniversary, April 10, 1935, to appear with Rooney in a special program at the Capitol Theatre. In February 1941, Rooney filed a voluntary petition for bankruptcy. Rooney never really retired; in 1950, he was featured in the original production of *Guys and Dolls*, and he was also to be seen in many early television shows. Between 1915 and 1948, Rooney appeared in a dozen or so relatively unimportant films, and he was also a songwriter, responsible for "I Got a Gal for Every Day in the Week" and "You Be My Ootsie, I'll Be Your Tootsie," among others. The Rooney marriage was not a happy one toward the end, and a year before Marion Bent's death, she and her husband separated.

Carrying on in the Rooney family tradition was Pat Rooney III, who was born in 1909 and who, as a child, was often carried onstage by his parents. After his mother's retirement, Pat Rooney III would usually work in a double act with his father, performing a precision dance routine with the two men working back to back. It was quite extraordinary and has never been successfully copied. After the Second World War, Pat Rooney III worked as a single act, although he and his father were reunited for a 1956 appearance at the Palace. After retiring from show business, Pat Rooney III ran a popular hot dog stand in Lake Blaisdell, New Hampshire. He died there on November 5, 1979.

Mattie Rooney (born in Baltimore in 1878) worked with Ken Murray in later years, appearing as one of the "Elderlovelies" in his *Blackouts* shows. Two other Rooney sisters, Julia and Josie, worked in vaudeville as a double act. Prior to the First World War, they made a successful tour of Europe, but they split up in 1915, when Julia married vaudevillian Walter Clinton. Julia continued to appear on an occasional basis through the 1970s; she died in Los Angeles on October 6, 1990.

In the annals of vaudeville, the Rooneys, along with the Cohans and the Foys,

were the most talented of its family, with the undoubted "head" of the family being Pat Rooney, Jr., "a mite of a man who refused to grow old."
BIBLIOGRAPHY
Kennedy, John B. "We've Forgotten How to Fight." *Collier's*, May 11, 1929, pp. 39–40, 42.

BILLY ROSE (New York, September 6, 1899—Jamaica, British West Indies, February 10, 1966)

A flamboyant showman who carried the vaudeville tradition through into the 1930s and 1940s, Billy Rose had many careers and did not fail in any of them. A product of the New York ghetto, Rose's life was a battle for wealth and power, and along the way, he became the ultimate American success story. "Without looking upwards to a Sistine ceiling, he was a Renaissance man," wrote Robert Hector in the *Saturday Review* (March 23, 1968). "His enormous vitality and successful defiance of odds give one hope." Billy Rose was a diminutive man, nicknamed the "Basement Belasco," the "Bantam Barnum," the "Egregious Effendi," the "Mad Mahout," the "Penthouse Caligari," the "Small Svengali," and the "Bantamweight Colossus," but there was nothing small about anything he did. He was brash and he was cocky—and he had the Midas touch.

A determined child, William Samuel Rosenberg excelled at sprinting and English. He was hired by the inventor of the Gregg system of shorthand to prove the speed and efficiency of the method, which he did. During the First World War, he was stenographer to Bernard Baruch, reorganizing the stenographic corps of the War Manpower Commission. There was nothing in Rose's early years to suggest an interest in show business, but after a brief period away from New York in 1920, he returned determined to become rich. Songwriters were wealthy, and so Billy Rose decided to become a composer. He studied the popular songs of the day, and then wrote "Barney Google," which became a hit and was followed by "That Old Gang of Mine," "You've Got to See Momma Every Night," "Does the Spearmint Lose Its Flavor on the Bedpost Overnight?," "I Found a Million Dollar Baby (in a Five and Ten Cent Store)," "Me and My Shadow," "It Happened in Monterey," "There's a Rainbow 'round My Shoulder," "I've Got a Feeling I'm Falling," "It's Only a Paper Moon," and many others.

Not content with writing popular songs, Rose decided to open a New York nightclub, the Back Stage. He wrote the lyrics for a couple of Broadway revues, *Padlocks of 1927* (1927) and *Harry Delmar's Revels* (1927), and also tried, unsuccessfully, to break into the film industry. On February 8, 1930, Rose married Fanny Brice, and he starred her along with George Jessel, James Barton, and Arthur Treacher in the musical comedy *Sweet and Low*, which he produced and wrote the music for, and which opened at New York's 46th Street Theatre on November 17, 1930. It ran for 184 performances, and Rose transformed it the following year into the touring revue *Crazy Quilt*.

Billy Rose was extraordinarily busy in the 1930s. At the start of the decade, in 1930, he opened the Casino de Paree, a combination theatre and restaurant. A second theatre-restaurant, the Billy Rose Music Hall, opened in 1934 at what was formerly the Manhattan Theatre and which was renamed the Ed Sullivan Theatre in 1967, in honor of another American showman. A third theatre-restaurant, the Diamond Horseshoe, opened at the former Paramount Hotel in 1938. He presented his variety show *Casa Mañana* in 1936 and 1937 at the Fort Worth, Texas, Exposition, and brought the *Casa Mañana* to New York on May 1, 1938, when it opened with Lou Holtz as the master of ceremonies, supported by Vincent Lopez and His Orchestra, Helen Morgan, and Harriet Hoctor. In 1937, Billy Rose presented his *Aquacade* spectacle for the first time at the Great Lakes Exposition in Cleveland; it came to New York in 1939 and 1940 as one of the highlights of the New York World's Fair.

The high point of Billy Rose's career in a hectic decade came on November 16, 1935, when *Billy Rose's Jumbo* opened at the New York Hippodrome. It had been postponed four times and ultimately lost money because of its size, despite running for 233 performances. The show was presented in two full-size circus rings and featured Jimmy Durante as ringmaster, with Paul Whiteman and His Orchestra, Barbette, A. Robins, Poodles Hanneford, and others. The credits read like a roster of the finest names in New York theatre history: book by Ben Hecht and Charles MacArthur, music and lyrics by Richard Rodgers and Lorenz Hart, book directed by George Abbott, and production numbers staged by John Murray Anderson. M-G-M produced a film version, starring Durante, in 1962.

In the 1940s, Billy Rose produced *Carmen Jones* (1943), followed by *Seven Lively Arts* (1944). Never a man to concern himself with ego, Rose purchased New York's National Theatre at 208 West 41st Street in 1959 and renamed it the Billy Rose Theatre. Outside of the entertainment world, he was equally successful as an inventor, and in 1964, it was reported that Rose was the largest individual owner of AT&T shares, his holdings valued at $11 million. Only in his marriages did Billy Rose falter. In 1939, he divorced Fanny Brice and married Eleanor Holm, the leading lady with the *Aquacade*. On July 15, 1951, Milton Berle's ex-wife Joyce Matthews tried to commit suicide in Rose's apartment. Five years later, on June 2, 1956, she married him after Rose had divorced Eleanor Holm. On March 3, 1964, Rose married Doris Warner Vidor, the widow of film director Charles Vidor. Subsequently, he married and divorced Joyce Matthews again, and at the time of his death, the couple expected to remarry once more.

The scrapbooks of Billy Rose are located at the New York Public Library Theatre Collection of the Performing Arts at Lincoln Center.

BIBLIOGRAPHY

"Billy Rose." *Current Biography*, August 1940, pp. 694–97.

Conrad, Earl. *Billy Rose: Manhattan Primitive*. Cleveland: World Publishing Co., 1968.

Gottlieb, Polly Rose. *The Nine Lives of Billy Rose*. New York: Crown, 1968.

Kilgallen, Dorothy. "The Thorn between the Roses." *The American Weekly*, November 25, 1951, pp. 4–5, 16.

Rayford, Julian Lee. "Billy Rose." *Theatre Arts* 19, no. 1 (January 1945), pp. 42–50.
————. "The Million Dollar Rose." *Coronet*, June 1945, pp. 37–41.
Rose, Billy. *Wine, Women and Words*. New York: Simon & Schuster, 1948.
Zolotow, Maurice. "The Fabulous Billy Rose." *Collier's*, February 15, 1947, pp. 11–13, 81–83; March 8, 1947, pp. 44, 52–53.

HARRY ROSE (Leeds, England, December 2, 1893—Los Angeles, December 10, 1962)

Harry Rose was a comedian who worked in the same somewhat effeminate style of Jack Benny and Lou Holtz. A typical Rose routine would have an offstage voice interrupting his act with the urgent summons, "Your best friend is making love to your wife." Eventually, a thoroughly irritated Rose would go off to investigate, only to return with a grin on his face, announcing, "Silly, that's not my best friend."

The comedian came to the United States in 1905 and made his vaudeville debut in Milwaukee in 1910; he was later active in burlesque and musical comedy. Rose's New York stage appearances include the 1921 edition of George White's *Scandals, The O'Brien Girl* (1921), and *The Merry Malones* (1927). He made his screen debut in one of the 1929 *Metro Movietone Revue* shorts, but he did not concentrate on a screen career—always as a bit player—until after the Second World War. One of his earliest film credits is Republic's *An Angel Came to Brooklyn* (1945). Harry Rose was also a songwriter, with his best known numbers being "Kitty from Kansas City," "Lonesome Hours," "Anna in Indiana," and "I've Got Some News for You." His wife, Eve, was also a vaudeville performer, and Rose claimed to be a nephew of Joe Weber (of Weber and Fields). He should not be confused with a younger actor and cinematographer of the same name.

Harry Rose is the subject of a classic vaudeville story. When he worked in vaudeville as a master of ceremonies, he would always have a platform built across the orchestra, onto which he would run as he came onstage for the first time. One night at Loew's Paradise Theatre, New York, the stagehands forgot to build the platform. Rose ran out onstage and fell into the orchestra pit. After a brief pause, the orchestra leader looked down at the injured Rose and asked, "You want me to play your entrance music again?"

JULIAN ROSE (1879—London, September 13, 1935)

Julian Rose was a Philadelphia accountant who perfected a stereotypical Jewish monolog titled "Levinsky's Wedding." He would appear in exaggerated costume, including a bald-headed wig and a long beard, and begin his discourse:

Then I got my invitation. It was printed on the back of her father's business cards. Old ones. On the invitation, it says, "Your presence is requested." Right away the presents they ask for. Sure, Feinberg was there. He stood up all evening. He borrowed a pair of pants and was afraid to sit down in them. He asked me to come over and see him the next night. I told him, I can't. I was going to see *Hamlet*. He says, "Bring him along, what's the difference?'' He thinks *Hamlet* is a man! Hamlet is a theatre. . . . And the supper! Everything was stylish. They had napkins—clean—some of them . . .

Julian Rose first appeared on the British music hall stage in 1905, and as his act became old-fashioned to American audiences, he found a new following in England, where he made his home, billing himself as ''Our Hebrew Friend.'' Two years before his death, he was one of the stars of the Royal Variety Performance at the London Palladium.

BABY ROSE MARIE (New York, August 15, 1923—)

Baby Rose Marie was a new type of child star who entered vaudeville in the late 1920s. She was not one of Gus Edwards's kiddies, but she was cute and cuddly, with jet black hair, a toothy grin, and a deep, husky voice. Through the years, she has developed into a television and stage personality of considerable verve and energy, with a quick wit that she is not reluctant to use against herself.

Born Rose Marie Curley, she won a talent contest in New York at the age of three, the first prize in which was a trip to Atlantic City and a pair of brocade-and-gold shoes. In Atlantic City, she was ''discovered'' by the manager of radio station WPG, and he had her sing on the city's famous Steel Pier. As a result of that Atlantic City engagement, Baby Rose Marie was signed by WMCA for *The Ohrbach Hour*, which led to a contract with NBC and her own fifteen-minute show on the Blue network in 1932. Baby Rose Marie's only rival on radio was Mary Small, a twelve-year-old who sang a good blues number but lacked Rose Marie's punchy delivery; in 1934, Small began singing on NBC on a program sponsored by Babbo household cleaner.

From radio, Baby Rose Marie—the ''Baby'' handle was given her by Evelyn Nesbitt Thaw and was not entirely justified, for there was nothing babyish about Rose Marie except her age—went into vaudeville, not because she was a great entertainer (which she was), but because radio listeners had become suspicious. Audiences wondered how one so young could sing so old, and there were many who claimed she was a forty-five-year-old midget. Whenever the child laws permitted, Baby Rose Marie sang and danced; when they did not, she mimed to recordings she had made for the Brunswick label. This possibly makes her the first variety artist to sing to a playback, an accepted procedure in contemporary show business.

At the age of twelve, as Rose Marie jokingly recalls, ''I became fat and ugly, so I retired from the stage.'' Happily, she returned to show business in 1947, and has been busy ever since. She began on television in the early 1950s as a guest on the shows of Milton Berle and Morey Amsterdam and on *Pantomime Quiz*. She has been a regular on *My Sister Eileen* (1960–1961), *The Dick Van Dyke Show* (1961–1966), *The Doris Day Show* (1969–1971), and *The Hollywood Squares* (1968–1980). In the early 1980s, she helped to bring back the spirit of vaudeville with the variety show *4 Girls 4*, featuring herself along with Margaret Whiting, Rosemary Clooney, and Helen O'Connell. One critic of the show described Rose Marie as a female Jimmy Durante, an affectionate and perhaps perfect title for a performer who never seemed to lose the vitality and zest for living she had displayed as one of vaudeville's youngest child stars.

BIBLIOGRAPHY

Ardmore, Jane. "Memories Are One Thing, But a Woman Needs a Man." *Photoplay*, January 1970, pp. 64–65, 78.

Durslag, Melvin. "She Goes Along." *TV Guide*, April 18, 1970, pp. 22–24.

Smith, Bill. "Rose Marie." In *The Vaudevillians*. New York: Macmillan, 1976, pp. 260–66.

ROSE'S ROYAL MIDGETS

While in no way as popular or as long-lived an act as Singer's Midgets, Rose's Royal Midgets was a standard act at neighborhood vaudeville houses in the 1920s. The troupe arrived from Germany in July 1922 led by Ike Rose, who was not a midget but a rather substantial individual. His company consisted of nine female and fifteen male "little foreign folk" with "quaint Teutonic accents." On arrival in the United States, the troupe was augmented with the addition of a Negro and a Javanese woman, supposedly of royal blood. The fast-paced act included dancing, acrobatics, juggling, a violin solo, and magic tricks. *Variety*'s critics were always impressed by the group's timing and always reviewed the act favorably; on September 14, 1927, "Meakin" described the midgets as "a sure bet in vaude houses," and on November 28, 1928, "Bige" called them "a fine turn."

LILLIAN ROTH (Boston, December 13, 1910—New York, May 2, 1980)

As a nine-year-old, Lillian Roth was teamed with her sister Ann in a double act in vaudeville which relied heavily on Roth's gift for mimicry. In 1920, she was featured in her first Broadway production, *Shavings*, which led to her becoming a vaudeville headliner and appearing again on Broadway in *Padlocks of 1927* and the 1928 and 1931 editions of Earl Carroll's *Vanities*. Roth began acting in films as an extra or bit player in 1916, but her screen career as a featured player began in 1929 with the Maurice Chevalier–Jeanette MacDonald vehicle *The Love Parade*. She appeared in a number of early 1930s feature films, including *Animal Crackers* (1930), *The Vagabond King* (1930), and *Madam Satan* (1930), and she was also the star of many short subjects produced between 1929 and 1939, including *Lillian Roth and Her Piano Boys* (1929), *Meet the Boy Friend* (1930), and *Ain't She Sweet* (1933). Tragically, Lillian Roth's premature success led to an alcoholic addiction in the 1930s, documented in her autobiography, *I'll Cry Tomorrow*. The book was filmed in 1956 with Susan Hayward portraying Roth.

Born Lillian Rutstein, the stage name of Lillian Roth was chosen by her mother, who named her daughter Lillian in honor of her idol, Lillian Russell. After Lillian Roth's career fell apart in the 1930s, a group of friends headed by Milton Berle helped in her rehabilitation, and in 1947 financed a nightclub act in which the performer returned to the spotlight. In the 1950s, Roth made a comeback as a nightclub singer, appearing at the Cafe Deauville in Los Angeles in April 1952 and at New York's Plaza Hotel in February 1956. She returned to the New York stage in March 1962 in David Merrick's musical *I Can Get It for You Wholesale* at the Shubert Theatre, where forty-five years earlier she had appeared in a minor role in Abraham Schomer's play *The Inner Man*. On February 4, 1953, Lillian Roth was the celebrity guest on *This Is Your Life*, but unlike other subjects on the program, she was told of her planned appearance in advance. She died in New York following a long illness.

BIBLIOGRAPHY

Coffin, Patricia. "God Helped Me Stop Drinking." *Look*, June 10, 1947, pp. 40, 42.
Roth, Lillian, with Mike Connolly and Gerold Frank. *I'll Cry Tomorrow*. New York: Frederick Fell, 1954.
————. *Beyond My Worth*. New York: Frederick Fell, 1958.
Smith, Cecil. "She Won't Cry Tomorrow; Lillian Roth's Star Rising." *Los Angeles Times*, January 8, 1956, part IV, pp. 1, 4.
Trow, Ursula. "Comeback of Lillian Roth." *The American Weekly*, June 15, 1947, p. 9.

S. L. ROTHAFEL (Stillwater, Mn., July 9, 1882—New York, January 13, 1936)

One of the great American showmen of the twentieth century, S. L. Rothafel's contribution to the presentation of both the motion picture and vaudeville is immeasurable. Affectionately known as "Roxy," Samuel Lionel Rothafel (alternate spelling, Rothapfel) moved with his family to New York at the age of twelve. Prior to his interest in the theatre, he served in the U.S. Marine Corps and also played minor league professional baseball. On December 25, 1908, he opened his first theatre, Rothafel's Family Theatre, in Forest City, Pennsylvania. It presented films accompanied by vaudeville acts, and while it might seem away from the mainstream of the entertainment world, it came to the attention of B. F. Keith. He was impressed by Rothafel's experimentation with novel presentations, and he hired the showman to tour the Keith circuit of theatres and advise on ways to improve the presentation of its vaudeville acts.

In October 1913, Rothafel was hired by Henry N. Marvin to operate the Regent Theatre in Harlem. The following year, he took over management of the Strand Theatre at Broadway and 47th Street, and in 1917 added the Rivoli Theatre at Broadway and 49th Street and the Rialto Theatre at Broadway and 42nd Street to his operation. The latter was advertised as the "Temple of the Motion Picture" and the Rivoli as the "Triumph of the Motion Picture." When the fifty-three-hundred-seat Capitol Theatre opened in 1919, it was not a success; it was reopened by Rothafel on June 4, 1920, promising the "Newest, Latest Rothafel Motion Picture and Music Entertainment, under the Personal Supervision of S. L. Rothafel."

Radio station WEAF began broadcasting *The Capitol Family Hour* from the stage of the Capitol Theatre in 1922. The show was hosted by Rothafel, who began each broadcast with "Hello, Folks. Well, here we are again," and concluded with "Goodnight! God bless you!," and featured the theatre's stage show. From 1927 to 1931, Rothafel presented *Roxy and His Gang* on the NBC-Blue network.

In 1925, Rothafel left the Capitol, and on March 11, 1927, he opened the Roxy Theatre. According to critic Robert E. Sherwood, writing in *The Film Daily*, "It means that Roxy is to have his own temple, in which he himself is the supreme high priest, at liberty to conduct services in his own way." Rothafel's philosophy at the Roxy was simply "Don't give the people what they want— give them something better than they expect." It had been his rallying cry for more than a dozen years.

S. L. Rothafel was the natural choice to head Radio City Music Hall, which opened on December 27, 1932. Unfortunately, he was taken seriously ill the day after the theatre opened. He returned as director general, but owing to major conflicts with the management, he quit in 1934. A few days after Radio City Music Hall opened, the RKO Roxy Theatre opened as part of the complex at 49th Street and Avenue of the Americas. Because of confusion with the extant Roxy Theatre, its name was changed to the Center Theatre. Used as a live theatre, the Center was demolished in 1954.

At the time of his death, Rothafel was paid tribute by Terry Ramsaye in *Motion Picture Herald*, who noted what happened to the showman after he left Radio City Music Hall:

Roxy went elsewhere, on the air, to Philadelphia to do things with a downtown house. Nothing seemed to come off. He went on the air for Castoria. Recently he had been building hopes on a big comeback. He was close, it is said, to a quarter of a million dollar settlement with RKO, close to a new contract on the air. And he left, so they say, insurance, worth about $286,000.

BIBLIOGRAPHY

Alicoate, Jack, ed. *Roxy: A History*. New York: The Film Daily, 1927.
Bush, W. Stephen. "The Theatre of Realization." *The Moving Picture World* 18, no. 7 (November 15, 1913) pp. 714–715.
Ramsaye, Terry. " 'Roxy': An Appreciative Account of His Life and Works." *Motion Picture Herald* 122, no. 3 (January 18, 1936), pp. 13–16.
Reynolds, Walter. "Don't Give the People What They Want." *The Green Book Magazine*, August 1914, pp. 225–30.
Wilchinski, Martha L. "Here's Roxey [sic]." *Photoplay* 25, no. 2 (January 1924), p. 80.

ADELE ROWLAND (Washington, D.C., July 10, 1883—August 8, 1971)

Adele Rowland was a solo performer specializing in "story songs," often with a Pollyana-type theme. "Sheer personality dominates her specialty," commented Wynn in *Variety* (July 13, 1917). She was at the Palace the week of May 16, 1921, and her act consisted of an "operatic travesty," a balled titled "My Madonna," and an optimistic number, "Keep on Henry." "Con" in *Variety* (May 20, 1921) reported, "Miss Rowland has a fine knowledge of values for vaudeville." The trade paper was less enthusiastic when Rowland returned to the Palace after semiretirement for the week of July 9, 1928. Abel Green in the July 11, 1928, issue described the singer as "a well-preserved woman" who "needs an act." As in earlier years, Rowland was accompanied by a female pianist, for the first time identified as Rose Vanderbosh. The high spot of her performance was the singing of "Among My Souvenirs," which Green described as "once the disease of the music business and now a scourge." Adele Rowland also appeared in the 1922 revue *Spice of 1922*, and made occasional film appearances, including *Short Stories in Song* (a 1928 short), *The Blonde from Singapore* (1941), and *For the Love of Mary* (1948). She was first married to actor Charlie Ruggles and later to silent screen star Conway Tearle.

BIBLIOGRAPHY

Tinee, Mae. "Headaches and Smiles." *The Green Book Magazine*, February 1913, pp. 235–240.

RUTH ROYE

Ruth Roye was a bright star of vaudeville, a singer of ragtime songs who dominated the vaudeville scene in the mid teens, and then disappeared as quickly as she had appeared. Born in Philadelphia, Roye moved with her family to New York in 1912 and made her debut a year later, in the summer of 1913, at the Union Square Theatre. Subsequently, she toured the vaudeville circuits and quickly became known as "The Princess of Ragtime." She played the Palace the week of June 15, 1914, and was held over for a second week by popular demand. "Miss Roye is a bunch of magnetism and she has the art of getting a song over 'down pat.' . . . Miss Roye is a phenomenal acquisition to vaudeville," reported *The New York Dramatic Mirror* (June 24, 1914).

Ruth Roye was still at the Palace in July 1914, sharing top billing with Belle Baker. A friendly feud developed between the two women in that both sang ragtime, and both had songs written for them by Irving Berlin. While at the Palace, Roye introduced "Abba Dabba Honeymoon." She returned again to the Palace in March 1916, at which time Frederick James Smith in *The New York Dramatic Mirror* (March 11, 1916) reported that she was as "irrepressibly grimacing as ever."

BIBLIOGRAPHY

"How Ruth Roye's Dreams Came True." *The New York Dramatic Mirror*, July 1, 1914, p. 17.

BENNY RUBIN (Boston, February 2, 1899—Los Angeles, July 15, 1986)

Benny Rubin was a Jewish-dialect comedian of considerable talent who became a reliable character comedian on screen in the 1930s. He made his vaudeville debut at the age of fourteen, and also around the same age began to appear in tab shows in the Boston area. From Boston, he moved to New York and to burlesque, in which he worked for a couple of years before returning to vaudeville in the early 1920s in partnership with Charles Hall. Rubin made his debut as a single in the fall of 1923 (although he did have a partner in the shape of child performer Norman Gast, who exchanged some gags with the comedian and also played the violin). Seeing Rubin at the Alhambra, *Variety* (November 29, 1923) commented that he had the makings of another Fanny Brice and continued, "Rubin is set for any kind of time with his present offering."

In addition to his comic Jewish monologue, Rubin also played the trombone and was a skillful tap dancer, attributes that helped get him hired frequently as a master of ceremonies in the late 1920s and early 1930s. He was also egotistical and sometimes difficult; in 1925, Rubin was signed by Florenz Ziegfeld to appear in *No Foolin'*, but he argued with the producer about his material and was fired. Rubin appeared at the Palace as early as September 1927, but in July 1930, he returned not only presenting his own act but also acting as master of ceremonies. *Variety* (July 30, 1930) reported, "Rubin has jumped to the top flight of stage comics, with dancing and gag-writing abilities added to his comic delivery. He's welcome anywhere vaude can play him." He was back at the Palace in December 1930, and in April 1932, he appeared there teamed with Jack Haley. The two comics parodied the song "Pals," as performed by Eddie Cantor and George Jessel, proving their friendship by giving each other the shirts off their backs and then by exchanging trousers. Another teaming, in July 1934, was with Max Baer at the Paramount. *Variety* (July 3, 1934) commented, "Max Baer, without Benny Rubin, might have been catastrophic, but with the aid of the experienced comic he gets over. . . . Sufficiently well handled, but Rubin is earning his salary."

Between 1928 and 1969, Benny Rubin appeared in more than forty feature films and short subjects, including *Seven Minutes of Your Time* (1928), *Naughty Boy* (1929), *Marianne* (1929), *It's a Great Life* (1930), *George White's Scandals* (1935), *Sunny* (1941), *Here Comes Mr. Jordan* (1941), *Torch Song* (1953), *A Hole in the Head* (1959), *Pocketful of Miracles* (1961), *The Errand Boy* (1961), *The Patsy* (1964), *Thoroughly Modern Millie* (1967), and *Airport* (1969). One film that very clearly demonstrates Rubin's talents is a 1929 Universal short subject titled *The Delicatessen Kid*, in which the comedian gives impersonations of Pat Rooney and Bill Robinson, and proves he is as good a dancer as comedian. On radio in the 1930s and 1940s, Rubin was a regular on Jack Benny's program. He was an early performer on television, starring in *Stop Me If You've Heard This One* (NBC, 1948–1949) and *The Benny Rubin Show* (NBC, 1949). In the 1960s, he was also a semi-regular on the NBC situation comedy *I Dream of Jeannie*.

Benny Rubin was forced to retire his Jewish-dialect character in 1938, as the situation in Nazi Germany helped create an environment in which such humor was considered offensive. An added problem for Rubin was that he *looked* too much like a stereotypical Jew for an audience to feel comfortable with his put-downs of Jewish society. Rubin became considerably bitter and in a 1961 television interview commented, "It wasn't a case of my giving up the business, it was the business that gave me up. Dialect comics were considered out. This was announced at a meeting of the entertainment bigs back in 1938. Pressure within banished us, not the general public. Ethnic groups were becoming hypersensitive, and a section of the industry thought it knew what was best for the nation."

He quit show business for a spell, running a dress shop on Hollywood Boulevard and managing the Victor Hugo Restaurant in Beverly Hills. Orson Welles offered Rubin some work with his Mercury Theatre, and the comedian even became a stockbroker. Eventually, he returned to films and to television. On a February 1963 episode of *77 Sunset Strip*, Rubin revived his Jewish-dialect character. Shortly before his death, he considered the question of his obituary: "I never was a one-line comic and I don't want to be dismissed with a one-liner."

BIBLIOGRAPHY

Rubin, Benny. *Come Backstage with Me*. Bowling Green, Oh.: Bowling Green University
    Popular Press, 1972.
Smith, Bill. "Benny Rubin." In *The Vaudevillians*. New York: Macmillan, 1976,
    pp. 169–78.

RUBINOFF (Russia, 1897—Columbus, Oh., October 6, 1986)

A violinist who was somewhat arrogant in his attitude toward his audience, David Rubinoff began on the vaudeville stage in the 1920s, but he was more successful in the following decade thanks to his newfound fame on radio. He started playing at the age of five and graduated from the Royal Conservatory of Music in Warsaw at the age of fourteen. Composer Victor Herbert brought him to the United States, where Rubinoff attended Forbes School in Pittsburgh. *Variety* (February 22, 1928) heard Rubinoff play at New York's Capitol Theatre and reported, "He knows technique and everything that goes with the strings, but because he knows his public equally as well is why Rubinoff can stop any picture stage performance."

Rubinoff's career might have faltered had it not been for CBS's hiring him for *The Chase and Sanborn Hour*, which began broadcasting on September 13, 1931, with Eddie Cantor as the star. Radio brought Rubinoff to a wider audience, and as a result, he was a desirable headliner at presentation houses in the 1930s, earning a reported $6,000 a week. He made a number of cameo appearances on-screen, notably in *Thanks a Million* (1935) and *You Can't Have Everything* (1937).

YVETTE RUGEL (Philadelphia, 1899–   )

Yvette Rugel was a pretentious semi-operatic singer, popular on the vaudeville stage in the 1920s, who had a penchant for dressing up in wigs and period costumes. She appeared at the Palace in November 1922 with Leo Feiner at the piano, billed as the "Miniature Prima Donna." Returning to the Palace in November 1927, with Marie Franklin at the piano, she had changed her billing to "The Distinguished Prima Donna." Rugel was featured in the 1926 edition of Earl Carroll's *Vanities*, and also headlined at the Palace in 1928 and 1929.

LILLIAN RUSSELL (Clinton, Oh., December 4, 1861—Pittsburgh, June 6, 1922)

The phenomenon that was Lillian Russell is not easy to explain. She was described by her biographer as "the most gorgeous and desirable woman on the American stage." From all accounts, her beauty was matchless, and yet photographs of her do not show a woman of stunning beauty. Similarly, her voice was said to make grown men cry, and yet extant recordings of her most famous song, "Come Down, My Evenin' Star," which she first sang in 1899 at the Weber and Fields Music Hall, are far from impressive. They give the impression of a somewhat cracked, semi-operatic voice, far from lilting and far from emotionally enthralling. Perhaps it is that, as a 1915 magazine writer commented, "Lillian Russell's beauty is of our mother's generation and not ours." It was Mark Twain who wrote, "God has gifted only a choice few with literary talent to withstand the ravages of time," and perhaps the same applies to those whose voices are preserved on phonograph recordings. If it does, Lillian Russell is not among the choice few.

Born Helen Louise Leonard, Lillian Russell came to New York with her mother and eventually obtained a position in the chorus of one of the pirated versions of Gilbert and Sullivan's *H.M.S. Pinafore*. While appearing in this operetta at the Brooklyn Academy of Music, she met and married her first husband, Harry Braham, the company's conductor; there were two later marriages, to Don Giovanni Perigini in 1894 and to Alexander P. Moore in 1912. Tony Pastor heard her sing in 1879, and he renamed her Lillian Russell, at the same time paying her $50 a week to sing in his theatre. In 1881, Lillian Russell played the role of Mabel in Pastor's travesty on *The Pirates of Penzance*, titled *The Pie Rats of Penn Yann*; she was later to star in straight versions of Gilbert and Sullivan's *Patience* and *The Sorcerer*. Russell remained with Tony Pastor through 1893, becoming, as *The Spirit of the Times* (October 29, 1881) called her, "a bright particular star of opera bouffe."

From 1883 through 1885, Lillian Russell was in England, appearing in a number of successful shows together with a few failures. In 1888, she signed a contract to appear at New York's Casino at a salary of $20,000 a year; her reputation was made, and the Casino became the site of some of her greatest successes, including *The Princess Nicotine* (1893) and *An American Beauty* (1896), a title that was soon to become her soubriquet. During the 1890s, Lillian Russell developed her famous—and apparently platonic—friendship with Diamond Jim Brady, and she also began to have weight problems that were to plague her for the remainder of her life. When Fay Templeton quit the Weber and Fields Music Hall, Lillian Russell replaced her, making a courageous step from opera to burlesque. When Weber and Fields reunited in 1912, she happily joined them in their production of *Hokey-Pokey*, along with Fay Templeton and George Beban.

Lillian Russell's vaudeville debut did not come until 1905, when she signed a contract with F. F. Proctor, calling for her to be paid $100,000 for a thirty-three-week engagement. She opened with unqualified success at Proctor's 23rd Street Theatre on October 2, 1905, and Diamond Jim Brady purchased a box for the entire run. Of Lillian Russell's first vaudeville appearance, Acton Davies wrote in the *New York Sun* (October 3, 1905), "Songs may come and songs may go, but age cannot wither not variety custom stale Miss Russell. She is the same old Lillian, and her voice is the same old voice." From this point on, Lillian Russell alternated vaudeville appearances with performances on the legitimate stage, and she could do no wrong as far as the critics were concerned. When she played the Palace in 1915, *Variety* (November 12, 1915) commented, "What matters how she sings or why she sings, she's Lillian Russell, and there's only one," a statement that seems to imply that perhaps the lady was indeed past her prime and succeeding only because of the fond memory in which she was held. When she was back at the Palace in 1918, Sime Silverman in *Variety* hailed her as "a feminine freak of loveliness," while the distinguished critic Alan Dale noted, "Lillian Russell is one of the very, very few women who never needed advertising."

The vaudeville act would, of course, include a rendition of "Come Down, My Evenin' Star," written by John Stromberg and Robert Smith, and Russell was not above reminding herself and the audience of the era from which they both came. In a 1919 Palace engagement, she told the audience that she had first introduced the song 150 years ago. It is doubtful that Lillian Russell would have continued with such frequent stage appearances had it not been for financial problems, which she blithely told *The New York Dramatic Mirror* (November 23, 1918) were caused by her buying too many Liberty Bonds. However, she was still able to draw a four-figure salary in vaudeville, and that was all that mattered.

Lillian Russell made one feature film appearance, in a 1915 World Film production of *Wildfire* (in which she had first played on the stage in 1907), partnered by Lionel Barrymore. When the film was released on January 25, 1915, both the critics and the public were only mildly excited.

The performer's third husband, Alexander P. Moore, was an ardent Republican and presumably had something to do with his wife's becoming increasingly involved in political matters. In 1921, she was appointed by President Warren G. Harding to investigate immigrant problems, and her findings showed a markedly conservative viewpoint. Following her death, a daughter, Dorothy, had a brief fling in vaudeville.

There can be no doubt that Lillian Russell was very much loved and admired in her day, and, in fact, had become a living legend. As one obituary noted, she was "a woman who left a trail of affection wherever she passed."

BIBLIOGRAPHY

"Lillian Russell: Her Path to Fame." *Literary Digest*, June 24, 1922, pp. 40–41.

Morell, Parker. *Lillian Russell: The Age of Plush*. New York: Random House, 1940.

O'Connor, Richard. *Dust in Diamonds: The Flamboyant Saga of Lillian Russell and Diamond Jim Brady in America's Gilded Age*. New York: G. P. Putnam's Sons, 1972.

Russell, Lillian. "Lillian Russell's Reminiscences." *Cosmopolitan* 72, no. 2 (February 1922), pp. 12–18; no. 3 (March 1922), pp. 25–29; no. 4 (April 1922), pp. 23–26, 90, 92, 94; no. 5 (May 1922), pp. 69–72, 92, 94; no. 6 (June 1922), pp. 81–83, 98, 100, 102; 3, no. 1 (July 1922), pp. 93–96, 110, 112; no. 2 (August 1922), pp. 80–82; no. 3 (September 1922), pp. 72–75, 106, 108.

RUSSIAN ART CHOIR

The Russian Art Choir was organized by Alexander U. Fine from the chorus of the Otto Harbach and Oscar Hammerstein II operetta *The Song of the Flame*, which opened at New York's 44th Street Theatre on December 30, 1925. The fifteen-man ensemble made its vaudeville debut in January 1927 at the Hippodrome, closing the bill with a seventeen-minute Russian cabaret routine, described as "A Human Pyramid of Voices." "Fred" in *Variety* (January 26, 1927) was not impressed: "As it is, the act isn't there for vaudeville. As a concert attraction it would serve nicely, for the voices alone would satisfy."

In 1930, the Russian Art Choir was featured in a one-reel Vitaphone short with George Jessel. In between inane commentary by Jessel (including the immortal line, "I'll never forget how the Russians shot my Uncle Sol"), the choir sang "Nightingale," "Cossack Farewell Song," "Down by the Neva River," and "Schilnichky." The film concludes with the choir performing a Negro spiritual, which is unbelievably, and unintentionally, funny because of the men's mispronunciation of the English words and Jessel's participation in the chorus.

S _____

ST. LOUIS

In 1906, there were five vaudeville theatres in St. Louis: the Gaiety, the Columbia, the Globe, the Empire, and the Standard. By 1921, at which time the city's population was 772,897, there were four major vaudeville houses: the Columbia, the Garrick, the Grand Opera House, and the Orpheum.

CHIC SALE (Huron, S.D., August 25, 1885—Hollywood, Ca., November 7, 1936)

With his bucolic humor, Chic Sale was almost unique among vaudeville monologists. He would present as many as twenty-seven types of country characters, from the head of a cultural group trying to bring a little theatre to his town to the moronic yokel, the old maid, and the preacher. Sale's favorite character was Gran'pa Summerill, a testy old veteran of the Union Army in the Civil War, who could provide both knee-slapping humor and heartrending pathos. If his characters had anything in common, aside from their lives away from the city, it was that much of the humor was earthy, involving outside lavatories and old ladies who burned their bottoms on the church pipes bringing in that new-fangled steam heat. "I never try to be funny," said Chic Sale in 1931:

I present my types going seriously through their routines and the comedy takes care of itself. It would be fatal for me to think "Now I'm going to be funny." Golly, I just couldn't! I just act out familiar people—and there you are. Folks don't like exaggeration, and I'll tell you why. When you make fun of a person, you hurt his feelings, and you make the folks around you uncomfortable. I aim to offend nobody, at any time, in any way. As long as you're entertaining, as long as you can make people laugh without making them uncomfortable, you're sure to get ahead.

Sale's comedy was wisecracking humor, and "wisecrack" was a term he originated. It was aggressively down-to-earth, and he always claimed to abhor sophistication.

Soon after his birth, Charles "Chic" Sale and his family moved to Urbana,

Illinois, and there Sale worked up an act with his brother Dwight. It was "hometown stuff," and as part of the act, Sale would borrow a pair of false teeth from his dentist father's surgery. A flyer advertising a performance by Charles Patlow Sale, "reader and impersonator," survives from this period, and indicates that as part of his burgeoning act, Sale gave recitations on "The Village Gossip," "A District School Program," and "Saving a Seat for a Friend."

In 1907, Dwight died, and Chic, who had been working as a mechanic, decided to leave Urbana and try his luck in Minneapolis. At first, he worked as a waiter, but he was discharged after serving water in a cup. However, at the restaurant, he met a waitress with whom he created a comedy act, which the couple tried out in Lafayette, Indiana. The girl decided Sale was better than she and joined a burlesque show, whereupon Sale changed his name to Chick Earle and played the Gus Sun circuit at $25 a week.

Gradually, Chic Sale began to make a name for himself. In September 1916, he headlined at the Palace with his "Rural Sunday School Benefit" sketch, in which he appeared as a rube preacher announcing an entertainment to celebrate the installation of "the steam heat." He also played the janitor and various country entertainers in the sketch. As a character comedian in vaudeville, Sale was one of the greatest, and in *Variety* (September 15, 1916), Sime Silverman suggested that a play could be built around the performer. Sale stopped the show at the Palace, and even the orchestra was whistling its appreciation. He paid so many visits to its stage that, by January 1917, he was hailed as "almost a Palace permanency." Reviewing a 1920 appearance there, *The New York Dramatic Mirror* (August 21, 1920) wrote, "Sale is an artist to his fingertips and he strives to make natural the types he portrays. None is overdone. He characterizes types that are familiar to most Americans with telling realism and humor."

One staple Chic Sale prop was the organ, behind which he would hang the clothes for his various character changes. Sale always maintained that a performer could make all the clothing changes he wanted onstage, provided the audience could see what he was doing. His timing was always perfect, something his sister Virginia believes he learned from playing the drums.

Sale usually wrote his own material and would often improvise during a performance. One character for whom he did not provide his own script was that of Billy Brown, a friend of President Lincoln, based on the Ida M. Tarbell story "He Knew Lincoln." Sale would tell of going to Washington to meet the president and talk about the Civil War. After he returns home, he learns of the president's assassination, and says, "I want to think of him as I knew him. The front door will open and in will walk Mr. Lincoln and say, 'Heard any new stories, Billy?' " In later years, Sale played Abraham Lincoln in a vaudeville sketch and an early M-G-M talkie short.

From vaudeville, Sale went into revues and then moved on to films. He worked continually in that medium from 1929, although he had made at least two earlier films in 1922 and 1924. Among his features are *The Star Witness* (1931), *The Gentleman from Louisiana* (1936), and *You Only Live Once* (1937). In 1932,

Warner Bros. starred him in *The Expert*, in which he played a crotchety, sentimental old grandfather who lives with his son, realizes that youth and old age have little in common, and goes off to reside in an old men's home. It was a typical Chic Sale characterization, pure corn, and audiences loved it. In Hollywood, he was something of a curiosity, with his high-pitched, rasping voice and his use of such phrases as "my gosh" and "land sakes." Equally unusual was his penchant for keeping a goat at his Beverly Hills mansion. "I like to have a little livestock around," he explained. "We always did have, back in Urbana."

In 1929, Sale wrote and published his "masterwork," a thirty-one-page booklet titled *The Specialist*, which was the ostensible story of Lem Putt, "the champion privy builder of Sangamon County." It sold more than two million copies, and is a classic of what is commonly referred to as "outhouse humor," with such lines as "I built fer him just the average eight-family three-holer" and "It's a might sight better to have a little privy over a big hole than a big privy over a little hole." The bathroom humor of the 1980s and 1990s has its origin in *The Specialist*, and after its publication, Sale participated in a series of magazine advertisements for Ex-Lax.

Virginia Sale (1900–1992), the comedian's sister, had a lengthy career as a character actress on-screen from 1927 onward, and appeared often in Chautauqua with her collection of "Americana" character sketches. From 1938 to 1945, she was the voice of Martha, the housekeeper on the radio series *Those We Love*.

BIBLIOGRAPHY

Costello, Terrence. "Chic Sale—the Actor Who's Never Himself." *Motion Picture* 42, no. 5 (December 1931), pp. 42, 95.
"Interview with Charles (Chic) Sale." *Commentator* 1, no. 22 (October 19, 1935), p. 2.
Kennedy, John B. "We're All Hicks." *Collier's*, March 19, 1927, pp. 16+.

"SALOME" DANCE CRAZE

A craze for "Salome" dances hit vaudeville in 1908 to such an extent that the United Booking Office was unable to keep up on demands coming from theatres across the United States. The fascination with the theme is generally assumed to have originated with Maud Allan, but in the 1907 edition of the Ziegfeld *Follies*, there were two "Salomes": "the one who sings," played by Helene Gordon, and "the one who dances," played by Mlle Dazie. Wearing a see-through costume and barefooted, Maud Allan (1879–1956) first danced "The Vision of Salome" to music by Archibald Joyce at London's Palace Theatre in March 1908. Allan did not make it to the United States until 1910, and so "The Vision of Salome" was first seen by American vaudeville audiences in the summer of 1908 as performed by Gertrude Hoffmann. Willie Hammerstein presented Hoffmann at his Victoria Theatre in July 1908, and Sime Silverman in *Variety* (July 18, 1908) reported:

"The 'Salome' dance is a dignified 'cooch.' It is 'cooch' from the instant of Miss Hoffmann's descent down a flight of stairs with a most perceptible wriggle to the finish, when she creeps along the floor to take the head of St. John, the Baptist, unawares. As incidentals, there are wavy moments when the dancer does several corkscrews with her arms; other times when she is waltzing with St. John's head, and again when Miss Hoffmann, by swirling her diaphanous skirts, lets loose the fact she is undressed beneath excepting for short white pantalets. . . . It's not even naughty, and Miss Hoffmann's dressing scheme isn't as inviting to unsophisticated bachelors as many of the chorus girls' costumes nightly on view along Broadway. Miss Hoffmann's 'Salome' may be a magnet for the curiosity seekers if it is properly 'boomed,' but it's not sensational—nor is it risqué."

Sime Silverman was unimpressed, but audiences flocked to see Hoffmann, and vaudeville managers hastened to find other "Salome" interpreters. Mlle Bianca Froelich, who had performed "The Dance of the Seven Veils" at the Metropolitan Opera House, gave her version of "Salome" at the Lincoln Square Theatre in September 1908. Sime Silverman, writing in *Variety* (September 12, 1908), considered it "a very effective and well-presented number." In the same issue of *Variety*, he was less impressed with Clara Berg's version of "Salome." He was equally displeased with Lotta Faust's "Salome" in the August 8, 1908, edition of *Variety*: "Salome is resolving itself into a question of nudity. How much does this or that 'Salome' wear—and where does she wear it?"

If nothing else, the "Salome" craze was bringing employment to a number of former "cooch" dancers, including Rajah and Mlle Millias. The latter appeared at the Asbury Park Casino in August 1908, but she was asked to leave by the local authorities; according to *Variety* (August 15, 1908), "Many of the seashore's feminine population entered the Casino, placed their hands before their eyes during Millias' performance, then peeked through. Others walked out."

At least one black performer, Laura Bowman, who usually worked with her husband, Sidney Kirkpatrick, offered her version of "The Vision of Salome." In the summer of 1909, a 250-pound fortune teller named Elsie Martin played vaudeville in the guise of Countess Amelia doing a "Salome" dance. Her tour lasted for two performances, at Bloomfield, New Jersey, and Roslyn, Long Island.

"The Vision of Salome," of course, opened itself up to parody. Female impersonator Malcolm Scott appeared as "Salome" with the object of his desire being a bottle of whiskey, rather than the head of John the Baptist. In September 1908, for the first time in New York, E. Merian presented his Kennel of Canine Players in "The Elopement of Salome." On the same bill was the greatest parody artist of the "Salome" craze, Eva Tanguay.

Percy G. Williams signed Tanguay for a twelve-week vaudeville tour in July 1908, beginning at New York's Alhambra Theatre. Sime Silverman saw her there, and commented in *Variety* (August 8, 1908):

The stage looks pretty as Miss Tanguay appears at the head of a flight of stairs. She gets down to business at once. Before her appearance four minutes are "stalled" along for the entrance. A portion of this time the audience is allowed to read a synopsis of the dance, thrown upon the moving picture sheet. What it says is immaterial since, perhaps,

Miss Tanguay hasn't read it herself. She does more "dancing" than all the other "Salomes" bunched, and intermingled is some dialogue and some dramatics. Miss Tanguay's recitation or whatever it was, came as a shock almost, she being the first to acknowledge "Salome" had the power of speech. After talking, Miss Tanguay had a couple of moments of emotionalism, sobbing and wringing her hands, but Eva always has had a smiling countenance, and while as pure acting, this portion may be liked, some could not be quite sure whether Miss Tanguay was simulating crying or simply laughing. St. John, The Baptist, had his head on the stage, not like the other "heads" with a flimsy make-up, but this was the real thing, and it liked Eva's dancing, for when she uncovered it, the head turned around to look her over. This was too much for "Salome," and she dropped to the floor, but evidently misjudged the spot she should fall upon or thought herself outside the range of the "spot-light" for Eva gave a sudden twist of her body, taking a fresh hold on the flooring. The audience thought it was part of the dance. As to costuming, Miss Tanguay did not meet expectations, although there's no-one with anything on Eva in the undraped scheme. But there is one thing Miss Tanguay has on every "Salome" dancer who has so far appeared. She can go on playing her "Salome" after the others will have been forgotten, for aside from its freshness and originality, Eva Tanguay's "Salome" might become an excellent vaudeville act.

Melville Gideon provided the music for Eva Tanguay's performance, which soon became billed as "The Sensation of the Year."

Maud Allan did not make it to the United States until 1910, by which time the "Salome" craze was over, although she did appear at Carnegie Hall. In 1918, Allan appeared in a private London production of Oscar Wilde's *Salome*. She was seriously injured in an automobile accident in Pasadena, California, in 1938, ending her dancing career. During the Second World War, Allan drove an ambulance in London, and in 1941 returned to the United States, working as a draftsman at the Douglas Aircraft Company in Santa Monica, California. She continued to live in the Los Angeles area until her death.

BIBLIOGRAPHY
"All About Salome." *Variety*, August 1, 1908, p. 7.
"A Few More Salomes." *Variety*, August 15, 1908, p. 8.

RAE SAMUELS (Youngstown, Oh., 1886—New York, October 24, 1979)

Billed as "The Blue Streak of Lightning," Rae Samuels had her own curtain in vaudeville depicting a flash of silver lightning against a dark background. Dressed in elegant attire, she would perform comedy songs and "rube" numbers with great force and energy, often ending her act by punching the scenery, a gesture she claimed Milton Berle adopted after seeing her act.

Born Rachel Samuels of Welsh descent, Rae Samuels entered vaudeville as a child, performing with her sister and her sister's husband in an act titled "Musical Hearts." In 1911, she was signed to perform on the Orpheum circuit and, as a result, was approached by Florenz Ziegfeld to appear in the 1912 edition of his *Follies*. She sang "I Should Worry and Get a Wrinkle" and "Down in Dear Old New Orleans." In the summer of 1914, Samuels made her first appearance at the Palace; she was to return as a headliner in 1923, 1927, 1930, and 1931. While appearing at the Palace in 1918, she was the first performer to sing Irving Berlin's "Oh! How I Hate to Get Up in the Morning." "I learned the thing in five minutes," she recalled. "That night Berlin was in the box right off the stage and when I got to the line 'Someday I'm gonna murder the bugler,' the soldiers went crazy. Izzy Berlin came back and said, 'Rae, that was marvelous. You couldn't have done it better if you wanted to.' "

The songs that Rae Samuels performed at New York's Alhambra in November 1924 indicate her versatility: "Have a Good Time While You're Here," "See If I Care," "You Never Find Out 'til You're Married," "Love is a Wonderful Thing," "Midnight Choo Choo Honeymoon," and "Never Too Times No Time." As "Con" in *Variety* (November 17, 1924) pointed out, "This without a 'wop' or 'Hebrew' song in the singing of which she is second to none." The critic concluded that Samuels was "one of the sure-fire headliners of vaudeville and as fine an artist in her specialty as the American stage boasts of." In 1928, Rae Samuels was touring with a female pianist and working at film presentation houses. *Variety* (February 22, 1928) caught her at the Chicago Theatre and commented, "She's a class name for picture houses. . . . All numbers had a strong element of comedy and went over big with the racy Samuels delivery." Samuels made her last Broadway stage appearance in *Here Goes the Bride* (1931) and retired from vaudeville in the early 1930s. She was married to her manager, Marty Forkin.

BIBLIOGRAPHY
Smith, Bill. "Rae Samuels." In *The Vaudevillians*. New York: Macmillan, 1976, pp. 188–94.

FRED SANBORN (Massachusetts, November 23, 1899—Cupertino, Ca., March 9, 1961)

Fred Sanborn entered show business as a drummer while still a teenager; from the drums he graduated to the xylophone, utilizing it as a prop in his comedy act. For a period in the 1920s, Sanborn worked as a stooge for Ted Healy, and between 1943 and 1946, he worked with Ken Murray in the *Blackouts*. Sanborn retired in 1954.

JULIA SANDERSON. See FRANK CRUMIT AND JULIA SANDERSON

EUGENE SANDOW (Konigsberg, Germany, April 10, 1867—London, October 14, 1925)

Eugene Sandow was not the only strongman to perform on the vaudeville circuit, but he was certainly the best known, although he was—and is—far more famous in the United Kingdom than in the United States. He made his first appearance outside of his native Germany in London on October 29, 1889, challenging the greatest strongman of the day, Samson, who billed himself as "The Most Powerful Man on Earth." After besting Samson and a number of Samson's protégés, Sandow came to America, appearing at New York's Casino Theatre in 1893. There he was seen by Florenz Ziegfeld, who starred the strongman at the Chicago World's Fair in August of the same year. Sandow is said to have held a grown man in the palm of his hand, lifted a piano upon which sat several men, and finally had three horses walk across a plank over his stomach. Ziegfeld had the notion of exploiting Sandow's body by having him appear in the briefest of costumes, sometimes nothing more than a fig leaf, thus creating a sensation with the ladies, who would actually pay to feel his muscles. Sandow was also exploited on-screen, when, in 1896, the American Mutoscope and Biograph Company produced a study of him flexing his muscles.

Sandow retired in 1907, involving himself in a number of business interests, including the Sandow Corset and Sandow Health Oil. Even before his retirement, competitors in vaudeville were utilizing his name. Young Sandow and Lambert, whom *Variety* described as "the regulation physical culture act," in which the two used each other as weights, played New York's Union Square Theatre in October 1906. Sandow died as a result of a stroke suffered by his single-handedly lifting an automobile out of a ditch.

BIBLIOGRAPHY

"How the World Went Mad over Sandow's Muscles." *Literary Digest*, October 31, 1925, pp. 46–48.
"Sandow the Strong Man." *Playground*, December 1925, p. 518.

EPES WINTHROP SARGENT (Nassau, Bahamas, August 21, 1872—Brooklyn, N.Y., December 6, 1938)

One of vaudeville's most influential critics and commentators, Epes W. Sargent utilized the pen name of "Chicot." According to Joe Laurie, Jr., "He 'called 'em as he saw 'em' and played no favorites." Douglas Gilbert opined, "Chicot combined a natural skepticism with a venomous pen, a dangerous alliance that sometimes warped his judgment and carried him headlong." Sargent's parents came to the United States in 1878, and his first job in show business was as an usher at Pat Harris's Bijou Theatre in Washington, D.C. Moving to New York, Sargent worked as a writer for the *Daily Mercury* and the *Germanic News* and began the first of his vaudeville reviews. In the mid 1890s, he joined the staff of the *New York Morning Telegraph*. He first used the name "Chicot" either at the *Daily Mercury* or the *Morning Telegraph*, and for a while also published his own trade paper, *Chicot's Weekly*. When Sime Silverman founded *Variety* in 1907, Sargent became the paper's first reporter/reviewer, and his reputation helped *Variety* gain in stature. Unfortunately, Silverman and Sargent quarreled, and the latter left to work as a press agent for F. F. Proctor, William Morris, the Vitagraph Company, and others. Epes W. Sargent returned to *Variety* in 1928 and remained there until his death.

JIMMY SAVO (New York, 1895—Terni, Italy, September 6, 1960)

With his baggy pants and pixie-like grin, Jimmy Savo was a unique comedy talent, whom mere words cannot describe. He was the darling of intellectual society. Charlie Chaplin called him "the world's greatest pantomimist." In 1938, e. e. cummings wrote an incomprehensible and unreadable poem in his honor. Savo was of diminutive stature but vast talent.

Savo learned to juggle at the age of six. He won a number of amateur competitions, and by the age of twelve was appearing on the Orpheum circuit, billed as "The Child Wonder Juggler." While he continued to rely in part on pantomime in the years to come, Savo gradually added rope-walking, singing, dancing, and joke-telling to his repertoire. His early use of pantomime was due in part to his faltering ability to juggle stones and colored balls. As *Vanity Fair* commented in September 1930, "Eventually he became established in 'big-time' vaudeville where his craftsmanship so improved that he was able to discard all facial contortions—only to replace them hastily when he discovered that audiences laughed harder at him as a pantomimist than as a juggler."

Savo's humor is difficult to appreciate in hindsight:

"Lady Godiva was the world's greatest woman gambler. She put everything she had on a horse." Or, "When I asked her for something that would warm my heart and remind me of her she presented me with a hot-water bottle."

His puns, of which he was particularly fond, are equally grating. In response to the question, "How are you?," he would respond, "Like a stove—grate" or "Like a bundle of wood—all broke up."

As Matt Weld wrote in *Pageant*, "In action, Jimmy's pantomime is as wistful as that of a tot who discovers the face of a truant officer behind a Santa Claus beard. He can provoke more hilarity by rolling his eyes than other comedians do with their jokes. And he's hard to pin down on paper because his wit is not only in words but in his entire personality."

Obviously, Jimmy Savo was a vaudevillian who had to be seen to be appreciated. As Eddie Cantor once remarked, "With his pixie face he could do more than many comedians could with a thousand words." Savo made only four feature film appearances—in *Exclusive Rights* (1926), *Once in a Blue Moon* (1936), *Merry-Go-Round of 1938* (1937), and *Reckless Living* (1938)—and while *Once in a Blue Moon* is not without interest, they fail to provide the viewer with the essence of the performer's strength and character.

Savo made his first New York professional appearance at the bottom of the bill at Hammerstein's Victoria Theatre in 1912. It took six years in vaudeville and burlesque before he became a headliner. He made his Broadway debut in 1924 in *Vogues*, in which he appeared with Fred Allen in a sketch titled "In Front of the Curtains." Savo told Allen, "I would rather be Chaplin than Shakespeare." Allen asked why, and Savo replied, "Because Shakespeare's dead." In 1929, he was featured in *Murray Anderson's Almanac*, in which he sang to buxom Trixie Friganza "I May Be Wrong (But I Think You're Wonderful)," and the following year, he costarred in Earl Carroll's *Vanities of 1930*. His greatest stage success came with the Richard Rodgers–Lorenz Hart musical *The Boys from Syracuse*, which opened at the Alvin Theatre on November 23, 1938, and in which Savo appeared with Teddy Hart as the two comic Dromios. On December 5, 1940, he opened in his own one-man mime revue, *Mum's the Word*, at the Belmont Theatre, and in 1943, he appeared in the first of the Alan Jay Lerner–Frederick Loewe musicals, *What's Up?*

In 1946, his right leg was amputated, but Jimmy Savo continued to perform—this time for nightclub audiences, appearing primarily at the Persian Room of New York's Plaza Hotel. He used pantomimic gestures to heighten the comic effect of songs such as "River Stay 'way from My Door," "Black Magic," and "One Meatball." The last, written by Hy Zaret and Lou Singer, concerned a little man with just enough money for one meatball. When the man asks the waiter for bread, he replies, "You get no bread with one meatball!" The song was, as one critic noted, "one of the theme songs of the depression," and one that only an artist such as Jimmy Savo, who understood the value of pathos, could perform.

Jimmy Savo was born in the Bronx, but he died in Italy while on vacation there, checking up on one of his family's properties.

BIBLIOGRAPHY

Crichton, Kyle. "Clowning." *Collier's* 95, no. 24 (June 15, 1935), pp. 22, 48.

"Little Man, Big Heart." *Coronet*, November 1949, p. 16.

Mastin, Mildred. "All the World's His Stage." *Photoplay* 47, no. 2 (January 1935), pp. 76–77, 108.

Russell, Frederick. "It's Jimmy Savo!" *Silver Screen* 5, no. 2 (December 1934), pp. 24, 66.

Savo, Jimmy. "I Own a Castle." *Los Angeles Times: This Week Magazine*, December 20, 1943, pp. 18–19.

————. "I Love Nelly." *Los Angeles Times: This Week Magazine*, June 16, 1952, pp. 7, 20.

————. *I Bow to the Stones: Memories of a New York Childhood*. New York: Howard Frisch, 1963.

Weld, Matt. "Witticitizen: Jimmy Savo." *Pageant*, January 1945, p. 15.

(BERT) SAVOY (Boston, 1888—Long Beach, N.Y., June 26, 1923) and **(JAY) BRENNAN** (Baltimore, 1883—Brooklyn, N.Y., January 14, 1961)

Afficionados of female impersonation still remember one act from the heyday of vaudeville with relish and affection, Savoy and Brennan. Jay Brennan was the straight man—no pun intended—dressed in dapper male attire, while Bert Savoy was the "female" member of the troupe. Unlike other female impersonators of the day, Savoy was outrageously "camp" in his speech and mannerisms, both onstage and off. He would refer to all effeminate men of his acquaintance as "she," while everyone else was "dearie." His pet phrases were "You must come along," "I'm glad you asked me," "You don't know the half of it," and "You must come over." It is claimed that Mae West borrowed not only her famous walk from Bert Savoy, but also the last phrase, with all the insinuation that Savoy put into it, and, of course, it became, "Come up and see me sometime."

In the act, Savoy was forever talking about his friend Margie and her gossip. It might be the story of the girl who took a man out to dinner where the lights were dim, the music soft, and the wine well chilled. The man said, "I've never been in a place like this before," to which the girl answered, "My God! I'm out with an amateur.'' Or Bert might tell of the showgirl who, after seeing Douglas Fairbanks in *The Three Musketeers*, passed a shop with the Dumas novel in the window and commented, ''Ain't that printing press wonderful— they've got the book out already.'' Margie's dialogue, as reported by Bert Savoy, would go something like this: ''I'll never forget, dearie, the time a baroness or somethin' ast me if I knew Sir Herbert Tree, an' I answered, 'No, but I knew his younger brother, Frank Bush.' ''

Without his wig, Savoy was slightly bald and might have been mistaken, provided he kept his mouth closed, for the president of a flourishing business. Unlike other female impersonators, Savoy did not remove his wig onstage, feeling it would ruin the audience's interest in the character. Jay Brennan was tall and good-looking, with blue eyes that he fluttered at his partner. In fact, theatre critic Ashton Stevens noted that Brennan would have made a more ladylike female impersonator.

Bert Savoy was born Everett McKenzie, and he claimed his first stage appearance was in a ''freak'' museum in Boston, where he was paid $6 a week to perform twelve times a day as a ''cooch'' dancer, alternating with a deaf mute. He later teamed with the deaf mute girl, and the two worked in a carnival until the owner left town without paying them. According to Savoy, this was so great a shock to the deaf mute that it restored her voice and she cried, ''Oh, my Gawd!'' After a term as a chorus boy, he was stranded in Montana, where he began to work as a female impersonator. After entertaining in the Yukon and Alaska, he returned to the United States, and, in Chicago in 1904, he met and married a showgirl named Ann, who was later to run a boarding house on New York's West 49th Street. According to *Variety* (July 16, 1930), the marriage was purely platonic and ended in 1922 when Bert returned home to find Ann and the furniture missing. The next day, he telephoned his bank and discovered that, like the furniture, their joint account was gone. Ann Savoy was last heard of in Chicago in July 1930, when she was arrested on a robbery charge.

In 1914, when James Russell of the Russell Brothers, a popular female impersonation act in which the two men appeared as Irish servant girls, died, Savoy replaced him. The previous year, Savoy had met chorus boy Jay Brennan on a streetcar traveling down Broadway. After a short period impersonating James Russell impersonating a woman, Savoy decided to team up with Brennan.

By 1916, the two were appearing at the Palace, and their combined salary quickly rose to $1,500 a week. While Irving Berlin was preparing his First World War revue *Yip Yap Yaphank*, he invited Savoy and Brennan to coach some of the soldiers in the art of female impersonation. The pair trained a couple named Bauman and Fitzgerald to present a more than adequate impersonation of Savoy and Brennan. In 1919, Bauman changed his name to Bamm and entered vaudeville with an act called Bard and Bamm, which was such an obvious copy of the Savoy and Brennan routine that the latter were forced to take action to prevent its continuation.

In 1920, Savoy and Brennan starred in the second edition of John Murray

Anderson's *The Greenwich Village Follies*. They remained firm favorites in the revue for the next three years, performing everything from a Bohemian number, with Savoy as Lady Nicotine and Brennan as an Apache, to a "Naked Truth" routine, with Savoy as the model for Inspiration and Brennan as the sculptor. Savoy took great care with his dress and employed a wardrobe mistress named Mrs. Jones. He explained, "They tell me Mary Garden's got a valet, but as for me, I contend it takes a woman to understand a woman's clothes. Mr. Eltinge had a Jap for years, but now that he's tried a woman he wouldn't have any other sex in his dressing room. Besides, you can't depend on a man. Just when you want him to lace you up he's out in the wings with the women. And why put temptation in the poor devil's way? Anyway, I always feel safer in a woman's hands."

Bert Savoy's end was as theatrical as his camping. On the sultry afternoon of Tuesday, June 26, 1923, he and a fellow vaudevillian, Jack Vincent, were walking on Long Beach, Long Island. A thunderstorm suddenly swept across that part of New York State, and after a particularly strong clap of thunder, Savoy supposedly said, "Mercy, ain't Miss God cutting up something awful?" Immediately, there was a lightning bolt from the sky, and both Savoy and Vincent were killed instantly.

At the time of Bert Savoy's death, critic Edmund Wilson wrote, "When he used to come reeling on the stage, a gigantic red-haired harlot, swaying her enormous hat, reeking with corrosive cocktails of the West Fifties, one felt oneself in the presence of the vast vulgarity of New York incarnate and made heroic."

After Savoy's death, Jay Brennan teamed up with Stanley Rogers, and they made their New York debut at the Palace in January 1924, after six months of trying out their act on the road. Rogers adopted all of Savoy's mannerisms and catchphrases, while Brennan wrote new dialogue which, according to *Variety* (January 31, 1924), "fits Rogers just as smoothly as the new gown which drew gasps from the feminine portion of the audience." The review continued, praising "Jay Brennan as the same, suave, sleek, straight man cuing his new partner admirably, feeding him at just the proper moments and regulating the tempo of the crossfire in his usual flawless manner." The seventeen-minute act ended with a song, "You Should Have Been with Us," and was a tremendous success.

Brennan went solo in 1929, playing the role of Caponetti in the Earl Carroll musical revue *Fioreta*, which opened at the Earl Carroll Theatre on February 5 and ran for 111 performances. Also in the cast were Fanny Brice, Leon Errol, Lionel Atwill, and Louise Brooks. Brennan and Rogers were reunited at the Palace Theatre in January 1930. It is interesting to note that seven years after Savoy's death, his performance was so well remembered that another vaudeville act, Ann Butler and Hal Parker, was having a success with impersonations of Savoy and Brennan.

In the mid 1930s, Brennan entered the film industry as a scriptwriter and dialogue director, but the only film on which he appears to have received credit, as cowriter, is *Expensive Husbands*, released in 1937. He continued to perform until his retirement in 1945. He remained a bachelor his entire life.

BIBLIOGRAPHY

Savoy and Brennan. "The Mutterings of Margie." *Variety*, December 28, 1917, pp. 13, 40.

Slide, Anthony. *Great Pretenders: A History of Female and Male Impersonation in the Performing Arts*. Lombard, Il.: Wallace-Homestead, 1986.

Stevens, Ashton. "Consistently Savoy and Brennan." In *Actorviews*. Chicago: Covici-McGee, 1923, pp. 113–18.

FRITZI SCHEFF (Vienna, August 30, 1879—New York, April 8, 1954)

Opera singers were no vaudeville novelty, but they were distinctly in the minority on vaudeville bills. Rosa Ponselle was reasonably successful, as were Vinnie Daly and Alice Zeppill, whom *Variety* considered the "prettiest of all opera primas." It was *Variety* (January 11, 1922) that noted only one out of fifty opera singers made it in vaudeville, but one who did and became a major headliner was Fritzi Scheff. Paderewski called her "The Little Devil of Grand Opera," and it was a title that she wore proudly when Charles Dillingham was her manager and building her as one of the biggest names on the American operatic stage.

Fritzi Scheff was born Fredericka Scheff Yarger and was the daughter of prima donna Hortense Scheff Yarger, noted for her Wagnerian roles with Vienna's Imperial Opera. At the age of eight, Fritzi Scheff was hailed as a prodigy, and in 1897, she made her professional debut with the Frankfurt Opera, singing Juliet in Gounod's *Romeo and Juliet*. Two years later, Scheff was singing at the Royal Opera in Munich, and there she was heard by Maurice Grau, director of the Metropolitan Opera. He was impressed by Scheff's light, high soprano and invited her to sing at the Metropolitan, where she made her U.S. debut in Beethoven's *Fidelio* on December 28, 1900. According to Janet M. Green, "She was received with much warmth, not only for her pure, high soprano of bird-like brilliancy but because of her youthful vivacity and piquant beauty of face and form."

The opera singer spent three seasons at the Met and also appeared at Covent Garden and gave a command performance for Queen Victoria shortly before the latter's death. Charles B. Dillingham heard Scheff sing at Covent Garden and was quick to recognize her potential for comic opera. Dillingham starred her in the 1903 production of Victor Herbert's *Babette*, which she sang for the first time in Washington, D.C., on November 9 of that year. On October 7, 1905, Victor Herbert's *Mlle Modiste* opened in Trenton, N.J., starring Fritzi Scheff in the role of Fifi. It was to become the singer's best known part and the song "Kiss Me Again" virtually her signature tune. By 1908, critic Janet M. Green was able to comment, "There is no other singer on the American stage today who ranks with her in the field of comic opera."

Scheff was also noted for her temperament, something she was never quite able to overcome. In his 1927 book *Behind the Curtains of Broadway's Beauty Trust*, Will A. Page recalled:

Miss Scheff was charming and unaffected at first, but as her name went up in electric lights and adulation was poured upon her, she became more and more temperamental. She surrounded herself with a retinue of servants and maids. She would not let the chorus girls walk across the stage while she was rehearsing. She made excessive demands on hotels for suites where her nerves could rest in absolute quiet. She carried her own cook to prepare her meals after declaring that hotel food was impossible. She once had her maid telephone to my room at the Congress Hotel in Chicago at three o'clock in the morning in great excitement. Johanna, the maid, said Madame insisted that I must come to her apartment. I awoke from a sound slumber, dressed, and responded to the call with the alacrity of a fireman sliding down the brass pole. Johanna met me at the door. ''Madame says'' (she spoke with a German accent) ''will you be so good as to take the dog out for a walk?''

Fritzi Scheff's vaudeville debut was at the Palace in September 1913 in an act wherein she sang three numbers accompanied by Eugene Bernstein at the piano. Sime Silverman wrote in *Variety* (September 5, 1913), ''To those who want to see Fritzi Scheff and pay vaudeville price, she's probably worth the money. Otherwise her act is a classy straight singing number.''

Perhaps because of *Variety*'s no-nonsense approach to her performance, within a month, Scheff was announcing she was tired of vaudeville, but nonetheless she continued to be active on the vaudeville stage through the 1920s. She was back at the Palace in the summer of 1916, and a far more sympathetic and intellectual critic, Frederick James Smith, wrote in *The New York Dramatic Mirror* (July 15, 1916), ''Fritzi Scheff is always trim and chic. At the Palace she was in good form and wore black with black spangled somethings-or-other for trimmings. She trilled through a repertoire which includes everything from 'They Wouldn't Believe Me' and 'Hickey Hoy' to 'Mighty Lak' a Rose.' '' Two years later, Scheff was again at the Palace, billed in July 1918 as ''The Brilliant Prima Donna.''

The final Fritzi Scheff engagement at the Palace was in April 1930, with a twenty-minute, revue-style act in which she was assisted by twelve male dancers and singers. Naturally, she sang ''Kiss Me Again.'' *Variety* (April 30, 1930) reported, ''Her reception at the Palace was long and sincere, as her appearance was, in the language of the billing, 'ever glorious.' . . . Miss Scheff has a neat, pretty and diverting turn. With her own presence and reputation to top it.''

The petite singer was featured in later years in Billy Rose's *Barbary Coast Show* at the 1940 New York World's Fair, and, in 1946, she appeared at Rose's Diamond Horseshoe. She was as temperamental as ever, demanding a hotel room in which to change and dictating who was to design her costumes. She died in her New York apartment within a month of being featured on television's *This Is Your Life*.

BIBLIOGRAPHY

Green, Janet M., compiler. "Fritzi Scheff." In *Musical Biographies*. Toledo, Oh.: Irving Squire, 1908, p. 274.

Bell, Archie. "When Fritzi Scheff Stars in a 'Polite Little Comedy.' " *The Green Book Magazine*, April 1914, pp. 665–667.

JOE SCHENCK. SEE VAN AND SCHENCK

MALCOLM SCOTT (London, March 7, 1872—London, September 7, 1929)

A female impersonator who specialized in grotesque characterizations and was known as "The Woman Who Knows," Malcolm Scott was the son of Admiral Sir Percy Scott and the younger brother of Robert Scott (better known as "Scott of the Antarctic," which he was the second man to reach). He made his first stage appearance, in legitimate drama, at the Theatre Royal, Margate, in the south of England in 1886, and first appeared on the variety stage at the London Pavilion in 1903. Utilizing his rubber-faced features, Scott would appear as Catherine Parr, Boadicea, Nell Gwyne, the Gibson Girl, and Salome, and it was in the last characterization that he first appeared before American vaudeville audiences at the American Roof Garden in August 1909. The object of his adoration was not the head of John the Baptist but rather a bottle of whiskey, and *The New York Dramatic Mirror* (August 14, 1909) commented:

"Creeping upon it stealthily as the usual Salome approaches the head of John the Baptist, Scott makes sure of its identity and then breaks forth into a mad, whirling dance of joy, throwing himself upon the object of his affection and hopping ecstatically about. Nothing funnier than this moment has been seen in a New York vaudeville theatre. The burlesque is pure artistry, subtle and screamingly funny."

After successful tours of South Africa and Australia, Malcolm Scott returned to the United States, appearing at the Winter Garden Theatre in 1916. The Shuberts considered engaging him for their next production, but they considered his weekly salary of $750 to be excessive.

BLOSSOM SEELEY (San Pablo, Ca., July 16, 1891—New York, April 17, 1974) and **BENNY FIELDS** (Milwaukee, June 14, 1894—New York, August 16, 1959)

They called her the "Queen of Syncopation" and the hottest gal in town, for Blossom Seeley could belt out a song like no one else. Sophie Tucker came close, in the 1930s Mae West adopted a style on-screen that was similar, but when all was said and done, there was only one Blossom Seeley. As *Variety* commented in 1911, "When Blossom starts those hands agoing, and begins to toddle, you just have to hold tight for fear of getting up and toddling right along with her." Her style of singing was brassy, earthy, and sexy without being crude, as she delivered, with smoldering yet relaxed intensity, such numbers as

"Somebody Loves Me," "Way Down Yonder in New Orleans," and "I Cried for You." As Ruth Etting once remarked, "She had a way with a song." And from 1921 onward, Seeley was backed up by Benny Fields, generally credited with being one of America's first crooners, whose easy style of delivery perfectly complemented that of his wife.

Blossom Seeley was already a stage performer at the age of ten, billed as "The Little Blossom." She added sex appeal to song salesmanship, wrote one reviewer. *Variety* (October 1, 1910) saw her at the Washburton in Yonkers and predicted, "Miss Seeley ought to be a hit anywhere." After some success in burlesque and vaudeville, singing "Put Your Arms around Me, Honey" and "Toddlin' the Todalo," she was spotted by Lew Fields, who put her in the cast of his 1911 production *The Henpecks*. She followed this with appearances in *Whirl of Society* (1912) with Al Jolson, *The Charity Girl* (1912), *Maid in America* (1915), and *Ned Wayburn's Town Topics* (1915), among others. In 1913, Seeley made her first appearance at the Palace, supported onstage by her second husband, Rube Marquand, a baseball player. Late in 1916, she was working with Bill Bailey and Lynn Cowan, with the trio billed as Seeley's Syncopated Studio.

Benny Fields had been playing and singing with a trio in a small Chicago night spot when Blossom Seeley first saw him in 1921. She asked him to join her act, and a year later—in March 1922—the two were married. It was Seeley's third marriage. As both were quick to admit, it was a very unequal partnership, for there was no question that Seeley was the star. Later, when Benny Fields worked solo, he recalled, "When I arrived at the theatre there was the marquee. In tiny letters it said 'Benny Fields,' and below in letters a foot high, it said, 'Formerly with Blossom Seeley.' "

Blossom Seeley and Benny Fields were popular headliners in the 1920s. They headlined at the Palace in July 1921, March 1923, April 1925, May and September 1926, September and October 1927, November 1929, and April 1931. Fields would handle the comedy and assist with the vocalizing, but Seeley was the main attraction, giving new life to such ballads as "You Left Me out in the Rain" and "A New Kind of Man with a New Kind of Love for Me." Sime Silverman saw them at the Palace and reported in *Variety* (April 22, 1925), "The turn now has songs, speed, music, and comedy, well placed and well timed. A review of it in *Variety* from out of town (Kansas City) a few weeks ago said, 'It is the best act Blossom Seeley has ever had—it is all of that.' "

Seeley and Fields were in the last (1928) edition of *The Greenwich Village Follies*. A few years earlier, for the 1922 edition of George White's *Scandals*, George Gershwin had composed a twenty-five-minute jazz opera, "Blue Monday," for Seeley and Fields, but it was pulled from the show after opening night. On December 29, 1925, the opera reappeared at Carnegie Hall, under the title *135th Street*, and the leading roles were sung by Blossom Seeley and Benny Fields, accompanied by Paul Whiteman and His Orchestra.

In 1936, Blossom Seeley decided to bow out of show business. "When Benny clicked," she wrote, "I went on to being Mrs. Benny Fields, not Blossom

Seeley. Singing was his career, and *he* was *my* career. That's the way it's got to be in any successful marriage. You don't have to be in show business to know that a husband must be the headliner. Second billing is good enough for the wife. And why not—as long as the act is a smash hit?'' Fields was featured in two films, *Big Broadcast of 1937* and *Minstrel Man* (1944). Aside from a couple of short subjects, Seeley appeared in only two films, *Blood Money* and *Broadway thru a Keyhole*, both released in 1933.

Blossom Seeley came out of retirement in 1952 when Paramount filmed the couple's life story under the title *Somebody Loves Me*, with Betty Hutton as Seeley and Ralph Meeker as Fields. She recorded three long-playing discs of her most famous songs for Mercury, M-G-M, and Decca, and she and Fields embarked on a successful engagement at the Cocoanut Grove in Los Angeles in November 1952. Soon, both became regulars on *The Ed Sullivan Show*. Fields died shortly after he and his wife had completed another successful engagement, at the Sands in Las Vegas. Blossom Seeley made her last public appearance on *Ed Sullivan* in 1966.

LARRY SEMON (West Point, Ms., July 16, 1889—Victorville, Ca., October 8, 1928)

Primarily known as a silent film comedian—if Chaplin, Keaton, Lloyd, and Langdon represent the top level of pre-talkie comedians, he is at the head of the second level—Larry Semon began his career in vaudeville as a cartoonist, rather than as a comic. He was the son of a professional magician, ''Zera the Great,'' and perfected his technique as an artist working as a cartoonist for New York's *Evening Sun*. One of Semon's earliest known vaudeville appearances was at New York's Fifth Avenue Theatre in November 1913. *Variety* (November 14, 1913) was not overly enthusiastic: ''With all due respect to Lawrence Seamon's [sic] ability and cleverness to entertain with the chalk and crayon and incidentally make the gift of drawing pay, a sigh of relief will go up when all of the New York newspaper artists have made their debut on the local vaudeville stage. A likable chap, with a pleasing voice, Seamon is able to make himself heard without tripping up any of the footlights.''

In 1916, Larry Semon joined a major early film company, Vitagraph, as a comedy writer and director. He began appearing in front of the cameras in July 1917, with a one-reel comedy titled *Boasts and Boldness*. It led to a series of one-reel comedies with similar titles: *Slips and Slackers, Romans and Rascals, Hindoos and Hazards, Big Boobs and Bathing Beauties*, etc. The following year, the comedian began starring in two-reelers. The comedies were notably crude, slapstick affairs in which Semon was always center stage, wearing heavy white makeup.

As his comedies gained in popularity, Semon's ego similarly expanded. Eventually, Vitagraph let the comedian go, and his stature declined as he began appearing in minor productions, including a 1925 version of *The Wizard of Oz* (in which he was supported by his wife, Dorothy Dawn). In February 1928,

Semon appeared in debtors' court in Los Angeles, and in an effort to repay the monies he owed, he embarked on a nationwide vaudeville tour. However, in August 1928, he suffered a complete nervous and physical breakdown, and he died shortly thereafter of tuberculosis at a health ranch on the outskirts of Los Angeles.

BIBLIOGRAPHY
Slide, Anthony. *The Big V: A History of the Vitagraph Company*. Metuchen, N.J.: Scarecrow Press, 1987.

MIKE SHEA (St. Catherines, Canada, 1859—Buffalo, N.Y., May 16, 1934)

Mike Shea was a small-time, independent theatre owner who always insisted on paying vaudevillians what he thought they were worth, rather than what the agreed salaries were. He was an influential figure in Buffalo, New York, opening his first theatre there, Shea's Music Hall, in 1883. It burned down in 1895, but Shea built twelve more vaudeville houses in the city, as well as two in North Tonawanda and one in Toronto. He was raised in Buffalo and had been a sailor, a stevedore, and an employee in an iron foundry before opening the Music Hall, which he initially operated single-handedly. The theatres generally offered a mix of supporting vaudeville acts and a motion picture presentation, and Shea would insist on booking the acts himself, making an average of two trips a month to New York until his death. Unlike his colleagues, who sold their theatres to the major circuits, Mike Shea retained ownership of his Buffalo empire, although he did go into partnership with the Publix circuit in 1931.

ELLA SHIELDS (Baltimore, September 26, 1879—Lancaster, England, August 5, 1952)

Although noted as one of the most prominent British male impersonators, Ella Shields was, in fact, born in the United States. She had a brief career here as a singer of "coon" songs—making her debut in Altoona, Pennsylvania, on April 28, 1898—before making her British stage debut at London's Forester's Music Hall on October 10, 1904. Shields quickly acclimatized herself to the English music hall scene, and her soft Southern accent became indistinguishable from a British west country accent. Her male impersonation closely resembled that of Vesta Tilley, relying heavily on either evening dress or a military uniform to make, as one critic wrote with unconscious humor, "a charming and gay figure."

The one exception to elegant attire was in the singing of her most famous number, "Burlington Bertie from Bow" (written by her one-time husband William Hargreaves, and not to be confused with an earlier Vesta Tilley song, "Burlington Bertie"). Shields would appear onstage in tattered clothing, a worn top hat, and white gloves, singing of the starving, broken-down swell too proud to accept invitations to dine:

> I'm Burlington Bertie,
> I rise at ten-thirty and saunter along like a toff.
> I walk down the Strand with my gloves on my hands,
> Then I walk down again with them off.

I'm all airs and graces, correct easy paces,
Without food so long,
I've forgot where my face is.
I'm Bert, Bert, I haven't a shirt,
But my people are well off, you know!
Nearly ev'ry one knows me,
From Smith to Lord Roseb'ry.
I'm Burlington Bertie from Bow.

Ella Shield's greatest triumph was her appearance at the opening of the London Palladium on December 26, 1910. Her second was surely her first American comeback, after the years in England, in January 1920 at the Palace. *The New York Dramatic Mirror* (January 15, 1920) reported, "Miss Shields to most of that Palace crowd Monday was an unknown—a complete stranger—yet before she was half through the audience sat up and took notice of everything she did. It couldn't help it; Miss Shields was giving the folks an act worthy of their attention and appreciation. True, she reminded us of the day of Vesta Tilley when she sauntered on in male attire, but her style, voice, unaffected way of working and gracefulness when tripping a few steps à la light fantastic were such that she was accepted as an artist worth while." *Variety* (January 9, 1920) thought her "an artist through and through. . . . We haven't had anything like such a turn in America in years."

Other American engagements followed. In January 1924, she was back at the Palace, again singing "Burlington Bertie from Bow" plus "I'm a Steward on an Ocean Liner," accompanied by a hornpipe.

"Before a discriminating audience she's a cinch," reported *Variety* (January 31, 1924). In January 1928, Shields appeared with Ada Reeve and Lily Morris on an all-English bill at the Palace, although it was Lily Morris who was the hit of the program. While in the United States at this time, Shields was filmed singing "The Queen's Navy" for the film short *Metro Movietone Revue No. 4*, released in 1929.

Ella Shields officially retired in 1929, but she made endless returns to the stage. Indeed, only days before her death, she was appearing at a holiday camp in Morecambe, a seaside resort in the north of England. She should not be confused with the American male impersonator Ella Fields.

BIBLIOGRAPHY

Slide, Anthony. *Great Pretenders: A History of Female and Male Impersonation in the Performing Arts.* Lombard, Il.: Wallace-Homestead, 1986.

SHOWBOATS

No major vaudevillian ever appeared on a showboat, but these vessels generally did present vaudeville turns between acts of their staple fare of melodrama or musical comedy, and were also frequently home to obscure minstrel shows. Showboats first appeared on the Mississippi in 1817, and the first custom-built showboat, designed by William Chapman, Sr., was launched at Pittsburgh in the summer of 1831. William Chapman, his wife, and children were regarded as America's first showboat family. The Civil War halted operation of all showboats, but Dan Rice revived showboat entertainment on the steamboat *Will S. Hayes* in 1869. The major post–Civil War showman was Augustus Bryan French, who built his first showboat, *French's New Sensation*, in 1878. French specialized in magic, ventriloquism, and banjo playing, and he employed a company of seven, including his wife. As late as 1931, at least four showboats were still plying the Mississippi.

The story of life on board a showboat was told in a form as melodramatic as any offering on board a real showboat in Edna Ferber's 1926 novel, *Show Boat*. The musical version by Jerome Kern and Oscar Hammerstein II opened at the Ziegfeld Theatre, New York, on October 27, 1927. The show was filmed in 1929, 1936, and 1951.

BIBLIOGRAPHY

Graham, Philip. *Showboats: The History of an American Institution*. Austin: University of Texas Press, 1951.
Kreuger, Miles. *Show Boat: The Story of a Classic American Musical*. New York: Oxford University Press, 1977.

SHUBERT ADVANCED VAUDEVILLE

A major American theatrical institution, the Shubert Organization (previously known as the Shubert Theatre Corporation) was founded in Syracuse, New York, at the end of the nineteenth century by three brothers: Sam (1876–1905), Lee (1875–1954), and Jacob J. (1880–1963). The organization's first involvement with vaudeville was with the United States Amusement Co. (q.v.) in 1907. In 1920, the Shuberts again decided to enter vaudeville with the so-called Shubert Advanced Vaudeville, booked through the Shubert Vaudeville Exchange, created in the spring of 1920 with Lee Shubert as president, J. J. Shubert as vice president, and Arthur Klein, who had previously been with B. F. Keith, as general manager. Shubert Advanced Vaudeville opened as a two-shows-a-day, seven-days-a-week entertainment in Boston, Dayton, Detroit, Cleveland, Chicago, Philadelphia, and New York in September 1921.

The organization announced that the following of its theatres were available to present vaudeville: 44th Street, New York; Crescent, Brooklyn; Rialto, Newark; Chestnut Street Opera House, Philadelphia; Academy of Music, Baltimore; Belasco, Washington, D.C.; Shubert, Pittsburgh; Euclid Avenue Opera House, Cleveland; Liberty, Dayton, Ohio; Shubert, Cincinnati; Strand, Louisville; Detroit Opera House, Detroit; Apollo, Chicago; Majestic, Boston; and Capitol, Springfield, Massachusetts. In an obvious reference to the B. F. Keith organization, Lee Shubert commented in a 1922 press release:

Shubert vaudeville is here to stay. . . . In these two seasons of uphill work and struggle and fighting against odds, Shubert Vaudeville has done more for the variety artist than has been accomplished in the last 25 years. It has opened the door for all professionals to become independents and not be dependents. It is an oft quoted but true saying that competition is the life of trade. . . . It was not and is not now my intention to start a fight because a fight means that one or the other must be vanquished.

In competing with B. F. Keith, Shubert had the advantage not only of owning a theatre chain, but also having many stars under contract in connection with its musical comedies and revues. As part of its Advanced Vaudeville program, it could send out on tour former Broadway revues such as *Make It Snappy*, starring Eddie Cantor, in the last week of the tour of which (in Philadelphia), Cantor introduced "Yes, We Have No Bananas" (written by Frank Silver and Ernest Cohn).

In April 1922, Shubert joined forces with I. H. Herk and E. Thomas Beatty to form the Affiliated Theatres Corporation, whose purpose was to book Shubert Advanced Vaudeville. However, by February 1923, competition from B. F. Keith was so strong that the Shuberts decided to end their vaudeville activities. In October 1923, the organization did file suit against B. F. Keith, charging "unlawful combinations in restraint of trade" and asking for $10,500,000 in damages. The suit was settled out of court, and in March of the following year, Shubert Advanced Vaudeville's Arthur Klein rejoined B. F. Keith.

BIBLIOGRAPHY

Wyma, Anne B., and Barbara Parisi. "Shubert Vaudeville." *The Passing Show* 5, no. 2 (Summer 1961), pp. 3–4.

SIME SILVERMAN (Cortland, N.Y., May 19, 1873—Los Angeles, September 22, 1933)

The colorful and individualistic founder and editor of *Variety*, Sime Silverman was one of the first prominent vaudeville critics, who would often take performers aside and suggest ways in which their acts might be improved. He had worked as the vaudeville critic for the *New York Morning Telegraph*, under the title "The Man in the Third Row," and when he was fired in 1905, Silverman determined to found his own trade paper. With a loan of $1,500 from his father-in-law, George Freeman, Silverman first published *Variety* on December 16, 1905. In its early years, the paper was financially unstable, but its printer, C. J. O'Brien, covered an initial debt of $2,000 and also loaned Silverman a further $5,000.

Silverman was proud of his paper's independence, and he was often embroiled in fights with E. F. Albee and others. In 1919, an angry member of the White Rats organization tried to shoot Silverman as he sat at his rolltop desk at *Variety*'s offices at 154 West 46th Street. In July 1923, Silverman took over publication of the *New York Clipper*, which he once described as "the worst newspaper in the world." On Wednesday, September 6, 1933, he began publication of a daily version of his trade paper, *Daily Variety*, out of Hollywood.

In later years, the publisher took to spending his summers in California. He arrived in Los Angeles for the last time on September 19, 1933, and died there three days later. In February 1944, Warner Bros. announced plans to film Silverman's life story, but nothing came of the project.

BIBLIOGRAPHY
Lait, Jack. "Sime Silverman." *Variety*, September 26, 1933, p. 51.
"Sime Dies at 60 in Hollywood." *Variety*, September 26, 1933, pp. 1, 50.
Stoddard, Dayton. *Lord Broadway, Variety's "Sime": The Man Who Made the Gay White Way Gayer*. New York: Wilfred Funk, 1941.

PHIL SILVERS (Brooklyn, N.Y., May 11, 1912—Century City, Ca., November 1, 1985)

A comedian whom one critic described as "the living image of what most of his fellow Brooklyn fans think a baseball umpire looks like," Phil Silvers was more a product of burlesque than vaudeville, although he did spend a number of years in the latter medium. Born Philip Silversmith into a Russian immigrant family, Silvers began singing at a local movie theatre at the age of eleven and was discovered a year later by a representative of Gus Edwards while singing on the beach at Coney Island. He was signed to appear in Gus Edwards's *School Days Revue*, and he toured with the act for three years until his voice broke. At the age of sixteen, Silvers entered vaudeville as a fresh-faced kid comedian. He worked the Borscht Belt, and from 1934 to 1939 played burlesque for the Minsky Brothers. During the years in burlesque, he began wearing his trademark lensless, horn-rimmed glasses onstage.

In 1939, Silvers left burlesque to appear on Broadway in *Yokel Boy*. As a result of his performance in that show, he was signed to a film contract with M-G-M, but the studio let the contract expire before featuring him in a production. He made his screen debut in 1940 in *Hit Parade of 1941*; subsequently, he appeared in many films, including *Lady Be Good* (1941), *Roxie Hart* (1942), *Coney Island* (1943), *Something for the Boys* (1944), *Diamond Horseshoe* (1945), *It's a Mad, Mad, Mad, Mad World* (1963), *A Funny Thing Happened on the Way to the Forum* (1966), and *The Cheap Detective* (1978).

On October 9, 1947, Phil Silvers opened on Broadway in *High Button Shoes*, playing the role of Harrison Floy, who engineers a fraudulent real estate boom. Silvers was hailed as a new theatrical star, and Brooks Atkinson in *The New York Times* (October 10, 1947) described him as "an uproarious comic." An even greater success was *Top Banana*, which opened on Broadway on November 11, 1951, and ran for 350 performances. Silvers also toured in this tribute to burlesque and starred in the 1954 movie version. His last Broadway appearance was in *Do Re Mi* in 1960 to 1961.

Phil Silvers was first featured on television as the host of the comedy-variety series *The Arrow Show* (NBC, 1948–1949), but he is best known as Sergeant Ernie Bilko on *The Phil Silvers Show* (CBS, 1955–1959), which began airing under its original title, *You'll Never Get Rich*. The series won four top awards at the 1955 Emmy Awards presentation on March 17, 1956: best comedy series, best actor in a continuing performance, best comedian, and best director of a film series (Nat Hiken). Silvers was also seen in *The New Phil Silvers Show* (CBS, 1963–1964) and *The Beverly Hillbillies* (CBS, 1969–1971).

The comedian once pointed out that his formula for success was the same as his formula for survival in Brooklyn as a child: "I may have been funny, but who ever said I was nice?" According to Maurice Zolotow in *The Washington Post* (February 26, 1956), in real life, Phil Silvers was "a keen intelligent man who reads a great deal and can talk articulately on a variety of topics including politics, literature and the drama."

BIBLIOGRAPHY

Drury, Michael. "Backstage with Phil Silvers." *Collier's*, May 11, 1956, pp. 40–46.

Gehman, Richard B. "The Comic's Comic." *Theatre Arts* 35, no. 12 (December 1951), pp. 36–37, 90.

Goldberg, Hyman. "Top Banana to Top Kick." *Cosmopolitan*, February 1956, pp. 123–27.

Klemensrud, Judy. "A Funny Thing about Phil." *The New York Times*, April 16, 1972, pp. D1, D3.

Martin, Pete. "I Call on Phil Silvers." *Saturday Evening Post*, September 7, 1957, pp. 28–29, 56–57.

Minoff, Philip. "Top Banana to Top Kick." *Cue*, January 22, 1955, pp. 20, 46.

Paul, David. "ooh, what she said! ooh, what he answered." *Photoplay* 54, no. 1 (July 1958), pp. 52–53, 94–96.

Silvers, Phil, with Robert Saffron. *This Laugh Is on Me: The Phil Silvers Story*. Englewood Cliffs, N.J.: Prentice-Hall, 1973.

Zolotow, Maurice. "Phil Silvers: The Soft Side of Sgt. Bilko." *The American Weekly*, February 26, 1956, pp. 8–9, 11.

SINGER'S MIDGETS

The best known troupe of midgets on the American vaudeville stage, Singer's Midgets consisted of between fifteen and twenty performers, all from Austria or Hungary, under the supervision of Leo Singer (who died on March 5, 1951). Singer brought the troupe to the United States in the mid teens. Marcus Loew booked them on his vaudeville circuit, and they are often cited as being responsible for his financial success. So popular did the troupe become that, when they played the Pantages circuit in 1917, other acts cancelled rather than compete on the same bill. The act was a vaudeville show in itself, including baby elephants, ponies, and dogs, a boxing match, the legend of Lady Godiva, and a musical playlet titled "A Little Touch of Paris." In the 1920s, Singer split the troupe into two, with one group of "twelve midgets and two girls" presenting the "Toyland" revue and the other a revue titled "Models and Music" with the Imperial Russian Balalaika Orchestra.

When the troupe played the New York area, they lived as a family in a brownstone in the West 70s, building their own furniture, making their own costumes, etc. Charlie Beeker was the cook, and Emily Garanyi was the seamstress. Others in the troupe were Franz Steingruber; Christine, Lydia, and Eddie Buresh; Sandor Roka; Vincent and Fritz Tarabula; Gabor Bagi; and Hattie Angerer, who at three feet, one inch, claimed to be the smallest of Singer's Midgets.

With the demise of vaudeville in the 1930s, Singer's Midgets combined with an English troupe, Roper's Midgets, to form "the world's greatest show of little people," touring circuses and fairgrounds throughout the world until the outbreak of the Second World War.

While popular with most performers with whom they worked, Singer's Midgets gained little praise from the critics. Robert Benchley wrote in *Life* (November 20, 1924), "If the Ku Klux Klan will include thespian midgets in their list of undesirables we will promise to take out a two-weeks' guest card in the order."

BIBLIOGRAPHY

Mok, Michael. "High-and-Low Hunt on for Vanished Little People." *New York World–Telegram*, December 7, 1959, p. 21.

(NOBLE) SISSLE (Indianapolis, July 10, 1889—Tampa, Fl., December 17, 1975) and **(EUBIE) BLAKE** (Baltimore, February 7, 1883—Brooklyn, N.Y., February 12, 1983)

Noble Sissle and Eubie Blake were two black Americans whose individual careers were phenomenal, and who together were a successful vaudeville team, playing the Palace in 1919. Eubie Blake was one of America's great songwriters, responsible for "I'm Just Wild about Harry," "Love Will Find a Way," "You Were Meant for Me," "Memories of You," and "You're Lucky to Me." Noble Sissle contributed the lyrics to many songs and also founded the Negro Actors' Guild.

James Hubert Blake was the son of former slaves and a child prodigy at the organ and piano. He began playing piano professionally at the age of fifteen. In 1915, he met Noble Sissle for the first time, and the two formed a partnership. Sissle had toured for two years with the Thomas Jubilee Singers and was a protégé of Negro bandleader James Reese Europe. One of the first songs the two men wrote, "It's Your Fault," was bought and performed in vaudeville by Sophie Tucker. Blake was too old for active service in the First World War, but Sissle enlisted and helped Europe create an all-black regimental band.

After the First World War, Sissle and Blake reunited, and in June 1919, they played the Harlem Opera House. "Ibee" from *Variety* saw their act, and reported on June 27, 1919:

Sissle and Blake was colored entertainers, but wholly different in style from acts of its class. Although of straight appearance they might be expected to unload a section of jazz, but instead the men offered a routine of special songs which might be termed as being of high class order, not, however, anything of the classical. The pair have been writing songs for some time. Recently they returned from overseas and were members of the widely known Jim Europe's band. Sissle, who possesses a good voice and to whom most of the singing is allotted, held a commission as lieutenant. The turn opens with Blake at the piano, he using a lusty touch. Singing from the wings Sissle enters with "Good Bye Angeline," which drew attention. There followed the only bit of rag, it being "Doggone Baltimore Blues," with Blake duetting at times. "Affectionate Dan" by Sissle went but fairly, but his rendition of "Mammy's Little Chocolate Colored Child," a corking melody, sent the going upwards again, with nifty returns. Blake had a session with a specialty using one of the melodies with an Asiatic label. The orchestra joined for the finish, going full blast, but Blake's playing could be plainly distinguished above all. For a closer the men gave "No Gal as Sweet as Mirandy," and exited in "high yallow" fashion. But they reappeared for a demand encore. Sissle explained it was a number they wrote while in France (the only mention of overseas service) and was to their mind descriptive of action in going over the top. The number is probably called "Patrol in No Man's Land." Sissle acted the number, getting down on all fours for the most time. The house got real excited over it and the heaviest returns of the show were registered. The finale number is going to be of aid for it is well worked up. The turn should land in big time for the men are able entertainers and their work is a contrast from others.

What perhaps helped Sissle and Blake become headliners in mainstream vaudeville was their refusal to be stereotyped as Negro performers. They appeared in evening attire and never resorted to the type of humor usually associated with blackface minstrels.

In 1920, Sissle and Blake met Miller and Lyles, and the four men collaborated on the creation of *Shuffle Along*, which opened at New York's 63rd Street Theatre the following year. A second Sissle and Blake show was produced in 1924 under the initial title *In Bamville*, but opened in New York in September 1925 as *The Chocolate Dandies*. Aside from Sissle and Blake, the show also featured Josephine Baker and Elizabeth Welsh. After touring with the show, the two men brought their vaudeville act to Europe in 1926, where Sissle remained, while Blake created a road show called *Shuffle Along, Jr.* Blake followed this with *Blackbirds of 1930*, for which he wrote the music, and in 1932 reteamed with Sissle for *Shuffle Along of 1933*.

In Europe, Noble Sissle had formed his own orchestra, and in 1932, Blake also formed an orchestra. The latter retired for the first time in 1942 but returned the following year, touring with the U.S.O. He retired for a second time in 1951, but a revival of interest in his music resulted in a second return to entertaining in the 1970s. He made a number of recordings of his compositions, played jazz festivals, and in 1977 appeared in the NBC television movie *Scott Joplin: King of Ragtime*, with Billy Dee Williams in the title role. Following the death of his wife, Marion, in 1982, Blake ceased making public appearances and died the following year, a few days after celebrating his one hundredth birthday.

BIBLIOGRAPHY

Sampson, Henry T. *Blacks in Blackface: A Source Book on Early Black Musical Shows.* Metuchen, N.J.: Scarecrow Press, 1980.

SISTER ACTS. See BOSWELL SISTERS, BROX SISTERS, CHERRY SISTERS, ROSIE AND JENNY DOLLY, DUNCAN SISTERS, VIOLET AND DAISY HILTON, JANE AND KATHERINE LEE, LOCUST SISTERS, THREE X SISTERS, KITTY AND FANNY WATSON

ROY SMECK (Reading, Pa., February 6, ?—   )

A virtuoso of the guitar, banjo, ukelele, and Hawaiian guitar, Roy Smeck was active on the vaudeville stage in the 1920s, but would be unknown today were it not for his place in film history. When *Don Juan* premiered at the Warner's Theatre, New York, on August 6, 1926, it was accompanied by a selection of short subjects highlighting the Vitaphone sound-on-disc system. The program opened with an address by Will H. Hays, president of the Motion Picture Producers and Distributors of America, and all the other shorts featured classical music except for *Roy Smeck, "The Wizard of the String," in "His Pastimes," Popular Solo on Hawaiian Guitar and Ukelele.* The short was filmed on July 14, 1926.

In 1983, producer Alan Edelstein and director Peter J. Friedman made a thirty-minute, 16mm documentary on Smeck, titled *Wizard of the Strings: A Film Portrait of Roy Smeck.*

In 1930, Smeck played both the Palace in New York and the Palladium in London. He was back at the Palace in October 1933, and at that time, *Variety* (October 10, 1933) commented, "Those trip-hammers Roy Smeck has instead of the fingers of ordinary mortals rat-a-tat their rhythmic messages on banjo, guitar, and uke. A unique experience." As a composer as well as a performer, Smeck remained active through the 1980s. The titles of some of the songs he composed are indicative of his interests: "Banjo Shuffle Boogie," "Steel Guitar Hop," "Magic Ukelele," and "Rockin' the Uke."

(JOE) SMITH (New York, February 16, 1884—Englewood, N.J., February 22, 1981) and **(CHARLIE) DALE** (New York, September 6, 1881—Teaneck, N.J., November 16, 1971)

Thanks largely to Neil Simon's *The Sunshine Boys*, with its version of the classic "Dr. Kronkhite" sketch, Smith and Dale are as well known today as they were at the height of their fame. And, of course, for all those millions who saw Smith and Dale's comedy routines live or on television, the two have never been forgotten. Their timing was immaculate, and the jokes, often corny by today's standards, were always funny. Joe Smith would ask Charlie Dale, "How could a low life like you have high blood pressure?" and the joke would become as classic—and certainly funnier—than any line from Shakespeare.

Joe Sultzer (Smith) and Charles Marks (Dale) met in December 1898 while riding their bicycles on New York's East Side. They got into an argument and were told that their verbal sparring was reminiscent of Weber and Fields, and that they should get together. Sultzer and Marks began to sing and dance in the saloons of the Bowery, working in blackface, and during the day they would work as waiters at Child's Restaurant. Smith and Dale became their names when Joe's brother found a printer who had made up calling cards for a vaudeville act of that name which had subsequently decided to change its billing. In 1900, the pair joined the Imperial Vaudeville and Comedy Company, which played the Catskills area of New York State around Roundout, and in which Smith and Dale first conceived one of their best-known sketches, "The New Schoolteacher."

When the Imperial Vaudeville and Comedy Company ran out of funds, Smith and Dale returned to New York and decided to perfect the schoolteacher act with two new partners, Will Lester and Jack Coleman, who were working as singing waiters at the Avon Cafe on 116th Street. From the name of the saloon, the new partners took their new billing, the Avon Comedy Four. The group's sketch was set in a schoolroom and appears to have had various names through the years—in the early years of the century it was called "The Private Tutor"—but the characterizations always remained the same: a Hebrew type, a German, a tough guy, and a sissy. "There are not dull moments during its presentation and numerous laughs accompany it from start to finish," reported the *New York Clipper* (August 20, 1904). In addition to appearing on the vaudeville stage, the Avon Comedy Four made a number of phonograph recordings in the teens, not only of comedy sketches but also songs.

Joe Smith often recounted the story of how vaudeville performers were first allowed to work Sundays. Performers could entertain on the Sabbath, but New York's Blue Laws forbade makeup, talking, tumbling, or emoting. Despite the law, the Avon Comedy Four were told by Willie Hammerstein to go ahead with their usual act on a Sunday—and they were promptly arrested. The next day in court, the judge asked the arresting officer to describe the act. The detective explained, "The sissy comes out and says he is going to call the role—all those who are absent say 'absent.' Then he asks the Yid to use the word 'delight' in a sentence, and he hits him on the head with a stick." After listening to this account, the judge responded, "They don't have an act—case dismissed." From then on, performers were allowed to work unhindered on Sundays.

In time, the members of the comedy and singing quartet changed, with Irving Kaufman and Harry Goodwin replacing Lester and Coleman. Others who were members of the Avon Comedy Four include Charlie Adams, Eddie Rasch, Eddie Miller, Frank Corbett, Paul Maul, Lou Lawrence, Mario Palermo, Alan Chester, Al Evans, Eddie Nelson, Al Walden, Al Rauth, Al Greene, Fred A. Ahlert (the composer, for one day at the Palace), Ben Edwards, Mike Kelly, Tom Dillon, and Arthur Fields. In 1914, the Avon Comedy Four headlined at London's Finsbury Park Empire. In the spring of 1929, Joe Smith and Charlie Dale, together with Mario Palermo and Lou Lawrence, headlined at the London Palladium. In 1919, the group added a restaurant sketch, with Smith playing the chef who feigns illness when he gets too many orders. The waiter would ask, "Where's the water?," and back would come the answer, "In the milk." "It's an elastic act that might be worked up to almost any limits," reported Sime Silverman in *Variety* (October 13, 1916). "While the new turn does not yet compare with the old one as a laugh maker, it may in time, and is at least a departure from a routine the Avons made very familiar to big-time audiences."

Irving Kaufman left the Avon Comedy Four in January 1919 and was replaced by Dale's brother, Lou. The Avon Comedy Four was ending its comedy reign, to be replaced by Smith and Dale. The "Dr. Kronkhite" sketch—*kronk*, of course, is both German and Yiddish for sick—had originated while the two were still billed as the Avon Comedy Four, but it was perfected when Smith and Dale took top billing in the act now called Smith and Dale and Their Avon Comedy Four. Smith would ask, "Is this the doctor's office?" The nurse would reply, "Yes, I'm his nurse." Back would come Smith, "His nurse? Is the doctor sick too?" "No, I'm a trained nurse." "Oh, you do tricks?" And so on. Circa 1926, Smith and Dale dropped "Dr. Kronkhite" from their vaudeville routine, but they reintroduced it in 1928, and the sketch and the team remained inseparable in the years to come.

One twenty-minute sketch that Smith and Dale featured, introduced at the Palace in September 1925, was titled "Battery to the Bronx," in which they were supposedly on a subway train traveling the length of Manhattan. The sketch opened with a song, "Canal Street," and then moved to a scene in the office of lawyer U. R. Stuck (played by Dale). The next stop was Harlem, where Smith and Dale were two firemen, too busy playing pinochle to leave the station and respond to an alarm. "How big is your house?" they ask. "Three stories." "Is it brick?" "Yes." "Then you've got plenty of time. Brick takes longer to burn." (The sequence was later adapted into a full-length vaudeville sketch in its own right, and also into a 1929 Paramount film short, *The False Alarm Fire Company*.) The Bronx sequence had the husband coming home to find his wife in the arms of his partner, Wolf, leading to the line, "While I'm down struggling to keep the wolf from the door, you let him come in the house." The husband shoots both his wife and Wolf and walks off with the maid. "The turn in its present form is sure fire for anywhere," reported *Variety* (September 16, 1925).

Smith and Dale's continuing success was due in no small part to the constant changing of the dialogue and the endings of the sketches. As late as June 5, 1934, *Variety* was still reviewing them under the heading of "New Acts."

Aside from vaudeville, the pair appeared in a number of revues and in several short films and three features, *Manhattan Parade* (1931), *The Heart of New York* (1932), and *Two Tickets to Broadway* (1951). They made frequent television appearances and participated in the fabulous Judy Garland show at the Palace which opened on October 16, 1951. Smith spent his last years as a resident of the Actors Fund Home in Englewood, New Jersey, and was always quick to point out that, despite the obvious similarities between Smith and Dale and the vaudeville partners in *The Sunshine Boys*, he and Dale only argued for the betterment of the act, never on a personal level. When Smith attended a Friars Club roast of Neil Simon, he commented, "Neil Simon didn't plagiarize Smith and Dale—he Simonized them."

Of Joe Smith's last years, his close friend Terry McGrath writes:

Eleven years ago I invited Joe to guest lecture at Hackensack High School. The lectures expanded into faculty variety shows, and before long other schools were asking Joe to lecture. At the time Charlie was almost totally deaf, so I was doing his part. In 1971 the Hackensack Board of Education awarded Joe a high school diploma—he had only finished the fourth grade. We then began to perform at colleges. Drama departments go ape over Joe showing the students how to do a take or take a fall. Last year [1980] one of the local colleges wanted to give Joe an honorary degree, but he turned it down out of loyalty to his alma mater, Hackensack.

For more than fifty years, Smith and Dale ended their act with a verse:

Over fifty [sixty, seventy] years together,
With a bond that never tore,
And if somebody up there likes us,
We'll make it more and more.

After Charlie Dale's death, Joe Smith changed the ending:

Over seventy years together
As close as two peas in a pod,
And the only one that could
Separate us—(pause)—
Was God.

As Terry McGrath comments, it was a hell of an ending. But, then, Smith and Dale was a hell of an act.

BIBLIOGRAPHY

Smith, Bill. "Joe Smith." In *The Vaudevillians*. New York: Macmillan, 1976, pp. 239–51.

Smith, Joe, and Charlie Dale. "Spawned in the Catskills, Christened in Harlem." In *The Spice of Variety*, ed. Abel Green. New York: Henry Holt, 1952, pp. 252–58.

KATE SMITH (Greenville, Va., May 1, 1909—Raleigh, N.C., June 17, 1986)

Franklin Delano Roosevelt once introduced Kate Smith with the words, "This is Kate Smith. And Kate Smith is America." So it is appropriate that the performer who first introduced Irving Berlin's "God Bless America," on November 11, 1938, should have played a meaningful part in the history of that particularly American institution, vaudeville. She came to the medium late in its career but early in her own, making her first professional stage appearance at the B. F. Keith Theatre in Washington, D.C., in the mid 1920s and her first New York vaudeville appearance in February 1926, at which time *Variety* prophesied a bright future for her. In 1931, Kate Smith starred in the stage show at the Capitol Theatre and later that same year had her own revue at the Hippodrome. The following year, she made vaudeville history by being the only performer to play ten consecutive weeks, from August 1 through October 9, at the Palace. Those Palace audiences never tired of hearing that familiar phrase which was to be part of show business for the next forty years, "Hello everybody, this is Kate Smith." Indeed, Smith returned to the Palace again in November 1932 with her *Swanee Revue*. (She had first appeared at the Palace in April 1929.)

Kathryn Elizabeth Smith was a daughter of the South—hence her title "Songbird of the South"—and she was raised in Washington D.C. As a child, she won amateur contests and eventually persuaded her family to permit her to try for a career in show business. Her first break came when she was signed for a small part in the musical *Honeymoon Lane*, which opened in Atlantic City on August 29, 1926, and subsequently ran for two years on Broadway. Writing of Smith in the New York *Daily News* (September 24, 1926), Burns Mantle commented, she "Charlestons desperately and also gracefully." Also in 1926, Kate Smith made her first released recordings for Columbia Records: "The Little White House" and "Mary Dear." When *Honeymoon Lane* closed in 1929, she went into the road company of *Hit the Deck*, playing the blackface "mammy" role and singing "Hallelujah." From *Hit the Deck*, Smith went into *Flying High*, which opened on March 3, 1930. Of "Kate Smith whose proportions are mountainous and whose singing voice lacks cathedral tone," Brooks Atkinson wrote in *The New York Times* (March 4, 1930), "She bellows in such volume that the orchestra swoons in despair." In all three stage shows, Smith played a plump, jovial character, and in *Flying High*, as Pansy Sparks, she was the foil for Bert Lahr and the brunt of jokes such as, "That girl is sitting on top of the world— nothing else could bear her weight."

Kate Smith became more and more self-conscious about her size—at the height of her fame, she weighed 212 pounds—until she met a recording manager for Columbia Records named Ted Collins. Collins (who was born in New York on October 12, 1900, and died at Lake Placid, New York, on May 27, 1964) taught Kate Smith self-confidence, became her manager in 1931, and was to be her lifelong friend and confidant. As Smith wrote in her autobiography, "Ted was more than a manager, more even than a friend. . . . Without Ted there would have been no Kate Smith." Collins introduced Smith to radio, and the singer made her first broadcast for CBS on May 1, 1931, singing "By the River St. Marie," "I Surrender, Dear," "Please Don't Talk about Me When I'm Gone," "Dream a Little Dream of Me," and the number that was to become her theme song, "When the Moon Comes over the Mountain." It was Collins who suggested the simple self-introduction and her closing words, "Thanks for listening." Her radio program soon became the most popular on the air. Her evening series was heard on CBS through 1947; in 1949 and 1950, she had a program on ABC titled *Kate Smith Calls*; and from 1957 to 1958, she was heard on Mutual Radio. Additionally, a daytime program, *Kate Smith Speaks*, was heard on CBS from 1938 to 1947.

The singer never learned to read music. In 1938, when she sang with Leopold Stokowski and the Philadelphia Orchestra, she asked the maestro to whistle the music for her. He reportedly told Smith, "Don't ever take a lesson. Your voice is a gift from God and should never be spoiled."

Smith made her television debut on September 25, 1950, with *The Kate Smith Hour*, seen on NBC through June 1952, and in 1960, she had a short-lived television variety program, *The Kate Smith Show*, on CBS. By 1956, she claimed to have made some eight thousand radio broadcasts, recorded two thousand, two hundred songs, and earned as much as $38,000 in a single week. She continued, "There's really nothing I've missed I'd care to do." Kate Smith officially retired in 1979.

BIBLIOGRAPHY

Collins, Frederick L. "The Answer to the Kate Smith Riddle." *Liberty* 17, no. 23 (June 8, 1940), pp. 45–48.

"Kate Smith." *Current Biography*, November 1965, pp. 390–93.

Pitts, Michael R. *Kate Smith: A Bio-Bibliography*. Westport, Ct.: Greenwood Press, 1988.

Smith, Kate. *Living in a Great Big Way*. New York: Blue Ribbon Books, 1938.

————. *Upon My Lips a Song*. New York: Funk & Wagnalls, 1960.

SONG PLUGGERS

Working for individual music publishers, it was the job of the song plugger to persuade a vaudevillian to sing a particular song. In order for the public to purchase a piece of sheet music, it was necessary to get that song sung and heard, and it was up to song pluggers to "sell" the song to a vaudeville act. Sometimes, but not always, vaudevillians were paid by music publishers to perform particular numbers as regular features in their acts. In the late 1880s or early 1890s, Lottie Gilson was probably the first vaudevillian to accept payments in return for singing specific songs. Grace Kahn, the wife of composer Gus Kahn, began her career as a song plugger and recalled, "A song plugger went to the theatres and saw the people who sang and practically dragged them back to the office to hear some songs they were working on. And you had to make them like it. And if they liked it, then you taught it to them. Got the key, got the orchestration, and then they would put it in their act. I was probably the only girl song plugger in the world."

CHUNG LING SOO (New York, April 2, 1861—London, March 23, 1918)

A New Yorker born William Ellsworth Robinson, Chung Ling Soo shaved his head and, with the use of Oriental makeup, had audiences believe he was of Chinese origin. He never spoke onstage, but instead used a Korean assistant, posing as a Chinese, to introduce his magic tricks. He began his career in vaudeville in the 1880s as "Robinson, the Man of Mystery," and later worked as an assistant to Harry Keller and Alexander Herrmann. In 1899, he returned to vaudeville with his own act, billed as Chung Ling Foo, and as Chung Ling Soo, he opened at London's Alhambra Theatre in May 1900. In 1904, he introduced his death-defying trick in which he would supposedly catch a bullet fired at him by his assistant. At London's Wood Green Empire on March 23, 1918, the assistant fired the gun, but the mechanism that was supposed to hold the bullet in the muzzle failed to work. Chung Ling Soo was shot in the right lung and died a few hours later.

AILEEN STANLEY (Chicago, 1893—Los Angeles, March 24, 1982)

To a generation of record collectors, Aileen Stanley was "The Victrola Girl," and her recordings are still prized today. She sold a reported 25 million records of 215 recordings, of which her greatest hits were "My Little Bimbo Down on the Bamboo Isle," "Singin' the Blues," "Look What You've Done with Your Doggone Dangerous Eyes," "Whatcha Gonna Do When There Ain't No Jazz?," "I'm Looking for a Bluebird (To Chase the Blues Away)," "Bimini Bay," "Lovin' Sam (The Sheik of Alabam')," "You May Be Fast, but Mamma's Gonna Slow You Down," "Everybody Loves My Baby," "Ain't That a Grand and Glorious Feeling," "When My Sugar Walks Down the Street," and "Here Am I—Broken Hearted."

Aileen Stanley was born Maude Elsie Aileen Muggeridge and began entertaining with her brother Stanley at the age of five, helping to augment the income her mother obtained from renting rooms. When they split circa 1911, she took his first name as her stage name. In 1919, she won a contest organized by the *Chicago Herald and Examiner* to find the most beautiful bathing girl in the city. From that contest, she went on to vaudeville. As early as September 26, 1919, *Variety* wrote of her:

Aileen Stanley is the syncopated goddess of jass [sic]. Jass music originated as the expression of an impulse. Today it is a science. Miss Stanley is a post graduate and carries all the degrees. Her unique method of delivering syncopated melody is rendered most effective by a demure and sedate personality which offers a charming and unusual background for this school of song. There are scores of young women in vaudeville who sing jasual songs. Miss Stanley stands alone with her individual talent.

She came to New York in 1920, initially for a vaudeville engagement, but she was almost immediately signed to appear in the revue *Silks and Satins*. She also appeared in two other Broadway revues: *Pleasure Bound* (1929) and *Artists and Models* (1930). Stanley made her Palace debut in October 1920, and also headlined at the Palace in March 1926, August 1930, and January 1931. Her contract for vaudeville tours required that she be permitted to return to New York on a regular basis in order to continue making recordings. Often she would perform her act in vaudeville and immediately take a cab to the recording studio, studying the sheet music en route. Her early recordings were acoustic, requiring that she sing directly into a horn, but in the mid 1920s, with the introduction of electrical recording, she began singing to a microphone. In 1926, she was officially given the title "The Victrola Girl" by the Victor Record Company.

Aileen Stanley continued as a popular vaudevillian through the early 1930s. At the New Palace Theatre in Chicago in 1931, she sang "Just Like Jimmy and Me," "Some Pigs, a Hen and a Cow," and "Walkin' My Baby Back Home." At that time, *The Billboard* (February 28, 1931) commented, "There's a graciousness and charm about Aileen Stanley that is hard to put into words, and it fits perfectly with the sort of heart-throb songs she sings." She appeared onstage in the United Kingdom from 1925 to 1937, playing the London Palladium in

1934. Stanley was a guest artist on a number of radio programs in the 1930s, notably working with Rudy Vallee and Paul Whiteman. She retired at the end of the decade.

BIBLIOGRAPHY

Burian, Grayce Susan. "Aileen Stanley, Her Life and Times." In *Women in American Theatre*, ed. Helen Krich Chinoy and Linda Walsh Jenkins. New York: Theatre Communications Group, 1987, pp. 107–13.

STATE THEATRE

The flagship of the Marcus Loew theatre circuit, the State was located at Broadway and 45th Street. It opened as a vaudeville house on August 29, 1921, with a program hosted by Will Morrisey that concluded with a triumphant march by the showgirls from the Ziegfeld *Follies*, led by Loew and actor David Warfield. Only after the theatre was built was it discovered that the architect had forgotten to include any dressing rooms, and initially, performers had to change at the New York Theatre across the street; later, Loew purchased the building at 160 West 46th Street, where dressing rooms were located, and a bridge was built linking the two buildings. The State Theatre continued to present vaudeville long after other vaudeville houses had closed, but eventually it accepted the inevitable, and on December 23, 1947, the last vaudeville bill was presented there. The final bill consisted of trampoline artists Jack and Charlie Brick, George Andre Martin, Molly Picon, Dave Apollon, Jack Carter, and Harold and Lola with their snake charmer's dance. George Jessel also appeared onstage and commented, "I wasn't invited here. I heard vaudeville is finished here tonight. So I thought I'd drop in and tell you folks that talent never can die."

BIBLIOGRAPHY

Laurie, Joe, Jr. "The State Theatre." In *Vaudeville: From the Honky-Tonks to the Palace*. New York: Henry Holt, 1953, pp. 499–503.

JULIUS STEGER (Vienna, March 4, 1870—Vienna, February 25, 1959)

During the first two decades of the twentieth century, Julius Steger was a popular favorite on the vaudeville stage with a playlet, of which he was also the author, titled *The Fifth Commandment*. It concerned a music teacher forced to earn a living as a street musician and saved from poverty by a daughter who did not know his identity. Apparently, Steger always demanded absolute silence when he was appearing in vaudeville and was nicknamed by his fellow vaudevillians "Shhhhh" Steger. Julius Steger also appeared on the legitimate stage in *The Algerian* (1893), *The Geisha* (1897), *Yankee Doodle Dandy* (1898), *It Happened in Nordland* (1904), *A Modern Girl* (1914), and other productions. In 1915, he filmed *The Fifth Commandment*, the first of many silent features in which the actor appeared. Between 1920 and 1923, he was a production executive with the William Fox Company in New York.

STEP BROTHERS

The Step Brothers were a quartet of unrelated black acrobatic tap dancers, formed in 1926 by Al Williams (who died in 1985 at the age of seventy-four). The other members of the group were Prince Spencer, Maceo Anderson, and Rufus "Flash" McDonald. They appeared in vaudeville and were frequent entertainers at the Cotton Club in the 1920s. The high spot of their act was a "challenge dance," in which each member performed a solo and challenged the other members to do better. The Step Brothers appeared as cameo performers in a number of films, including *It Ain't Hay* (1943) and *Carolina Blues* (1944). The act disbanded in 1959, Al Williams became a personal manager for a number of performers, including Sarah Vaughan and Scatman Crothers.

BIBLIOGRAPHY

Huber, Melba. "Maceo Anderson: An Original Step Brother." *Dance Pages* 10, no. 1 (Summer 1992), pp. 16–17.

ASHTON STEVENS (San Francisco, August 11, 1872—Chicago, July 11, 1951)

"The Dean of American Drama Critics" and a good friend to vaudeville and vaudevillians, Ashton Stevens began his career as a writer with the *San Francisco News Letter* in 1894, succeeding Ambrose Bierce as the "Town Crier." Later, he wrote for the *San Francisco Examiner* and the *New York Journal* before joining, in 1910, the *Chicago Herald-American*, where he was to remain for the remainder of his career. Stevens published his last column, posthumously, on July 15, 1951. In 1927, he married his second wife, actress Katherine Krug. "Ash," as he was known among his many friends, was a great lover and advocate of the banjo, and Fred Allen once commented, "Mr. Stevens claims that if 140 million Americans will start playing banjos, Utopia is around the corner."

Stevens's only book, *Actorviews: Intimate Portraits* (Chicago: Covici-McGee, 1923), contains chapters on the following vaudevillians: Nora Bayes, Irene Bordoni, Fanny Brice, the Duncan Sisters, Raymond Hitchcock, Elsie Janis, Al Jolson, Fay Marbe, Savoy and Brennan, Sophie Tucker, and Bert Williams.

FRED STONE (Valmont, Co., August 19, 1873—Hollywood, Ca., March 6, 1959)

An all-around entertainer, Fred Stone was an accomplished acrobat, tightrope walker, song-and-dance man, and actor. The chief reason for his versatility was that he started early, learning to walk the tightrope as a child in his mother's backyard and touring in circuses with his brother Eddie before either was in his teens. Because of this expertise, Stone worked in all areas of entertainment: the circus, minstrel shows, vaudeville, musical comedy, the legitimate stage, and motion pictures.

Born in a log cabin in Valmont, Colorado, Fred Stone was christened Val by his father, until an angry grandmother changed the name to Frederick. He spent his early years traveling around with his father, an itinerant barber, and at the age of eleven, with his brother, joined a circus. From then on, he seldom returned home. On April 19, 1894, he teamed up with a young man from St. Joseph, Missouri, David Montgomery, who had previously worked as Montgomery and Wilson with an act called "Pullman Car Porters." The new team of Montgomery and Stone worked in blackface and appeared together on the vaudeville stage for the first time at Keith's Theatre, Boston. Within a relatively short space of time, they became headliners, and in 1900 appeared at London's Palace Theatre. Montgomery and Stone made their first musical comedy appearance together, under Charles Frohman's management, in *The Girl from up There*, which opened at the Herald Square Theatre on January 7, 1901.

Their greatest success was in *The Wizard of Oz*, with book and lyrics by L. Frank Baum and music by Paul Tietjens and A. Baldwin Sloane, which was first seen at the Grand Opera House, Chicago, on June 16, 1902. Stone appeared as the Scarecrow, and the cyclone scene in which the straw man is torn to bits was one of the most famous trick sequences on the legitimate stage. Montgomery appeared as the Tin Woodsman and introduced a popular song of the period, "Must You Have Meat with Your Mustard?" Eventually, *The Wizard of Oz* opened in New York at the Majestic Theatre and ran for a magnificent 293 performances. Also in the production, playing Lady Lunatic, was Allene Crater, whom Fred Stone married in 1904 and by whom he had three daughters, Paula, Dorothy, and Carol, all of whom entered show business.

The Wizard of Oz was followed by the Victor Herbert operatta *The Red Mill*, which opened at the Knickerbocker Theatre, New York, on September 24, 1906, and ran for 274 performances. In the role of Con Kidder, Stone had another hit, and the show marked the beginning of his long association with producer Charles Dillingham. In 1909, Stone toured in the George Ade comedy *The Old Town*, in which he introduced his famous lariat dance. To teach him how to use a rope, Stone looked for someone familiar with a lasso and found such a person in Will Rogers, with whom he had a close friendship until the latter's death. The death of Dave Montgomery at the age of forty-seven on April 20, 1917, broke up one of the great theatrical partnerships of the early twentieth century. It was, as *Variety* commented, "firm and fast from the outset." Stone wrote:

> For twenty-five years we had been together. We had built our careers together, so closely that they seemed like one career. We had in common a whole lifetime of shared experiences, and deep-rooted friendship and trust. We supplemented each other, as is the case with all enduring partnerships. He had a gayety and sparkle and love of life that aroused a response in his audience and his friends. No one will ever know how I missed him. The most difficult thing I ever had to do was to go ahead alone. For one thing I decided—I would never take another partner. No one should have Dave's place.

After Montgomery's death, Stone appeared in the title role of *Jack o' Lantern*, which opened at New York's Globe Theatre on October 16, 1917. This "musical extravaganza" was claimed to be the most expensive production in terms of seat prices to play Broadway up to that time. A year later, he went to Hollywood to appear in his first film—for Famous Players—Lasky—*Under the Top*, directed by Donald Crisp and written by John Emerson and Anita Loos. Stone was advertised as "the marvel of musical comedy," and the film, set in a circus, gave him ample opportunity for wire walking and acrobatics. He appeared sporadically in films through the 1940s, and among his features are *Broadway after Dark* (1924), *Smiling Faces* (1932), *Alice Adams* (1935), and *The Trail of the Lonesome Pine* (1936). He also continued to appear onstage, in *Tip-Top* (1920), *Stepping Stones* (1923), *Criss-Cross* (1926), *Ripples* (1930), *Smiling Faces* (1932), and *Jayhawker* (1934). In 1928, Stone was about to go into rehearsals for a new show, *Three Cheers*, when he was involved in a plane crash that broke both his legs. His friend Will Rogers took over the part, sending his weekly paycheck to Stone.

Stone's last major stage appearance was as Grandpa Martin Vanderhof in *You Can't Take It with You* at New York's City Center in 1945; he also essayed the same role in a small 1950 Hollywood production at the Las Palmas Theatre. Fred Stone died following a long illness. He had experienced a remarkable career, and as he wrote in his autobiography, "The world has been good to me. I have been a happy man."

BIBLIOGRAPHY
Stone, Fred. *Rolling Stone*. New York: Whittlesey House, 1945.

STRIPTEASE

While striptease is generally associated with the burlesque theatre, it had its origins in vaudeville and has embraced virtually all areas of the entertainment world. As critic George Jean Nathan wrote in 1941, "Despite the occasional interferences by various municipal authorities, by the police, and by moralists in mufti, the striptease has thrived in burlesque, which is its current home, in musical shows, in nightclubs, in pleasure parks, honky tonks and carnivals, and, Will Hays or no Will Hays, even to a degree in the movies."

Striptease had as its seed the vaudeville acts of the 1840s later known as "Living Models" or "Tableaux Vivants," in which women, and men, would strike artistic poses while clad only in body stockings. As the nineteenth century gave way to the twentieth, the body stockings were replaced by body makeup, tights, and breast coverings. Florenz Ziegfeld adapted and modified such acts for his *Follies*, in which scantily clad showgirls would remain carefully posed and motionless. The first performer not only to move her body but also remove an item of clothing was, as far as can be ascertained, Millie de Leon, who, during the first two decades of the twentieth century, would end her dance with removal, and throwing to the audience, of her garters.

The striptease acts in the burlesque theatres of the 1930s developed from the "cootch" dancers of the 1890s and early years of this century, who exposed tantalizing inches of flesh as they danced with eroticism and teasing movements. One of the first strippers on the burlesque circuit in the 1920s was Edna Victoria. She was followed later in the decade by Carrie Finnell, who billed herself as

"The Girl with the Million Dollar Legs." Finnell has the distinction of introducing the popular stripper's routine of using the pectoral muscles to twirl tassels attached to the dancer's nipples. Ann Corio recalled, "She could make one go slow, the other fast. She could spin the left in one direction and the right in an opposite direction. . . . She could attack tassels to her derrière and have them spinning every which way while the bosom tassels revolved merrily on their own."

Striptease came to the revue stage on September 1, 1930, when the latest edition of Earl Carroll's *Vanities* featured the fan dancing of Faith Bacon, an act similar to that of Sally Rand. The New York police closed the show but permitted its reopening after Bacon acquired a larger fan. The Minsky Brothers brought striptease to Broadway in 1931, when they took over the leases of the Central and Republic theatres. The Minskys were nothing if not patriotic in their hiring practices. On February 24, 1937, Herbert and Morton Minsky appeared before an immigration committee of the House of Representatives and pledged themselves to employ only American strippers in their theatres. Off the record, the congressmen on the committee asked that the Minsky Brothers send some of their strippers to appear at the following week's hearings.

The late 1930s saw the appearance of the three best known exponents of the art of striptease, Gypsy Rose Lee, Margie Hart, and Ann Corio. Lee's weekly salary in the 1940s was $2,000, with Corio earning $800 and Hart $600. The three women represented a new generation of strippers, more glamorous, self-controlled, and anxious to build a legitimate career in a medium which, up to that time, had seemed illegitimate. Both Lee and Hart were featured in Broadway revues; the latter in the Shubert Brothers's *Wine, Women and Song* (1942), and Gypsy Rose Lee in Mike Todd's *Star and Garter* (1942). Corio enjoyed a brief career in films, as did another well-known stripper, Lili St. Cyr. Lee gained a reputation as an intellectual, and her character was parodied in the 1940 Richard Rodgers and Lorenz Hart musical *Pal Joey*.

Striptease died with burlesque. It was killed by self-inflicted boredom, as the supporting comedic acts were replaced by additional strippers until the all-male audience had nothing to relieve the monotony of G-strings and naked nipples. With the advent of hard-core film pornography in the 1960s and home video in the late 1970s, there was no reason for the male population to frequent a striptease show. Curiously, the demise of the female striptease acts was followed in the 1980s by the rise of male striptease performances, geared toward female audiences, but with their origins a decade or more earlier in all-gay establishments. The all-male Chippendales dancers in Los Angeles grew from one nightclub to an industry, which embraced books and calendars as well as theatrical tours throughout the Western world.

See also GYPSY ROSE LEE, SALLY RAND.

BIBLIOGRAPHY

Alexander, H. L. *Striptease: The Vanished Art of Burlesque*. New York: Knight, 1938.
Corio, Ann, with Joe DiMona. *This Was Burlesque*. New York: Grosset & Dunlap, 1968.
Grubb, Kevin. "How the Chippendales Survived the Eighties." *Dance Magazine*, September 1987, pp. 64–65.

Crichton, Kyle. "Strip to Fame." *Collier's* 98, no. 25 (December 19, 1936), pp. 13, 47.

Nathan, George Jean. "The Strip-Tease Industry." *Liberty* 18, no. 32 (August 9, 1941), pp. 56–57.

Newquist, Roy. "Ann Corio." In *Showcase*. New York: William Morrow, 1966, pp. 44–56.

Sobel, Bernard. "Striptease." In *A Pictorial History of Burlesque*. New York: G. P. Putnam's Sons, 1956.

Toll, Robert C. "The Girlie Show: From Statuary to Striptease." In *On with the Show*. New York: Oxford University Press, 1976.

STRONGMEN

Despite being little more than "freak" attractions, strongmen were fairly popular entertainers on vaudeville bills in the teens and early 1920s, but never as headliners. Their appeal was primarily to the women in the audience, who enjoyed seeing the men pose in skimpy costumes that accentuated their physiques. Sandow (q.v.) was the most famous of all strongmen, and he posed for contemporary photographs wearing nothing more than a fig leaf. Like Sandow, many strongmen preferred one-name billing. There were, for example, Kronas, Medevedeff, Bertishe (who could hold three men on a bar with his teeth), and Breitbart (whose 1923 act at the Orpheum, Brooklyn, included immobilizing a miniature carousel with six horses on which sat six members of the audience).

Alan Corelli entered vaudeville in the mid 1920s with an act that would begin with his wearing a white leotard and striking various Greek poses, and would continue with his inviting members of the audience to come onstage and try to lift him. As many as six volunteers would attempt unsuccessfully to disprove Corelli's billing as "The Man Nobody Can Lift." He recalled, for Bill Smith in *The Vaudevillians*, that at the Golden Gate Theatre, San Francisco, he invited Houdini to witness his act, and the great escape artist reported, "I have been on the stage and watched Alan Corelli. He is not a fraud."

In 1924, Francisco Pantilon, known as "The Lion," was popular with audiences. Wilfred Cabana could lift an automobile, while Ben Meyer lifted a man with his teeth. The act of the Francelias would consist of one using his teeth to hold his partner by the hair while performing a cakewalk. In 1927, a strongman who wore a hood and was billed as "The Masked Athlete" was touring the vaudeville circuits. Female "strongmen" acts included Mary Arniotis, Alba, and Martha Farra, who could hold up an automobile in which were seated twelve men.

EVE SULLY. See BLOCK AND SULLY

GUS SUN (Toledo, Oh., October 7, 1868—Springfield, Oh., October 1, 1959)

Gus Sun was a name synonymous with minor league vaudeville; to play small-time vaudeville was to play Gus Sun time. As the head of his own booking agency, he once claimed to book more theatres than B. F. Keith, but they were never major establishments. He introduced the concept of the split week, with the entertainer playing three days at one theatre and, if he was lucky, three days at another. Many performers were willing to work Gus Sun time while breaking in a new act, but probably the only vaudevillian discovered by Gus Sun was Chic Sale.

The son of German immigrants named Klotz, Gus Sun changed his name while working in a juggling act with his brothers, because the family name was confusing to the audience. In 1889, he joined the Summerville and Lee Circus as a juggler; he later worked as a vaudevillian, an Indian medicine show impressario, and head of his own minstrel troupe. In October 1904, Sun opened a makeshift vaudeville/motion picture theatre in Springfield, Ohio, and from that one theatre Sun expanded, within five years, to eleven other theatres and also purchased the building in which the first venture was housed.

A lack of acts for his theatre forced Sun to open his own agency, the Gus Sun Booking Agency, in 1906, providing performers for small-time vaudeville theatres across the midwest and later throughout most of the country, excluding the Western seaboard. There was some aggressive competition with the B. F. Keith organization, except for a period of agreement between 1914 and 1920, but Sun managed to survive and prosper, perhaps because his operation was ultimately too small to be a threat to Keith. Following Sun's death, the agency continued under the management of Gus Sun, Jr., who joined the company in 1934. In later years, the agency prospered more from booking acts for fairs and amusement parks.

BIBLIOGRAPHY

Hanford, Edgar C. "Gus Sun—Showman 50 Years." *The Billboard*, April 29, 1939, pp. 28–33, 67.

VALESKA SURATT (Terre Haute, In., June 28, 1882—Washington, D.C., July 2, 1962)

Just as Theda Bara exemplified exoticism in her role as the screen's most famous vamp, so did Valeska Suratt represent a similar quality in vaudeville. It is no coincidence that Suratt had a brief, relatively unsuccessful film career, playing parts similar to those of Bara and trying to eclipse the cinema's reigning vampire (female variety).

Details of Valeska Suratt's early life are sketchy. Her first job was apparently as an assistant in a millinery shop at $5 a week. Eventually, she became an actress in Chicago and may also have appeared in vaudeville at the turn of the century, but it is not known in what capacity. She was spotted by song-and-dance man Billy Gould shortly after he had broken up with his first partner, Nellie Burt, and he teamed up with her to form a highly successful act, which included exotic dancing by Suratt and an Apache dance by the two of them. The couple split up in 1908, and Suratt embarked on a solo career in vaudeville, singing, dancing, and displaying her figure in a variety of stunning costumes. By 1909, she was advertising herself as "Vaudeville's Greatest Star" and "The Biggest Drawing Card in New York." Sime Silverman wrote in *Variety* (November 20, 1909), "In the show world Valeska Suratt occupies a little niche all to herself. There is no one who can look as Miss Suratt does when costumed as only she can dress."

In December 1910, Suratt starred in her own thirty-minute mini-revue at Hammerstein's Victoria Theatre, titled "Bouffe Variety." Her leading man was Fletcher Norton (Suratt's one-time husband), and with him she had a brief romantic interlude onstage, performed a comedy routine which included her singing "When Broadway Was a Pasture," and closed with her as the bride. *Variety* doubted the piece was good enough for "The Belle of Broadway," Suratt's new self-given title.

The chief importance of "Bouffe Variety" is that it appears to have been the first time Valeska Suratt performed any type of playlet on the vaudeville stage, and from this time on, that was to be her chief claim to fame, as a sultry and exotic leading lady of generally tawdry melodramas. Typical of the playlets in which Suratt appeared was *The Purple Lady* (1917), in which she portrayed a young lady of dubious background who lures a former Russian governor to a Greenwich Village cafe and then strangles him with the scarf with which he had strangled her brother. "She has now done everything in the acting line" was the comment from *Variety* (December 7, 1917).

Popular plays were condensed into forty minutes for Suratt's vaudeville act. Jack Lait adapted his successful *One of Us* for Suratt and retitled it, as befitted her image, *Scarlet*. She played a cabaret singer loved by a society type (Eugene Strong) who pretends to be a tough guy in order to win the singer's affections. "Miss Suratt gives a subtle impersonation of a woman of the slums who feels the urge of finer things," commented *The New York Dramatic Mirror* (November 6, 1920).

Between 1915 and 1917, Valeska Suratt starred in eleven feature films: *The Immigrant* (1915), *The Soul of Broadway* (1915), *Jealousy* (1916), *The Straight Way* (1916), *The Victim* (1916), *The New York Peacock* (1917), *A Rich Man's Plaything* (1917), *She* (1917), *The Siren* (1917), *The Slave* (1917), and *Wife Number Two* (1917).

Suratt reached the peak of her vaudeville career in 1920, when, as "The Dynamic Force of Vaudeville," she headlined at the Palace, moving Sime Silverman to write in *Variety* (February 20, 1920), "There are two wonders in and of vaudeville. They are Eva Tanguay and Valeska Suratt." Just as her rise to fame had been sudden, so was Valeska Suratt's departure from vaudeville. By the end of the 1920s, the woman who "wore her clothes as a flower its petals" had vanished from the scene.

In the 1930s, she lived in one room in a shabby New York hotel. Novelist Fannie Hurst heard of her plight and arranged a benefit performance, which netted a couple of thousand dollars for Suratt. After receiving the money, the performer disappeared for a couple of weeks. Upon her return to the hotel room, she was carrying six eggs and a bouquet of roses. She had lost the $2,000 gambling and was back where she started. Suratt also tried to interest the Hearst newspapers in publishing her autobiography, but when a reporter finally read the lengthy manuscript, he discovered that Suratt now believed herself to be the Virgin Mary, and what he was reading was the autobiography of the mother of God. "She was completely batty," remembered one newspaperman.

SWAYNE'S RATS AND CATS

A novelty animal act of the teens, Swayne's Rats and Cats featured rodents dressed as jockeys which would ride around a miniature racetrack on the cats' backs. "They must have fed the cats before the show," comments Joe Laurie, Jr., in his book *Vaudeville*. He does not explain how Swayne trained these natural enemies to perform together, nor how an animal as small as a rat could be seen by a vaudeville audience. Groucho Marx told the story of Fanny Brice, who was on the same bill as Swayne's Rats and Cats, finding a rat in her dressing room. She screamed, Swayne entered, and retrieved the rat, which he declared was not one of his. The next year, that rat was the star of the show. Almost the same story is told by Fred Allen in his autobiography *Much Ado about Me*, except he calls the act Nelson's Cats and Rats.

A similar act from the late 1920s was Lady Alice's Pets, featuring trained cats, mice, and dogs. *Variety* (January 18, 1928) reported, "A couple of these babies were accomplished wire-walkers."

SWEDISH COMEDIANS. See EL BRENDEL, KNUTE ERICKSON

FREDERICK CHASE SWEENEY. See DUFFY AND SWEENEY

T

TABLEAUX VIVANTS

Tableaux vivants or "living pictures" were a curiosity on the vaudeville stage during much of the nineteenth century and early in the twentieth. These acts consisted of individuals striking various static poses, often in scanty or flesh-colored costuming. The earliest recorded tableaux vivants artist on the New York stage was Mrs. Ada Adams Barrymore, who appeared as "The Soldier's Widow" in September 1831. Barrymore's pose was perfectly respectable, but tableaux vivants quickly degenerated to nothing more than an excuse for seminudity, with poses such as "The Three Graces" from 1847, in which three women appeared virtually nude on a revolving platform, and in the 1840s, there was much legal activity directed against such forms of entertainment.

The most prominent producer of "living pictures" was Hungarian-born Edward Kilanyi, whose work was first seen in the United States in the 1894 production of *1492*. Because Kilanyi refused to go to Koster and Bial's Music Hall in 1894, Oscar Hammerstein produced his own "living pictures" there in May of that year. Among the tableaux were "The Three Muses," "General Grant at the Battle of the Wilderness," "The Gladiator," and "Custer's Last Stand." "Living pictures" enjoyed a considerable vogue in the mid through late 1890s, involving large numbers of models and various novelty devices such as "Miss Pygmalion," from 1895, in which Jane May was a sculptress whose statue of Pierrot came to life.

BIBLIOGRAPHY

McCullough, Jack W. *Living Pictures on the New York Stage*. Ann Arbor, Mi.: UMI Research Press, 1983.

TAB SHOWS

The tab show takes its name from a tabloid, or half-size newspaper, and refers to a shortened version of a full-length show. Many musical comedies were condensed to tab show format for presentation at vaudeville theatres in the 1920s and 1930s.

EVA TANGUAY (Marbleton, Canada, August 1, 1878—Hollywood, Ca., January 11, 1947)

To her generation, Eva Tanguay *was* American vaudeville, and for almost its entire existence, she was the medium's greatest female star. She was overweight and ugly and her costumes were deliberately outrageous—one dress was covered in memo pads and pencils—and yet for more than twenty years, Eva Tanguay was adored by critics and audiences alike. The former were always searching for new ways in which to describe her. In 1914, *Variety* wrote that she was "vaudeville's single greatest drawing 'card'"; on December 25, 1914, she was on that trade paper's front cover with the description, "The Girl Who Made Vaudeville Famous"; in 1915, Tanguay was called "The Evangelis of Joy"; in 1920, she was "The Dynamic Force of Vaudeville"; that same year, *The New York Dramatic Mirror* hailed her as "Vaudeville's Greatest Box Office Attraction" and described her as "The Man-o-War of Vaudeville."

Eva Tanguay's appeal for those who never saw or heard her is, of course, difficult to explain. Phonograph recordings do not do her justice. Photographs seem to be deliberately posed to show her at her most outrageous or repellant, with bosoms bursting out of bras and thighs rippling with fat. Writing in *American Vaudeville*, Douglas Gilbert thought it easy to analyze her act: "It was assault and battery." And that, to a large extent, does sum up the secret of Tanguay's success. She *did* have boundless energy. She sang suggestive songs in an inimitable fashion, with a blatant delivery which proved the point of her most famous number, "I Don't Care." She really didn't care what people thought of her, be they critics, audiences, or theatrical managers.

Above all, Eva Tanguay was a perennial youngster; she was ever youthful, and audiences who had grown up with her could forget the passing years, watching her changeless, ageless, frantic gyrations. As Marian Spitzer wrote in her study of the Palace, "Eva had the fizz and taste of a not-very-good brand of champagne," but even mediocre champagne can seem good and fizz well for an unsophisticated taste, and that was what comprised much of vaudeville's audience. Cheap champagne she may have been, but she was never cold duck.

On October 6, 1915, *The New York Dramatic Mirror* reviewed her act and noted, "We can't imagine anyone sitting back in his theater chair and placidly observing Eva Tanguay. There's no passive way of watching the Cyclonic One. When the spotlight centers upon the corner of the stage and the trombones blare, as the Tanguay moment comes, you have such a feeling as we suspect a staid resident of London harbors when a Zeppelin hovers in the English evening mists. There's a tingling sensation of electrical expectancy. . . . If ever the United States becomes involved in war, we recommend Miss Tanguay as recruiting sergeant extraordinary." (The trombones, by the way, were always used to announce her entrance.)

Apart from "I Don't Care," none of Tanguay's songs have achieved lasting fame, perhaps because no one could sing them as she did. One might listen in vain today to hear "I'd Rather Be a Rooster Than a Knocker" (1916), "Tune in on Eva" (1921), "I May Be a Nut, but I'm Not a Crossword Fan" (1921), "I Want Somebody to Go Wild with Me" (1913), "It's All Been Done Before, but Not the Way I Do It" (1913), and "Go as Far as You Like" (1913). As *The New York Dramatic Mirror* noted in 1915, all her numbers were "Tanguayesque, distinctly and thunderously personal."

Offstage, Eva Tanguay was equally tempestuous. She argued with everyone, totally ignored E. F. Albee's puritanical dictates on the type of material that could be used in his theatres, constantly walked out on engagements because of real or imagined slights, and once threw a stagehand down a flight of stairs because he was in her way. In a 1908 article in *Variety*, Tanguay admitted that her success relied in part on the fact that she did behave in a crazy fashion, and because she was a terrible and crazy actress, who acted like an insane person, audiences flocked to see her.

Canadian-born Tanguay sang in the church choir at the age of ten—although no one would have guessed it from her later career—and appeared in amateur nights at Parson's Hall, Holyoke, Massachusetts, to where her parents had emigrated. Later, she played child parts with the Rose Stahl Repertoire Company, and for five years, she toured as Cedric Errol in *Little Lord Fauntleroy*. On February 11, 1901, she opened at Hammerstein's Victoria Theatre in *My Lady*, and as she recalled, "Several musical numbers were given me that had been promised a favorite chorus girl and that settled it. Obstacles of all sorts were put in my way to prevent my success, but I started to fight and discovered I had a temper that had been given me to carry me through life." By 1903, she was starring with her own Eva Tanguay Comedy Company, and she was acclaimed as the youngest star on the American stage as she appeared in *The Office Boy* (1903), *The Sambo Girl* (1904), and *A Good Little Fellow* (1906). In March 1904, she returned to Hammerstein's Victoria Theatre to make her vaudeville debut.

The mass of frizzy blond hair, animated arms and legs, and a big voice singing lyrics that no one believed could be produced by a sane person was vaudeville's newest hit. In 1908, she introduced the story of Salome to vaudeville audiences and created a sensation, not to mention a host of imitators. By 1910, she was asking, and getting, $3,500 a week, making her the highest salaried star in vaudeville, beating out Ethel Barrymore, who could ask for only $3,000 for a week's engagement. There was more than a hint of truth in a song introduced by Tanguay in 1915:

> There's method in my madness,
> There's a meaning for my style;
> The more they raise my salary,
> The crazier I'll be.

In 1916, she demanded a weekly salary of $10,000 and a guarantee of three years work before she would agree to star in films. There were no takers, and as a result, she formed her own production company, starring in two feature films: *Energetic Eva* (1916), directed by Joseph Smiley, and *The Wild Girl*

(1917), directed by Howard Estabrook. The latter was advertised with the slogan, "Eva Tanguay's dynamic personality generates more energy than Niagara Falls."

Ted Waldman worked with Eva Tanguay in her early days, playing the harmonica while she changed clothes and exchanging crosstalk with her from the stage box. He remembered her as a complex personality, a mixture of eccentricity and warmth. Often she would send him across the road from whichever theatre she was playing to take a $100 bill to a beggar, with strict instructions not to divulge its origin. As part of her act, Tanguay used a pet monkey, and when it died in San Francisco, she had Waldman bury it in Golden Gate Park. That night, she worried that the monkey would be cold, so she ordered Waldman to return and dig it up.

The years did not dim Tanguay's popularity. When she appeared at the Palace in January 1921, she had to admit she was not the Eva of her prime—Tanguay never lied about her age—but a year earlier, on December 13, 1920, she had appeared at the Coliseum Theatre and played to the biggest matinee audience since the theatre opened. Reviewing Tanguay's January 1924 Palace appearance, *Variety* (January 17, 1924) wrote, "What Ruth is to baseball, Dempsey to pugilism and Chaplin to pictures, Tanguay is to vaudeville. She embodies the spirit of youth in her work, her personality is elusive and baffling as ever, and she has the color that penetrates beyond the four walls of a theatre and cashes in at the box office."

Eva Tanguay returned to vaudeville in May 1930 after a three-year absence. For an opening number, she sang "Back Doing Business at the Same Old Stand," followed by "Mae West, Texas and Me," a comedy number about the mob's having dubbed her, West, and Texas Guinan as "The Unholy Three." "Edba," writing in *Variety* (May 14, 1930), saw her at the 58th Street Theatre and commented, "Although not the tempestuous Sambo girl of other days, Miss Tanguay still retains plenty of zip and good sense of showmanship that should still keep her around." In 1931, Tanguay toured with the Fanchon and Marco unit.

As the years went by, vaudeville died, and Eva Tanguay dropped from the public eye, becoming more and more reclusive in her Hollywood, California, home. (In March 1917, she had announced that henceforth she would make her home and her headquarters in Los Angeles.) By 1933, she was destitute and reliant upon charity from the National Vaudeville Association and former colleagues. On her sixty-eighth birthday, she gave an interview to a reporter from the *Los Angeles Times*, and told of her hopes for a film based on her life. This came to reality after her death with the release in 1952 of the dismal George Jessel production *The I Don't Care Girl*, with Mitzi Gaynor in the title role. Tanguay died after years of ill health, with the last fifteen years of her life in pitiful contrast to the fabulous era of vaudeville through which she had lived and with which her name was synonymous.

BIBLIOGRAPHY

Smith, Frederick James. " 'I Do Care!,' Says Eva Tanguay." *The New York Dramatic Mirror*, January 27, 1915, p. 30.

Tanguay, Eva. "Success." *Variety*, December 12, 1908, p. 34.

⸻. "I Care at Last." *Liberty* 10, no. 6 (February 11, 1933), pp. 43–44.

JULIUS TANNEN (New York, May 16, 1880—Hollywood, Ca., January 3, 1965)

Generally considered a brilliant comedy monologist, Julius Tannen entered vaudeville in 1902 as an impressionist, and early in his career gained fame for his impersonations of Raymond Hitchcock and George M. Cohan. As a monologist, he was second only to Will Rogers, with the ability to tell a humorous story of either topical or personal interest. Often he would deliver a gag and leave the last line to the audience's imagination, and he is credited with introducing the line, "My father thanks you, my mother thanks you, my sister thanks you, and I thank you." Tannen was particularly noted for his quick wit and ability to improvise. Once while appearing at the Palace, the theatre's black cat walked across the stage and settled at his feet; the comedian looked down and said, "This is a monologue, not a catalogue." On another occasion when he was heckled, he responded, "Save your breath, you may want it to clean your glasses later."

In 1920, he wrote and starred on Broadway in *Her Family Tree*. Tannen served as master of ceremonies for the 1925, 1926, and 1927 editions of Earl Carroll's *Vanities*, and he was also master of ceremonies at the Palace in July and October 1929. (He had made his first appearance at the Palace in September 1913.) Julius Tannen was often billed as "The Chatterbox," and under that name he also wrote an occasional column for *Variety*.

Between 1935 and 1958, Julius Tannen appeared in many films, including *Dimples* (1938), *Christmas in July* (1940), *The Dolly Sisters* (1945), *Mad Wednesday* (1947), *Unfaithfully Yours* (1948), *Singin' in the Rain* (1952), and *The Last Hurrah* (1958).

BIBLIOGRAPHY

Tannen, Julius. "The Monologist—and Why." *Variety*, December 26, 1919, p. 19.

TAP DANCING

Tap was a dance phenomenon that came along rather late for vaudeville. The Nicholas Brothers (q.v.) were the greatest exponents of acrobatic tap dancing. Another brother act was the Condos Brothers, Nick and Steve (who were sometimes joined by older brother Frank), who performed precision tap dancing in vaudeville in the 1930s and 1940s and also appeared in a number of films, including *Wake Up and Live* (1937), *In the Navy* (1941), *Pin-Up Girl* (1944), and *She's Back on Broadway* (1953). Donald O'Connor is better known as a song-and-dance man on screen (from 1937), but he also appeared as a tap dancer in vaudeville in the 1930s. Like many tap dancers, Leonard Reed was black, but so fair-skinned that he could often pass as white. He began his career in 1922, inventing the "Shim Sham Shimmy," a four-step tap routine, and later worked in vaudeville in partnership with Willie Bryant. Another black tap dancer, Ralph Brown, worked with many big bands on the vaudeville stage in the 1930s, most notably Cab Calloway. Charles (Honi) Coles enjoyed his greatest success late in his career; he costarred in the 1983 musical *My One and Only*, and Lena Horne once described him as "so graceful, he made butterflies clumsy." Coles had worked in vaudeville in the 1930s and in the mid 1940s teamed with another dancer, Cholly Atkins.

George Tapps, a white American whose real name was Mortimer Alphonse Becker, was given a three-year dance scholarship by Ned Wayburn at the age of seven. He toured vaudeville, and in 1932, he had his big break, performing "Brother, Can You Spare a Dime," in *Americana*. He retired in 1967, when no longer able to obtain work, but in May 1981, along with Hal Le Roy, Charlie "Cookie" Cook, and Ernest "Brownie" Brown, he tap danced at the Smithsonian Institution as part of the Museum of American History's festival of American popular entertainment.

Eddie Rector was a major black soft-shoe and tap dancer of the 1920s, but he is little known today because he worked in vaudeville almost exclusively on the black TOBA circuit and in Europe.

BIBLIOGRAPHY

Ames, Jerry, and Jim Siegelman. *The Book of Tap: Recovering America's Long-Lost Dance*. New York: David McKay, 1977.

Atwater, Constance. *Tap Dancing*. Rutland, Vt.: E. E. Tuttle, 1971.

Battiata, Mary. "Tales of a Tapping Trouper." *The Washington Post*, May 2, 1981, pp. F1, F7.

Draper, Paul. *On Tap Dancing*. New York: Marcel Dekker, 1978.

Frank, Rusty E. *Tap!: The Greatest Tap Dance Stars and Their Stories, 1900–1955*. New York: William Morrow, 1990.

FAY TEMPLETON (Little Rock, Ar., December 25, 1866—San Francisco, October 3, 1939)

One of the great, old-time favorites of the legitimate and vaudeville stages, actress, singer, and comedienne Fay Templeton enjoyed a career that was crammed with excitement and controversy. She was the daughter of John Templeton, a theatrical manager and former editor of the *Tammany Times*, and in his Templeton Opera Company, Fay toured as a child. Before that she had made her first stage appearance, as a cupid singing fairy songs, on August 16, 1869. On August 19, 1873, she first appeared as Puck in Augustin Daly's production of *A Midsummer Night's Dream* at New York's Grand Opera House.

By the age of fifteen, Fay Templeton had a national reputation as a light opera singer and had also eloped with and separated from minstrel singer Billy West. In 1886, she made her first London appearance at the Gaiety Theatre, in *Monte Cristo, Jr.* It was in this production that she sang "I Like It, I Do," wearing what was, for the day, a daring costume featuring tights that showed off the elegance of her legs. The Lord Chamberlain, the British stage censor, objected to both the costume and the song, and Fay Templeton fought his decision in the English courts. Her second marriage was to Howell Osborn, known as "The King of the Dudes," and it was kept secret until his death in 1895, when he left her $100,000.

After a number of successful stage appearances in *Madame Favart* (1893), *Excelsior, Jr.* (1895), and other shows, Fay Templeton joined the Weber and Fields Music Hall Company for the season of 1898–1899. Weber and Fields biographer Felix Isman described her as "the finest feminine talent ever given to American burlesque," and with such songs as "Keep Away from Emmeline" and "What? Marry Dat Girl?," not to mention parodies of legitimate stage actress Ada Rehan, she took New York by storm. By 1903, she was hailed as "The Queen of American Burlesque." Fay Templeton reached even greater heights in 1905 when she starred in George M. Cohan's *Forty-Five Minutes from Broadway* and introduced the song "Mary's a Grand Old Name."

On August 1, 1906, Fay Templeton made her third and final marriage, to the wealthy Pennsylvania industrialist William Patterson, and announced her retirement from the stage, preferring, perhaps not unnaturally, to be one of the wealthiest women in America. However, in 1911, Fay Templeton returned for a vaudeville tour, but she refused to play her hometown of Pittsburgh or any other town on the Eastern seaboard. By 1913, she had changed her mind and was headlining at Willie Hammerstein's Victoria Theatre with an act that included songs from her Weber and Fields days, "Fishing" and "Rosey Posey." She also performed "So Long Mary" from *45 Minutes to Broadway*, "Poor Little Buttercup" from Gilbert and Sullivan's *H.M.S. Pinafore* (in a 1911 revival of which she had starred), and a song indicative of her weight problem, "Though I'm Stouter Than I Have Been, Still I'm Thinner Than I Was." *Variety* (February 28, 1913) hailed her as a "great old-time favorite—and artist."

In 1912, Fay Templeton reunited with Weber and Fields, playing Peachie Mullen in *Hokey-Pokey* and Bunty Biggar in *Bunty Bulls and Strings*. She came out of retirement again for Weber and Fields in June 1925 to headline with them in an old-timers bill at the Palace. She sang Lillian's Russell's famous song, "Come Down, My Evenin' Star," after being wheeled out in a wheelchair by Weber and Fields—part of a gag about her massive weight. After performing some of her own hits of two decades earlier, including "Ma Blushin' Rose," "Dinah," and "Lou," Templeton broke down and wept. "There was many a dim eye in the audience that lighted with a new fire at the thoughts that came crowding back." commented *Variety* (June 10, 1925).

There was one other glorious theatrical moment reserved for Fay Templeton when, as Aunt Minnie in the original 1933 production of *Roberta*, she introduced Jerome Kern's haunting melody "Yesterdays." And what yesterdays they had been for Fay Templeton, one of the great comic ladies of the American stage.

BIBLIOGRAPHY

Crichton, Kyle. "Lady in the Wings." *Collier's* 93, no. 16 (April 21, 1934), pp. 18, 59–60.

"Queen of American Burlesque." *Munsey*, December 1903, pp. 460, 465–66.

Templeton, Fay. "Grease Paint and Glory." *Pictorial Review*, September 1926, pp. 26 + ; October 1926, pp. 4, 64, 69–70, 72–73; November 1926, pp. 26, 36, 60, 62, 64, 66.

EVELYN NESBIT THAW (Tarentum, Pa., December 25, 1884—Santa Monica, Ca., January 18, 1967)

Had it not been for the sensational murder of architect Stanford White by Evelyn Nesbit's husband, millionaire Harry K. Thaw, the vaudeville stage would not have known of Evelyn Nesbit Thaw, whose career prior to her marriage was exclusively that of a chorus girl. But Evelyn Nesbit Thaw became more than a mere vaudevillian; she was the "freak" act of all time, proving Willie Hammerstein's claim that vaudeville audiences would pay good money to see newspaper headliners, particularly when sex and violence was involved.

Evelyn Nesbit came to New York with her mother circa 1900 and became an artist's model—notably as Charles Dana Gibson's "The Eternal Question"—and eventually a chorus girl in *Florodora*, from which came the popular song "Tell Me Pretty Maiden, Are There Any More at Home Like You?" Like many other chorus girls before her, Evelyn Nesbit met Stanford White, who seduced her, and one of whose favorite relaxations was to place the naked Evelyn on a red velvet swing in his studio apartment. Evelyn Nesbit was not averse to such activities, and while seeing Stanford White, she was also enjoying a tempestuous affair with actor John Barrymore. She also met Philadelphia millionaire Harry K. Thaw, who was obviously mentally unstable and who became infatuated with the chorus girl. On April 5, 1905, Thaw and Nesbit were married. Thaw had learned of Stanford White's role in his wife's losing her virginity and brooded constantly upon the matter until, on June 25, 1906, during a performance of *Mamzelle Champagne* at the Roof Garden of Madison Square Garden, he shot White to death. Naturally, the murder and trial, or to be more precise, the two trials that followed, caused a sensation. "Stanny White was killed," Evelyn Nesbit reportedly said once, "but my fate was worse. I lived."

As early as October 1908, Evelyn Nesbit Thaw was offered $3,000 a week to appear in vaudeville. All that was required was that she be seated in a box during an audience song, but Mrs. Thaw declined, stating, "I will not consider the vaudeville stage under any circumstance." However, by 1913, her circumstances had changed. Harry Thaw's mother was determined that her daughter-in-law should return to the gutter, from which she was sure she had come, and Evelyn was having financial problems.

H. B. Marinelli, the highly successful international agent, arranged for her to appear in the 1913 revue *Hello Ragtime* at the London Hippodrome. Marinelli found her a partner in the person of Jack Clifford (whose real name was Virgil Montani), who had been teaching English society how to dance the fox-trot and one-step. After her success in *Hello Ragtime*, Nesbit was booked by William Hammerstein into his Victoria Theatre (New York) at $1,750 a week. He did not believe the publicity would sustain Evelyn Nesbit Thaw's appearances at the theatre for more than two weeks, but she insisted on a four-week guarantee and, in fact, had no problem in filling the theatre for that length of time. The management netted a profit of $100,000, which established Nesbit as the biggest single drawing card in any vaudeville theatre.

As for the act itself, which, incidentally, marked Mrs. Thaw's first Broadway appearance in ten years, it consisted of three dances, which she performed in a transparent, yellow, ankle-length dress with her hair hanging down her back. In the final dance, Nesbit clung around Clifford's neck while he swung her—shades of that red velvet swing! "It's a nice act if you don't stop to analyze too closely," reported *Variety* (August 8, 1913).

Still later in 1913, Nesbit toured for Comstock and Gest at a salary of $3,250 a week. In April 1914, she announced she would drop the name of Thaw. The Thaw family was giving her a number of problems. Not only had Harry K. Thaw an annoying habit of escaping from the mental institutions in which he was confined, but his mother had financed an organization of civic-minded women and religious leaders who demanded that Evelyn be arrested for immoral dancing wherever she appeared.

In September 1917, Evelyn Nesbit dropped Jack Clifford, whom she had married when her divorce from Thaw become final, from her act, and took a new dancing partner in Bobby O'Neill. She made occasional film appearances, beginning in 1914 with *Threads of Destiny*, followed by *Redemption* (1917), *Her Mistake* (1918), *I Want to Forget* (1918), *The Woman Who Gave* (1918), *A Fallen Idol* (1919), *My Little Sister* (1919), *Thou Shalt Not* (1919), *Woman, Woman!* (1919), and *The Hidden Woman* (1922). The plots might be fictional, but all exploited Evelyn Nesbit's image as a fallen woman. "I just have to succeed. I must make money for myself and my little boy. There's his education and all the years to come. I *must* be successful," she pitifully told a 1919 fan magazine reporter.

Nesbit's vaudeville career ended in the 1920s, although occasionally she appeared at such night spots as Chicago's Moulin Rouge, where, in 1925, she sang "I'm a Broad-Minded Broad from Broadway." During the prohibition era, she was involved in various roadhouses as a hostess and entertainer. In 1955, 20th Century–Fox produced a feature about her life, *The Girl in the Red Velvet Swing*, starring Joan Collins in the title role. It was not successful.

The last years of Evelyn Nesbit Thaw's life were spent in a downtown Los Angeles hotel room. She told a reporter in 1962, "I'm registered here under my maiden name, Evelyn Nesbit. I'm still reading and trying to understand, just as I did when I was a girl. I'm still interested in that world of art and music and beauty which Stanford White first showed me, so long ago." Harry K. Thaw died in Miami, Florida, in 1947. Evelyn Nesbit died in a Santa Monica, California, nursing home. She had become "The Tired Butterfly," the title of a famous photograph for which Nesbit posed on Stanford White's bearskin rug. Totally forgotten, Evelyn Nesbit Thaw's funeral was attended by only a handful of mourners.

BIBLIOGRAPHY

Haskins, Harrison. "Evelyn Nesbit, the Ambitious." *Motion Picture Magazine* 16, no. 12 (January 1919), pp. 38–39, 108.

Macdonald, Michael. *Evelyn Nesbit and Stanford White: Love and Death in the Gilded Cage*. New York: William Morrow, 1976.

Nesbit, Evelyn. *Prodigal Days: The Untold Story*. New York: Julian Messner, 1934.

THEATRE OWNERS BOOKING ASSOCIATION (TOBA)

The Theatre Owners Booking Association (TOBA) was organized in Chattanooga, Tennessee, in 1920 by a group of Southern and midwestern theatre owners to book Negro entertainers for all-black vaudeville theatres. From an initial group of thirty-one theatres, it grew to a circuit of more than eighty, booking black acts for entire seasons. In 1924, *The TOBA Revue* was produced by Albert Gibson, featuring the Gibson Trio, "Grasshopper" (a comedian), and Wilton Crawley (who was billed as "The Human Worm"). The Theatre Owners Booking Association was a powerful group which was much disliked by the Negro performers forced to work with it, and it was generally stated within the vaudeville fraternity that TOBA was, in reality, an acronym for "Tough on Black Asses."

BIBLIOGRAPHY

Sampson, Henry T. *Blacks in Blackface: A Source Book on Early Black Musical Show.* Metuchen, N.J.: Scarecrow Press, 1980.

"THINK-A-DRINK" HOFFMAN

The vaudeville act of "Think-a-Drink" Hoffman is not discussed in any of the volumes on vaudeville and its history, but it is one remembered fondly by many in the audience. Novelist Robert Bloch recalls:

Think-a-Drink Hoffman's act was primarily a patter-and-magic routine built around an old gimmick—a container which pours liquids of several different colors. But Hoffman expanded it by producing "drinks"—either introduced by himself or in response to requests from members of his audience. Thus, beer, champagne, red or white wine, martinis (probably with palmed olives), Bloody Marys, crème de menthe, and—the almost-inevitable grand finale of the now almost-forgotten—*pousse café*. Whether some of the "requests" came from stooges planted in the audience I don't know: one would assume so when Hoffman did his act in a long-running Broadway revue. But it's obvious, of course, that his container was "prepared"—with a series of compartments, each holding its individual concoctions, and operated most like by push-buttons in the handle of the pitcher or whatever was used—pressure causing release of compartment contents into the tube connected with the spout. (I imagine Hoffman used thick glassware with thick bases, so a minimal amount of liquid filled them and appeared larger.) The multi-layered *pousse café* was probably achieved by releasing the liquids in proper sequence, as in ordinary preparation; the heaviest and thickest first. I'm told it takes a skilled hand, and I'm sure Shemp Howard [of The Three Stooges] never prepared one in The Black Pussy Cafe.

LYDIA THOMPSON (London, February 19, 1836—London, November 17, 1908)

Lydia Thompson is generally dubbed "The Burlesque Queen," the woman responsible for introducing the "leg show," or modern version of burlesque, to the United States, although the description may be somewhat exaggerated. What she and her troupe of female performers brought to America was nothing more than the typical costumes worn by the female performer playing the principal boy in English pantomime.

The entertainer made her stage debut in 1852 as a dancer in a fairy ballet at London's Her Majesty's Theatre. The following year, Thompson made her debut in pantomime, and she became extremely popular in that medium, notably as Ali Baba in *The Forty Thieves*. In 1856, Lydia Thompson toured Europe, but it was not until the fall of 1868 that she came to the United States with what were billed as her "British Blondes," although many of the ladies were not blond. Among those in the troupe were Pauline Markham and Ada Harland (who married the distinguished drama critic Brander Matthews). It was the first time that a woman had brought a theatrical company to the United States, although her group was under the management of Thompson's husband, Alexander Henderson (whom she married in 1867, and who died in 1886). Thompson and her company returned on three other occasions to the United States, the last time in 1886, appearing in productions of *The Forty Thieves* and *Sinbad the Sailor*. As a solo performer, Thompson came back in 1892 with the musical comedy *The Dazzler*.

Despite the fact that Thompson and her company were not scantily clad and even their legs were clothed in flesh-colored tights, the critics and some members of the public were outraged. Writing in *Before the Footlights and Behind the Scenes* (1870), Olive Login complained of the "disgraceful spectacle of padded legs jiggling and wriggling," and wrote of Lydia Thompson's company: "They do not either act, dance, sing, or mime; but they habit themselves in a way which is attractive to an indelicate taste, and their inefficiency in other regards is overlooked." The editor of the *Chicago Times* denounced Thompson, calling the women of her company "ladies of the evening." Accompanied by her husband and various members of the troupe, the actress went to the editor's home and horse-whipped him. She was fined $100 for the assault.

Lydia Thompson formally retired in 1899, and something of the high esteem in which she was held in her native England may be understood by the fact that the farewell benefit in her honor at the Lyceum Theatre was chaired by Sir Henry Irving. Thompson's daughter Zeffie Tilbury (1863–1950) lived in the United States and ended her acting career in Hollywood films.

BIBLIOGRAPHY

Moses, Marlie. "Lydia Thompson and the 'British Blondes.' " In *Women in American Theatre*, ed. Helen Krich Chinoy and Linda Walsh Jenkins. New York: Theatre Communications Group, 1987, pp. 88–92.

BONNIE THORNTON (New York, circa 1871—New York, March 13, 1920)

Noted for her performance of sentimental and comic songs, Bonnie Thornton was one of vaudeville's first headliners. Born Elizabeth Cox, she made her vaudeville debut at the age of seventeen, and one of her first New York appearances was in August 1890 with the Henry Burlesque Company at the London Theatre. She was extremely popular in the late 1890s and early 1900s, often billed as "The Original Tutti-Frutti Girl," a title she acquired as a result of posing for Adams's Tutti-Frutti Chewing Gum wrappers.

Bonnie Thornton took her stage name from her husband, composer James Thornton (Liverpool, England, December 4, 1861—Astoria, N.Y., July 27, 1938), who appeared in vaudeville as a solo act and occasionally with his wife. She helped popularize his songs, including "She May Have Seen Better Days," "My Sweetheart's the Man in the Moon," "The Streets of Cairo," and "When You Were Sweet Sixteen." James Thornton was a notorious alcoholic, and much of his wife's time was spent in trying to keep him sober, usually to no avail. "I like the idea of being drunk continuously. It eliminates hangovers!" Thornton once explained.

Bonnie semiretired in 1915, running a millinery establishment in New York. She made one final vaudeville appearance with her husband in the fall of 1919.

THREE KEATONS

While they toured vaudeville circuits for many years and were fairly popular with audiences—but never as major headliners—the chief interest in the Three Keatons lies in the fact that the youngest of them was Buster Keaton (Piqua, Ks., October 4, 1895—Los Angeles, February 1, 1966). Buster Keaton's birth occurred while his parents, Joe (1867–1946) and Myra Keaton (1877–1955), were on the road with the Mohawk Medicine Company. Joe was an eccentric dancer and acrobat, while Myra danced and played the cornet. The Two Keatons were best known for an act titled "The Man with the Table," which consisted of Joe's performing strenuous and violent acrobatics on a kitchen table with Myra entertaining the audience during the intervals while he rested.

The young Keaton may have joined his parents' act at the age of six months, and it is often stated he became an official member of the act in 1898. However, it would appear that, in reality, he did not become a permanent member of the company until October 23, 1900, when the Three Keatons came into being in Easton, Pennsylvania. By this time, Buster had been given his familiar nickname by family friend Harry Houdini. As the comedian recalled in a 1921 interview, "Up to the time I was six months old, I had the somewhat dignified name of Francis Joseph. And then, one day, I fell downstairs; all the way down; from the top to the landing. 'What a buster,' said Harry Houdini, when he found I wasn't hurt. And, 'Buster's his name!' said my father; so I've been Buster even since!"

When Buster Keaton first joined the act, his contribution consisted of imitations and burlesque dancing. The *New York Clipper* (July 20, 1901) reported, "The tiny comedian is perfectly at ease in his work, natural, finished, and artistic, and his specialties have proved a fetching addition to the favorite act of the Keatons." In time, the whirlwind comedy of The Three Keatons became more violent, centering on a savage, knockabout sketch between a father and his rebellious son. A 1905 advertisement for the act read, "Maybe you think you were handled roughly when you were a kid. Watch the way they handle Buster!"

The beatings that Buster took onstage bothered many in the audience. The comedian recalled, "When we were in England, the manager of the theatre insisted that I must have been stolen, or adopted, or something. He said that no parents would treat their own son as my father and mother treated me! And on another occasion in New York, I had to be carried before the Governor of the state and stripped in order to prove that I had no broken bones! As a matter of fact, I didn't even have any bruises."

The Three Keatons toured the Kohl and Castle, Hopkins, Keith, and Proctor circuits. They wore grotesque costumes, with the men sporting baggy pants and coats, fuzzy black wigs with skin masks over the fronts of their heads, and pasty-face makeup. The act broke up in February 1917, when Keaton alone was signed by the Shubert Brothers for the 1917 edition of *The Passing Show*. However, while walking down Broadway, Keaton met a fellow vaudevillian, Lou Anger (who was later to become his manager), and comedian Roscoe "Fatty" Arbuckle, who persuaded Keaton to appear in films with him. Keaton never went into *The Passing Show*, but instead worked with Arbuckle in *The Butcher Boy* (1917), the first of fifteen films in which the two were teamed. He enjoyed his greatest successes on-screen in the 1920s in such classics as *Our Hospitality* (1923), *The Navigator* (1924), *Seven Chances* (1925), *The General* (1926), and *Steamboat Bill, Jr.* (1928). Curiously, the films offered a comedic style that was all Keaton's own and owed little to his early years in vaudeville. The important elements that Keaton did bring from vaudeville to films were his impassive style and stone-face demeanor. As he recalled in his autobiography, "I learned as a kid growing up with an audience that I just had to be that type of comedian—if I laughed at what I did, the audience didn't."

The same dependence upon alcohol that had hurt his father's career also hurt Buster's. But he did continue to appear on-screen, in lesser roles, through the 1960s, by which time a new generation of filmgoers had discovered his silent comedies. A 1957 film biography, *The Buster Keaton Story*, starred Donald O'Connor.

BIBLIOGRAPHY
Anobile, Richard J., ed. *The Best of Buster: The Classic Comedy Scenes Direct from the Films of Buster Keaton*. New York: Darien House, 1976.

Benayoun, Robert. *The Look of Buster Keaton*. New York: St. Martin's Press, 1983.

Bishop, Christopher, "The Great Stone Face." *Film Quarterly* 12, no. 1 (Fall 1958), pp. 10–22.

Blesh, Rudi. *Keaton*. New York: Macmillan, 1966.

Coursodon, Jean Pierre, ed. *Keaton et Cie: Les Burlesques Americains du "Muet."* Paris: Editions Seghers, 1964.

Cuenca, Carlos Fernandez. *Buster Keaton*. Madrid: Filmoteca Nacional de España, 1967.

Dardis, Tom. *Keaton: The Man Who Wouldn't Lie Down*. New York: Charles Scribner's Sons, 1979.

Friedman, Arthur B. "Buster Keaton: An Interview." *Film Quarterly* 19, no. 4 (Summer 1966), pp. 2–5.

Gillett, John, and James Blue. "Keaton at Venice." *Sight and Sound* 35, no. 1 (Winter 1965/66), pp. 26–30.

Keaton, Buster, with Charles Samuels. *My Wonderful World of Slapstick*. Garden City, N.Y.: Doubleday, 1960.

Lebel, J.-P. *Buster Keaton*. New York: A. S. Barnes, 1967.

Moews, Daniel. *Keaton: The Silent Features Close Up*. Berkeley: University of California Press, 1977.

Mulligan, W. E. "The Man Who Never Smiles." *Pantomime* 1, no. 2 (October 5, 1921), p. 5.

Peltret, Elizabeth. "Poor Child!" *Motion Picture Classic* 12, no. 1 (March 1921), pp. 64, 96–97.

Robinson, David. *Buster Keaton*. London: Secker & Warburg, 1969.

Turconi, Davide, ed. *Buster Keaton*. Venice, Italy: Edizioni M.I.A.C., 1963.

Wead, George, and George Lellis. *The Film Career of Buster Keaton*. Pleasantville, N.Y.: Redgrave, 1977.

THREE X SISTERS

A sister act similar in style and delivery to the Boswell Sisters and the Pickens Sisters, the Three X Sisters enjoyed minor popularity in the early 1930s on radio and recordings and in vaudeville. To add an air of mystery to their work, Jessie, Pearl, and Violet Hamilton decided to bill themselves as the X Sisters, and they worked in England in the early 1930s before becoming steady entertainers on CBS radio in 1932; they were starred in programs sponsored by Tydol, Hellmann, Ford, Chase & Sanborn, and Bab-O, and also appeared in short film subjects for Paramount and Warner Bros. According to *Radio Digest* (November 1932), "The question as to whether they can harmonize or not is pretty well known, as they had not been on CBS a week before they were sought for records and movies. They had to go to Europe to gain their first recognition. There they were acclaimed in a whirlwind tour of harmony and cross-fire chit-chat."

BIBLIOGRAPHY

"X & X & X." *Radio Digest*, November 1932, p. 9.

THURSTON (Columbus, Oh., July 20, 1869—Miami Beach, Fl., April 13, 1936)

Howard Thurston, billed always simply as "Thurston," was the successor to American vaudeville's first great magician, Harry Kellar, whose show he purchased in 1908. As a child, he ran away from home and worked in circus sideshows, perfecting the card manipulation for which he was to become highly regarded. No one could present the trick of the rising card better than Thurston. Influenced by Alexander Herrmann, the first magician whom he saw perform, Thurston developed a vaudeville act that he took to Europe, Australia, and the Orient. He joined Harry Kellar's vaudeville tour on his return to the United States, and on May 16, 1908, at Ford's Theatre, Baltimore, Kellar introduced Thurston as his successor.

He developed a number of specialties, including making an automobile disappear onstage and the Indian rope trick, in which a boy climbed to the top of the rope and vanished. *Variety* (May 16, 1913) reviewed his two-hour show at the New National Theatre on New York's Second Avenue and commented, "Thurston has developed into a magician of much expertness, some originality, and considerable showmanship. Neither of these things were predicted for him upon the Great Kellar, when retiring a few years ago, placing his Kingly Magical mantle upon Thurston.''

In December 1924, he appeared at the White House before President Calvin Coolidge, and the high spot of his act was destroying Coolidge's pocket watch before making it disappear, then reappear intact in the middle of a loaf of bread. In 1925, he introduced what Ricky Jay in *Learned Pigs and Fireproof Women* describes as "what was then the largest illusion in the world: the disappearance of 'Beauty,' the Arabian steed. Beauty and his robed rider were hauled high above the stage on a swinging platform. The platform was covered for an instant and the horse and rider seemed to vanish in midair.'' The illusion was sold the following year to another magician, Dante.

Thurston was, apparently, somewhat arrogant toward his audiences and his fellow performers, and he lacked a sense of humor. Film historian Jack Spears recalled:

Thurston didn't seem very warm in his personality, not like Blackstone later on, and lacked humor. He also did mind-reading, using a woman on the stage who was blindfolded and presumably read his mind. I was in an aisle seat, Thurston placed his hand on my head and said, "What color is the kid's hair?" When the mindreader said, "Red" (which was right), Thurston said, "No—it's auburn!" And everybody laughed but me—I didn't know what auburn meant! Maybe Thurston did have a sense of humor!

The magician remained active through the 1930s, often revising his act in order to present a full evening of entertainment. He was perhaps one of the first magicians to understand the need for glamour in presentation, replacing those who had assisted Kellar with attractive showgirls.

VESTA TILLEY (Worcester, England, May 13, 1864—London, September 16, 1952)

Arguably the greatest of all male impersonators, Vesta Tilley was certainly the best known. She was a slightly built, flat-chested woman, and her male characterizations, played in evening dress or military attire, were more reminiscent of boys than men. Tilley played a dapper little man—as one critic wrote, "the dandiest fellah turned sixteen.'' There was little spontaneity to her characterization, for every movement and inflection had been carefully rehearsed. There are probably few alive today who saw Vesta Tilley on the stage, and thus it is hard to explain her fame, which is perhaps based chiefly on the fact that she was the first woman to adopt totally masculine dress in her act. Prior to Tilley's appearance on the scene, female performers had usually portrayed male characters in tights and strictly feminine versions of male clothing. But once she arrived, there was no one who would argue with the statement in *Variety* (December 18, 1909), "For male impersonations Vesta Tilley is the standard.''

By all accounts, Tilley's voice was not particularly strong, but she had clear enunciation. "Master of her characters, she was mistress of herself,'' wrote the distinguished British theatre critic James Agate. It was not particularly her voice that made her a star, but rather her manner and the style in which she comported herself. As Will M. Cressy wrote in *The Green Book Magazine* (March 1916), "If Vesta Tilley could not sing a note nor speak a word, she could *walk* her songs successfully. There has never been a player who could paint a character more clearly by word or note than she can by her walk."

Born Matilda Alice Powles, she was the daughter of Harry Ball, who was the chairman (or master of ceremonies) at St. George's Music Hall in Nottingham, England, and it was on the stage of her father's theatre in 1868 that Vesta Tilley made her debut. She first appeared in male attire at the age of five and continued to adopt that guise for the rest of her career. In her autobiography, she wrote, "I concluded that female costume was rather a drag. I felt I could express myself better if I were dressed as a boy." By 1876, she was fairly popular in provincial British music halls; appearing with her father, she was billed as "The Great Little Tilley." Her London debut came on March 25, 1878 at the Royal Theatre, Holborn. She sang "The Pet of Rotten Row" and "Near the Workhouse Door," and thereafter she became known as "The London Idol."

Tilley made her first American appearance at Tony Pastor's on April 16, 1894, and was hailed by critic Alan Dale as "The Irving of the Halls," a reference to the great theatrical star Sir Henry Irving. "Chicot" saw her at the Colonial Theatre in May 1906 and wrote in *Variety* (May 5, 1906), "She is the one male impersonator on the stage today who really looks like a boy; her costumes are exact and she wears a wig that might well be her own hair. . . . But Miss Tilley is something more than a clotheshorse. She is a leader of style and every detail of dress is merely the complement to her detail of rendition. She is an artist."

The entertainer returned to the United States in 1905, beginning with an engagement again at the Colonial Theatre on April 5. She was invited to return for a vaudeville tour in 1912, but she turned down $4,000 a week rather than work on Sundays.

The songs for which Vesta Tilley is most famous are "After the Ball" (the title of a 1957 British film loosely based on her life, with Pat Kirkwood as the star), "Following in Father's Footsteps," and "Algy" ("the Piccadilly Johnny with the Little Glass Eye"). During the First World War, she sang "Jolly Good Luck to the Girl That Loves a Sailor," which became a recruiting song, as did her "I Joined the Army Yesterday, So the Army of Today's All Right." She was the first male impersonator to appear at a royal command performance—in 1912—but legend has it that Queen Mary was so offended by the idea of a woman's dressing as a man that she turned her back on the star.

On June 5, 1920, Vesta Tilley gave her farewell performance at the London Coliseum. She sang "Jolly Good Luck to the Girl That Loves a Sailor" and took seventeen curtain calls. Ellen Terry presented her with "The People's Tribute to Vesta Tilley," a number of volumes containing two million signatures of her admirers. She had married Walter de Frece, who managed many British music halls, on August 6, 1890. Between 1920 and 1931, he was a member of

Parliament, and his wife actively helped promote his career. He died in Monaco in January 1935. Vesta Tilley never returned to the stage after her 1920 farewell, preferring life as Lady de Frece.

At that farewell performance, she sang the line "Girls, if you'd like to love a sailor, you can all love me." Back from the gallery came the shout, "We do!"

BIBLIOGRAPHY

Slide, Anthony. *Great Pretenders: A History of Female and Male Impersonation in the Performing Arts*. Lombard, Il.: Wallace-Homestead, 1986.

Tilley, Vesta. *Recollections of Vesta Tilley*. London: Hutchinson, 1934.

HERMAN TIMBERG (1892—New York, April 16, 1952)

A comedy monologist, Herman Timberg would often leave the stage, at the end of his act, walking on all fours. Aside from his verbal humor, Timberg was also agile and would perform trick violin playing. He first came to prominence in the role of an immigrant boy in *School Days*, a musical play in three acts by Aaron Hoffman, with music by Gus Edwards, which opened at New York's Circle Theatre on September 14, 1908. He appeared in *The Passing Show of 1916, Doing Our Bit* (1917), and *Tick-Tack-Toe* (1920, which he also wrote). Timberg provided material for other vaudevillians, wrote but did not appear in *Crazy Quilt* (1931) and *You'll See Stars* (1943), and was also active in motion pictures and radio. He headlined at the Palace in June 1929, January 1931, and April 1932. On that last occasion, he appeared in an act with Pat Rooney, and each man was supported by his son. "Tim" Timberg had initially billed himself as Herman Timberg, Jr., but later, as Tim, he performed a double act with Don Saxon. Despite being nearly blind, Herman Timberg made one final appearance at the Palace in 1951.

FRANK TINNEY (Philadelphia, March 29, 1878—Northport, N.Y., November 28, 1940)

Arguably the best of vaudeville's blackface comics, following in the footsteps of George "Honey Boy" Evans, Frank Tinney was described by Joe Cook as "the greatest natural comic ever developed in America." He would appear onstage with a cigar in his mouth and would often indulge in impromptu chatter with the orchestra director. His humor was, on the whole, dreadful. At the Palace in June 1915, he told the story of the goat without a nose. "How does he smell?" asked the orchestra director. "Awful" was the reply. Other comic lines from Tinny include:

"Lend me a dollar for a week, old man."

"Who is the weak old man?"

and

"Why is an old maid like a green tomater?"

"Because it's hard to mate her."

"Tinney is elemental, but he is funny—now and then" was the opinion of

Frederick James Smith in *The New York Dramatic Mirror* (June 16, 1915). Perhaps the humor was as much in Tinney's delivery as in itself, for "Wynn" in *Variety* (June 4, 1910), reviewing one of Tinney's first vaudeville appearances at the Fifth Avenue Theatre, wrote, "His material consists of a bunch of nothingness moulded together into seventeen minutes of original and rare humor. . . . Tinney's is the most original offering brought to Broadway this season." When not chatting with the orchestra director, Tinney would confide in the audience, perhaps telling them that the leading lady was so crazy about him she couldn't answer when he spoke to her, but simply looked at him without a word.

Tinney claimed to have made his first stage appearance, in blackface, at the age of four at Philadelphia's Bijou Theatre. From Philadelphia, his mother took him to Texas, where he perfected his blackface comedy routine, and where he was spotted by a vaudeville agent named Max Hart, whose clients included Eddie Cantor, Fred Stone, the Avon Comedy Four, and Blossom Seeley. Hart brought Tinney to New York and introduced him to big-time vaudeville. By 1913, the comic was earning $1,000 a week at Hammerstein's Victoria Theatre. That same year he made his London debut at the Palace and was an immediate success, described as "the most irresistible entertainer that America has sent us." Tinney returned to London in 1914, 1919, 1924, and 1925.

The year 1913 marked a changing point in Tinney's career, in that he also made his first appearance in the Ziegfeld *Follies*, where his ad-libbing made him as much a success as the *Follies'* other comedian, Leon Errol. Throughout his early career, Frank Tinney alternated vaudeville with appearances in Broadway shows such as *Watch Your Step* (1914), *The Century Girl* (1916), and *Doing Our Bit* (1917). In the 1920s, he dropped the blackface, but as he had never adopted a Negro voice, it meant relatively little change in his material. He did reintroduce a novelty from the early years of vaudeville, making his navel whistle, a performance reminiscent of a French act from the turn of the century in which an entertainer named Le Petomane would play tunes and perform various stunts with his anus.

In 1924, Frank Tinney made headlines when he consistently beat up a *Follies* showgirl named Imogene Wilson, with whom he was romantically involved. One sordid story had Tinney's taking a pair of scissors and cutting off one of the girl's nipples in a drunken rage. Wilson fled the country, obtained film work in Germany, and subsequently became a fairly popular American film star under the name of Mary Nolan (Louisville, Ky., December 18, 1905—Los Angeles, October 31, 1948). In 1926, Tinney suffered a complete breakdown, in part brought on by the Imogene Wilson scandal, and retired from the stage. His service as a captain in the Quartermasters Corps during the First World War made him eligible to enter the Veteran's Hospital at Northport, Long Island, and there he died.

BIBLIOGRAPHY

Mullett, Mary B. "Frank Tinney's Job Is to Make People Laugh." *American Mercury*,
        February 1921, pp. 34–35, 122–27.
Vane, Timothy. "From Funeral to Fun." *Everybody's*, June 1921, pp. 30–31.

LYDIA YEAMANS TITUS (at sea between Sydney and Melbourne, Australia, 1866—Glendale, Ca., December 30, 1929)

A busy character actress on stage and screen, Lydia Yeamans Titus also enjoyed an extensive career in vaudeville, where she helped popularize the song "Sally in Our Alley." Married to actor Frederick Titus, Lydia Yeamans Titus ended her career after suffering a stroke two years before her death.

TORONTO

In 1906, there were only two vaudeville theatres in Toronto, the Star and Shea's. By 1921, at which time the city had a population of 801,000, there were three: the Pantages, Shea's, and Shea's Hippodrome.

TOTO (Genf, Switzerland, 1888—New York, December 15, 1938)

One of the few circus clowns who became a regular feature on the vaudeville stage, Toto would always make his entrance in a toy car that was far too small for him, let alone his dog, Whiskey, who came along for the ride. After starring in a series of comedy shorts for Hal Roach, Toto (whose real name was Alfonso Novello) made his vaudeville debut in San Francisco in September 1918, sponsored by male impersonator Kathleen Clifford. "Toto goes through various contortion stunts, which in his fantastic and grotesque makeup are more agreeable, and does not appear as unattractive as the usual contortion turn," commented *Variety* (September 6, 1918).

In the 1920s, Toto might have been considered a fixture of the New York Hippodrome were he not equally at home on the stage of the Palace. He headlined at the Hippodrome in February 1924 and April 1926, and was at the Palace in June 1926, September 1929, and June 1932. He retired in the 1930s and operated the Greenhaven Inn at Mamaroneck, New York.

Toto's death was a virtual comedy of errors. On November 27, 1938, the New York *Daily Mirror* printed a false story that Toto had died. His lawyer prepared a libel action against the newspaper, but just as it was about to be served, Toto developed peritonitis and died. His death came just as he was planning a comeback, having been booked, at $650 a week, to play the Christmas season at the Oriental Theatre, Chicago.

ARTHUR TRACY (Philadelphia, June 3, 1903—   )

"Radio's Voice of Romance," Arthur Tracy had a fine baritone voice with the hint of a rich Irish brogue. He was at his best singing sentimental ballads such as "Trees," "It's My Mother's Birthday Today," "In a Little Gypsy Tea Room," "Danny Boy," and, of course, his theme song, "Marta" (the "ramblin' rose of the wildwood" who rambled through radio, vaudeville, and films with considerable success in the 1930s). Tracy always took himself very seriously, and that helped with the type of material he had to sing. British actress Margaret Lockwood, who was Arthur Tracy's leading lady in the 1937 film *The Street*

Singer, remembered that he would sit for hours in his dressing room, listening to his own recordings with tears of emotion in his eyes.

"I started singing when I was about six years old," recalled Tracy. "I sang in churches, synagogues, at weddings and parties, wherever I could get a dollar in those days." Initially, he took lessons at $4 a week, and he also learned a lot from his father. In addition, he would listen to the recordings of Caruso, buy sheet music of the arias, and mark Caruso's nuances. As far as Tracy is concerned, Caruso was his teacher, although he also acknowledges a great debt to Horatio Connell, "a fine baritone," one of his instructors at Philadelphia's Curtis Institute. In Philadelphia in 1927, Tracy was booked into the Logan Theatre on North Broad Street and played there for eleven months. He sang the type of songs with which he has always been associated, and notes, "The audience itself teaches you how to behave onstage." At this time, Tracy was approached by the Philadelphia Opera Society to perform with them at $200 an appearance, but, as he admitted later with regret, he turned the offer down because he was making $300 a week in vaudeville at the Logan.

On July 31, 1931, he was heard on 187 CBS stations with his own program, in which he was billed simply as "The Street Singer." "Overnight, I'm happy to report, it was sensational," he commented with pride, and soon Tracy had four fifteen-minute shows a week on CBS and was earning a weekly salary of $3,000. "I liked to be known as the Street Singer," he recalled:

I loved the air of mystery on the program, with its closing announcement of "There he goes, your Street Singer, to pick new melodies for your entertainment." I was only known to the trade, the music men. By the third week of my appearances on the air I was getting 2,000 letters a week, the majority asking who the Street Singer was. When Mr. Bill Paley gave me six weeks to do or die, as he said, I had six weeks in which to prepare my program. I worked to conceal my identity. I finally decided because of the international scope of my work—ten languages—and the types of songs that I would call myself the International Balladeer. These days prior to my first program, I picked up *The New York Times*, turned to the theatre page, and found an item which said Freddie Lonsdale had just arrived with a new play titled *The Street Singer*. I thought "My God, why didn't I think of that?" For fear of being accused of plagiarism I appended the phrase "of the air"—calling myself the Street Singer of the Air—but then a lawyer told me I didn't need that because you can't copyright the English language.

After five months on radio, the identity of "The Street Singer" was revealed.

"Marta" became Arthur Tracy's theme song in August 1931. He recalled, "Having adopted the title of Street Singer, I temporarily adopted 'East Side, West Side' as my theme song, but as I went on for some three or four weeks doing it, I realized it did not fit into my type of singing, my type of program. I went around in search of some beautiful melody to adopt, something new. I walked into Marks Music one day when I heard this beautiful strain coming from behind a closed door. I walked in, and there was a little Cuban—he was so tiny his feet didn't even touch the floor—and he was playing this beautiful strain. I wanted to buy the song, but Mr. Marks said, 'No, songs that are demonstrated in my office, I buy them.' So he bought it. Millions have been made off that song. The Cuban had peddled the song for eight years and no one would buy it.'' Arthur Tracy has recorded ''Marta'' many times in a recording career that began in 1931 with ''I'm All Dressed Up with a Broken Heart'' for RCA, and by 1990 included some 750 recordings.

One of Tracy's earliest major vaudeville bookings was as ''The Mystery Man of the Air'' at the New York Hippodrome in December 1931. *Variety* was not impressed by his act, describing Tracy as a neutral performer who used no showmanship. ''What suggests a splendid voice is spoiled by a cold style of presentation,'' commented ''Rush'' at the end of his review. As Arthur Tracy's radio fame grew—in 1932 he was featured along with Ruth Etting and the Boswell Sisters on Chesterfield's *Music That Satisfies*—his vaudeville career expanded. Vaudeville offered radio listeners an opportunity to meet their favorite singers in person, and it also provided Tracy with the means to polish and perfect his act.

In 1935, Tracy went to England for a seven-week vaudeville tour and remained there for six years, starring in five films: *Flirtation* (1935), *Limelight* (1935), *The Street Singer* (1937), *Command Performance* (1937), and *Follow Your Star* (1938). He had earlier appeared in the 1932 Paramount film tribute to radio, *The Big Broadcast*, and also made a few short subjects. Tracy's style seemed to suit the English mood; well into the 1980s, he still had a fan club in England, and Tracy's recordings continue to be available there. Interestingly, Tracy's singing style is very similar to that of the British Cavan O'Connor, who began his career as a mystery singer on the BBC in the early 1930s, billed as ''The Vagabond Lover.''

Arthur Tracy returned to the United States in 1941 and continued his career. The accordion he once used was dropped because, as he was quick to admit, he was not a good accordionist, and without being tied to the instrument, he is able to make eloquent use of his hands.

The singer enjoyed something of a comeback—although he would argue he had never been away—in 1982, when his 1937 recording of ''Pennies from Heaven'' was used by M-G-M in the musical of the same title, lip-synched on-screen by Vernal Bagneris. Audiences were taken by Tracy's emotional rendering of the song, and he was booked for a cabaret engagement at New York's Cookery in February and March 1982. ''What may have seemed mawkish, sentimental, and stiff to young Crosby fans half a century ago now has a delightful patina of period charm,'' wrote John S. Wilson in *The New York Times* (February 28, 1982). ''At the Cookery, Mr. Tracy is a spellbinder, setting a mood and scene, disarming the doubters by admitting that 'I always put all the schmaltz I had into my songs.' '' He was accompanied on the piano by Elliot Finkle, son of Yiddish actor Fyvish Finkle.

After a thirty-five-year absence from the stage, Arthur Tracy was hired by director Mike Nichols to appear as a ninety-eight-year-old artist in the 1987 touring version of *Social Security*. There were a number of publicized problems between Tracy and the play's star, Lucie Arnaz, who did not appreciate her fellow performer's need to sing at backstage parties or his long-winded speeches.

While there is no question that Arthur Tracy was possessed of a considerable ego, there is no doubt as to his appeal to his audiences. With his unsophisticated songs, he is a pleasant throwback to an earlier, simpler, unamplified time in show business when, as Tracy pointed out, audiences recognized that what came from the heart goes to the heart.

BIBLIOGRAPHY

Smith, Bill. "Arthur Tracy." In *The Vaudevillians*. New York: Macmillan, 1976, pp. 219–28.

THE TROUPERS CLUB

A Hollywood based, fraternal, theatrical organization, the Troupers was founded in 1925, with the original primary requisite for membership being thirty years in the profession. By 1926, the original membership of nine had grown to 100; they called themselves The Cast and attended meetings dubbed "Rehearsals." For many years, the small Troupers Theatre was a familiar site on La Brea Avenue in Hollywood, but today the organization gives showcase performances for actors, producers, and directors at the Women's Club of Hollywood.

Address: 7080 Hollywood Boulevard, Suite 809, Hollywood, CA. 90028.

SOPHIE TUCKER (Boston, Poland, or Russia, January 13, 1887—New York, February 9, 1966)

As the lyrics of her theme song, "Some of These Days," explain, Sophie Tucker was the "red-hot mama" who, with age, became everybody's "big fat mama." And along the way, as she added the pounds, Tucker became an American institution. The plump Sophie Tucker of later years was described by one critic as "a glistening iceberg cut loose from its foundation"; to an earlier generation, to her vaudeville and burlesque audiences, she was slim, not exactly beautiful, but certainly not unattractive, and she had a sexy, vibrant way with a song. She claimed to have originated jazz on the stage, and, who knows?, perhaps she did, for she had a flair for songs such as "We Are Simply Full of Jazz" and "When Fan Tan Takes Her Jazz Band to Tokyo." A writer in *Life* captured the essence of her style when he wrote, "Her exuberance and racy songs made people feel wicked without the wear and tear of being so." But there was a gentler side to her singing, a side that she exhibited less and less as she grew older. Mrs. Gus Kahn recalled, "She could sing a ballad beautifully. She could sing anything—anything at all." Who else could have put such feeling into "My Yiddishe Mama"? The style was brassy and loud, and Tucker talked a song as much as she sang it; there was a worldliness in her voice, but there was also kindness and compassion.

As she grew older—and fatter—Sophie Tucker realized the need for glamorous clothes and for songs that poked fun at her girth and her age, songs like "Life

Begins at Forty.'' She would still sing the old standards, such as ''Some of These Days,'' written in 1910 by Shelton Brooks, and ''After You've Gone,'' written in 1918 by Henry Creamer and Turner Layton, but she added new, saucy numbers to her repertoire. With the advancing years came ''I'm the 3-D Momma with the Big Wide Screen,'' ''I May Be Getting Older Every Day (But Getting Younger Every Night),'' ''There's No Business Like That Certain Business—That Certain Business Called Love,'' and, of course, ''I'm the Last of the Red Hot Mamas.'' The title was self-given, but it was certainly deserved, summing up her vitality and zest for living.

As she wrote in her autobiography, Sophie Tucker was born on the road, not on a vaudeville circuit, but the road between Russia and the United States while the family was emigrating. Her parents' name was Kalish, but her father changed it to Abuza for fear of the Russians discovering that he was a deserter from the military. Sophie Abuza was born probably in Poland on January 13, 1887, although in early years she claimed the year to be 1888, and in later life to be 1884. Anyway, whatever the year, Sophie Tucker arrived in the United States at the age of three months.

Sophie's parents opened a restaurant in Hartford, Connecticut, and there she began to sing for the customers. At the age of thirteen, she was singing in amateur concerts, and also while still in her teens she was married, albeit briefly, to Louis Tuck, from whose last name her stage name originated. In 1906, she told Willie Howard—who was playing Poli's Theatre in New Haven with his brother Eugene—that she was determined to enter show business, and he gave her a letter of introduction to composer Harry Von Tilzer (''Wait 'til the Sun Shines Nellie,'' ''A Bird in a Gilded Cage,'' ''I Want a Girl Just Like the Girl That Married Dear Old Dad,'' etc.). He was unable to help her, but at least Sophie was in New York, and eventually she got a job singing at the Cafe Monopol. ''I worked on Second Avenue in one place where I not only sang but had to wash dishes and make knishes,'' she recalled. ''Not many young performers of today would be willing to sacrifice their lives for their profession as we did in those days.''

More amateur nights followed at the 125th Street Theatre, where Sophie Tucker performed her act in blackface for the first time. Blackface became an established part of her early act, and she was soon billed as ''The World-Renowned Coon Shouter.'' Following her first professional New York vaudeville appearance at the 116th Street Music Hall, Tucker became a regular in small-town houses. She appeared at Tony Pastor's 14th Street Theatre, and *The New York Dramatic Mirror* (April 18, 1908) commented, ''On the whole, the impression she created was distinctly favorable.'' She was booked on the Manchester and Hills burlesque circuit, and while playing a theatre in Holyoke, Massachusetts, she was seen by Marc Klaw of the theatrical concern Klaw and Erlanger, and he offered her a part in the second edition of the Ziegfeld *Follies*.

There is some confusion as to what happened when Sophie Tucker went into the 1909 Ziegfeld *Follies*. During the tryout in Atlantic City, she claims in her autobiography that her songs went over too well for the comfort of the star, Nora Bayes, who ordered the newcomer's numbers cut to one. This statement is not substantiated by *Variety*, which in its issue of June 12, 1909, reported that the *Follies* had opened the previous Monday and that "Sophie Tucker received little chance." Certainly, when the *Follies* opened in New York at the Jardin de Paris on June 14, 1909, Sophie Tucker was performing only one number in a Kermit Roosevelt jungle sketch. *Variety* made no specific comment on Tucker's song, but in mentioning her and another burlesque star new to the *Follies*, a Miss MacMahon, it noted that "both the burlesquers made good." If Nora Bayes did best Sophie Tucker in 1909, then Tucker certainly got the best of Bayes in 1927, when both were on the bill at a National Vaudeville Association benefit at the Palace. An argument erupted between the two as to who would appear first; Bayes announced that she was the headliner and would not permit Tucker to go on in advance of her, but Tucker won the fight largely because the Palace booker, Eddie Darling, was tired of Bayes's temperament and inconsiderateness. Bayes was publicly humiliated, and Sophie Tucker was, as usual, the hit of the show.

After the brief, unproductive spell in the *Follies*, it was back to vaudeville and the slow climb to headliner status. *Variety* first reviewed Sophie Tucker on September 4, 1909, reporting, "The young woman has a way of ingratiating herself at once, and possesses not only good looks but magnetism to back it." *The New York Dramatic Mirror* (September 11, 1909) reviewed Sophie Tucker's vaudeville act at the same time:

> From the small time to the big time is a long jump and many there are who have slipped or stumbled in the attempting of it. Sophie Tucker is another recruit from the lower rungs of the vaudeville and amusement ladder, who is about to find her own. She certainly deserves it! Seldom is such a vivacious, intense and entertaining personality found in one body. Miss Tucker fairly lifts a person out of his seat. She has a very powerful voice of the "coon shouting" calibre, but which she used to such good advantage that the harshness of it is forgotten and her higher and lower notes are quite pleasing. But it isn't her voice—it's her ability to act. Musical comedy will undoubtedly soon take her away from the variety stage and we will then no longer hear her sing "The Cubanola Glide," "My Southern Rose," "Carrie and Harry" and "The Wild Cherry Rag." On Thursday afternoon she received five bows and was then forced to given an encore. But her gown! Whoever designed it must have thought the main idea is to get everything in the trimming line on one gown. " 'Nuff said!''

Under the guidance of William Morris, Sophie Tucker's fame and popularity grew. When she appeared at the American Music Hall in Chicago, Ashton Stevens wrote of her, "If Julian Eltinge's singing voice was as virile as Miss Tucker's, he would be executing a long overdue male impersonation. . . . Miss Tucker can move an audience or a piano with equal address." On July 24, 1914, Tucker made her debut at the Palace, on a bill that also included Joseph Santley, Chic Sale, and Sam Barton, "the cycling pantomimist." *Variety* (July 31, 1914) reported, "Sophie let loose her 40-h.p. voice and sang six songs," including "There's a Girl in the Heart of Maryland," "The International Rag," and "Who

Paid the Rent for Mrs. Rip Van Winkle (When Rip Van Winkle Went Away)?''
In her study of the Palace, Marian Spitzer wrote, "If any one person could be
said to have symbolized the Palace in its greatest days, that person was Sophie
Tucker." But Tucker did not merely symbolize the Palace—she symbolized,
and indeed was, vaudeville.

In the summer of 1916, Sophie Tucker added five young men to her act,
billing them as the "Kings of Syncopation." They would add to the performance
of such songs as "I've Got a Bungalow," with its lyric:

> My bills are shocking,
> But I've got a Santa Claus,
> Who fills my stocking.

The boys were also featured with Tucker on the cover of the sheet music for
"Ev'rybody Shimmies Now."

Around this time, Tucker was taking credit for the introduction of the shimmy
to vaudeville, and she explained to *The New York Dramatic Mirror* (February
1, 1919), "When I was known as a coon shouter, I executed a Jazz and Shimmie
rhythm with every song. As inventors of Jazz and Shimmie, these other birds
are wonderful aviators—their imagination takes such long flights. But don't wake
them up. Just let them dream, for I'm getting the stuff that buys Liberty Bonds."

Sophie Tucker deserted vaudeville late in 1918 for an extended engagement
at Reisenweber's, a popular restaurant and cabaret at Eighth Avenue and 58th
Street. Here she introduced one of her most famous blues numbers, "A Good
Man Is Hard to Find," singing it nightly for ten consecutive weeks. From
Reisenweber's, Tucker went into the McIntyre and Heath Show *Hello Alexander*,
and from there returned to vaudeville at the Colonial, singing "Vamp a Little
Lady," "The Wonderful Kid from Madrid," and "Won't You Bless Everybody
That's Worth Blessing in My Suwanee Home?," among others. "It's a great
act," reported *The New York Dramatic Mirror* (December 25, 1919). "Here's
hoping vaudeville doesn't let her get away again."

There have been many jokes about Tucker's endless farewell performances,
but there might have been just as many jokes about her returns to vaudeville in
the teens and 1920s, each return accompanied by a new act and new songs.
There were many personifications, but when all was said and done, there was
only the same, beloved Sophie Tucker. In 1922, she was appearing onstage with
two male piano players, discussing her private life with the audience. One of
those pianists was Ted Shapiro, who remained with Sophie Tucker as her accompanist for the rest of her life; the other was Jack Carrol. In 1925, Tucker
billed herself as Dame Sophie Tucker and sang "It's How Young You Feel"
and "Polly, the Pest of Hollywood." Before billing herself as Dame Sophie
Tucker, she had adopted the title of Madame, causing *Variety*'s Sime Silverman
to note, "There's a $2 Madame at the Palace this week." In 1928, Tucker's
son Bert was part of the act, together with six Tivoli Girls; it featured her rendition

of "I'm Not Taking Orders from No One," "Nobody Loves a Fat Girl," and a Yiddish rendering of "Bye, Bye, Blackbird" titled "Bye, Bye, Greenberg."

In addition to vaudeville, Sophie Tucker found time to play nightclubs and to become popular in England through frequent appearances at the London Palladium. She made her first British appearance in April 1922 at the Stratford Empire, in the East End of London, singing "There's More Music in a Grand Baby Than There Is in a Baby Grand" and "When They Get Too Wild for Everyone Else, They're Perfect for Me." She made her last London appearance in 1965. Tucker also made many British recordings, notable for the risqué quality of the lyrics, the number of "hells" and "damns," and the hint of rhyming a word not used in polite society with the singer's last name. In 1934, she starred in a British feature film, *Gay Love*, which was not as suggestive as its title implies and did not introduce a later Tucker number, "I Picked a Pansy in the Garden of Love."

In the United States, Sophie Tucker appeared in six feature films: *Honky Tonk* (1929), *Broadway Melody of 1938* (1937), *Thoroughbreds Don't Cry* (1937), *Follow the Boys* (1944), *Sensations of 1945* (1944), and *Atlantic City* (1944). She was seen on Broadway in *Leave It to Me* (1938) and *High Kickers* (1941). In 1949 M-G-M announced plans for a film of her life story to be called *Some of These Days*, but nothing came of the project.

As she got older, it became obvious that Sophie Tucker's singing ability was questionable, but she remained above criticism. As Leo Guild commented in *The Hollywood Reporter* (July 23, 1954), after seeing her act at Ciro's nightclub in Los Angeles, "She's a tradition and woe betide the disbeliever who sees the king walking the street with no clothes."

In recognition of Sophie Tucker's five decades in show business, *The New York Times* (August 31, 1953) editorialized, "To a versatile and generous trouper, we say thanks for the half-century of songs, some sad, some comic, but always entertaining." Tucker never retired, and only months before her death, she had been working in an act with George Jessel and Ted Lewis.

Her funeral was evidence of her popularity, attended by more than three thousand mourners. Even the Teamsters Union, whose hearse drivers were on strike, called off its picketing in deference to her memory. She herself once explained one of the reasons for her popularity: "It may sound corny to some, but I also have a deep love and respect for my audiences. I have a file of seven thousand names, persons I've met on my travels, and never fail to send each of them a handwritten note telling them I'll be appearing in their communities. They also receive Christmas cards from me—handwritten, because I do not employ a secretary." Only Joan Crawford was as attentive to her fans as Sophie Tucker.

BIBLIOGRAPHY

Engle, William. "The Magnificent Sophie Tucker." *The American Weekly*, April 16, 1950, p. 12.

"How Sophie Tucker Ran Away to Become a Star." *The New York Dramatic Mirror*, August 26, 1914, p. 18.

"I Love Them All." *Newsweek*, February 21, 1966, p. 91B.

Roberts, Katherine. "Your Gal Sophie." *Collier's* 10, no. 8 (February 19, 1938), pp. 26–29.

"Sophie Tucker." *Current Biography*, April 1945, pp. 626–30.

Tucker, Sophie. *Some of These Days*. Garden City, N.Y.: Doubleday, 1945.

————, as told to Dan Senseney. "The Most Wonderful Thing That Ever Happened to Me." *The American Weekly*, October 4, 1953, p. 4.

TWO-A-DAY

The leading vaudeville theatres that presented only two complete shows a day were known as two-a-day houses. The demise of vaudeville is often dated from May 1932, when the Palace theatre ceased to be a two-a-day house.

U _____

UNITED BOOKING OFFICE

A predecessor of B. F. Keith's Vaudeville Exchange, the United Booking Office of America (U.B.O.) was incorporated in Maine in 1906. It worked as a "trust," controlling the booking of all vaudeville acts into East and Midwest vaudeville houses and charging a commission to the acts it booked. Any act that did not book through the U.B.O. was blacklisted and could not work in U.B.O. houses. By 1907, the organization controlled all the theatres on the Eastern Seaboard, with the exception of those owned by Percy G. Williams (who later contracted with the U.B.O.). It had also negotiated an agreement with Oscar Hammerstein to limit his vaudeville activities to Manhattan, and with the Shuberts, Klaw and Erlanger, and the United States Amusement Company, whereby those companies agreed for a ten-year period not to become involved in vaudeville production.

In 1914, the words "of America" were dropped from the organization's title, and in 1918, it changed its name to B. F. Keith's Vaudeville Exchange. The name change signified what everyone knew all along: that U.B.O. was synonymous with the B. F. Keith vaudeville circuit and that it was headed, as was B. F. Keith's, by E. F. Albee (q.v.). Aside from the United Booking Office, B. F. Keith's operated a subsidiary, B. F. Keith New York Theatres Company, as a holding company for its theatres in New York City. A second subsidiary company, the Vaudeville Collection Agency, collected a 5 percent commission from all acts playing the B. F. Keith circuit.

UNITED STATES AMUSEMENT CO.

The United States Amusement Co. was incorporated in New Jersey on April 28, 1907, by two major names in theatrical production, Klaw and Erlanger and the Shuberts. The latter was to provide theatres to be converted to vaudeville, with Klaw and Erlanger booking the performers. Naturally, there was immediate opposition from the B. F. Keith interests, which initially tried to blacklist any vaudeville acts signing with the new concern. On November 9, 1907, an agreement was signed between B. F. Keith and the United States Amusement Co., whereby the latter's contracts with vaudevillians were taken over by B. F. Keith for a reported $1.5 million, and with payment of an additional $250,000, Klaw and Erlanger and the Shuberts agreed not to enter the vaudeville field again for a ten-year period.

BIBLIOGRAPHY

Gilbert, Douglas. "The Shuberts vs. Albee." In *American Vaudeville: Its Life and Times*. New York: Whittlesey House, 1940, pp. 238–39.

V ————————————————

RUDY VALLEE (Island Pond, Vt., July 28, 1901—North Hollywood, Ca., July 3, 1986)

Rudy Vallee was a multitalented entertainer, something of a phenomenon in show business. He had been a major figure in the field of popular music, one of the top stars of radio in the 1930s, a delightful character comedian in films of the 1940s and 1950s, a Broadway star in the 1960s, and in the waning years of his life, Vallee continued to entertain with his one-man show. Like Jack Benny, he exploited a reputation for stinginess, but in Vallee's case, it was probably true. At the same time, he always remained amiable and retained a sense of humor that was often directed against himself.

Hubert Prior Vallee was born in Island Pond, Vermont, the son of the local druggist, but it was in Westbrook, Maine, that he developed his charming New England style of delivering either a song or a line of dialogue. At the age of fifteen, he decided that he wanted to be a musician, joined a local band as a drummer, and adopted the first name of his idol, saxophonist Rudy Weidoeft. He paid his own way through Yale, working with various dance bands, and after graduation in June 1927, he toured for a while with the Yale Collegians. In January 1928, he put his own group together, the Connecticut Yankees, and with them he obtained an engagement at the Heigh-Ho Club in New York. As saxophonist and director of the group, Vallee had almost instantaneous success, and his familiar greeting of "Heigh-Ho, everybody!," first used at the club, soon became known to a new audience on radio and in vaudeville.

Vallee was first heard on radio over New York's WABC, broadcasting from the Heigh-Ho Club in February 1928. After a year on local radio, Vallee was picked up by NBC, and *The Rudy Vallee Show*, also known as *The Fleischmann Hour*, was first heard nationally on October 24, 1929. It was the first major network variety show, and with its announcer, Graham McNamee, and Vallee's theme song, "My Time Is Your Time," it became one of the most enduring programs on radio. Vallee was noted for introducing such new talent as Alice Faye, Frances Langford, Phil Baker, Joe Penner, and Bob Burns, and in the early 1940s, the program was known for the outrageous appearances of John Barrymore. Vallee left his radio program in July 1943, when he joined the coast guard to become conductor of its band. He returned after the war, but he did not enjoy the same success as had been his in the previous decade.

Thanks to his New York radio broadcasts, Vallee was able to embark on a short vaudeville tour in the spring of 1929. He opened at Keith's 81st Street Theatre, broke all the house records, and, as Vallee himself noted, quoting publicity of the time, created "an explosion in the theatrical world." From there, he moved to the Coliseum, then to the Palace, ending his initial vaudeville tour at Proctor's 86th Street Theatre. Vallee and His Connecticut Yankees performed such numbers as "Deep Night," "Sweetheart of My Dreams," and "Sweet Lorraine." Reviewing them at the 81st Street Theatre, *Variety* (February 13, 1929) commented, "With silly little props such as an assortment of carnival hats and simple hokum pantomimic business to further stress the lyric significance of their ditties, theirs proved a pleasantly unique style of popular entertainment. The chief appeal is the quiet simplicity of their music. There is no fanfare, no heavy arrangements, no hullaballoo. They rely strongly on their vocal interludes, with some comedy derived from a couple of saucy lyrics. The keynote of their instrumentation is charming softness, with plenty of rhythm from piano and traps." At the Palace, Rudy Vallee and His Connecticut Yankees appeared on the same bill with the Duncan Sisters, Van and Schenck, and Joe Laurie, Jr. They easily stole the show and were held over for a second week (which also happened at the 81st Street Theatre). It was, as *Variety* (March 6, 1929) noted, an amazing achievement "for an act that hadn't seen the back of a vaude stage a month ago."

From today's viewpoint, the most delightful, and still entertaining, of the Vallee songs from this period are what he described as "nut" songs, such as the somewhat risqué "You'll Do It Someday, So Why Not Now?" Vallee and his men would perform the song complete with appropriate gestures; when they sang "You may be kissing," they blew kisses in the air; when they sang of the land "where men are men," they would flex their muscles. The eight members of the Connecticut Yankees had considerable personality, as evidenced by their work on songs such as this, but that personality completely fails to come across in the group's first feature film, *The Vagabond Lover*, produced by RKO in 1929, which Vallee was quick to brand as the worst film ever made.

"Vaudeville was not important to my career, but it was a delightful experience," said Vallee. "I had always enjoyed vaudeville as a child, and to be appearing on the stage with these people was really something. . . . I learned more than anything, from watching the other acts perform, about what an audience would accept and how to gain audience approval."

Vallee felt this was particularly true of his second vaudeville engagement, a long-term stint at the Brooklyn Paramount presentation house in 1930. Here, Vallee conducted a twenty-four piece orchestra onstage and also acted as master of ceremonies. Built over a two-year period at a cost of $5 million, the Brooklyn

Paramount, when it opened on November 24, 1928, with its four thousand five hundred seats, was one of the largest theatres in the country. Vallee's act there was basically a revue titled "A Night at the Villa Vallee," and although, as *Variety* (March 12, 1930) noted, "Vallee's voice has a tough time with it even by the aid of a big megaphone," his thousands of devoted fans greeted the crooner's appearances with enthusiasm. Had he wished, there is no question that Rudy Vallee could have continued on in vaudeville for many years.

Vallee's film career did not end with *The Vagabond Lover*, but continued with *George White's Scandals* (1934), *Sweet Music* (1935), *Second Fiddle* (1939), *It's in the Bag* (1945), *The Bachelor and the Bobby-Soxer* (1947), *I Remember Mama* (1948), *Gentlemen Marry Brunettes* (1955), and many others. He was at his best under Preston Sturges's direction in *The Palm Beach Story* (1942), *Mad Wednesday* (1947), *Unfaithfully Yours* (1948), and *The Beautiful Blonde from Bashful Bend* (1949). He served as narrator for the 1968 film *The Night They Raided Minsky's*.

He made a triumphant return to Broadway in 1961 with the Frank Loesser musical *How to Succeed in Business without Really Trying*, which Vallee filmed in 1967. In the last years of his life, he toured with a one-man show, *Something Different*, often surprising audiences with some outrageously risqué stories and one of his favorite songs, "He's Screwing Dolores Del Rio." The show would always end with "Let's Put Out the Lights and Go to Sleep," while Vallee flashed a slide on the screen, showing him and his fourth wife, Eleanor Kathleen Norris, in bed together. (Vallee was previously married to Leonie Cauchois, Fay Webb, and Bettyjane Greer.)

Rudy Vallee died while watching the Statue of Liberty centennial celebration on television. At his death, he was eulogized by President Ronald Reagan: "He was a dedicated patriot who interrupted his career to serve in the U.S. Coast Guard, and it was appropriate that Rudy's last moments were spent watching the illumination of the Statue of Liberty."

BIBLIOGRAPHY

Gellhorn, Martha. "Rudy Vallee, God's Gift to Us Girls." *The New Republic*, August 7, 1929, pp. 310–11.

Kiner, Larry F. *The Rudy Vallee Discography*. Westport, Ct.: Greenwood Press, 1985.

"New Rudy Vallee Voice Is Catnip." *Literary Digest*, October 19, 1929, pp. 46–50.

"Rudy Vallee." *Current Biography*, June 1947, pp. 652–54.

St. Johns, Adela Rogers. "The Private Life of Rudy Vallee, Part One—He *Did* See a Dream Walking." *Liberty* 11, no. 14 (April 7, 1934), pp. 4–9.

————. "The Private Life of Rudy Vallee, Part Two—The Girl on the Magazine Cover." Ibid, no. 15 (April 14, 1934), pp. 18–22.

————. "The Private Life of Rudy Vallee, Part Three—His Dream and His Doubts." Ibid, no. 16 (April 21, 1934), pp. 32–38.

————. "The Private Life of Rudy Vallee, Part Four—Conclusion." Ibid, no. 17 (April 28, 1934), pp. 46–49.

Scullin, George. "How to Succeed in Show Business by Being Rediscovered." *Saturday Evening Post*, June 23, 1962, pp. 24–27.

Strakosch, Avery. "Vagabond Lover." *Liberty* 7, no. 21 (May 24, 1930), pp. 18–26.

Vallee Rudy. *Vagabond Dreams Come True*. New York: Grosset & Dunlap, 1930.

————, with Gil McKean. *My Time Is Your Time*. New York: I. Obolensky, 1962.

————. *Let the Chips Fall*. Harrisburg, Pa.: Stackpole Books, 1975.

BILLY B. VAN (Pottsdam, Pa., August 3, 1878—Newport, N.H., November 11, 1950)

Billy B. Van worked in vaudeville as a single comedian and also teamed with straight man James J. Corbett and with Rose and Nellie Beaumont, "The Clever, Fascinating Beaumont Sisters." With the latter, he appeared at the Palace in January 1916. He began his stage career in 1893, and aside from vaudeville, he was active on the New York stage in many musical productions: *Jersey Lily* (1903), *The Errand Boy* (1904), *Little Nemo* (1908), *Have a Heart* (1917), *Adrienne* (1923), *The Dream Girl* (1924), *Artists and Models* (1925), *Gay Paree* (1925), *The Great Temptations* (1926), and *Sunny Days* (1928).

He was the husband of musical comedy performer Grace Walsh, and with her he appeared in *The Rainbow Girl*, which opened at the New Amsterdam Theatre on April 1, 1918. He costarred with Raymond Hitchcock in the 1922 screen version of the musical comedy *The Beauty Shop*. Billy B. Van retired in the late 1920s and became a successful businessman.

(GUS) VAN (Brooklyn, N.Y., August 12, 1887—Miami Beach, Fl., March 12, 1968) and **(JOE) SCHENCK** (Brooklyn, N.Y., 1891—Detroit, June 28, 1930)

"The Pennant Winning Battery of Songland"—a phrase invented by publicist Jack Lait—was the billing of Van and Schenck, one of vaudeville's favorite singing teams from the late teens onward. Gus Van was the slightly overweight member of the team who specialized in dialect songs, while Joe Schenck played the piano, often using only one hand. The two sang in close harmony and also performed comedy dialect songs in Italian or Yiddish, numbers like "Pasta Vazoola" or "Hungry Women." The latter is usually associated with Eddie Cantor, but Gus Van's rendition with a pronounced Yiddish accent is a delight, particularly as he complains of a magic act in which a woman is cut in half and, of course, he gets the half that eats. The act was, as *The Billboard* commented on March 3, 1928, "the best of its kind in the business."

August Van Glone (Gus Van) and Joseph T. Schenck were both born in Brooklyn and first met when they attended the same public school. As children, they appeared at Brooklyn's Myrtle Avenue Picture House and also performed at the Lenore Club, which was later to become the Van and Schenck Club, located at 12 Cypress Hill Street, Glendale, Queens. While planning a professional act, Van and Schenck landed jobs as trolley car operators, with Schenck as the conductor and Van as the pilot. Eventually they entered vaudeville, but not as a team, for Gus Van initially appeared as part of the Edwards, Ryan, and Keeney act. Around 1910, the two men finally became a vaudeville team. At first, Schenck only played the piano until his voice changed to a pleasant tenor which blended well with Van's rich baritone. As early as August 30, 1912, *Variety* wrote of them, "Van and Schenck need never worry about anything as long as they stick together and their voices stick with them. . . . Van and Schenck form one of the best teams of its kind in vaudeville." By 1916, the two were fairly well known, and when in May of that year the couple headlined at the Royal Theatre, New York, *Variety* (May 5, 1916) noted, "They set a pace rather difficult for others to follow. The pianist makes a strong bid for popular favor with a well trained tenor voice of commercial proportions, while the dialect singer stands out conspicuously as one of the best in his line. The boys have chosen a sensible repertoire, closing with 'Good Old Days Back Home,' although the pianist might have picked a better ballad for his solo. . . . They scored a decisive hit."

In 1916, Florenz Ziegfeld and Charles Dillingham hired Van and Schenck to appear in their production of *The Century Girl*, which opened at the Century Theatre on November 16, 1916, with music by Victor Herbert and Irving Berlin. The stars of the show were Hazel Dawn, Elsie Janis, Leon Errol, and Frank Tinney. The following year, Van and Schenck went into Ziegfeld's *Midnight Frolic* on the New Amsterdam Theatre roof, but they quit in April 1918, apparently after overhearing Ziegfeld make a disparaging remark about their being "cabaret hams." That comment notwithstanding, Van and Schenck were back with Ziegfeld in 1919 as two of the stars of that year's edition of the *Follies*. They were featured in the minstrel show sequence in the second half of the program, which included an impersonation of famed minstrel George Primrose by Marilyn Miller. Van and Schenck sang perhaps their most famous song, "Mandy," written by Irving Berlin, and also performed a song routine with Eddie Dowling and John Steel. Through the 1921 edition of the *Follies*, Van and Schenck were regulars in the Ziegfeld company.

Radio's *The EverReady Hour* made its debut on New York station WEAF on December 4, 1923, and Van and Schenck were the stars of this pioneering variety show. After Schenck's death, Van was to be heard on radio for a while as the interlocuter on *The Sinclair Minstrel Show*.

Aside from vaudeville, the team appeared in nightclubs and also went to Hollywood to appear in short subjects and one feature for M-G-M, *They Learned about Women*. In this 1930 film, they played major league baseball players, supported by Bessie Love and Benny Rubin. Billed as "The Shahs of Songland," Van and Schenck made their last Palace Theatre appearance together the week of June 7, 1930. While appearing at the Fischer Theatre, Detroit, Schenck suffered a heart attack and died in Van's arms at the Book Cadillac Hotel. As a partnership, Schenck and Van had been unique in that they had remained friends since childhood and even owned homes within a block of each other.

After Schenck's death, Van went solo, making his New York debut at the Albee Theatre, Brooklyn, early in September 1930. He opened with "Why Kentucky Bids the World Good Morning" and then spoke briefly about the trolley route that he and Schenck had before entering vaudeville. Afterward, he performed a number of dialect songs, one Irish, one Italian, and a Yiddish number titled "Is Dat Religion?" Two straight numbers, "That's the Kind of Baby I Am" and "I Like to Stay After School," completed the program. As *Variety* (September 3, 1930) reported, Gus Van closed the show and stopped it. He explained that he always sang his numbers to the spirit of his dead partner: "I am uncertain as every mortal about what happens to the soul after death, but if I didn't know absolutely that Joe Schenck's spirit was listening to my every note—that he is keeping me in pitch, so to speak—as he always did when we were partners, I would never make another public appearance."

Later in September 1930, Van returned, as a solo, to the Palace. *Variety* (September 17, 1930) reported:

Palace audience Saturday afternoon had its first chance in a long while to go sentimental, and it did even more so than Gus Van, the subject of the demonstration, who appeared to have difficulty with his emotions. Gus kept as straight-faced as possible while the reception lasted but was said to have broken down sobbing in his dressing room. No wonder. . . . It was a great tribute to this remaining member of vaudeville's greatest singing team. He did not mention the name of Joe Schenck at any time, an immediate sign of good taste, with the lamented Joe suggested only faintly by lyric. Announcing he had learned it the day before, thinking it particularly suited to this house, Gus sang that he's not so much alone. Gus was right when, while thanking the audience, he said that from the Palace response he sees a bright future for himself as a single entertainer. There is no doubt he will. This singer as a single is a jewel character man, a neat, smart-acting showman. No one in vaude so well versed in the various dialects. In the course of one number, wherein reference was made to the old car barn days by a nicely written introduction, Van does Hebe, Irish, Cockney, Wop, Dutch and Coon, the latter as a colored preacher delivering a sermon and the rest mainly snatches from the old repertoire. He impressed as a singer and single act despite the audience's sob. Van will not have any trouble with his single.

Gus Van returned again to the Palace in February 1931 and September 1932. He remained active through the 1940s and was seen on the New York legitimate stage in 1946 in *Toplitzky of Notre Dame*. He served as president of the American Guild of Variety Artists and was made a life member in 1949. Retiring to Miami Beach, he died after being struck by a car.

GERTRUDE VANDERBILT (Brooklyn, N.Y., 1880—New York, December 18, 1960)

Gertrude Vanderbilt was both a talented singer and dancer, but it was for the latter talent that she was best known and a favorite on the vaudeville stage. Caroline Caffin wrote glowingly of her in *Vaudeville* (1914):

"Whatever nationality may claim her descent, Gertrude Vanderbilt may fairly be admitted to be a typical American girl. The long straight limbs, alert and yet a little drooping in their lines; the free and unafraid carriage of the head; the arms rather long in proportion; the shoulders a trifle broad and carried erect,— all these may be duplicated many times any fine winter afternoon on Fifth Avenue or the main thoroughfare of almost any city in the Union. And not only in physical makeup but in the spirit of her performance we find the epitome of much that characterizes the American girl. For she is in high spirits, carried along by a flood of youth and energy that makes for the joy of life. And added to this are a natural grace and the audacity that comes from never having met with defeat. Difficulties she may have encountered, yet one is convinced that they proved but a source of stimulation and were eventually overcome. So now she faces you with laughing cordiality, pleased that you are pleased with her, but never doubting for a moment that you would be. She sings with frank, unpretentious simplicity, not over-anxious to make points but by no means without a sense of humor. And then she dances and all the world seems young. So gay, so happy, so pleased with herself and with everything else that her good humor is infectious! The long limbs are compact of suppleness and agility, and swirl in quite surprising orbits. The sinuous figure bends and turns and skims over the ground, bounding with long, boyish strides, carefree, laughing, joyous.''

She began her career at the age of fourteen and was a frequent star of the Broadway stage during most of the first two decades of the twentieth century: *The American Idea* (1908), *The Jolly Bachelors* (1910), *A Skylark* (1910), *Our Miss Gibbs* (1910), *The Happiest Night of His Life* (1911), *The Red Widow* (1911), *Maytime* (1917), *Listen, Lester* (1918), *Fifty-Fifty, Ltd.* (1919), *Oh! Oh! Nurse* (1925), and *Tabloid* (1929). She was featured in the 1914 edition of the Ziegfeld *Follies* and appeared at the Palace as late as April 1926. In vaudeville in the teens, Gertrude Vanderbilt was often partnered by George Moore, with the two appearing in a dance parody of the burlesque melodrama *The Villain Still Pursued Her*. In later years, Vanderbilt worked in summer stock, but she was primarily a business executive.

FRANK VAN HOVEN (Sioux City, Ia., 1887—Birmingham, England, December 1929)

Frank Van Hoven was billed as ''The Mad Magician,'' and according to Joe Laurie, Jr., ''this guy was really mad.'' His act did not contain too many magic tricks but relied heavily on Van Hoven's endless commentary and a stunt involving two large and heavy cakes of ice. Two stooges would be asked to hold the blocks of ice, and while they staggered under the weight, Van Hoven would ponder what to do with them. After a while, he would beg the audience to be patient while he went offstage to think about it. He would walk through the audience and out of the theatre door, returning a few minutes later with a glass of beer in his hand and foam around his mouth. Once Van Hoven performed this stunt at the Palace, and on his way back into the auditorium through the lobby, he met E. F. Albee, who was scandalized at Van Hoven's lack of professional ethics. Supposedly, Van Hoven looked straight at Albee and said, ''Look, Bud, if you don't like it, just go to the box office and get your money back. Then you can get the hell out of this theatre.''

Van Hoven began his career, working for Gus Sun in Springfield, Illinois, at

$25 a week. Sun fired him, and Van Hoven would take great pride in advertising this fact in later years, when Sun had to pay him $1,000 a week to work the same theatre. Much of the last ten years of his life was spent in England, although he did play vaudeville again in the United States between 1926 and 1928. He was noted for his practical jokes, a favorite of which was to claim that one of his colleagues had died. When news of his own near-death situation—pneumonia and "creeping paralysis"—reached the United States, no one believed it was true.

VARIETY

The leading American entertainment trade paper, *Variety* is known as the "Bible of Show Business." It is a major source of research and reference for all areas of entertainment, including vaudeville. It began on December 16, 1905, as a trade paper for vaudeville and related areas such as minstrel shows, fairs, amusement parks, burlesque shows, and circuses. It also covered the legitimate stage and the motion picture industry. Founded by Sime Silverman with the support of Epes W. Sargent, *Variety* was welcomed by vaudevillians, who appreciated its honest and forthright commentary on their performances. As Douglas Gilbert wrote in *American Vaudeville*, "It hit Broadway like a thousand of brick: an honest publication whose summaries of acts and plays were fearless and uncompromising, one that flayed an act with a left-hook critique, often printed in the same issue containing the act's paid advertisement."

The cover of the first issue announced "Chicot and Sime's Reviews of the Week," "Chicot" being the nickname of Epes W. Sargent, and inside was an article by Acton Davies on "What I Don't Know about Vaudeville." In an editorial, Sime Silverman explained:

Variety in its initial issue desires to announce the policy governing the paper.

We want you to read it. It will be interesting if for no other reason than that it will be conducted on original lines for a theatrical newspaper.

The first, foremost and extraordinary feature of it will be FAIRNESS. Whatever there is to be printed of interest to the professional world WILL BE PRINTED WITHOUT REGARD TO WHOSE NAME IS MENTIONED OR THE ADVERTISING COLUMNS.

"ALL THE NEWS ALL THE TIME" and "ABSOLUTELY FAIR" are the watchwords.

The news part of the paper will be given over to such items as may be obtained, and nothing will be suppressed which is considered of interest. WE PROMISE YOU THIS AND SHALL NOT DEVIATE.

The reviews will be written conscienciously, and the truth only told. If it hurts it is at least said in fairness and impartiality.

We aim to make this an artists' paper; a medium; a complete directory; a paper to which anyone connected with or interested in the theatrical world may read with the thorough knowledge and belief that what is printed is not dictated by any motive other than the policy above outlined.

The first vaudeville act reviewed was of monologist Tod Sloan at Hammerstein's Victoria Theatre. His act, "Monologue of Race Track Stuff," was written by George M. Cohan.

The reviews in *Variety* were always signed with abbreviations or nicknames of the critics. "Sime" was Silverman. "Chicot" or "Chic" was Sargent. "Rush" was Alfred Greason, whose middle name was Rushford. "Jolo" was Joshua Lowe. "Abel" was Abel Green. "Con" was Jack Conway. "Kauf" was Wolfe Kaufman. "Ibee" was Jack Pulaski. "Mark" was Mark Vance. "Fred" was Fred Schader. "Bige" was Joe Bigelow.

Aside from its use of nicknames to identify its writers, who were dubbed "muggs" by Silverman, *Variety* also created its own language, transforming nouns into verbs and inventing new words, such as "hoofology" for dancing and "torso-tosser" for striptease artist.

Sime Silverman and *Variety* had a number of disputes with E. F. Albee, resulting in the mid 1920s in the paper's being banned by the B. F. Keith organization and vaudevillians threatened with blacklisting if they advertised in *Variety*. In 1916, the White Rats filed a suit against the paper, claiming discrimination, and in 1918, a complaint was filed with the Federal Trade Commission, claiming that vaudevillians were forced to advertise in *Variety* to ensure satisfactory reviews. Neither complaint was proven, although there is no question that *Variety* solicited advertising from performers as they came offstage and were informed that a *Variety* reviewer was at that show.

With the growth of the film industry in the 1920s, it was given prominence in the front section of *Variety*, and vaudeville news and reviews of "New Acts" were moved to the center of the paper. Even with the demise of vaudeville per se, *Variety* continued to review new acts, but these were relegated to the back pages.

Variety is available on microfilm from Kraus-Thomson.

Address: 475 Park Avenue, New York, N.Y. 10016.

See also JACK CONWAY, ABEL GREEN, ISMA BERLINGER (JACK) PULASKI, EPES WINTHROP SARGENT, SIME SILVERMAN.

BIBLIOGRAPHY

Landry, Robert J. "Variety's Four-Letter Signatures the Dog-Tags of Its Critics." *Variety*, January 9, 1974, p. 26.

Slide, Anthony. "Variety." In *International Film, Radio, and Television Journals*. Westport, Ct.: Greenwood Press, 1985, pp. 363–67.

Stoddard, Dayton. *Lord Broadway, Variety's "Sime": The Man Who Made the Gay White Way Gayer*. New York: Wilfred Funk, 1941.

VASCO (England, 1871—England, May 9, 1925)

Vasco was billed as "The Mad Magician," his act consisting of playing some twenty-eight different musical instruments, a routine that Charles "Buddy" Rogers was to adapt later, albeit with far fewer instruments. Educated at a military orphanage in England, Vasco (whose full or real name is unknown) learned his craft at the British Army Academy of Kneller Hall. He toured South Africa with an opera company and also worked with a circus before making his American debut at New York's Alhambra Theatre in 1897. He made a number of U.S. appearances and on April 13, 1907, *Variety* wrote of him, "Not only does Vasco play each [instrument] in a manner to indicate his ability, but finds time to inject comedy and acrobatics." Vasco continued to perform until the spring of 1923, when he made his last appearance at a circus in Madrid.

VAUDE

Vaude is the slang term for vaudeville, popularized by *Variety*. When *Variety*'s Abel Green and vaudeville's Joe Laurie, Jr., collaborated on a history of entertainment, it was titled *Show Biz: From Vaude to Video* (New York: Henry Holt, 1951).

VAUDEVILLE COMEDY CLUB

A fraternal organization, the Vaudeville Comedy Club was organized by Louis Simon and held its first meeting at New York's Empire Hotel in 1906. Will Cressy was the first president, James J. Morton the first secretary. The following year, the club moved to headquarters at 147 West 45th Street. In 1909, it moved again to 224 West 46th Street, where it originated "Clown Nights" with Morton as master of ceremonies. The club did demonstrate some concern for the betterment of working conditions for vaudevillians, but its activities were primarily social in nature. It was later reorganized as the Jesters, but it ceased operations in 1914.

VENTRILOQUISM

Ventriloquism is the art of throwing one's voice so that it appears to come from an inanimate object, usually a wooden dummy. As an acceptable form of entertainment, it would appear to date from the mid 1700s. The earliest practitioners on the vaudeville stage were Ed Reynard and A. O. Duncan. They were followed by "Coram," Cole Travis, Fred Russell, Jay W. Winton, and many others.

W. E. Whittle would appear onstage as Teddy Roosevelt and discuss concerns of the day with his dummy. Leo Bill was a French-born entertainer with an act somewhat similar to that in later years of Señor Wences. The Great Lester influenced vaudeville's best known ventriloquist (in large part thanks to his years on radio), Edgar Bergen. Charlie Prelle's Ventriloquial Dogs featured canines with human masks over their faces, Prelle providing the voices for each. Some performers, including William Ebbs in the United States and Sandy Powell in England, specialized in parodies of vaudeville acts, with the dummies often falling apart and it being obvious they were utilizing another person offstage to provide their voice.

Among female ventriloquists were Ella Morris, Winona Winter, Hilda Hawthorne, Mabel Johnson, and Grace Wallace. The best was probably Grace De

Winters, who would appear initially as a bellboy paging her dummy. The dummy would go through a variety of costume changes as De Winters impersonated vaudeville headliners such as Harry Lauder and Raymond Hitchcock. "A girl ventriloquist is something of a novelty in itself," and "Miss De Winters . . . displays splendid showmanship," reported Mark in *Variety* (March 4, 1919) after seeing the lady's act at New York's American Roof.

The paucity of female ventriloquists led to a curious situation as a number of female impersonators embarked on new careers as vaudevillians. Lydia Dreams (real name Walter Lambert) was one such performer in vaudeville. The best known, and a superb ventriloquist in his own right, was British music hall performer Bobbie Kimber, who grew his hair long and styled it as a woman. He was active from the 1930s through the 1960s and never revealed his sexual identity onstage.

One of the first ventriloquists to become a vaudeville headliner was black American Frank Rogers, who worked with two dummies, one black and one white. He enjoyed considerable success in 1910, but he was not the first Negro ventriloquist in mainstream vaudeville, having been preceded by J. W. Cooper.

See also EDGAR BERGEN, THE GREAT LESTER, MARSHALL MONT-GOMERY, SEÑOR WENCES.

VESTA VICTORIA (Leeds, England, November 26, 1873—London, April 7, 1951)

Vesta Victoria was a plump character songstress with a toothy smile, noted for her low-pitched voice, clear diction, and energy, who became as popular in the United States as she was in her native England. Her songs were generally concerned with some misfortune, of which she was the victim. "Waiting at the Church" told of her as a stranded bride at the altar. "Poor John," its successor, which became an instant hit when she first sang it at New York's Colonial Theatre in 1907, was the sad lament of a girl's first meeting with her prospective mother-in-law:

> John took me round to see his mother!
> His mother! His mother!
> And while he introduced us to each other,
> She weighed up everything that I had on.
> She put me through a cross-examination,
> I fairly boiled with aggravation,
> Then she shook her head, looked at me and said,
> Poor John! Poor John!

Other songs associated with Vesta Victoria include "I've Told His Missus about Him," "Just Because They Put Him into Trousers," "He Calls Me His Own Grace Darling," "You Can Do a Lot of Things at the Seaside (That You Can't Do in Town)," "Now I Have to Call Him Father," "Our Lodger's Such a Nice Young Man," "See What Percy's Picked Up in the Park," "Some

Would Marry Anything with Trousers On," "The Next Horse I Ride On," and one that will last forever, "Daddy Wouldn't Buy Me a Bow-Wow." "It's All Right in the Summertime" had her as a sign painter's wife; he longed to paint portraits in "the altogether," for which she was required to pose:

It's all right in the summertime,
In the summertime it's lovely.
While my old man's a' paintin' 'ard,
Standin' 'ere a' posin' in the old back-yard.
But, oh my, in the wintertime;
It's a different thing, you know,
With a red, red nose, and very few clothes
And the stormy winds do blow.

Vesta Victoria was the daughter of a music hall performer named Joe Lawrence, who appeared in blackface and was billed as "The Upside Down Comedian," because he sang songs standing on his head. She made her first stage appearance at the age of four as "Baby Victoria." Subsequently, she was frequently billed as "Little Victoria," and under that name she made her first London appearance at the Cambridge Music Hall on October 22, 1883. Quickly she became a favorite of London music halls, with her first hit song being "Good for Nothing Nan." In 1893, she introduced "Daddy Wouldn't Buy Me a Bow-Wow," which she sang that same year on her first U.S. vaudeville tour.

In 1906, Vesta Victoria returned to America after an eight-year absence, opening at New York's Colonial Theatre in February. She performed five songs, changing her costume before each, and writing in *Variety* (February 24, 1906), Sime Silverman noted, "Miss Victoria 'made good' easily. She is the truly blown-in-the-bottle music hall artist of the first grade." Within a year, Vesta Victoria was back in the States for a ten-week tour at $3,000 a week. At that time, Silverman in *Variety* (January 19, 1907) called her "the magnetic, pretty, buxom character songstress, the idol of the New York public, unexcelled and impossible of imitation."

Vesta Victoria announced her retirement from the stage at the end of the First World War, but she still made a number of highly successful returns to vaudeville. At London's Victoria Palace in 1926, she revived the songs she had made famous. In April 1927, she headlined at the Palace, and Sime Silverman was in the audience again, noting in *Variety* (April 6, 1927), "There's something magic in the Vesta Victoria name in America." In the early 1930s, Vesta Victoria toured in a British review titled *Stars Who Never Failed to Shine*, and in 1932, she appeared in the Royal Variety Show at the London Palladium. At the height of her fame, she was the highest paid star in American vaudeville.

VICTORIA THEATRE

Located at the corner of 42nd Street and Seventh Avenue in New York, the Victoria Theatre was built by Oscar Hammerstein and opened on March 2, 1899, with *The Reign of Error*. Its roof garden, which extended from the Victoria to the adjoining Republic Theatre, opened in 1900 and was named the Paradise Roof Garden. The Victoria was noted for its bar, which served drinks throughout the performances, and for its vaudeville bills featuring "freak" acts. It was Oscar Hammerstein's son Willie who was responsible for both of the theatre's claims to fame. Willie Hammerstein was always seeking unusual acts and the names from newspaper headlines to be the headliners at the Victoria, which he managed for his father. As Douglas Gilbert commented in *American Vaudeville*, "Hammerstein's [Victoria] was the most topical theatre in America. A headline in the news led directly to a headline at the Victoria. Any outstanding contemporary figure in the public prints could obtain a week's booking."

The last vaudeville program presented at the Victoria was on April 26, 1915. The theatre was subsequently taken over by S. L. Rothafel and remodeled as the Rialto movie theatre. It was further rebuilt in 1935.

VITAPHONE

Vitaphone was a pioneering sound-on-disc system sponsored by Western Electric and first used by Warner Bros. in 1926. *The Jazz Singer* (1927), starring Al Jolson, which is often erroneously described as the first "talkie," utilized the Vitaphone system. Vitaphone is important to vaudeville history in that many early vaudevillians recorded their acts on Vitaphone for Warner Bros. between 1926 and 1930. In many respects, the Vitaphone system helped "kill" vaudeville, as audiences turned away from the medium to the entertainment of sound motion pictures, and vaudevillians discovered that one performance of their act for Vitaphone meant that it was no longer "fresh" for vaudeville audiences. B. F. Keith actively discouraged vaudevillians from signing contracts with Vitaphone and Warner Bros., and in March 1927 banned "name acts" from appearing in talking pictures under penalty of blacklisting by the Keith circuit. Vitaphone and Warner Bros. responded by offering one-year contracts to vaudeville acts willing to appear in Vitaphone shorts. In late March 1927, a minor harmony musical act, the Four Aristocrats, was offered a one-year, $52,000 contract by Vitaphone, which also promised to book the act in vaudeville houses during the year as well as feature it in four or five short subjects. "Vitaphone is out to fight vaudeville hammer and tongs," reported *The Billboard* (April 2, 1927).

Because the Vitaphone system utilized separate picture and sound, one element or the other has been lost for a number of short subjects. The copyright is controlled by Turner Entertainment. The Vitaphone shorts are housed in the form of negatives, discs, or composite prints primarily at the Library of Congress and the UCLA Film and Television Archive, and both have been active in preserving and restoring the films.

W _____

TED WALDMAN (BIRMINGHAM, AL., FEBRUARY 12, 1899—LOS AN-
geles, February 1, 1987)

Typical of the many vaudevillians who were the backbone of the industry but
never became household names was Ted Waldman. Borrah Minevitch may be
the best known harmonica player in vaudeville, but Ted Waldman is more
symbolic of what vaudeville was all about, and his career playing the harmonica,
or mouth organ, lasted far longer than that of Minevitch.

Waldman taught himself to play while still a child, and at the age of sixteen,
he was performing while working as a waiter at Brown's Cafe in Charlotte,
North Carolina. The restaurant was next to the Piedmont Theatre, and a number
of the entertainers there heard Ted play and urged him to join their shows, but
he was too familiar with stranded companies and other blights affecting entertainers to leave the security of Brown's Cafe. However, circa 1911, he saw a
tab show called *Yankee Doodle Doos* and was impressed by its producer, Harry
Feldman, and his soubrette wife, Agnes Gary. Waldman agreed to join the
company, and recalled: "We played all the oil fields, and a gusher would come
in and fill the theatres with oil; sometimes we'd have to sleep in the dressing
rooms."

When the tab show played two-a-day vaudeville houses such as the Majestic
Theatre in Dallas, Waldman's harmonica playing received such attention that
quickly he had offers to join mainstream vaudeville. He teamed up with Ned
Norworth and the two played together for three years. In the teens, Waldman
reached New York, and while playing one evening for fun at Lindy's Restaurant,
he was seen and heard by Eva Tanguay, who invited him to join her act, playing
the mouth organ while she changed costumes and engaging in repartee with her
from the stage box. He remained with Tanguay for four years, earning an average
yearly salary of $25,000.

In the 1920s, Waldman created an act titled "Blu-O-Logy" with his brother
Al. Both appeared in blackface, and Ted played the mouth organ or, to be more
precise, eleven different mouth organs of varying sizes. He claimed to be the
first individual to play blues on harmonica. Ted Waldman played the Palace in

July 1927 and March 1929. After fourteen years together, Al retired from show business in 1938, and Ted's wife, Priscilla, joined the act. During the Second World War, the two worked with the U.S.O. touring Australia. After their retirement, both worked as volunteers at the Motion Picture Country House and Hospital in Woodland Hills, California.

FLORENCE WALTON (Wilmington, Del., 1890—New York, January 7, 1981)

Florence Walton was a "class" dancing act in vaudeville in the teens and 1920s, who always appeared in expensive clothes which she advertised as coming directly from Paris. With her husband, Maurice Mouvet, and later with Allan Fagan and Leon Leitrim, she helped popularize the tango, fox-trot, and other forms of ballroom dancing. With Mouvet, she appeared at the Palace in 1913, 1914, and 1917, and claimed to be the first American to entertain troops in the war zone during the First World War. At the November 1914 Palace appearance, Walton and Mouvet announced they had just returned from Europe, where they claimed to have taught the tango to King George V and Queen Mary; the image of the latter doing the tango is hard to contemplate.

Prior to teaming with Mouvet, Florence Walton was featured in *The Soul Kiss* (1908, and Adeline Genée's first American appearance), *The Bachelor Belles* (1910), and *The Pink Lady* (1911). In 1920, she returned to the Palace with her new dancing partner, Allan Fagan. *The New York Dramatic Mirror* (October 16, 1920) reported, "Miss Walton and Mr. Fagan have evolved an up-to-date fancy dancing routine that runs mainly to the waltz and one step. Miss Walton does a solo that shows the artist to have exceptional ability. Miss Walton carried two musicians, a violinist and a pianist. During breathing spells two violin solos are offered. American vaudeville thrice welcomes Miss Walton back upon its stages. She certainly spells and dances class." The week of September 17, 1923, Walton headlined at the Palace, partnered by Leon Leitrim. The couple also danced in 1924 at New York's Club Ostend and at the New York Hippodrome.

Swiss-born Maurice Mouvet also danced with Joan Sawyer and Eleanora Ambrose. The "Valse Maurice" was written in his honor by Sylvester Belmonte, and he and his wife danced it at the Winter Garden Theatre. In 1912, Maurice was the subject of three published dance numbers: the "Maurice Glide" by Gustav Haenschen, the "Maurice Tango" by Silvio Hein, and the "Maurice Rag" by William H. Penn. There were few occasions such as these when Mouvet was recognized in his own right, for the billing of the vaudeville act was always Florence and Maurice Walton. In 1922, Maurice wrote "The Talmadge Foxtrot" for silent screen star Constance Talmadge. Mouvet died in Lausanne, Switzerland, on May 18, 1927, at the approximate age of forty.

FANNIE WARD (St. Louis, February 22, 1871—New York, January 27, 1952)

It may sound trite, but the best description available for Fannie Ward is that of the Marlene Dietrich of her era. Like Dietrich, Ward was ageless, as beautiful at sixty as she had been at twenty, and without the aid of a face-lift. She once commented, "I posted a standing offer of $50,000 for anyone who could prove I ever had my face lifted." She kept her money. She was known as the "Eternal Flapper," but her career began long before that age—in fact, back in the nineteenth century in the era of the soubrette.

Born Fannie Buchanan, Fannie Ward made her first stage appearance at New York's Broadway Theatre on November 26, 1890. It was theatrical impressario Daniel Frohman who changed her name to Ward, and under his guidance she quickly became a popular favorite on the New York and London stages. It was in London in 1898 that she married her first husband, "Diamond" Joe Lewis, a South African millionaire. She divorced him in 1913 and married Jack Dean, who had been named correspondent in the divorce action and who became her leading man onstage and in films. Dean died on June 23, 1950, at the age of seventy-five.

Fannie Ward probably made her vaudeville debut in the 1890s. Certainly, she toured the vaudeville circuits as early as 1910, first in a thirty-minute playlet titled *Van Allen's Wife*, a somewhat sordid tale along the lines of her 1915 film success, *The Cheat*, but without the racial angle. *Variety* (January 15, 1910) was not impressed: "Miss Ward . . . will leave behind no yearning devotees of light entertainment to long for her return." Her second vaudeville playlet, *An Unlucky Star*, which she introduced in April 1910, proved more popular. It concluded with its author appearing onstage to reveal that the audience was supposedly only watching a dress rehearsal; then followed a vigorous argument with the star, Ward. Writing in *Variety* (April 2, 1910), "Rush" found *An Unlucky Star* "an immensely refreshing sketch for the jaded vaudeville habitué."

Between 1915 and 1919, Fannie Ward starred in twenty-three American silent feature films: *The Marriage of Kitty* (1915), *Each Pearl a Tear* (1916), *For the Defense* (1916), *A Gutter Magdalene* (1916), *Tennessee's Pardner* (1916), *Witchcraft* (1916), *The Years of the Locust* (1916), *Betty to the Rescue* (1917), *The Crystal Gazer* (1917), *Her Strange Wedding* (1917), *On the Level* (1917), *A School for Husbands* (1917), *Unconquered* (1917), *The Winning of Sally Temple* (1917), *Innocent* (1918), *A Japanese Nightingale* (1918), *The Narrow Path* (1918), *The Yellow Ticket* (1918), *Common Clay* (1919), *The Cry of the Weak* (1919), *Our Better Selves* (1919), and *The Profiteers* (1919). Her most important film was her first one, *The Cheat*, released by Paramount in 1915, in which she was an American businessman's wife branded by a Japanese (Sessue Hayakawa) from whom she borrowed money. After the film's release, the Japanese government protested the film, and the character was changed to a Chinese. "I cannot . . . omit words of unqualified praise for Fanny [sic] Ward, whose impersonation of the social butterfly with the singed wings was a masterly performance,'' wrote W. Stephen Bush in *The Moving Picture World* (December 25, 1915).

Fannie Ward returned to vaudeville in December 1926 with a twenty-four-minute playlet titled *The Miracle Woman* at the Palace. The plot had her as a seemingly young woman with a daughter who looked as old as she. Ward showed her legs, appeared in a negligée, and apparently received more floral tributes than the Palace stage generally saw in an entire season. One reason for this appearance was to promote Ward's beauty shop. She was back at the Palace in February 1928, billed as ''the most remarkable looking woman for her age of our age,'' singing ''Grandma Blues,'' ''Flapper Fannie,'' and ''My Marine'' (dressed as a French war bride).

In 1929, Fannie Ward appeared in a six-minute Vitaphone short titled *Miracle Woman* (apparently not related to the playlet of the same name), in which she sang ''Flapper Fannie'' and ''Radio Widow,'' accompanied by a male pianist.

The actress never officially retired, although from the 1930s onward, she was more concerned with her social life as the mother of Lady Plunket than with her stage career. At the age of forty-five, she could still pass for a fourteen-year-old onstage, and at the age of sixty, she was proud to report that her legs were still slim and handsome. Reporters noted that a year before she died, Fannie Ward's face retained an unbelievable babylike softness. There were many explanations for how she kept her youthful appearance. One had it that she had learned of a secret facial treatment from the French actress Gaby Deslys; other secrets were a ''Siberian snow face mask,'' a young husband, and a diet of green vegetables.

BIBLIOGRAPHY

Holland, Larry Lee. ''Fannie Ward.'' *Films in Review* 36, no. 12 (December 1985) pp. 590–595.

FREDERICK WARDE (Warrington, England, February 23, 1851—Brooklyn, N.Y., February 17, 1935)

Frederick Warde was a florid Shakespearian actor who found lucrative employment in vaudeville on chautauqua, working both as a monologist and a performer in playlets. He made his first stage appearance at the Lyceum Theatre, Sunderland, England, on September 4, 1867, in *Macbeth*. He came to the United States in 1874, and on August 10 of that year, he made his New York debut at Booth's Theatre in *Belle Lamar*. Warde made his vaudeville debut at Proctor's, New York, in June 1898 as Marc Antony in a scene from Shakespeare's *Julius Caesar*. In 1921, the actor appeared in an experimental sound film produced by Orlando Kellum, in which he reads one of his poems, ''A Sunset Reverie,'' an ode to a sunset over the Golden Gate from California's Berkeley shores. Warde also appeared in a handful of feature films in the teens and early 1920s.

GEORGE DEWEY WASHINGTON (Rock Island, Il., May 1, 1898—   )

Black American George Dewey Washington was a fine bass-baritone who played vaudeville in the 1920s and 1930s, usually appearing as a well-dressed gentleman tramp and singing such unlikely melodies as "On the Road to Mandalay." He was featured in a couple of all-black musical shows, *Old Kentucky* (1932) and *Rhythm Hotel* (1935), and made at least one screen appearance, in *Metro Movietone Revue No. 4* (1929).

ETHEL WATERS (Chester, Pa., October 31, 1897—Los Angeles, September 1, 1977)

The early life of Ethel Waters was one of squalor and degredation. She was married at thirteen, the same age as when her mother had been raped. Yet from those sordid beginnings, Waters emerged as perhaps the greatest popular black singer of this century, a performer who was equally at home with songs of pathos and wit. "I'm Coming Virginia," "Am I Blue?," "You're Lucky to Me," "Harlem on My Mind," "Taking a Chance on Love," "Cabin in the Sky," and "Honey in the Honeycomb" are just a few of the songs that only she could sing to perfection. She would break your heart with a sentimental ballad such as "Cabin in the Sky" and the next moment have you sniggering at the out-and-out bawdy lyrics of "My Handy Man." It is little wonder that *Variety* hailed her in 1938 as "the prima donna of all colored warblers."

Ethel Waters entered vaudeville at the age of seventeen, making her debut at the Lincoln Theatre, Baltimore, teamed with the two Hill Sisters and billed as "Sweet Mama Stringbean." She recorded her first song in 1921, and by the mid 1920s, she was a popular entertainer on the Theatre Owners Booking Association Negro vaudeville circuit. In 1925, Waters replaced Florence Mills at the Plantation Club and then signed a contract with Columbia Records. She made her Broadway debut in *Africana*, a musical review by Donald Heyward, which opened at the Daly Theatre on July 11, 1927, and ran for seventy-two performances.

Her "white" vaudeville debut came in September 1927 at the Palace Theatre. *Variety* (September 21, 1927) liked her act and noted, " 'Shake That Thing' is to Ethel Waters what 'I Don't Care' is to Eva Tanguay. It's her trademark." In May 1928, Ethel Waters was headlining at the Chicago Palace, after taking *Africana* on the road. *Variety* (May 23, 1928) reported, "Miss Waters's first appearance was in a tattered plantation outfit, singing 'I'm Coming Virginia.' She had a friendly house and her handling of this number brought considerable extra recognition. Later she shocked the family customers by wearing almost nothing and going through a series of gyrations and grinds identified as B. B. It seemed a little too Harlem for the local momma and the kiddies down front. . . . There's no doubt as to this girl's ability with blues. Her husky voice and understanding delivery can make an ordinary number full of torrid implications or profound melancholy."

The singer returned to Broadway for Lew Leslie's *Blackbirds*, which opened at the Royale Theatre on October 22, 1930, and ran for a disappointing 57 performances. The cast included Mantan Moreland, Buck and Bubbles and Flourney Miller. In that show she introduced "You're Lucky to Me." Three years later, at the Cotton Club, Ethel Waters introduced "Stormy Weather," and that same year, 1933, she sang "Heat Wave" for the first time in *As Thousands Cheer*. Also in the 1930s, Ethel Waters was seen on the New York stage in *Rhapsody in Black* (1931), *At Home Abroad* (1935) and *Mamba's Daughters* (1939).

She was by now an established star; New York *Times* critic Brooks Atkinson described her as "the gleaming tower of dusky regality, who knows how to make a song stand on tiptoe." Waters had appeared in the 1929 Warner Bros. feature *On with the Show*, capturing on film her renderings of two of her greatest songs, "Am I Blue?" and "Birmingam Bertha." Even in an unpretentious 1933 short like *Bubbling Over*, she transforms the screen with her rendition of "That's Why Darkies Never Dream." Waters's other films include *Cabin in the Sky* (1943), based on the "hit" Broadway show of 1940 in which she starred, *Pinky* (1949), and *The Member of the Wedding* (1952), based on her 1950 Broadway play, in which she cradled Julie Harris and Brandon De Wilde in her arms and sang "His Eye Is on the Sparrow":

> Why should I feel discouraged?
> Why should the shadows come?
> Why should my heart be lonely?
> And long for heaven and home?
> When Jesus is my portion,
> My constant friend is he.
> His eye is on the sparrow
> And I know he watches Me.

In 1947, plans were announced for a film of Waters's life, titled *Am I Blue?*, with Suzet Harbin to play the singer at eighteen and Ethel Waters to portray himself in later years. The project was abandoned.

Despite her success, Ethel Waters suffered from racial discrimination. In March 1937, when she played Kansas City with her own vaudeville show *Swing, Harlem, Swing*, the audience was segregated, and Negroes were required to pay an extra admission fee to attend a midnight, all-Black audience show. Angry Blacks picketed the theatre, and it was reported Ethel Waters "was visibly shaken by the affair."

In the last years of her life, Ethel Waters devoted herself to religion. She would sing only religious numbers, a tragic loss for later generations who had never had the opportunity to witness an Ethel Waters performance. She was, as critic Ashton Stevens described her, "The Yvette Guilbert of her race."

BIBLIOGRAPHY

DeKorte, Juliann. *Ethel Waters: Finally Home*. Old Tappan, N.J.: Fleming H. Revell, 1978.
"Ethel Waters," *Current Biography*, April 1941, pp. 899–901.

Knaack, Twila. *Ethel Waters: I Touched a Sparrow*. Waco, Tx.: Word Books, 1978.

Rankin, Allen. "The Three Lives of Ethel Waters." *Reader's Digest*, December 1972, pp. 81–85.

Vick, Marsha. "Ethel Waters." In *Notable Black American Women*, ed. Jessie Carney Smith. Detroit: Gale Research, 1992, pp. 1225–1229.

Waters, Ethel, with Charles Samuels. *His Eye Is on the Sparrow*. Garden City, N.Y.: Doubleday, 1951.

————. *To Me It's Wonderful*. New York: Harper, 1972.

KITTY WATSON (1886—BUFFALO, N.Y., MARCH 3, 1967) AND **FANNY WATSON** (Rochester, N.Y., 1885—Albany, N.Y., May 17, 1970)

Writing in *Vaudeville: From the Honky-Tonks to the Palace*, Joe Laurie, Jr., described Kitty and Fanny Watson as the Smith and Dale of sister acts. Fanny was the comedienne and Kitty the straight woman in a routine that had developed from a singing act to a comedy turn. The sisters had entered vaudeville as children, playing the burlesque circuits for many years before becoming headliners for B. F. Keith. They first played the Palace in 1915 and made their last appearance there in 1949. Generally, the two women wrote their own material and regarded the high spot of their career to be a 1927 royal command performance in London. Although she was married many times, Kitty was living with Fanny at the time of her death.

NED WAYBURN (Pittsburgh, March 30, 1874—New York, September 2, 1942)

A prolific director of revues, musical comedies, and dancing shows, Ned Wayburn produced countless mini-revue-style acts for vaudeville, and his school of dancing in New York was considered by many as a gateway to a professional career in show business. Ned Wayburn claimed to have persuaded W. C. Fields to add dialogue to his juggling act; Eddie Cantor to drop blackface; and Will Rogers to talk more and spend less time on his rope tricks. At the time of his death, *Motion Picture Herald* (September 12, 1942) described Wayburn as "the most prominent director in the development of the modern American musical comedy with its emphasis on color, dancing and tuneful melody."

Born Edward Claudius, Ned Wayburn began his career as a theatre usher at the Chicago Opera House. In the 1890s, he became a vaudevillian, singing and playing ragtime piano under the sponsorship of May Irwin. In 1901, he staged his first two shows, George M. Cohan's *The Governor's Son* and George Ade's *The Night of the Fourth*. Oscar Hammerstein hired him as stage director for the Paradise Roof Garden on top of the Victoria and Republic theatres, but Wayburn soon returned to the musical stage. He staged *The Ham Tree* (1905) for McIntyre and Heath, *The Time, the Place and the Girl* (1907), Victor Herbert's *The Rose of Algeria* (1909), Sam Bernard's *The Girl and the Wizard* (1909), and the Victor Herbert/Irving Berlin musical *The Century Girl* (1916). Wayburn staged the

1912 and 1913 editions of *The Passing Show*, the 1922 and 1923 editions of the Ziegfeld *Follies*, and nine editions of Ziegfeld's *Midnight Frolic*. He staged Al Jolson's *The Honeymoon Express* in 1913 and also staged the London production, the first of many in that city.

As his fame increased, Wayburn's name would appear as part of the title of the show. The earliest example of this is *Ned Wayburn's Town Topics* in 1915, which featured Lew Hearn, Trixie Friganza, Blossom Seeley, and Clifton Webb. For the vaudeville stage, he produced short musical comedies or revues, longer than the average vaudeville act but generally less than forty-five minutes in length. For example, the Palace program for the week of April 15, 1928, featured *Ned Wayburn's Promenaders*, "a miniature follies," with lyrics by Morrie Ryskind and music by Walter G. Samuels. Peggy Hanlon and John Byam headed the cast of ten, which included acrobatic dancers Blanche and Elliott. A vaudeville presentation, "Buds of 1927," featured "young ladies and gentlemen . . . developed under the personal direction of Mr. Wayburn at the Ned Wayburn Studios of Stage Dancing, 1841 Broadway, New York City." Acts such as this helped promote the dance school and also provided cheap talent for Wayburn's presentations. Founded in the early years of the century, the Ned Wayburn Studios of Stage Dancing was still in operation at its founder's death.

With his pince-nez glasses and business suit, Wayburn always appeared in public looking more like a bank manager than a dance director. In 1956, Charlotte Greenwood recalled Wayburn's working methods during the rehearsals for *The Passing Show of 1912*:

Mr. Wayburn, as always, wearing his ornamental sweaters and bedecked with his silver whistle, had a habit of perching in the topmost peak of the gallery to watch the show during dress rehearsals. He felt that if he could see and hear everything from this pinnacle, he had done his best by his customers; and he was a stickler for clarity of speech.

As I finished my first song, feeling very well pleased with myself, the whistle shrilled. It sent icy shivers down my spine. There was deadly silence for a moment. I strained my eyes to see what was happening in the gallery. Wayburn, who had a fine sense of the dramatic, was making a leisurely descent to the lower floor. You could hear his feet in a measured clump-clump. Each footfall crushed me. Finally he reached the last row in the orchestra section and came slowly and majestically forward like an avenging god. With each leisurely step, he hurled imprecations at me.

"I don't know what you're here for" clump-clump. "The Shuberts are intelligent men" clump-clump. "They evidently had some idea you could do something" clump-clump. "They must have been told you had talent" clump-clump . . . "else you wouldn't be here" clump-clump . . . "or be getting this salary" clump-clump. "But I don't know how the public is going to find out unless they can hear you."

Now he was directly in front of me, just behind the orchestra leader. I expected every moment to see fire spurt from his nostrils, like the chromos I had seen of bull fights.

"I can see you all right, MISS Greenwood," he roared at me. "But that is not quite enough, MISS Greenwood. I'll be damned if I can hear you, MISS Greenwood."

BIBLIOGRAPHY

Kutner, Nanette. "Ned Wayburn Shows the Way." *Dance Magazine*, October 1928, pp. 26–27, 60.

Patterson, Ada. "Broadway's King of the Chorus." *Theatre*, December 1923, pp. 22–23, 62.

(JOSEPH) WEBER (New York, August 11, 1877—Los Angeles, May 10, 1942) and **(LEW) FIELDS** (New York, January 1, 1867—Beverly Hills, Ca., July 20, 1941)

Weber and Fields not only represent old-fashioned knockabout comedy; they were its creators. Almost every corny joke of the twentieth century would seem to have its origin with Weber and Fields. The trick of apparently poking your finger in a partner's eye, so beloved of Laurel and Hardy, the Three Stooges, and Dean Martin and Jerry Lewis, originated with Weber and Fields. Circa 1887, Weber asked Fields, "Who is that lady I saw you with last night?" and back, for the first time, came that hoary response, "She ain't no lady; she's my wife." Another favorite gag was to inveigle a valuable violin away from its owner, handle it roughly, get into an argument over it, and eventually smash it over the partner's head.

Joseph Weber and Lew Fields made their stage debuts together at New York's Chatham Square Museum in 1877, opening with a chorus of "Here we are, a jolly pair," before embarking on their comedy act. For $3 a week, the couple presented eight or nine shows a day. From the Chatham Square Museum, they took to appearing at other dime museums, vaudeville theatres, and beer gardens. Their entrance would change with the ethnic nature of the act. For blackface, they sang, "Here we are, a colored pair." For an Irish act, "Here we are, an Irish pair." And so on. As their biographer Felix Isman wrote, "They fit any figure, as did the second-hand suits in the Broadway schlockshops."

In was not until the 1880s that Weber and Fields became firmly established with a Dutch knockabout act called Mike and Myer. Tall and bullying Fields was Myer, while the "knockee" was small and plump, trustful and innocent Weber as Mike. Sporting goatees and destroying the English language in a parody of German immigrants new to this country, the routine would include the following dialogue:

Mike: I am delightfulness to meet you.

Myer: Der disgust is all mine.

Mike: I receividid a letter for mein goil, but I don't know how to writteninin her back.

Myer: Writteninin her back! Such an edumucation you got it! Writteninin her back! You mean rotteninin her back. How can you answer her ven you don't know how to write?

Mike: Dot makes no nefer mind. She don't know how to read.

Myer: If I'm cruel to you, Mike, it's because I luff you. (As he gouges Mike's eyes.)

Mike: If you luffed me any more, I couldn't stand it.

The classic Mike and Myer sketch involving a pool table was introduced in 1889. Myer, the pool shark, is showing Mike how to play pool, occasionally hitting him over the head with the cue while telling him, ''Ven I'm away from you, I cannot keep mein mind from off you. Ven I'm mit you, I cannot keep mein hands from off you. Oh, how I luff you, Mike!'' The game ended with the innocent Mike winning the betting money. The pool table sketch was new to vaudeville—W. C. Fields was a decade or so away—and with their act, Weber and Fields offered a burlesque of reality. Felix Isman wrote, ''The pool table skit told a story and held a mirror up to life; a farcical story and a distorted mirror, it is true, but a long step beyond the belled cap, the bladder, the stuffed club, and the topical joke.''

It is interesting to note the sadomasochism in the Weber and Fields routines which was carried through into the twentieth century, not so much on the vaudeville stage as in circuses with their aggressive and passive clowns. In more recent times, Laurel and Hardy have come closest to the violent nature of the Weber and Fields routines, but had their sketches been written by the latter, portly Hardy would have borne the brunt of the violence. Certainly, audiences have a need for violence, as evidenced by boxing matches, ice hockey, and soccer games in the area of sports, and Weber once commented that ''all the public wanted to see was Fields knock the hell out of me.'' Fields explained, ''I don't know why it was, but the audiences always seemed to have a grudge against him.''

On September 5, 1896, the two opened their own theatre, the Weber and Fields Music Hall, which had formerly been New York's Imperial Theatre, at 29th Street and Broadway. It was the world's first burlesque theatre when burlesque did not mean ''girlie'' shows, but rather burlesques of popular theatrical productions such as *The Heart of Maryland* (in which Mrs. Leslie Carter was then starring), with which the theatre opened. *The Art of Maryland*, as the Weber and Fields burlesque was called, ran for six weeks and was followed by *The Geezer*, a burlesque on a recent musical comedy import from Europe, *The Geisha*. Among the shows that followed were *Under the Red Globe*, *Barbara Fidgety*, *Quo Vass Iss?*, *Fiddle-dee-dee*, *Pousse-Café*, *Hurly-Burly*, *Hoity-Toity*, and *Higgledy-Piggledy*. Aside from the introduction of burlesque, the Weber and Fields Music Hall also introduced, or increased the popularity of, some of the era's most famous vaudeville and light opera stars, including Lillian Russell, DeWolf Hopper, Fay Templeton, Bessie Clayton, David Warfield, and Sam Bernard. The *New York Clipper* (December 27, 1900) described Weber and Fields as ''among the most popular actor-managers in this country,'' adding, ''They have placed their cozy little house not only in the front rank of amusement resorts in the metropolis but in the world.''

For seven years, the Weber and Fields Music Hall prospered, until the Iroquois

Theatre Fire in Chicago caused New York City to revise its theatre building codes. The Weber and Fields Music Hall would have to be rebuilt or close down; Weber and Fields chose the latter course, and on January 30, 1904, it gave its last performance. A few months later, on April 25, Weber and Fields dissolved their partnership, with Joe Weber paying Lew Fields $40,000 for the rights to the name of Weber and Fields Music Hall. May 29, 1904, was the date of their final performance in *Whoop-dee-doo* at the New Amsterdam Theatre and the final appearance of Weber and Fields onstage together for a number of years. "We can only say that we are sorry," said Weber, to which Fields added, "I can only echo Mr. Weber's sentiment."

Lew Fields leased a theatre on West 42nd Street and renamed it Fields Theatre, moving in 1906 to the Herald Square Theatre, where he continued to produce burlesques, beginning with *It Happened in Nordland*. Other productions included *The Music Master* (1905), *About Town* (1906), *The Girl Behind the Counter* (1907), *Old Dutch* (1909), *The Henpecks* (1911), and *The Never-Homes* (1911). Joe Weber also continued with burlesques at Weber's Music Hall, which reopened in the fall of 1904.

In January 1912, Lew Fields's father died, and Weber and Fields attended the funeral together. Weber confirmed that he was giving up the Music Hall, and Fields suggested that they get back together again. Lillian Russell, Fay Templeton, George Beban, Bessie Clayton, and others joined Weber and Fields for the reunion which took place at the Broadway Theatre on February 8, 1912. The Weber and Fields Music Hall reopened at the 44th Street Theatre on November 21, 1912, but survived only one season, because, Felix Isman claims, it was too large for burlesque.

Following the engagement at the Broadway Theatre, Weber and Fields embarked on a five week, thirty-six-city tour, playing one day at each location. The spring tour was in the tradition of tours that Weber and Fields had made at the turn of the century, and which they last made together in 1904. The New York Central Railroad provided a special train for the tour, consisting of two baggage cars, one dining car, two sixteen-section cars, one ten-room compartment car, and two private cars. Among those participating were William Collier, George Beban, Lillian Russell, Fay Templeton, Fay Tincher, Ada Lewis, and Bessie Clayton.

Weber and Fields continued to appear separately and together in musical comedy and revue. In February 1914, they appeared in the thirty-minute sketch "Mike and Myer's Trip Abroad" at the Auditorium, Chicago, assisted by Nora Bayes, George Beban, and Harry Clark. The sketch required Weber and Fields to pose as statues and be subjected to all types of annoyance and humiliation. *Variety* (February 27, 1914) reported, "The comedy is fast and furious. Some of it is new and some old. . . . It is an act such as suits the people in it, but demands just such people to put it over." On August 9, 1915, Weber and Fields made their debut at the Palace, receiving a weekly salary of $3,800, compared to the $40 they had earned weekly in 1883.

The team appeared in a number of films from 1915 onward, including *Two of the Finest* (1915), *The Worst of Enemies* (1916), *Friendly Enemies* (1925), and *Blossoms on Broadway* (1937). Additionally, Lew Fields appeared as himself in *The Story of Vernon and Irene Castle* (1939). In 1912, they were paid $10,000 to make a phonograph recording of their "Dutch Sidewalk Conversation," containing this classic exchange:

Mike: Do you have any money?

Myer: No.

Mike: Well, all I have is a nickel—just enough for one beer.

Myer: Why don't you have one. I don't want a drink just now.

Mike: Oh good. But it wouldn't look good if we both went in and I ordered a beer without offering one to you. Tell you what we'll do. We'll go into this bar. I'll ask you if you want a beer, and you say, "I don't care for any."

Myer: Okay, I'll do that. (There is the sound of a door opening. A pause. Then the sound of the door opening as they come out.)

Mike: Oh, you idiot! Now see what you've done.

Myer: Why, I just done what you told me. When you asked me if I wanted a beer . . .

Mike: You said, "I don't care if I do." And the bartender gave you the beer, and I had to pay my last nickel.

In 1925, Weber and Fields headlined on the Palace Theatre's old-timers bill. Their popularity never really waned, and they were the star attraction on the opening night program at Radio City Music Hall on December 27, 1932. The couple chose to close the show, but unfortunately, it was by then so late in the evening that *The New York Times* critic, Brooks Atkinson, decided not to wait for the act before filing his column. In 1930, both comedians took up residence in Los Angeles, where they spent their final years.

The Weber and Fields catchphrase, "Don't poosh me, Myer," was one of the most famous in early vaudeville history. As Douglas Gilbert wrote in *American Vaudeville*, "Theirs was an inherent aptness for the ridiculousness of pseudo pomp and they laid bare many a fool in their latter day clowning."

BIBLIOGRAPHY

Fields, Armond, and L. Marc Fields. *From the Bowery to Broadway: Lew Fields and the Roots of American Popular Theatre*. New York: Oxford University Press, 1993.

Isman, Felix. *Weber and Fields*. New York: Boni and Liveright, 1924.

Patterson, Ada. "Interview with Weber and Fields." *Theatre*, April 1912, pp. 113–14, 116.

"When Weber and Fields Were Youngsters." *Literary Digest*, April 25, 1925, pp. 42, 44.

BEN WELCH (?—Smithstown, N.Y., September 2, 1926)

Ben Welch was the cheerful Jewish comic whose typical dialogue began: "I vas to meet her here at halluf past six. It is now five o'clock. Vile I'm vaiting for her, I'll go home! How do you like my suit? A fine piece of merchandise. I got it in a restaurant. The fellow is still eating!"

In 1921, while appearing in a show called *Jimmie*, Welch began to go blind, but for the last five years of his life, he continued to work in vaudeville, relying on his straight man, Frank Murphy, to lead him on- and offstage, assuming that the audience would not notice his condition. It was rumored that he had insurance, but the company refused to pay up, claiming he could still work—and he did. As Welch might have said, "Vould a situation like this exist today?!"

Ben Welch's brother Joe (1869–1918) was also a popular comedian, but he always played a mirthless Jewish character, opening his act with the line, "Mebbe you t'ink I am a heppy man." In 1908, Joe Welch introduced an Italian immigrant character in the sketch "Ellis Island." One month prior to his death, he entered a mental institution.

SEÑOR WENCES (Peñaranola de Bracamonte, Spain, April 17, 1899—   )

Arguably the greatest of all comic ventriloquists, Señor Wences entered vaudeville in its waning years, but he brought vaudeville to new audiences thanks to some twenty-three separate appearances on *The Ed Sullivan Show* and many, many live performances through the 1980s. To call him simply a ventriloquist is comparable to stating that Eddie Cantor was just a comedian or that Belle Baker was nothing more than a popular songstress, for the ventriloquism act of Señor Wences was unique and incomparable to any other performer's routines before or since. The act usually featured two characters. The first was a doll, created by painting a mouth with lipstick and adding two onyx rings for eyes and a tiny red wig to Wences's left hand. The result was a character both impudent and funny. The other "dummy" was nothing more than the head of a Moorish-type man in a wooden box. The head was always arguing and threatening, and so wonderful was Wences that as he began to close the box, the voice of the head would gradually become muffled. Often, a three-way argument would develop between Wences, the doll, and the disembodied head.

Señor Wences was born Moreno Wenceslao, the son of an artistic Spaniard who played violin in a local orchestra and also restored paintings. The young man spent four years as a bullfighter prior to three years in the army. On his return home, he watched matinees at his father's theatre and decided he wanted to enter show business. Earlier, at school, he had worked on his ability to throw his voice and made hand puppets with which to entertain his friends. A mischievous boy, he based the hand puppet characterization on himself. An injury while bullfighting resulted in a doctor's advising him to exercise his arms and fingers, and thus Señor Wences took up juggling, with which he began his show business career.

In 1928, while playing at the Casino Theatre in Buenos Aires, the management issued an order that only acts not requiring musical accompaniment might appear. As a result, Wences adapted the ventriloquism routine that he had last performed at school at the age of eleven. After a successful European tour, Wences came to New York in 1936 and made his first appearance there at the El Chico Club in Greenwich Village. The London *Times* (November 10, 1937) had already reported on his act, when Wences played the Holborn Empire, commenting, "Wences is a ventriloquist who had a dummy of individuality, a dummy who not so much departs as strides away vigorously from the methods of his master." In 1938, Señor Wences toured with Chester Morris and the Frazee Sisters in *Ice Carnival*.

Wences made his vaudeville debut in an eleven-minute act at the Paramount Theatre, New York, in November 1938, billed incorrectly as "The Wences," which, as *Variety* noted, made him sound like a dance team. He was an instant hit with the audience, with the high spot of his act being the drinking of a glass of water and the smoking of a cigarette while the doll sang a high soprano. In *Variety* (November 2, 1938), Abel Green reported, "He walks off the Par. stage with a resounding personal score, working hard, fast and effectively. . . . Act is a happy blend of comedy and generally good pacing." (On the same bill was a young tap dancer named Ann Miller, but she did not make the same audience impact as Señor Wences.)

After his New York vaudeville debut, Señor Wences was booked on a lengthy tour with Martha Raye, which opened at the Earle Theatre, Philadelphia, on October 14, 1939. The act went over well, although there were complaints from the Midwest that Wences's foreign accent was confusing to cornbelt audiences. However, on August 26, 1942, *Variety* hailed him as "one of the best ventriloquists around."

Around this time, the head in the box developed. He had an engagement at the Chicago Theatre, Chicago, but when his dummy arrived, it had been damaged in transit. Wences got the idea of cutting off the head and using that alone. In 1939, he met his wife at the San Francisco World's Fair, and she helped with his act, translating his ideas from Spanish into English. In 1942, Wences appeared in New York at the Alvin Theatre in *Laugh, Town, Laugh*, but because of the situation in Europe and Spain's pro-Nazi stance, he was billed as "From Portugal, a Gentleman of Originality." When Judy Garland opened at the Palace in the fall of 1951, Wences replaced one of her supporting acts, British singer Max Bygraves, in December.

As the years went by, Señor Wences tended to spend more time in Europe— he was seven years at the Crazy Horse Saloon in Paris—but he did film his act for posterity, as a cameo, in the 1947 Betty Grable vehicle *Mother Wore Tights*. While working in Egypt in the 1950s, Wences created a third character, Cecelia Chicken, who made her U.S. debut on the television series *Your Show of Shows*. One of his last major television appearances was in *One-Man Show*, which aired on February 14, 1970. Its finale consisted of Wences juggling four plates on sticks while speaking in four separate voices. It was, as *Variety* (February 18, 1970) commented, "a reminder that great vaude turns are getting scarce."

One of Señor Wences's last stage appearances was in Los Angeles in November 1983, in the show *It's Magic*. One reporter described the entertainer as surreal, and in a sense that is true. He is a surrealistic artist of the theatre as much as his fellow Spaniard Luis Buñuel is a surrealistic filmmaker.

BIBLIOGRAPHY

Ormsbee, Helen. "Señor Wences Has Seven Voices but Audiences Believe Only Five."
   New York Herald Tribune, September 26, 1943, p. 2.
Wallace, Ed. "Look Who's Talking!" *New York World–Telegram and Sun*, May 26,
   1953, p. 21.

MAE WEST (Brooklyn, N.Y., August 17, 1892—Hollywood, Ca., November 22, 1980)

Reviewing Mae West's vaudeville act in 1912, *Variety* (January 20, 1912) noted that "Miss West is a lively piece of femininity" and went on to report, "The girl is of the eccentric type." As a criticism of West, it could have been applied to any period of her career, from vaudeville through musical comedy and her sex-related dramas to her classic feature films of the 1930s.

Mae West began appearing onstage in amateur productions as a child circa 1901, and by the age of eleven, she had played with stock companies in New York and on the road. In September 1911, she appeared in Ned Wayburn's revue *A la Broadway* at the Folies Bergere cabaret, and a few months later, she was in the revue *Vera Violetta*, which starred Al Jolson and Gaby Deslys. By January 1912, she had teamed with Billy O'Neal and Harry Laughlin (The Girard Brothers) for a vaudeville tour, but the obvious appreciation of the audiences for her body movements persuaded her to return to solo work. She was in Florenz Ziegfeld's *A Winsome Widow* when it opened at the Moulin Rouge, New York, on April 11, 1912, but obviously she did not stay very long with the show because one month later, she was back in vaudeville. Sime Silverman saw her and commented in *Variety* (May 25, 1912), "Miss West is a 'single' now. She has been about everything else, from a chorus girl in the Folies Bergere and head of a 'three-act' to principal in a Ziegfeld show. . . . The girl is of the eccentric type. She sings rag melodies and dresses oddly, but still lacks that touch of class that is becoming requisite now in the first class houses."

In 1916, Mae West teamed with her sister Beverly in vaudeville. She sang "I Want to Be Loved in the Old Fashioned Way" and "They Call It Dixieland," then reappeared in male attire, complete with silk hat, to sing "Walkin' th' Dog." *Variety* (July 7, 1916) was not particularly impressed: "Mae West in big-time vaudeville may only be admired for her persistency in believing she is a big-time act and trying to make vaudeville accept her as such." To conclude the act, Mae West had made a speech saying, "I am very pleased, ladies and gentlemen, you like my new act. It's the first time I have appeared with my sister. They all like her, especially the boys, who always fall for her, but that's where I come in—I always take them away from her." In a put-down, *Variety* suggested that the entertainer would do better in vaudeville if she wore men's dress all the while onstage, and that with her sister she could then do a boy-and-girl "sister" act.

West came to prominence on the musical comedy stage when she opened as the star of the Rudolf Friml musical romance *Sometime* on October 4, 1918, at the Shubert Theatre. She was a big hit with a dance that was a combination of the cooch and the shimmy called "The Shimmy Shawabble." *Variety* (October 11, 1918) commented, "Miss West has improved somewhat in looks but is still the rough hand-on-the-hip character that she first conceived as the ideal type of a woman single in vaudeville." Two of Mae West's songs from this show, "Any Kind of Man" and "All I Want Is Just a Little Lovin'," typified the kind of material that was to be associated with the star in later years.

In September 1919, Mae West returned to vaudeville after an absence of two years, and *Variety* (September 19, 1919) was a little kinder to her, commenting that "Miss West shows a marked improvement in method and delivery since last appearing in vaudeville." She was on the bill of the opening program at the Capitol Theatre on October 24, 1919, with a burlesque shimmy dance and the song, "Oh, What a Moanin' Man." Also on the program were the Douglas Fairbanks feature film *His Majesty the American* and Muriel De Forrest singing George Gershwin's "Swanee," its first performance. Mae West was featured on the front cover of the December 25, 1919, issue of *The New York Dramatic Mirror*, described as a "Popular Broadway Comedienne featured in *Sometime* and Ned Wayburn's *Demi-Tasse Revue*." In August 1920, West opened at the Colonial with a new, eighteen-minute vaudeville act titled "Songalog," in which she performed "I Want a Cave Man," "I'm a Night School Teacher," and "The Mannikin," wearing a black, silver-jetted gown. "Miss West has acquired ease and a legitimate repose in character comedy since last seen around, getting every point over without the slightest effort and for full value. . . . Miss West looks set as a big-time feature," reported *Variety* (August 13, 1920).

During the 1920s, Mae West had little time for vaudeville. On August 15, 1921, she opened at the Century Theatre in *The Mimic World of 1921*, the high spot—or low spot, depending upon one's point of view—of which was her dancing a shimmy dressed as Our Lady of Fatima. She returned to vaudeville in 1922, touring with Harry Richman as her pianist, and when the two appeared at the Riverside Theatre, New York, *Variety* (June 23, 1922) reported, "She rises to heights undreamed of for her and reveals unsuspected depths as a delineator of character songs, a dramatic reader of ability, and a girl with a flare for farce that will some day land her on the legitimate Olympus." Richman departed in the fall of 1922, and West apparently turned her attention to sex and its possibilities as a dramatic subject. The result was her play *Sex*, which opened at the Daly Theatre on April 26, 1926, and which, according to the *New York Herald Tribune*, "wins high marks for depravity [and] dullness." West starred in *Sex*, but she did not appear the following year in her play *The Drag*, which dealt explicitly with homosexuality, or in her next production, a satirical comedy titled *The Wicked Age* (1927).

Mae West's most successful play was *Diamond Lil*, "a drama of the underworld," which opened at the Royale Theatre on April 9, 1928, and ran for 323 performances. It was followed by other productions of a lurid nature: *Pleasure Man* (1928) and *The Constant Sinner* (1931). Prior to starring in the latter, West had returned to vaudeville with a fourteen-minute act which made its debut at the Fox Audubon—where the cooch dance was ordered removed—in May 1930. Reviewing the act at the Academy, a presentation house, *Variety* (May 21, 1930) commented, "Miss West has been out of vaude since 1925 or thereabouts and in the interim has become an accomplished and at the same time notorious legitimate authoress, producer, and actress. In her new vaude act she mentions all of that legit career, including the shows and the trouble. In talking, she's the nearest to a female Jimmy Durante as, when talk-singing about the 'Pleasure Man' bunch, she pipes, 'They (the police) said these guys is fairies.' "

At that time, Mae West announced somewhat prematurely that she was departing for Hollywood. In reality, she did not enter films until 1932; her appearances in *Night after Night* (1932), *She Done Him Wrong* (1933), *I'm No Angel* (1933), *Goin' to Town* (1935), *Go West, Young Man* (1936), *My Little Chickadee* (1940), and others, precluded any further appearances on the vaudeville stage.

In the 1950s, Mae West developed a popular nightclub act in which she would appear with eight musclemen clothed only in loincloths. She rehashed all the old lines, such as "peel me a grape," from her films, and had Louise Beavers as her maid and Tito Coral as her lover make worthwhile contributions to the act. Reviewing her performance at Ciro's in Los Angeles, "Helm" wrote in *Daily Variety* (May 16, 1955), "Those who check their inhibitions at the door will have themselves a night; an experience they won't soon forget—Mae West." From this decade onward, Mae West slowly became a caricature of her former self, an old woman hopelessly clinging to youth and sex appeal in her last, desperate film appearances: *Myra Breckinridge* and *Sextette*.

(In 1911, Mae West was briefly married to a song-and-dance man, Frank Wallace, and toured with him. Billed as "Mister Mae West," Wallace opened in burlesque at the Eltinge Theatre on September 27, 1935, in an act with Trixie LeMae that he claimed he had performed with Mae West.)

BIBLIOGRAPHY

Arbus, Diane. "Mae West," *Show* 5, no. 1 (January 1965), pp. 42–45.

Bavar, Michael. *Mae West*. New York: Pyramid Books, 1975.

Calhoun, Dorothy. "Blondes Prefer Gentlemen." *Motion Picture Magazine* 52, no. 2 (September 1936), pp. 47, 84–85.

Cashin, Fergus. *Mae West: A Biography*. Westport, Ct.: Arlington House, 1992.

Clarke, Gerald. "At 84 Mae West Is Still Mae West." *Time*, May 22, 1978, pp. 65–66.

Condon, Frank. "Come Up and Meet Mae West." *Collier's* 93, no. 24 (June 16, 1934), pp. 26, 42.

Davis, George. "The Decline of Mae West." *Vanity Fair*, May 1934, pp. 46, 82.

Eells, George, and Stanley Musgrove. *Mae West: A Biography*. New York: William Morrow, 1982.

Eyman, William Scott. "I've Always Done Everything I Wanted: Mae West Interviewed." *Take One* 4, no. 1 (September-October 1972), pp. 19–21.

Hanna, David. *Come Up and See Me Sometime!: An Uncensored Biography of Mae West*. New York: Belmont Tower Books, 1976.

Jennings, Robert C. "Mae West: A Candid Conversation with the Indestructible Queen of Vamp and Camp." *Playboy*, January 1971, pp. 73–82.

Lane, Hester. "Mae Answers the Letter of Her New Boy Friend." *Shadowplay* 2, no. 5 (January 1934), pp. 30–31, 76.

"Mae West." *Current Biography*, November 1967, pp. 455–58.

Ringgold, Gene. "Mae West." *Screen Facts* 2, no. 1 (1964), pp. 1–25.

Sochen, June. *Mae West: She Who Laughs Last*. Arlington Heights, Il.: Harlan Davidson, 1992.

Troy, William. "Mae West and the Classic Tradition." *The Nation*, November 8, 1933, pp. 547–48.

Tuska, Jon. *The Films of Mae West*. Secaucus, N.J.: Citadel Press, 1973.

Ward, Carol M. *Mae West: A Bio-Bibliography*. Westport, Ct.: Greenwood Press, 1989.

Weintraub, Joseph, ed. *The Wit and Wisdom of Mae West*. New York: G. P. Putnam's Sons, 1967.

West, Mae. *Goodness Had Nothing to Do with It*. Englewood Cliffs, N.J.: Prentice-Hall, 1959.

WESTERN MANAGERS' VAUDEVILLE ASSOCIATION AND EASTERN MANAGERS' VAUDEVILLE ASSOCIATION

Founded in 1900 under the guidance of John J. Murdock, the Western Managers' Vaudeville Association and the Eastern Managers' Vaudeville Association were two branches of the same organization, created on the West Coast by Martin Beck and on the East Coast by B. F. Keith and E. F. Albee. The idea was to create a vaudeville circuit that would book performers directly, and require each act to pay a 5 percent commission to the relevant association. Out of these two associations grew the Orpheum circuit, covering the western United States, and the B. F. Keith vaudeville circuit, controlling the eastern states.

(BERT) WHEELER (Paterson, N.J., April 7, 1895—New York, January 18, 1968) and **(ROBERT) WOOLSEY** (Atlanta, August 14, 1888—Malibu Beach, Ca., October 31, 1938)

To most readers familiar with the films of Wheeler and Woolsey—*The Cuckoos* (1930), *Hook, Line and Sinker* (1930), *Cracked Nuts* (1931), *Diplomaniacs* (1933), *Hips, Hips, Hooray!* (1934), *The Nitwits* (1935), and the like—the funny man was the one with the lean face and glasses, Robert Woolsey. The baby-faced, better-looking one, Bert Wheeler, is often mistaken for the straight man of the team, and few realize that Wheeler's career prospered both before and after his teaming with Woolsey; if anything, this essay should be devoted entirely to Bert Wheeler.

Vaudevillian Ted Waldman recalled that Bert Wheeler would walk out onstage carrying a joke book and announce to the audience that he would read to them from the volume. So funny was Wheeler that when he proceeded to do precisely that, audiences were convulsed in laughter. The jokes might be corny—for example, "The headwaiter kept asking me if I had a reservation. What does he think I am? An Indian?"—but they never failed to amuse a vaudeville crowd.

Many times, Wheeler would simply sit on the edge of the stage, perhaps eating a sandwich, and just talking with the audience; sometimes he would cry and accidentally wipe his eyes on the sandwich and eat his handkerchief.

Albert Jerome Wheeler's early career included a spell with Gus Edwards's company and a vaudeville act with his first wife, Betty, whom he married while still a teenager. (She later married Clarence Stroud of the Stroud Twins, and Wheeler was to marry on three other occasions, with all unions ending in divorce.) In 1923, Wheeler was featured in the Ziegfeld *Follies*, and as a result of his success in that show, Florenz Ziegfeld offered Wheeler a five-year contract. It was Ziegfeld who teamed Bert Wheeler and Robert Woolsey for *Rio Rita*, which opened at the Ziegfeld Theatre on February 2, 1926. Wheeler played Chick Bean, while Woolsey was Ed Lovett; J. Harold Murray was Jim, and Ethelind Terry played the title role.

Robert Woolsey had been an exercise boy and a jockey before a riding accident forced him to change careers. He entered show business, playing in stock companies and performing in Gilbert and Sullivan operettas. Woolsey made his New York debut as Drake in *Nothing but Love* at the Lyric Theatre on October 14, 1919, and was later featured in *The Right Girl* (1921), *The Blue Kitten* (1922), *Poppy* (1923), *The Dream Girl* (1924), *Mayflowers* (1925), and *Honest Liars* (1926).

Rio Rita made the continuation of the Wheeler and Woolsey partnership inevitable, for as the 1929 film version indicates, the two interreacted with one another perfectly, with efficient, split-second timing. In addition, the film illustrates what a delightful singing voice Bert Wheeler had, particularly in the charming duet with Dorothy Lee, "Sweetheart, We Need Each Other." A film career for Wheeler and Woolsey followed, and the two starred in twenty-one features and some additional short subjects. "They were pretty bad, but they all made money," Wheeler once commented. The pair split up in May 1932, with Woolsey explaining, "I wish it understood that Wheeler and I never really formed a team at any time. He had his manager and attorney and I had mine." However, a reconciliation was worked out in July of the same year, and the two were immediately starred in their only film for Columbia, *So This Is Africa* (all the other Wheeler and Woolsey features were produced by RKO).

Robert Woolsey died at his Malibu, California, home in 1938, and after his death, Bert Wheeler made only a few additional films: *Cowboy Quarterback* (1939), *Las Vegas Nights* (1941), and *The Awful Sleuth* (1951). He returned to vaudeville and was also to be heard on radio and seen on early television. He took on several partners, including Betty Grable, Harry Jans, Sid Slate, and Jack Pepper, and for a number of years, he appeared in drag, as an elderly lady, with Tom Dillon playing his abusive son. On October 26, 1966, the small theatre inside New York's Dixie Hotel was named in his honor.

Wheeler's last years were spent on the borderline of poverty, but he always enjoyed participating in various entertainments at the Lambs Club, explaining, "I make all I need." His last public appearance was at the Garden City Hotel on Long Island in December 1966. At the time of his death, Lambs Club President Harry Hershfield said of him, "Bert had a pixie face and remained a pixie to the end."

BIBLIOGRAPHY
Cohen, Joe. "Bert Wheeler, 73, Always a Pixie." *Variety*, January 24, 1968, pp. 2, 70.
Drew, William M. "The Screwball Satirists: Wheeler & Woolsey." *American Classic Screen* 2, no. 4 (March/April 1978), pp. 34–37.
Maltin, Leonard. "Wheeler and Woolsey." In *Movie Comedy Teams*. New York: New American Library, 1970, pp. 85–104.

"WHEELS"

Dating back to the turn of the century, "wheels" was the name given to the various burlesque theatre circuits, of which the first was the Columbia Amusement Company. The burlesque shows revolved around the circuits rather like spokes of a wheel, hence the name.

ALBERT WHELAN (Melbourne, Australia, May 5, 1875—London, February 19, 1961)

Often billed, particularly in England, as "The Australian Entertainer," Albert Whelan was noted for his tuneful whistling as he elegantly removed his top hat, cane, and white gloves. Whelan began his career in his native Australia in the late 1890s and first appeared on the London stage in 1901 as an eccentric dancer. He made his U.S. debut in 1908 and alternated appearances in the United States, the United Kingdom, and Australia through the 1920s. His last U.S. vaudeville tour was probably in 1924 and 1925, on his way back from Australia to London. It began in San Francisco and reached its climax at the Palace in November 1925. At that time, Whelan was supported by a female tap dancer and introduced a new song to American audiences, "Show Me the Way to Go Home." Writing in *Variety* (November 11, 1925), Sime Silverman commented, "Whelan carries it along lightly in song and story."

While there is no documentation to back up the claim, Albert Whelan was supposedly the first performer to utilize a signature tune.

FRANCES WHITE. See WILLIAM ROCK AND FRANCES WHITE

GEORGE WHITE (Toronto, Canada, 1890—Hollywood, Ca., October 10, 1968)

The man who gave Broadway its *Scandals* began his career in vaudeville as a dancer. Born George Weitz, the showman began dancing while still a teenager with Bennie Ryan. The two men soon quarreled and parted, and George White made his first appearance at the Palace as a single turn in February 1914. He was back again in 1916, partnering Lucille Cavanagh. In 1915, White joined the Ziegfeld *Follies*, where he was teamed with Ann Pennington; she became his mistress and later joined him in the *Scandals*. Despite their close personal relationship, Pennington did not continue as White's partner outside of the *Follies*. In 1917, he was dancing in vaudeville with Emma Haig, and in September 1918, he was back again at the Palace, this time with four female dancers. "Mr.

White is a resourceful producer of high class dancing turns, also a skillful dancing instructor," commented Sime Silverman in *Variety* (September 6, 1918).

That 1918 vaudeville act would appear to have been the first time that White tried to produce any form of entertainment. It led to his deciding to produce his own revue-style show, the *Scandals*, the first of which opened in 1919. The second edition, in 1920, is more important in that it marked the first time George Gershwin became associated with the revue. He continued with the *Scandals* through 1924, composing some forty-five songs for the shows, including "I'll Build a Stairway to Paradise" (1922) and "Somebody Loves Me" (1924). In 1925, Gershwin was succeeded as company composer by Buddy DeSylva, Lew Brown, and Ray Henderson, who composed "Birth of the Blues" and "Black Bottom" for the 1926 edition.

George White's *Scandals* were produced on an annual basis through 1926, and revived again in 1928, 1929, 1930, 1931, 1935, and 1939. In 1927, White produced the popular Broadway musical *Manhattan Mary*, featuring Ed Wynn and Lou Holtz. In 1932, he produced *George White's Music Hall Varieties*, starring Harry Richman, Lili Damita, Bert Lahr, and Eleanor Powell. In September 1933, White signed a five-year contract with the William Fox Company as a film producer, and in 1935, he produced *George White's Scandals*, starring Alice Faye, James Dunn, Ned Sparks, Lyda Roberti, Eleanor Powell, Cliff Edwards, and Benny Rubin. The film introduced the song "You Nasty Man," sung by Faye. In 1945, he produced a second *George White's Scandals*, this time for RKO, with Joan Davis and Jack Haley.

From the 1940s onward, George White encountered myriad personal problems, many associated with his love of gambling on horses; indeed, *Variety*'s obituary of the producer is headlined, "Big Supporter of Broadway Revue & Racetracks." On June 9, 1942, he filed for voluntary bankruptcy, listing liabilities of $100,000. Four years later, White was arraigned on manslaughter charges in connection with the hit-and-run killing of a honeymoon couple on July 20, 1946, in Solano Beach, California; he served one year in country jail. On December 29, 1953, White again filed for bankruptcy, again listing liabilities of $100,000. Through the years, George White tried on a number of occasions to produce revue-style entertainments in the style of the *Scandals*, the last being at Jack Silverman's International Restaurant in New York in 1963.

BIBLIOGRAPHY

Baral, Robert. *Revue: A Nostalgic Reprise of the Great Broadway Period*. New York: Fleet, 1962.
White, George. "The Luck of George White." *The American Weekly*, November 30, 1947, pp. 22–23; December 7, 1947, pp. 24–25; December 14, 1947, pp. 6–7.
Woollcott, Alexander. "Rise of Swifty White." *Collier's*, May 19, 1928, pp. 12, 49–50.

PAUL WHITEMAN (Denver, March 28, 1890—Doylestown, Pa., December 29, 1967)

Paul Whiteman was not only the best known conductor of popular music in the world, but also the best known and most expensive to play vaudeville. He was paid $7,000 a week to headline at the New York Hippodrome in 1925, and the reason for that was not only the Whiteman name but also the fact that his act was an entire show in its own right.

Born into an affluent Denver family, Whiteman learned to play the violin as a child. He played first viola with the Denver Symphony Orchestra and in 1915 played with the San Francisco People's Symphony. After serving during the First World War as a bandmaster with the navy, he formed his own orchestra in 1919, introducing "symphonic jazz," with which he had first come into contact around 1915 on San Francisco's Barbary Coast. It can be argued that the Jazz Age arrived in 1920 when Whiteman and his orchestra played Broadway's Palais Royale. His jazz style was not improvisational, and so he gathered around him thirty of the finest musicians in the country, each of whom was a capable soloist. His arranger was Ferdie Grofé, whose "Grand Canyon Suite" Whiteman introduced. Of course, Whiteman also introduced George Gershwin's "Rhapsody in Blue" at New York's Aeolian Hall as part of a concert program titled "An Experiment in American Music." The concert took place on February 12, 1924, Lincoln's Birthday, an auspicious date for a new era in American music.

Paul Whiteman had earlier introduced Gershwin's "I'll Build a Stairway to Paradise" in the 1922 edition of George White's *Scandals*. That same year he played the Palace, earning a mere $2,500 a week. Of Whiteman's 1925 Hippodrome performance, *Variety* (May 13, 1925) wrote, "Whiteman's program is a happy medium. It is not musical hoke. It does not resort to moron appeal with blatant jazz, or so-called popular appeal with scenic back-ups, but gets to both, and beyond that, with a study in syncopation that distinguishes the orchestra as an individuality and not of a class."

Singer Al Rinker recalled: "Whiteman was a marvelous personality. He wasn't a great band leader. He wasn't a great musician, like Tommy Dorsey; he played fiddle, but he gave that up and all he did was carry it, and it had nothing to do with leading the band. But he was a marvelous personality. He paid big salaries. In those days, a top lead in that orchestra, a sax player, would make three hundred dollars a week. No one else paid three hundred dollars a week."

Aside from working with Whiteman, Al Rinker, Harry Barris, and Bing Crosby, as the Rhythm Boys, toured the vaudeville circuit in 1928. Rinker remembered the problems they encountered: "The younger people knew who we were, because they bought our records, but the average person who went to vaudeville was not used to seeing such a type of act as ours. We didn't go over at all at the Palace. We'd sing 'Mississippi Mud' and all these things, and the audience didn't know what the hell we were doing. They were probably waiting for Sophie Tucker to come on and sing 'Some of These Days.' We were too modern."

The Rhythm Boys would parody the old type of vaudeville entertainer with a dance performed to the tune of "Baby Face." They engaged in comic patter and, of course, they harmonized. *The Billboard* (August 18, 1928) saw them at Keith's 81st Street Theatre and commented, "The Paul Whiteman Rhythm Boys have personality, good voices and a way of putting their song numbers over effectively. . . . They have the art of rhythm perfected to a stellar degree.''

Paul Whiteman headlined at the Palace in December 1928 and appeared on Broadway in *Lucky* (1927) and the 1929 edition of Ziegfeld's *Midnight Frolic*. After completing his first film, *The King of Jazz*, for Universal in 1930, Whiteman prophesied that ''within two years you will see the bands and orchestras back in the picture houses again. The talkies drove them out, but they will make the people so music loving that they will have to put the bands back. I think that pictures with music will make the people demand big bands and good bands. They won't stand for four- and five-piece affairs again. They will be educated up to the big band class. And watch big bands come back to the theatres. A good band can make a house pay even if the picture is bad.'' Whiteman was proved correct in that, with the changeover from vaudeville houses to presentation houses featuring both movies and vaudeville acts, and big bands became a staple of the bill.

Whiteman had little reason to worry, as he was busy touring the country with his orchestra as the entire show. He made his radio debut in 1932, and on June 26, 1933, he began broadcasting as the star of *The Kraft Music Hall*. In 1943, *Paul Whiteman Presents* began airing on NBC, and on July 4 of that year, Harry Barris, Al Rinker, and Bing Crosby got together on the program to revive, albeit for one performance, and Rhythm Boys. In 1936, Paul Whiteman and his orchestra were featured in *Billy Rose's Jumbo* at the New York Hippodrome. Whiteman married for the fourth and last time in 1931—to actress Margaret Livingston, who wrote a book about her husband's attempt to reduce his sizeable figure.

Paul Whiteman's music was such that it struck the very soul of America, and the *Chicago Tribune* editorialized on April 7, 1925:

It is as racy of our soil as a Russian folk song is of Russia. It is the rush of our racing streets. It has all the bright contrasts of our racial conglomerate, but they are now forming in designs of real harmony and meaning. It has our moods and our spirit, our impudence and irreverence, our joy in speed and force. But it can sigh as well as laugh, and in the midst of its boisterous cynicism and surface brilliance it opens glimpses of quiet underdeeps and sudden sweeps of feeling which show how far its eventual achievements will go.

BIBLIOGRAPHY
DeLong, Thomas A. *Pops: Paul Whiteman, King of Jazz*. Piscataway, N.J.: New Century, 1983.
''Paul Whiteman.'' *Current Biography*, August 1945, pp. 671–74.
Whiteman, Margaret Livingston, and Isabel Leighton. *Whiteman's Burden*. New York: Viking, 1933.
Whiteman, Paul. ''The All-American Swing Band.'' *Collier's* 102, no. 11 (September 10, 1938), pp. 9–12, 63–64.
————. ''So You Want to Lead a Band.'' *Collier's* 104, no. 11 (September 9, 1939), pp. 14, 51–52.

WHITE RATS

The White Rats was the first union of vaudeville artists, founded in 1900 by
George Fuller Golden in response to the successful attempt by management to
form a syndicate or trust. Golden got the idea from the British fraternal orga-
nization the Grand Order of Water Rats, founded in the 1880s, which took care
of him financially after he was stranded in England in 1899. Along with Golden,
David Montgomery, Fred Stone, Sam Morton, Thomas Lewis, Sam J. Ryan,
Mark Murphy, and Charles Mason met at the Parker House bar on Broadway
on June 1, 1900. After an initial suggestion that the organization be called the
Vaudeville Artists of America, they opted for the name White Rats, after the
British society, and because "Rats" is "Star" spelled backward. Gypsy Dolan
was on tour at the time of the organizing meeting, but at the next meeting, his
name was added to the list of founders. The White Rats adapted "The Emblem,"
the song of the Water Rats, as their own, substituting "White" for "Water":

> And this is the emblem of our society,
> Each member acts with the greatest propriety,
> Jolly old sports, to us they raise their hats!
> A merry lot of fellows are The Real White Rats.
> Rats! Rats! Rats! RATS. Rats! Star!

The first test of strength for the White Rats came on February 22, 1901, when
its members struck the Western Vaudeville Managers' Association over the
latter's decision to charge vaudevillians a 5 percent commission upon their
signing a contract. The strike was settled within a week, with the rescission of
the 5 percent commission, but the White Rats had made a powerful enemy in
E. F. Albee, and failed to realize that he and his colleagues were only biding
their time before a showdown with the union.

The White Rats grew in size until, by 1910, it claimed a membership of eleven
thousand. A sister organization, Associated Actresses of America, was founded
in September 1910, and in 1912, the White Rats opened its clubhouse. For a
while, *Variety* published a weekly column prepared by the White Rats, but in
1916, the organization sued the trade paper for discrimination, claiming pref-
erential editorial treatment for those who advertised. Nothing came of the suit,
although there is a strong possibility that it was not without merit.

In 1907, a British music hall performer named Harry Mountford came to the
United States, and because of his involvement in labor relations in England, he
was asked to reorganize the White Rats. Mountford approached Samuel Gom-
pers, president of the American Federation of Labor, for a charter, and on
November 7, 1910, it was granted to the White Rats of America. In 1916,
Mountford called for a nationwide strike against the United Booking Office,
representing management, which had introduced a clause into its contracts with
vaudevillians requiring that the latter guarantee they were not members of the
White Rats. The strike began in Oklahoma City and spread to Boston and New
York. It was reported that vaudeville management, led by E. F. Albee, paid up

to $2 million to fight the strike, which was ultimately unsuccessful because of a lack of cooperation from the stagehands union (which had its own political agenda).

Reprisals against the White Rats were swift and vicious. Any vaudevillian known to be a member of the organization was denied a booking. In 1917, the White Rats was unable to meet the mortgage on its clubhouse, and it was acquired by E. F. Albee for his company union, National Vaudeville Artists, Inc. Membership in the White Rats dropped to less than six hundred. The White Rats survived as an organization until 1934, when it gave up its charter to Actors Equity.

BIBLIOGRAPHY
Golden, George Fuller. *My Lady Vaudeville and Her White Rats.* New York: White Rats of America, 1909.
Nugent, J. C. "Evolution of the White Rats." *Variety*, December 14, 1907, p. 22.

ANNABELLE WHITFORD (1878—Chicago, November 30, 1961)
A modern dancer with a style similar to that of Loïe Fuller, Annabelle Whitford was noted for her exceptional beauty. As early as 1896, she was filmed by the American Mutoscope and Biograph Company performing a flag dance. Artist Charles Dana Gibson selected her as the original "Gibson Girl," and Florenz Ziegfeld chose her to be featured in the first, 1907, edition of his *Follies*.

GEORGE WHITING (Chicago, August 6, 1884—Bronx, N.Y., December 18, 1943) and **SADIE BURT** (?—Great Neck, N.Y., December 6, 1966)
George Whiting was both a vaudevillian and a lyricist, whose songs include "My Blue Heaven," "West of the Great Divide," and "Strolling through the Park One Day." At the age of nineteen, he was brought to New York by boxer Kid McCoy to sing at the latter's rathskeller in the Hotel Normandie. While there, he was heard by Irving Berlin, who collaborated with him on the 1909 song "My Wife's Gone to the Country." George Whiting next worked in vaudeville as a pianist and singer, and while on tour, he met Sadie Burt in San Francisco. They teamed as a song-and-dance act with comedy patter and later married. Whiting and Burt played the Palace in April 1927.

MARSHALL P. WILDER (Geneva, N.Y., September 19, 1859—St. Paul, Mn., January 10, 1915)
Marshall P. Wilder was a curious character, a hunchbacked dwarf who came to vaudeville after lecturing successfully on the Chautauqua circuit. On the vaudeville stage, he told stories that were, according to Caroline Caffin in her 1914 book *Vaudeville*, full of "dry whimsicality." They were also apparently always stolen from other vaudevillians, who took no action against Wilder because of his physical deformities. Before opening at any theatre, Wilder would check the bill and omit stories he had "borrowed" from others working with him that week. Often, in an effort to protect himself from charges of plagiarism,

he would begin a story with the line, "As my friend so-and-so told me," or "As so-and-so related . . . " The monologist was reasonably popular with vaudeville audiences, earning a weekly salary of $600 shortly before his death.

BERT WILLIAMS (New Providence, Nassau, British West Indies, November 12, 1874—New York, March 4, 1922)

Bert Williams was one of the finest pantomimists and comedians that the vaudeville stage has ever known. *The New York Dramatic Mirror* (December 7, 1918) called him "one of the great comedians of the world." W. C. Fields described him as "the funniest man I ever saw." Eddie Cantor regarded Williams as both his teacher and his friend, "the man to whom I owe so much," and wrote of him: "In my seventy years, I've known many outstanding people in and out of the theater. A Will Rogers, an Al Jolson, comes once in a generation. Bert Williams . . . once in a lifetime."

Bert Williams was also black, and in an age when black performers were not welcome on the "white" vaudeville stage, he was very much a pioneer. He was the only black vaudevillian the Keith circuit could book on a white bill in Washington, D.C. In 1904, he played a command performance before King Edward VII. He was a Mason and had the distinction of being the first black to be buried by a white Masonic lodge. His humor did not poke fun at his race, as did the comedy of so many blackface comedians of the era. Rather, he found mirth in situations that might apply equally well to any poor folk. Yet he always performed—as was the style of the day—in blackface makeup, overemphasizing his racial background.

There is no question that his color did hurt him both commercially and emotionally. Some white vaudevillians would not appear on the same bill with Williams, while others objected when his material seemed superior to their own. He once told Eddie Cantor how much it hurt that he should be allowed to stay at the same hotels as his fellow white performers but be expected to take the back elevators: "It wouldn't be so bad, Eddie, if I didn't still hear the applause ringing in my ears."

The Williams family moved permanently from the British West Indies to Florida when Bert was eleven. As a teenager, he became fascinated with show business. In 1893, he joined Martin and Selig's Mastodon Minstrels, in which he met a black song-and-dance man named George Walker (circa 1873–1911). The two teamed up and became a highly popular act until Walker's death of syphilis diagnosed in 1909 during the run of a show called *Bandanna Land*. Williams and Walker made their New York debut in 1898 in a short-lived production titled *The Gold Bug* at the Casino Theatre. They entertained with songs and with a quick-paced patter act in which Walker was always trying to persuade the slower and more cautious Williams to participate in one of his get-rich-quick schemes.

When Walker became sick in 1909, Bert Williams embarked on a single act, which led to his being signed by Florenz Ziegfeld as one of the stars of the 1910 *Follies*. Williams played in the *Follies* almost continually from 1910 through 1919, taking breaks only in 1913 and 1918. He and Cantor first played together in the 1917 edition, in which the Jewish comedian played the black comedian's son in a sketch set in Grand Central Station. Cantor recalled:

As a performer, he was close to genius. As a man, he was everything the rest of us would like to have been. As a friend, he was without envy or jealousy. . . . A master of pantomime, he was a miser with gestures, never raising his hand six inches if three would suffice. Whatever sense of timing I have, I learned from him. Years later when I was in pictures that called for pantomime—*The Kid from Spain* and *Roman Scandals*—I'd ask myself, "How would Bert Williams handle this scene?"

Bert Williams's most famous pantomime act was that of a player in a poker game. His head and shoulders would be lit by a single spotlight as he mimicked all the gestures of the player, from the draw to losing the game. When he returned to vaudeville in 1918 to top the bill at the Palace, he climaxed his act with this sketch, and *The New York Dramatic Mirror* (December 14, 1918) noted that despite its familiarity, the pantomime "holds fresh interest with every resurrection."

In addition to the poker game, Williams introduced many popular songs of the day, including "You Ain't So Warm," "That's Harmony," "You Got the Right Church but the Wrong Pew," "He's a Cousin of Mine," "My Castle on the Nile," and his best known song, "Nobody." This writer's particular favorite is "Bring Back Those Wonderful Days," which Williams recorded for Columbia circa 1920, and in which he pleads at the dawn of prohibition for the saloon and "the ale that was always musty," and asks that we take back the income tax collector and the red flag agitator. Aside from the songs, Williams was a natural storyteller, with a calm deliberation to his delivery. A typical yarn, as recalled by Douglas Gilbert in *American Vaudeville*, concerned Williams's home:

Where I'm living now is a nice place, but you have to go along a road between two graveyards to get to it. One night last week I was coming home kind of late, and I got about halfway home when I happened to look over my shoulder and saw a ghost following me. I started to run. I ran till I was 'most ready to drop. And then I looked around. But I didn't see no ghost, so I sat down on the curbstone to rest. Then out of the corner of my eye I could see something white, and when I turned square around, there was that ghost sitting alongside of me. The ghost says, "That was a fine run we had. It was the best running I ever saw." I says, "Yes. And soon as I get my breath you're going to see some more."

Even without Williams's delivery, a simple reading of the tale confirms the comment by "Rush" in *Variety* (December 26, 1913) that "Williams has the story telling gift in a degree possessed by few."

Bert Williams even found time for a brief film career with the American Biograph Company in the summer of 1916. One of the films in which he appeared, and which is extant, is *A Natural Born Gambler*, released by the General Film Company on July 24, 1916. It was inspired by his celebrated poker game.

The critic for *The Moving Picture World* (August 12, 1916) reported, "The actors are all colored persons of the male sex and they are all addicted to gambling. Williams attempts to annex the role of a swell sport from the city, but the game is raided and when last seen the natural born gambler is sadly dealing out imaginary hands behind the bars of a prison. The business of some of the scenes could be improved, but Bert Williams's skill at pantomime shows up well on the screen."

In 1920, Williams left Ziegfeld and signed with the Shuberts. On February 21, 1922, while touring in their production of *Under the Bamboo Tree*, he collapsed onstage at the Shubert-Garrick Theatre in Detroit. He returned to New York, where he died a couple of weeks later in his home at 2309 Seventh Avenue. His death was the result of pneumonia, compounded by heart problems.

Despite all the black performers who have come along since, none has the appeal or the personality of the man who made vaudeville audiences accept black performers and, coincidentally, proved they could be better than many white entertainers of the era.

BIBLIOGRAPHY

Brown, Janet. "The 'Coon Singer' and the 'Coon Song': A Case of the Performer-Character." *Journal of American Culture* 7, nos. 1–2 (Spring-Summer 1984), pp. 1–8.

Cantor, Eddie. "Bert Williams—The Best Teacher I Ever Had." *Ebony* 13, no. 8 (June 1958), pp. 103–106.

Charters, Ann. *Nobody: The Story of Bert Williams*. New York: Macmillan, 1970.

Fauset, Jessie. "The Symbolism of Bert Williams." *Crisis*, May 24, 1922, pp. 12–15.

Feingold, Michael. "Bert Williams: The Clown Who Quoted Aristotle." *Village Voice*, January 14, 1971, pp. 55, 62–63.

"Genius Defeated by Race." *Literary Digest*, March 25, 1922, pp. 28–29.

Giorgiady, Nicholas P. *Bert Williams: American Negro Actor*. Milwaukee: Franklin, 1969.

Hirsch, William. "Bert Williams." *Negro History Bulletin*, no. 11 (1941), p. 45.

Monfried, Walter. "Bert Williams, the Modern Pagliacci." *Negro Digest* 11, no. 1 (November 1961), pp. 28–32.

Richards, Sandra. "Bert Williams: The Man and the Mask." *Mime, Mask and Marionette*, no. 1 (Spring 1978), pp. 7–24.

Rowland, Mabel. *Bert Williams—Son of Laughter*. New York: English Crafters, 1923.

Smith, Eric Ledell. *Bert Williams: A Biography of the Pioneer Black Comedian*. Jefferson, N.C.: McFarland, 1992.

Stowe, William M., Jr. "Damn Funny: The Tragedy of Bert Williams." *Journal of Popular Culture* 10, no. 1 (Summer 1976), pp. 5–13.

Walker, George. "The Real Coon on the American Stage." *Theatre Magazine* 6, no. 66 (August 1906), p. 224.

Walsh, Jim. "Favorite Pioneer Recording Artists—Bert Williams, a Thwarted Genius." *Hobbies*, September 1950, pp. 23–25, 36; October 1950, pp. 19–20; November 1950, pp. 19–22.

Washington, Booker T. "Interesting People: Bert Williams." *American Magazine*, September 1910, pp. 600–601, 603–604.

Williams, Bert A. "The Negro on the Stage." *Green Book Album*, December 4, 1910, pp. 1341–44.

———. "Comic Side of Trouble." *American Magazine*, January 1919, pp. 35–36.

———. "Keeping Up with the New Laughs." *Theatre Magazine* 29, no. 220 (June 1919), pp. 346–48.

Wolf, Rennold. "The Greatest Comedian on the American Stage." *Green Book Magazine*, June 1912, pp. 1173–84.

HERB WILLIAMS (Philadelphia, 1884—Freeport, N.Y., October 1, 1936)

Comedian Herb Williams relied for his act on a prop piano that fell apart while he played it, but which could also deliver beer or serve as a chicken coop. While performing, he would make loud and plaintive demands to the electrician for "Spotliiiiiiiight." Born Herbert Schussler Billerbeck, Williams graduated as a serious pianist from the Philadelphia Conservatory of Music. In the early years of the century, he teamed with and married Hilda Wolfus, with the act billed as Williams and Wolfus. When his wife took time out from vaudeville in 1915 to give birth to the couple's first daughter, Doris, Williams teamed with Tom Kennedy. He reteamed later with his wife, but circa 1926, the couple split up, and Williams teamed with and married a new female assistant, Jean Halpin.

Herb Williams made his first appearance at the Palace in 1915 and returned many times through the years. He headlined there in December 1926, February and December 1929, January and July 1931, and July 1932. He was featured in the 1930 edition of Earl Carroll's *Vanities* and made his legitimate stage debut in 1934 with *The Farmer Takes a Wife*. His last Broadway appearance was in *At Home Abroad* in 1935. He made only one feature film appearance, in Paramount's *Rose of the Rancho* (1936), but he had been slated to appear in the 1936 screen adaptation of *Anything Goes*.

PERCY G. (GARNETT) WILLIAMS (Baltimore, 1857—East Islip, N.Y., July 21, 1923)

An important figure in vaudeville management in the early years of the twentieth century, Percy G. Williams was one of the few in his profession who was well liked by the vaudevillians he hired. Williams was a kind and gentle man, and when he died, he left his thirty-acre estate at East Islip, Long Island, as a home for aged and indigent performers. In his will, he wrote, "I made my money from the actors; I herewith return it to them."

As a young man, Percy G. Williams (or P.G., as he was affectionately known) came to Brooklyn, where he took an interest in amateur theatricals. From there, his interest evolved into running medicine shows and also appearing as a blackface performer. In 1893, with the financial backing of Thomas Adams, Jr. (Adams's Tutti Frutti Gum), he created the Bergen Beach, New York, resort, featuring a dance hall, concessions, rides, and a pier. In 1896, he built a casino at the resort, which alternated vaudeville with musical comedies and stock company productions. Williams expanded his activities in 1897 by taking over the

Brooklyn Music Hall (later renamed the Gotham), and soon thereafter acquired a second Brooklyn vaudeville house, the Novelty. In 1901, with financial backing from Otto Huber Brewing, he built the Orpheum, Brooklyn.

Williams acquired his first Manhattan theatre, the Circle, in 1906, followed by the Colonial and the Alhambra. In 1908, he built the Greenpoint Theatre, Brooklyn, and that same year took over the Crescent, Brooklyn. Williams's last Brooklyn development was the Bushwick, opened in 1910. He also built the Bronx Opera House and acquired vaudeville houses in Boston and Philadelphia. The entire P. G. Williams empire was sold to the B. F. Keith vaudeville circuit in 1912 for $5 million.

BIBLIOGRAPHY

Laurie, Joe, Jr. "Percy G. Williams." In *Vaudeville: From the Honky-Tonks to the Palace*. New York: Henry Holt, 1953, pp. 353–59.

WILLIE, WEST AND McGINTY

Willie, West and McGinty were a popular trio in vaudeville from the mid 1920s through the late 1930s, and their act lingered on into television in the 1950s. The trio's slapstick routine was billed as "A Billion Builders Blunders" or "A Comedy of Errors," and in it they appeared as three workmen attempting to build a house, in the course of which everything went wrong. They were hit by buckets, planks of wood, and the like, and with perfect timing, the men would awkwardly manipulate the assorted paraphernalia with disastrous results. When Willie, West and McGinty played their first major New York engagement at the Hippodrome in August 1924, *Variety* (August 27, 1924) commented, "This manner of clowning made several Billy Reeves and Charlie Chaplins stars, and is sound, wholesome, and entirely welcome whenever it is efficiently done." It was slapstick, pure and simple, but it was also, as *Variety* (February 19, 1930) noted, "a good act with plenty of laughs," and it proved tremendously popular on variety stages in the United States and England. The act is still being copied today by countless circus clowns. Willie, West and McGinty reached their zenith in 1939 when they were one of the star attractions of Billy Rose's *Aquacade* at the New York World's Fair. Willie, West and McGinty played the Palace in July 1926, February 1929, and February 1930.

NAT WILLS (Fredericksburg, Va., July 11, 1873—Woodcliffe-on-Hudson, N.J., December 9, 1917)

Billed in vaudeville as "The Happy Tramp," Nat Wills was anything but happy in real life, and he died an apparent suicide. He would appear onstage as a genial bum with his front teeth blacked out, several days growth of beard on his chin, and hair awry. He was a monologist, notorious for the large sums of money he paid writers for fresh material. *Variety* claimed that he was willing to pay any sum for good, new jokes.

Originally, Nat Wills worked with a partner, Dave Halpin, who was incredibly thin and would conclude their act, "The Tramp and the Policeman," with a dance. The couple broke up around the turn of the century, and Wills brought his first wife, known as Madame Loretto, into the act. She died early, and Wills married May Montrief, who also worked in the act, but who died in 1909. The following year, Wills married for a third time; the new wife was Nellie Mc-Nierney, who appeared in vaudeville as "La Belle Titcomb," riding a white horse while singing grand opera. The couple were divorced in 1914, with Wills commenting, "I should have married the horse." His fourth wife was May Day, who had appeared in the Ziegfeld *Follies* under the name May Harrison.

Nat Wills appeared at the Palace as early as April 1913 and was a favorite on the stage at the New York Hippodrome. Despite an average weekly salary of $800, he became increasingly worried about his finances, in large part because of his alimony payments to "La Belle Titcomb." Also, he was constantly concerned that his material might become stale and there would be no money to pay for anything new. On December 9, 1917, he went into the garage of his New Jersey home, turned on the motor of his car, and sometime later was found dead of carbon monoxide poisoning by his wife. He left an estate valued at $23.

EDITH WILSON (Jefferson, In., 1906—Chicago, March 30, 1981)

A superb blues and jazz singer, Edith Wilson was born Edith Woodall, the great-granddaughter of a slave and (illegitimately) John Cabell Breckenridge, vice president of the United States from 1857 to 1861. Her grandmother escaped from slavery to Canada by crossing the frozen Ohio River, and her escape is supposedly the basis for the episode in Harriet Beecher Stowe's *Uncle Tom's Cabin*.

Wilson first began singing professionally at the Park Theatre, Louisville, in 1919, and the following year teamed up with the brother and sister act of Danny and Lena Wilson. In 1921, Danny Wilson and Edith Woodall were married. She made her New York debut at Town Hall in *Put and Take* and recorded "Nervous Blues" for Columbia, reportedly only the second black woman to record for a major label. Aside from continuing vaudeville appearances, Edith Wilson was featured in a number of black revues, including *The Plantation Revue* (1922), *Dover Street to Dixie* (London, 1923), *Dixie to Broadway* (1926), *Blackbirds of 1926* (London, 1926), *Hot Rhythm* (1930), *Shuffle Along of 1933* (1932), *Hummin' Sam* (1933), and *Blackbirds of 1934* (1933). In 1929, she starred with Fats Waller and Louis Armstrong in *Hot Chocolates*, in which the trio was billed as "The Thousand Pounds of Harmony," and in which Wilson introduced her best known song "(What Did I Do to Be So) Black and Blue."

In 1948, Edith Wilson was signed by Quaker Oats to make personal appearances as the character "Aunt Jemima," in which uncredited role she continued until 1965, when objections from the NAACP and the advent of the civil rights movement put an end to the public appearances of the bandannaed and aproned figure. She made her last public appearance at New York's Town Hall from May 1 to 24, 1980, in *Black Broadway*.

BIBLIOGRAPHY
Jewell, James C. "Edith Wilson: Aunt Jemima Plus. . . . " *The World of Yesterday*, no. 36 (April 1982), pp. 5–9.
Mercier, Denis. "Edith Wilson." In *Notable Black American Women*, ed. Jessie Carney Smith. Detroit: Gale Research, 1992, pp. 1264–66.

FRANCIS WILSON (Philadelphia, February 7, 1854—New York, October 7, 1935)

A major actor, writer, and manager of the legitimate theatre, Francis Wilson began his career as a child in vaudeville. With John B. Mackin, he teamed as the blackface act Mackin and Wilson on the minstrel stage and impressed audiences with his "wench" characterizations. He first appeared in New York in vaudeville at Tony Pastor's Music Hall and was a proficient song-and-dance man. It was the time spent in vaudeville that gave Wilson the training for his first major New York role, as Sir Joseph Porter in *H.M.S. Pinafore* at the Casino Theatre in 1882.

BIBLIOGRAPHY
Wilson, Francis. *Recollections of a Player*. New York: De Vinne Press, 1897.
————. *Francis Wilson's Life of Himself*. Boston: Houghton Mifflin, 1924.

WEE GEORGIE WOOD (Jarrow-on-Tyne, England, December 17, 1895—London, February 19, 1979)

Wee Georgie Wood was a comedian of dwarf-like physique who played children throughout his lengthy career, which began in his native England when he was six years old. Born George Bramlett, Wee Georgie Wood made his London debut in 1908, toured South Africa in 1909, and made his U.S. vaudeville debut in January 1915. He toured for thirty-four weeks on the B. F. Keith circuit in 1924 billed as "Vaudeville's Peter Pan," with the following year spent primarily in Australia and New Zealand. His best known sketch was titled "Mrs. Robinson and Her Son," with Dolly Harmer playing Mrs. Robinson from 1917 to 1956. Wood was a combative and difficult entertainer, traits which one fellow vaudevillian claimed were the result of his brain being too close to his bottom.

BIBLIOGRAPHY
Wood, Georgie. *I Had to Be "Wee."* London: Hutchinson, 1948.

ROBERT WOOLSEY. See WHEELER AND WOOLSEY

WRITERS

The popularity of monologists on the vaudeville stage encouraged a handful of writers to try their luck in the medium. One of the first was Captain Bruce Bairnsfather, author of *The Better 'Ole*, who made his American vaudeville debut at the Orpheum, Brooklyn, in September 1923. *Variety* reviewed his act on September 6, 1923. A number of critics and columnists appeared on the vaudeville stage, usually as masters of ceremony in the medium's closing years. Mark Hellinger was possibly one of the first, followed by Walter

Winchell, Earl Wilson, and others. Heywood Broun offered a ten-minute act at the Palace in May 1930; it was reviewed in *Variety* on May 21, 1930. Alexander Woollcott has been described by critic Brendan Gill as "a poor critic, an execrable actor, and a successful 'personality' on radio, where he peddled with breezy unction pipe tobacco and breakfast food." The summation is somewhat unfair in that Woollcott was extremely professional in his performances, with a formidable determination to entertain his listeners. He appeared on the vaudeville stage and was also *The Town Crier* on CBS radio from 1933 to 1943, presenting high-class Broadway gossip in his own inimitable style. *Variety* (September 19, 1933) wrote of him, "Woollcott is human in his address, chatty, soft-spoken, by no means bombastic or possessed of the awkward manner of trying to be impressive, such as pervades the [Walter] Winchellian school of ether dishing."

BESSIE WYNN (1876—Towaco, N.Y., July 8, 1968)

Billed as "The Lady Dainty of Vaudeville," Bessie Wynn was a popular singer on the vaudeville stage in the teens. *The New York Dramatic Mirror* (September 2, 1914) described her as "one of our best vocal singles." In May 1913, she supported Sarah Bernhardt when the French actress headlined at the Palace, and thirty-six years later, Wynn was back as an honored guest when vaudeville returned to the Palace in May 1949.

ED WYNN (Philadelphia, November 9, 1886—Los Angeles, June 19, 1966)

"A comic is a monologist who tells jokes but he isn't necessarily funny," explained Ed Wynn. "He's a man who doesn't do funny things but does things funny. He doesn't open a funny door, he opens a door funny." Known as "The Perfect Fool," after a 1921 musical comedy of that name in which he starred, and also known as "The Fire Chief," from the Texaco-sponsored radio show he began in 1932, Wynn was a comedian with a bespectacled baby face, a silly giggle, an effeminate walk, and expressive hands which always seemed to be on the move. In many respects, film comedian Harry Langdon was a mute version of Ed Wynn. As a vaudeville act onstage for ten minutes or so, Wynn could obviously be very entertaining, but based on surviving footage of Wynn and his humor, after a half-hour or more, he could become extremely tiresome.

Ed Wynn was famous for his silly inventions, such as an eleven-foot, four-and-a-half-inch pole for people you wouldn't touch with a ten-foot one. He invented a windshield wiper for use in eating grapefruit, and there was also a device for eating corn on the cob which was somewhat similar to a modified typewriter carriage. It was these inventions that led Fred Allen to describe Wynn as the greatest visual comedian of his time. Wynn's jokes were corny in the extreme. For example, in the 1930 Paramount film *Follow the Leader*, in which Wynn costarred with Lou Holtz, the latter announces, "A man was shot under my nose." Ed Wynn look's closely at Holtz's proboscis and comments, "That could happen.'' *Follow the Leader* was based on Wynn's 1927 Broadway musical success *Manhattan Mary*; it captures for posterity the classic, corny gag that has a gangster announcing to waiter Wynn, ''I'm so hungry, I could eat a horse!'' Wynn runs out of the restaurant and returns leading a horse and asking, ''Will you have mustard or ketchup?'' According to old-timers, that joke was the biggest clean laugh in the history of show business.

Wynn was a comedian who was idolized by his peers. George Burns said of him, ''Ed Wynn is the greatest of us all. Every comedian alive today has borrowed or learned something from him.'' Jack Benny noted, ''In more than fifty years he never used a naughty word or a suggestive line, yet he could keep you screaming for two hours and a half.'' To Red Skelton, Wynn was simply ''a funny, funny man.'' However, as the autobiographies by his son and grandson indicate, Wynn's personal life was not an entirely happy one, and Clara Beranger recognized this element of sadness in his style when she wrote in 1935, ''In all true comedy, there must be an undercurrent of pathos; and the pathos can only come from the comedian's intimate acquaintanceship with the heartbreak, the misery, and the elemental sadness of life.''

Born Isaiah Edwin Leopold, Ed Wynn was the son of a well-to-do millinery manufacturer who would have preferred that he become a businessman, rather than an entertainer. ''I was twelve when, at the People's Theatre in Philadelphia, I got on a stage for the first time,'' recalled Wynn.

Howard Thurston, the magician, called for volunteers to help him do a mind-reading act. Blindfolded, he would identify objects handed to his girl assistant down in the aisles. ''I know this trick. I can do this!'' I exclaimed, as I tied the scarf around Thurston's eyes. Thurston lifted the blindfold. ''You can?'' he cried, as though delighted to meet someone who shared his occult powers. ''Then you do it, by all means!'' Of course, I couldn't. It was done with a code of signals in the apparently innocuous patter of his girl assistant; the spacing of the words, their very tone—all had meaning. If she kept talking, Thurston could read the serial numbers on a dollar bill handed to her by anyone in the audience. It sounds naive today, but it was high drama then. Thurston gasped out the numbers, tortured by the intensity of his concentration. The applause was deafening when the owner of the money cried, ''By gosh, that's right!'' I think Thurston actually welcomed interruptions like mine, which challenged his power over an audience. For years he was, to me, the ideal showman.

Ed Wynn—taken from his middle name—made his first professional stage appearance in 1901. A year later, he teamed up with Jack Lewis, ten years his senior, to create an act titled the Rah, Rah Boys. ''I wrote an act around two college boys that required a fairly high level of intelligence from the audience. I had squirmed through too many low comedy acts. I knew I wasn't that dumb, and I didn't think other people were, either. We also agreed that we would use no 'blue' lines, no dirt,'' Wynn recalled years later. The two men persuaded ''Gentleman Jim'' Corbett to introduce their act, which he did, pretending that Wynn and Lewis were an act from the West, new to New York, and they were an instantaneous success. A typical Wynn and Lewis routine went something like this:

Lewis: Has your brother read the novels of Dickens and Thackeray?

Wynn: No, he hasn't.

Lewis: What has your brother read?

Wynn: He has red hair.

Wynn maintained, "We revolutionized the two-man comedy act. Up to then the straight man used to swat his partner with a bladder or rolled-up newspaper after every joke and chase him around the stage. We stood still and cut out swatting."

In 1904, Wynn split with Lewis and would sometimes work as a solo in vaudeville and sometimes with a partner. In 1909, he teamed with Al Lee for an act called The Billiken Freshmen, which Sime Silverman in *Variety* (July 12, 1909) thought "a good comedy number, Lee playing the 'straight.' " In 1910, P. O'Malley Jennings from the legitimate stage was Wynn's partner, playing an asinine Englishman. "It is a clever comedy turn worked out along familiar lines," reported *Variety* (December 17, 1910).

"Mr. Busybody" was a twenty-nine-minute vaudeville musical comedy sketch that Wynn introduced to audiences at Brooklyn's Greenpoint Theatre in October 1908. His leading lady in the sketch was Minerva Courtney, who in later years entertained on the vaudeville stage with her impersonations of Charlie Chaplin. Wynn was a department store customer named Appiuscanbee, while Courtney played "a superior shopgirl" named Navva Fitzhugh. Even *Variety* (October 31, 1908) had to admit that most of the jokes in the sketch, which like all material written by the star, were corny. "There is no novelty in the piece," complained the trade paper.

Wynn has the distinction of being, in hindsight, the best known name on the March 24, 1913, opening bill at the Palace Theatre. His fourteen-minute comedy routine titled "The King's Jester" had him in the title role trying to make the king (Frank Wunderlee) laugh. The premise was that if Wynn failed, he would die, a premise that led *Variety* (March 28, 1913) to note that the audience was not the king. Wynn played ragtime—badly—on the piano, and at the close of the act whispered in the king's ear. The king, who had remained silent throughout the act, roared with laughter, and Wynn asked, "Why didn't you tell me you wanted to hear that kind of a story?" While at the Palace, Wynn claimed to have been vaudeville's first master of ceremonies, announcing the acts when the electric sign on the proscenium arch, used for that purpose, failed to operate.

From 1914 onward, Wynn turned his back on vaudeville and devoted his energies to the musical comedy and revue stages. He was featured in the 1914 and 1915 editions of the Ziegfeld *Follies* and in the 1916 edition of *The Passing Show*. He starred in *Doing Our Bit* (1917), *Over the Top* (1917), *Sometime*

(1918), *The Shubert Gaieties of 1919*, *The Ed Wynn Carnival* (1920), *The Perfect Fool* (1921), *The Grab Bag* (1924), *Manhattan Mary* (1927), *Simple Simon* (1930), *The Laugh Parade* (1931), and many other shows. In the 1915 *Follies*, a well-known incident occurred when Wynn hid under W. C. Fields's pool table, making faces at the audience, until Fields discovered him and hit him with a billiard cue. From *The Grab Bag* came the gag with an inch-long harmonica, which Wynn swallowed and caused him to wheeze throughout the show. In a 1942 revue, *Boys and Girls Together*, Wynn entered in the middle of an Indian club throwing routine, climbed a ladder to catch one of the clubs, and then walked offstage without even acknowledging the audience.

In 1919, he was one of the leaders of the Actors' Equity strike. Although not a member of Equity, he was sympathetic toward the plight of his fellow performers, and it was he who suggested that Equity join the American Federation of Labor. He personally approached A.F. of L. founder Samuel Gompers for support. For his efforts, Wynn was blacklisted, but in some respects, the blacklist paid off for him in that it led to his writing, directing, producing, and starring in his own show, *The Ed Wynn Carnival*, which opened at the New Amsterdam Theatre in April 1920.

Ed Wynn's radio show, *The Fire Chief*, had its premiere on April 26, 1932, and the comedian and his catchphrase, "S-o-o-o-o," immediately caught on with listeners. He remained on radio through 1937, then retired from the air until 1944, when his fantasy program, *Happy Island*, had its debut. It was not a success and was cancelled in 1945. When told that the show was sponsored by Borden, makers of homogenized milk, Wynn quipped, "Why I have an uncle who used to go out every Saturday night to get homogenized." In the late 1940s, television provided Wynn with a new medium to conquer. He was a guest on many programs, hosted *All Star Revue* on NBC from 1950 to 1952, and starred in *The Ed Wynn Show* on NBC from 1958 to 1959. When television no longer wanted him, the comedian turned to motion pictures, in which he had made his debut in 1927 with *Rubber Heels*. In his early films, Wynn had been strictly a comic, but in the 1950s, he became a character actor in productions such as *The Great Man* (1956), *Marjorie Morningstar* (1959), *The Absent-Minded Professor* (1960), *Mary Poppins* (1964), *The Greatest Story Ever Told* (1965), *The Warning Shot* (1967), and his last film, *The Gnomemobile* (1967). He was nominated for an Academy Award for his role in *The Diary of Anne Frank* (1959); as early as 1956, he had appeared in a serious role on television, in *Requiem for a Heavyweight*, which also featured his son Keenan.

At the time of his death, Ed Wynn could look back on a career that had evolved from the perfect fool to the perfect character actor. On being told of Wynn's death, Jack Benny commented, "The reason he was also such a great dramatic actor was because he was what I call an 'honest comedian.' When he said anything was funny, you believed everything he said. It made no difference how ridiculous the joke was. If he said he had an uncle who was walking around without his head, you absolutely believed it because of the delivery. . . . Just like

Al Jolson was the world's greatest entertainer, Ed Wynn was definitely, in my opinion, the world's greatest comedian.''

BIBLIOGRAPHY

Beranger, Clara. "The Private Life of Ed Wynn." *Liberty* 12, no. 35 (August 31, 1935), pp. 38–39.

Colton, Henry E. "Ed Wynn Conquers His Fourth Dimension." *The New York Times Magazine*, October 23, 1949, pp. 20, 39–41.

"Ed Wynn." *Current Biography*, January 1945, pp. 698–700.

"The First Time He Ever Made Anyone Sad." *Time*, July 1, 1966, p. 37.

Green, Stanley. "Ed Wynn." In *The Great Clowns of Broadway*. New York: Oxford University Press, 1984, pp. 177–93.

Herndon, Booton. "So-o-o-o- Ed Wynn Fell Again." *The American Weekly*, December 15, 1946, p. 11.

Hill, Gladwin. "It's Ed Wynn Again—in Video." *Collier's*, October 15, 1949, pp. 22–23, 68–69.

Mahoney, Stephen. "The Master of Foolishness." *Life*, July 1, 1966, p. 69.

"Nice Man." *Newsweek*, September 22, 1944, p. 81.

Nichols, Lewis. "Ed Wynn: Up-and-Coming Actor." *The New York Times Magazine*, May 12, 1957, pp. 14, 16, 30.

Reese, John. "Grand Old Man's New Career." *Saturday Evening Post*, April 4, 1959, pp. 24–25, 112, 114, 117.

Sayre, Joel. "August Clown." *Life*, July 26, 1948, pp. 65–66, 69–70, 73, 76–78.

"Something Old, Something New." *Time*, October 17, 1949, p. 77.

Stumpf, Charles K., and James C. Jewell. "Ed Wynn—The Perfect Fool." *The World of Yesterday*, December 1980, pp. 13–21.

Wainwright, Loudon S. "A Warm Father and Son Story about the Wynns." *Life*, June 17, 1957, pp. 96–102.

Wynn, Ed. "The People I Have Laughed With." *Good Housekeeping*, February 1959, pp. 47, 197–200.

Wynn, Keenan, as told to James Brough. *Ed Wynn's Son*. Garden City, N.Y.: Doubleday, 1959.

Wynn, Ned. *We Will Always Live in Beverly Hills: Growing Up Crazy in Hollywood*. New York: William Morrow, 1990.

Y ━━━━━━━━━━━━━━━━━━━━━━━━━━

HENNY YOUNGMAN (Liverpool or London, England, January 12, 1906—)

Henny Youngman's career began as vaudeville died, but he was one of the few entertainers, and virtually the only comedian, who has carried on the vaudeville tradition through to the end of the twentieth century. He is noted for one joke in particular, "Take my wife, Please!," and for the speed of his delivery of gags that are seldom more than one line in length. As he explained, "I discovered . . . when I started in this business that if I told long jokes and they flopped I used up all the time I was on, so I made everything brief. . . . If it flops, I'm in the middle of telling another one anyway."

Youngman has always stated that he was born in London, but it seems possible that his actual birthplace was Liverpool. He grew up in the Bay Ridge section of Brooklyn, and at the age of eight began taking violin lessons—and like Jack Benny he has always used the violin as a prop in his act, although unlike Benny he seldom plays the instrument. In the mid 1920s, Youngman was a bandleader, billed as Hen Youngman and the Swanee Syncopaters. He worked in the Catskills as a master of ceremonies and was also associated with the New York Yacht Club in the early 1930s. The comedian played small-time vaudeville, and in 1934, he toured with a show titled *Vaudeville U.S.A.* In 1936, he was discovered by Kate Smith and Ted Collins and featured on the former's radio show.

For radio, his name was changed to Henry Youngman, and under that name the comedian appeared as a solo act and master of ceremonies at New York's State Theatre in March 1937. He was reviewed for the first time by *Variety*, whose critic "Scho" reported (in the issue of March 17, 1937):

Tall, skinny comedian, whose flair for gag-switching and ad-libbing is bringing him favorable comparison with Milton Berle, has not altered his intimate style of working. At times that style is too intimate, but Youngman will learn as he goes along that the customers further back in the theatre count much more than the fiddlers in the pit. Laughs from the latter won't add to his pay-check, which, incidentally, has grown considerably since his knock-around days of six months or so ago.

Youngman briefly left New York to try for a film career, but he found no interest in Hollywood. His occasional film appearances, generally consisting of nothing more than cameo parts, include *A Wave, a Wac and a Marine* (1944), *You Can't Run Away from It* (1956), *Nashville Rebel* (1966), *Won Ton Ton, the Dog That Saved Hollywood* (1976), *Silent Movie* (1976), and *The Comeback Trail* (1982).

Unlike his contemporaries, Henny Youngman never stopped working; like Milton Berle he was always performing—and enjoying every minute of it. In 1975, he was the first comedian on Dial-a-Joke and proved that a younger generation was equally at east with his humor. After fifty-eight years of marriage, Youngman's much-maligned wife, Sadie, died on March 18, 1987, at the age of eighty-two. Youngman was still working, his vitality and zest for entertaining audiences intact. As *Variety* had commented fifty years earlier, "How far he can go depends almost wholly upon himself."

BIBLIOGRAPHY

"Henry." *The New Yorker*, March 18, 1961, pp. 36–37.

Hiss, Tony. "Hurry, Hurry!" *The New Yorker*, September 12, 1977, pp. 46–48, 51–54, 56, 59, 60, 62–66, 68, 71–73, 77–78, 80, 85–88, 91–92.

"Take My Wife, Please." *Newsweek*, February 2, 1976, p. 75.

Tipmore, David. "Henny Youngman: Joke. Laugh. Pause. Stare." *Village Voice*, August 30, 1976, p. 94.

Youngman, Henny. *Take My Wife, Please!* New York: G. P. Putnam's Sons, 1973.

JOE YULE (Edinburgh, Scotland, April 30, 1894—Hollywood, Ca., March 30, 1950)

Joe Yule was a vaudeville and burlesque comedian who is better known as the father of Mickey Rooney, to whom he bore a startling resemblance. Yule was brought to the United States at the age of three months and made his stage debut in New York in 1904. Joseph Ninian Yule grew up in Brooklyn and developed a vaudeville act with his first wife, and Rooney's mother, Nell. Mickey Rooney was born Joe Yule, Jr., on September 23, 1920, in a Brooklyn vaudeville theatre, where his father was playing, and Rooney's mother returned to the act eleven months after her son's birth. At the age of two, Mickey Rooney became part of the act, known as "Sonny Yule." Joe Yule entered films in 1932, and his features include *Idiot's Delight* (1939), *Judge Hardy and Son* (1939, with son Mickey), *Go West* (1940), *Air Raid Wardens* (1943), and *Kismet* (1944). In 1946, he began playing the character of Jiggs in the "Bringing Up Father" series at Monogram. In 1948, he made his New York legitimate stage debut, playing the title role in the musical *Finian's Rainbow*.

Z

FLORENZ ZIEGFELD, JR. (Chicago, March 21, 1867—Los Angeles, July 22, 1932)

America's first great theatrical showman, Florenz Ziegfeld introduced glamour to the musical stage with his *Follies* and also used the revue form of entertainment to build up the careers of many vaudevillians in the first two decades of the twentieth century. The Ziegfeld Girl was the epitome of glamour and beauty to weary American businessmen for more than two decades, and the producer displayed an unfailing ability to select some of the best, upcoming performers of the day to be featured in his revues, from Lillian Lorraine and Grace LaRue to Bert Williams and Fanny Brice.

The first Ziegfeld *Follies* opened at the Jardin de Paris on the roof of the New York Theatre on July 8, 1907, staged by Julian Mitchell, and featuring Mlle Dazie, Annabelle Whitford, and Grace LaRue. The second edition, in 1908, featured Nora Bayes and Jack Norworth introducing ''Shine on Harvest Moon,'' along with Mae Murray, Annabelle Whitford, and Mlle Dazie. Lillian Lorraine was first featured in the 1909 edition of the *Follies*. Fanny Brice and Bert Williams were first seen in the *Follies* in the 1910 edition, which was also the only *Follies* in which Anna Held appeared—in a film clip only. The stars of the 1911 edition were Bessie McCoy, the Dolly Sisters, Bert Williams, Lillian Lorraine, and Leon Errol. Lorraine, Errol, and Williams were back in 1912. In 1913, the *Follies* cast included Ann Pennington, Leon Errol, Frank Tinney, Jose Collins, and Rosie Dolly, and the show moved from the Jardin de Paris to the New Amsterdam Theatre.

The 1914 edition featured Ed Wynn, Bert Williams, and Annette Kellermann. Wynn and Williams were back in 1915, along with Ina Claire, W. C. Fields, Mae Murray, George White, Ann Pennington, and Olive Thomas. Will Rogers made his first appearance with the *Follies* in 1916; also in the cast were Ina Claire, William Rock and Frances White, Marion Davies, Justine Johnstone, and Lilyan Tashman. Eddie Cantor made his *Follies* debut in 1917; also in the company were Fanny Brice, Bert Williams, Will Rogers, and Marion and Madeline Fairbanks. Marilyn Miller made her first appearance in 1918, and Lillian Lorraine made her last; others in the cast were Will Rogers, Ann Pennington, and Eddie Cantor. The 1919 *Follies* featured Bert Williams, Van and Schenck, Eddie Cantor, Marilyn Miller, Ray Dooley, and John Steel introduced the Irving Berlin song "A Pretty Girl Is Like a Melody," which became virtually a theme song for the *Follies* and its showgirls.

In 1920, the *Follies* cast featured Ray Dooley, W. C. Fields, Fanny Brice, Moran and Mack, and Mary Eaton (replacing Marilyn Miller). In 1921, the *Follies* left the New Amsterdam Theatre for the Globe, and the cast included Van and Schenck, Mary Eaton, Raymond Hitchcock, W. C. Fields, and Fanny Brice (who introduced "Second Hand Rose" and "My Man"). Gilda Gray, Gallagher and Shean, and Mary Eaton were featured in 1922, along with two groups from England, Nervo and Knox and the Tiller Girls; from this show came the phrase "Glorifying the American Girl." Fanny Brice made her last appearance in the *Follies* in 1923, supported by Ann Pennington, Lina Basquette, Bert Wheeler, Paul Whiteman and His Orchestra, Cissie Loftus, and Gertrude Hoffman. In 1924, the cast included Will Rogers, Ann Pennington, Imogene Wilson, George Olsen and His Band, Ethel Shutta, and the Tiller Girls. The last were back in 1925, along with W. C. Fields and Ray Dooley. The next *Follies* was not until 1927, when the stars were Ruth Etting, the Brox Sisters, the Ingenues, and Eddie Cantor. The last *Follies* to be presented by Ziegfeld was in 1931 and featured Harry Richman, Ruth Etting, Helen Morgan, Mitzi Mayfair, and Jack Pearl.

The father of the showman, Florenz Ziegfeld, Sr., was president of the Chicago Musical College, which he founded in 1867. His son first became interested in show business after witnessing Buffalo Bill's Wild West Show, which was probably the biggest influence in his early life. In 1892, Florenz Ziegfeld, Jr., was sent to Europe by his father to book musicians for the Columbian Exposition, to be held the following year in Chicago. Instead, Ziegfeld brought back vaudevillians, notably strongman Eugene Sandow, whom Ziegfeld popularized and with whom he toured the country. In 1896, Ziegfeld came to New York and persuaded Charles Evans and Bill Hoey to revive their popular play *A Parlor Match*. In search of a new leading lady for the play, Ziegfeld again went to Europe, where he discovered Anna Held. She and Ziegfeld entered into a common law marriage in the spring of 1897; she sued for divorce in 1912, citing Ziegfeld's love affair with Lillian Lorraine, and the divorce was declared absolute in January 1913. On April 11, 1914, Ziegfeld married actress Billie Burke, and despite a number of affairs (one was with Olive Thomas), Ziegfeld remained her husband until his death.

Aside from the Ziegfeld *Follies*, the showman also produced many musical comedies, as well as a 1919 play, *Caesar's Wife: The Pink Lady* (1911), *A Winsome Widow* (1912), *Miss 1917*, *Sally* (1920), *Kid Boots* (1923), *Annie* (1924), *Louie the 14th* (1925), *No Foolin'* (1926), *Betsy* (1926), *Rio Rita* (1927),

Rosalie (1927), *Show Boat* (1927), *The Three Musketeers* (1928), *Whoopee!* (1928), *Show Girl* (1929), *Bitter Sweet* (1929), *Simple Simon* (1930), *Smiles* (1930), and *Hot-Cha!* (1932). From 1915 to 1922, Ziegfeld also produced the *Midnight Frolic* on the roof of the New Amsterdam Theatre as a late-night entertainment for audiences of the *Follies* and also as a training ground for potential *Follies* stars.

On February 2, 1927, he opened his own theatre, the Ziegfeld, at 54th Street and Sixth Avenue with the musical comedy *Rio Rita*. It was demolished in April 1967. *Hot-Cha!* had a short run in 1932 and was not a financial success. Its failure, together with increasing ill health, forced Ziegfeld to flee to the West Coast, where he died. After his death, Billie Burke presented the 1933 *Ziegfeld Follies*, featuring Fanny Brice, Willie and Eugene Howard, Jane Froman, and Eve Arden. Burke also presented a 1936 edition, starring Fanny Brice, Josephine Baker, Bob Hope, Gertrude Niesen, Judy Canova, Eve Arden, and Edgar Bergen. In 1945, the *Follies* was again revived with Milton Berle, Arthur Treacher, and Ilona Massey. A 1956 version, starring Tallulah Bankhead, failed to make it to Broadway, closing on tour in Philadelphia. A final, 1957 edition starred Beatrice Lillie and Billy DeWolfe. There was also a 1945 film version of the *Ziegfeld Follies*, produced by M-G-M, which also produced the 1936 biographical film *The Great Ziegfeld*, in which William Powell played the showman.

BIBLIOGRAPHY

Baral, Robert. *Revue: A Nostalgic Reprise of the Great Broadway Period*. New York: Fleet, 1962.

"Beauty, the Fashions and the Follies." *Ladies' Home Journal*, March 1923, pp. 16–17.

Cantor, Eddie, and David Freedman. "Ziegfeld and His Follies," *Collier's* 93, no. 2 (January 13, 1934), pp. 7–9, 50–51; no. 3 (January 20, 1934), pp. 22, 26, 47–48; no. 4 (January 27, 1934), pp. 24–25, 45–46; no. 5 (February 3, 1934), pp. 18–19, 32–33; no. 6 (February 10, 1934), pp. 18–19, 44–45; no. 7 (February 17, 1934), pp. 22, 38, 40.

———— and David Freedman. *Ziegfeld: The Great Glorifier*. New York: King, 1934.

————. "Those Ziegfeld Days—And Nights!" *Variety*, January 6, 1954, p. 271.

Carter, Randolph. *The World of Flo Ziegfeld*. New York: Praeger, 1974.

Farnsworth, Marjorie. *Ziegfeld Follies*. New York: G. P. Putnam's Sons, 1956.

Hackett, Frances. "Musical Comedy Evolves." *The New Republic*, July 31, 1915, p. 336.

Higham, Charles. *Ziegfeld*. Chicago: Henry Regnery, 1972.

Morehouse, Ward. "The Ziegfeld Follies . . . a Formula with Class." *Theatre Arts* 40, no. 5 (May 1956), pp. 66–69, 87.

Samuels, Charles. "Ziegfeld: The Genius Who Owned Broadway." *Cavalier*, July 1958, pp. 48–51, 85–88.

Tittle, Walter. "Ziegfeld of the Follies." *World's Work*, March 1927, pp. 562–68.

Woollcott, Alexander. "The Invisible Fish." *Collier's* 84, no. 17 (October 26, 1929), pp. 24, 64–65.

Ziegfeld, Florenz, Jr. "Picking Out Pretty Girls for the Stage." *American Magazine*, December 1919, pp. 34–37.

Ziegfeld, Patricia. *The Ziegfelds' Little Girl*. Boston: Little, Brown, 1964.

CARL F. ZITTEL (Paterson, N.J., 1876—New York, January 30, 1943)

A colorful reporter and reviewer of vaudeville, C. F. Zittel began his career as a newsboy and worked for various newspapers before joining William Randolph Hearst's *New York Journal* in 1910 as vaudeville critic and solicitor of advertising from vaudeville performers (a somewhat dubious combination). In 1921, he founded his own vaudeville trade paper, *Zitt's Weekly*, in which he would grade vaudeville performers as if they were racehorses, a style he had developed at the *New York Journal*. The trade paper was relatively unsuccessful, but it did continue publication through 1938. In 1919, Zittel took over operation of the Central Park Casino, which he continued to run through 1929. At various times, he also handled publicity and booking for a number of vaudeville performers, including Lillian Russell and Eva Tanguay, and he was instrumental in establishing Belle Baker as a headliner.

Vaudeville Resources _____

Aside from the books listed in the general bibliography and the items listed in the bibliographies following many of the entries, the primary source for information on vaudeville remains the trade papers of the period: *The Billboard*, the *New York Clipper*, *The New York Dramatic Mirror*, and *Variety*. The following guide to libraries and other institutions notes relevant vaudeville-related collections, but should not be considered definitive.

CALIFORNIA

Margaret Herrick Library of the Academy of Motion Picture Arts and Sciences (333 South La Cienega Boulevard, Beverly Hills, Ca. 90211). The library's biographical files contain clippings on and photographs of vaudevillians who also appeared in films. Additionally, the library has three scrapbooks formerly belonging to Jeb and Audrey Dooley; volume 1 contains professional and personal photographs of the Dooleys and their colleagues; volume 2 contains film-related materials from 1926 to 1929 (specifically relating to Stern Bros. comedies); and volume 3 contains clippings and a two-page typed biography of Jeb Dooley.

Louis B. Mayer Library of the American Film Institute Center for Advanced Film Studies (2021 North Western Avenue, Los Angeles, Ca. 90027) holds a microfilm and hard-copy printout of Buster Keaton's personal scrapbook for the years 1902 to 1909.

Frances Howard Goldwyn/Hollywood Regional Library (1623 North Ivar, Hollywood, Ca. 90028) holds a small collection of clippings and photographs (personal and professional) dating from the teens and 1920s relating to Gladys and Bessie Bromley (the Bromley Sisters), a minor song and dance act.

Institute of the American Musical (121 North Detroit Street, Los Angeles, Ca. 90036) houses the archives of the Paramount Theatre, New York, 1934 to 1951.

Literature Department of the Los Angeles Central Library (630 West Fifth Street, Los Angeles, Ca. 90071) holds more than twenty-nine thousand theatre programs, together with local theatre scrapbooks and clippings on theatrical personalities.

Thousand Oaks Library/American Library of Radio and Television (1401 East Janss Road, Thousand Oaks, Ca. 91362) holds the papers of Rudy Vallee.

Department of Special Collections of the University of California at Los Angeles (405 Hilgard Avenue, Los Angeles, Ca. 90024). The Jack Benny Collection here includes 900 radio scripts, 269 television scripts, scrapbooks, business correspondence, still photographs, and radio transcriptions. The Eddie Cantor Collection includes radio and television scripts, correspondence, scrapbooks, music, and recordings. Ed Wynn's scrapbooks from 1923 to 1937 are also here.

Mandeville Department of Special Collections/University Library of the University of California at San Diego (La Jolla, Ca. 92037) holds a 130-page scrapbook of newspaper clippings on Will Rogers.

Cinema Collection/Doheny Library of the University of Southern California (University Park, Los Angeles, Ca. 90007). The George Burns and Gracie Allen Collection here consists of eighty-two volumes of radio scripts, fifty-seven volumes of television scripts, twelve scrapbooks, clippings, disc recordings, and more than two hundred 16mm prints of *The George Burns and Gracie Allen Show*. The Jimmy Durante Collection consists of scripts and radio transcriptions of the comedian's programs from 1943 to 1947. The Edgar Bergen Collection contains radio scripts, recordings, audio tapes, photographs, scrapbooks, and 16mm films. The Charlotte Greenwood Collection contains stage and screen photographs; stage, radio, and film scripts; clippings, correspondence; and the typed manuscript of an unpublished autobiography. The Joe Laurie, Jr., Collection contains sketches, radio transcriptions, joke files, and miscellaneous writings by the chronicler of vaudeville. The Benny Rubin Collection consists of sixty-seven photographs (most used in his autobiography), one "Mickey Finn" comic strip dated December 4, 1968, a plaque from the Masquers dated February 28, 1964, clippings, scripts for *Jack Benny's 20th Anniversary TV Special* (October 24, 1970), *Adam–12: Extortion* (April 27, 1971), and *The Partners: Have I Got an Apartment for You* (June 2, 1971), and four 16mm films: *Full Coverage*, *Guests Wanted*, *Dumb Dicks*, and *The Promoter*. The Paul Whiteman Collection consists of one box of photographs of Whiteman, his family, and friends. The unpublished autobiography *You Don't Have to Be Crazy to Be in Show Business but It Helps* by Edward Small, as told to Robert E. Kent, includes material on the Independent Booking Agency, Small's work as a vaudeville booking agent, vaudeville circuits, and minor vaudevillians.

The Magic Castle/Academy of Magical Arts, Inc. (7001 Franklin Avenue, Hollywood, Ca. 90028) contains a large library of magic-related books accessible only to working magicians. It also houses a library of vaudeville-related books, Eddie Cantor's gag files, the Earl Carroll Collection, and one of Buster Keaton's scrapbooks.

COLORADO

Denver Public Library (1357 Broadway, Denver, Co. 80203) houses material relating to vaudeville and Chautauqua in the western United States.

DISTRICT OF COLUMBIA

Channing Pollock Theatre Collection at Howard University (Washington, D.C. 20059). Not only are the papers of theatre critic and playwright Channing Pollock here, but also the Percy G. Williams Collection.

Library of Congress (Washington, D.C. 20540). As the nation's copyright depository, the Library of Congress has considerable holdings of vaudeville sketches and playlets, including those of W. C. Fields. Among its special collections are the papers of Irving Berlin, consisting of 750,000 items, including 42 scrapbooks, memorabilia, and handwritten scores.

IOWA

Special Collections and Manuscripts Division of the University Libraries, University of Iowa (Iowa City, Ia. 52242). The University of Iowa is an essential resource for vaudeville research with its B. F. Keith/E. F. Albee Collection. The collection includes twenty-four volumes of weekly reports on the bills of various theatres on the circuit, arranged chronologically; volumes of clippings from various theatres; five volumes of reviews of "New Acts" from *The New York Dramatic Mirror* and *Variety*; and eleven boxes of business files.

MARYLAND

Maryland Historical Society (201 West Monument Street, Baltimore, Md. 21201) houses the papers of Eubie Blake.

MASSACHUSETTS

Mugar Memorial Library of Boston University (771 Commonwealth Avenue, Boston, Ma. 02215) houses the papers of Fred and Adele Astaire, Jesse L. Lasky, Harry Richman, and Kate Smith.

Harvard Theatre Collection of Harvard College Library (Cambridge, Ma. 02138) has significant vaudeville holdings, including playbills, photographs, reviews, books, and manuscripts. Its holdings also include a large collection on minstrels; materials on burlesque; and an extensive sheet music collection. Most of the material relating to vaudeville has not been classified as such but is incorporated into the general theatrical holdings with most accessible by name of theatre, performer, or act.

NEW JERSEY

William Seymour Theatre Collection/Firestone Library of Princeton University (Princeton, N.J. 08544) holds the papers of female impersonator Vardaman. Covering the period 1883 to 1917, the papers are housed in six boxes and include diaries, correspondence, a scrapbook, photographs, playbills, clippings and sheet music.

NEW YORK

The American Museum of the Moving Image (34–12 36th Street, Astoria, N.Y. 11106) holds oral histories of Joe Smith and Rudy Vallee, but primarily relating to their film careers.

Oral History Research Office/Butler Library of Columbia University (116th Street and Broadway, New York, N.Y. 10027) holds oral histories of many personalities associated with vaudeville.

Department of Manuscript and University Archives/Cornell University Libraries (101 Olin Research Library, Ithaca, N.Y. 14853) holds the papers of Irene Castle.

Theatre and Music Collection of the Museum of the City of New York (103rd Street and Fifth Avenue, New York, N.Y. 10028) has some vaudeville materials.

The New York Public Library at Lincoln Center (111 Amsterdam Avenue, New York, N.Y. 10023) has possibly America's largest collection of clippings and scrapbooks relating to vaudeville, with files on all vaudeville personalities. Also here are collections as varied as the scrapbooks of Billy Rose and the papers and photographs of Fay Marbe.

Robert F. Wagner Labor Archives of the Tamiment Institute Library of New York University (70 Washington Square West, New York, N.Y. 10012) houses the records of the American Guild of Variety Artists (AGVA).

The Walter Hampden–Edwin Booth Theatre Collection and Library of the Players Club (16 Gramercy Park, New York, N.Y. 10003) houses the Chuck Callahan Collection of burlesque scripts and the John Mulholland Magic Collection.

The Shubert Archive (149 West 45th Street, New York, N.Y. 10036) has some scattered references to vaudeville. In the General Correspondence Series

1910 to 1926 are memos, telegrams, and letters between various vaudeville managers, booking agents, vaudeville attractions, etc. and the Shubert offices. The archive also has one box of vaudeville programs. The Shuberts produced many revues that featured vaudeville performers, and so the archive's production files may have information about performers or acts. Most of the material is organized or accessed either by a performer's name or production. The archive also has papers relating to Fanchon and Marco; the collection is unprocessed, unavailable to researchers, and consists of fifteen transfer files (about thirty linear feet) of correspondence and booking records (some photographs) for the period circa 1939 to 1949.

OHIO

Popular Culture Library at Bowling Green State University. (Bowling Green, Oh. 43403) houses the Leo S. Rosencrans Collection of Chautauqua.

OKLAHOMA

Will Rogers Memorial (Claremore, Ok. 74017). The former home of Will Rogers houses his personal papers, scripts, photographs, memorabilia, and scrapbooks, as well as the scrapbooks of his close friend Fred Stone. Microfilm copies of the scrapbooks are also on deposit with the University Library, Oklahoma University, Stillwater, Ok. 74074.

PENNSYLVANIA

Theatre Collection of the Free Library of Philadelphia (Logan Circle, Philadelphia, Pa. 19103) contains books, periodicals, photographs, programs, posters, and other memorabilia on vaudeville and minstrelsy. Minstrel programs date back to 1860, and most significant in this area are the manuscripts from Philadelphia's Dumont Minstrels.

TEXAS

Oral History Collection on the Performing Arts at Southern Methodist University (Dallas, Tx. 75275) includes oral histories of Steve Allen, Fred Astaire, Herbert Baker (son of Belle Baker), Ray Bolger, Imogene Coca, Pinky Lee, Rose Marie, Harold Minsky, Ken Murray, and Rudy Vallee.

General Bibliography _____

Allen, Robert. *Vaudeville and Film, 1895–1915: A Study in Media Interaction.* New York: Arno Press, 1980.

Altman, Sig. *The Comic Image of the Jews.* Rutherford, N.J.: Fairleigh Dickinson University Press, 1971.

Balaban, Carrie. *Continuous Performance.* New York: A. J. Balaban Foundation, 1964.

Baral, Robert. *Revue: A Nostalgic Reprise of the Great Broadway Period.* New York: Fleet, 1962.

Blesh, Rudi, and Harriet Janis. *They All Played Ragtime: The True Story of an American Music.* New York: Grove Press, 1950.

Browne, Walter, and E. De Roy Koch. *Who's Who on the Stage, 1908.* New York: B. W. Dodge, 1909.

Burton, Jack. *In Memoriam—Oldtime Show Biz.* New York: Vantage Press, 1965.

Busby, Roy. *British Music Hall: An Illustrated Who's Who from 1850 to the Present.* London: Paul Elek, 1976.

Caffin, Caroline, and Marius De Zayas. *Vaudeville: The Book.* New York: Mitchell Kennerley, 1914.

Cahn, William. *A Pictorial History of the Great Comedians.* New York: Grosset & Dunlap, 1970.

Clarke, Norman. *The Mighty Hippodrome.* Cranbury, N.J.: A. S. Barnes, 1968.

Csida, Joseph, and June Bundy Csida, eds. *American Entertainment: A Unique History of Popular Show Business.* New York: Watson-Guptill, 1978.

DiMeglio, John E. *Vaudeville U.S.A.* Bowling Green, Oh.: Bowling Green University Popular Press, 1973.

Dunning, John. *Tune in Yesterday: The Ultimate Encyclopedia of Old-Time Radio 1925–1976.* Englewood Cliffs, N.J.: Prentice-Hall, 1976.

Erenberg, Lewis A. *Steppin' Out: New York Nightlife and the Transformation of American Culture, 1890–1930.* Westport, Ct.: Greenwood Press, 1981.

Felstead, Theodore S. *Stars Who Made the Halls.* London: T. Werner Laurie, 1946.

Fisher, John. *Funny Way to Be a Hero.* London: Frederick Muller, 1973.

Golden, George Fuller. *My Lady Vaudeville and Her White Rats.* New York: The White Rats of America, 1909.

Grau, Robert. *The Business Man in the Amusement World.* New York: Broadway Publishing Company, 1910.

_____. *The Stage in the Twentieth Century*. New York: Broadway Publishing Company, 1912.

Green, Abel. *The Spice of Variety*. New York: Henry Holt, 1952.

_____, and Joe Laurie, Jr. *Show Biz from Vaude to Video*. New York: Henry Holt, 1951.

Henderson, Mary C. *The City and the Theatre: New York Playhouses, from Bowling Green to Times Square*. Clifton, N.J.: James T. White, 1973.

Hoyt, Harlowe R. *Town Hall Tonight*. Englewood Cliffs, N.J.: Prentice-Hall, 1955.

Hughes, Langston, and Milton Meltzer. *Black Magic: A Pictorial History of the Negro in American Entertainment*. Englewood Cliffs, N.J.: Prentice-Hall, 1967.

Jay, Ricky. *Learned Pigs & Fireproof Women: Unique Eccentric and Amazing Entertainers*. New York: Warner Books, 1986.

Jenkins, Henry. *What Made Pistachio Nuts?: Early Sound Comedy and the Vaudeville Aesthetic*. New York: Columbia University Press, 1992.

Laurie, Joe, Jr. *Vaudeville: From the Honky-Tonks to the Palace*. New York: Henry Holt, 1953.

Lloyd, Herbert. *Vaudeville Trails thru the West, "by one who knows."* Chicago: The Author, 1919.

Mander, Raymond, and Joe Mitchenson. *British Music Hall*. London: Studio Vista, 1974.

Marks, Edward B., as told to Abbot J. Liebling. *They All Sang: From Tony Pastor to Rudy Vallee*. New York: Viking Press, 1934.

Matlaw, Myron, ed. *American Popular Entertainment*. Westport, Ct.: Greenwood Press, 1979.

Mattfeld, Julius. *Variety Music Cavalcade 1620–1969*. Englewood Cliffs, N.J.: Prentice-Hall, 1971.

McLean, Albert F. *American Vaudeville as Ritual*. Lexington: University of Kentucky Press, 1965.

McNamara, Brooks, ed. *American Popular Entertainments: Jokes, Monologues, Bits, and Sketches*. New York: Performing Arts Journal Publications, 1983.

Midwinter, Eric. *Make 'Em Laugh*. London: George Allen & Unwin, 1979.

Odell, George. *Annals of the New York Stage*. New York: Columbia University Press, 1949.

Rust, Brian. *The Complete Entertainment Discography*. New Rochelle, N.Y.: Arlington House, 1973.

Samuels, Charles, and Louise Samuels. *Once upon a Stage: The Merry World of Vaudeville*. New York: Dodd, Mead, 1974.

Short, Ernest. *Fifty Years of Vaudeville*. London: Eyre and Spottiswoode, 1946.

Slide, Anthony. *The Vaudevillians: A Dictionary of Vaudeville Performers*. Westport, Ct.: Arlington House, 1981.

_____. *Selected Vaudeville Criticism*. Metuchen, N.J.: Scarecrow Press, 1988.

Smith, Bill. *The Vaudevillians*. New York: Macmillan, 1976.

Smith, Wallace. *Are You Decent?* New York: G. P. Putnam's Sons, 1927.

Snyder, Robert W. *The Voice of the City: Vaudeville and Popular Culture in New York*. New York: Oxford University Press, 1989.

Sobel, Bernard. *A Pictorial History of Vaudeville*. New York: Citadel Press, 1961.

Spitzer, Marion. *The Palace*. New York: Atheneum, 1969.

Stein, Charles W., ed. *American Vaudeville as Seen by Its Contemporaries*. New York: Alfred A. Knopf, 1984.

Toll, Robert C. *Blacking Up: The Minstrel Show in Nineteenth Century America.* New York: Oxford University Press, 1974.

————. *On with the Show: The First Century of Show Business in America.* New York: Oxford University Press, 1976.

Unterbrink, Mary. *Funny Women: American Comediennes, 1860–1985.* Jefferson, N.C.: McFarland, 1987.

Who Was Who in the Theatre, 1912–1976. Detroit: Gale Research Company, 1978.

Wilde, Larry. *The Great Comedians Talk about Comedy.* New York: Citadel Press, 1968.

Wilders, Alice. *American Popular Song: The Great Innovators, 1900–1950.* New York: Oxford University Press, 1982.

Wilmeth, Don B. *The Language of American Popular Entertainment: A Glossary of Argot, Slang, and Terminology.* Westport, Ct.: Greenwood Press, 1981.

————. *Variety Entertainment and Outdoor Amusements: A Reference Guide.* Westport, Ct.: Greenwood Press, 1982.

Index

About the Author

ANTHONY SLIDE is the author or editor of more than fifty books on the history of popular entertainment, including *Sourcebook for the Performing Arts* (1988), *The International Film Industry* (1989), *The American Film Industry* (1986), *The Television Industry* (1991), *International Film, Radio, and Television Journals* (1985), and *Before Video* (1992), all published by Greenwood Press. He has served as Associate Archivist of the American Film Institute and resident historian of the Academy of Motion Picture Arts and Sciences.